THE
ASIAN AMERICAN
ENCYCLOPEDIA

THE
ASIAN AMERICAN
ENCYCLOPEDIA

Volume 6

U.S. Immigration Commission – Zuzu Ben

Index

Editor
FRANKLIN NG

Managing Editor
JOHN D. WILSON

Marshall Cavendish
New York • London • Toronto

Published By
Marshall Cavendish Corporation
2415 Jerusalem Avenue
P.O. Box 587
North Bellmore, New York 11710
United States of America

∞ The paper in these volumes conforms to the American National Standard for Permanence of Paper for Printed Library Materials, Z39.48-1984.

Library of Congress Cataloging-in-Publication Data

The Asian American encyclopedia / editor, Franklin Ng.
     p. cm.
    Includes bibliographical references and index.
    Contents: v. 6. U.S. Immigration Commission—Zuzu Ben.
    1. Asian Americans—Encyclopedias. I. Ng, Franklin, 1947-   .
E184.O6A827 1995
973′.0495′003—dc20   94-33003
ISBN 1-85435-677-1 (set).   CIP
ISBN 1-85435-685-2 (vol. 6).

First Printing

PRINTED IN THE UNITED STATES OF AMERICA

Contents

THE
ASIAN AMERICAN
ENCYCLOPEDIA

U.S. Immigration Commission: Convened from 1907 to 1911 to determine immigration's effect on American life. The forty-two-volume report issued by the commission concluded that immigrants were vital to industrial expansion but caused poor working conditions. The report included testimony on immigration to Hawaii and the impact of Japanese immigrant labor in the Pacific Coast and Rocky Mountain states. The report's findings were partly responsible for the introduction and passage of restrictive immigration legislation, culminating in the IMMIGRATION ACT OF 1924.

U.S.-India maritime relations: U.S.-India maritime contact in the nineteenth century was subservient to the British mercantile interests in India. The BRITISH EAST INDIA COMPANY dominated India's trade for most of the century. U.S. exports to India consisted of tobacco, copper, and other metals. India's exports were wool, oilseeds, hide, indigo, and spices. One interesting luxury item exported from the United States had been bulk ice, first exported in 1833. The first U.S. consular service was established in Calcutta in 1792.

In the absence of other major seaborne traffic, trade has remained the basic point of contact between India and the United States. After India's independence from British rule (1947), the volume of trade between India and the United States showed hardly any growth. Besides a lack of trade interest, one inhibiting factor was that trade in grains was used by the U.S. government to promote American interests in the Cold War rivalry with the Soviet Union, making India particularly susceptible to U.S. pressure to change its policy of non-alignment especially in the 1950's and 1960's. Since 1947 three shipping conferences have handled a major share of the U.S.-India trade, two outbound conferences serving the east and west coasts of India and one inbound conference serving India and other South Asian countries.

Besides grain and milk, India has imported petroleum products, ferrous and other metals, machinery, chemicals, road and railroad vehicles, and fertilizers. Major U.S. imports have been tea, jute goods, metals, cotton and textiles, leather, crude minerals, and oilseeds. The balance of trade has been generally unfavorable to India, except in some isolated years, because of India's need for enhanced imports to implement its economic development plans since 1951 and to meet its food shortages of the 1950's and 1970's. The trade imbalance was especially glaring during the 1960's. In later years, however, the overall trade statistics have been favorable toward India, with the exports surpassing imports in terms of total dollar value. For example, of the country's total world trade between 1978 and 1985, imports constituted about 10 to 12 percent while exports occupied less than 20 percent.

India's share of Indo-U.S. shipping has been small, with Indian ships handling only about 10 percent of Indo-U.S. trade. Only two shipping lines, the Scindia Steam Navigation Company and the Shipping Corporation of India, are members of the conferences, which are dominated by the older American and continental shipping lines. The conferences operate under the U.S. Shipping Act of 1918 from a common secretariat located in New York. On the main functional committee of the conferences, all member countries are represented. Nevertheless, being a latecomer, Indian shipping interests have felt the competitive pressures of other entrenched interests.

U.S.-Japan relations: The origins of U.S.-Japan relations extend back to July of 1853, when Commodore Matthew C. Perry first sailed four U.S. "black ships" into Uraga seaport, at the entrance to Edo Bay. From that time forward both nations embarked on a relationship characterized by trust and mistrust, friendship and enmity, peace and war. This oscillating relationship has moved through several stages: historical opening in the 1850's; industrial modernization and Japanese immigration in the late nineteenth century; imperialist expansion in the 1930's; clash of interests in World War II; post-1945 occupation and strategic partnership in Asia; shocks and rifts in the partnership during the 1970's; the end of Japan's dependency and rising tensions in the 1980's; and global competitive partnership in the transition to the twenty-first century.

Historical Opening: 1850's. Perry anchored his squadron in Uraga in 1853. European powers had already secured commercial and diplomatic privileges in Asia by forcing China to accept the Treaty of Wangxia (1844). Given the four hundred miles across the Sea of Japan separating Japan from China, Perry saw the importance of Japanese ports for U.S. commercial interests in Asia. Thus with the Perry Treaty of 1854 and the Harris Treaty of 1858, the U.S. government obtained from Japan port facilities and coaling stations, thereby positioning itself for Asian market opportunities. The Harris Treaty also paved the way for U.S.-Japan diplomacy by stationing the first U.S. diplomatic envoy at Shimoda in 1858 and by establishing the first Japanese embassy and mission to Washington, D.C., in 1860.

During the 1860's major events occurred in both

Artist's rendering of Commodore Matthew Perry and his landing party meeting the Japanese imperial commissioners at Yokohama, Japan, March, 1854. (Library of Congress)

countries, momentarily focusing attention and resources on domestic issues and problems. The outcome of the two major events set the two nations on a path of industrial modernization that would find them meeting head-to-head in unexpected ways.

Industrial Modernization and Immigration. In 1868 the restoration of the emperor system, known as the MEIJI RESTORATION, had three important consequences for Japan's future. First, it accelerated the centralization of power and sense of nationhood, critical to the political modernization of Japan. Second, it produced leaders who abandoned isolationism, incorporated Western science and technology, and set Japan on a course to catch up with the West. Third, it launched Japan's industrial modernization based on an educated and skilled work force, resource acquisition, capital formation, and trade in exports.

On the American side the conclusion of the Civil War in 1865 solidified the American experiment in nation-building and accelerated industrial development, with implications for Japan. Propelled by the cotton gin and the steam engine, U.S. products welcomed Asian markets for trade and required domestic railroads for transporting goods. Factories and railroad-building brought Asian immigrants to the United States, first from China, then from Japan. Powered by the modernization of navies, weapons, and energy technology, the United States began to assert influence in Asia in the 1890's.

Concerned about Japan's growing power in Asia, the United States diplomatically intervened to limit Japan's territorial claims in China following the Russo-Japanese War of 1904-1905 (1905 Treaty of Portsmouth); Japan's economic concessions in China after World War I (Paris Peace Conference of 1919); and Japan's growing military power and naval tonnage (Washington Disarmament Conference of 1921-1922). Given the rapid economic and military modernization of the two nations, their interests in Asia would soon clash.

As early as 1869, but mainly in the mid-1880's, the first Japanese immigrants came to the United States, partly pushed by economic recession and avoidance of military conscription in Japan, and partly pulled by the opportunity of work, education, and hoped-for riches. The vast majority came as laborers to build the American railway system, work in the gold mines, run local retail stores, or till agricultural fields. Some would return to Japan; most would stay in the United States. By 1890 there were approximately 2,000 peo-

First Japanese mission to the United States. (National Archives)

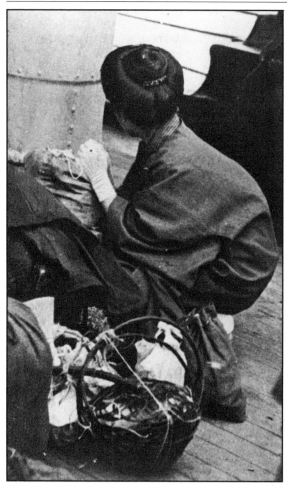

Kimono-clad Japanese woman aboard the deck of a ship, amid her belongings. The first Japanese immigrants to the United States sailed in search of a better life overseas. (California State Library)

SAN FRANCISCO SCHOOL BOARD CRISIS (1906) and U.S. laws were alleviated by the Root-Takahira Agreement of 1908 and the resignation of the U.S. ambassador to Japan, C. E. Woods, to protest the 1924 exclusion law. In the long term, however, anti-Asian U.S. laws touched raw nerves in Japan and served to increase mutual antagonism and mistrust.

In the early stages of Tokyo-Washington bilateralism, these episodes clearly marked a nadir in the oscillating U.S.-Japan relationship. As a rising power in Asia, confirmed in Japanese eyes by victories against China in 1894-1895 and against Russia in 1904-1905, Japan sought equal status in the world, only to be humiliated by American denial. These mutual perceptions did not augur well for the future.

Imperialism in Asia: The 1930's. If the storm clouds of war darkened in the 1930's, the clouds were politically seeded during the preceding two decades. By 1920 both the U.S. and Japan had critical industries and infrastructure requisite to industrial growth: iron and steel, shipbuilding, telephone, telegraph, rail transport systems, and large businesses for managing capi-

ple of Japanese ancestry in the United States, 24,300 by 1900, 72,000 by 1910, and 110,000 by 1920.

U.S.-Japan relations deteriorated in the early twentieth century. Serious problems rooted in mistrust, cultural misperceptions, and economic competition led to racial discrimination toward the first generation of immigrants (Issei) from Japan and their American-born children. In May of 1905 and October of 1906, the San Francisco School Board passed resolutions segregating Japanese, Chinese, and Korean children from white children in the city's schools. In 1913 and 1920 the California legislature passed ALIEN LAND LAWS that prevented Japanese from owning or leasing agricultural land in California. In 1924 Congress enacted an Immigration Act, which proscribed further Japanese immigration to American soil.

In the short term, racial tensions generated by the

U.S. secretary of state Elihu Root, winner of the Nobel Peace Prize in 1912. He helped engineer the Root-Takahira Agreement, which eased mounting tensions between the United States and Japan by recognizing the policies and influence of each government in the Pacific region. (AP/ Wide World Photos)

In the decades preceding World War II, escalating imperial Japanese military aggression in Asia and the Pacific region alarmed the U.S. government. The caption to this political cartoon from 1939 reads, "You are asking for an embargo, my Asiatic friend." (Library of Congress)

tal and production. A singular difference between the two nations was their comparative supply of and access to raw materials. Key territorial acquisitions and continental expansion gave the Americans a cornucopia of natural resources. By comparison the Japanese archipelago was barren of critical minerals and raw materials, save for coal deposits. This difference would lead to war.

Japan expanded into Asia during the first three decades of the twentieth century mainly to improve strategic and economic security. Secret negotiations with Russia in 1907 and concessions in the Treaty of Portsmouth gave Japan a sphere of interest in Korea, leading to the colonization of Korea from 1910 to 1945. The economic and logistic jewel was the South Manchurian Railway, attractive to business and military groups in Japan. By the end of World War I Manchuria had become the chief supplier of iron ores for Japan's domestic industries.

At the Versailles Peace Conference (1919) Japan secured important trading concessions in Shandong Province in China. In Southeast Asia, Japan sought access to rubber and oil to feed her industry and military. In Tokyo an ultranationalist, militarist officer fac-

tion and right-wing political groups rose suddenly to power. Driven by resentment over postwar military retrenchment, economic recession in the 1920's, and a festering dissatisfaction with party democracy, this right-wing coalition vented its frustration in political coups, assassinations, repression of Asian neighbors, and eventually war against the United States.

War: Japan Against the United States. World War II ushered in the atomic age, established Hiroshima and Nagasaki as metaphors of destruction and peace, and gave birth to a strategic partnership between former wartime enemies transformed into peacetime friends.

War between Japan and the United States resulted from a failure in diplomacy to reconcile fundamental, conflicting interests as perceived by leaders. Triggered by Japan's attack on U.S. forces at Pearl Harbor, Hawaii, on December 7, 1941, other fundamental causes included the U.S. embargo on strategic materials to Japan beginning in the summer of 1940; U.S worries about Japan's encroachment on U.S. interests in China; Japan's search for oil, tin, and rubber in Dutch, French, British, and U.S. colonial possessions throughout Southeast Asia, the East Indies, and the South Pacific; Japan's assessment that success in war required the elimination of U.S. naval capability, especially the Pa-

Months before Japan's unconditional surrender in September, 1945, the USS Bunker Hill *aircraft carrier sustains hits by two kamikaze assaults off Kyushu in May. The combined attack—the second arriving thirty seconds after the first—killed 372 Americans.* (National Archives)

A dense mushroom cloud of smoke rises more than sixty thousand feet into the air over the Japanese port of Nagasaki—the result of an atomic bomb, the second ever used in warfare, dropped on the industrial center on August 9, 1945, from a U.S. B-29 airplane. (National Archives)

Battered religious figures are among the debris scattered across a tattered valley in Nagasaki in September, 1945. (National Archives)

cific Fleet at Pearl Harbor; and diversion of Soviet and Allied troops away from Europe to fight Japan's military forces in Asia.

Japan, a tiny island nation, eventually lost the war for several reasons: a crippling defeat suffered by the Japanese Imperial Navy at the Battle of Midway in June, 1942; overextension of military capabilities to defend its perimeter strategy; the high cost of securing access to critical raw materials and minerals; irreparable damage to production capability inflicted by the Allied bombing raids; and ultimately, the superior numbers and firepower of the Allied forces.

In spite of initial success in the Dutch East Indies and the Philippines and in spite of a strategic triumph at Pearl Harbor, Japan lacked a sustained war capability. Each battle, each passing month, led inexorably to a strategic defeat for Japan. On August 6, 1945, an atomic bomb was detonated over Hiroshima; three days later, on August 9, another bomb was dropped on Nagasaki.

Five days later, on August 14, Emperor Hirohito urged his people to "endure the unendurable" as he agreed to Allied terms of unconditional surrender.

The Far Eastern Agreement, signed by U.S. President Franklin D. Roosevelt, Soviet Premier Joseph Stalin, and British Prime Minister Sir Winston Churchill at Yalta in February, 1945, contained two key, controversial provisions that set the stage for U.S.-Japan relations in the post-1945 era. First, the Soviet Union agreed to enter the war on the Allied side against Japan, three months after Germany's surrender. Second, the Soviet Union regained key territory lost to Japan after Russia's defeat in the Russo-Japanese War, notably southern Sakhalin, railroad rights in Manchuria, access to the commercial port of Dairen, and control of the Kuril Islands. On the premise that Soviet forces were necessary to subdue Japan, Allied leaders made concessions that radically changed Japan's role in post-1945 Asia: Enemy was transformed into friend, conflict into cooperation, adversary into ally.

In the United States one war episode illustrated the changing meaning of the U.S.-Japan relationship—the evacuation and incarceration of 120,000 Americans of Japanese ancestry. Based on the assumption that people of Japanese ancestry would commit espionage and sabotage, Roosevelt issued EXECUTIVE ORDER 9066, (1942), authorizing the removal of Japanese Americans from their homes to ten isolated campsites from late spring of 1942 to the end of the war in 1945.

Yet despite the humiliation of incarceration, Japanese Americans—first-generation immigrants (Issei), their second-generation children (Nisei), and their third-generation grandchildren (Sansei)—remained loyal to the United States. No act of sabotage or espionage was ever proved in a U.S court of law. Young Nisei men in the camps volunteered for military duty in the famous 442ND REGIMENTAL COMBAT TEAM, 100TH INFANTRY BATTALION. At a staggering cost in casualties, the 442nd fought heroically in European campaigns, provided intelligence services for the U.S. command in Asia, and emerged as the most decorated unit in American military history.

Occupation and Strategic Partnership in Asia. World War II has influenced U.S.-Japan relations in

Soviet premier Joseph Stalin, one of three signatories to the Yalta compact that set the stage for U.S.-Japan relations in the postwar period. (Library of Congress)

The Ninomiya family in its barracks at the Granada relocation center, southeastern Colorado. More than 120,000 Japanese evacuees would pass through the internment camps by the war's end. (National Archives)

four fundamental ways. In the first case the Cold War and enhanced Soviet power in Asia shaped Japan's new role in containment strategy. In the second case the war set Japan on a course of mandated democracy, with a U.S.-imposed constitution proscribing the use of military force abroad. In the third case, ravaged by war and faced with economic collapse, post-1945 Japan ascended as the proverbial phoenix reborn from the ashes of war and launched an economic miracle that would eventually challenge the United States. In the fourth case total surrender reinforced Japan's historic memories of dependency on the West and rekindled Japan's ambition to catch up with the West to achieve equal status.

In the immediate aftermath of the war, Japan's business, political, and military leaders were punished by economic reforms and by the Tokyo War Crimes Tribunal. Reform and punishment were aimed at laying down a new road to democracy by controlling Japan's economic and military base of power. Under U.S. Army General Douglas MacArthur, Supreme Commander for the Allied Powers (SCAP), the Allied forces occupied Japan. SCAP staff members wrote and imposed the 1947 Peace Constitution, famous for its no war, Article 9 clause. Events in Asia, however, soon reversed these reforms.

In the post-1945 Asian security environment, the overriding factor that influenced U.S.-Japan relations was Soviet power. Allied perception of Soviet power and intentions changed dramatically from expedient ally during the war to ideological foe after the war. In addition to territorial gains from the Yalta agreement, the Soviet Union was seen as the linchpin in an international communist coalition against Western democracies. George Kennan, as "Mr. X," authored his celebrated assessment of Soviet capabilities and goals in July, 1947, articulating the basis for the American Cold War containment policy. Global events supported this image of the Soviet threat: the creation of communist regimes in Eastern Europe after 1945; the Berlin blockade in June, 1948; communist seizure of power by MAO ZEDONG in China in 1949; and the KOREAN WAR of 1950-1953.

The upshot of this Cold War mindset was the integration of Japan into a U.S.-Japan security arrangement that dominated the post-1945 years. Nowhere is this better seen than in NSC-48/1 and NSC-48/2, two top-secret documents issued by the U.S. National Security Council outlining the Allied priority of containing and reducing Soviet power and influence in Asia. Only four years after Japan's unconditional surrender, the SCAP

resurrected business leaders of powerful wartime conglomerates (*zaibatsu*) to lead Japan's postwar economic recovery. In August of 1950 the SCAP established a National Police Reserve, which in 1954 was reorganized into Japan's Self-Defense Forces. In September of 1951 Prime Minister Yoshida Shigeru signed the Security Treaty. Revised in 1960 as the Treaty of Mutual Cooperation and Security, this bilateral security arrangement has served as the cornerstone for U.S-Japan containment of Soviet influence in Asia.

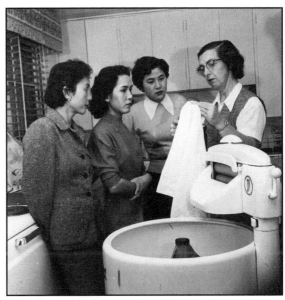

Japanese women learning the rudiments of domesticity in American-occupied Japan. (National Archives)

With U.S. occupation forces and the nuclear umbrella protecting Japan from external threats, Japan concentrated on rebuilding the national economy. Stimulated by the Korean War, Japan's economy was poised for an amazing recovery and phenomenal growth. From the mid-1950's through the decade of the 1960's, Japan's economy grew at a rate slightly in excess of 9 percent per year. Mass affluence and prosperity created optimism and worker security.

With voter sentiment bouyed by an expanding economy, the conservative and probusiness Liberal Democratic Party consistently won elections, thus lending a degree of stability to the U.S.-Japan bilateral arrangement. This mood of good times was enhanced by U.S.-Japan negotiations resolving territorial issues stemming from World War II. In 1968 and 1969 control of the Bonin Islands and Okinawa reverted back to Japan. Few observers in 1950 could foresee that thirty years down the road, Japan's economic giant would challenge the United States for global economic leadership.

Shocks and Rifts in the Partnership. Both sides of the U.S.-Japan partnership could point to evidence of success and mutual benefits flowing from cooperation. Yet the success and stability of this relationship masked some fundamental changes in interest and power. If political, economic, or military arrangements are to work effectively, they must accommodate the shifting structure of power and interest of its members. Cumulative postwar changes surfaced in the 1970's in the form of rifts with major implications for the future of the U.S.-Japan relationship.

As the decade of the 1970's opened, the United States faced two major concerns with Japan: a growing trade imbalance and an emerging view that Japan should assume a larger share of the Pacific defense burden. In the United States escalating costs for welfare programs and the Vietnam War (1965-1975) increased political concerns about U.S. revenue sources and mounting deficits. U.S. export businesses, faced with increasing competition in textiles, steel, electronics, cars, and shipbuilding, began to blame restrictive market practices in Japan.

Variations of the military free-ride criticism appeared in the media, suggesting that Japan prospered economically and unfairly because the U.S. government

U.S. secretary of state Henry Kissinger is greeted by Chinese government officials at a Beijing airport in 1971. His secret negotiations with the Chinese paved the way for U.S. president Richard Nixon's historical visit in 1972—a move that deepened the rift in U.S.-Japan relations. (National Archives)

paid for Japan's military protection. These kinds of criticisms mirrored a more fundamental, structural change. The success of Japan's economic recovery had altered the bilateral structure of economic power and generated new interests and tensions in the U.S.-Japan relationship.

Four shocks jolted the general stability and goodwill of U.S.-Japan relations. The first shock centered on the textile dispute of 1969-1970. Pressured by the closure of American textile mills and Southern electoral votes, President Richard M. Nixon demanded a textile agreement favorable to U.S. textile industries in the South. Prime Minister Sato Eisaku failed to get a consensus on export limits because of opposition from the powerful Ministry of International Trade and Industry (MITI) and the Japanese textile industry. Failed negotiations escalated acrimony and inflexibility on both sides of the bargaining table and damaged the bilateral relationship.

The second shock to the U.S.-Japan relationship was Nixon's resumption of diplomatic relations with the People's Republic of China in 1971-1972. Japanese leaders were chagrined, but not by Secretary of State Henry A. Kissinger's secret diplomacy or by the U.S. initiative to seek new opportunities in the Sino-Soviet rift. Instead the disquietude in Tokyo was caused by the virtual absence of U.S. prior consultation with Japan, especially on a matter of such geopolitical importance to Japan. This China shock drove home the central message: In the eyes of Washington, Japan was not an equal in the Tokyo-Washington partnership.

Shock number three occurred in mid-1971, when the U.S. unilaterally aborted the gold standard and initiated currency revaluation in an effort to counter mounting U.S. trade deficits and inflation. A burgeoning trade surplus made Japan a principal target, but in truth the U.S. decision was directed more at the European Common Market's preferential system. U.S. officials hoped that a floating exchange rate and dollar devaluation would increase U.S. exports to Japan's domestic markets and halt the drain on U.S. gold. Washington's unilateral action unraveled currency markets in Tokyo, shifted blame for U.S. economic woes to Japan, and affronted Tokyo's expectation of prior consultation.

A fourth shock that strained U.S.-Japan relations was the oil embargo associated with the Yom-Kippur War of October, 1973. Arab members in the Organization of Petroleum Exporting Countries (OPEC), reacting to U.S. support for Israel, implemented a cutoff of oil supplies to the United States. For Japan this first oil-shock created a major dilemma. If Japan, highly dependent on Middle Eastern oil imports, backed the U.S.'s pro-Israeli policy, it would risk oil cutoffs by antagonizing Arab oil producers. Japan opted for continued access to Iranian and Iraqi oil supplies. From Japan's point of view, U.S. policy put Japan's interests at risk by threatening oil deliveries, pushing energy prices upward, and creating inflationary pressures inimical to Japan's economic growth.

For Japan the four shocks drove home the lesson that domestic and global changes were driving a wedge between Tokyo and Washington. In both countries the four shocks caused reactions that ranged from angst to anger. Increasingly, audible concerns were voiced by business and political leaders about the purpose and necessity of the U.S.-Japan partnership.

End of Japan's Dependency and Rising Tensions. Although the security alliance remained on solid footing, strains in U.S.-Japan relations intensified in the 1980's, mirroring economic and political changes in both countries. Dubbed by the media as the "Ron-Yasu" connection, the two heads of state, President Ronald Reagan and Prime Minister Nakasone Yasuhiro, projected an image of U.S.-Japan cooperation. Both shared a conservative ideology and a Cold War worldview supported by their respective military establishments and defense industries. Behind this appearance of cooperation, disputes grew increasingly acrimonious over trade, defense cost-sharing, and global diplomacy.

The trade balance between any two countries is a function of several factors: savings, investment, productivity, transport costs, market access, currency exchange rates, and government policies. For a variety of cultural and economic reasons, the quantitative and qualitative measures of these factors vary considerably for the United States and Japan. Trade imbalances began to show up in the late 1970's, growing to huge trade deficits for the United States in the 1980's. The U.S. bilateral trade deficit with Japan, slightly under $16 billion in 1980, more than doubled to $33.5 billion in 1984, escalated to $55 billion in 1987, decreased to $38 billion in 1990, but then edged up again over the next two years to $43.6 billion in 1992. Politicians, labor unions, impacted industries, and xenophobic groups in both countries hurled blame and invective across the ocean, diverting attention away from underlying systemic causes.

As U.S. trade deficits (or conversely Japan's trade surplus), business bankruptcies, plant closures, and unemployment rose, mutual recrimination grew more

President Ronald Reagan and Japanese prime minister Nakasone Yasuhiro projected an image of U.S.-Japan cooperation and goodwill during the latter's visit to Washington, D.C., in April-May of 1987 to discuss trade issues with Reagan and members of Congress. (AP/Wide World Photos)

shrill. Both sides perceived unfair trade practices or restrictive policies by the other. In Japan rice and citrus farmers burned American cars. In the United States, Congress passed restrictive legislation, such as the Omnibus Trade and Competitiveness Act of 1988, including a section that targeted Japanese exports to the United States. In Japan, Ishihara Shintaro, a member of the Japanese Diet, argued in a controversial book in 1988 that Japan was strong enough to take care of its own defense and to stand up and say no to the United States. The incidence of anti-Asian hate crimes rose in the United States, a phenomenon which, the U.S. Civil Rights Commission concluded, was associated with trade and economic friction. In this climate of mistrust, Japan bashing and America bashing made front-page headlines in both countries.

Political tensions escalated, even in areas formerly defined by cooperation, such as military programs. The U.S. government adamantly argued that Japan was getting a free ride on defense and demanded that Japan pay for more of the cost of U.S. troops in Japan. Weapons coproduction efforts barely survived several rounds of testy negotiations. U.S.-Japan relations came under fire in late 1989 and early 1990 during the Persian Gulf War. In spite of Japan's contribution of some $9 billion, U.S. officials scored Japan for failing to contribute more money and actual troops. Japan's leadership was especially stung by the criticism that characterized Japan's help as "checkbook diplomacy" hiding behind the no war clause.

Global Competitive Partnership. Japan and the United States are two economic giants going head-to-head, competing for leadership in a world undergoing economic transformation. In 1985-1986 Japan edged slightly ahead of the United States as the world's leading creditor nation while the latter became the world's leading debtor nation. Since 1987 the two countries have been vying for the title of number one donor in overseas development assistance measured in absolute dollars. Globally the two countries rank first and second in gross national product (GNP), with Japan's GNP running about 65 percent that of the U.S. GNP. Both nations are the envy of the world in terms of leading-edge technology, higher education, and product research and development.

Looking ahead the United States will continue to lead the world in GNP, but Japan will narrow the gap. Both nations face economic slowdowns because of limited resources, environmental pollution, and social demand for improved health and welfare. Both nations are so economically integrated in trade, direct investments, and finance that the resulting degree of interde-

pendence will override friction and maintain the partnership. Both nations will, however, seek out new regional arrangements in their national interest.

Japan's continuing effort to catch up with the West is reflected in Tokyo's search for an expanded role in the global community (*kokusaika*). Japan's search for diplomatic status commensurate with its economic power will look to a permanent seat on the United Nations (UN) Security Council and a greater voting role in international economic organizations. The Japanese emperor's apology to China in 1992, participation in UN peace-keeping operations in Cambodia, and goodwill trips to Association of Southeast Asian Nations (ASEAN) countries all point to the importance that Japan assigns to a greater regional role in the Pacific Basin and Southeast Asia. The United States also has made commitments to regional integration in North America and Mexico.—*David T. Yamada*

World leaders attending a Tokyo summit of industrialized nations in 1986 pose for a group photograph. Approaching the twenty-first century, the United States and Japan are the envy of the world because of their technological capability, higher education, and product research and development. (AP/Wide World Photos)

SUGGESTED READINGS:

- Finn, Richard B., ed. *U.S.-Japan Relations: Learning from Competition.* New Brunswick, N.J.: Transaction Books, 1986. *This book is part of a continuing, annual series under the auspices of the Harvard Program on U.S.-Japan Relations. Essays focus on industrial policy, defense and security issues, and financial liberalization. This particular annual edition is interesting because it was published at a time when Japan's burgeoning trade surplus preoccupied analysts' attention.*

- Iriye, Akira, and Warren Cohen, eds. *The United States and Japan in the Postwar World.* Lexington: University Press of Kentucky, 1989. This collection of essays addresses three themes in the U.S.-Japan relationship: an overview of post-1945 relations dominated by the United States; the role of trade in a changing world economy; and issues and problems stemming from the transformation of national power and global roles.

- Kawai, Kazuo. *Japan's American Interlude.* Chicago: University of Chicago Press, 1960. The chief value of this volume is the author's explanation of the Allied occupation and the SCAP's economic and political reforms in post-1945 Japan from the Japanese point of view. Highly readable, this book offers many psychological and cultural insights.

- Morley, James W., ed. *The Pacific Basin: New Challenges for the United States.* New York: Academy of Political Science, Columbia University, 1986. Although this volume of essays does not focus specifically on the U.S.-Japan relationship, it provides a useful reminder that bilateral relations take on significance when seen in larger, geographical frameworks. In this case the larger framework is the Pacific Basin, with a section that addresses U.S. economic and security interests.

- Nagai, Yonosuke, and Akira Iriye, eds. *The Origins of the Cold War in Asia.* New York: Columbia University Press, 1977. This volume presents differing views by specialists from the United States, Japan, and Europe on the root causes of Cold War thinking and policies in Asia. Based on papers presented at a Kyoto conference in 1975, this book reflects scholarly thinking at an important point in the transition of U.S.-Japan relations.

- Patrick, Hugh T., and Ryuichiro Tachi, eds. *Japan and the United States Today.* New York: Center on Japanese Economy and Business, Columbia University, 1986. This book brings together the views of policymakers and academic specialists from Japan and the United States, who cover three important areas that impact U.S.-Japan relations: financial markets, exchange rates, and macroeconomic policy. There are some useful tables and graphs. Comments on future implications are insightful.

- Vogel, Ezra F. *Japan as Number One: Lessons for America.* Cambridge, Mass.: Harvard University Press, 1979. As one of the first major books that stimulated U.S. preoccupation with Japan's postwar success, it examines key factors that explain Japan's economic miracle: state guidance, group solidarity, educational system, corporate productivity, and social support systems. Vogel suggests that Japan's success provides a model for the United States to emulate.

- Weinstein, Franklin B., ed. *U.S.-Japan Relations and the Security of East Asia.* Boulder, Colo.: Westview Press, 1978. Asian specialists address issues that go to the heart of the U.S.-Japan security arrangement: defense capabilities for Japan and the role of the U.S. nuclear umbrella. This volume is noteworthy because it raises questions about the unity of the mutual security pact and the importance of Korea to Japan's security strategy.

- Wolferen, Karel van. *The Enigma of Japanese Power.* New York: Vintage Books, 1990. Although unsympathetic to the Japanese point of view, the author presents some intriguing arguments about Japanese society, cultural myths, and the role of state guidance and industrial policy. By critically examining Japanese society, power, and policy-making, this readable book raises questions about misperceptions that affect the U.S.-Japan relationship.

U.S.-Japan trade conflict: Like the classic film *Rashomon* (1951), trade conflict between the United States and Japan is often a matter of perception, and it is sometimes difficult to know who is telling the truth. Ambiguity is compounded by the complex structure of trade, the adversarial management of trade issues, and transformation of the global economy and international power. World stability may well depend on whether these two economic giants pursue a course of collision or cooperation.

Structure of Trade Conflict. Export markets have been vital to the political and economic development of the two nations. External trade is a strategy of earning hard currency for capital investment and economic growth at home. As long as export markets are expanding and nonconflicting, bilateral trade proceeds without incident; but when export markets contract and threaten domestic constituents, then hostility and con-

Ford Motor Company workers picket a suburban Detroit, Michigan, Toyota dealership in February, 1992, to protest Japanese auto imports. (Jim West)

flict are likely to arise. Usually this threat is defined in terms of market and policy obstacles to exports; product or sectorial competition seen as the cause of declining home industries and rising unemployment; and structural shifts in power and status. All three of these conditions define U.S.-Japan trade relations and, hence, the escalation of trade conflict.

Beginning in the 1960's Japan mass-produced and distributed quality products at prices at or below those of its competitors. On the one hand this comparative advantage dramatically expanded Japanese exports to U.S. markets, especially in textiles, steel, motor vehicles, electronic products, computer chips, and machine tools, but at the cost of growing American resentment. On the other hand the U.S. comparative advantage in some sectors (such as rice, construction trades, and financial services) has yielded minimum market access and maximum American frustration.

Consequently each side views the other as the trade culprit. The United States perceives Japan's governmental protection of noncompetitive industries, complex bureaucratic requirements, and retail practices as

rooted in culture, as unfair barriers that deny American businesses access to Japan's domestic markets. Japan perceives U.S. laws, such as the Omnibus Trade and Competitiveness Act of 1988, as protectionist and retaliatory. The U.S. government sees Japanese markets as an unfair playing field and Japanese exports to the United States as a cause of plant closings, business foreclosures, and loss of jobs. Japan views American trade efforts and policy as a combination of whining, impatience, failure to reform deficits and infrastructure, a threat to Japanese culture (as in the case of traditional rice-farming), and latent racism.

At bottom, trade hostility and conflict between the two countries are linked to the transformation of the two economies. Japan's economic growth and the United States' declining infrastructure have substantially narrowed the gap in economic power, but Japan's subordinate diplomatic and political status remains problematic. U.S. bilateral trade deficits, media bashing, xenophobia, and protectionism are symptomatic of this economic transformation.

Management of Trade Conflict. Trade disagree-

U.S. president Bill Clinton (left) and Japan prime minister Kiichi Miyazawa exchange words during a session of delegation leaders at Akasaka Palace, Tokyo, in July of 1993. The two were part of a summit conference of the G-7 industrialized nations that gathered to discuss global economic issues. (AP/Wide World Photos)

ments can be handled bilaterally or multilaterally. At either level success in resolving trade conflict depends mainly on three factors: corporate goals and strategies, domestic political pressures, and the ability of negotiating parties to reach common definitions of ends and means.

U.S.-Japan trade talks are locked into a tradition of goals, strategies, and values that generate clashing perceptions. First, when a Japanese company lowers unit cost to increase market share, this sort of trade action inevitably conflicts with an American company that wants to protect higher profit margins driven by quarterly accountability to shareholders. Second, domestic political forces exert major constraints on the ability of policymakers to achieve consensus on conflicting trade issues. Rice, citrus, textiles, electronics, steel, or autos represent much more than jobs and industry; they are subcultures, institutions, and a way of life in both countries. Third, trade problems are exacerbated by different economic philosophies: The United States advocates privatization and deregulated free markets, but Japan practices a neomercantilist policy of protecting selected industries.

In spite of these difficulties several bilateral and multilateral strategies have evolved to deal with U.S.-Japan trade conflict. Among the major instruments are the General Agreement on Tariffs and Trade (GATT);

market-oriented, sector-selective talks; economic summit meetings of the five and seven industrial nations, dubbed "G-5" and "G-7," respectively; government studies and white papers, such as Japan's Mayakawa Report of 1985; and bilateral talks by heads of state and by the Office of the U.S. Trade Representative and Japan's ministerial counterparts. All these strategies seek to liberalize trade, reduce trade barriers, and increase market access.

Collision Course or Cooperation? The U.S. trade deficit with Japan was in the $15-20 billion range between 1981 and 1983, ballooned to $55-56 billion in the mid-1980's, and receded to the $38-42 billion range in the early 1990's. Citing Japan's unfair market barriers, Congress retaliated with the Omnibus Trade Act of 1988 and the Trade Expansion Act of 1992. Three of Japan's key government ministries on trade issues—the Ministry of Trade and Industry (MITI), Construction Trades, and Agriculture and Fisheries—have shown little willingness to back down from protecting their constituent industries. Compounded by recession and economic slowdown during the early 1990's, the war of words has escalated.

Both the United States and Japan realize how economically interdependent they are. As of 1993 about 31 percent of Japan's exports go to the United States and 12 percent of U.S. exports end up in Japan. Other factors mitigate trade conflict. For example the highly publicized U.S. trade deficit with Japan measures only trade in merchandise. This deficit goes down by as much as 28 percent if the U.S. trade surplus is subtracted. Between 1985 and 1992 the United States has run a trade deficit with every major trading country (Canada, Hong Kong, South Korea, Singapore, Taiwan, and China) except the European Community. Trade policymakers also realize that Japan's direct investment in the United States generates American jobs and that Japan's purchase of U.S. government bonds and other debt instruments helps to pay for U.S. domestic programs.

Graffiti on a Detroit freeway overpass in 1992. (Jim West)

Undeniably U.S.-Japan trade conflict is substantial and serious. Adjusting trade imbalances will require compromise and reform in several areas: savings, investment, productivity, transportation, market access, government policies, and currency exchange rates. Time-consuming Japanese consensus will try American impatience, but if pragmatism prevails, a much-feared collision between these two economic giants may be averted.—*David T. Yamada*

SUGGESTED READINGS: • Blaker, Michael, ed. *The Politics of Trade: U.S. and Japanese Policymaking for the GATT Negotiations.* New York: Columbia University, 1978. • Cohen, Stephen D. "United States-Japanese Trade Relations." *Current History* 90:555 (April, 1991): 152-155, 184-187. • Inoguchi, Takashi. *Japan's International Relations.* Boulder, Colo.: Westview Press, 1991. • Inoguchi, Takashi, and Daniel I. Okimoto. *The Political Economy of Japan.* Vol. 2. Stanford, Calif.: Stanford University Press, 1988. • Lincoln, Edward J. *Japan's Unequal Trade.* Washington, D.C.: Brookings Institution, 1990. • Yamamura,

Kozo, ed. *Policy and Trade Issues of the Japanese Economy.* Seattle: University of Washington Press, 1982.

U.S.-Japan Treaty of Amity and Commerce (Mar. 31, 1854): Treaty between the United States and Japan in which the Japanese agreed to open two isolated Japanese ports to American ships for supplies and limited trade. The two ports were Shimoda, on Izu Peninsula, and Hakodate, on the island of Hokkaido, the northernmost of the four main Japanese islands. The Japanese also agreed to allow an American consulate to be stationed at Shimoda and to treat well American sailors shipwrecked in Japan. The treaty, which was negotiated by Commodore Matthew C. Perry shortly after his arrival in Japan, marked the end of the seclusionary policy of the Tokugawa shogunate.

U.S.-Japan Treaty of Commerce and Navigation (1894): Stipulation giving citizens of both countries the right to "enter, travel, or reside" anywhere in the territory of the other and while there to "enjoy full and perfect protection for their persons and property." The treaty also gave them the privilege of conducting trade there as well. Yet it also reserved to the United States the right to deny entry to Japanese immigrants.

U.S.-Korea relations: Only since about 1950 have relations between the United States and Korea been "meaningful." The relationship between the two countries is therefore relatively young. Yet their recent relations have been most intense and eventful largely because the United States saw the Korean peninsula from different angles depending upon the former's own international standing. The relationship has been a strategic partnership that has had to overcome disadvantages of notable geographical distance and cultural differences. Arguably such a relationship has reflected more global undertones than bilateral issues.

The "Hermit Kingdom" of Korea. Until the waning moments of the nineteenth century, the Hermit Kingdom of Choson maintained foreign relations with only China, its longtime cultural and political ally. Even when the region was engulfed by the wholesale Western incursion, Taewon-gun, who ruled as a regent the ancient kingdom for the pivotal period of 1863 to 1873, resolutely insisted on remaining isolated from the "barbarian" Western world. Lacking both a progressive spirit and knowledge of international affairs, the inward Choson court refused to open its doors to foreign powers until forced to do so by outsiders. Even after it signed, under duress, a treaty with Japan in 1876, the court of King Kojong signally rejected Western overtures.

The West did not leave Korea alone in that time of high mercantilism; the United States was the first Western power that extracted from the Korean court a concession of normal diplomatic relations. In 1882, the Choson and U.S. governments signed a treaty, thus commencing their eventful relations. Although the United States was a distant nation of which the Choson court did not have even a basic understanding, the treaty was typical of the time. It was not the nature of the treaty but the way that it materialized that effectively set an atypical tone in early U.S.-Korea relations.

It was the Choson court that rejected the United States' repeated overtures for normal treaty relations after the Choson-Japan treaty. Spurned by the Choson court, the American delegation sought Chinese help. The Qing court, desperately in need of a counterbalance for rapidly growing Japanese influence in Korea, readily offered its assistance. Qing officials not only advised the Choson court to enter treaty relations with the United States but itself initiated negotiations with the American delegation without even seeking the Choson court's sanction. Only after the two parties had completed the negotiations did the Chinese inform the Koreans of what had transpired. Handicapped by its almost total lack of diplomatic experience with the West, the Choson court was obliged to sign the treaty.

Korea's Open-Door Policy. The new treaty was a product of the Chinese ploy to bring the American presence into Korea, where China faced a stiff challenge from the Japanese. The Qing court insisted throughout the negotiations on inserting a clause establishing China's suzerainty over Korea. China was obsessed with obtaining American consent for this attempt to gain sovereign control of the Choson court. American negotiators successfully foiled the blatant Qing attempts by categorically rejecting the clause. Nevertheless, by negotiating the treaty with the Chinese officials and not with the Koreans, the rightful negotiation party, the Americans did implicitly acknowledge the existence of the uncommon Chinese influence in Korea.

Li Hongzhang, representing the Qing court in Korea, failed to achieve his primary goal in the treaty. Yet China managed to bring the United States, a growing Pacific Western power, into Korea's already unruly political landscape, intending to use the Americans as a counterweight to the Japanese in Korea. Qing policymakers were unable to dissuade Western powers from exploiting China for commercial gain, but they adhered to the unrealistic Middle Kingdom mentality in Korea. China made a pivotal concession to the Americans by agreeing that Korea was a free, independent nation, yet it had no intention of allowing Choson to exercise freely its sovereign rights.

The American government was eager to sign a treaty with Korea to prevent naval accidents such as the one encountered by the merchant ship GENERAL SHERMAN, which was burnt by the Koreans in 1856 in Pyongyang. Furthermore, the United States was convinced that only an independent Korea could assume the responsibilities imposed by the treaty for similar naval accidents. Thus the United States thwarted Li Hung-chang's ploy largely for its own good rather than for Korea's political integrity. Yet despite its objection of Qing encroachment in Korea, the United States had no intention of sacrificing its growing commercial interests in China for the sake of Korea, a virtual economic insignificance in the late 1880's. The American Korean policy at this juncture was merely the maintenance of normal relations. It attached neither political nor commercial significance to this small, curious kingdom. Pursuing such a limited objective the Americans intended to remain aloof so as not to side with any of the Asian powers in their incessant competition for a supreme political influence in Korea.

A Noncommittal American Government. King Kojong, the young and innocent monarch, was very much interested in enlisting American support in his longtime desire to curb the ever-worsening power struggle among the Asian powers in his kingdom. The king placed high hopes on the United States in his discreet campaign to restore the kingdom's political integrity. His personal attempt at American diplomacy was neither refined nor effective, for the king and his close advisers understood little of the highly complex diplomatic maneuver the Americans undertook to navigate the delicate regional politics of the time. Furthermore, whenever the king was able to secure a communication channel to Washington, itself a considerable feat under the circumstances, the Chinese often managed to spoil his efforts. The Hermit Kingdom of Korea was hardly a match for the Middle Kingdom of China in Washington politics.

In spite of Washington's passive political posture in Korea, many Americans were active in organizing various social institutions for the kingdom. Horace ALLEN greatly assisted in founding the kingdom's first Western-style medical clinic, while Horace Underwood started the systematic propagation of Protestantism in Korea. Many Christian churches soon began to offer educational programs introducing the Western cultures systematically for the first time. Those pioneering Americans' unselfish contributions quickly turned America into the trusted friends of the Koreans. Still, the American government remained pro-China and pro-Japan, distancing itself from the small kingdom, which was suffering from the most hazardous geopolitics of the region. Washington's cool, aloof treatment of Korea at this time was based on the former's near-sighted diplomacy calculated to safeguard its political interests in the region.

King Kojong's failure to enlist the United States' political support in his desperate attempt to check the Japanese aggression allowed the rivalry between China and Japan to reach the boiling point 1884. The Gapsin Jungbyun, a bloody skirmish between the Japanese-backed reformists and the Chinese-backed conservatives in the Choson court, furnished the two rivals with a timely excuse for military intervention. China managed to overshadow Japan to some extent, yet neither won a decisive round. The sole loser was Choson, as the two aggressors made a truce at its expense. The United States remained neutral but generally went along with the Western ministers stationed in Seoul.

U.S.-Japan Alliance in Korea. With its war victory over China in 1895, Japan effectively eliminated China as a contender in Korea. Once its domination

Staunchly pro-Japanese, the U.S. government refused to recognize nationalist Syngman Rhee (shown here) and the Korean Provisional Government in exile until after World War II had begun. (The Korea Society/Los Angeles)

was secured, Japan led the Western powers in expropriating commercial rights from the Choson court. Although Japan was taking the lion's share, the United States also participated in the commercial exploitation of Korea. When the initial division was over, Japan

While the rest of the world looked on with indifference, Korean nationalists living in America continued the fight against the Japanese occupation. Korean-established flight schools such as this one in Willows, California, in 1920 existed to train aviators for service to the mother country back home. (University of Southern California East Asian Library)

Korean Americans sympathetic to the plight of Japanese-occupied Korea urged the U.S. government to resist the Japanese war machine. (University of Southern California East Asian Library)

began to purchase the rights secured by the Western powers to further its overwhelming holding. Japan's incessant aggression drove the Choson court to seek the political support of the Russians, who enthusiastically assumed the role of the new Japanese competition in Korea. Still, the United States maintained a stand favorable to Japan, overlooking Japan's open aggression in Korea.

Shocking the world community, Japan was victorious in its war against Russia in 1904-1905. The outcome of the Russo-Japanese War most of all signaled the arrival of a mature and powerful Japan, which had been the product of extensive Westernization efforts for the last four decades. It also meant that Japan had eliminated its last foreign competition in Korea. After the war Japan wasted no time in undertaking procedures for open annexation of Korea. An American government that pursued similar expansion policies at home willingly acknowledged the presence of Japan's

profound interests in Korea. In 1905 the United States and Japan signed the Taft-Katsura Agreement, in which the United States guaranteed Japan's free hand in Korea in exchange for Japan's recognition of American hegemony in the Philippines. The same year U.S. president Theodore Roosevelt condoned the Japanese takeover of Korea's diplomatic functions. Shortly thereafter Japan forced Korea to sign a treaty of protection, the first step toward the eventual annexation of Korea in 1910. By then Korea had become a lost member of the world community, which conveniently overlooked Japan's glaring violation of international law and order. Like all other foreign countries, the United States withdrew its legation in Seoul after the annexation.

For most of Japan's long colonial rule of Korea (see CHOSON), the United States sided with the Japanese. The Americans objected to Japan's aggression in China but maintained a long silence in the matter of

Korea. In spite of lobbying by religious leaders who went to Korea and observed the Korean people's undying aspiration for independence, Washington did not alter its pro-Japan stand. Even Syngman RHEE's persistent lobbying was not enough to persuade the U.S. state department to receive him as a representative of the Korean Provisional Government in exile. The United States steadfastly valued the Japanese friendship more than the Korean people's inherent right to decide their own fate, to have their own government. Even Korea's phenomenal MARCH FIRST MOVEMENT of 1919, inspired by U.S. president Woodrow Wilson's famous "Fourteen Points" doctrine, did not have much effect on Washington's indifference to the Korean plight.

Pacific War and Korea. The American honeymoon with Japan ended abruptly when war between the two broke out in 1941. Only then did the United States rediscover the strategic value of the Korean peninsula, which served not only as a vital source of raw materials and labor for the Japanese military machine but also as a convenient operational base for Japan's China front. In 1943, the United States and its allies announced that at the conclusion of the war all Japanese territories acquired since 1894 would be returned to their rightful owners. The Allies made clear that Korea should "in due time" become a free and independent nation. Thus was born an American progressive postwar Korea policy that was radically different from the prewar period, perhaps more than anything reflecting the fact that the U.S. sphere of influence now extended to the East Asian mainland for the first time.

The United States' new Korea policy was based on the ultimate goal of establishing a free, independent nation. Yet the policy was a part of the postwar solution for Japan rather than a solution for sovereign Korea. The difference was not subtle; as a solution with Japan in mind, the plan proposed to divide the

American naval and Marine personnel of the battle cruiser USS Guam *pose for a photograph beneath an archway welcoming them to Inchon in U.S.-occupied southern Korea, December, 1945.* (AP/Wide World Photos)

Korean peninsula into two spheres of influence even before the anticipated liberation. As an apparent reward for its entry into the war against Japan, the United States allowed the Soviet Union to occupy Korea north of the thirty-eighth parallel. The United States was to occupy the southern part upon a Japanese surrender. For Washington planners this would have been a temporary arrangement needed to form a central government in Seoul. From the outset, however, the Soviet Union did not share this objective.

It was the Soviet Red Army that arrived in Korea first; a dispirited Japanese army offered only light resistance. In fact, the Red Army had enough time to occupy the whole peninsula. By the end of August, 1945, the Soviet Union had completed the occupation of the northern half, stopping its southward thrust at the prearranged thirty-eighth parallel. On September 8 the U.S. Eighth Army began to arrive under the command of General John R. Hodge. Upon accepting official surrender from the Japanese forces in southern Korea, the Americans set up an occupation government. The American military's early goal of maintaining strict political neutrality was quickly abandoned when the Communists' sweeping infiltration throughout the southern half of Korea was revealed. As a result, the occupation government's main task for the

period 1945 to 1947 was eradication of Communist cells by force. Forming a de facto alliance with the anti-Communist faction led by Syngman Rhee, the occupiers collaborated with the newly born Korean national police to suppress Communist activities in the South. As the nationwide anti-Communist campaigns began, a negotiated settlement between the North and South became a mere mirage. The United States resorted to the creation of a government for the South, while the Soviet Union did the same for the North. This officially occurred in 1948, when the country was partitioned into South Korea and North Korea. Rhee (South Korea) and KIM IL SUNG (North Korea) assumed control over the new governments both with the same hope of reunifying the land, but each hoped to do so under the banner of his own respective regime.

Two Koreas and the War. The American Korea policy during the postwar period was so fluid in nature that it is difficult even to characterize it. U.S. policy was formulated with little reflection or strategy. Its early plan, a United Nations (UN) trusteeship for a lengthy period, was met coolly by its allies, even before it was categorically rejected by the Koreans. The trusteeship drive was a clear indication that American planners did not understand the Korean temperament and, even more important, the rich political tradition in

General Douglas MacArthur (center) confers with a South Korean official while in South Korea to inspect American defenses, July, 1950. (AP/Wide World Photos)

At Inchon, U.S. Marines (foreground) inspect the trenches of the late and departed North Korean troops in September, 1950. (U.S. Marine Corps Photo)

the region. Even after the Rhee government had been installed in the south, Washington did not attach much strategic significance to the peninsula; the United States was most reluctant in providing the South with the financial resources necessary to build a national defense force comparable to that of the North. As an American official's open remarks indicated, Korea was merely a small legacy of Japanese imperialism and not within the U.S. defense perimeter for that region.

On June 25, 1950, the North launched a full-scale invasion of the South. The well-planned Communist war machine quickly overran the utterly unprepared, lightly equipped, and numerically inferior forces of the Rhee government. This sudden turn of events forced Washington to transform its Korea policy from reluctant aloofness to active involvement. The Americans characterized the war from the outset as the international Communist camp's active challenge to the Free World. Such a hasty conclusion was possible because Washington was by then extensively preoccupied by a looming East-West confrontation, one that would be based on ideological incompatibility. Thus, it moved quickly to denounce the aggression from the interna-

tional perspective. Kim Il Sung's likely motive for the war, unification of the nation under his banner, was conveniently buried by U.S. officials. Instead the conflict was elevated to a great Communist conspiracy to conquer the world.

Under the circumstances, the United States had to utilize all available resources to repeal the aggression. Military intervention was a foregone conclusion. Yet the way in which the United States intervened militarily was to have broad ramifications for the course of the war. Washington, in conducting the Western war effort, wanted the authorization of the UN. The UN Security Council readily backed the American move, thus assuming legal authority to use force against the Communists as a police action. Although neither the North nor the South was a member of the UN, the conflict between them became a matter on which the UN authorized the use of arms. Washington instructed General Douglas MacArthur, the Supreme Commander for the Allied Powers (SCAP) in Japan, to dispatch his own forces to Korea while steps were being taken for a major transpacific mobilization of forces. Immediately MacArthur brought small contingents to the Korean front to bolster the South Korean forces' defense ef-

High explosives rip through several spans of a railroad bridge outside Hamhung, North Korea, in December, 1950. UN forces withdrawing from the region destroyed the bridge to prevent its use by Chinese Communist troops. (AP/Wide World Photos)

forts. Yet MacArthur's forces, drawn from mostly non-combat personnel of the occupation command, were largely symbolic; their presence failed to slow the momentum of the North's near-blitz advance.

The UN forces, from the United States and sixteen other UN member nations, continued their retreat under the relentless pressure. By August the defenders had reached the Naktong perimeter, the last defendable front that enclosed the small southeastern region. Along the front U.S. and South Korean forces waged a desperate campaign against determined Communist forces, who may have sensed imminent victory. While reinforcements were arriving from the United States, the defenders held the front, barely escaping total collapse time after time. While the North was unable to inflict a fatal blow overrunning the front completely, the tide of the war was slowly turning. Using the standoff at the front, MacArthur's forces made a daring landing at Inchon, the port city twenty miles from Seoul, effectively ending any hope of Kim's swift military victory. By the end of September, UN forces had recaptured Seoul and extended their operation north of the thirty-eighth parallel, inflicting heavy casualties on the retreating Communist forces.

The Inchon landing aside, the UN forces had enjoyed prohibitive advantages over the North Korean forces ever since the front had moved to the southern region. UN troops secured total air superiority from the outset, gradually limiting the invasion forces' battle capability as the front's southern location exposed the invaders' long, difficult supply lines. Soon the Communists were forced to depend solely on nighttime supply efforts to avoid UN warplanes. Another major handicap the invaders encountered was that the whole campaign was designed to last no more than several weeks; UN military leaders were confident that their highly mechanized forces would capture the entire nation quickly, eliminating any opportunity for the foreign forces to intervene. In addition, the North's planners erroneously expected that the South would be sympathetic to the North and would provide local logistical supports. Much to their dismay, however, the South Korean public was militantly against the Communists.

As the combined UN forces made rapid progress, chasing the invaders into North Korea in the winter months of 1950, Washington made a major shift in policy by ordering the takeover of the North. It did not wish to limit its military campaign to recovering the territory south of the thirty-eighth parallel. Instead, Washington was hopeful of achieving a Korean unification under the UN banner, a likely prospect at the time. This revised objective was near to becoming a reality in November, 1950, as UN and South Korean forces reached the banks of the Yalu River, the China-Korea boundary. Then, however, MAO ZEDONG's Communist China entered the war to save Kim from imminent and certain defeat. Under the sudden pressure of numerically superior, fresh forces, the UN undertook costly retreat from the North, surrendering Seoul to the Communists in January, 1951. A war of attrition followed for the next two years among the Communist forces, which ultimately did not have the resources to defeat the UN forces.

With the presence of Chinese forces in Korea, Washington quickly lost its zeal to defeat the Communist forces in Korea. American domestic public opinion was not favorable toward continuing the costly war for this scarcely known nation. In addition, there was a growing concern that U.S. preoccupation with Korea would encourage the Soviet Union and its allies to launch similar, much more consequential military invasions in Europe. Under the circumstances, the United States regarded a status quo in Korea as an acceptable solution. South Koreans were unable to comprehend the United States' sudden unwillingness to seek a military solution after a phenomenal victory only a few months earlier. Regardless, the decision was made in Washington to terminate the war; the UN and North Korea signed a truce in 1953, ending without a firm verdict the civil war that had been elevated to an international ideological war. Kim's intentions aside, the Americans made this conflict the launching point for the ensuing Cold War.

The United States signed a mutual defense treaty with South Korea to diffuse the fear among the South Koreans of another military conflict. With the arrangement South Korea became a key link in the United States' vast containment ring of the Soviet Union. South Korea was now the United States' key military frontier, indispensable in checking international so-

U.S. artillerymen load a shell into a cannon while bombarding North Korean or Chinese Communist troops entrenched along the west-central front of South Korea in March, 1951. (AP/Wide World Photos)

Heavily fortified gateway inside the demilitarized zone, or DMZ, separating North and South Korea. (AP/Wide World Photos)

cialist expansionism. South Korea accepted the role eagerly, painfully realizing the fact that an effective national defense could be guaranteed only by American military might and political support. After the truce the American government reduced its combat troops stationed in South Korea, but it never altered its defense commitment to the Korean people. In addition to the military umbrella it furnished, the United States delivered significant economic aid packages for South Korea's reconstruction efforts. Since the 1950's the United States has been a staunch political supporter of South Korea, and there is no indication that this will change any time soon. South Korea has matched American support with a faith and loyalty that it shares with no other nation in the world.

Military-Political Alliance. When General PARK CHUNG HEE staged a military coup in 1961, evicting the democratically elected government of Prime Minister Chang Myon, the United States experienced a severe setback in its efforts to rebuild South Korea as it had Japan following World War II. Washington was against such interruption of a constitutional government, yet it reversed itself later, providing the new

military regime with the economic and political support needed to complete South Korea's ambitious economic development programs. The military regime's serious efforts toward the normalization of its relations with Japan did not hurt its image in Washington. In spite of its open stand, the United States remained handicapped in pushing South Korea's democratization as long as the latter was expected to serve the American global containment of Communism. As a result, in South Korea military matters became more important than political democracy because of the greater concern for avoiding another military conflict with the North. Washington desired but could not demand South Korea's political democratization at the cost of providing a military opportunity for the Communists.

The Park Administration was the contributor of the largest military contingent to the Vietnam War after the United States. Washington's financial coaxing was a factor, as well as the close cooperation between South Korea and the United States since the liberation. At the same time, however, South Korea's participation reflected its growing confidence over its own destiny, which was drastically improved under the energetic, driving military leadership. It was the Park Administration that adopted an export-oriented growth model influenced by Japan, a notable departure from the consumption-oriented economy from which the Rhee Administration had been unable to escape. Park undertook extensive industrial programs aimed at elevating the nation to an industrial power.

Park's desire to strengthen the nation's industrial capacity turned to desperation when U.S. president Richard M. Nixon issued his Guam Doctrine in 1969. The doctrine, which shocked most American allies in Asia, including the South Koreans, called for a major revision of the American defense commitment in the region. Under the new doctrine the United States would furnish only the military materials and economic assistance but not the troops to help U.S. allies defend themselves against Communist aggression. Although Nixon enunciated the continuation of the American nuclear umbrella in the region, the new doctrine was quickly interpreted as the process of total American withdrawal from Asia. South Korea felt the most vulnerable under the new doctrine because the country had not yet completed the needed modernization of its armed forces. As the Nixon doctrine was being implemented with the withdrawal of one additional combat division from Korea, Park's drive to develop his country's own armament industry became the national obsession.

President Gerald Ford's reassurance calmed South Korea's anxiety somewhat. Yet Park by then was pushing hard for the industrial developments that were needed to build quickly not only the country's armament industry but also its nuclear program. Only under Ford's intense pressure did the Park Administration agree to abandon its nuclear program. Park, however, continued the nation's drive to achieve a self-sufficiency in arms production. By the 1980's South Korea had become a producer of many quality arms except for highly technical items.

President Jimmy Carter's Korea policy was the source of the most serious conflict the two traditional allies have experienced in recent years. During the presidential campaign Carter advocated the withdrawal of all combat troops from South Korea. South Koreans interpreted this chilling message as the United States' intention to abandon its defense commitment to South Korea. They were fully aware of the fact that the North still possessed a significant military superiority over the South. Carter's withdrawal plan collapsed as the Congress and military leaders successfully resisted the idea. Yet Carter remained critical of Park over human rights issues. Carter's concerns were genuine, but the way the demands were made pleased few people in South Korea; most South Koreans believed that their country could not afford the political environment to which Americans were accustomed because of South Korea's unique military-political circumstance.

Although Washington exerted pressure on Seoul for its democratization, Park was succeeded by General CHUN DOO HWAN. President Ronald Reagan adopted more indirect prodding rather than the direct confrontation Carter had applied. As a result, bilateral relations found more harmony in the 1980's. Washington was aware of the changing geopolitical landscape of northeast Asia. A phenomenal success in global mercantilism gave South Korea unprecedented confidence in conducting its foreign affairs. For the first time in history South Korea was reaching the world, even initiating aggressive "northern diplomacy" contacts with Eastern Bloc countries, including the Soviet Union and the People's Republic of China.

New Partnership. By the middle of the 1980's, South Korea's economy had improved, becoming one of the world's most energetic and briefly running a sizable trade surplus against the United States. As South Korea rose as a major trade partner, Washington faced another major adjustment that was necessary but highly delicate. Washington believed that it should uphold its defense commitment as South Korea remained vulnerable to the North militarily. Yet at the same time Washington had to address preventive methods so that South Korea would not become another Japan in trade imbalance. While mutual cooperation in defense matters continued to be amicable, the alliance experienced growing trade frictions during the 1990's. Washington's other serious concern, South Korea's political democratization, remained an irritation for both countries until the installment of the Kim Young Sam government in 1993.

In March, 1993, North Korea announced its intention to withdraw from the Nuclear Non-Proliferation Treaty rather than submit to on-site inspection. This raised worldwide suspicion over the true nature of the North's nuclear program. A prolonged cat-and-mouse game followed, with North Korea alternately making and withdrawing concessions to International Atomic Energy Agency (IAEA) inspectors, leaving the extent of its nuclear arms capability unclear.

In 1994, following a visit to South and North Korea by former U.S. president Jimmy Carter, tentative arrangements were made for meetings between repre-

Unidentified North Korean nuclear facility, seen in undated film footage broadcast on television in 1994. The Communist state announced in June of that year its immediate withdrawal from membership in the International Atomic Energy Agency, the UN nuclear watchdog agency. Pyongyang also vowed that its nuclear program would henceforth remain closed to agency inspection. (AP/Wide World Photos)

sentatives of the two Koreas. The picture was complicated, however, by the death of Kim Il Sung in July of that year. The death of Kim—the only leader North Korea had known during its entire history—marked the end of an era both in relations between the two Koreas and in U.S.-Korea relations, demanding a reassessment of positions on all sides.—*Byung I. Jung*

SUGGESTED READINGS:

• Alexander, Bevin. *Korea: The First War We Lost.* New York: Hippocrene Books, 1986. A comprehensive coverage of the Korean War, mostly from a military standpoint. It includes detailed accounts of military decisions and their outcomes with analysis of key wartime Washington politics.

• Bridges, Brian. *Korea and the West.* New York: Routledge & Kegan Paul, 1986. A confident description of Korea's political culture, its recent economic success, and inter-Korea relations.

• Dennett, Tyler. *Americans in Eastern Asia.* New York: Barnes & Noble Books, 1941. Explains American approaches to East Asia from the late nineteenth century to the early twentieth century.

• Kim, Gi Pal. *The Third Republic.* Seoul: Hyundai Culture, 1986. A detailed account of the rise of Park's Third Republic in Korea. South Korea's close relations with Washington, the role of the U.S. military in Korea during the coup, and Park's responses to America's political-economic pressure are documented.

• Koo, Youngnok, and Sung-joo Han, eds. *The Foreign Policy of the Republic of Korea.* New York: Columbia University Press, 1985. It reveals South Korea's political decision-making process and its implications for South Korea-U.S. relations. It also describes the nature of South Korea's diplomacy in general.

• Lee, Sun K. *Korean History, Modern Times.* Seoul: Eul U Publishing, 1963. A most comprehensive description of Korean history. The eight-volume book includes most detailed accounts of Korea's internal events as well as external relations from the beginning to modern times.

• Mazarr, Michael J., ed. *Korea 1991: The Road to Peace*. Boulder, Colo.: Westview Press, 1991. Includes Korea's changing geopolitical environment, the role of the four powers in the Korean settlement, South Korea's recent "Nordpolitik," and defense cooperation with the United States.

• Ohn, Chang-Il. "The Basic Nature of U.S.-Korean Relations." *Korea and World Affairs* 12 (Fall, 1988): 580. Explains the nature of U.S.-South Korea relations, examining South Korea's military, its security

Presidents Kim Young Sam (left) of South Korea and Bill Clinton of the United States walk through the grounds of the Blue House presidential mansion in Seoul, South Korea, in July of 1993. At a news conference a day earlier, Clinton denounced North Korea for raising the specter of "nuclear annihilation" and seeking to develop long-range missiles that could threaten Japan. (AP/Wide World Photos)

needs, and America's intention to defend the East Asian frontier.

• Sunoo, Harold H. *America's Dilemma in Asia: The Case of South Korea*. Chicago: Nelson-Hall, 1979. Discusses America's involvement in the Korean War, South Korea's postwar economic modernization drives, and South-North relations.

U.S.-Laos relations: Since the eighteenth century, Laos has been trapped in the rivalries of stronger neighbors. After years of exploitation by France, which crept into the isolated, ethnically fragmented backcountry of Indochina in the late nineteenth century, the confused and complex situation in Southeast Asia after World War II (1939-1945) began to attract the involvement of the United States. Despite thirty years of effort, the United States learned that the various peoples of Indochina could not be "developed" and were probably better left to determine their own historical fates.

The Later Days of the French. In the 1940's, the Lao, Hmong, and Yao peoples in Laos were rather indifferent to struggles waged around them to determine the future of the region. In March, 1945, the Japanese, as they were being forced out of Southeast Asia, sought to establish an independent Laos. Elements of the traditional Lao ruling family rejected the maneuver in favor of remaining a protectorate of France. Over the next few years, Laotian radicals organized an armed movement, the Pathet Lao, with Communist tendencies and the support of the Viet Minh, then resisting French rule in Vietnam. In May, 1954, an international conference in Geneva met to discuss the political situation in Indochina. While defending Laos from a Pathet Lao-Viet Minh "invasion," French forces were defeated at Dien Bien Phu, the news of which changed the complexion of the Geneva negotiations and the fate of the whole region. The Geneva accords removed French power from Indochina and created independent states—a divided Vietnam, Laos, and Cambodia. The terms of the accords allowed the Pathet Lao, probably no more than a couple of thousand people, to "regroup" in two northern provinces, awaiting promised elections that would determine the future of Laos.

Early U.S. Involvement. Accepting the French departure from the region but fearing a power vacuum, the United States created the Southeast Asia Treaty Organization (SEATO) in September, 1954, to resist Communist movements throughout Southeast Asia, including Laos. The move enveloped Laos in the Cold War and exacerbated the struggle between the various

The threat of encroaching communism in Laos triggered U.S. involvement in that region, beginning in the post-World War II period and continuing through the end of the Vietnam War. Here a crowd of Laotians gathers in the capital city of Vientiane to receive rice flown in from the United States in December, 1960. (AP/Wide World Photos)

political factions within Laos. Initially, Americans went to Laos on technical-aid missions seeking to promote Westernization through programs of economic and political development. Increasingly, the Pathet Lao claimed leadership of the nationalistic aspirations of the Laotian people and began to exploit both the weaknesses of the central government and what the Pathet Lao portrayed as the American preoccupation with military aid programs creating a "neo-colonial" climate.

American Involvement in Laotian Politics. After Laos received its independence in 1954, nationalist leader Souvanna Phouma attempted to organize a neutralist coalition government that included members of the pro-Communist Pathet Lao. Washington found this unacceptable and stepped up its military aid program to the Laotian army. In May of 1958, the victory of leftists in elections alarmed pro-Western and neutralist elements in the Laotian government and the Eisenhower Administration. With American aid, the radical

U.S. military advisers train Lao soldiers in firing mortar, at a camp inside Laos in May, 1962. (AP/Wide World Photos)

rightists formed the Committee for the Defense of National Interests (CDNI). In 1958, the Central Intelligence Agency (CIA) helped engineer the CDNI's displacement of Souvanna and the Pathet Lao faction in the government. In 1960, Souvanna managed a brief return to power and, in the process, sought economic aid and support from Moscow and North Vietnam to counter American influence. This seemed to justify American fears of his leadership and the crusade against Communism. With increased support, the American-sponsored right-wing elements of Laos were able to force Souvanna to flee again in December, 1960.

The Kennedy Years. The Kennedy Administration accepted the same "Domino Theory" that had shaped the Eisenhower Administration's policies. In March, 1961, facing a predicted collapse of the American-sponsored government, President John F. Kennedy ordered American troops to be ready to intervene. The

American military advisers already in Laos, who had been wearing civilian clothes to cover their presence and direct intervention, were ordered to wear their uniforms in an attempt to parry increased Soviet support to the Pathet Lao. The Soviets did not relish a fight in Laos and proposed a cease-fire tentatively accepted by Kennedy in April, 1961. In June, 1961, Kennedy discussed Laos when he met with Soviet leader Nikita S. Khrushchev at Vienna, and bargaining over Laos' future continued until June, 1962, when the major powers reached agreement. Laos would receive a new neutralist government headed again by Souvanna. This government ironically included more Communists than his 1957 government.

The Pathet Lao Continues the Struggle. Unfortunately, the Soviets could not control their clients, and the Laotian Communists continued to fight. The Pathet Lao had grown from a poorly equipped force of a few thousand fighters to a much larger army of as many as

A Vientiane street vendor sells fish to a Pathet Lao soldier (left) in early 1976. Once the Communists began to rule Laos, troops of the Pathet Lao became a common sight throughout the capital. (AP/Wide World Photos)

ten thousand, supplied with Soviet weapons. By the end of 1962, Washington again began secret arms shipments to the right-wing elements of Souvanna's government.

The Larger Indochina War. As the United States invested more power and prestige in the Vietnam War (1965-1975), in early 1964 secret air strikes began to pound both Vietnamese supply routes that ran through Laos and Pathet Lao bases. This escalation broadened the war and both the Vietnamese and the Laotian response to it. By 1970, as many as seventy thousand Vietnamese were operating in or through Laos. Thousands of Laotians had been incorporated into these activities or had become refugees in Laotian cities as they fled the battle zones. American advisers in the Laotian capital of Vientiane recruited, trained, and supplied the Hmong, living in the Laotian highlands, to attack and fight the Pathet Lao. In early 1971, President Richard M. Nixon encouraged a Vietnamese invasion of Laos to destroy the Vietnamese staging areas. The North Vietnamese forces stood their ground and forced the South Vietnamese army to retreat quickly.

The American Withdrawal. The Paris peace talks of 1973 produced an armistice between the United States and North Vietnam to allow the orderly withdrawal of American military forces from Indochina. The Viet-

These two Laotian children wear the tattered, castoff rags of refugees of war, in a photograph taken in 1971. (AP/Wide World Photos)

Street scene in Vientiane, where in 1979 the bicycle remained virtually the only mode of transportation. This once-lively capital, its boulevards lined with French cafes and nightclubs, was practically deserted after the Communist takeover of Laos in late 1975. (AP/Wide World Photos)

In 1988, at least, business appeared to be good in the markets of Vientiane, the capital of Communist Laos. Recent lifting of many controls on the economy created a miniboom, which was also triggered partly by refugees abroad sending money back to relatives in Laos. (AP/Wide World Photos)

namese, not wanting anything to delay the American departure, imposed a cease-fire on their allies in Laos. For two years, things remained relatively peaceful in Laos, and the power of the non-Communist government gradually eroded. In 1975, a crescendo of Communist victories, first in Vietnam and then in Cambodia, encouraged the Pathet Lao to increase its pressure on the government in Vientiane, which peacefully collapsed. By the end of 1975, the Laotian monarchy had been abolished, and a Laotian Communist government, closely aligned with Vietnam but maintaining more open relations with the outside world, began to rule Laos. By the 1980's, American policy objectives in Laos no longer included geopolitical strategic gambits but were limited to efforts at suppressing the supply of drugs that were flowing out of the region.— *P. Scott Corbett*

SUGGESTED READINGS: • Dommer, Arthur J. *Conflict in Laos: The Politics of Neutralization.* New York: Praeger, 1971. • Goldstein, Martin E. *American Policy Toward Laos.* Rutherford, N.J.: Fairleigh Dickinson University Press, 1973. • Horn, Robert C. "Southeast Asian Perceptions of U.S. Foreign Policy." *Asian Survey* 25, no. 6 (June, 1985): 678-691. • Rudolph, Lloyd I., et al. *The Regional Imperative: The Administration of U.S. Foreign Policy Towards South Asian States Under Presidents Johnson and Nixon.* Atlantic Highlands, N.J.: Humanities Press, 1980. • Stevenson, Charles A. *The End of Nowhere: American Policy Towards Laos Since 1954.* Boston: Beacon Press, 1972.

U.S. military bases in Asia: World War II (1939-1945) brought about a dramatic rise in the international political, economic, and military power of the United States. The war in Asia fostered a U.S. military presence on islands such as Guam and Okinawa, in the Philippines, and on the mainland in countries such as Korea. Since World War II, the U.S. government has maintained and used its Asian bases to support military actions in Korea, Vietnam, and the Persian Gulf. Half the approximately 20,000 Marines stationed on the Japanese-ruled island of Okinawa were sent to Saudi Arabia during the Persian Gulf War of 1991.

Proponents of American global power have argued that bases are a necessary part of U.S. "big stick" diplomacy to protect U.S. interests and democracy worldwide. Critics charge the bases have pernicious social effects, damage host countries' economies, and infringe on national sovereignty. With the end of the Cold War and the 1991 lapsing of a long-standing treaty between the United States and the Philippines, many began rethinking the role and future of U.S. military bases, and host countries such as the Philippines began attempting to mitigate the economic effects of base closings.

Origins—World War II. The December 7, 1941, Japanese attack on American ships in Pearl Harbor, Hawaii, brought the United States into the largest war in human history. The U.S. role in Asia and the Pacific over the next three and a half years was decisive in the Allied victory. The war greatly hastened the demise of European colonial empires in Asia and elsewhere. In the war's wake, with a new international political order beginning to arise—with countries such as Indonesia, the Philippines, Malaysia, and Vietnam gaining independence—many strategists saw a need for a "Pax Americana"—a peace enforced by a strong U.S. military presence. Over the next decades, the U.S. government maintained a military presence on Okinawa, in South Korea (which since the end of the Vietnam War has been the only U.S. military presence on the Asian mainland), in Thailand, and in the Philippines.

Bases in U.S. Military and Political Strategy. Military bases in Asia have supported what U.S. leaders have judged to be the interests and principles of the world's most powerful nation. Walden Bello, executive director of the San Francisco-based Institute for Food and Development Policy, claims that what he calls the "garrison state" of U.S. military power is meant for "power projection into Northeast Asia, the Chinese heartland, and Southeast Asia. More recently, it has also served to project U.S. power to the Persian Gulf and the Indian Ocean," he notes. The U.S. military presence amounts to "an integrated and extremely secretive complex composed of mobile forces and fixed bases over which the host states in the western, central, and south Pacific exercise merely nominal sovereignty," he asserts.

Bello calls Japan the "keystone" of U.S. power in Asia, "its contributions consisting not only of numerous bases and facilities but also of its military, which is supported by the third-largest military budget in the world; its pro-US political leadership, which has . . . obediently subordinated its foreign policy to US strategy; and its industry, which . . . provides the Pentagon with critical high-tech components such as advanced microchips for weapons systems."

Social and Economic Effects. Military apologists point to enhancement of local economies by U.S. bases; these proponents claim that $500 million has been added to the economy of the Philippines. Critics point to what they call economic distortions and social problems. U.S. bases have "spawned a subeconomy and subculture that has had distorting effects on the larger economy and culture of the host societies," writes Bello. The "subeconomy" wrought by U.S. bases in the Philippines, he argues, has consisted mainly of "the purchase of sexual labor, entertainment, smuggling of arms, drugs, and extortion." Prostitution has flourished around U.S. bases in Korea, Okinawa, and the Philippines, as shown by the essays and oral histories in the book *Let the Good Times Roll: Prostitution and the US Military in Asia* (1992.) In Thailand, where troops fighting in Vietnam during the 1960's went for rest and recreation, the coastal resort town of Pattaya continues to thrive on regular visits from U.S. Navy ships. "The sale of women's sexual labor is at the base of the complex economy surrounding the bar areas around the bases," write editors Saundra Pollock Sturdevant and Brenda Stoltzfus in *Let the Good Times Roll.* "The bar and brothel owners gain financially

from the sale of liquor and food and . . . from the women's sexual labor. The grocery, liquor, and Mom-and-Pop stores in the area are also dependent on the bar traffic. Restaurants, short-order takeout places, ice-cream parlors, T-shirt and hat shops, and pool halls also abound."

The End of the Cold War. With the easing of East-West tensions caused by the demise of the Soviet Union, U.S. military bases' economic importance to host countries replaced strategic interests as an urgent issue, notably in negotiations for the renewal of the Military Base Agreement (MBA), in force between the United States and the Philippines since 1947. Many Filipinos had chafed at what they saw as a compromise of their national sovereignty. For their part, "US officials in the 1990-91 bases negotiations were unabashed in their candid linking of renewal of the treaty with foreign economic assistance to the Philippines," asserts Philippine writer Aida F. Santos.

The 1991 eruptions of volcanic Mount Pinatubo hastened the U.S. decision to close Clark Air Base and Subic Bay Naval Station on Luzon. The MBA's September 16, 1991, expiration ended an era, and it left the former host country struggling to find economically viable new uses for the land. In August, 1993, the Philippine government approved a plan to sell off a state-owned shipyard near Subic Bay and agreed to receive a loan of 23.5 million U.S. dollars from Taiwan to develop the base into an industrial park.—*Ethan Casey*

Suggested Readings: • Enloe, Cynthia. *Bananas, Beaches and Bases: Making Feminist Sense of International Politics.* Berkeley: University of California Press, 1990. • Karnow, Stanley. *In Our Image: America's Empire in the Philippines.* New York: Random House, 1989. • Sturdevant, Saundra Pollock, and Brenda Stoltzfus, eds. *Let the Good Times Roll: Prostitution and the U.S. Military in Asia.* New York: The New Press, 1992. Includes the essays "From American Lake to a People's Pacific" by Waldo Bello, "Gathering the Dust: The Bases Issue in the Philippines" by Aida F. Santos, "Okinawa Then and Now" by Saundra Sturdevant, and "Disparate Threads of the Whole: An Interpretive Essay" by Saundra Sturdevant and Brenda Stoltzfus.

U.S.-Philippines relations: Political relations between Filipinos and Americans began on the eve of the twentieth century. The United States had declared war against Spain over the issue of Cuban independence, while the Filipinos were in the second year of their

WHAT WILL HE DO WITH IT?

This political cartoon published in the New York Herald *on June 3, 1898, raises the ponderous issue of American ownership of the Philippines.* (Library of Congress)

revolt for independence against Spain. As a result of the Spanish-American War (1898), the United States stripped Spain of its colonies: Cuba, the Philippines, and Puerto Rico. The United States gave Cuba its independence but annexed the Philippines and Puerto Rico as U.S. territories. Nationalist Filipinos who had already declared independence from Spain and established a republican government opposed the imposition of U.S. colonial rule and resisted the United States in a second war—the Philippine-American War (1899-1902)—that actually lasted nearly a decade. The United States would prevail in this war, but Filipinos would persist in seeking independence. Filipinos gained political independence on July 4, 1946, but only after allowing the United States to retain its military bases in the Philippines and extending to Americans rights equal to those of Filipinos in the exploitation of Philippine natural resources. On September 16, 1991, the Philippine Senate rejected a proposed treaty that would extend U.S. military base rights beyond 1991. This forced the United States to close down its bases in the Philippines, ending almost a century of U.S. military presence in the Philippines.

The Spanish-American War and the Philippines. A few days after the United States declared war on Spain in April of 1898, American naval forces under the command of Commodore George Dewey were instructed to proceed to the Philippines to neutralize the Spanish naval fleet stationed there. On the morning of May 1, Dewey arrived in Manila Bay and engaged ten Spanish ships in battle. Barely seven hours later Dewey defeated the Spanish and could have then sailed back to the United States a war hero; instead, he sent word of his victory over the Spanish to U.S. president William McKinley and stayed at Manila Bay awaiting further instructions. Apparently confident of a Dewey victory, McKinley, meanwhile, had already asked General Wesley Merritt to lead an Army expedition to the Philippines.

The Americans sought out Filipino revolutionary leaders, especially General Emilio Aguinaldo, who was in exile in Hong Kong, and brought him back to the Philippines to intensify the war against Spain. Soon after his return to the Philippines, Aguinaldo met with Dewey aboard the flagship *Olympia*, where the former was accorded the honors due a general. Aguinaldo was unsure of American intentions in the Philippines; he later said that at this meeting Dewey assured him that the United States needed no colonies and that there was no doubt that the United States would recognize Philippine independence. In congres-

sional hearings much later, Dewey denied that he ever gave Aguinaldo such assurances.

The return of Aguinaldo buoyed Filipino nationalist troops, who renewed their struggle against the Spanish troops in the Philippines. By June of 1898, the Philippine nationalist army had established control over the whole of Luzon, save for the port cities of Cavite and Manila. Taking full advantage of the American blockade of Manila Bay, which prevented the Spanish from replenishing their forces, Aguinaldo laid siege to the city, forcing the Spanish to withdraw to the walled fortifications of Intramuros. To make his siege effective, Aguinaldo's troops cut off food and water to the city, and it was only a matter of weeks before Spanish authorities would surrender to the Filipinos. As Spanish garrisons fell to Filipino nationalist troops throughout the Philippines, Aguinaldo consolidated nationalist gains by establishing a government. On June 12, Aguinaldo proclaimed independence from Spain, and decrees were issued calling for the formation of a congress and the election of delegates to this congress. American naval and army officers were invited to the ceremonies, but no one came. Despite the absence of American recognition of the new government, consolidation continued. The first Philippine congress convened on September 15, 1898, and immediately took up the task of drafting a constitution. This was completed on January 21, 1899, and on January 23, the Philippine Republic was inaugurated in the city of Malolos, amid colorful ceremonies.

In the summer of 1898, as Filipino nationalists were busy consolidating their government while keeping the Spanish confined to Intramuros, American ground troops under General Merritt began to arrive. To enable these troops to establish a position against the fortified Spanish forces, U.S. officers requested permission to establish a beachhead. Despite misgivings Aguinaldo consented and instructed his troops to abandon positions from the bay side of Intramuros so that the Americans could occupy it. As the Americans established their beachhead, Dewey began secret negotiations with the Spanish for the surrender of Manila. The Spanish agreed, but to save face they insisted that there should be a mock battle prior to surrender. They also demanded that Filipinos be excluded from participating in the surrender of Manila and not be allowed to enter the city. Dewey and Merritt agreed to these terms even if it meant betrayal of their Filipino allies. The mock battle of Manila was staged, giving the Americans the foothold they needed to stake a claim on Philippine territory, while denying the Filipinos their final victory over the Spanish. The satisfaction of a final victory over the Spanish was not the only thing that the Filipinos would lose to the Americans in 1898. The Filipinos would also be denied the independence for which they had so bitterly fought the Spanish. Americans would soon take over from the Spanish as the new colonial rulers of the Philippines.

American duplicity during the siege of Manila was merely the first step in the American betrayal of Filipino aspirations for sovereignty and independence. The Filipinos would be excluded from the Paris peace negotiations between Spain and the United States that would decide the future of the Philippines. When the Filipinos learned of these negotiations the Philippine government sent its chief diplomat, Felipe Agoncillo, a lawyer, to Washington to see McKinley and request Filipino representation at the talks. McKinley refused; nor would he allow the American negotiators to hear the Filipino's case, claiming that Agoncillo's command of English was inadequate. As it turned out, McKinley wanted total acquisition of the Philippines and had so

instructed his negotiators, in disregard of the fact that the Filipinos had already declared independence from Spain and had already established a republican form of government. In the end, the Spanish agreed to cede a colony that they had already lost to the Filipinos in exchange for $20 million in compensation. The peace treaty was signed on December 10, 1898, but its provisions would not be valid until ratified by the U.S. Senate. McKinley could not wait for Senate ratification. On December 21, he issued an executive order annexing the Philippines as a U.S. territory and instructing his military commanders to extend U.S. sovereignty over the entire Philippines by force.

McKinley's proclamation enraged the Filipinos and prompted Aguinaldo to issue a counterproclamation denouncing the forcible seizure of Philippine territory and warning of open hostilities against the Americans should these actions continue. General Elwell Otis of the United States regarded Aguinaldo's proclamation as a virtual declaration of war and placed his troops on alert. Finally, on the evening of February 4, 1899, two

Rebel troops at an insurgent outpost in the Philippines, 1899. American intransigence over the issue of Philippine independence ignited a second war between Filipino revolutionaries and U.S. forces for control of the islands. (Library of Congress)

American infantrymen in the Philippines, 1899, hunkered down in their trenches while preparing to advance their position. (Library of Congress)

days before the U.S. Senate vote on the ratification of the Treaty of Paris, Private Willie W. Grayson, a soldier under the command of General Arthur MacArthur, fired on Filipino soldiers guarding a bridge leading to the village of San Juan. The Filipinos returned fire. The next day, without even attempting to investigate the incident, MacArthur ordered his men to advance against Filipino troop positions. The Philippine-American war was on, and the Senate, which until then had been pretty much divided over the annexation of the Philippines, closed ranks and voted to ratify the Treaty of Paris.

The Philippine-American War. The Philippine-American war, by most accounts, was as brutal and cruel as any in the annals of imperialism. Although the war would drag on for most of the first decade of the twentieth century, U.S. president Theodore Roosevelt officially declared it over on July 4, 1902, a few months after the capture of Emilio Aguinaldo. At this juncture, some 126,500 U.S. troops were involved, with 4,234 killed and 2,818 more wounded. In addition, the war cost the U.S. treasury $400 million—

roughly $4 billion by today's standards. American costs and losses, however, pale into insignificance beside even a conservative tally of Filipino losses.

From the very beginning, superior American training and firepower took a heavy toll on the Philippine nationalist army. As it became evident that the Filipinos would not prevail if they continued to confront American forces in fixed-position set-piece battles, Philippine military planners quickly switched to the tactics of mobile guerrilla warfare, which would enable them to use their superior knowledge of the terrain and the universal support of the civilian populace to their advantage. The response of American generals to this shift in tactics was to wage scorched-earth campaigns that obliterated towns and villages. One American general described this tactical response to guerrilla warfare as follows: "It may be necessary to kill half of the Filipinos in order that the remaining half of the population may be advanced to a higher state of life than their present semi-barbarous state affords." These scorched-earth campaigns devastated large areas of the Philippines. Estimates of the death toll for Filipinos resisting American occupation range from 600,000 to one million. Many more were to die of starvation and diseases brought about by the ravages of war.

As U.S. involvement in the Philippines became more and more public, political opposition to the war increased. Leading this opposition was the Anti-Imperialist League, which had been organized in Boston in November, 1898, by individuals active in the antislavery struggle. The core of the league's political activities consisted of opposition to the acquisition and the colonial conquest of the Philippines. The league enjoyed the adherence of many outstanding intellectuals such as Mark Twain, William James, and Jane Addams and conducted three Philippine-related campaigns that received massive public support. It opposed Senate ratification of the treaty annexing the Philippines; it also opposed the Philippine-American War and mounted a sustained campaign against American military atrocities in the Philippines that led to a Senate investigation in 1902. Public revelations during these hearings later led to the indictment and conviction of Brigadier General Jacob F. "Jake" Smith for

Such well-known American personalities as Mark Twain publicly opposed the U.S. government's deepening involvement in the Philippines. (Library of Congress)

ordering the execution of everyone "ten years and older" and that the island of Samar be turned into a "howling wilderness."

The determination of Filipinos to resist the imposition of American rule led U.S. military leaders to complement military operations with programs of attraction that would encourage defections from the leadership of the nationalist army and/or undermine popular support for the resistance. Two programs that proved successful were the education and the "Filipinization" programs. The education program involved the winning of the "hearts and minds" of Filipinos through the establishment of schools. General Elwell Otis, the second military governor of the Philippines, initiated the practice by detailing soldiers to act as teachers and even selecting the textbooks to be used. General Arthur MacArthur affirmed the practice of establishing schools in pacified areas as a matter of policy when he replaced Otis as military governor in 1900. In his budget request, MacArthur recommended a large appropriation for schools, indicating that "this appropriation is recommended primarily and exclusively as an adjunct to military operations calculated to pacify the people."

American-Style Colonial Education. Much is often made of the American contribution to the system of public education in the Philippines, and Americans are even credited with establishing the system. Teodoro A. Agoncillo, an eminent Filipino historian, considers it "the greatest contribution of the United States to Philippine civilization." This assessment, however, is rather overblown. Filipinos were definitely not "unschooled savages," as was often suggested by annexationist propaganda. By the middle of the nineteenth century, the Spanish colonial administration had established a system of schools throughout the Philippines—the Schurman Commission formed by McKinley to evaluate the Philippine situation in 1899 counted 1,914 Filipino teachers scattered throughout the archipelago. The Philippines even boasts of having the oldest European-style university in the Far East, the University of Santo Tomas, which was established in the 1600's. Colleges and universities established by Spanish friars enabled the Philippine elite to be one of the most modern, sophisticated, and Westernized in Asia. The public school system, however, was hobbled by inadequate funding and ill-prepared teachers, and by the Spanish friars, who regarded public schools as competing with their own system of parochial schools.

The American contribution to the Philippine educational system lies in two areas. The first is the aggressive expansion of the public school system, making primary education accessible to almost everyone. The second is in the curriculum. In marked contrast to the Spanish curriculum, which emphasized the study of religion and the use of regional languages as the medium of instruction, the Americans instituted a curriculum that was similar in many ways to the curriculum developed for schools in Native American and new immigrant communities. This curriculum was designed "to Americanize and Anglicize" the children of these communities and emphasized "the Anglo-Saxon conception of righteousness, law and order, and popular government, and . . . reverence for our democratic institutions and for those things which [Americans] as a people hold to be of abiding worth."

Initially, American military authorities tried to preserve what they found of the Spanish system of public schools. First, Filipino teachers were paid to continue their curriculum even though U.S. soldiers were enlisted to teach English. As American curriculum materials became available, these and the use of English as the medium of instruction gradually supplanted the Spanish curriculum. The use of English speeded up the introduction of the American curriculum. Since attendance was mandatory, Filipinos soon began learning a new language and a new culture. Philippine history was all but ignored, and heroes of the Philippine revolution were regarded as bandits (*ladrones*), as the curriculum emphasized American history and civilization.

The adoption of English in schools gave the colonial power tremendous advantage in education and government administration. In government, the use of English ensured closer supervision since business was conducted in the language of the colonizer. Competence in English served as a litmus test to ensure that aspiring government service applicants had at least begun their own process of cultural Americanization. Proficiency in English also became an important qualification for advancement, giving the process of Americanization a powerful impetus.

Ironically, the establishment of a public school system with an American colonial curriculum had a democratizing effect on Philippine society. By greatly improving access to schools, Americans paved the way for the development of a Filipino middle class consisting of college-educated professionals, which was largely nonexistent in Spanish colonial society. No longer would higher education be the sole domain of the elite and their children. Under the Americans even children of farmers and small landowners could get beyond a primary education to become doctors, law-

yers, teachers, and other professionals. The rise of this professional, college-educated class would later create a glut of highly skilled and educated individuals that the economy could not effectively absorb. To get beyond entry-level positions, they would aspire for opportunities beyond Philippine borders and fuel Filipino immigration to the United States.

Filipinization. The program that directly undercut the leadership of the Philippine nationalist movement was the Filipinization of the government infrastructure and its leadership. Under Spain, the highest public office that Filipinos could occupy was that of town mayor. Under American rule, to encourage defections from the independence movement, Filipino collaborators were given charge of local governments and of provincial governments as well. When general conditions of peace could be established, Filipinos were promised an opportunity to elect their own legislature. The Filipinization policy effectively thinned out the leadership ranks of the nationalists; in 1907 governor-general James L. Smith reported to U.S. president William Howard Taft that, as a tool of pacification, the policy of Filipinization "charmed the rifle out of the hands of the insurgent and made the one time rebel chief the pacific president of a municipality or the staid governor of a province."

The field successes attributed to Filipinization were not the only factors that led to its continued use. In the United States the policy became a foil against the critics of annexation and was promoted as evidence of benevolent intentions toward Filipinos, despite frank admissions by Republicans that they wanted the Philippines for commercial gain. Two recommendations in the Schurman Commission Report of 1900 also gave further impetus to Filipinization. One recommendation was that the civil government in the Philippines be supported solely by its own treasury. This made it more economically expedient to employ Filipinos in the business of civil government than to employ Americans, who had to be assured free transportation to and from the islands as well as leave privileges. The other recommendation was that the U.S. Congress enact a law creating a bicameral legislature for the Philippines. This led to the passage of the Philippine Bill of 1902, which became the first organic act of the Philippines. This law gave executive powers of governance to the Philippine Commission, to be headed by a civilian governor-general, and provided that its legislative powers be shared with an elective Philippine Assembly. In bicameral fashion, the Philippine Commission functioned as the "Senate" of the legislature while the Philippine Assembly acted as the "House of Representatives."

Three conditions, however, had to be satisfied before the Philippine Assembly could be established: complete restoration of peace and order, the completion of a nationwide census of the Philippines, and a condition of complete peace and quiet for two years after the completion and publication of the census. A census of the Philippines was conducted from 1903 to 1905. On March 25, 1905, the governor-general announced the publication of the last volume of the census. On March 28, 1907, the Philippine Commission certified to President Roosevelt that the conditions of peace and order required by the act of 1902 had continued for two years since the publication of the census in 1905. Although the certification of peace and order was rather strained because several pockets of anti-American resistance continued to flourish even at the late date of 1907, the commission nonetheless requested that the president call for the immediate election of members of the Philippine Assembly. Subsequently, the first Philippine national elections were held, and eighty delegates to the Philippine Assembly were elected to serve two-year terms.

The inauguration of the Philippine Assembly in October, 1907, marked the real end of the Philippine-American War. The election of representatives to the Philippine Assembly initiated the ascendance of a new order of leadership for the Philippines. While pockets of armed resistance to American rule still existed, henceforth the most organized struggle for sovereignty and independence would be through the Assembly, its leaders, and various political organs that it created.

Republican Autocracy. There was also an ironic twist to the Filipinization process. American tutelage in self-government, instead of leading to the eventual democratic empowerment of Filipinos, resulted in the development of an autocracy in republican form. Because the Filipinization of the Philippine government was, at bottom, a component of the pacification campaign, the extension of the right of political suffrage to Filipinos was a carefully calibrated process designed to undermine Filipino nationalism and resistance to American empire. Initially, when Filipinos were given control over municipal and provincial governments, political suffrage was given only to those who might be favorably disposed toward U.S. colonial rule. Thus, only males at least twenty-five years or older who held a local position in the municipal government prior to American occupation, owned real property valued at five hundred pesos or paid annual taxes worth thirty

pesos, and could read, speak, and write English or Spanish were given the right to vote. These restrictions on the exercise of political suffrage ensured that only a small percentage of the total national population would qualify as electors. These were the members of the *principalia*, the privileged class of nineteenth century Filipino-Spanish society who made up the economic elite. American-sponsored elections deprived the masses of Filipinos of the right of suffrage as even provincial governors were initially elected by a conference of town mayors. The subsequent removal of economic requirements to suffrage did not correct the problem. By then, the autocracy was already well established, and elections for the Philippine Assembly served only to tighten the economic elite's grip on political power. Philippine electoral politics to this day continues to be dominated by families whose ancestry dates back to the first Philippine Assembly and the first governors of provinces.

Moving Toward Self-Government. McKinley's official rationale for colonizing the Philippines was to tutor Filipinos in the ways of "civilized" self-government. Republicans and Democrats would generally accept this rationale but disagreed on how long the period of tutelage would take. Republicans favored indefinite retention, while Democrats favored Philippine independence if a stable government could be established. From 1899 to 1912, while the Republicans controlled the White House, they refused to consider the issue of Philippine independence. When the Democrats took over in 1912, Filipinos found more sympathy for independence. One of President Woodrow Wilson's first acts was to send a colleague, Henry Ford Jones, to conduct a confidential investigation of conditions in the Philippines. Ford gave a glowing report on the Filipinos' capacity for government; he recommended the abolition of the Philippine Commission since its retention was a source of discord and friction in the government. In his first message to Congress, Wilson indicated that he wished to see a process of withdrawal of U.S. supervision over the Philippines that was coupled with a process where Filipinos were given more and more control over the social instruments of their life. In 1916 Congress affirmed Wilson's policy with the passage of the Jones Act (after William Atkinson Jones, its sponsor). Although the act did not set a definite date for Philippine independence, it made a commitment to grant independence to the Philippines "as soon as a stable government [could] be established."

The Jones Act kept the executive branch of government under American control but reorganized the Philippine legislature into the bicameral structure that it retains today: a Senate and a House of Representatives. The Senate replaced the American-dominated Philippine Commission, and the House superseded the Philippine Assembly. Although all legislation was still subject to the review and approval (or veto) of the American governor-general, Filipinos now had full control of their legislature.

In addition to the Jones Act, Filipino nationalists found an invaluable American ally in Francis Burton Harrison, governor-general of the Philippines during the Wilson presidency. Harrison favored increased Filipino participation in the government. One of his first reforms, prior to the passage of the Jones Act, was to make Filipinos the majority in the Philippine Commission, breaking the legislative deadlock between the commission and the assembly. Harrison also targeted executive bureaus for Filipinization and by 1919 had transformed the colonial government of the Philippines from a government of Americans "assisted by Filipinos to a government of Filipinos aided by Americans." The one exception was the office of secretary of public instruction. The Jones Act reserved the portfolio of public instruction for the vice governor, and even as late as 1935, an American continued to preside over the educational affairs of Filipinos.

Harrison's efforts to give Filipino executives all possible opportunity to exercise their own judgment and discretion went beyond the intentions of the Jones Act. In 1918, he created the Philippine Council of State to advise the governor-general on "matters of public importance." This consisted of the governor-general as ex-officio chairman, the Speaker of the House, the president of the Senate, and the members of the cabinet. This council soon acquired broad powers that made it more than merely an advisory body. Through a process of "local legislation," the Philippine legislature passed laws that gradually made the Council of State nearly as powerful as the governor-general's office. Harrison could have vetoed these laws, but he chose not to, practically abdicating his powers to the Filipino leadership. Harrison gave the Filipinos a chance to develop their key leaders, since the establishment of the council created the opportunity for centralized leadership to flourish.

To give the Filipinos' newfound political power an economic base, Harrison established the Philippine National Bank to serve as the official depository of the government and facilitate the issuance of credit to Filipino economic enterprises. At first, the bank flourished because of the high demand for Philippine ex-

port products, but the lack of trained administrators soon led to failure. American and Filipino administrators squandered its assets on questionable loans and transactions, forcing the bank to draw from its deposits with the Currency Reserve Funds that were set aside to protect Philippine currency and facilitate foreign exchange. As these reserves declined, the bank became unable to meet its obligations, and the Philippine currency depreciated. The scandal associated with the Philippine National Bank would haunt Harrison and the Filipino leadership when it came time to raise the issue of independence. The scandal would be used by the Republicans to cast doubts about Filipino capability for self-rule.

The Republican Party returned to power in the 1920 elections, capturing the presidency through Warren Harding and gaining a majority in both houses of Congress. As a Senator, Harding had been opposed to Philippine independence; he also felt that Harrison, in virtually abdicating his powers as governor-general to the Filipinos, had seriously undermined American sovereignty over the Philippines. On the eve of his inauguration he revealed his views on the Philippine question to the pro-Republican *New York Sun*, which then ran a front-page story that headlined: "Philippines in Chaos; Big Harding Task; Governor Harrison Blamed for Misrule." During Harrison's term, the story points out, "American sovereignty in the island had been undermined, Filipino demagogues and adventurers who urge independence for their own selfish purposes have come to the front, American authority has been sadly impaired, the fiscal affairs of the islands have been thrown into chaotic shape, and things have gone backward instead of forward." It was clear to anyone that under Harding the question of Philippine independence would not receive a positive hearing. What remained was for Filipinos to buckle down and protect their gains.

Independence from the Philippines. It was not until the late 1920's that debate over Philippine independence began to intensify once again. This time the economic arguments for keeping the Philippines as an economic outpost and a market for U.S. goods began to turn on themselves. As the U.S. economy fell into hard times, an increasing number of groups in the United States began to see in the Philippines a scapegoat for their woes, and they became the loudest advocates of Philippine independence. U.S. tobacco producers resented the competition presented by Philippine tobacco, which could enter the country duty-free from the colony. Falling world sugar prices led American sugar beet growers to denounce Philippine sugar, even though the real competition was with Cuban sugar. Philippine cotton exports, though never very substantial, were described as a "millstone about the necks of cotton producers." Even dairy and farm lobbies denounced Philippine coconut oil as a major ingredient in margarine—even though most coconut oil went into making soap. With the deepening economic depression, even labor unions joined the anti-Philippine chorus, demanding curbs on the flow of Filipino labor.

Filipino laborers had come to the United States in increasing numbers as the flow of cheap labor from China and Japan was halted by a series of restrictive immigration laws, culminating in the IMMIGRATION ACT OF 1924. As unemployment from the economic depression proliferated, however, Filipinos began to be resented, and the American Federation of Labor (AFL) joined the American Legion and other self-styled patriotic movements in demanding that Filipinos, too, be excluded or that U.S. ties with the Philippines be cut. These self-styled patriotic groups maintained that the influx of Filipino immigrants, like the Chinese and Japanese before them, was "like a cancer in American private and public life, destroying American ideals and preventing the development of a nation based on racial unity."

There were still many who favored retention. These included the big American corporations with investments in the Philippines, the American importers of Philippine commodities, the U.S. exporters of American products—since they enjoyed a monopoly of the Philippine market—and the American community in Manila. The cry for Philippine independence was now louder than that for retention, but the Filipinos no longer held the initiative; it was now Americans who wanted to be "independent" of the Philippines.

In the United States, the clamor to become independent of the Philippines led to the passage of a bill that defeated the long-time advocates of Philippine retention. The HARE-HAWES-CUTTING ACT OF 1933 provided that Filipinos be granted independence in ten years, with the Philippines to be governed by a commonwealth in the interim. The United States would retain its army and navy bases, and American goods would enter the Philippines duty-free while Philippine goods would enter the United States under generous quotas but with gradually increasing tariffs. The bill also imposed an annual Filipino immigration quota of fifty. President Herbert Hoover, a Republican, vetoed the bill, but the House overrode his veto in a matter of

hours by a huge margin, and four days later the Senate did likewise. The vote signaled the end of thirty years of Republican policy in the Philippines.

There was one more hurdle before the Hare-Hawes-Cutting Act could become fully enforceable: The Philippines had to approve it. Debate over the bill in the Philippine legislature brought to the fore the intense political rivalry between Manuel Quezon, president of the Philippine Senate, and Sergio Osmena, Speaker of the House. Previously, Quezon and Osmena had been able to work as allies toward the common goal of independence. When the Congress was considering the bill, Quezon, who had earlier led various independence lobby efforts, became ill, and so in his place Osmena was sent to Washington to head the Philippine lobby. Quezon realized as soon as the bill had passed that Osmena would come home a conquering hero and would most likely win the election for president of the soon-to-be-established commonwealth. Quezon immediately set in motion a campaign to reject the bill, by focusing on its shortcomings. In October, 1933, the Philippine legislature rejected the Hare-Hawes-Cutting Act, noting that the provisions on trade relations would "seriously imperil the economic, social, and political institutions" of the Philippines; the immigration clause was objectionable and offensive; and the retention of military, naval, and other reservations was inconsistent with true independence, in violation of national dignity, and subject to misunderstanding. The legislature then appointed Quezon to head another effort to get a better bill. Quezon would return home with an essentially repackaged legislation sponsored by Senator Millard Tydings of Maryland and Representative John McDuffie of Alabama. The two bills were essentially the same save for the provision on the retention of military bases. This was replaced by language calling for the settlement of this issue on terms mutually agreeable to both at the time of the grant of Philippine independence. Quezon's triumphant return with a new act assured his election as commonwealth president.

The Philippine Commonwealth. What lay immediately ahead for Philippine leaders was to prepare their country for independence in the brief span of ten years. The TYDINGS-MCDUFFIE ACT OF 1934 contained very specific steps that had to be undertaken for the establishment of the commonwealth. The act required the convening of a constitutional convention with elective delegates, then ratification of the constitution through a national plebiscite. Only then would Filipinos be allowed to choose, in general elections, the officers of the commonwealth. The act further dictated the inclusion of certain "temporary" provisions in the constitution, such as granting to American citizens civil rights equal to those of Filipino citizens and reserving to the United States control on all matters pertaining to Philippine currency, coinage, trade, immigration, and foreign affairs until the grant of independence. Finally, the act required that the constitution be approved by the president of the United States. Filipinos had no choice but to include these provisions if they were to move toward self-rule. The convention completed the constitution in February, 1935; the latter received Roosevelt's approval in March and was ratified in a plebiscite held in May. After the election of officers in June, the Philippine Commonwealth was inaugurated on November 15, 1935, with Quezon and Osmena as its president and vice president, respectively.

The most difficult problem for the commonwealth was the readjustment of the Philippine economy to an independent status. The economic development of the Philippines and the prosperity it brought were tied directly to the American market via free-trade agreements. When free-trade relations were first proposed in the early decades of American colonial occupation, Quezon and Osmena opposed it, knowing that dependence on American markets would, in the long run, endanger political independence. Americans, however, were eager to capture the Philippine market for their commodity exports, and free-trade relations were instituted. When the restrictions on the exportation of sugar, tobacco, coconut oil, and hemp began to take effect as provided by the 1934 act, severe dislocations in the economy resulted. Surplus products that could no longer be exported to the United States had difficulty finding other foreign markets. The virtual monopoly that American commodities enjoyed in the Philippines also discouraged the development of local manufacturing and commodity production. The result was that the Philippine economy was totally dependent on the United States.

The commonwealth government recognized the necessity to wean the Philippine economy from the American market and adopted an economic readjustment program to diversify and increase agricultural production, expand and increase the domestic market by encouraging consumption of local products and by industrialization, and develop foreign markets outside the United States. This program, however, continued to be severely hampered by the economic provisions of the act, which provided that while Philippine exports to the United States would be subject to an increasing schedule of tariffs and quotas, American com-

modities would continue to enter the Philippines duty-free even beyond the date of complete Philippine independence. Even then, the minimal gains that were achieved by this economic readjustment program were soon to be totally destroyed by World War II (1939-1945) and the Japanese invasion of the Philippines.

It is sometimes debated whether the Philippines might have been spared an invasion by Japanese imperial forces if the country had not harbored U.S. military bases (as the Spanish presence in the Philippines had provided a pretext for the U.S. invasion a half-century before). What is not debatable is that the Philippines was turned into a major battleground by the United States and Japan. The battle of the Philippine Sea and the battle for Leyte Gulf are remembered as among the greatest naval encounters in the history of the world. General Douglas MacArthur's campaign to reclaim the Philippines resulted in incalculable damage. Manila was second only to Warsaw as the most devastated city during the war.

Restoration of the Autocracy. As soon as the fires of Manila and the surrounding provinces subsided, the Philippine Commonwealth government set about the task of rebuilding and restoration. Quezon had died in exile during the war, and Osmena had succeeded to the presidency. One of Osmena's first orders was the restoration of executive departments of the government. New cabinet members were appointed to coordinate the process of relief and reconstruction. Amid the confusion, chaos, frustration, and anguish during the months that immediately followed the liberation of the Philippines, MacArthur started a pattern of covert intervention in Philippine affairs that would continue for decades.

As Osmena and his cabinet set about the task of restoring civil order, one of the biggest dilemmas they faced was what to do with those who had collaborated with the Japanese. U.S. president Franklin D. Roosevelt had decreed that anyone from the prewar Philippine government who had collaborated with the Japanese had to be removed from authority. Osmena was also warned that the United States would withhold relief unless he "diligently and firmly" punished the collaborators. This posed a major dilemma for Osmena, who knew that most of the nation's elite had served under the Japanese. To banish the landlords and big-business families from politics would not only estrange him from his colleagues, associates, and compadres; it would also create a power vacuum. General MacArthur also valued the *ilustrados* as friends and was hesitant to "run them to the ground" as he had

General Douglas MacArthur and his aides wade ashore after landing at Leyte, the Philippines, in the fall of 1944. (Library of Congress)

promised during the war. As commander of American forces in the Pacific, MacArthur had certain prerogatives under conditions of war. First, he exonerated a close friend, Manuel Roxas, by issuing a statement that cleared Roxas of any taint of collaboration. Then he contrived a distraction. Instead of trying Filipinos, he prosecuted Japan's senior officers in the Philippines as war criminals to draw attention away from the collaborators. Finally, he pressured Osmena, as commonwealth president, to convene the prewar legislature. This body had been elected only as of 1942 and had never had the chance to convene. Most of its surviving members had collaborated with the Japanese puppet government of Jose Laurel. When Osmena caved in to MacArthur and reinstated these men, he and Mac-Arthur instantly reactivated the political oligarchy of the Philippines and in the same stroke reconstituted the autocratic form of government that the United States had created when it first tried to pacify the Filipinos

and tutor them in the ways of "Western democracy."

In the years following the grant of political independence, the United States continued to be deeply involved in Philippine affairs. Some of this involvement was benign, such as the grant of economic aid to help the Philippine government correct problems that were the result of U.S. colonial policies. In other forms, it was insidious, as when the Central Intelligence Agency (CIA) engineered the rise of Ramon Magsaysay to the Philippine presidency. While the purpose of avowed U.S. policy in the Philippines has been to assure a government that is pro-American, the tenure of the United States' military bases in the Philippines became a key determinant of that policy. During the period of the 1970's, for example, a rising nationalist movement threatened to undermine the especially favorable relationship existing between both governments. When Philippine president Ferdinand Marcos made a bid to maintain himself in power indefinitely by declaring martial law and assuming dictatorial powers, the U.S. government condoned and even supported his actions since he was able to assure the tenure of the American military bases. Throughout Marcos' fifteen years of dictatorship, the United States continued to provide him with huge amounts of military and economic aid, ignoring evidence that his government was responsible for numerous cases of extrajudicial executions and human rights violations. When Marcos finally lost his grip on power, the U.S. government rescued him from certain execution and gave him safe haven in the United States until his death in Honolulu in 1989.

Independence with Chains. Instead of using the postwar reconstruction period to set the Philippine economy on an independent path, the United States took the opportunity to draw it closer to its fold. In April, 1946, a few months before independence and

after considerable debate, Congress approved the Philippine Trade Act of 1946, whose intent was clearly to preserve American economic control over the Philippines. The act pegged the value of Philippine currency to the U.S. dollar, protecting American businesses in the Philippines against currency fluctuations regardless of the financial needs of the Philippines. It also provided for free-trade relations between both countries until 1954, after which goods coming from either country would receive a 5 percent tariff increase each year until the specified tariff ceiling was reached. This meant a return to the prewar system, where American business interests enjoyed a virtual monopoly in the Philippine market. The most onerous provision was the parity provision, which entitled Americans to the same rights as Filipinos in the ownership of business and in the exploitation of mines, forests, and other resources—without extending Filipinos the same

An estimated three thousand Philippine citizens march through Manila in February, 1986, to protest President Ferdinand Marcos' declared victory in the alleged rigged special election held earlier in the month. The demonstrators also visited the U.S. embassy briefly to protest American support of the Marcos government. (AP/Wide World Photos)

Marcos' ironfisted regime ended in disgrace in February, 1986, when he was forced by the Philippine people to leave office. Here he addresses a joint session of the U.S. Congress in Washington, D.C., 1966. (AP/Wide World Photos)

rights in the United States. The parity provision violated the Philippine Constitution; amending the latter would have required ratification by the Philippine legislature and a referendum. To coerce Filipinos into accepting the provisions of this act, Congress linked Philippine ratification of the Trade Act to the Tydings Rehabilitation Act, which promised to provide direly needed funds to rebuild the damage suffered from the war. Congress thus warned that the Rehabilitation Act would become effective only upon amendment of the Philippine Constitution to give "parity rights" to Americans. Fortunately for Filipinos, the "parity rights" amendment to their constitution was only a temporary amendment, expiring after twenty-five years.

Besides the parity rights amendment, the other indignity that Filipinos had to suffer as a price for political independence was the extension of U.S. military base rights in Philippine territory via the U.S. Military Bases Agreement (1947). The right to establish military bases overseas had earlier been extracted from Germany and Japan as a consequence of their defeat in war. The Filipinos had been American allies during the war, yet some of the terms imposed upon the Philip-

pines were even harsher than those imposed on Japan. The U.S. government obtained ninety-nine-year leases to twenty-two sites including Subic Bay Naval Station and Clark Air Base, two of the largest overseas U.S. military installations in the world. The access provisions of the agreement gave the United States virtually unlimited access to and use of these base areas, with only a courtesy notification to the Philippine government. In theory, this meant that these bases could be used to launch attacks on other countries with whom the Philippines might be friendly, and the Philippines would be powerless to intervene since all that was required was a simple notification. The Philippines was also forced to cede legal jurisdiction over offenses and crimes committed by American personnel outside the base areas even as it gave U.S. authorities jurisdiction over Filipinos committing offenses inside the bases.

The ninety-nine-year lease for American military bases in the Philippines was revised in 1966 to expire in 1991. On the expiration date of the agreement, the Philippine Senate refused to ratify a proposed treaty that would have extended the lease for another twenty-five years, forcing the United States to vacate its military facilities in the Philippines. The removal of the bases from the Philippines marked the end of almost a century of U.S. military occupation in the archipelago and brought U.S.-Philippine relations to a crossroads. During the height of the Cold War, the presence of the bases assured the Philippines of a high level of attention among Washington policy makers, especially those responsible for ensuring U.S. national security. With the end of the Cold War and the removal of the bases, the relationship between these two countries is redefined.—*Enrique de la Cruz*

SUGGESTED READINGS:

• Agoncillo, Teodoro A. *History of the Filipino People*. 8th ed. Quezon City: R. P. Garcia, 1990. The dean of Filipino historians, Agoncillo provides an engaging account of Philippine history while focusing on the main currents of Filipino resistance to Spanish and American colonial rule in the Philippines. A valuable basic account of Philippine history.

• Agoncillo, Teodoro A. *A Short History of the Philippines*. New York: New American Library, 1975. An abridged version of Agoncillo's *History of the Filipino People*, available as a Mentor Paperback.

• Broad, Robin. *Unequal Alliance: The World Bank, the International Monetary Fund, and the Philippines*. Berkeley: University of California Press, 1988. A thoroughly researched case study of how the structural adjustment model of development used by the World

The military hospital at Clark Air Base, the Philippines. The U.S. government was forced to vacate its military installations in the islands by order of the Philippine government. (Library of Congress)

Bank and the International Monetary Fund (IMF) has ravaged the Philippine economy and soured its development. Broad, a U.S.-trained economist, shows how U.S.-espoused and -supported economic development policies in the Philippines have led to economic decline.

• Constantino, Renato. *The History of the Philippines: From the Spanish Colonization to the Second World War.* New York: Monthly Review Press, 1975. Constantino provides a nationalist account of Philippine history and describes the various popular struggles of Filipinos against both Spanish and American colonial rule. Constantino shows the continuities and discontinuities in these struggles as a unified historical progression.

• Constantino, Renato. "The Miseducation of the Filipino." *Weekly Graphic* (June 8, 1966). An essay on American colonial education in the Philippines and its effects on Filipinos.

• Constantino, Renato, and Letizia R. Constantino. *The Philippines: The Continuing Past.* Quezon City: The Foundation for Nationalist Studies, 1978. Sequel to Constantino's *The History of the Philippines*, in which the authors continue Constantino's nationalist analysis of Philippine history and demonstrate that the past colonial relations with the United States persist despite political independence.

• Karnow, Stanley. *In Our Image: America's Empire in the Philippines.* New York: Random House, 1989. A Pulitzer Prize-winning account of U.S.-Philippine relations focusing on the major personalities that directed U.S. policy toward the Philippines. Although critical of overall U.S. policy towards the Philippines, Karnow nonetheless tries to put a progressive polish on some of these policies. The book contains as appendices a useful chronology and thumbnail sketches of the principal characters in his study.

• Miller, Stuart Creighton. *"Benevolent Assimilation": The American Conquest of the Philippines, 1899-1903.* New Haven, Conn.: Yale University Press, 1982. A thorough and well-researched account of the Philippine-American war, utilizing a wealth of primary sources. Miller also provides a good account of the American opposition to the war, particularly the Anti-Imperialist League.

• National Security Council. "A Report to the President on the Position of the United States with Respect to the Philippines." A secret National Security Council policy report recommending U.S. policies toward the Philippines. Declassified, October 10, 1975. This document provides an excellent illustration of U.S. interventionist policies in the Philippines during the 1950's.

• Paredes, Ruby R., ed. *Philippine Colonial Democracy*. New Haven, Conn.: Yale University, Southeast Asia Studies, 1988. A collection of essays by distinguished scholars on Asia. Each essay examines an aspect of Filipino elite collaboration with their American colonial rulers. The essays provide valuable insight and understanding of the peculiarities of Philippine colonial politics and demonstrate that behind the rhetoric of independence was collaboration that led to the establishment of an autocratic government in republican form.

• Schirmer, Daniel B. *Republic or Empire: American Resistance to the Philippine War*. Cambridge, Mass.: Schenkman, 1972. This is an extensive study of the Anti-Imperialist League and American opposition to the Philippine-American War. A most valuable study of what is normally considered as a minor tendency during the beginnings of America's global expansionist era.

• Schirmer, Daniel B., and Stephen Rosskamm Shalom, eds. *The Philippines Reader: A History of Colonialism, Neocolonialism, Dictatorship, and Resistance*. Boston: South End Press, 1987. An extensive collection of primary and secondary sources on U.S.-Philippine relations from 1898 to the end of the Marcos era in 1986. Includes a bibliography of selected readings and is a good source book for anyone wishing to study the many and complex aspects of U.S.-Philippine relations.

• Shalom, Stephen Rosskamm. *The United States and the Philippines: A Study of Neocolonialism*. Philadelphia: Institute for the Study of Human Issues, 1981. An engaging study of the impact of U.S. policy on the Philippines in the post-World War II period. Through careful and extensively documented analysis, Shalom demonstrates that U.S. postwar policy in the Philippines was established in pursuit of U.S. strategic and economic interests with negative consequences for the great majority of Filipinos.

• Simbulan, Roland G. *The Bases of Our Insecurity: A Study of the US Military Bases in the Philippines*. 2d ed. Metro Manila: BALAI Fellowship, 1985. Simbulan's study documents the role of U.S. bases in the maintenance of U.S. interests in the Philippines and their importance to American global strategy. Simbulan also demonstrates escalating U.S. involvement in Philippine affairs as the tenure of the bases was threatened.

U.S.-South Asia relations: South Asia, the Indian subcontinent, is peripheral to the Asian landmass. Historically it had limited political, economic, and cultural ties with other Asian societies. Of the seven nations that compose South Asia, India is the central power, dominating the region with its size, military, natural resources, and economy. Pakistan, India's traditional enemy, is the only other state in the region that has significant relations with the United States and the Western world. Two others—Bangladesh and Sri Lanka—have had limited relations with the United States. The remaining three—Bhutan, which is half the size of Indiana and which made its first diplomatic links with non-Asian countries in 1985; Maldives, which became independent in 1965 and had a 1992 population of 30,000; and Nepal, a landlocked country the size of Arkansas between India and Tibet, whose external dealings have mainly been with its two giant neighbors, India and the People's Republic of China—are of marginal importance to the United States and the Western world. Therefore, this article will focus on U.S. relations with India and Pakistan.

South Asia has a rich mosaic of religions, cultures, races, and languages. This diversity has resulted in ethnic, religious, and linguistic conflicts within these states and has, at times, affected relations with other states in the region. The heterogeneity of the region has prevented the South Asian states from taking a regional stand on international issues.

Official relations between the United States and the South Asian states, which had been under British rule or control for two centuries, developed in the period following World War II, especially after the independence of India and Pakistan in 1947. The United States' relations with countries in the region have been shaped primarily by its global security and economic interests. During the Cold War, U.S. policy toward the subcontinent reflected America's global strategic and superpower considerations. The strategic location of South Asia, which is a continuation of the Middle East and is south of the two largest Communist countries, China and the Soviet Union, made the region a vital security interest to the United States. The hostility between India and Pakistan has, however, complicated America's role in South Asia. Yet the end of the Cold War and of superpower rivalry in world politics has diminished the importance of South Asia for America's security.

U.S.-India Relations. Observers of U.S.-India relations have described the relations between the two to be generally uneasy, ambiguous, uncertain, and fragile though cooperative and friendly at times. The United States, the oldest democracy in the world, and India, the world's largest democracy, were expected to be natural friends; the two have, however, differed over international issues and especially over Pakistan. Whereas U.S. policy toward Pakistan during the Cold War reflected its global strategy of containment and of encircling the Soviet Union with a ring of friendly nations through a system of military alliances, India perceived the American military alliance and its arms sale to Pakistan to be a serious threat to India's security and destabilizing to the region's balance of power.

Before India's independence America had limited interest in and contact with South Asia. During India's nationalist struggle the image that most Americans received of its most prominent leader, Mahatma GANDHI, was a confused one. Though U.S. president Franklin D. Roosevelt was sympathetic with the Indian aspiration for greater autonomy, he had never pressed that cause. After India's independence in 1947, however, India's images of contemporary international society and perception of its interests clashed with those of the United States. Whereas the United States, which emerged as the strongest power in the alliance—economically and militarily—at the end of World War II, defined its interests as a superpower globally and in terms of the ideology of anticommunism, India, which was the largest British colony in Asia to become independent, emphasized anticolonialism and antiracism in its foreign policy and took a position on the threat of communism to international peace that diverged from that of the U.S. government.

With the onset of the Cold War, India and the United States found themselves to be at cross purposes in international affairs. The U.S. government held communism as a threat to the security of the free world and justified its military arrangements for the containment of the communist powers as a defensive measure. Though India did not deny the expansionist nature of communism, it held the view that there was a greater threat to the peace and security of the world from

India prime minister Jawaharlal Nehru (left), being met on arrival at Washington, D.C.'s National Airport in 1949 by Mrs. Vijaya Lakshmi Pandit, his sister and India's ambassador to the United States, and by U.S. president Harry S Truman. (National Archives)

military pacts and the isolation of the communist powers than from the ideology of communism as such. Hence India supported the admission of China to the membership of the United Nations and opposed all Western-sponsored military pacts such as the South East Asian Treaty Organization (SEATO) and Central Treaty Organization (CENTO).

The United States viewed India's policy of non-alignment—of not formally aligning with either power bloc and reserving the right to side with either in an international crisis based on the merits of each particular case—to be immoral in a world that was sharply divided along ideological lines. Moreover, Indian prime minister Jawaharlal NEHRU's self-righteous, moralizing rhetoric and pontifications about Western (American, in particular) responsibilities and obligations in the postcolonial world irritated Americans. India's stand on international issues (Nehru's proposal

in the wake of the Korean War that China be given a seat in the U.N. Security Council in order to facilitate a solution, and India's advocacy for the creation of a New International Economic Order in the 1970's, for example) drew India and the United States further apart. America, therefore, tried to build up Pakistan to outflank Nehru's India.

Pakistan, which considered India as a major threat to its existence as a nation, had the ambition of attaining parity in military strength with India. In pursuit of this ambition Pakistan joined the American-sponsored alliance system in 1954 and started receiving American military aid under a mutual security arrangement. India resented Pakistan's participation in the Western alliances that had involved the subcontinent in the Cold War. Nehru, in fact, believed that Pakistan's motive in joining SEATO and CENTO had more to do with India than with the Soviet Union or China.

U.S. food aid to India increased during the Johnson Administration. Here U.S. vice president Hubert Humphrey (third from left) and U.S. ambassador to India Chester Bowles (right), accompanied by Indian officials, inspect wheat crops in Ludhiana in 1966. (National Archives)

In 1956 the U.S. government stepped up its economic assistance to India, partly in response to the growing influence of the Soviet Union in India; the United States gave economic assistance in the form of loans and grants. America provided $92 million in emergency military aid to India after the Indo-Chinese border war of October, 1962. Indo-U.S. relations reached a low point in 1965, however, when Pakistan and India went to war for the second time, mainly over Kashmir, in which Pakistan had used American arms in utter disregard of the assurance that U.S. president Dwight D. Eisenhower had given to Nehru that American arms would never be used against India. As a result of the Indian protest, the United States cut off its assistance to Pakistan and India, an act that both resented.

There were, however, signs of the beginning of better relations between India and the United States when Indira Gandhi, India's new prime minister, visited Washington, D.C., in March, 1966, and succeeded in securing an emergency 3.5 million tons of food on top of the 6.5 million tons approved for 1966 to help meet India's serious food shortage. Yet a series of events—most notably the decision of the Indian government to devalue its currency under the pressure of the World Bank (which actually meant American pressure), and the Johnson Administration's effort to use food aid as a weapon against India's criticism of American involvement in the war in Vietnam—stirred up widespread anti-American sentiment in India. Relations between the two countries returned to the low point of earlier years.

The Bangladesh crisis of 1971, in which U.S. president Richard M. Nixon and Henry Kissinger adopted the policy of "tilt" toward Pakistan in spite of the opposition by the administration's own bureaucracy and criticism in the American press and the Congress, brought Indo-U.S. relations to an all-time low. There is an extensive literature on the Nixon-Kissinger policy toward the South Asian crisis of 1971 that attributes the U.S. "tilt" policy toward Pakistan variously to Nixon's personal distaste for Mrs. Gandhi and regard for Yahya Khan; America's preoccupation with forging a new relationship with China in which Pakistan would facilitate America's effort; and the U.S. effort to reward an old ally and punish India, which had signed a Friendship Treaty with the Soviet Union in early 1971. Following the liberation of Bangladesh, Nixon abruptly terminated $82 million in authorized aid to India in 1972, to which India responded by closing the AID establishment in October, 1973. The United States, however, recognized India's enhanced position

India prime minister Indira Gandhi, 1966. (AP/Wide World Photos)

in South Asia after the dismemberment of Pakistan. In March, 1973, the United States relaxed the embargo on arms supplies to India and Pakistan (the United States could sell non-lethal equipment and spare parts). In short, the U.S. government gave low priority to India.

Under President Jimmy Carter the United States made an effort to reorder its priorities in South Asia. Carter, who had a personal interest in India, visited New Delhi in January, 1978, and Prime Minister Desai visited Washington later that year. Yet the issue of nuclear nonproliferation and India's refusal to sign the Non-Proliferation Treaty (NPT) prevented any significant improvement in relations between New Delhi and Washington. The Soviet invasion of Afghanistan in 1979 made Pakistan once again a country of geostrategic importance to the United States. Moreover, when the U.S. government resumed military aid to Pakistan, this became a major source of tension between India and the United States in the 1980's. Yet unlike the 1970's, India downplayed areas of disagreement and emphasized the areas of cooperation. Since India had started liberalization of its economy in the early 1980's under Indira Gandhi, which was later accelerated by Rajiv Gandhi in 1985-1986, it was interested in improving trade (two-way trade between India and the

United States stood at $7 billion in 1990) and economic relations and acquiring sophisticated technology from the United States rather than emphasizing areas of disagreement.

U.S.-Pakistan Relations. Since its inception as a separate state in 1947, Pakistan has perceived India to be a major threat to its continuation as an independent state, and this perception has dominated its foreign-policy agenda. In contrast with India's policy of non-alignment, Pakistan started searching for a powerful ally from the beginning. For example, in 1947 Governor-General Mohammad Ali Jinnah requested $2 billion in military and economic aid from the United States in return for Pakistani alignment during the Cold War. Though Pakistan's request was not given serious consideration in 1947, by 1953 Eisenhower and John Foster Dulles focused on Pakistan as a fulcrum of American security design in the Near East and South Asia, and Washington was ready to strengthen ties to Karachi.

In its quest for military and technical assistance, Pakistan joined the Western power bloc by signing a Mutual Defense Assistance Agreement with the United States in 1954. On September 8, Pakistan joined Australia, France, New Zealand, the Philippines, Thailand, the United Kingdom, and the United States in SEATO, which was designed to prevent communist expansion throughout the area. The following year Pakistan joined CENTO with Iran, Turkey, and the United Kingdom for collective defense and for promotion of economic well-being of the regional countries. (The United States was not a full member of CENTO but sat in on its meetings as an observer.)

Pakistan's alliance with the U.S. government brought $1.2 billion in military aid from America between 1954 and 1965. In return Pakistan allowed the U.S. Central Intelligence Agency (CIA) to set up listening posts in its northern provinces to monitor the land-based missile sites in the Soviet Union and provided secret bases for U-2 spy plane flights. Under President Ayub Khan, Pakistan became America's "most allied ally." When Washington adopted a neutral position in the 1965 Indo-Pakistani war over Kashmir and suspended military aid to Pakistan (and India), however, Pakistan considered the American act as a betrayal by an ally, and relations between the two

U.S. military supplies, requested by India prime minister Nehru for use by Indian forces against Chinese Communist aggression, are unloaded at Calcutta airport in November, 1962. (National Archives)

countries became tense. Ayub Khan, who had earlier opposed simultaneous American military assistance to India, especially the emergency aid after the Indo-Chinese war in 1962, believed that America's neutrality in the war had tilted the military balance in the region against Pakistan.

Though the U.S. government resumed the sale of nonlethal military items to Pakistan (and India) in 1966, American prestige in Pakistan was seriously diminished. Pakistan modified its foreign policy and turned to communist states for military aid and economic cooperation. Zulfikar Ali Bhutto, Ayub's foreign minister, was instrumental in bringing about this shift in Pakistan's foreign policy. Believing that his country's overdependence on one superpower was not in its best interest, Bhutto advocated close relations with all powers with interests in the region. As a result of his effort Pakistan concluded economic cooperation agreements with both China and the Soviet Union (from China it also received military aid) while remaining aligned with the United States.

U.S.-Pakistani relations remained strained in the late 1960's and the 1970's. In the 1971 Bangladesh war, in which the Pakistani military government was committing genocide in order to prevent the secessionist movement in East Pakistan from succeeding, the United States did not assist Pakistan against India even though the Nixon Administration had taken a pro-Pakistan stand in recognition of Pakistani help in opening American relations with China. The U.S. embargo on arms shipments to Pakistan remained in place until lifted by U.S. president Gerald Ford in 1975. In the 1970's Pakistan formally ended its association with the Western alliance; Pakistan withdrew from SEATO in November, 1972, and from CENTO in March, 1979—months before it joined the Nonaligned Movement. U.S.-Pakistan relations reached a low point in 1979 when the anti-American sentiment was very strong and a Pakistani mob sacked the American embassy in Islamabad in November. Yet shortly after this incident there was a renewed interest in arming Pakistan because of its strategic importance after the Soviet invasion of Afghanistan in December, 1979.

Pakistan, being a frontline state facing the Soviet Union, was recognized as being of great strategic importance to the United States in its covert war against the Soviet occupation of Afghanistan. Toward that end, President Ronald Reagan gave Pakistan a six-year $3.2 billion package in military and economic aid in 1981. (Pakistan had earlier rejected Carter's offer of $400 million in military aid as insufficient.) In the "New Cold War" environment of the early 1980's, the U.S. strategy was to fight the Soviet Union in a clandestine war; therefore, Pakistan was given the responsibility of disbursing the aid to Afghan *mujahideen* resistance forces and of running the war. In the 1980's Pakistan emerged as one of the largest recipients of U.S. military assistance—the fourth largest in 1985 and the second largest in 1987. Yet the Soviet withdrawal from Afghanistan and the United States' growing concern over Pakistan's nuclear program resulted in the suspension of significant U.S. aid to Pakistan in 1990.

India and Pakistan at the Nuclear Crossroads. The advent of nuclear power in South Asia has been a major concern for the United States since the 1980's. After detonating a "peaceful nuclear device" in May, 1974, India became part of a select group that until then had comprised only the five permanent members of the U.N. Security Council. India's effort to develop nuclear capability, if not nuclear weapons, was mainly in response to the perceived threat from China, which had achieved nuclear capability in 1964. Yet India's decision to "join the nuclear club" was precipitated by the new regional and global realignments between and among major and lesser powers in the early 1970's. The U.S. "tilt" policy toward Pakistan in the 1971 Bangladesh war, which produced a sense of vulnerability on the part of India, brought India and the Soviet Union closer and led to the signing of the twenty-five-year Indo-Soviet Friendship Treaty in 1971. Moreover, the growing Sino-American diplomatic and economic ties following the visits of Secretary of State Kissinger and President Nixon to China in 1971 and 1972, respectively, were viewed by India to have significantly altered the strategic balance of power in the region.

After testing its nuclear device, India resisted American pressure and refused to sign the Non-Proliferation Treaty (NPT) of 1968, adhered to by 155 countries, on the ground that the treaty was discriminatory since the signatory was required to give up its symbolic sovereignty (embodied in nuclear capability) while nuclear-weapon states were not subject to such restrictions. As a result, India was denied certain kinds of international cooperation, which led it to become technologically more self-reliant. The country has since developed an enormous civil and military nuclear program. Spread across the country on sixteen sites, India's nuclear program is sophisticated and employs thousands of scientists and technical personnel. Though the government of India has consistently maintained that it has not yet assembled a nuclear bomb, India's nuclear capability makes it a "threshold power," that is, it only needs to "turn a screwdriver" to start production of nuclear weapons.

Pakistan's response to the development in neighboring India was to develop a nuclear program of its own. Throughout the late 1970's and 1980's Pakistan relentlessly pursued a covert nuclear program, which became a major issue in its relations with the United States. The U.S. government made an earnest effort to stop a nuclear arms race in South Asia. For example, Carter's national security adviser made an offer of $250 million in aid to Pakistan in return for the latter's commitment to dismantle its nuclear program. The offer was rejected by Pakistan, however, and it also refused to sign the NPT on the ground that Pakistan would do so only if India signed the treaty. In April, 1979, Carter terminated aid to Pakistan, in accordance with the Glenn amendment to the Foreign Assistance Act. Yet the Soviet invasion of Afghanistan in December, 1979, brought the United States and Pakistan closer again.

Reagan, unlike Carter, ignored the development of Pakistan's nuclear technology that enabled the latter to pursue the development of its nuclear program without much hindrance. It is ironic that despite the Solarz-Pressler amendment on foreign assistance and nuclear proliferation, Pakistan bought millions of dollars' worth of restricted high-tech materials in the United States in its pursuit of the bomb. Though the State Department and the CIA had information that Pakistan's uranium-enrichment plant at Kahuta had been enriching weapon-grade uranium at a 90 percent level, Reagan and later President George Bush certified to Congress, as required by the Pressler amendment to the Foreign Assistance Act, that Pakistan did not possess a nuclear explosive device. Thus Pakistan continued to receive American military and economic aid. The Soviet withdrawal from Afghanistan, however, allowed the Bush Administration to reestablish the link between military aid and nuclear nonproliferation. In October, 1990, the U.S. government suspended the $4.02 billion economic and military aid package to Pakistan that had been offered by Reagan in 1986 and was to be disbursed over fiscal years 1988 and 1993.

The Pakistani military leaders, including President Zia ul-Haq, considered the development of the country's program to be vital to its defense against India. Pakistan acknowledges India's military superiority and knows, after Pakistan's defeat in the Bangladesh war, that it could never withstand a full-scale Indian assault. The Pakistani military doctrine, therefore, is based on the belief that the best way to avoid a war with India is to have nuclear weapons as a deterrent against war. The proponents of this doctrine have dominated the Pakistani military establishment in the 1980's and 1990's. They have pursued the nuclear program zealously, so much that they even kept information about the development of the nuclear program and nuclear planning from Prime Minister Benazir Bhutto (1988-1990), who was never allowed to visit the nuclear facility at Kahuta.

In May, 1990, India and Pakistan came to the brink of a nuclear exchange, and the United States played an important role in defusing the crisis. After Bush read the intelligence report that Pakistan was preparing to launch a nuclear first strike against India, he sent personal envoy Robert Gates, then-deputy national security adviser, to Pakistan and India. Gates first met President Ghulam Ishaq Khan and General Beg in Islamabad and convinced them that in the event of a war between India and Pakistan the latter had no chance of winning. He then brought President Khan's assurance to India's Prime Minister V. P. Singh that Pakistan had agreed to shut down its training camps for Kashmiri insurgents. As a result of the American effort India and Pakistan moved their troops away from the borders, and by the end of June the crisis was over.

The 1990 crisis demonstrated that the acquisition of nuclear capability by India and Pakistan, South Asia's two traditional enemies, was potentially dangerous for the region and the world. "The upsurge of the Hindu-Muslim animosity throughout South Asia following the destruction of Ayodhya mosque," the 1993 Carnegie Report warns, "has heightened the danger of a war between India and Pakistan that could escalate to the nuclear level." The Indian and Pakistani refusal to allow international inspection of suspected weapons facilities is a further cause of concern for the United States. Though both deny the possession of nuclear weapons, experts believe that by 1991 India had enough weapons-grade plutonium to manufacture sixty weapons while Pakistan had enough highly enriched uranium to assemble six to ten nuclear weapons. Both countries have acquired or are in the process of acquiring ballistic missiles able to deliver nuclear weapons.

Outside the industrialized world, India's space program, which started in the 1970's, is the most developed. It has developed an antitank missile, surface-to-air missiles and in the early 1990's has tested and is

U.S. deputy national security adviser Robert Gates (left) meets with India prime minister V. P. Singh in New Delhi in May, 1990. Gates was leading a high-level American delegation to both India and Pakistan in hope of diffusing tensions between the two countries over the issue of Kashmir. (AP/Wide World Photos)

developing a short-range missile and a medium-range ballistic missile; the latter would boost the country's military capabilities. In July, 1993, India launched an indigenously made multipurpose satellite, INSAT-2B, which would enhance its communications, weather forecasting, disaster warning, and broadcasting services. In the same year India launched its Polar Satellite Launch Vehicle (PSLV), which launched a remote sensing satellite into a circular orbit around the earth at a height of eight hundred kilometers with a payload comparable to that of an intermediate-range ballistic missile.

The United States has tried, when possible, to slow the nuclear and missile race in South Asia. In 1991 it imposed a two-year ban on the export of high technology to the Indian Space Research Organization (ISRO), and in 1993 Russia canceled, under American pressure, the $350 million cryogenic rocket deal for India's space program. (The U.S. government warned that its $1.8 billion aid package to Russia would be seriously jeopardized if the latter sold the rocket technology to

India.) The U.S. government contends that the transfer of cryogenic technology, barred by the twenty-one-country Missile Technology Control Regime (MTCR) that seeks to control exports of technologies or components that have dual applications in civilian and military space industries, could be used by India to build long-range ballistic missiles. India had already mastered the solid-booster and liquid-fuel- engine technology and declared its intent to develop the cryogenic technology. In 1993 the United States also threatened to take action against China, which was alleged to have transferred M-11 missiles to Pakistan.

U.S.-South Asia Relations After the Cold War. The end of the Cold War, which fundamentally changed the global strategic balance, produced instability in India and Pakistan: Pakistan found that its Cold War ally (the United States) did not need it, and India's policy of nonalignment was disoriented after the collapse of the Soviet Union. As the strategic importance of Pakistan declined, America straightened its tilt toward Islamabad, and since 1991 its policy toward South Asia has been to stay equidistant from India and Pakistan. In the new international reality of the 1990's, India has taken the initiative and tried to develop close ties, especially economic, with the United States. After the cancellation of American military aid to Pakistan in 1990, no major obstacles to closer relations between the two existed. America began to recognize India as a regional power—the former backed India's military intervention in the Sri Lankan civil war and its employment of force in the Maldives coup, and it has given tacit support to India's role as security manager for South Asia.

America's relations with Pakistan were tense following the cancellation of aid in 1990. The tension subsided by the end of 1992, however, and a relaxed working relationship between the two developed. In 1992 Pakistan declared that it had the capability to produce nuclear weapons but did not actually possess those weapons. The tension between India and Pakistan continued over Kashmir and Punjab. Yet America's position on Indo-Pakistan issues—Kashmir and Punjab, in particular—has shifted in favor of India.

On the proliferation issue the administration of U.S. president Bill Clinton is more realistic, although there has been no basic change in America's stand. In a comprehensive report submitted to Congress in May, 1993, Clinton recognized that for India and Pakistan "domestic considerations are a vital factor in their deliberations" on the nuclear issue. The report noted that an opinion poll in India showed that 85 percent of those polled supported keeping India's nuclear option open. Similarly, there is a strong national consensus in Pakistan that its nuclear program is essential to national security. The report, which will form the basis of future legislation toward curbing proliferation in South Asia, stresses that proliferation in South Asia is a regional problem and in the end will require a regional solution—a direct, high-level dialogue between India and Pakistan.

The U.S. government has shown a willingness to facilitate talks between India and Pakistan over regional security and nonproliferation issues. It has been suggested by some in the Clinton Administration that the United States should push strongly for the establishment of a nuclear-weapon-free zone in South Asia. Concerned about rising tensions on the Asian subcontinent, the Clinton Administration renewed a proposal in July, 1993, which had been proposed with no success by the Bush Administration, for security talks between India and Pakistan involving Americans, Chinese, and Russians. The South Asian response to this proposal was not encouraging: Whereas the Pakistanis agreed to hold talks, the Indians did not. Though America remains interested in stopping the spread of nuclear weapons in the region and in creating conditions that would avert the possibility of a future war between India and Pakistan—which might involve the use of nuclear weapons—it lacks a strategic framework for South Asia; the region is not a top foreign policy priority for the Clinton Administration. Other regions and issues—the Middle East, the Bosnian conflict, and the problems in Russia, for example—are consuming the attention of senior officials. Unless there is a new crisis, it is unlikely that the U.S. government will get deeply involved in the regional security matters in this part of Asia as it did in the case of the Arab-Israeli conflict in the Middle East.

America has vital economic interest in South Asia that it will continue to promote and protect. The subcontinent, containing more than one billion people (estimated to rise to about two billion by the year 2025), offers significant trade, investment, and other economic opportunities to American business. India, with a 1992 population of almost 900 million, of which 125 million are middle class and have the income to make consumer choices, provides significant business opportunities to American corporations. After the Rao government introduced a most ambitious economic reform program in mid-1991 aimed at dismantling most government regulations and controls, there has been a substantial increase in American private investment in India, making the United States its leading foreign investor. Realizing the potential of the Indian market—a megamarket of the future—American corporations have rushed to invest in India. In computers, for example, all major American manufacturers— IBM, Apple, Dell, Hewlett Packard, and Compaq— were present in India by 1992. Nonresident Indians living in the United States have contributed to the development of the Indian economy by repatriating foreign exchange and investing in India. Since India is moving toward a globally oriented, competitive market economy, the outlook of Indo-U.S. economic relations is bright.—*Sunil K. Sahu*

SUGGESTED READINGS:

• Brands, H. W. *India and the United States: The Cold Peace*. Boston: Twayne, 1990. A good introductory book in the Twayne's *International History* series on Indo-U.S. bilateral relations. Brands provides a chronological and perceptive analysis of relations between the world's largest democracy and the world's oldest—which have been marked by disputes, misunderstandings, and near crises—within the framework of U.S. dealings with Asia and the Third World.

• Bratersky, M. V., and S. I. Lunyov. "India at the End of the Century: Transformation into an Asian Regional Power." *Asian Survey* 30 (October, 1990): 927. A Russian perspective on the emergence of India as a regional power in the 1970's and as a regional naval power in the 1980's. The authors argue that in the 1990's India will emerge as a major regional power in Asia.

• Carnegie Task Force on Non-Proliferation and South Asian Security. *Nuclear Weapons and South Asian Security*. Washington, D.C.: Carnegie Endowment for International Peace, 1988. This Task Force Report, which is a collective effort of eighteen experts on South Asia, examines the question of whether and how nuclear proliferation in the subcontinent can be slowed. It also examines the role of the United States, the Soviet Union, and China in the South Asian security equation.

• Ganguly, Sumit. *The Origins of War in South Asia: Indo-Pakistani Conflicts Since 1947*. Boulder, Colo.: Westview Press, 1986. Provides a comprehensive study of the forces that made Indo-Pakistani relations prone to conflict. Ganguly examines the factors—domestic, regional, and global—that led to three armed conflicts (1947-1948, 1965, and 1971) between India and Pakistan. The book also provides an analysis of the impact of the Soviet invasion of Afghanistan on the security of the subcontinent.

• Harrison, Selig S. "South Asia and the United States: A Chance for a Fresh Start." *Current History* 91 (March, 1992): 97-105. In this perceptive and prescriptive essay Harrison argues that the end of the Cold War, which has produced instability in India and Pakistan, presents the United States with an opportunity to make a fresh start in its relations with India. Arguing for closer relations with India, Harrison makes the following recommendations: Give India the same treatment that the United States gives to China, avoid getting involved in the Indo-Pakistani military rivalry, enlarge multilateral economic support for India, promote a regional rapprochement, encourage nuclear restraint, and support Indian membership in the UN Security Council.

• Hewitt, Venon Marston. *The International Politics of South Asia*. New York: Manchester University Press, 1992. An excellent comparative introductory textbook for undergraduate and graduate students on the international politics of seven South Asian states: India, Pakistan, Bangladesh, Bhutan, Nepal, Sri Lanka, and Maldives. Hewitt provides a comprehensive analysis of the internal factors—the legacy of colonialism, religious and ethnic conflict, and developmental objectives—that have important consequences for foreign policy. The book examines the bilateral relations—diplomatic, trade and economic—among South Asian states and between them and China, the United States, and the Soviet Union. Hewitt makes a strong connection between domestic and international politics and shows that the functioning of the liberal international economy has set a definite limit on the domestic policy options of the South Asian states. He argues that the 1990's will make or break these states.

• "India and Pakistan: Collision or Compromise?" In *Great Decisions*, edited by the Foreign Policy Association. New York: Foreign Policy Association, 1993. Provides a brief but clear account of the complex problems in Indian and Pakistani politics and the relations between the two—which have been marked by tension, three wars, and a nuclear and missile race in the 1990's—since the partition of India in 1947. The article is very informative and written for nonexperts. It covers, among other things, the nuclear arms race in South Asia, the future of India's policy of nonalignment, the Kashmir problem, the role of the U.S. government in the region, and the impact of domestic politics in India and Pakistan on their bilateral relations.

• Jackson, Robert. *South Asian Crisis: India, Pakistan and Bangla Desh: A Political and Historical Analysis of the 1971 War*. New York: Praeger, 1975. Provides a detailed account of the civil war in East Pakistan that led to its secession and the creation of a separate state, Bangladesh, in December, 1971. Sixteen important documents related to this crisis are appended to this book.

• Malik, Iftikhar H. "The Pakistan-U.S. Security Relationship." *Asian Survey* 30 (March, 1990): 284. A Pakistani perspective that analyzes the ups and downs in U.S.-Pakistani bilateral security relations from the 1950's until 1989.

• Palmer, Norman D. *The United States and India: The Dimensions of Influence*. New York: Praeger, 1984. A scholarly and detailed study of Indo-American relations that explains why relations between India, the largest democracy in the world, and the United States, the oldest democracy, have had their roller-coaster character. Palmer argues that the two democracies have perceived and pursued interests that are simultaneously divergent and convergent.

- Perkovich, George. "A Nuclear Third Way in South Asia." *Foreign Policy* no. 91 (Summer, 1993): 85. A perceptive analysis of the nuclear race between India and Pakistan. Of the three policy options discussed in the article—that both countries should eliminate their nuclear weapons capabilities and sign the NPT as a nonnuclear weapons state; that the U.S. government should help to manage overt nuclear proliferation in South Asia; and that the United States should seek to construct a nonweaponized deterence regime—Perkovich advocates the third option for the United States.

- Rudolph, Lloyd I., et al. *The Regional Imperative: The Administration of U.S. Foreign Policy Towards South Asian States Under Presidents Johnson and Nixon.* Atlantic Highlands, N.J.: Humanities Press, 1980. An in-depth study of the capacity of the Johnson and Nixon administrations to maintain coordination among a large number of policies affecting South Asian states. The book contains a lengthy introductory essay by the Rudolphs that, apart from commenting on the case studies that follow, makes a number of important recommendations. The Rudolphs argue that in the policy-making process, regional considerations were given less consideration by both the Johnson and the Nixon administrations than they require; they suggest organizational modifications, among other things, to improve the policy-making process. The ten case studies included in this volume provide detailed analysis of topics ranging from diplomatic-strategic and economic policy to people-to-people diplomacy.

- Thomas, Raju G. C. *Indian Security Policy.* Princeton, N.J.: Princeton University Press, 1986. A comprehensive study of India's security policy. Thomas analyzes the factors—strategic environment, domestic political system, economic issues, technological capability, and so forth—that influence India's security policy.

- Ziring, Lawrence, ed. *The Subcontinent in World Politics: India, Its Neighbors, and the Great Powers.* Rev. ed. New York: Praeger, 1982. This edited volume contains nine essays written by leading experts in the field; they provide a comprehensive and learned view of world politics in South and Southwest Asia. The book describes the rearrangement of power relationships in the "arc of crisis." Topics addressed in the volume range from superpower politics in South and Southwest Asia and the regions' security and military policy to the future of Afghanistan and the importance of Iran and Saudi Arabia in world politics. Since the book was published at the time of renewed hostility, or

"new cold war," between the United States and the Soviet Union, the articles focus on the superpower rivalry in South and Southwest Asia and the implications of the Soviet occupation of Afghanistan for the United States and the world. The main conclusion of the book is that the Soviet Union had moved into an advantageous position in this part of the world. Therefore, it recommends that the U.S. government must "reappraise its previous policies" and "evolve new strategies capable of defining its interests in an area of critical concern."

U.S. Supreme Court and internment: In 1944 in *Korematsu v. United States*, the U.S. Supreme Court, in a 6-3 vote, sustained the constitutionality of the federal government's exclusion of all persons of Japanese descent from the Pacific Coast and their internment in RELOCATION CENTERS in the interior. The majority of the justices found reasonable the assumption of the president, Congress, and military authorities that some Japanese Americans were disloyal and would likely aid the enemy in case of a Japanese invasion of the West Coast. Although discrimination on racial grounds must be subjected to rigid scrutiny, said the Court, the Constitution does not protect citizens against such discrimination when national security is at stake.

The Exclusion Order. Following the attack on Pearl Harbor, in February, 1942, President Franklin D. Roosevelt, fearing a Japanese invasion of the West Coast, issued EXECUTIVE ORDER 9066, authorizing the secretary of war to prescribe military areas from which any person might be excluded in order to prevent espionage and sabotage. In March the U.S. Congress enacted Public Law 503, providing criminal penalties for violation of any exclusion order that the military authorities might issue. In May, 1942, Lieutenant General John L. DeWitt, Western Defense commander, issued civilian exclusion order 34, which provided that "all persons of Japanese ancestry, both alien and nonalien, be excluded from" the western coast of the United States. The evacuation program initially required that about 112,000 Japanese Americans in the prescribed zone (two-thirds of whom were natural-born U.S. citizens) leave their homes, report to assembly points, and be transported under military control to relocation centers. (Ultimately, more than 120,000 Japanese Americans were interned.) The military authorities had earlier imposed a curfew, requiring all persons of Japanese origin living in the coastal area to remain in their homes between 8 P.M. and 6 A.M., but such confinement was judged to provide an insufficient degree of public safety.

The Constitutional Challenge. The Supreme Court unanimously sustained the curfew order in *Hirabayashi v. United States* (1943). Hirabayashi had contended that the Fifth Amendment of the Constitution prohibits discrimination between citizens of Japanese descent and those of another ancestry. Chief Justice Harlan Fiske Stone stated the Court's opinion that the Constitution gave wide scope to Congress and the president in the selection of the means for waging war. The exigencies of war, he concluded, override individual rights.

The *Hirabayashi* decision gave little hope to Fred Toyosaburo KOREMATSU as he sought to overturn his conviction under Public Law 503 for violating civilian exclusion order 34. Korematsu claimed that he was a loyal American citizen, that Northern California was not under martial law (temporary rule by military authorities imposed upon a civilian population in time of war), and that, contrary to the Fifth Amendment's prohibition against deprivation of liberty and property without due process of law, he had been seized, removed from his home, detained in a stockade, banished from the military area and imprisoned in a concentration camp, without benefit of trial or accusation of crime being brought against him.

In his opinion for the Court, Justice Hugo Black said that even in May, 1942, there was still some danger of a Japanese invasion and that the curfews and exclusion were well designed to prevent espionage and sabotage. The president and Congress, he said, were correct in concluding that there were disloyal members of the Japanese American population in California and that there was no easy way to isolate such individuals at a critical moment.

Although the exclusion was inconsistent with basic American governmental institutions, Black acknowledged, the power to protect the country must be commensurate with the threat. Justice Black emphasized the fact of congressional authorization for the president's order but did not say whether the president could have ordered the exclusion in the absence of such support. Strongly motivating the justices was the tradition of judicial deference to the president in the exercise of his war powers and to the expert judgment of military authorities.

The most enduring portion of Justice Black's opinion has proven to be his statement that "all legal restrictions which curtail the civil rights of a single racial group are immediately suspect [and] Courts must subject them to the most rigid scrutiny." This "strict scru-

tiny" standard, although of no avail to Japanese Americans during the war, was employed by the Court to dismantle the policy of racial segregation in the 1950's and 1960's, beginning with *Brown v. Board of Education* (1954).

The most memorable of the three dissenting opinions in *Korematsu* was that of Justice Frank Murphy, who characterized the exclusion as the product of racism. The exclusion order was unreasonable, he urged, because it was based on the assumption that *all* persons of Japanese ancestry had a dangerous tendency to commit sabotage and espionage and to aid the Japanese enemy in other ways. The military's commanding general referred to all individuals of Japanese descent as "subversive," as belonging to "an enemy race." The general testified that persons of Japanese ancestry "are a dangerous element" and that "we must worry about the Japanese all the time until he is wiped off the map."

The exclusion reflected the racial and economic prejudices of white Americans, said Justice Murphy. Examples of individual disloyalty do not prove group disloyalty. Under the American system of law, individual guilt is the sole basis for deprivation of rights. In the case of persons of German and Italian ancestry, he showed that individual investigations and hearings were conducted to separate the loyal from the disloyal. In Justice Murphy's opinion, if time had been of the essence, martial law would have been declared and the exclusion order would have been issued soon after the bombing of Pearl Harbor.

Aftermath. Although no Japanese American was ever found guilty of espionage or sabotage, the Supreme Court has never admitted that its decisions in *Hirabayashi* and *Korematsu* were wrong. Congress, however, following a presidential commission's condemnation after the war of the forced evacuation, passed the JAPANESE AMERICAN EVACUATION CLAIMS ACT OF 1948, under which Japanese Americans recovered more than $37 million—amounting, however, to only a small fraction of what they had lost. In 1984 a U.S. district court vacated Korematsu's conviction, based on the revelation that the government had deliberately withheld and falsified evidence during his trial. Finally, Congress passed the CIVIL LIBERTIES ACT OF 1988, legislation offering the nation's apology for the wartime treatment of Japanese Americans and providing $20,000 to each survivor of the internment (see REDRESS MOVEMENT).—*Kenneth Holland*

SUGGESTED READINGS: • Ball, Howard. "Politics Over Law in Wartime: The Japanese Exclusion Cases." *Harvard Civil Rights-Civil Liberties Law Re-*

view 19 (Summer, 1984): 561-574. • "Fancy Dancing in the Marble Palace: Internment of Japanese Americans During World War Two." *Constitutional Commentary* 3 (Winter, 1986): 35-60. • Irons, Peter. *Justice at War: The Inside Story of the Japanese American Internment Cases.* New York: Oxford University Press, 1983. • Kutler, Stanley. "At the Bar of History: Japanese Americans Versus the United States." *American Bar Foundation Research Journal* (Spring, 1985): 361-373. • Potts, Margaret. "Justice Frank Murphy: A Reexamination." *Supreme Court Historical Society: Yearbook* (1982): 57-65. • U.S. Congress. House. Committee on Interior and Insular Affairs. *Personal Justice Denied: Report of the Commission on Wartime Relocation and Internment of Civilians.* 102d Congress, 2d session, 1983. Washington, D.C.: Government Printing Office, 1992.

U.S.-Taiwan relations: U.S.-Taiwan contacts were neither extensive nor significant prior to the end of World War II (1939-1945). Subsequently the relationship became very important, especially for the Nationalist Chinese government, which made Taiwan its base of operations in 1949, when CHIANG KAI-SHEK fled mainland China. When the KOREAN WAR (1950-1953) started the United States became Taiwan's protector and provider of economic aid. The relationship changed, however, with the waning of bipolarity and particularly when the U.S. government sought better relations with the People's Republic of CHINA after 1969. Relations hit a low point in 1979, when the United States broke off diplomatic relations with Taiwan and established formal ties with China.

Relations Before 1950. In the mid-1800's Commodore Matthew C. Perry and several other American notables in the Far East recommended a U.S. presence on Formosa, as Taiwan was then called in the West; some even suggested colonizing the island. Top officials in Washington, D.C., however, rejected the idea. In 1895, when Japan made the island part of the Japanese Empire following war with China, the U.S. government did not object.

During World War II, in the Cairo Declaration of 1943, the United States promised that Taiwan would be returned to China. Following Japan's defeat the United States helped the Japanese evacuate the island and the Nationalist Chinese government of Chiang Kai-shek assume political control. Subsequently, however, the United States was embarrassed by the dictatorial rule of Nationalist Governor-General Chen Yi and his brutal repression of a rebellion in February, 1947.

In 1949 Washington changed its policy of helping Chiang Kai-shek fight the Communists. Losing the struggle, Chiang and his government and military fled to Taiwan. In early 1950 MAO ZEDONG's forces were poised to invade Taiwan after the U.S. government "washed its hands" of involvement in China's civil war and announced that Taiwan was not within its "defense perimeter."

Relations from 1950 to 1959. When the Korean War started in June, 1950, U.S. President Harry S Truman reversed U.S. China policy and ordered the 7th Fleet into the Taiwan Strait to block an invasion of Taiwan. The U.S. government also resumed aid, both economic and military, to Chiang Kai-shek. In 1954 Washington signed a military alliance with the Nationalist Chinese government on Taiwan as part of an effort to contain Communism in East Asia.

Crises occurred when Mao's forces attacked the Nationalist-held islands of Quemoy and Matsu off the coast of China in 1954-1955 and again in 1958. In both cases the U.S. government came to Taipei's rescue.

The United States, however, feared that Chiang Kai-shek would start a conflict with China that would expand into a broader war. Washington thus warned Chiang and sought to limit his offensive military capabilities. In 1959 Chiang acquiesced and declared that "liberating the mainland" would be a largely political endeavor.

Relations from 1959 to 1969. With the military situation stalemated and hopes for recovery of the mainland diminishing, Chiang put more emphasis on economic development. With the help of American aid this proved very successful. Taiwan's economic "take-off," which followed the termination of U.S. economic assistance in 1964, was facilitated by exports and access to the U.S. market.

Meanwhile U.S. diplomatic support for Taipei faded, and a two-China policy, or more accurately a one-China, one-Taiwan policy, seemed to be evolving in Washington. The development of such a policy, however, if this were the case, was stalled by the escalation of the war in Vietnam in 1964 and the Cultural Revolution in 1966, which evoked a self-imposed isolation by China.

Taiwan provided bases for the U.S. military during the Vietnam War and proved to be a loyal U.S. ally. Nevertheless, when American support for the war declined, the Nixon Administration, in 1969, sought détente with Beijing to help extricate the U.S. presence from Vietnam. As a consequence Taiwan's geostrategic importance to the United States diminished.

A shipment of military supplies is loaded onto a U.S. Air Force C-124 cargo plane in Richmond, Virginia, in 1958 for delivery to besieged Nationalist Chinese forces in Taiwan. (AP/Wide World Photos)

Relations from 1969-1979. Threatened by the Soviet military buildup, both the United States and China sought to improve relations with each other. In 1972 President Richard M. Nixon visited China. There he concluded the SHANGHAI COMMUNIQUÉ, which stated that Chinese on both sides of the Taiwan Strait believe that there is but one China and that the U.S. government does not challenge China's position that Taiwan is part of China. While it contained ambiguous language, it seemed to reverse any two-China stance.

Taiwan, as a result, lost formal diplomatic ties with more countries. Relations with the United States became cool. Yet Taiwan needed ties with the United States and the latter proved unwilling to abandon Taiwan completely for better relations with Beijing. Also, because of Watergate and Mao's death in 1976, Sino-U.S. relations did not progress further.

In mid-December, 1978, President Jimmy Carter announced that the United States would break diplomatic ties with Taipei and establish formal relations with China on January 1, 1979. He also announced the termination of the U.S.-Republic of China Defense Treaty. Taiwan was stunned.

Relations from 1979 to 1989. Carter's "abandoning" of Taiwan was countered by Congress' writing into law the Taiwan Relations Act in April, 1979. The act in essence returned to Taipei its sovereignty and reestablished U.S. security guarantees. It also created what observers said were two China policies (one by the administration and one by Congress, the former a one-China policy, the latter a one-China and one-Taiwan policy).

Taiwan responded, after a period of shock, by democratizing, parrying offers by Beijing to reunify the country, and establishing a flexible foreign policy. Taipei also increased its defense spending, seeking to maintain its own deterrence—to prevent Beijing from using military force against the island or to ensure that the United States would keep its security promises to Taiwan if this happened.

In the late 1980's trade relations between Washington and Taipei became a source of tensions—with Taiwan sending almost half of its exports to the U.S. market, adding considerably to the American trade deficit. Taipei made strenuous efforts to diversify its exports and in other ways cut the surplus. In 1988 the U.S. government ended Generalized System of Preferences (GSP) trade benefits to Taiwan. The U.S. deficit with Taiwan remained but became a less serious problem.

Relations After 1989. In 1989 Beijing reversed its democratic reforms, killing protesting students in Tiananmen Square with machine guns and tanks. Tai-

Into the 1990's, Taiwan's increasing financial clout has helped propel the country into the ranks of the world's economic superpowers. As a result, U.S.-Taiwan relations have improved considerably. (Taiwan Coordination Council)

wan, meanwhile, continued and even accelerated its decade-long period of democratization. Observers noted that Taiwan's government was no longer viewed as an authoritarian dictatorship in the United States and had shed its pariah-state image—almost as if it had passed such an image to China. This, plus Taipei's increased financial clout in the context of a new economic world order, where economic power was perceived as more important than military might, also helped improve Taiwan's influence in the United States, thereby setting U.S.-Taiwan relations on a much improved course.

In 1992 the United States pushed for Taiwan's admission to the General Agreement on Tariffs and Trade (GATT). Washington also reversed a policy set in a 1982 communiqué with Beijing of not selling Taiwan more arms when President George Bush authorized the sale of F-16 fighter planes to Taiwan.

On the one hand Washington's determination to maintain a balance of power in the Taiwan Strait in the face of Beijing acquiring new arms from Russia and the former republics worked to Taiwan's benefit in other ways. On the other hand Taipei expressed new concern with the Clinton Administration over growing protectionist and isolationist sentiments in the United States and with the American plan to withdraw its military from the region.—*John F. Copper*

SUGGESTED READINGS: • Copper, John F. *China Diplomacy: The Washington-Taipei-Beijing Triangle.* Boulder, Colo.: Westview Press, 1992. • Downen, Robert L. *The Taiwan Pawn in the China Game: China to the Rescue.* Washington, D.C.: Centre for Strategic and International Studies, 1979. • Gregor, A. James, and Maria H. Chang. *The Republic of China and U.S. Policy: A Study in Human Rights.* Washington, D.C.: Ethics and Public Policy Center, 1983. • Lasater, Martin L. *Policy in Evolution: The U.S. Role in China's Reunification.* Boulder, Colo.: Westview Press, 1988. • Myers, Ramon H., ed. *Two Chinese States: U.S. Foreign Policy and Interests.* Stanford, Calif.: Hoover Institution Press, 1978. • Wheeler, Jimmy W., and Perry L. Wood. *Beyond Recrimination: Perspectives on U.S.-Taiwan Trade Tensions.* Indianapolis: Hudson Institute, 1987.

United States v. Bhagat Singh Thind (1923): Unanimous U.S. Supreme Court ruling that aliens from India were ineligible to become naturalized American citizens. The Court reaffirmed that Congress had vested citizenship rights only in "free white persons" and persons of African descent. Since Asian Indians were not commonly considered to be white, the statute therefore did not apply to them. Empowered by this opinion, the U.S. government then proceeded to strip seventy Asian Indian Americans of their status as naturalized citizens. Over the next two decades Asian Indians in the United States would be denied naturalization and property rights. This injustice was finally rectified with the passage of the LUCE-CELLER BILL OF 1946, restoring naturalization and fixing a quota of one hundred immigrants from India to the United States annually.

Nativism on the Rise. In the period leading up to the case, states such as California—the destination of many Asian Indian immigrants—enacted laws restricting property ownership among aliens. The state's Alien Land Law, first passed in 1913, strengthened in 1920 and 1923, and intended to curb Japanese expansion into California agriculture, was applied to Asian Indians beginning in 1923. Under the 1913 version of the statute, aliens ineligible to citizenship, as well as companies the majority of whose members or stockholders were aliens, were prohibited from purchasing agricultural land and from leasing such land for longer than three years. Nor could an alien owner of agricultural land sell or bequeath it to another immigrant. Those caught violating the act were subject to strict penalties, such as confiscation of the property in question.

Such restrictive codes had been prompted by the public concern over increasing immigration into the Western states. Between 1899 and 1920 some seventy-three hundred immigrants from India, mostly agricultural laborers, relocated primarily to California. Many came from Canada to escape Canadian immigration restrictions or because the climate was better. In the first decade of the twentieth century, the popular opposition to the entire Asian influx included considerable opposition to that arriving from India. One extensive government study of the growing Indian community in 1910 concluded that Indians were the most undesirable of all Asians and that Americans residing in the Western states were unanimous in their desire to rid the region of Indian immigrants.

Federal Legal Appeals. Thind, born in Amritsar, Punjab, India, emigrated to the United States in 1913. During World War I, he was drafted into the U.S. Army, served six months, then was honorably discharged. He subsequently went to an Oregon federal

In the Thind *case the U.S. Supreme Court (pictured here in 1921) ruled that immigrant Asian Indians did not qualify for U.S. citizenship.* (Library of Congress)

district court and applied for U.S. citizenship. The Immigration and Naturalization Service (INS) of the U.S. Justice Department moved to cancel his petition based on the BARRED ZONE ACT OF 1917, under which virtually all nonwhite immigration from South Asia was excluded. While acknowledging the issue to be controversial, the district court in 1920 granted Thind's application after deciding that he was white. After the U.S. Ninth Circuit Court of Appeals upheld the lower court's findings, the INS, against the backdrop of popular nativist sentiment, appealed the case to the nation's highest court.

The major issues before the Court were whether to classify Thind, a high-caste Hindu, as a white person and, if so, whether he was therefore beyond the grasp of the exclusionary Barred Zone Act. Thind's lawyers argued that their client, like other Indians but especially those from the Punjab, was a member of the Aryan race—a Caucasian. Moreover, the terms "Caucasian" and "white person" were synonymous. Hence, they contended, an Indian is a white person eligible under U.S. law for naturalized citizenship. The justices, however, countered that the act of 1790, extending the right of citizenship only to "free white persons," was intended to benefit principally aliens from the British Isles and northwestern Europe. Additionally, the designation "white person" as it reappears in the act of 1917 must be taken to mean whatever the "common man" would understand it to mean. Such a construction excluded the obviously nonwhite peoples of Asia. The Court dismissed the term "Caucasian" as not being scientific or accurate and "Aryan" as having to do with linguistic rather than physical characteristics. Thind, the justices declared, plainly was not white.

The opinion further noted that federal legislation passed in 1790 and 1870 (which extended citizenship to aliens of African birth or descent) and subsequent hearings conducted in Congress clearly revealed a national policy of restricting citizenship exclusively to whites and blacks. Children of English, French, German, Italian, Scandinavian, and other European ancestry easily "merge into the mass of our population and lose the distinctive hallmarks of their European origin." Indian children, by contrast, retain the distinctive features of their ancestry and do not blend with the rest of society. Explained the Court: "It is very far from our thought to suggest the slightest question of racial superiority or inferiority. What we suggest is merely racial difference, and it is of such character and extent that the great body of our people instinctively recognize it

and reject the thought of assimilation."

It is interesting to note that the Court's reasoning in *Thind* flies in the face of its opinion in the earlier case of *Ozawa v. United States* (1922), which denied naturalization to a Japanese alien because he was not Caucasian. The Court in *Thind* agreed that the defendant was indeed Caucasian—but was still ineligible for citizenship because he was not white within the usual meaning of that term.

Consequences. Federal authorities in the United States used the *Thind* decision to annul previous grants of citizenship. Between 1923 and 1926, the INS cancelled the naturalization certificates of some fifty Indians. The ruling also disenfranchised some Euro-American women married to Sikhs and rendered these women stateless. As a result of *Thind* and California's ALIEN LAND LAWS, the number of Indian immigrants declined. Between 1920 and 1940 nearly three thousand immigrants returned to India, of whom only a few hundred were actual deportees. By 1940 the Asian Indian population in the United States was only twenty-four hundred.—*Hari Vishwanadha*

SUGGESTED READINGS: • Jacoby, Harold S. "More Thind Against Than Sinning." *Pacific Historian* 11, no. 4 (1958): 1-2, 8. • Leonard, Karen. *Making Ethnic Choices: California's Punjabi Mexican Americans.* Philadelphia: Temple University Press, 1992. • Leonard, Karen. "Punjabi Farmers and California's Alien Land Law." *Agricultural History* 59 (1985): 549-562. • Melendy, H. Brett. *Asians in America: Filipinos, Koreans, and East Indians.* Boston: Twayne, 1977. • U.S. Reports. *Cases Adjudged in the Supreme Court at October Term 1922.* Vol. 261. Washington, D.C.: Government Printing Office, 1923.

United States v. Ju Toy (1905): U.S. Supreme Court ruling that denied an American-born Chinese the right to reenter the United States. Ju Toy left the country to travel to China. Upon returning, he sought readmission on the basis of his American citizenship. After immigration officers rejected his application, he appealed to the U.S. secretary of commerce and labor, who affirmed the earlier decision. Ju Toy then took the case before a federal district court, seeking a writ of *habeus corpus*, a federal constitutional right that allows an individual held in some form of custody to allege that he or she is being detained unlawfully and to have the courts decide the matter quickly. Based on Toy's proof of U.S. citizenship, the district court ruled in his favor, and the government filed for an appeal.

The primary issue before the Supreme Court concerned the right of a Chinese U.S. citizen to claim the benefit of *habeus corpus*—a privilege to which any American citizen would ordinarily be entitled. The Court's response was that Chinese did not have this right even when such a petition was supported by a claim to citizenship. Legal precedent on this question, the opinion stated, had already been established a year earlier in the case of *United States v. Sing Tuck* (1904), which applied the ban to all individuals governed by the Chinese Exclusion Acts. Moreover, prior Supreme Court opinions had affirmed the established legal principle that decisions handed down by immigration officers affecting alien admissions are binding unless overturned by the secretary of commerce and labor. Finally, the justices, in dismissing Toy's petition for *habeus corpus*, saw no infringement of his federal constitutional right to due process of law, which guarantees to every citizen a fair and timely court hearing.

United States v. Jung Ah Lung (1888): U.S. Supreme Court ruling that allowed a lawful Chinese resident of the United States to reenter the country despite having no federal certificate of identification as specified by law. Chinese immigrant laborer Jung Ah Lung lived in San Francisco between 1880 and 1883, when he left the country to travel to China. A year earlier, the U.S. Congress had passed the CHINESE EXCLUSION ACT OF 1882, which among other things required all Chinese leaving the United States to present the certificates to immigration officers as a condition to being readmitted upon return. The act did not, however, explicitly make these certificates the only acceptable evidence for reentry — as an amendment to the act would in 1884. Before departing, Jung Ah Lung obtained a certificate.

Jung Ah Lung tried to reenter the United States in 1885 upon his return but was instead detained by customs officers when he could not produce the certificate. When the officers rejected his claim that the affidavit had been stolen, he filed a court petition for *habeus corpus* seeking his release from custody. After a federal appeals court accepted the petition and issued a decision in his favor, the government appealed to the Supreme Court.

The year before the Court had handed down an opinion in the similar case of *Chew Heong v. United States* (1884). That ruling involved a resident Chinese who had left the country prior to the passage of the 1882 act and who was denied readmission for lack of the necessary identification papers. There the Court recognized the unfairness of penalizing the petitioner

when prevailing conditions rendered compliance with the law physically impossible.

Reviewing the facts in the case at hand, the Court found that Jung Ah Lung had complied with all legal requirements regarding the certificates of identification and reentry. The act of 1882 could not, however, be read to stipulate that the only permissible means of identification were the affidavits. Moreover, although congressional lawmakers closed this loophole in the 1884 amendment, Jung Ah Lung was still out of the country and therefore not bound by its terms for the time that he was away. In any event, the amended law did not apply retroactively. The government could not therefore bar him from coming back into the United States.

United States v. Wong Kim Ark (1898): U.S. Supreme Court ruling that under the Constitution's Fourteenth Amendment a person born in the United States is a U.S. citizen, regardless of his or her ethnic background. Wong Kim Ark was born in San Francisco in 1873 of Chinese resident aliens. In 1890 he accompanied his parents on a trip to their homeland but subsequently returned to the United States. In 1894, after making another visit to China, he was denied reentry into the United States on the basis that he was not an American citizen.

The issue in *Wong Kim Ark* was whether a person born in the United States of alien parents was a citizen by virtue of the first clause of the Fourteenth Amendment, which declared that "[a]ll persons born . . . in the United States . . . are citizens." The court's majority opinion, written by Associate Justice Horace Gray, found this provision to be consistent with English common law. Gray pointed out that unless the father was a foreign ambassador or the parents were enemy aliens, a child born in England was the king's subject. The same rule applied in the American colonies and in the United States after the revolution. It followed, therefore, that the framers of the Fourteenth Amendment intended that "persons," irrespective of race or color or lineage, were citizens by birth and that Congress, even though it may bar Chinese aliens from entering the country and prohibit them from becoming naturalized citizens, may not legislate to restrict the effects of being born in the United States.

There was also a dissenting opinion in *Wong Kim Ark*. Chief Justice Melville W. Fuller, joined by Associate Justice John Marshall Harlan, argued that the English common law was inapplicable in the United States, that the effect of the American Revolution was to reject the English doctrine of indissoluble allegiance and to replace it with the right of expatriation. Rather than the English common law, international principles should prevail; the country of the father was the country of his children.

The importance of the Supreme Court's opinion in *Wong Kim Ark* was revealed in a startling manner during World War II. In *Regan v. King* (1942) there was an attempt to deny Japanese Americans the right to vote on the basis that they were not American citizens. The Federal District Court for the Northern District of California dismissed the suit, citing *Wong Kim Ark* as precedent, and the U.S. court of appeals affirmed that decision.

U.S.-Vietnam relations: Although U.S. relations with Vietnam began on a positive note in 1945, Cold War concerns soon overshadowed other considerations, and American soldiers entered Vietnam to defend the non-Communist south against the Communist north. After withdrawing U.S. troops in 1973, Washington failed to provide reconstruction aid to the north as promised in the Paris accords and made no effort to stop Khmer Rouge genocide and war against Vietnam. Despite Washington's policy of tying down Hanoi in an unwinnable military operation in Cambodia during the 1980's, Vietnam was increasingly cooperative from 1985, while Washington imposed one condition after another to the normalization of relations. In 1994, however, the United States lifted its trade embargo on Vietnam, and the two nations took the first steps toward normalizing relations.

Earliest Relations. In 1945, a small U.S. force arrived to aid Ho Chi Minh in a joint effort to defeat Japan. One month later, when Ho read Vietnam's independence declaration, modeled on the American Declaration of Independence of 1776, to the assembled citizens of Hanoi, a U.S. airplane dipped down and showed its insignia, and the crowd cheered joyously.

Although President Franklin D. Roosevelt wanted a United Nations (UN) trusteeship for Vietnam after World War II (1939-1945), Great Britain's prime minister Winston Churchill, eager to regain dominion, vetoed the idea. France tried to reassert colonial authority, and in 1953 President Dwight David Eisenhower imposed an embargo on Ho's forces and provided aid to France, but the support came too late. After the Geneva Conference of 1954 divided Vietnam into Ho's Democratic Republic of Vietnam in the north and the State of Vietnam (later, the Republic of Vietnam) in the south, American secretary of state John Foster Dulles drafted a collective security treaty that formed the basis for the Southeast Asian Treaty Organization (SEATO) to provide a legal basis for intervention to hold back the Communist north. Although the Geneva accords called for parliamentary elections in 1956 for a unified Vietnam, Dulles urged Saigon not to sign the agreement, as Ho was the likely winner. Thereafter, Washington backed a series of unpopular regimes in the south.

Entry into War. In 1965, President Lyndon B. Johnson was persuaded that only U.S. military forces could prevent the fall of the south; otherwise, he believed, non-Communist states in Southeast Asia and ultimately Japan might fall like a "row of dominoes" into the Communist orbit. When U.S. troops pushed aside the army of the south, rather than bolstering its fighting capabilities, Vietnamese saw the new war as the "American War," and opposition to the United States soon exceeded the will to resist forces allied with Hanoi.

From 1968, Johnson sought to negotiate a withdrawal of U.S. troops, but the north anticipated an inevitable victory. In 1973, the two parties signed accords at Paris. Washington promised aid to reconstruct the north; in exchange, Hanoi agreed never to annex the south. When Congress blocked aid to the north, Hanoi sent troops to the south, which surrendered in 1975. U.S. embassy personnel and Vietnamese on the American government payroll fled the country in a panic during the last days before the fall of Saigon. A flow of refugees, escaping on boats into the South China Sea, brought even more Vietnamese from the country, and about a million eventually arrived in the United States.

Normalization Scuttled. Upon taking office in 1977, President Jimmy Carter launched a peace offensive that might have normalized relations between the two countries, but Hanoi was unwilling to proceed as long as the U.S. government withheld reconstruction aid, as promised at Paris. Meanwhile, Khmer Rouge claims to annex the territory of southern Vietnam to Cambodia, punctuated with KHMER ROUGE atrocities on civilians inside Vietnam, prompted Hanoi to respond by unifying the two parts of Vietnam under a single government, the Socialist Republic of Vietnam. As the Khmer Rouge secured backing from the People's Republic of China, Hanoi complained in the UN and elsewhere that Vietnam was a victim of unprovoked aggression. U.S. envoys refused to act. Vietnam became desperate as some thirty thousand civilian Vietnamese were butchered by the Khmer Rouge, more than had lost

Villagers of Da Nang, South Vietnam, bid farewell to departing U.S. troops in March, 1973, in the wake of the Paris peace accords signed in January. (AP/Wide World Photos)

their lives in fighting against the French for more than a century. Although unwilling at first to allow the Soviet Union to use military facilities in Vietnam, Hanoi agreed to this price for Moscow's support, launching a counteroffensive into Cambodia in late 1978 and early 1979 to drive the Khmer Rouge to the Mekong. When the Cambodian people greeted the People's Army of Vietnam (PAVN) as saviors from the "killing fields," the army proceeded to the Thai border.

During the next decade, Vietnam called for an international arrangement that would permit the PAVN to leave Cambodia. China, Thailand, and the United States, however, arranged to assure a steady flow of military supplies to the Khmer Rouge and its allies, which occupied camps inside Thailand as bases for aggression against Vietnam's army in Cambodia. Knowing that the PAVN's unilateral withdrawal would mean the return of POL POT to power, Washington continued the earlier embargo on trade, with the aim of "bleeding

Vietnam white," in order to keep Vietnam tied down in Cambodia.

Improving Relations. In 1985, Hanoi announced that by 1990 the PAVN would withdraw from Cambodia, as by then the Phnom Penh government's army would be able to handle the Khmer Rouge unassisted. Hanoi also began to cooperate more fully in allowing Amerasians and immigrants to leave for the United States under the Orderly Departure Program, but Washington believed that Vietnam was refusing to account for soldiers missing in action (MIAs) from the war.

Pressure mounted in academic and business circles to normalize relations with Hanoi, but Washington insisted that Vietnam must first leave Cambodia. In 1989, when the PAVN marched out of Cambodia, Washington changed its policy, telling Hanoi that normalization of relations awaited a multilateral peace agreement regarding Cambodia, a condition that de-

U.S. presidential adviser Henry Kissinger (right) confers with North Vietnamese delegates following the signing of the peace agreement in Paris in January of 1973. North Vietnamese chief negotiator Le Duc Tho stands just left of Kissinger. (AP/Wide World Photos)

pended more on an end of U.S. support for the Cambodian resistance than on any action by Vietnam, which played a much lesser role in Phnom Penh. In the spring of 1991, Washington promised normalization only after free elections in Cambodia based on an international peace treaty. In October, 1991, after Australia, France, and Indonesia prevailed on China and the United States to be reasonable to Vietnam, a Cambodian peace treaty was signed in Paris. In 1992, U.S. government officials demanded more information on MIAs, yet another new precondition for normalization, and Hanoi opened more archives, resolving the matter, whereupon Washington insisted that Hanoi release all political prisoners.

A breakthrough came on February 3, 1994, when President Bill Clinton ordered an end to the nineteen-year U.S. trade embargo on Vietnam. The lifting of the embargo permitted unrestricted commercial ties between the United States and Vietnam. (Beginning in 1992, commercial sales to Vietnam had been permitted, but only in the case of products that were considered to meet basic human needs.) In May, 1994, the United States and Vietnam announced an agreement to open diplomatic missions in each other's capitals—a key step toward full normalization of relations.—*Michael Haas*

SUGGESTED READINGS: • Haas, Michael. *Genocide by Proxy: Cambodian Pawn on a Superpower Chessboard*. New York: Praeger, 1991. • Kahin, George McT. *Intervention: How America Became Involved in Vietnam*. New York: Alfred A. Knopf, 1986. • Kissinger, Henry S. *Years of Upheaval*. London: Weidenfeld & Nicolson, 1982. • McCoy, Alfred W. *The Politics of Heroin in Southeast Asia*. New York:

Harper & Row, 1972. • Sheehan, Neil. *A Bright Shining Lie: John Paul Vann and America in Vietnam*. New York: Random House, 1988.

Uno, Edison (Oct. 19, 1929, Los Angeles, Calif.—Dec. 24, 1976): Political and community activist. To many Japanese American activists, Uno was the father of the redress movement. He was the son of George and Riki Uno. In 1942, at the age of twelve, he and his family began a journey that changed not only their lives but also the lives of all Japanese Americans living at the time on the West Coast. Because of the war with Japan and the racist policies of U.S. government officials, Uno and other Japanese Americans were imprisoned in the various internment camps run by the federal WAR RELOCATION AUTHORITY (WRA) and the U.S. Justice Department. He spent more than four years in camps located at Santa Anita Racetrack, California, at Granada, Colorado, and at Crystal City, Texas. In his writings he professed to hold the record as the person interned the longest by the government.

Uno's camp experience left a deep impression on his life. At the age of eighteen, he became president of the JAPANESE AMERICAN CITIZENS LEAGUE'S (JACL's) East Los Angeles chapter and later married Rosalind Kido, daughter of wartime national JACL president Saburo Kido. While in his early twenties, Uno attended Hastings College of the Law in San Francisco and suffered a serious heart attack. Following the advice of his doctors, he abandoned his ambition of becoming a lawyer and instead focused his energy into causes concerning the Japanese American community. He worked on numerous issues through the years, including the repeal of Title II of the Internal Security Act of 1950 and the pardon for Iva Toguri d'Aquino ("TOKYO ROSE"). His most memorable crusade, however, was his tireless push for redress in the early 1970's. His dedication to the redress movement inspired a countless number of other activists to join the cause and fight for justice. Unfortunately, on December 24, 1976, he died of a heart attack and was deprived of seeing his goal accomplished. His legacy, however, will continue to live through the young activists he inspired.

Uno, Roberta (b. May 12, 1956, Honolulu, Hawaii): Theatrical producer and director. Founding and artistic director of the New World Theatre in Amherst, Massachusetts (1979), she championed the rights of artists of color by creating a performance forum in which their voices could be heard. Along with editing one of the

first anthologies devoted to Asian American women playwrights, *Unbroken Thread: An Anthology of Plays by Asian American Women* (1993), she has developed and directed world premieres of plays by Hispanic American, African American, and Asian American dramatists.

Urasenke School of Tea: Located in Kyoto during the Tokugawa era (1600 to 1867), the school was founded by Shoshitsu Sotan and was one of the components of the Seke School of Tea, which also included the Omotosenke School founded by Shoshitsu Sotan's brother Sosa. Because of the TEA CEREMONY's growing popularity among the rising merchant class, the brothers could devote full time to the art. They practiced a looser style than their father and tea master, Sen no Sotan.

Urdu: The national language of Pakistan and one of the sixteen official languages of India. It is spoken by approximately fifty million speakers in the subcontinent of India and Pakistan. It is a descendant of the Sanskrit language and belongs to the Indo-European language family. The term "Urdu" is Turkish in origin. Both Hindu and Urdu have their origins in the mixed speech spoken around the area of Delhi, North India, which gained currency during the twelfth and thirteenth centuries as a contact language between native residents and Arabs, Afghans, Persians, and Turks. In time, this mixed speech called *khari bili* developed its own variety, Urdu.

In many respects, Urdu and Hindi are mutually intelligible, and at other levels they are quite unintelligible. Muslims often report their speech variety as Urdu, and Hindus and other non-Muslim speakers tend to report their speech variety as Hindi.

Urdu is particularly known for its separate script. It is written in the Perso-Arabic script. Like Arabic, it is written from right to left, and short vowels are usually not written. It is because of Urdu that the Arabic script underwent maximum modification and that some new symbols were added to it.

Although Hindi and Urdu are written in two different scripts, the two languages differ from each other in minor ways in their grammatical systems and vocabulary. Urdu tends to borrow its vocabulary from Perso-Arabic sources, whereas Hindi borrows from indigenous Sanskrit sources. This tendency has resulted in the admission of some new sounds into Urdu and in the development of its distinct literary style.

Hindi and Urdu have a common form known as

"Hindustani." This was the variety that was adopted by Mahatma GANDHI and the Indian National Congress as a symbol of national identity during the struggle for freedom from England. Urdu literature flourished both in India and Pakistan. The literary history of Urdu can be traced back to the thirteenth century.

Uyeda, Clifford (b. Jan. 14, 1917, Olympia, Wash.): Pediatrician and civil rights activist. A Nisei reared and educated in Tacoma, Washington, Uyeda was accepted as an undergraduate at the University of Wisconsin, where he majored in English. After graduating cum laude with a bachelor's degree in 1940, he was accepted into medical school at Tulane University. Unlike most Japanese Americans, who were interned during World War II, he was able to continue his studies during the war. Completing his pediatric internship at Harvard Medical School and Boston's Massachusetts General Hospital, Uyeda went on to serve as a medical officer with the U.S. Air Force during the Korean War from 1951 through 1953. He established a private practice upon his return and eventually settled in the San Francisco Bay Area.

During the 1970's, Uyeda became active with the JAPANESE AMERICAN CITIZENS LEAGUE (JACL). He helped found the Golden Gate chapter of the JACL, campaigned vigorously for a presidential pardon to be given to accused collaborator Iva Toguri d'Aquino (known as "TOKYO ROSE"), and worked to ease tensions between JACL supporters and Japanese Americans who had resisted the draft during World War II. Uyeda served as the organization's president from 1977 to 1980 and served as chair of the JACL committee established to obtain redress from the federal government for indignities suffered by Japanese Americans during World War II. Concerned about preserving the rich cultural heritage of Japanese Americans, Uyeda worked with the National Japanese American Historical Society (NJAHS), serving as editor of the

Clifford Uyeda. (Asian Week)

society's newsletter *Nikkei Heritage* and acting as president of the society between 1988 and 1992.

Uyemoto, Holly: Novelist. She was still in her teens when her first novel, *Rebel Without a Clue*, was published in 1989. Residing in Northern California, she had decided at the age of fifteen to become a writer. The characters in her novel are not explicitly Asian American; she touches on issues facing youths of all races, including love, friendship and family relationships, going off to college, popular culture, and AIDS.

V

Vang Pao (b. 1932?, Laos): Military officer, politician, and Hmong refugee leader. During the Laotian Civil War (1960-1975), he commanded a major military force that was allied with the United States' government and the rightist government of Laos. Laos fell in 1975, and Vang fled with a substantial portion of his army and the fighters' families to Thailand. That same year, he went to the United States, while his supporters remained in Thai refugee camps. In the United States, he founded the social service agency Lao Family Community, which played a major role in the resettlement of HMONG refugees during the 1980's. During this time, he also founded the United Lao National Liberation Front (NEO HOM), which supported the overthrow of the Communist government in Laos.

Vang's military career started in 1945 at age thirteen, when he was an interpreter for anti-Japanese French commandos. By 1954, he had risen to become the commander of a force of 850 men that took heavy casualties in a futile attempt to rescue the French garrison at Dien Bien Phu during the First Indochina War (1946-1954). By about 1960, he had a commission in the Royal Lao Army. In this role, he established a special relationship with the U.S. Central Intelligence Agency (CIA), which was interested in him because of his reputation as a military leader willing to take risks and suffer casualties in the pursuit of military objectives.

Defeats in the remote mountains along the North Vietnamese border resulted in the retreat of Vang's army into the Plain of Jars in central Laos in 1969-1972. There, a refugee camp and a military base with up to one hundred thousand people were established near Long Tien. Hmong were perhaps the largest ethnic group in this camp, but there were also substantial populations of KHMU and other groups allied with the rightists. This population remained in Long Tien under the command of Vang until 1975, when the Laotian government fell to the Communists. In 1975, Vang and about fifty thousand of his Hmong followers fled to Thailand, where large refugee camps were established on the Mekong River border. Tens of thousands more left Laos in the late 1970's and 1980's. Vang himself continued to the United States in 1975.

In 1978, Vang established the grass-roots social service agency Lao Family Community. This agency administered government contracts to provide social services for the approximately one hundred thousand Hmong refugees who followed him to the United States in the 1980's. Vang was the president of this agency until 1988, when he resigned as a result of factionalism within the Hmong community. Despite the loss in practical administrative authority, he continued to be the charismatic head of the Hmong in the United States and Thai refugee camps. During the 1980's, he also continued to be involved with resistance forces fighting the Communist government in Laos. For a short time in the 1980's, he held a portfolio as deputy minister of defense in a rightist government-in-exile.

Van Reed, Eugene Miller (?—1873, Pacific Ocean): Businessperson and public official. Van Reed was the American responsible for the recruitment of the first

General Vang Pao, 1971. (AP/Wide World Photos)

group of Japanese laborers to Hawaii. A businessman living in Japan, he was appointed as Hawaii's consul general to Japan in 1865. He was instructed to secure a treaty of friendship and commerce between Japan and the kingdom of Hawaii and gain permission to recruit laborers for the sugar plantations. There was a dire need for laborers because the Native Hawaiian population was greatly diminished and because the Chinese, first to be brought over as laborers, tended to leave the plantations when their first contracts expired.

Although Japan seemed a promising source of laborers, it was in a period of instability. Having been a closed country until forced open by Commodore Matthew C. PERRY of the United States in 1853-1854, Japan was uncertain on how to deal with foreign demands. Nevertheless, Van Reed did manage a tentative agreement on a treaty with the Japanese. At the crucial moment, however, the Japanese government claimed that as a merchant, he was not a person of high enough rank to sign the treaty.

Van Reed had gained permission from the Tokugawa government to recruit laborers for the sugar plantations of Hawaii. Because Van Reed shipped out the recruits without the permission of the Meiji government, which had come into power in the interim, however, Japanese officials were furious and believed that their government's honor was at stake. Nevertheless, they were advised by foreign diplomats of the extraterritorial rights (the rights of foreigners to be subject only to the laws of their own country) provided for in treaties signed by Japan. The American minister argued: "I cannot see Van Reed has been guilty of the breach of any of the laws of the United States."

In February, 1871, Van Reed resigned his commission as consul general but was asked to continue as acting consul general. In 1873 he died at sea on his way back to the United States. Previously a treaty between Japan and the kingdom of Hawaii had been signed in August, 1871.

Varna: Hindu caste system. The Sanskrit term *varna* literally means "color" and is used in India for the social-class system known in English as "CASTE." Since ancient times, Indian society has been organized as a hierarchy of four social classes, each hereditary and ranked according to status. The earliest reference to this social system is found in the text *Rgveda*, or *Rig Veda.* This text is the foundation for the Hindu religious tradition and can be dated at about 1200 B.C.E. It presents a way of organizing society as divinely created and as part of the order of the cosmos. Later legal texts specify the rights and duties of each *varna.*

The usual description of the *varna* groups is as follows: The group highest in status is the brahmin class, which consists of priests and scholars of the religious tradition and their female family members. The second group in the hierarchy is the warrior class, the professional warriors and their female family members. The third group is the commoners, who are farmers, business owners, and artisans. The fourth group is the servant class, whose members serve the other classes as manual laborers, servants, and the like. The first three groups are descendants of the Aryan people who conquered India beginning about 1500 B.C.E., while the fourth *varna* includes those who were conquered. In addition to these four *varna* groups, there is a fifth one called the "untouchables," which consists of tribal peoples and others who are regarded as being of such low status that they are not part of this *varna*, or caste system. *Varna* ideally functions as a system for the division of labor, with each group having its clearly defined role. Although the system is based on heredity, there have been many cases of marriage across *varna* lines.

The constitution of India, adopted in 1950 shortly after India achieved independence, declared all forms of discrimination based on the *varna* system illegal in India. Many people in India, however, continue to describe themselves in terms of one or another of the *varna* groups.

Varona, Francisco: Political appointee and labor mediator. In 1920, Varona was selected by Francis B. HARRISON, governor-general of the Philippines, to investigate labor conditions endured by Filipino workers on Hawaiian sugar plantations and determine a plan of action for assisting those laborers unable to return to the Philippines upon completion of their contracts. During his visit, Varona negotiated an agreement known as the "Honolulu Contract," calling for plantation owners to provide means by which laborers whose contracts did not guarantee their return passage could earn funds to return home. After completing an extensive tour of labor camps on the Hawaiian Islands, Varona submitted a report to Harrison that provided details of camp conditions and placed the blame for labor unrest on racial tensions between Filipino laborers, Japanese laborers, and white plantation owners. In his report, Varona provided several recommendations for alleviating these tensions. In 1939, Varona was appointed to serve as chief of the national division of the Philippine Resident Commissioner's Office reporting to Commissioner Joaquin M. Elizalde. As part of his duties, Varona was responsible for mediating various labor disputes between Filipino laborers and their employers.

Varsity Victory Volunteers (VVV): Labor battalion formed by Nisei volunteers in Hawaii during World War II. In the wake of the Japanese attack on PEARL HARBOR in 1941, many Japanese Americans were forced out of the Hawaii Territorial Guard because their ancestry caused their loyalty to be placed in doubt. Many former guard members signed a petition addressed to the territory's commanding general, Delos EMMONS, in January of 1942 requesting that their loyalty be recognized and that they might be allowed to serve their country in some capacity. As a result of their efforts, the Varsity Victory Volunteers were formed as an auxiliary to the 34th Combat Engineers Regiment in February of that year. The group's volunteer members made heroic contributions to the civil defense of Hawaii by performing manual labor, undertaking construction projects, and supporting local war bond drives. Their visible support for the American war effort allayed many fears and defused tensions that had mounted between Japanese American and Caucasian communities on the islands. In January of 1943, the group was officially disbanded; since the armed forces' ban on Japanese American inductees had been lifted, many former VVV members went on to join the all-Nisei 442ND REGIMENTAL COMBAT TEAM and fought with distinction during the remainder of the war.

Vedanta: Orthodox system of Indian philosophy. The Sanskrit term "Vedanta" means the "end " (*anta*) of the Vedas, the sacred texts of the Hindus, or the culmination (*anta*) of all knowledge (*veda*).

Vedanta is one of six Hindu philosophical systems that are grouped in three complementary pairs: Nyaya and Vaisheshika, Sankhya and Yoga, Purva-Mimamsa (early study) and Vedanta (later study). The Purva-Mimamsa, attributed to the Indian philosopher Jaimini (fl. c. 200 B.C.E.), recognizes the authority of the Vedas (especially the Brahmanas), which teach *dharma* (right action).

The central concern of Vedanta is the inquiry into the nature of "Brahman," which is ultimate reality, the true nature of all existence. The main Vedanta texts are the *Upanishads*, the Bhagavadgita, and the *Brahma-sutra* (or Vedanta-sutras) of Badarayana (c. fourth century B.C.E.). There are three philosophical schools of Vedanta: the Advaita (Nondualist) school of the seventh

or eighth century philosopher Sankara, the Visistadvaita (Qualified Nondualist) school of the eleventh or twelfth century thinker Ramanuja, and the Dvaita (Dualist) school of the thirteenth century thinker Madhva.

According to Sankara, the world as it is normally perceived is merely a manifestation of Brahman that is neither absolutely real nor absolutely unreal. The ordinary world exists in the sense that it is a manifestation of ultimate reality; it is illusory because it itself is not ultimate reality. People perceive this manifestation of Brahman rather than the ultimate nature of Brahman because their ignorance (*avidya*) prevents them from perceiving what is ultimately real. Sankara describes the ultimate Brahman, or *nirguna* Brahman (Brahman without qualities), as consisting of being (*sat*), consciousness (*cit*), and bliss (*ananda*). This ultimate Brahman produces the illusion of the everyday world, which is known as *saguna* Brahman (Brahman with qualities). When one perceives directly (experientially rather than intellectually) that one's individual soul (*atman*) is in fact one with ultimate Brahman, one becomes liberated in this lifetime, and one's soul attains complete freedom at death.

Ramanuja, a Vaisnava scholar, claims that the individual soul and the concrete world are like one body of Ishvara (God), who is none other than Brahman. Thus, everything is contained within Brahman, but individual souls do exist. Ramanuja's theistic doctrine is known as Visistadvaita—a complex organic unity of God, soul, and matter.

Another Vaisnava scholar, Madhva, is a dualist in that he accepts the reality of the material world but regards Brahmin, or God, as the controller of an immense variety of different entities that exist throughout the universe. Ramanuja's qualified nondualism is a compromise between Sankara's radical monism and Madhva's fundamental dualism.

Venice celery strike of 1936: Labor strike by eight hundred Mexican, two hundred Japanese, and a small number of Filipino celery pickers against Japanese American celery growers in Venice, California, to demand better wages and collective bargaining rights. The California Farm Laborers Association, formed by Japanese laborers in 1935, allied with the Farm Workers of America for the protest. Growers, through the eight-hundred-member strong Southern California Farm Federation, received assistance from the police, the U.S. Immigration Service, and the Japanese consulate. Moreover, in quelling the strike, growers gained the support of Japanese American community institutions, such as the Japanese American Citizens League (JACL), the *Rafu Shimpo* newspaper, banks, and the Japanese Association. The strike lasted from April 17 until June 8, when Mexican workers compromised on wages and dropped the demand for collective bargaining.

Vera Cruz, Philip Villamin (Dec. 25, 1904, Saoang, Philippines—June 11, 1994, Bakersfield, Calif.): Labor union official. Vera Cruz served as the highest-ranking Filipino American officer of the United Farm Workers (UFW) union from 1971 to 1977, second only to César Chavez and Dolores Huerta in the union leadership. A tireless organizer and militant activist, Vera Cruz helped bring about national awareness of the plight of California's farmworkers during the tumultuous 1960's, participating in the famous protests against growers in California's Central Valley that led to the formation of the UFW in the early 1970's. Vera Cruz also campaigned for the restoration of political free-

Philip Vera Cruz. (San Francisco Chronicle)

doms in the Philippines when that country came under a dictatorship in 1972. He represents the last in a long line of militant Filipino labor organizers since the 1920's, part of the generation of pioneering immigrants called the MANONGS. Through his activism, Vera Cruz linked the varied concerns of the old and the new immigrants.

Early Life. Vera Cruz was born in a small town in the northern Philippine province of Ilocos Sur. He grew up in small farming communities, reared by his parents and by his grandmother. As the oldest of three children, the young Vera Cruz obtained a limited education in schools run by the American colonial government, spending most of his time working in the fields.

In 1926 Vera Cruz came to the United States with dreams of working, saving money, and then going back to his family in the Philippines. As it turned out, he never saw his parents again. His father died two years after his arrival, while his mother died in 1972, at the height of Vera Cruz's involvement in the farmworkers' struggles. Vera Cruz supported himself and his family in the Philippines by working at farming and low-wage occupations in various cities, from Cosmopolis, Washington, to Manville, North Dakota, experiencing firsthand the class exploitation and racism directed toward Filipinos—which included laws against racial intermarriage—to which he would attest in his later political life. During this time he plowed through high school and attended some classes at Gonzaga University in Spokane, while supporting his younger brother and sister through college in the Philippines, an achievement from which he took considerable pride.

In 1943 Vera Cruz moved to Delano, a city in California's San Joaquin Valley, to work in the area's vineyards. He remained there until the Delano grape strike (1965). In the interim he participated in a number of farm labor organizing efforts. He joined in the Stockton asparagus strike of 1948, led by Chris Mensalves and Ernesto Mangaoang, two prominent Filipino union leaders who fought the U.S. Immigration and Naturalization Service's attempt to deport them and break the strike. In the late 1950's Vera Cruz joined and served as leader of the fleeting National Farm Labor Union (NFLU). In the early 1960's he joined what came to be one of the parent organizations of the UFW, the AGRICULTURAL WORKERS ORGANIZING COMMITTEE (AWOC), a predominantly Filipino union founded by members of the AMERICAN FEDERATION OF LABOR-Congress of Industrial Organizations (AFL-CIO).

The Formation of the UFW. Vera Cruz took part in

Vera Cruz's increasing disenchantment with the administration of UFW head Cesar Chavez (shown here at a union gathering in 1974), including Chavez's support of the Marcos regime in the Philippines, resulted in Vera Cruz resigning his union post in 1977. (AP/Wide World Photos)

the historic AWOC grape strikes in Coachella and Delano in 1965 that began the largest and most successful agricultural protests in California in the twentieth century. Chavez' National Farm Workers Association, a predominantly Mexican American group, immediately joined the strike. Both the strike and the efforts to force growers to sign union contracts drew national attention. They attracted the support of numerous religious denominations, ethnic movements, and prominent figures such as Martin Luther King, Jr., and Robert F. Kennedy. At the instigation of AFL-CIO leaders, Chavez, Vera Cruz, and others pushed for the merger of the two groups. An interim UNITED FARM WORKERS ORGANIZING COMMITTEE was soon founded. It was not until the 1971 National Convention, however, that the union organization was formally launched and Vera Cruz was elected as second vice president.

Disagreements with UFW Leadership. During his tenure as vice president, Vera Cruz became increasingly frustrated by the predominantly Mexican American leadership, particularly in relation to its handling of relations with the aging Filipinos in the union. First, Vera Cruz criticized what he saw as the UFW leadership's neglect in organizing Filipinos, who had become a minority in a predominantly Mexican union. Second, he took issue with the union's conducting of meetings in Spanish, which excluded Filipinos, who spoke mostly Ilocano and other Philippine languages. Third, though he supported Chavez' idea of building a retirement home for retiring farmworkers, Vera Cruz criticized what he perceived as the exclusive fees set by the leadership, which adversely affected many elderly Filipinos.

Moreover Vera Cruz voiced his disaffection with the concentration of power and initiative upon Chavez, which made the farmworker movement dependent upon a central authority. Several incidents highlight Vera Cruz's concerns. First, he was often the only dissenting vote in arbitrary firings of volunteers that involved red-baiting charges and personality clashes. Second, he found troubling the blurring of distinctions the leadership had made between the leaders and the farmworkers' movement—Vera Cruz felt strongly that the grass roots had to be given more authority and initiative, which the personality cult around Chavez had eroded. Last, Vera Cruz strongly criticized Chavez for visiting the Philippines and lending his stamp of approval to the dictatorship of Ferdinand MARCOS, which had suppressed human rights.

All the above factors led to Vera Cruz's decision to resign from the UFW during its 1977 National Convention.

Later Activism. In his post-UFW years, Vera Cruz continued to speak out against the Marcos dictatorship in various conferences. He spoke especially to numerous Chicano and Asian American student and youth organizations. In 1987 Vera Cruz received the first Ninoy M. Aquino Award, named after the slain Philippine oppositionist, for his lifelong service to the Filipino community in America.

Despite his criticisms of Chavez and the UFW leadership, Vera Cruz was often critical of himself and other Filipinos for their failure to play a more effective role in the multiracial union. Indeed, Vera Cruz, greatly influenced by Marxism, valued and advocated internationalism and working-class solidarity. He remained supportive of the UFW and the cause of labor even after he left. He died in his hometown of Bakersfield, California, from emphysema, at the age of eighty-nine.—*Augusto Espiritu*

SUGGESTED READINGS: • Cordova, Fred. *Filipinos: Forgotten Asian Americans, A Pictorial Essay, 1763-1963.* Edited by Dorothy L. Cordova and Albert A. Acena. Dubuque: Kendall/Hunt, 1983. • Kushner, Sam. *Long Road to Delano.* New York: International Publishers, 1975. • Scharlin, Craig, and Lillia Villanueva. *Philip Vera Cruz: A Personal History of Filipino Immigrants and the Farmworkers Movement.* Edited by Glenn Omatsu and Augusto Espiritu. Los Angeles: UCLA Labor Center Institute of Industrial Relations and UCLA Asian American Studies Center, 1992. • Vera Cruz, Philip. "Sour Grapes: Symbol of Oppression." In *Roots: An Asian American Reader,* edited by Amy Tachiki. Los Angeles: Continental Graphics, 1971.

Vesak: Buddhist festival to mark the birth, enlightenment, and death of the Buddha (Siddhartha Gautama). This most important of Theravada Buddhist celebrations is a national holiday across much of Southeast Asia. The day typically features special ceremonies and charitable acts—releasing captive birds and fish, for example—that symbolize the Buddha's compassion. The holiday falls on the day of the full moon in April/May (corresponding to the lunar month Vesakha).

Vibora Luviminda: Filipino labor union that organized the first successful strike of a sugar plantation in Hawaii in 1937. This nationalistic organization was led by Manuel Fagel, who previously had been active in organizing Filipino farmworkers in California. Fagel had worked there with Pablo MANLAPIT, another Filipino labor leader who had been banished from Hawaii for his organizing activities.

The name "Vibora Luviminda" indicated the union's nationalist orientation. "Vibora" (serpent) was the nickname of a Filipino military leader during the Philippine war of resistance against American annexation (1899-1902). "Luviminda" is a combination of the names of the three major island groups in the Philippines: Luzon, Visayas, and Mindanao.

The Vibora Luviminda led an unplanned strike of Filipino plantation workers at Puunene, Maui, in April, 1937, after the pay rate for cutting cane had been substantially reduced. The workers demanded a wage increase, but the plantation management responded by firing those who refused to return to work. The management also evicted striking workers from plantation housing and declined to negotiate with their union. To keep them from directing strike activities, as in previous strikes, the union leaders, including Fagel, were arrested, in this case on charges of conspiracy to kidnap a nonstriker. Another arrested leader was Carl Damaso, who later became president of the Hawaii chapter of the INTERNATIONAL LONGSHOREMEN'S AND

WAREHOUSEMEN'S UNION (ILWU), the union that would organize all Hawaii plantation workers in 1946.

More than fifteen hundred Filipinos joined the strike before it was settled after nearly three months. Fearful of a possible investigation by the National Labor Relations Board (NLRB) of a complaint of unfair labor practice (the beating of Fagel), the plantation agreed to raise wages and to meet with the union's representatives in future disputes. Both of these concessions were the first such victories ever won by a plantation union. The Vibora Luviminda also was the last ethnically based union to lead a major labor dispute in the sugar industry and was a significant part of the Filipino contribution to the labor movement in Hawaii.

Viet and World (Nguoi Viet The Gioi): First international magazine published in the Vietnamese language, founded in 1994 and based in Westminster, California. Its contents emphasize Vietnamese traditions, history, and personalities. Other sections (including a smaller English-language section) provide news and features from around the world as well as the various Vietnamese enclaves existing in other countries. The magazine's overall purpose, according to UniMedia Corporation, the publisher, is to instill in Vietnamese youths a greater appreciation for their native culture and to unite the exiled world community of Vietnamese. Among the more prominent board members of UniMedia attached to the magazine are Kieu CHINH, a popular Vietnamese actor who appeared in the 1993 feature film *The Joy Luck Club*; editor-in-chief Viet Khanh Nguyen (well known under his pen name, "Son Dien"); Yen Do, editor of *Nguoi Viet Daily*; and novelist Nha Ca and poet Da Tu Tran, husband and wife.

Viet Cong: Phrase meaning "Vietnamese Communists." It was a derogatory label first used by South Vietnamese President Ngo Dinh Diem for the South Vietnam National Liberation Front (NLF), which was formed in 1960 to bring together all elements who opposed the South Vietnamese government. Viet Cong forces identified themselves as the People's Revolutionary Army and were organized under the Central Office for South Vietnam (COSVN), referred to in Vietnamese as the "Truong Uong Cuc."

The Viet Cong were guerrilla fighters who harassed both South Vietnamese and American forces and carried out terrorists activities against civilians in an attempt to bring communist revolution to South Vietnam. Lacking the skill and experience to wage conventional warfare, the Viet Cong nevertheless exacted a heavy toll in South Vietnam. The number of South Vietnamese government officials assassinated by them in 1959 alone was 1,200, and the count increased to 4,000 killed in 1961.

Both the People's Republic of China and North Vietnam gave military support to the Viet Cong. During 1962, China supplied more than ninety thousand rifles and machine guns. By late 1964, the North Vietnamese were infiltrating South Vietnam and buttressing Viet Cong units with commanders, political commissars, and a variety of technical experts.

Viet Cong strength doubled during 1964, drawing most new adherents from South Vietnam and reaching a total force of 170,000 troops. Thirty thousand fighters were organized into fifty battalions of elite troops trained in the use of modern weaponry and bolstered by veterans from North Vietnam. By the spring of 1967, American forces in South Vietnam estimated Viet Cong strength at 250,000.

The Tet Offensive of 1968 both proved the mettle of Viet Cong forces and accelerated their demise relative to North Vietnamese troops. Although their multifront offensive against South Vietnamese cities shocked Americans and Vietnamese alike, many Viet Cong units were badly decimated or dispersed during or after the operation. North Vietnamese fighters were deployed to replace these troops, and by early 1970, approximately two-thirds of the estimated 125,000 Communists regulars in the south were northerners. By the time the Communists began their decisive invasion of South Vietnam in 1972, the initial wave consisted of 120,000 North Vietnamese regulars and only several thousand Viet Cong guerrillas.

Viet kieu: Vietnamese term meaning "overseas Vietnamese," referring to the Vietnamese diaspora.

Viet Minh: Term for the Vietnam Independence League, or Viet Nam Doc Lap Dong Minh Hoi. The Viet Minh was formed in 1941 out of the Indochina Communist Party in Vietnam for the purpose of achieving independence from the French. Under the leadership of Ho Chi Minh, the organization developed a political and fighting force that would rout French and later American forces in its effort to dominate all Vietnam.

The Viet Minh, although fundamentally a political organization, garnered international recognition primarily through its military successes. Soon after its foundation, the Viet Minh began developing an army

Ho Chi Minh (right) at a reception in France in 1946. (National Archives)

under the leadership of Vo Nguyen Giap. By September of 1944, Viet Minh troops numbered five thousand and controlled three of Vietnam's northernmost provinces. When the Japanese, who had occupied Vietnam during World War II (1939-1945), capitulated to the Allies, the Viet Minh entered Hanoi, demanding the abdication of the last Vietnamese emperor, Bao Dai. The emperor relinquished his sword and seal to the Viet Minh in 1945, and Ho Chi Minh proclaimed the birth of the Democratic Republic of Vietnam (DRV) in September of that year.

No country officially recognized the DRV as the legitimate government of Vietnam in 1945. The Allies agreed that Nationalist Chinese troops would occupy the north, and British troops the south, to facilitate the capitulation and repatriation of Japanese troops. Ultimately, control of Vietnam was returned to France, and the Viet Minh pursued its opposition through guerrilla warfare and terroristic violence against the French and their Vietnamese collaborators. By 1946, Viet Minh forces in the north numbered more than forty thousand. Giap and his troops challenged French control and expanded their popular support during the ensuing years. Viet Minh ability to defy the French improved significantly in 1949 when the Chinese Communists gained control of the China mainland and began equipping the Viet Minh with automatic weapons, mortars, howitzers, and trucks. The Viet Minh's most decisive victory against the French took place in 1954 at Dien Bien Phu, where they destroyed the French forces. At the Geneva conference of the same year, the Viet Minh reluctantly agreed to a temporary division of Vietnam along the seventeenth parallel. Thereafter, control of the north remained in their hands.

When the regrouping of Viet Minh forces was carried out according to the Geneva accords in 1954-1955, a force of five to ten thousand Viet Minh cadres remained in the south. These veterans became the nucleus of the National Liberation Front (NLF) of South Vietnam, which the Communists organized at the end of 1960. Through collaboration with the guerrilla fighters of the VIET CONG in the south, the Viet Minh achieved control of Vietnam in 1975.

Vietnam, Socialist Republic of: Republic created in 1976 when North Vietnam and South Vietnam were reunified. It is bordered to the north by the People's Republic of China, to the east by the Gulf of Tonkin and the South China Sea, to the south by the South China Sea and the Gulf of Thailand, and to the west by Laos and Cambodia. Its capital, HANOI, is located in the north. Vietnam is 127,813 square miles in size; its population was estimated in 1992 to be about 69,052,000. Though mainly Vietnamese in ethnicity, Vietnam contains a variety of minority groups. Its four-thousand-year history includes Southeast Asian patterns, Chinese domination and influence, and European conquests, all capped by a civil war in the twentieth century.

Geography and People. Plains, rivers, and mountains make up the landscape of Vietnam. A 1,200-mile coastline runs from the Gulf of Tonkin to the South China Sea and to the Gulf of Thailand. Into these seas run the Red River, the MEKONG RIVER, and many smaller streams in between. The two large deltas, formed by the Red and Mekong rivers, and the many lesser ones are the sources of wet-rice agriculture, which provides substantial employment for the Vietnamese. To the north and west, running down three quarters of the country, lie the Long Mountains (Truong Son), also known as the Chaine Annamitique or Annamite Chain, separating Vietnam from China, Laos, and northeast Cambodia. These mountains are the sources of the rivers and the home of different ethnic groups and a variety of upland resources.

The majority (85 percent) of the people in Vietnam are ethnic Vietnamese, though some are of Chinese descent. Tai and HMONG groups live in the northern hills, while Mon-Khmer and Malayo-Polynesian peoples dwell in the Central Highlands of the south. CHAMS, from the old pre-Vietnamese state of Champa, still live along the south central coast, while the Mus-

Vietnamese troops stationed in Cambodia wave goodbye to bystanders while leaving the war-torn country in 1989. Since invading Cambodia in late 1978 to battle the Khmer Rouge, the occupation forces had remained there. (AP/Wide World Photos)

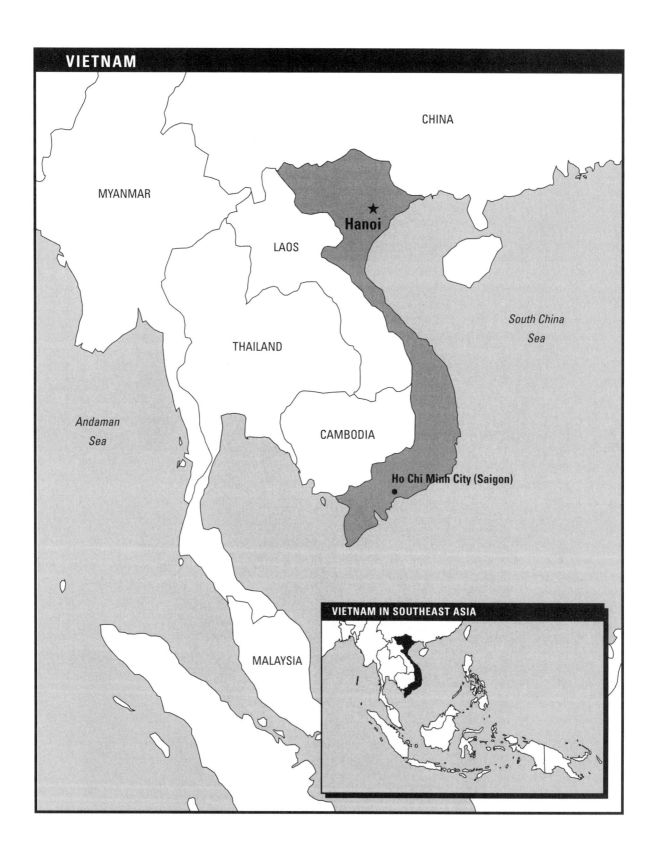

VIETNAM

CHINA

MYANMAR

LAOS

★
Hanoi

THAILAND

South China Sea

Andaman Sea

CAMBODIA

Ho Chi Minh City (Saigon)
●

MALAYSIA

VIETNAM IN SOUTHEAST ASIA

Street scene in Ho Chi Minh City, 1992. (Eric Crystal)

lims live on the southwest border, near Cambodia. Theravada Buddhist KHMER groups also continue to reside in the Mekong Delta area, which was taken over by the Vietnamese. The other major ethnic group is made up of the urban Chinese, who live mainly in Cholon, next to HO CHI MINH CITY (formerly called Saigon), and in the port of Haiphong, east of the capital city of Hanoi.

Culture and History. Vietnamese civilization developed in the north, near what is now Hanoi, and had a strong continuity over several millennia. The language was a mixture of MON-KHMER, Tai, and Chinese elements. Early Vietnamese culture had Southeast Asian elements within it and a heavy overlay of Chinese influence, which began more than two thousand years ago. The kinship was originally bilateral, as women held a relatively high place in society. Spirit cults were characteristic of Vietnamese religion, and blood oaths took place in political activities. Wet-rice agriculture and fishing formed the economic basis of the society. Mahayana Buddhism came to Vietnam in the first millennium C.E. from both India and China, and neo-

Confucianism arrived from China in the second millennium.

For more than a thousand years, Vietnamese society changed within a fluctuating Chinese domination (111 B.C.E.-939 C.E.). The Han Dynasty (206 B.C.E.-220 C.E.) brought basic Chinese elements to Vietnam, and the Tang Dynasty (618-907) showed it an imperial model. Local elements survived and in the tenth century kept a reunified China from returning. For four centuries (1000-1400), Earlier Le (980-1009) and Tran (1225-1400) dynasties of Vietnam maintained a Buddhist state that repulsed Mongol invasions in the late thirteenth century but that was weakened by CHAM invasions a century later and by the Ming Chinese occupation (1407-1427).

The fifteenth century saw the Later Le Dynasty (1428-1788) establish the Chinese Confucian model— a bureaucracy based on texts, scholars, and examinations. It brought a heavier emphasis on Chinese social elements, particularly male dominance, and reached its peak with the Nguyen Dynasty (1802-1945). At the same time, Vietnamese society was expanding south

The Vietnamese in the twentieth century have had to struggle not only for their political future but also for their national identity in the modern world. (James L. Shaffer)

down the coast, moving from central Vietnam, the old Cham realm, into the Mekong Delta and KHMER territory. Civil war in the Vietnamese state pushed the expansion, as did the commercial dynamism of the South China Sea.

Vietnam became united in its present extent at the beginning of the nineteenth century under the Nguyen Dynasty. Yet only when the French took control later in the century did Saigon and the far south become developed. The French separated the country into three *pays*: north (Tonkin), center (Annam), and south (Cochinchina), joining them to Cambodia and Laos to form Indochina. They encouraged an already existing Catholicism until about 10 percent of the population followed it, and in the twentieth century American missionaries brought Protestantism to some upland groups. The colonial period fragmented Vietnamese society as it established an exploitative economic presence. The Vietnamese in the twentieth century have had to struggle not only for their political future but also for the meaning of being Vietnamese in the modern world. A variety of answers appeared in the 1920's and 1930's: pro-French and anti-French, conservative, liberal, radical, and religious. The Japanese control during World War II (1939-1945) opened areas of activity for the Vietnamese. Vietnamese communists acted against the Japanese in concert with the American Office of Strategic Services. The Vietnamese equivalent of Chiang Kai-shek's Nationalist Party was the Viet Nam Quoc Dan Dang (VNQDD). Other groups also became active, such as the southern religious sects Hoa Hao and Cao Dai.

Uprising, Independence, and War. By mid-1945, these groups were ready to act. The surrender of Japan led directly to the August Revolution of the communist-led VIET MINH, a coalition of Indochinese nationalists led by the revolutionary Ho Chi Minh. The August Revolution resulted in the declaration of independence from France, the dethroning of the emperor, and the establishment of the Democratic Republic of Vietnam, led by Ho Chi Minh. Sixteen months of contention among these forces led to the outbreak of the First Indochina War in December, 1946, between France and the Viet Minh.

The Viet Cong-led Tet Offensive of 1968 was one of the bloodiest and most telling encounters of the Vietnam War. Here refugees cross the Perfume River in Hue to escape the Tet assault. (National Archives)

What began as a colonial struggle became, in 1949-1950, an anticommunist crusade, as MAO ZEDONG and his forces took China. The French were unable to crush the Viet Minh and its guerrilla warfare. Now, with the latter supported by China and the French by the United States, battles occurred. Finally, the French drew the Viet Minh into the battle of Dien Bien Phu and were decisively defeated. The Geneva Conference brought the war to an end in July, 1954.

Two zones of military disengagement, north and south, were to be united in a 1956 election. The anticommunist forces established themselves in the south, bolstered by the southern religious sects and almost a million northerners, mainly Catholics. With American support and under Ngo Dinh Diem, they soon established the Republic of Vietnam, centered in Saigon. The Democratic Republic in the north, with its capital at Hanoi, worked to reconstruct the land and build socialism.

No unifying elections were held, and severe pressures fell on the anti-Diem forces in the south, now called the VIET CONG (Vietnamese Communists). The latter moved into resistance and, in 1961, formed the National Liberation Front (NLF). The Vietnam conflict had begun. For four years, the NLF grew in strength, and the Saigon government weakened in a classic guerrilla struggle. Finally, in 1965, the United States bombed the north and inserted troops to block defeat. Eight years of heavy fighting led to a stalemate and to the withdrawal of the United States. Two more years of conflict resulted in the collapse of Saigon and in formal reunification a year later.

The Socialist Republic of Vietnam. Vietnam has suffered grave difficulties and two waves of refugees, totaling between a half million and a million people. The first wave was immediate, as Saigon supporters left following their defeat. Vietnam tried to establish itself on the international scene, but growing difficulties with China led to conflict with Cambodia and no relations with the United States. Internal economic problems brought urban reform and trouble with Chinese residents. The year 1978 was a disaster. The second wave of refugees began with resident Chinese and

Deteriorating relations between Vietnam and the People's Republic of China triggered China's invasion of Vietnam in early 1979. Here Chinese troops seal the doors and windows of an emporium in captured Cam Duong to protect the property. (AP/Wide World Photos)

Into the 1990's, Vietnam has experienced renewed economic prosperity and a growth in tourism. (Eric Crystal)

continued for years, becoming increasingly Vietnamese. Driving POL POT from Cambodia soured international relations further, and the United States continued its embargo. These events, together with the winds of change in the socialist world, led to reform in the 1980's. The 1990's have been marked by economic growth and increased trade. Tourism has also increased significantly. In 1994, the United States ended its nineteen-year embargo and took steps toward full normalization of relations.—*John K. Whitmore*

SUGGESTED READINGS: • Jamieson, Neil. *Understanding Vietnam*. Berkeley: University of California Press, 1993. • Karnow, Stanley. *Vietnam: A History*. New York: Viking Press, 1983. • Nguyen Trieu Dan. *A Vietnamese Family Chronicle: Twelve Generations on the Banks of the Hat River*. Jefferson, N.C.: McFarland, 1991. • Whitfield, Danny J. *Historical and Cultural Dictionary of Vietnam*. Metuchen, N.J.: Scarecrow Press, 1976. • Woodside, A. B. *Community and Revolution in Modern Vietnam*. Boston: Houghton Mifflin, 1976.

Vietnam Veterans Memorial. *See* **Lin, Maya Ying**

Vietnam War and Asian Americans: The Vietnam War (1965-1975) is one of several examples of American military involvement in an Asian country during the twentieth century. Roughly 1 percent of U.S. forces who served during the Vietnam War were Asian Pacific Americans. Unlike other racial groups in the military, Asian Pacific Americans looked like the Vietnamese, and many of them reported instances of being viewed, mistaken, and used as the enemy during the war. Although the Vietnamese were dehumanized in racial terms, the ambivalence of Asian Pacific American soldiers toward viewing the Vietnamese as less than human may have led to particular forms of post-traumatic stress disorder (PTSD). In 1982, amid much controversy, the Vietnam Veterans Memorial, designed by a Chinese American, Maya Ying LIN, was dedicated in Washington, D.C. The wall has symbolized healing and reconciliation for many U.S. veterans and their families. A further legacy of the war is the exodus and resettlement of more than one million refugees from Vietnam, Laos, and Cambodia since 1975. They form significant portions of the Asian Pacific American population.

Demographics. There are no exact figures for the numbers of Asian Pacific American Vietnam veterans because military records included Asian Pacific Americans in an "Other" category. The U.S. Depart-

ment of Defense estimates that 34,600 Asian Pacific Americans served in the Vietnam theater. The Veterans Administration estimates that 85,000 Asian Pacific Americans served in the U.S. military during the Vietnam era throughout the world.

A review of the 58,000 names that appear on the Vietnam Veterans Memorial in Washington, D.C., honoring U.S. soldiers killed in Vietnam, reveals at least 250 Asian Pacific Americans. About 80 percent were from Hawaii, Guam, or California, and most were Chinese, Japanese, and Filipino, reflecting the regional character and the ethnic profiles of the Asian Pacific American population prior to the dramatic waves of new immigrants during the 1970's and 1980's.

Looking Like the Enemy. Perceptions that the enemy was everywhere and nowhere at the same time, shaped both by experience with the guerrilla tactics of the VIET CONG and by historic stereotypes of Asians as evil and cunning, reinforced views that Asians could not be trusted. Dehumanization of the Vietnamese along racial lines profoundly affected the experiences of Asian Pacific American men and women in Vietnam

In 1981 Maya Ying Lin (right) and Jan Scruggs of the Vietnam Veterans Memorial Fund unveil the inscriptions that will be affixed to the not-yet-completed memorial. (AP/ Wide World Photos)

Asian American participants at a Veterans Day parade in New York City. (Richard B. Levine)

who, themselves, looked like the enemy. Each of these individuals was easily identifiable. For many, the combination of being the only Asian Pacific American in their units and the war's racial character led to frequent situations where they were used in training to represent the enemy.

Asian Pacific Americans were also placed tactically in the field to infiltrate enemy territory. Team Hawaii, a combat and reconnaissance team assembled in 1969, was composed of Japanese American, Chinese American, Filipino, and American Indian U.S. Army Rangers who could all pass for Vietnamese. Army intelligence revealed that the Viet Cong put prices on these troops' heads, knowing that they would be harder to spot than white or black soldiers in the jungle.

Asian Pacific American Vietnam veterans, regardless of rank, have described numerous incidents of being mistaken as the enemy, such as being fired on or left behind as wounded. Asian Pacific American women serving as nurses in Vietnam were also mistaken as Vietnamese and were treated sometimes as if they were prostitutes. Many developed strategies to minimize situations where they might be mistaken or

questioned as the enemy. For example, by staying in sight of sergeants or platoon leaders who recognized them, some were saved from being fired on when their identities were questioned. Others only went out in the company of white or black soldiers, always having a visible "shadow" for protection.

Trauma and Healing. In Vietnam, Asian Pacific Americans faced not only the trauma of war but also the stresses of their own identities being used, mistaken, and dehumanized as the enemy. Significant mental health research, social services, and advocacy efforts on behalf of Vietnam veterans have been dedicated to facilitating their readjustment and enabling their healing process. Many Asian Pacific Americans have remained silent about their war experiences and the incidence of posttraumatic stress disorder.

Politicization served as a healing process for some. Those returning to the United States in the late 1960's and early 1970's found newly formed Asian contingents in the growing antiwar movement as well as a burgeoning ASIAN AMERICAN MOVEMENT demanding political power in the communities and ethnic studies on campus. Radicalized Asian Pacific American Vietnam veterans offered firsthand testimony about the character and conduct of the war through the Winter Soldier Investigations and the pages of Asian American Movement publications such as GIDRA and GETTING TOGETHER.

For others, military service continued after the war and became their career. Still others, perhaps most of the population, returned to their communities and reestablished their lives, drawing on the strengths and maturity as well as the educational benefits that they gained through their military service. Many were children of Nisei veterans or Filipino and Chinese American veterans from World War II (1939-1945), growing up with military service as a part of family life.

The healing process for many Vietnam veterans has been facilitated by Maya Ying LIN, the Ohio-born Chinese American who designed the Vietnam Veterans Memorial. Since its dedication in 1982, its healing power for Vietnam veterans, their families, and the United States as a whole has been movingly described in words and photographs. The selection of her design, however, sparked controversy, perhaps in part because she also looked like the enemy.

Southeast Asian Refugee Resettlement. Beginning in April, 1975, with the fall of the Cambodian, Lao, and south Vietnamese governments, and continuing in waves throughout the 1980's, more than one million Southeast Asian refugees fled their homelands and

Vietnamese vendor, 1960's. The end of the Vietnam War eventually displaced more than a million refugees from Southeast Asia who fled their homelands for other parts of the continent or the world. (James L. Shaffer)

were resettled in the United States. By 1990, they accounted for nearly 15 percent of the Asian Pacific American population. Their presence, contributions, and needs in the United States also represent a significant legacy of the Vietnam War.—*Peter Nien-chu Kiang*

SUGGESTED READINGS: • Engelmann, Larry. *Tears Before the Rain: An Oral History of the Fall of South Vietnam.* New York: Oxford University Press, 1990. • Freeman, James M. *Hearts of Sorrow: Vietnamese-American Lives.* Stanford, Calif.: Stanford University Press, 1989. • Hayslip, Le Ly, with Jay Wurts. *When Heaven and Earth Changed Places.* New York: Doubleday, 1989. • Kiang, Peter N. "About Face: Recognizing Asian and Pacific American Vietnam Veterans in Asian American Studies." *Amerasia Journal* 17, no. 3 (1991): 22-40. • Kulka, Richard A., et al. *Trauma and the Vietnam War Generation.* New York: Brunner/Mazel, 1990. • Scruggs, Jan C., and Joel L. Swerdlow. *To Heal a Nation: The Vietnam Veterans Memorial.* New York: Harper & Row, 1985.

Vietnamese Amerasians: Widely defined, any person who has one American parent (of any race and ethnicity) and one Vietnamese parent. The following description will focus specifically on those who are the offspring of a Vietnamese mother and an American father, conceived in Vietnam during the United States' involvement in the Vietnam War (1965-1975).

Historical Background. When the Vietnam War ended in April of 1975 with the fall of Saigon to the Vietnamese Communists, American troops fled the city in a frantic, last-minute flurry. Left behind were some thirty to sixty thousand Amerasians and their mothers. With the subsequent severing of all diplomatic ties between the United States and Vietnam, most of these separations became permanent, as it was impossible for Americans to send for even legal spouses and children and communication between the two countries was virtually halted for several years.

Most of the American fathers of Amerasians were members of the military, but many others were civilians working in Vietnam as journalists, photographers, and businessmen. Many of the Vietnamese mothers were employed by the U.S. military as secretaries, translators, and janitors; others worked in the service industries catering to the military in occupations such as sales, waitressing, bank telling, and nursing; and some became prostitutes. Many Americans and Vietnamese alike tend to imagine that all Amerasians are the product of unions between servicemen and prostitutes, but research has shown that this stereotype is incorrect. The mothers of Amerasians represent a wide variety of occupational backgrounds and education levels. Many, and perhaps even most, of the relationships from which Amerasians were born were long-term and committed ones. One study, focusing on an early sample of Amerasian immigrants and their mothers, found that the parents of Amerasians lived together for an average of two years and that many were either legally married or had filed common-law marriage documents.

After the Communist takeover of South Vietnam, rumors of torture and death for Amerasians and their mothers because of their association with the enemy led many women with Amerasian children to destroy all pictures, documents, and keepsakes that could connect them to their American lovers or husbands. Because of the racial differences of most of the Amerasian children, however, these women's "disloyalty" was usually obvious to others. For this reason, some women kept their children hidden at home; others tried to disguise the racial differences of their children by cutting off or dyeing their hair; others sent their children to live with relatives or friends, often in rural areas less likely to be purged by the VIET CONG; and some women abandoned their children on the streets or on doorsteps of houses and hospitals. Most women, however, openly kept and raised their Amerasian children as best they could, and while the torture and murder threats were never realized, Amerasians and their mothers were frequently singled out, removed from their homes, and sent to the New Economic Zones for years of hard labor.

Life in Vietnam for Amerasians. While life in war-torn Vietnam has been difficult for all people there, it has been especially difficult for Amerasians and their mothers. In Vietnamese culture, as in many Asian cultures and cultures around the world, children inherit much of their social identity from their fathers. The father's family lineage, education level, occupation, and social position largely decide that of his children. By having an absent father, and an American one at that, an Amerasian is said to be "a house without a roof." In addition, the stereotype that all mothers of Amerasians are prostitutes has stigmatized both the women and their children as social outcasts. They are expected to be impure and immoral—oversexed and prone to criminal behavior—as well as stupid and uncouth.

Amerasians are also racial minorities in a relatively racially homogeneous society. This both lends itself to discrimination, as racial minorities in most societies are singled out as different and inferior, and makes it easy for others to identify Amerasians for discrimination based on the reasons mentioned before—that they are presumed to be illegitimate, criminal, and the children of prostitutes. There is no question that Amerasians have been and are discriminated against in Vietnam, but research shows that individual experiences vary as to the form and the level of severity. Those Amerasians who are part black seem to experience the highest degree of discrimination. The vast majority of Amerasians have experienced some form of prejudice and verbal harassment for being Amerasian, and recognize that they are viewed with disdain by other Vietnamese.

Amerasians in Vietnam, as a group, find themselves with few job opportunities, because of both discrimination and low levels of formal education. Research on Amerasians arriving in the United States has shown them to have less education, on average, than their monoracial refugee counterparts. This seems to arise from a combination of factors, including social harassment and institutionalized racism, but is mostly attributable to economic disadvantages: Amerasians tend to have fewer economic resources because a larger number of Amerasians than other Vietnamese come from single-parent and female-headed households, which, in Vietnam as in the United States, are more likely to be low-income.

The conditions of being poor, uneducated, and despised function to fulfill and reinforce many of the negative images of Amerasians. Because some were orphaned and others were searching for ways to make money for their families, populations of Amerasians formed in the big cities, and many became homeless and/or involved in prostitution or criminal activities. They were labeled *bui doi*, which means "dust of life" and which is a commonly used epithet similar to the American-English epithets "scum" or "lowlife." Both the label and the image of *bui doi*, at some point, was extended to all Amerasians, increasing social and institutional discrimination against them and further lowering their self-esteem. These factors, in turn, have in-

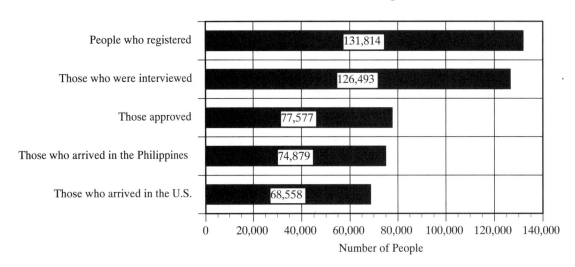

The Resettlement Program as of 1993

	Number of People
People who registered	131,814
Those who were interviewed	126,493
Those approved	77,577
Those who arrived in the Philippines	74,879
Those who arrived in the U.S.	68,558

Source: Government Accounting Office, *Vietnamese Amerasian Resettlement.* PEMD-94-15.

creased the possibility that an Amerasian will become involved in begging for money, in prostitution, or in criminal behavior. While only a small percentage of Amerasians have ever been involved in "street life," the assumption that they all have has made them even more vulnerable to exploitation in a variety of ways.

The United States and Amerasian "Policy." Meanwhile, in the United States, Americans had been trying hard to forget about the Vietnam War, which had been long, bloody, and very controversial, and which was the first lost war in the nation's history. With all diplomatic ties to Vietnam severed, it was easy for most Americans to forget that the Amerasians existed, if Americans were aware of them at all. Moreover, as was true with the United States' earlier wars in Japan and Korea, the unwritten policy of the American government and military regarding Amerasians is, as one expert from the Pearl S. Buck Foundation stated, "a silent policy of child abandonment."

In 1979, the ORDERLY DEPARTURE PROGRAM (ODP) was established by the Office of the UNITED NATIONS HIGH COMMISSIONER FOR REFUGEES (UNHCR) to offer a safe and legal option for those wanting to leave Vietnam. In 1981, Amerasians and their families were written into ODP policy as a "top priority." In late 1982, the first Amerasians began to arrive in the United States. These Amerasians represented the small percentage whose American fathers had filed papers to bring them over, and who therefore arrived in the United States as American citizens. In 1984, the Viet-

namese government accused the U.S. government of failing to take responsibility for the Amerasians; in September of the same year, a subprogram of the ODP was created especially to deal with Amerasians, and ODP policy was expanded to include Amerasians without firm documentation but who physically appeared to be part "American." These Amerasians were admitted as refugees, receiving refugee benefits, rather than as U.S. citizens. In total, the ODP brought some forty-five hundred Amerasians with seven thousand accompanying relatives to the United States between September, 1982, and August, 1988—only a small fraction of the total Amerasian population in Vietnam.

Investigation into the Amerasian situation revealed that a much larger number of Amerasians wanted to immigrate to the United States, but that the ODP was not enabling them to do so for a variety of reasons. For example, in order to leave Vietnam through the ODP, a Vietnamese citizen must first obtain an exit permit from the Vietnamese government. This is a slow and lengthy process, however, involving a large amount of administrative paperwork, which is routinely negotiated and accelerated through the offering of fees, favors, or bribes—resources that Amerasians and their families are the least likely to have. Another example of why the ODP was not reaching Amerasians is that, as mentioned earlier, Amerasians and their mothers generally have low social status and little access to the people and the institutions in power; therefore, information about the ODP's special priority for Amerasians and how to go about utilizing it was simply not reaching most of them.

On October 28, 1987, a bilateral agreement between the U.S. and Vietnamese governments, the AMERASIAN HOMECOMING ACT, was passed by the U.S. Congress specifically giving Amerasians in Vietnam the opportunity to immigrate to the United States. The fact that this act separated Amerasian emigration and immigration from the rest of Vietnamese emigration and immigration made an enormous difference in its ability to reach Amerasians and their families and facilitate their departure. For the first time, both the U.S. and Vietnamese governments were committed to making Amerasians a priority, and money and staff were allocated specifically to work with them. For example, the Vietnamese government, with cash assistance from the United States, organized a public information campaign to advertise the act, communicating through such readily accessible forms of information as public billboards. Through the act, the U.S. government "pays" the Vietnamese government to process the paperwork on each Amerasian, so as to relieve Amerasians from having to raise the money themselves. (Unfortunately, experts in the area and Amerasians themselves say that fees and bribes are still routinely required of the Amerasians, sometimes motivating Amerasians to participate in the "fake family" frauds discussed below.)

The Emigration and Immigration Process. The process, for an Amerasian, of leaving Vietnam for the United States varies from case to case, but in general, upon deciding to emigrate, an Amerasian first goes to the local office of the government in his or her town or village and begins the application process. In small or rural villages, the local government might consist of one person who is the community representative, while larger towns might have several staff members—a variable that often affects the length of time that an Amerasian waits for the paperwork to be completed. As the Amerasian's application passes through the various reviews of the Vietnamese and American governments, the Amerasian undergoes interviews and medical exams. There are opportunities for many problems to arise throughout the review process, such as health issues, child custody issues for Amerasians with children, and questions regarding the validity of accompanying family members. The entire process may take from six months to two or three years.

Since January, 1990, Amerasians and their family members who live away from HO CHI MINH CITY (formerly Saigon) can stay at the nearby Amerasian Transit Center while their last minute paperwork is being completed and travel arrangements are made. The center was built and is run by the Vietnamese government with U.S. funding and provides food, accommodations, and English-language classes. Prior to the construction of the center, many of the Amerasians and their families who had traveled to Ho Chi Minh City from outlying areas had no place to stay while their paperwork was being completed, and so they would spend their days and nights in the park in front of the Ministry of Foreign Affairs. The Vietnamese government proposed the Transit Center to the U.S. government as a way to get Amerasians "off the streets" and also to simplify and speed up the paperwork process and to obtain information on the Amerasians and their families for use by the social service agencies in the United States.

After completing all paperwork and interviews, and after all the travel arrangements are made (airfare is paid for by the International Organization for Migration), the Amerasians and their families travel by plane to the Philippine Refugee Processing Center (PRPC) in Bataan City, the Philippines, for a six-month (or more) stopover.

The PRPC is a large encampment surrounded by barbed wire and can house up to eighteen thousand immigrants and refugees at once. It is, technically, run by the United Nations (UN) but is staffed mostly by Filipino citizens and also by American social workers, counselors, and volunteers. In the PRPC, Amerasians and their family members, as well as other immigrants and refugees from Vietnam, Laos, and Cambodia, undergo extensive interviews and physical exams, attend English-language classes and classes on American culture, and have the option of attending discussion and counseling groups. The stated purpose of the PRPC is the "acculturation" of Southeast Asian immigrants and refugees to American ways, but the information gathered through the interviews provides important data that is sent ahead to the future resettlement site of the immigrant/refugee so that the resettlement agency can make arrangements according to that person's (or family's) specific needs.

Over the months that these individuals live in the PRPC, problems with other individuals or between family members sometimes surface, at which time social workers intervene, sometimes suggesting or requiring that the involved parties attend group, family, or individual counseling. The counseling services at the PRPC have been criticized by social workers in the United States for failing to give sufficient information on birth control and abortion, presumably because the counseling services are run by a Catholic agency and because the majority of the staff is Catholic.

Conditions in the PRPC have led to the growth of a population of Amerasian and monoracial Vietnamese "gangsters" who harass and demand money from other immigrants/refugees. As these gangsters are awaiting trial in the Philippine court system, they cannot be sent back to Vietnam, sent ahead to the United States, or let out of the camp in the Philippines, so they simply remain in the PRPC for many months and even for years.

Another problem that exists at the PRPC is the sexual harassment and rape of women, especially Amerasian women, both by fellow immigrant/refugees and by male members of the Filipino staff. Frequently, a woman who has been raped or otherwise sexually abused will not report it because awaiting the trial might hold back her departure to the United States. Social workers in the United States tell how these women arrive traumatized and sometimes pregnant.

The PRPC will be closing in the year 1994. After this, Amerasians will come directly to the United States.

"Fake Families." While there are always instances of fraud where immigrant/refugee arrivals are concerned, in more recent years social workers believe that fraud has become the rule rather than the exception. The common scenario, they say, is that an Amerasian in Vietnam "sells" himself or herself to a family who hopes to immigrate to the United States (through the AMERASIAN HOMECOMING ACT) by posing as the real or adopted family of the Amerasian. The Amerasian uses the money obtained from "selling" these slots to finance the completion of the paperwork and/or to give to his/her real family. Frequently, the Amerasian assumes that he or she can send for his/her real family after settling in the United States.

"Fake families," say social workers, were simply not an issue in the earlier years of the program, but had become more and more of a problem in the early 1990's: In 1992, social workers at the PRPC and in the United States estimated that somewhere between 50 to 75 percent of the Amerasians were arriving with "fake families." The Office of Refugee Resettlement (ORR) responded with stricter criteria for application approval. While in the beginning years of the program, 80 to 90 percent of applications were approved, in the fiscal year 1992, out of 29,796 cases reviewed, only 11,740 were approved. Between October, 1992, and September, 1993, of the 18,481 applications considered, only 3,749 were approved. Unfortunately, this "crackdown" on applicants has most likely caused legitimate families as well as illegitimate ones to have been turned down.

Resettlement in the United States. Each Amerasian and his or her family leaves the PRPC to go to his or her new home in the United States, at one of the fifty-five "cluster sites." A cluster site is a city that has been designated by the ORR as a place to settle Amerasians (and other immigrants and refugees) because it has an organization(s) with experience in resettling Southeast Asians. These organizations, which are usually connected to a religious institution, are called voluntary agencies, or VOLAGS. Social workers working for the VOLAGS provide services such as obtaining a place for a family to live; processing the paperwork needed to receive government assistance, foodstamps, and medical care; and enrolling individuals in English-language classes. The VOLAGS also operate support and social programs especially tailored to Amerasians and their needs. These services are funded by the federal government and thus must be nonreligious in orientation. The three VOLAGS most involved in Amerasian resettlement are the International Rescue Committee, United States Catholic Charities, and Lutheran Immigration and Refugee Services.

The VOLAGS are required to keep in contact with the immigrants and refugees that they assist for a minimum of 90 to 180 days, although sometimes an immigrant/refugee will leave without contacting his or her VOLAG. Frequently, Southeast Asian immigrants and refugees will leave their cluster sites to move closer to an established ethnic community. For example, many Amerasians and their families initiate a "secondary resettlement" to cities such as San Jose or Huntington Beach, California, which have large Vietnamese communities. Researchers and social workers have found that while Amerasians are not accepted by the larger Vietnamese community in the United States much more readily than they were in Vietnam, they tend to adjust better to American life if they have access to a Vietnamese community and its resources.

A Profile of the Amerasians in America. The Amerasian population is a very diverse one, including men and women who are urban and rural, completely illiterate and highly educated, married and unmarried, Afro-Asian and Eurasian. There are, though, certain generalizations that can be made based on the information gathered about Amerasians from social workers and researchers.

Vietnamese Amerasians immigrating to the United States represent about equal numbers of females and males. They were born between 1962 and 1976, so they arrive in the United States as young adults. Approximately 15 to 25 percent are considered "Afro-Asian" (black and Asian); most of the rest are "Eurasian" (white and Asian), although there are also Amerasians who are Latino-Asian, Native American-Asian, and Asian-Asian (for example, Asian Indian and Vietnamese). Amerasians tend to have relatively few years of schooling and high rates of illiteracy or limited literacy. Most have very few "transferable job skills," which means that their occupations in Vietnam did not train them in ways that make them marketable for jobs in the American economy. Those who have had schooling in Vietnam usually wish to continue school in the United States, whereas those who received little or no schooling want to train for a job.

The Amerasians who arrived in the earlier years of the AMERASIAN HOMECOMING ACT were more likely to be traveling with their mothers and/or other close family members, biological or adopted. In the past few years, as "fake family" frauds have become more widespread, more and more Amerasians are traveling with people who are little more than strangers and who are likely to leave the Amerasian soon after arriving in the United States.

Also, as Amerasians get older, a growing percentage of them bring over their own children and spouses. Amerasians marry both within the community of Amerasians and with members of the larger Vietnamese community. It has been noticed that Afro-Asians fre-quently marry one another, Eurasian women frequently marry monoracial Vietnamese men, and Eurasian men marry less often than others. One theory for this pattern is that the racism against Afro-Asians isolates them from other Amerasians and Vietnamese in the marriage market, and that Eurasian men have a difficult time finding marriage partners because of their difficulties in the job market.

Issues and Problems in the Amerasian Community. As early as 1983, shortly after the first groups of Amerasians arrived through the ODP, social workers reported that Amerasians and their family members exhibited more than the average number of "problems," such as depression, long-term unemployment, concentration of medical complaints, child abuse/neglect, and "disruptive behavior." Involvement of Amerasians in "criminal" activities such as drug dealing and abuse, prostitution, theft, and gang activities have increased throughout the years since the act, as have instances of unmarried pregnancies and family violence.

These "adjustment problems" have frequently been attributed to low levels of education and low levels of Vietnamese and English-language literacy, "unrealistic expectations" about life in the United States, discrimination experienced in the Vietnamese American community and in the larger American society, low self-esteem, poverty, and "intense" family relationships. The "unrealistic expectations" found to be common among Amerasians include a belief that they will automatically "fit in" with American society because they

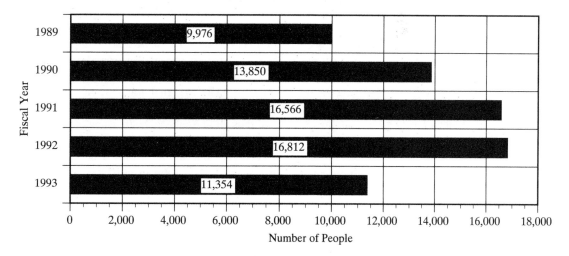

Arrivals of Amerasians and Family Members, 1989-1992

Fiscal Year	Number of People
1989	9,976
1990	13,850
1991	16,566
1992	16,812
1993	11,354

Source: Government Accounting Office, *Vietnamese Amerasian Resettlement.* PEMD-94-15.

"are" American. When they arrive in the United States, however, they soon realize that their lack of English-language skills and unfamiliarity with American culture and lifestyle make them unable to leave the past behind. In fact, they usually find themselves living in and depending on the Vietnamese American community, which still sees them as *bui doi*. Another common expectation among Amerasians is that they will be reunited with their father in the United States. In reality, only between 1 to 2 percent reunite with their fathers because of factors such as a lack of information with which to find them and fathers who are no longer alive or who do not wish to make contact with their Amerasian child or children. Interestingly, the majority of media coverage of Amerasians in the United States has centered on these very unusual reunions.

Broadly stated, Amerasians arrive in the United States expecting their lives to change drastically for the better. While their lives do change in many ways, they usually still find themselves to be very poor, with little or no education and few job options, fatherless, and interacting almost exclusively in a community where they are not accepted as equals. Many of these Amerasians exhibit what social workers call "adjustment problems" such as depression, criminal behavior, and abusive family relations. The growth of "fake families" has led to a growth in the problems mentioned above as more and more Amerasians are involved in exploitive relationships with strangers and then are left alone, frequently realizing for the first time that they may never be able to bring their real family members to the United States.

Vietnamese Amerasians have tended to have harder-than-average lives in Vietnam and seem to be experiencing harder-than-average lives in the United States. As victims of international politics and an American "silent policy of child abandonment," they have not been given the options that many people believe they should have. Yet they are survivors who have found creative ways to make their lives livable, and they have found comfort in the company of one another.— *Cynthia Nakashima*

SUGGESTED READINGS: • *Amerasians' Special Needs Report*. Sacramento: State of California, Health and Welfare Agency, Department of Social Services, 1989. • Felsman, J. Kirk, Mark C. Johnson, Frederick T. L. Leong, and Irene C. Felsman. *Vietnamese Amerasians: Practical Implications of Current Research*. Washington, D.C.: Office of Refugee Resettlement, Family Support Administration, Department of Health and Human Services, 1989. • Lacey, Marilyn. *In Our Father's Land: Vietnamese Amerasians in the United States*. Washington, D.C.: Migration and Refugee Services, United States Catholic Conference, 1985. • Newell, Jean F. *Vietnamese Amerasians: A Needs Assessment*. Ann Arbor, Mich.: University Microfilms International, 1993. • U.S. Department of State. Bureau of Public Affairs. *Amerasians in Vietnam*. Washington, D.C.: Government Printing Office, 1988. • Valverde, Kieu-Linh Caroline. "From Dust to Gold: The Vietnamese Amerasian Experience." In *Racially Mixed People in America*, edited by Maria P. P. Root. Newbury Park, Calif.: Sage, 1992.

Vietnamese Americans: The history of Vietnamese Americans in the United States began with the end of the Vietnam War in 1975. On January 28, 1973, after having spent years and millions of dollars financing the war, the U.S. government reluctantly agreed to withdraw its financial and military assistance after signing the Agreement on Ending the War and Restoring Peace in Viet Nam. The peace agreement was signed by representatives of the U.S., South Vietnam, and North Vietnam governments in Paris. The main features of the agreement committed the United States and other signatories to respect the independence, sovereignty, unity, and territorial integrity of Vietnam, called for prisoners of war to be exchanged, and declared an immediate cease-fire.

The Exodus Begins. Soon after the withdrawal of U.S. military and economic support, however, the military situation deteriorated rapidly for the government of South Vietnam. The flight of Vietnamese refugees from within the country began with the North Vietnamese military offensive of mid-March, 1975, resulting in South Vietnamese defeats at Pleiku, Kontum, and Ban Me Thuot. As a result, about one million refugees poured out of these areas and headed for Saigon and the coast. Most traveled by foot; a few were fortunate enough to travel by car, truck, or motor bike. On April 30, 1975, the capital of South Vietnam, and thus all of South Vietnam, came under the control of the Provisional Revolutionary Government.

The Vietnamese emigration is generally divided into two periods, each with several "waves." The first period began in April, 1975, and continued through 1977. This period included the first three waves of Vietnamese refugees to the United States.

Massive Emigration. The first wave of refugees, involving some ten to fifteen thousand people, began at least a week before the collapse of the government. The second wave, and probably the largest in numbers, in-

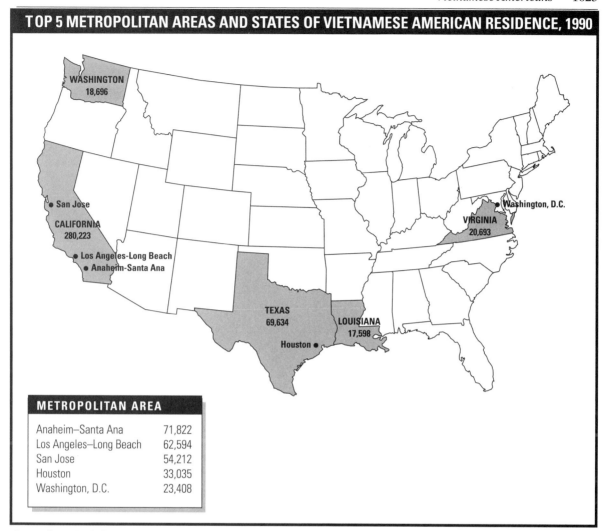

TOP 5 METROPOLITAN AREAS AND STATES OF VIETNAMESE AMERICAN RESIDENCE, 1990

WASHINGTON
18,696

San Jose

CALIFORNIA
280,223

Los Angeles-Long Beach
Anaheim-Santa Ana

Washington, D.C.

VIRGINIA
20,693

TEXAS
69,634

LOUISIANA
17,598

Houston

METROPOLITAN AREA	
Anaheim–Santa Ana	71,822
Los Angeles–Long Beach	62,594
San Jose	54,212
Houston	33,035
Washington, D.C.	23,408

Source: Susan B. Gall and Timothy L. Gall, eds., *Statistical Record of Asian Americans.* Detroit: Gale Research, 1993.

volved some eighty thousand, who were evacuated by aircraft during the last days of April. The evacuation of American personnel, their dependents, and Vietnamese affiliated with them was achieved through the use of giant helicopters under "Operation Frequent Wind."

These individuals were relatively well educated, spoke some English, had some skills that were marketable, came from urban areas, and were Westernized. Members of these two waves were primarily Vietnamese who worked for the U.S. government, American firms, or the Vietnamese government. All were thought to be prepared for life in the United States on the basis of their contact with the U.S. government and association with Americans.

The final wave during this period involved forty to sixty thousand people who left on their own in small boats or ships or who commandeered aircraft during the first two weeks of May, 1975. They were later transferred to Subic Bay in the Philippines or Guam Island after having been picked up, in many cases, by U.S. Navy and cargo ships standing off the coast.

The second period of the Vietnamese refugee migration began in 1978. Since the fall of South Vietnam in 1975, many Vietnamese have tried to escape the political oppression, the major social, political, and economic reforms instituted by the authoritarian government of North Vietnam. Although the influx continues steadily, the numbers are no longer as massive as they once were. A significant characteristic of this period, especially between the years 1978 to 1980, is the large number of ethnic Chinese leaving Vietnam and Cambodia.

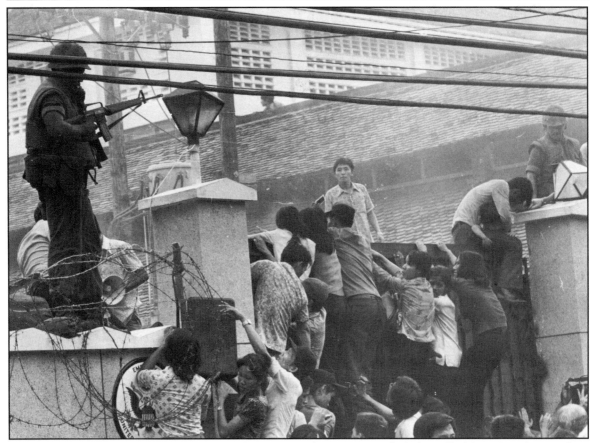

With Saigon having fallen to the Communist North Vietnamese, frantic citizens climb the wall of the U.S. embassy in hope of boarding American helicopters leaving the city. (AP/Wide World Photos)

In addition to the ethnic Chinese, there were many Vietnamese who left during this period. These individuals have been called "BOAT PEOPLE" because the majority of them escaped in homemade, poorly constructed boats. Because of their often-flimsy craft, their poor navigation skills, the limited amount of provisions that they were able to bring, and numerous attacks by Thai sea pirates, the death rate of the boat people has been very high. Many of them are awaiting their fate in refugee camps throughout Southeast Asia. In addition, since 1979 many countries previously open to refugees are turning them away because of the economic, political, and social strains that have resulted domestically.

The United States Response. At the end of the war, the general atmosphere of the American public toward the Vietnamese refugees was hostile. A Gallup Poll taken in May, 1975, showed that "54% of all Americans [were] opposed to admitting Vietnamese refugees to live in the United States and only 36% were in favor with 12% undecided." A common concern of the American public was one of economic self-interest—a fear of having jobs taken away by refugees as well as too much public assistance and welfare given to them.

In order to minimize the social impact of the large influx of Vietnamese refugees on an American public that was largely opposed to the Vietnam War, the U.S. government adopted the Refugee Dispersion Policy. This policy served four purposes: to relocate the Vietnamese refugees as quickly as possible so that they could achieve financial independence; to ease the impact of a large group of refugees on a given community, an accommodation that might avoid increased competition for jobs; to make it logistically easier to find refugee sponsors; and to prevent the development of an ethnic ghetto. If this policy was carried out successfully, the Vietnamese refugees would quickly assimilate into the American society.

The Role of VOLAGS. As a result, an assortment of voluntary agencies (VOLAGS) were contracted by the government's Interagency Task Force to handle the resettlement of the refugees in the United States. The agencies included the United Hebrew Immigration and Assistance Service, the Lutheran Immigration and Refugee Service, the International Rescue Committee, Church World Service, the American Funds for Czechoslovak Refugees, the United States Catholic Conference, the Travelers Aid International Social Service, and the Council for Nationalities Service. Each refugee family was asked to choose a resettlement agency. If the refugee did not have a preference, one was assigned.

The primary task of these agencies was to find sponsors who could fulfill both financial and moral responsibilities and to match them with the refugee families. In short, the sponsors would serve as a resource to introduce the refugees into the society while the latter became economically self-supporting. Sponsors found by voluntary agencies consisted of church congregations, parishes or affiliates, individual families, corporations, and companies with former Vietnamese employees.

This policy enabled many Vietnamese to be relocated throughout the United States. A few years after

Scores of refugee children found new homes in America through the help of assorted resettlement agencies. (James L. Shaffer)

this dispersion, however, many Vietnamese began to participate in a secondary migration. That is, since their initial resettlement, many have moved to other states. The 1980 census data on the Vietnamese in the United States indicated that the states having the largest refugee populations are California, with 34.8 percent; Texas, with 11.3 percent; Louisiana, with 4.4 percent; Washington, with 3.7 percent; Virginia, with 3.9 percent; Pennsylvania, with 3.3 percent; and Florida, with 2.9 percent. The 1990 census data also reflected this pattern. The states in which the refugees concentrated their secondary migration are still those states most populated with Vietnamese. California is still the state most preferred by the total number of Vietnamese refugees living in the United States, with 45.4 percent of the total Vietnamese American population. Texas is still second at 11.3 percent. Washington, with 4.8 percent, and Virginia, with 3.3 percent, have moved ahead of Louisiana's 2.9 percent. Florida is still fifth, with 2.65 percent, while Pennsylvania is now sixth, with 2.57 percent. These seven states together combine for almost 73 percent of the total number of Vietnamese refugees living in the United States. The attractions of these states reflect the need for Vietnamese to migrate to those states that have an established Vietnamese community for support, a warmer climate similar to their homeland, and job opportunities.

As a result of the original resettlement, the secondary-migration process, and the length of time since their first arrival in 1975, Vietnamese refugees have been able to establish communities throughout the United States. Such communities are generally located in metropolitan and urban areas where the majority of Vietnamese reside.

Vietnamese refugees, many in makeshift shelters, crowd the deck of the freighter Hai Hong *as it remains anchored off Port Klang, Malaysia, in late 1978.* (AP/Wide World Photos)

Vietnamese American Statistical Profile, 1990

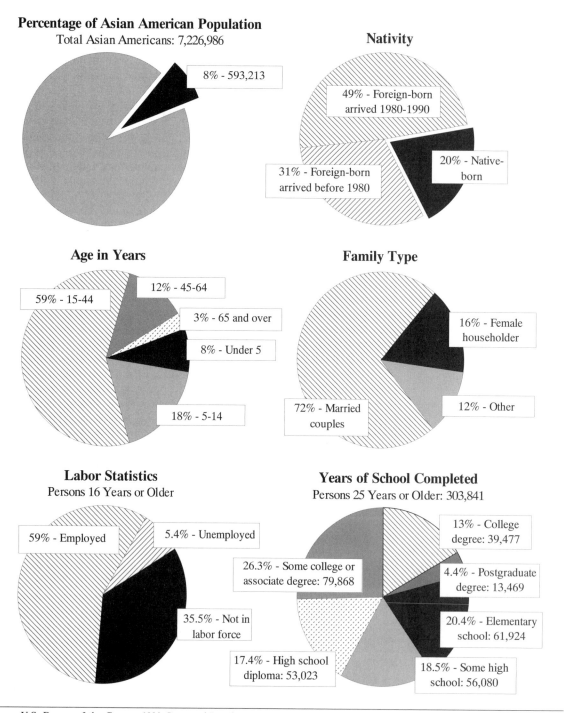

Percentage of Asian American Population
Total Asian Americans: 7,226,986

8% - 593,213

Nativity

49% - Foreign-born arrived 1980-1990

31% - Foreign-born arrived before 1980

20% - Native-born

Age in Years

12% - 45-64

59% - 15-44

3% - 65 and over

8% - Under 5

18% - 5-14

Family Type

16% - Female householder

72% - Married couples

12% - Other

Labor Statistics
Persons 16 Years or Older

59% - Employed

5.4% - Unemployed

35.5% - Not in labor force

Years of School Completed
Persons 25 Years or Older: 303,841

13% - College degree: 39,477

26.3% - Some college or associate degree: 79,868

4.4% - Postgraduate degree: 13,469

20.4% - Elementary school: 61,924

17.4% - High school diploma: 53,023

18.5% - Some high school: 56,080

Source: U.S. Bureau of the Census, *1990 Census of Population: Asians and Pacific Islanders in the United States,* 1993.

The Process of Acculturation. Like many of the other recent immigrant and refugee communities, Vietnamese Americans face many adjustment issues, ranging from personal adjustment, occupations and employment, family relations, social adaptations, and international differences.

Since the Vietnamese were forced to leave their country as a result of the war, personal adjustments pertaining to English proficiency, separation from families, and war memories were the issues that were most pressing. Since many Vietnamese did not know English, learning a new and different language became an important criteria for adjusting to new living conditions in the United States. In addition, because many extended families were forcibly separated because of the Dispersal Policy, some Vietnamese found themselves in

Vietnamese girls use a globe to point out their homeland to classmates at a Pennsylvania elementary school. (David S. Strickler)

Occupation	
Employed Persons 16 Years or Older	Percentage
Managerial and professional specialty	17.6%
Technical, sales, and administrative support	29.5%
Service	15.0%
Farming, forestry, and fishing	1.4%
Precision production, craft, and repair	15.7%
Operators, fabricators, and laborers	20.8%

Income, 1989	
Median household income	$29,772
Per capita	$9,033
Percent of families in poverty	24%

Household Size	
Number of People	Percentage
1	10.2%
2	15.6%
3	16.7%
4	19.0%
5	15.0%
6	10.5%
7 or more	13.0%

Source: U.S. Bureau of the Census, *1990 Census of Population: Asians and Pacific Islanders in the United States,* 1993.

unfamiliar communities without the family or community support networks that were so important in Vietnam. Finally, because of their traumatic experiences while leaving their homeland, some were plagued by depression, anxiety, alienation, a sense of helplessness, and recurring war nightmares.

In order to assimilate economically into the United States as quickly as possible, many Vietnamese were forced to obtain low-paying jobs. Those who had been professionals in their country often found that their credentials were neither transferable to nor accepted in the United States. The large number of people who had been members of the military also indicate that they had skills that were no longer marketable. In addition, since many refugees did not have the skills necessary to land high-paying jobs, they were forced to accept whatever employment they could find.

Changing Roles. Since it was easier for women to find employment, however, especially in the service and low-skill sectors, women began to occupy positions traditionally held by men. As a result, these women have succeeded in achieving a degree of economic independence through their employment outside the home. In some cases, women support the entire family while the men receive technical or educational training for occupations with specific skills. As a result, family conflicts between husbands and wives have emerged. Since women were more likely to find jobs than men and in some instances became the only income earners, the traditional family roles, authority, and patterns were changing. Men were no longer the sole provider for the family, and the ladder of authority is no longer as clear as it was in Vietnam. In sum, the fact that women began to work outside the home created tension because it eroded the husband's traditional role as the sole provider and his authority within the family.

In general, it is easier for immigrant children to adapt to a new country. This is also true in the Vietnamese American community. After an initial period of confusion, alienation, uncertainty, and difficulty, most Vietnamese children have resumed their education. Many have been successful and have continued onto higher education. There are a substantial number of Vietnamese Americans who are attending the most prestigious colleges and universities in America. Upon

graduation, these individuals have also become members of the professional or skilled working class in America.

Other problems. Yet despite some success in education, there are many younger Vietnamese Americans who have had problems in school adjustment. Those who seem to be having the hardest time adjusting are those who came either as unaccompanied minors or with the refugee arrivals of the late 1980's or early 1990's. After the fall of Vietnam in 1975, only a small group of children there were allowed to continue their education. These individuals primarily immigrated af-

Educational Attainment, Labor Status, and Occupation of Vietnamese American Women, 1990

Education of Women 25 Years or Older	
	Percent
High school graduate	19%
Some college or associate degree	22%
College graduate	10%
Advanced or professional degree	2%
Total high school graduate or more	53%

Women 16 Years or Older	
	Percent
In labor force	56%
(Unemployed	9%)
Not in labor force	44%

Employed Civilian Women 16 Years or Older

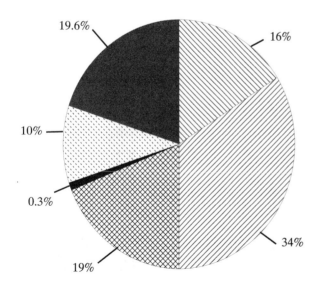

Managerial and professional specialty

Technical, sales, and administrative support

Service

Farming, forestry, and fishing

Precision production, craft, and repair

Operators, fabricators, and laborers

Source: U.S. Bureau of the Census, *1990 Census of Population: Asians and Pacific Islanders in the United States,* 1993.

This Vietnamese refugee found work as a seamstress after resettling in Pennsylvania. (David S. Strickler)

ter 1975 and most likely came at an age when it was difficult to learn a new language and adjust to a new society; in America, some have turned to gangs and illegal activities. The formation of these youth gangs might have resulted from their inability to catch up with their peers in school, their unfamiliarity with a strange land, and perhaps their alienation from their families because of cultural gaps.

For the elderly Vietnamese Americans, depression, isolation, loneliness, loss of family and homeland, and a feeling of helplessness are among the most prevalent problems. Because of their inability to speak English and their age, many have experienced difficulties finding jobs in America that match their skills. In addition, many are frustrated by their loss of status and authority and their inability to speak with their children and grandchildren. For them, younger Vietnamese Americans have acculturated too quickly and seem to have discarded many of the values of their parents and homeland and have substituted new American values in their place. As a result, the traditional authority and status accorded to the elderly have all but disappeared. Finally, elderly Vietnamese Americans are disappointed at not being able to contribute to the welfare and well-being of their families in the way that they had done in Vietnam. The traditional Vietnamese family structure has drastically changed for them.

Stabilization. There is evidence that things are stabilizing in many Vietnamese American communities. After a period of social, economic, and familial adjustment, the communities have turned their attention to

interaction with the larger society. The young Vietnamese Americans who have spent most of their lives in the United States have come of age and are beginning to exert some of their influence. Since the older generation has sacrificed so that the younger generation can receive a good education and/or obtain the necessary skills for professional employment, many of the latter have returned to build their own communities. Even though they are building their ethnic communities, these individuals are also participating in the larger society through their participation in political, economic, and social processes.

Despite their recent arrival, Vietnamese Americans have contributed greatly to the American cultural mosaic. Vietnamese communities located throughout the United States do not exist in isolation from the larger society. These communities not only serve as a place of cultural preservation for the next generation of Vietnamese Americans but also provide Vietnamese and non-Vietnamese alike the chance to participate in a variety of cultural activities. These activities include

Elderly Vietnamese Americans have experienced a variety of problems since immigrating to new lives in America. (James L. Shaffer)

For these Vietnamese Americans in Garden Grove, California, celebrating the traditional Tet holiday includes competing in a volleyball tournament. (David Fowler)

which the war and its aftermath are seen from a Vietnamese perspective.

• Rutledge, Paul James. *The Vietnamese Experience in America*. Bloomington: Indiana University Press, 1992. This survey includes an anthropological study of the formation of Vietnamese communities in Oklahoma and Texas.

• Strand, Paul J., and Woodrow Jones, Jr. *Indochinese Refugees in America: Problems of Adaptation and Assimilation*. Durham, N.C.: Duke University Press, 1985. An overview of Vietnamese immigration to the United States.

Vietnamese in Westminster: The economic and cultural capital of Vietnamese refugees and immigrants in the United States is located in the city of Westminster in Southern California's Orange County, the seat of the largest Vietnamese community outside Vietnam. Little Saigon, or "Bolsa," as it is commonly referred to in the Vietnamese community, is a business district of about two miles that runs along Bolsa Avenue between Magnolia and Ward streets. Formerly bean fields and half-empty minimalls, this stretch of Bolsa Avenue has been transformed into a bustling business area that serves approximately three hundred thousand customers annually. It has grown from three Vietnamese-owned businesses in 1978 to more than fifteen hun-

lunar New Year, the Mid-Autumn Lantern Festival, new forms of Vietnamese American arts, and other religious and cultural ceremonies. Finally, with the rapid growth of Vietnamese restaurants throughout America, Vietnamese cuisine is quite popular and is readily enjoyed by many.—*Hien Duc Do*
SUGGESTED READINGS:

• Caplan, Nathan, et al. *The Boat People and Achievement in America: A Study of Family Life, Hard Work, and Cultural Values*. Ann Arbor: University of Michigan Press, 1989. A framework for understanding the educational, social, and familial experiences of younger Southeast Asian students and their families.

• Freeman, James A. *Hearts of Sorrow: Vietnamese-American Lives*. Stanford, Calif.: Stanford University Press, 1989. A wonderfully warm, candid, lively, and insightful series of narratives on the adaptation processes of ordinary Vietnamese.

• Hayslip, Le Ly, with Jay Wurts. *When Heaven and Earth Changed Places: A Vietnamese Woman's Journey from War to Peace*. New York: Doubleday, 1989. Hayslip's personal account of her upbringing in Vietnam, her suffering during the Vietnam War, and her return there twenty years later. One of the few works in

CALIFORNIA

dred establishments in 1993, selling everything from live catfish to designer clothing. The person most responsible for Little Saigon's successful commercial development is Frank JAO, a Vietnamese American of Chinese descent. His Bridgecreek Development Company owns and manages many properties in the area, including the Asian Village and Asian Garden malls, the heart of the Bolsa business district.

This growth of businesses, Asian-owned and directed primarily toward an Asian clientele, in a predominately white, middle-class area, generated a brief community protest in 1981. A citizens' petition, however, asking that no more business licenses be issued to people of Vietnamese descent was unanimously rejected by the Westminster City Council. Another clash occurred in 1989 when a Westminster city councilman tried to deny ex-Vietnamese veterans seeking a parade permit. The councilman later apologized to the Vietnamese community.

Dental offices staffed by Vietnamese American professionals, located along well-known Bolsa Avenue in Little Saigon, Westminster. (Eric Crystal)

In 1988, the Westminster Redevelopment Agency designated the Bolsa business district as the "Little Saigon Tourist Commercial District." This action acknowledged the area's commercial potential and also brought about special directional Little Saigon signs on nearby freeways. According to the 1990 census, the Vietnamese are the fastest growing ethnic group in Orange County, increasing in population by 271 percent since 1980. The 1990 census gives Orange County's Vietnamese population as 71,822. This figure, however, has been questioned by the Vietnamese Chamber of Commerce and other community groups, who estimate the Vietnamese population as at least 120,000. The largest Vietnamese populations in Orange County are found in the adjoining towns of Westminster, Garden Grove, and Santa Ana: In each, Vietnamese constitute about one-fifth of the population.

The 1992 elections were a turning point for Westminster's Vietnamese community. Two Vietnamese American candidates, Tony LAM and Jimmy Tong Nguyen, ran for positions on Westminster's City Council. Lam, a local restaurateur and community activist, won a seat by 132 votes, making him the first Vietnamese American to be elected to political office in the United States.

Vietnamese literature: Expressive writing in Vietnam may be divided between the pre-1900 period, which used Chinese characters and local variants (called *chu nom*), and the twentieth century, which employed a romanized script (*quoc-ngu*). Vietnamese literature goes back more than a thousand years and was originally based on the Chinese literary style. Poetry was the major form taken, and in the first centuries of independence (tenth-twelfth centuries) through the Ly Dynasty (1009-1225), the verse was Buddhist. The subject was otherworldly. In the following two centuries, under the Tran Dynasty (1225-1400), there emerged as central the style of the Chinese Tang Dynasty (618-907)—stanzas of four or eight lines, usually with seven words per line, sometimes five, tightly regulated. The subjects became naturalistic and historical. The CHAM invasions of the late fourteenth century led to poetic involvement in the politics of the age. Prose took the form of tales, as the Vietnamese sought to construct a new cultural base.

The poetic form continued in the fifteenth century as the Le Dynasty (1428-1787) adopted the moralistic Neo-Confucianism of Ming China. This style remained the central one for more than four centuries, into the twentieth. During the same centuries, a folk style, of alternating six- and eight-word lines (*luc bat*) and using *nom*, grew in popularity. This form reached its peak in the Vietnamese classic by Nguyen Du, *The Tale of Kieu*, of the early nineteenth century.

French colonization and Vietnamese nationalism joined in the twentieth century to establish *quoc-ngu*. The early decades saw the gradual development of prose in the Western style as the short story and the novel arose. Then in the 1930's the "New Style" of poetry appeared, using a freer form. Strong themes of individualism and romanticism emerged among the French-educated writers and ran through the fiction and poetry of that decade, reacting to the traditional forms then in existence. Both the novelists of the Tu Luc Van Doan (Self Strengthening Literary Group) and the New Poets struggled against old social and cultural forms. Quickly, literature became intertwined with the politics of the age. The discussion of "art for art" versus "art for life" was tied into liberal versus radical responses to the colonial regime.

With World War II, a strong split occurred between those supporting the Communist-led VIET MINH and those opposing it. The former group of writers centered in Hanoi and their writing focused on social discipline. The anti-Viet Minh group centered in Saigon and their literature expressed personal spontaneity. Eventually, with the fall of Saigon in 1975, the anticommunist writers took refuge abroad.

Vietnamese special events: Facing resettlement difficulties, personal anguish, and cultural nostalgia, the celebrations of traditional festivals have become the most meaningful way for Vietnamese refugees to re-create their cultural heritage, to cope with their uncertain present, and to work for their bright future. The four most important festivals that have been celebrated in the United States are the "Ngay Quoc Han" (day of national mourning), the "Tet Trung Thu" (mid-autumn festival), the "Le Gio To" (memorial rites for primal ancestors), and the "Tet Nguyen Dan" (New Year celebration).

Ngay Quoc Han. This festival has become the most important political commemoration for the Vietnamese refugees in the United States because it marks the fall of their former Republic of Vietnam to the Communists on April 30, 1975, and the historically unprecedented exodus that followed. For this purpose, community and student organizations have normally organized political seminars to learn the lessons of modern Vietnamese history. They have also organized musical entertainment programs that normally consist of singing patriotic songs, anti-Communist satires, historical dramas, and fashion shows as main commemorative activities. Anti-Communist political groups have instead preferred more politically charged activities such as demonstrations, candle vigils, and the broadcasting of radio messages back to Vietnam calling for the establishment of civil rights and democracy. Despite great efforts made by political groups to transform the day of national mourning into the day of national resistance (Ngay Quoc Khang), this celebration has declined somewhat during the 1990's because of political normalization and also because thousands of Vietnamese in the United States are more inclined to go back to Vietnam as tourists rather than to demonstrate on that fateful day.

Tet Trung Thu. This festival is celebrated on the fifteenth day of the eighth month of the Eastern calendar primarily as the biggest annual festival for children. The familiar Trung Thu symbols are the delightful mooncakes and colorful lanterns. The celebration of the Tet Trung Thu has become a culturally significant way for Vietnamese children in the United States to enjoy a festive taste of their heritage. Unlike the more socially collective form of celebrating the Tet Trung Thu in Vietnam, its celebration within the Vietnamese American communities has become more fragmented, since most Vietnamese religious organizations, community associations, and school teachers have organized their own separate festivals. These festivals normally feature Trung Thu cakes, lion dances, musical shows, marital arts competitions, fashion shows, art exhibitions, and lantern parades.

Le Gio To. This festival is commemorated on the tenth day of the third Eastern month at the sacred national Shrine of Hung Kings (northern Vietnam). Modern archaeological evidence from northern Vietnam tends to support the possibility that this celebration had originally been a cosmically sacred rite that originated with the kings of the Hung Dynasty (2879-258 B.C.E.) to commemorate the primal ancestors of the entire human race. Prior to the reunification of the land in 1975-1976, the Le Gio To was observed by the two Vietnamese regimes in their separate regions. The Vietnamese in the United States have now entrusted to their elders the responsibility for conducting the festival to commemorate the Hung kings and all subsequent Vietnamese heroes and heroines who dedicated their lives to building and defending Vietnam. The conduct of the Le Gio To normally includes setting up the ancestral altar in a school hall, reading commemorative stanzas, making food offerings (fresh fruits, food dishes, a pair of round and square cakes) and burning incense to the spirits of the Hung kings and national heroes and heroines, performing worshiping rituals, and feasting together with the other celebrants at the end.

Tet Nguyen Dan. The term "Tet Nguyen Dan" literally means "festivity on the first morning" of the new year because it marks the "very auspicious beginning" of time and fortune or misfortune to come. The Tet Nguyen Dan, commonly called "Tet" (festivity), is the biggest national holiday, and culturally and spiritually the most sublime, in comparison with all other Vietnamese festivals. For the Vietnamese, Tet is like Christmas, Easter, Thanksgiving, and one's own birthday all rolled into one. Even though the origin of Tet is

Vietnamese American dancers welcome the New Year. (James L. Shaffer)

still shrouded in mystery, the Chinese are known to have celebrated the new year since the third century B.C.E. The Vietnamese have, however, traced Tet to their own ancient cultural source (c. third millennium B.C.E.) when the sixth Hung king initiated the New Year celebration and the common people then followed his example.

Tet, which was traditionally accompanied by Hoi Xuan (spring festival), is meant to be the happiest time for family reunion, harmony, rest, and celebration before the world turns to a new cycle of cosmic renewal and human productive activities. The final preparations for Tet in Vietnam normally begin in earnest early in the last month of the preceding year and reach their climax on the Tet's Eve shopping day (December 30 on the Eastern calendar). Therefore, most Vietnamese overseas make sure that their Tet gifts reach their

relatives or that they themselves arrive in Vietnam with gifts in time for Tet. The Tet season begins with the "rite of sending the kitchen lord (Tao Quan) to Heaven" on the twenty-third day of the last Eastern month so that he will have sufficient time to travel to Heaven to report to the Jade Emperor and return on time for the New Year's Eve family feast. At dusk on New Year's Eve, all preparations should be complete and all family members including returnees must be inside their own homes. The family feast begins with the holy ANCESTOR WORSHIP rituals to welcome the return of the deceased members to celebrate Tet with all the living. The feast is normally prolonged until midnight so that the whole family can celebrate the "Gio Giao Thua" (hour of cosmic transition), which marks the end of the old year and the beginning of the new year as the long string of firecrackers (sometimes

Tet celebrants bring gifts to the altar inside this church. (James L. Shaffer)

accompanied by drums and gongs) are carefully timed to explode wildly exactly at the "Zero Hour!"

The new year is celebrated with a sense of awe on the first three Tet days, which normally fall between January and February in the Western calendar. The "original morning" of the first Tet day is considered to be extremely auspicious because it is "the holy beginning" of the new year and must therefore be observed with the spirit of absolute goodness, purity, and reverence. Tradition-minded Vietnamese make sure that every aspect of their family is truly genuine, positive, and elevating like the purity of the rays of sun shining brightly in the morning of the new year. All family members wear their new clothes to welcome the new year and wish one another the best. Children and grandchildren are expected to thank their parents and grandparents and wish for them the three best wishes

of "Phuc, Loc, and Tho" (happiness, good fortune, and longevity). In return, parents and grandparents congratulate their young children and grandchildren for being a year older and give them "lucky" money in red envelopes (mung tuoi and li xi).

Gift-giving (Tet) is another well-established New Year tradition that serves different social purposes such as thanking benefactors, renewing or strengthening friendships, and healing old wounds. The gift-giving tradition is expressed in this popular dictum, "Tet one's parents on the First Day, and one's teacher on the Third Day!" One has therefore the second day or any other convenient day of the new year to "tet" in-law parents and any other important benefactors. The magical words of Tet greetings are: "Chuc Mung Nam Moi (happy New Year)!"

To obtain "good luck" throughout the new year for

happiness, good fortune, longevity, tranquillity, and security, the head of a household normally invites (pre-Tet) favorite friends, especially those who are morally good, wealthy, successful, and influential, to visit the families of the particular household first during the late morning of the first Tet day. People in mourning usually abstain from making Tet visits.

Tet festivals (Hoi Tet) have become the cultural form of Vietnamese American New Year celebration. Most well known are the Tet festivals in San Jose (Northern California), Orange County (Southern California), and Houston (Texas). These Tet festivals have served as the focal points for Vietnamese identity enhancement, friendship making, friendship renewal, community cooperation, community leadership build-

ing, and cultural preservation. The Tet festival in San Jose, which has been successfully organized at Santa Clara Fairgrounds (1982-1993), is considered to be the biggest among all the Tet festivals outside Vietnam. The 1993 Tet festival in San Jose, which attracted more than forty thousand Vietnamese participants, featured community agency information booths, food bazaars, games, outdoor concerts, Karaoke contests, ballroom dances, a Miss Vietnam pageant, martial arts competitions, table-tennis championships, Vietnamese fashion shows, lion dances, and Asian chess matches.

In short, the Tet Nguyen Dan and the Le Gio To are culturally and spiritually important for adult Vietnamese since the former symbolizes their culture and the latter bonds them to their ancient mythical roots. The

Tet festival performers in Garden Grove, another Vietnamese American enclave of Orange County, California. (David Fowler)

Ngay Quoc Han reminds them of the humiliating fall of their homeland to the Communists and the Vietnamese American desire to return to national liberation and renewal. The Tet Trung Thu helps the children maintain their ethnic and cultural identity through meaningful personal participation and festive enjoyment.— *Chánh Công Phan*

SUGGESTED READINGS: • Cohen, Barbara. "Holidays and Festivals." In *The Vietnam Guidebook*. Teaneck, N.J.: Eurasia Press, 1990. • Crawford, A. C. *Customs and Culture of Vietnam. Rutland, Vt.: Charles E. Tuttle, 1966.* • Huynh Dinh Te. *"Tet, The Vietnamese New Year Festival." In Introduction to Cambodian Culture*. 2d ed. San Diego: Multifunctional Service Center, San Diego State University, 1989. • Le Quang Vinh. *Moon Festival (Tet Trung Thu)*. Bassendean, Western Australia: Avery Publishing Company, 1990. • "Nguon Goc Cac Le Tet Co Truyen Viet-Nam" (Origins of the Traditional Vietnamese Tet Holidays). In *Van Hoa Viet Nam* (Vietnamese Culture), compiled by Tran Do, et al. Hanoi: Ban Van Hoa Van Nghe Trung Uong, 1989. • Phan Công Chánh. "Tet: Nguon Goc va Y Nghia" (Tet: Origins and Meanings). In *Quan Doi* (San Jose, 1991). • *Tet: The Vietnamese New Year*. Compiled and edited by Kim-Anh Nguyen Phan. San Jose: San Jose Unified School District, 1986.

Vijayadashmi: Tenth day of DIWALI, the Hindu festival of lights celebrating the return of Rama (an incarnation of the Hindu god Vishnu) to Ayodhya (one of the seven holy places of HINDUISM, located in Uttar Pradesh) and his delayed coronation as king following a long exile—the triumph of good over evil. On this day, effigies of Rama are built throughout the country and filled with firecrackers. The fourth day—the principal Diwali festival day—marks the start of the new year according to the Vikrama calendar. This and other Hindu festivals are observed with equal fervor in communities throughout the diaspora in an effort to maintain traditional Asian Indian culture.

Villa, José García (b. Aug. 5, 1914, Manila, Philippines): Writer. Villa, a self-exile from the Philippines for decades, has earned an international reputation for both his poetry and his short stories. He became, in 1973, the first Filipino writer in English to be declared a National Artist, receiving a lifelong government pension.

The son of a physician-father who had once served under Emilio AGUINALDO, the Philippine revolutionary, Villa attended the University of the Philippines, intent for a time on becoming a lawyer. In 1929, however, the school temporarily suspended him for writing the sexually explicit poem "Man Songs." The same year, his story "Mir-i-Nasa" won a prize in what later became a prestigious annual contest. Shortly thereafter, he used the prize money to travel to America.

Villa graduated with a B.A. degree from the University of New Mexico in 1932. As an undergraduate he founded the literary magazine *Clay*. He also wrote numerous short stories, many of which appeared in his magazine. As these works garnered positive critical attention, Villa was encouraged enough to move to New York City to pursue his writing further.

Although Villa kept writing, amid the Great Depression a steady income was tough to manage; he also claimed that his Filipino nationality was a source of discrimination when job hunting. Nevertheless, his stories and poems were accepted for publication. *Have Come, Am Here* (1942), his third published volume of verse, was mentioned as worthy of the Pulitzer Prize.

Part of World War II was spent in Washington, D.C., where Villa was a clerk at the Philippine embassy. Eventually, he returned to New York, married, and published more books. In addition, he was an associate editor with the avant-garde New Directions Publishing Corporation of New York and led poetry workshops at various schools. Since the 1940's his verse has been reprinted regularly in anthologies the world over.

Visayan Islands: Central island group of the Philippines. Clustered in a ring about the Visayan Sea, the Visayas comprise the sizable, inhabited islands of Negros, Panay, Leyte, Cebu, Bohol, Samar, and Masbate plus innumerable isles. Altogether they total a majority of the Philippine archipelago's islands. The Visayan Islands' land area of about twenty-two thousand square miles contained a 1990 population exceeding thirteen million.

The Visayas constitute nearly nineteen percent of the Philippines land area but contain mostly mountains with some coastal lowlands. Three exceptions to the rugged interiors are Panay's Iloilo Plain, the Leyte Valley, and the level sections of western and northern Negros. The fertile alluvial soils of the Iloilo area and Leyte Valley promote wet rice farming because of their composition and moisture retention.

Since the Philippine climate is tropical, the seasonal rainfall of the eastern Visayas is heavy through the winter but limited and variable during the summer and fall. The interior of the Visayan Islands is protected from the brunt of precipitation-carrying air masses, and its reduced rainfall is conducive to corn cultivation. Unfortunately the eastern Visayan region is prone to earthquakes and tropical cyclones; it experienced a series of damaging shakes in 1955. Typhoons usually arrive in October or November.

The Visayan economy is mainly primary. Besides corn and rice, farmers produce large quantities of bananas. The eastern Visayas grow coconuts while the western islands operate sugarcane plantations.

The Philippines is recognized for its mineral wealth, and Visayan copper was the country's principal ore in the 1970's. Huge deposits were mined at Toledo in Cebu and on Samar and Negros. Additional Visayan minerals are iron ore, nonmetallic coal, and sulfur.

Because the greatest population densities are located in the center of the Visayas, the most populous provinces are Cebu, Iloilo, and Negros Occidental. The important cities of Cebu and Iloilo are situated in Cebu and Iloilo provinces, respectively.

Other Filipinos perceive Visayans as courageous and hedonistic. Eating, drinking, and music are Visayan pleasures. The region's inhabitants speak a variety of dialects, the most common being Cebuano. Visayans of note are Cebu's Sergio Osmeña, second president of the Philippine Commonwealth, and Leyte's Imelda Marcos, wife of former president Ferdinand MARCOS.

Pivotal events of the Philippine past took place in the Visayas. Cebu and Mactan Islands are the celebrated landfalls of Ferdinand Magellan, and U.S. Army general Douglas MacArthur's 1944 invasion of Leyte signaled the fulfillment of his vow to return to the Philippines during World War II.

Visual Communications: Community-based media resource and production facility, founded in 1970, that strives to portray the history and culture of Asian Pacific Americans through its various works. The organization began in Los Angeles when a group of young Asian Americans decided to produce a photo exhibit on Japanese Americans alive during World War II. These visionaries, Robert Nakamura, Eddie Wong, Alan Ohashi, and Duane Kubo, were part of the new generation of activists dedicated to social change and responsible for building up the ever-widening ASIAN AMERICAN MOVEMENT. They produced artwork for the Asian American community, including posters, photos, and leaflets, but soon realized that they needed to expand their vision of the group to meet their broader objectives.

In 1971 Visual Communications became a nonprofit corporation. This made it easier to both serve the community and pursue filmmaking. As a nonprofit organization, the group was eligible to receive funding from programs such as the Comprehensive Employment and Training Act (CETA) and the Emergency School Aid Act (ESAA). For the next few years, through 1977, the group was able to produce ten films on the Asian American experience and even published a book of photos, *In Movement* (1974). In 1980 Visual Communications completed its first full-length movie, *Hito Hata: Raise the Banner*, featuring an all-star Asian American cast. It was the first project of its type ever attempted by Asian Americans, and it came close to becoming a victim of its ambition. Problems with the budget almost sank the project and the organization as well. The nonprofit group Friends of Visual Communications was organized soon after in Los Angeles to help provide community support for the group.

Affiliated with Visual Communications is the Asian Pacific American Photographic Archives, a collection of several hundred thousand photographs and slides.

Visual Communications has inspired a number of other Asian American media groups around the country, including ASIAN CINEVISION (ACV) (1976) in New York City, the ASIAN AMERICAN RESOURCE WORKSHOP (1979) in Boston, and Asian American Arts and Media (1985) in Washington, D.C. In 1980 the NATIONAL ASIAN AMERICAN TELECOMMUNICATIONS ASSOCIATION (NAATA) was formed from members of these other organizations to provide support for Asian Americans working in the media.

Vivekananda (Narendranath Datta, also Narendranath Dutt; Jan. 12, 1863, Calcutta, West Bengal, India— July 4, 1902, Calcutta, West Bengal, India): Hindu spiritual leader and reformer. Vivekananda was RAMAKRISHNA's disciple and hand-picked successor who spent his life spreading the teachings of his former master. Vivekananda also taught that work performed in the service of others was the most noble of human endeavors.

Born into an upper-middle-class family, Vivekananda received a university education that exposed him to Western philosophy, Christianity, and science. Dedicating his life to social reform, he began to labor for laws to end illiteracy and upgrade education, while urging the modernization of Indian tradition—advocating spiritual enlightenment as the key by which all of this could be obtained. To the Americans and the British he introduced the tenets of VEDANTA, articulating his beliefs at the World's Parliament of Religions in Chicago in 1893 and winning many converts. He also started several Vedanta societies throughout the United States. In 1897 Vivekananda organized the Ramakrishna Mission along the Ganges River near Calcutta to teach the ideas of the late Hindu ascetic and mystic and perform social service. The Vedanta Society of the City of New York, incorporated in 1898, is the oldest branch of the mission in the United States.

VOLAGS (voluntary agencies): Organizations that have played a critical role in assisting refugees in Southeast Asia and the United States. Such agencies are not a part of any government and are therefore also known as "NGOS" (nongovernmental agencies). Often such agencies have contracts with government agencies of the United States or the United Nations to provide services to refugees using the personnel and facilities of the VOLAG. Most agencies also do private nongovernmental fund-raising as well. Sometimes VOLAGS are the charity arms of church organizations. Examples of church-affiliated VOLAGS include Catholic Relief Services, the American Friends Service Committee (Quaker), and World Vision (Prot-

estant). Examples of nonsectarian VOLAGS that have been active in the provision of assistance to Indochinese agencies include the International Rescue Committee, the Joint Voluntary Agency, and the Cooperative for American Relief to Everywhere (CARE).

Large national and international agencies such as the Office of the UNITED NATIONS HIGH COMMISSIONER FOR REFUGEES (UNHCR) and the U.S. Department of State often prefer to contract with VOLAGS to provide services to refugees. VOLAGS are able to provide services to refugees more quickly than large government agencies. Unlike the latter, VOLAGS do not have the many bureaucratic regulations governing purchasing, hiring, and staff that can slow responses to the quickly changing conditions under which refugees often live.

In Southeast Asia the UNHCR has often contracted with VOLAGS to provide medical, sanitation, drug treatment, and some education services in refugee camps. Also in Southeast Asia the U.S. Department of State has contracted with VOLAGS to provide English language instructional programs and to do the legal work required for the preparation of refugee resettlement cases.

Vietnamese boat people at Sungei Besi refugee camp, Kuala Lumpur, Malaysia. (A. Hollmann/UNHCR)

Resettled Vietnamese refugees, such as this San Diego, California, lab technician, have made valuable contributions to their new society. (Ph. Théard/UNHCR)

In the United States the Department of Health and Human Services has contracted with a large number of voluntary agencies to provide resettlement and retraining programs for Southeast Asian refugees. Among the more well-known of these resettlement agencies are church-based groups such as Catholic Social Services and the Lutheran resettlement agencies. The largest nonsectarian contractor is the International Rescue Committee.

VOLAGS are often the first contact that refugees have with Americans and the American government.

Voorhees, Donald (July 30, 1916, Leavenworth, Kans.—July 7, 1989, Seattle, Wash.): Federal judge. Appointed by President Richard M. Nixon to the federal district court, based in Seattle, Washington, he presided in the 1988 *coram nobis* rehearing of the Gordon HIRABAYASHI wartime internment and curfew case of 1943, in which he ruled in favor of Hira-bayashi. A graduate of Harvard Law School, he also ordered a forced busing plan to achieve racial balance in the Seattle school system.

Sponsored by a Catholic church group, this Vietnamese family arrives at an airport in Dubuque, Iowa. (James L. Shaffer)

W

Wah Chang Trading Company: Corporation that operated various mining concerns and metal refineries, founded in New York in 1916. It was started by metallurgical engineer Li K. C., who had attended England's Royal School of Mines. By 1953 the corporation ran the world's largest tungsten refinery. Its roster of companies acquired through takeovers continued to grow, as did its combined assets. Li also established a scholarship foundation in his name to assist international students who want to study and work in the United States.

Wah Ching: Chinese youth gang, originating in San Francisco's Chinatown during the mid-1960's. After the passage of the 1965 immigration law, San Francisco's Chinatown became home for newly arriving Chinese families from Asia, especially Hong Kong. Although these families came with visions of a better life, many found themselves confined in a congested, densely populated area. Immigrant youth faced numerous problems. There were few recreational and job opportunities. The American-born Chinese (ABC) youth scorned them for their language and cultural differences and mocked them as FOBs (fresh off the boat). The young immigrants joined together for protection and called themselves Wah Ching (Chinese youth).

The Wah Ching began to organize formally, becoming incorporated in 1968. They operated as a self-help group with the goal of improving conditions for youth in Chinatown. In addition to holding fund-raising activities, they approached the political structures of the city and Chinatown for help. Their pleas were denied at meetings with the Economic Opportunity Council, San Francisco Human Rights Commission, and Chinatown's powerful Chinese Six Companies.

Wah Ching members grew frustrated with their inability to access legitimate institutions for assistance. Their youth movement was dying, and ironically they moved in a different direction. The group split off. Some members joined the Hop Sing Tong and worked as guards for the protection racket and gambling houses. They retained the name Wah Ching. Other members of the original youth group went to work for the rival Suey Sing Tong and took the name Suey Sing Boys.

By 1969 the Wah Ching and Suey Sing Boys had become embroiled in gang warfare, resulting in several killings and serious injuries. As the conflict continued into 1970, one Wah Ching member, Joe Fong, left the Hop Sing Tong and created the group Chung Yee. In 1971 Wah Ching in alliance with Chung Yee drove the Suey Sing Boys out of San Francisco and into Oakland. Members of Chung Yee and Wah Ching organized the group Yau Lei but argued over several issues, particularly extortion practices. Wah Ching and Chung Yee (later known as the JOE BOYS) fought for six years. The conflict culminated in the GOLDEN DRAGON RESTAURANT MASSACRE. Wah Ching continues to exist but is believed to be loosely organized.

Waihee, John David, III (b. May 19, 1946, Honokaa, Hawaii): Governor of Hawaii. A Native Hawaiian, Waihee received his bachelor's degree in history and business from Andrews University in Michigan in 1968 before entering the field of education. He worked as the coordinator of community education for the Benton Harbor, Michigan, school district from 1968 to 1970 before serving as the program's assistant director from 1970 through 1971. Waihee returned to Hawaii in 1971 to work with the planners and directors of the

Governor of Hawaii, John David Waihee, III.

Honolulu Model Cities Program. In 1973, he was hired as a senior planner for the city and county of Honolulu and was promoted to program manager for the city's Office of Human Resources the following year. During his stint as a city planner, Waihee had returned to school at the University of Hawaii and earned his J.D. degree in 1976. Upon graduation, he was admitted to the Hawaii state bar and joined the law firm of Shim, Sigal, Tam & Naito before becoming a partner in his own Honolulu firm in 1979. Waihee launched his political career in 1980, when he ran as a Democratic candidate and was elected to the Hawaiian House of Representatives for a two-year term. He was elected to serve as the state's lieutenant governor in 1982. At the end of his four-year term, Waihee ran for election as governor. His election victory in 1986 made him the state's first governor of Native Hawaiian descent; he was reelected to a second term in 1992.

Waipahu Cultural Garden Park: The first multicultural public park in the United States, founded in 1972. As the sugar industry was gradually phased out in Hawaii, a growing nostalgia for the plantation era affected many people in the state. Although labor conditions were often harsh, former sugarcane laborers remembered the sense of community that developed among the immigrant plantation workers, ultimately transforming Hawaii into a paragon of ethnic harmony. Accordingly, in the early 1970's the idea arose to build a model village, with appropriate botanical and ethnic artifacts of the major ethnic groups that worked alongside one another over the past century.

The City and County of Honolulu developed a site for the park on 45.4 acres of land in Waipahu, not far from the smokestack of a sugar mill (now abandoned) in the flat flood plain of Waikele Stream, fourteen miles from downtown Honolulu, east of Pearl Harbor. Three components were planned: a replica of a multiethnic plantation village, a community education and information center, and a botanical garden.

When the park opened in 1972, fundraising ensued to construct authentic housing replicas. Beginning in 1973 the Friends of Waipahu Cultural Garden Park sought corporate and individual donations, as well as county and state government financing.

The plantation village, which officially opened in September, 1992, consists of a plantation store, a union meeting hall, and twenty-eight replicas of the houses, recreational sites, and religious temples of eight ethnic groups (Chinese, Filipino, Hawaiian, Japanese, Korean, Okinawan, Portuguese, and Puerto Rican). Heritage societies representing each group have provided clothes, furniture, and other artifacts that were actually used on the plantations from 1875 to 1975. The community education and information center has a small museum, meeting room, and administrative offices. The botanical park is to consist mainly of plants introduced to Hawaii by plantation immigrants.

Wakabayashi, Ron (b. Nov. 13, 1944, Reno, Nev.): Administrator and activist. Executive director of the Los Angeles City Human Relations Commission, he was previously the national director of the JAPANESE AMERICAN CITIZENS LEAGUE (JACL) and also served in a key capacity with the United Way.

Administrator and activist Ron Wakabayashi. (Asian Week)

Wakamatsu Tea and Silk Farm Colony: Tea and silk farm established at Gold Hill near Placerville, California, by Japanese immigrants in 1869. It is derived from what is now the city of Aizu-wakamatsu, near the northern end of the Mikuni mountain range, about one hundred miles north of Tokyo. During the civil war that ushered in the MEIJI period (1868-1912), Aizu-wakamatsu was a part of Hoshina Han, a feudal fief held by Matsudaira Katmori, a *DAIMYO*, or great lord. Matsudaira was the family name of many of the collateral houses collectively called "Shimpan," or "related *han*." There were twenty-three such collateral houses related to the Tokugawa shoguns by blood or marriage. The Shimpan's loyalty was unquestioned. They were often referred to as "treasures among men." So deeply trusted were the Shimpan that three houses had the right to provide an heir in the event that the main Tokugawa family could not. Given such loyalty it is understandable that Aizu-wakamatsu would support the Tokugawa against the imperial forces during the civil war.

When the Tokugawa were defeated, Aizu-wakamatsu was confiscated in the name of the emperor, and the many warriors became masterless samurai.

Among Matsudaira's advisors was a German, John Henry Schnell, who had married a Japanese woman. It was Schnell who apparently developed the idea of emigrating to California to establish a tea and silk colony. Exactly how the small band of travelers received permission to leave Japan is not known; technically it was still against the law.

The small party arrived in San Francisco on May 27, 1869. They journeyed to Sacramento and then to Placerville and nearby Gold Hill. They arrived on June 8, 1869, at Gold Hill, where they were planning to buy the Granger ranch. The deed for the six-hundred-acre site was recorded some two weeks later.

The fledgling colony arrived with some fifty thousand mulberry trees for silk farming, along with assorted tea seeds and other plants and seeds. It is not known where Schnell obtained the tea seeds. The Aizu-wakamatsu area is not a tea-producing area.

Despite the best of intentions the colony was short-lived. It was dissolved in 1871. The red lateritic soils of the Gold Hill-Placerville region were not suitable, and the colony was established in the hot, dry California summer at a time when irrigation was not yet well-developed.

In July, 1870, the names of twenty-two Japanese were recorded at Gold Hill, including Schnell's wife. Schnell and his wife and children left the colony in 1872. A year before, in 1871, a nineteen-year-old Japanese girl had died of a fever and was buried nearby. In the 1930's her grave was discovered and restored. The other members of the colony were apparently assimilated into the larger population. In Sacramento a mixed family of white, black, Indian, and Japanese ancestry claim Masumizu Kuninosuke as one of their forebears. Masumizu died in 1915 and is buried in Colusa.

In 1969 the state of California placed a State Historical Plaque on the site of the Wakamatsu Tea and Silk Farm Colony. The plaque reads: "Site of the only tea and silk farm established in California. First agricultural settlement of pioneer Japanese immigrants who arrived at Gold Hill on June 8, 1869. Despite the initial success, it failed to prosper. It marked the beginning of Japanese influence on the agricultural economy of California."

The plaque is on the grounds of the Gold Trail Elementary School in El Dorado County.

Wakayama: Is located on the southern part of Honshu, the largest of the Japanese islands, and was the region of origin of many Japanese who emigrated to the United States from the 1880's to 1924. It occupies an area of about 1,824 square miles, and its population exceeded one million in 1991. Among its major products, manufactured mostly in the northwest, are petroleum, textiles, and steel. The capital city is Wakayama.

Wake, Lloyd (b. Jan. 12, 1922, Reedley, Calif.): Pastor. Incarcerated at POSTON, Arizona, during World War II, he became the first Asian American pastor (1967-1989) to serve at Glide Memorial United Methodist Church in San Francisco, California. A member of the Asian American United Methodist goodwill team to South Korea (1974) and Taiwan (1980), he has served on the boards of the Bay Area Asian American Service Committee (1976-1978), the Ohana Cultural Center of Oakland, California (1985-1987), and the ASIAN LAW CAUCUS (since 1976).

Wakukawa, Seiei (b. Aug. 18, 1947, Okinawa, Japan): Journalist. He was the former editor of the *HAWAII TIMES* and the executive director of the Okinawa Relief and Rehabilitation Foundation. He taught the Japanese language at the University of Chicago and wrote a book about TOYAMA KYUZO, a pioneer Okinawan who emigrated to Hawaii.

Walsh, Richard J. (Nov. 20, 1886, Lyons, Kans.— May 28, 1960, near Doylestown, Pa.): Writer and co-founder of Welcome House. A Harvard graduate, Walsh worked as a reporter for the *Boston Herald* from 1907 to 1909. He joined the Curtis Publishing Company in 1912 and worked as promotion manager until 1916. During the next five years, he was an advertising writer. From 1917 to 1949 he served consecutively as editor for *Collier's Weekly, Judge, Asia Magazine,* and *United Nations World.* Meanwhile he wrote and published his own books: *Kidd* (1922), *The Making of*

Pearl S. Buck, author of The Good Earth, *founded Welcome House with her husband Richard Walsh.* (AP/Wide World Photos)

Buffalo Bill (coauthor 1928), and *The Adventures and Discoveries of Marco Polo* (1948).

In 1927 Walsh and his friend Earl Newsom bought a foundering publishing firm named after John Day, a sixteenth century printer known for his courage in publishing unpopular papers. Two years later, as John Day's president, Walsh decided to print Pearl S. BUCK's first book, *East Wind: West Wind* (1930), when other publishers had turned her down because they believed that American readers were not interested in China. His decision made it possible for the ordinary Chinese as depicted in Buck's novels to be introduced to American readers.

Walsh married Buck in 1935, a second marriage for both. The two devoted much of their time to promoting Americans' understanding of Asia and advocating racial equality. They campaigned tirelessly in the early 1940's for the repeal of the racially discriminatory CHINESE EXCLUSION ACT in effect since 1882. They helped to found the Citizens Committee to Repeal Chinese Exclusion in 1943, and Walsh served as its chairman until its mission was accomplished six months later.

In 1949, with Buck, Walsh founded Welcome House in Bucks County, Pennsylvania, to care for and find foster homes for children of mixed blood who has been abandoned by their parents and rejected by many well-equipped institutions. Soon the House began to place for adoption hundreds of unwanted children fathered by American servicemen overseas in such places as Japan and Korea. Walsh's humanitarian work helped to end the discrimination and ill treatment suffered by these children in their places of birth.

Wang, An (Feb. 7, 1920, Shanghai, China—Mar. 24, 1990, Boston, Mass.): Scientist, philanthropist, and entrepreneur. As a child Wang was taught Confucian ideas of moderation, patience, balance, and simplicity. The eldest of five children of a middle-class family, Wang entered prestigious Jiaotung University in Shanghai at the age of sixteen. In 1945 he came to the United States as one of hundreds of Chinese engineers selected to study American technology. Harvard University enrolled Wang as a master's degree candidate. Sixteen months after acceptance at Harvard, Wang was gradu-

Dr. An Wang, founder of Wang Laboratories, speaks at the dedication ceremonies for the Wang Center for the Performing Arts in Boston. (AP/Wide World Photos)

ated with a Ph.D. in applied physics. In 1949 he married Lorraine Chiu. They had two sons and a daughter.

In the spring of 1948 Wang became a research assistant in the Harvard Computer Laboratory. His work with Howard Aiken, a pioneer in computer development, eventually led to the establishment of Wang Laboratories. That year Wang helped develop magnetic core memory—essential to the development of modern computers.

In 1951 Wang began Wang Laboratories with $600 in savings and one employee—himself. Through the development and sales of electronic calculators, word processors, and office automation systems, Wang Laboratories became a company with sales of $2.4 billion and hundreds of thousands of employees worldwide.

Wang was among the pioneers who developed the desktop calculator industry in the 1960's, the computer-based word processor in the 1970's, and the minicomputer. He was an inventor who held more than forty patents.

Wang received many awards, including twenty-three honorary degrees. He received the Medal of Liberty, awarded by former President Ronald Reagan, in 1986 and enshrinement in halls of fame erected by journals and universities. Wang's community contributions were many: $4 million to create Boston's premier center for performing arts; $4 million to Harvard; $6 million to establish the Wang Institute, which awards master's degrees in software engineering; and $4 million to build the Massachusetts General Hospital outpatient clinic. Wang also funded scholarships and student exchange programs with the People's Republic of China. Yet he lived a quiet, simple life, never owning more than two suits at a time.

Wang, Art (b. Feb. 4, 1949, Boston, Mass.): Politician. Elected in 1981 to the Washington State House of Representatives (Twenty-seventh District), he has served on a number of committees, including Revenue, Capital Facilities and Financing, and House Appropriations. He holds a B.A. degree in mythology from Franconia College, New Hampshire, and a J.D. degree from the University of Puget Sound's law school in Washington, where he returned to teach courses on legislation and state and local taxation.

Wang, L. Ling-chi: Scholar. Wang is chair of the Department of Ethnic Studies and has served as coordinator of ASIAN AMERICAN STUDIES at the University of California, Berkeley. He received a bachelor's degree in music from Hope College, a bachelor's degree in Old Testament studies from Princeton Seminary, and a master's degree in Semitic studies from the University of California. Author and lecturer on Asian American history, civil rights, and educational issues affecting Asian Americans, he cofounded CHINESE FOR AFFIRMATIVE ACTION (CAA), a civil-rights group based in San Francisco.

Wang, Taylor Gunjin (b. June 16, 1940, Shanghai, China): Physicist, inventor, and science administrator. Wang was a Space Shuttle astronaut-scientist for the National Aeronautics and Space Administration (NASA) from 1983 to 1985. He invented the acoustic levitation and manipulation chamber and holds twenty other patents in his field. Wang served as a manager of the microgravity science and applications program at the Jet Propulsion Lab in Pasadena, California, from 1972 to 1988 and afterward served as director of the Center for Microgravity Research and Applications at Vanderbilt University in Nashville, Tennessee.

Wang, Wayne (b. Jan. 12, 1949, Hong Kong): American film director. In 1993, Wang completed what has

Educator and politician Art Wang. (Asian Week)

Wayne Wang directed the film The Joy Luck Club. (Asian Week)

become his most critically and commercially successful film, *The Joy Luck Club*, based on the 1989 bestseller of the same title by Chinese American novelist Amy TAN. Wang's father was a businessman and motion picture enthusiast who named his son after popular American film star John Wayne. After schooling in Hong Kong, Wang came to the United States to study photography and painting—against the wishes of his parents, who wanted him to become a physician or an engineer. At the California College of Arts and Crafts in Oakland, he earned a master's degree in film and television.

Returning to Hong Kong, Wang worked on the American film *Golden Needles* (1974), directing the Chinese sequences. He went back to the United States, however, and worked as a community activist in San Francisco. In 1982, with help from the American Film Institute (AFI) and the National Endowment for the Arts (NEA), he shot *Chan Is Missing*—the first American feature film with a completely Asian American cast. A detective story set in San Francisco's Chinatown, it explores the Chinese experience in America and was a critical hit. *Dim Sum: A Little Bit of Heart*

(1984) and *Eat a Bowl of Tea* (1989) similarly depict Chinese Americans caught between competing cultures. In 1987, Wang, whose work has been linked almost exclusively with Chinese themes, directed the poorly received *Slamdance*, to date his only picture not to deal with anything Chinese. The offbeat *Life Is Cheap . . . but Toilet Paper Is Expensive*, made in Hong Kong, appeared in 1990.

The Joy Luck Club explores the relationships between four Chinese mothers and their American daughters. Executive produced by American filmmaker Oliver Stone and Janet Yang, the film was one of five major studio releases in the United States in 1993—*Rising Sun, Dragon: The Bruce Lee Story, Map of the Human Heart*, and *The Wedding Banquet* were the other four—in which Asian American characters or actors enjoyed center stage.

War Brides Act of 1945: U.S. legislation that granted American soldiers unrestricted permission to bring foreign-born wives to the United States. World War II (1939-1945) transformed China from a source of "YELLOW PERIL" to an important ally in the United States' struggle against the Japanese. Reflecting this altered position, the U.S. Congress ended more than sixty years of Chinese exclusion with the IMMIGRATION ACT OF 1943. The new law, however, limited immigration from China to an annual quota of 105, preventing Chinese Americans from rapidly reversing the effects of past discrimination.

Most devastating in the United States' legacy of anti-Chinese immigration laws was the prolonged shortage of immigrant women that they created. Starting in the 1870's, the United States blocked Chinese families from establishing themselves by restricting female immigration. On December 28, 1945, Congress enacted legislation that, though not specifically aimed at correcting this problem, was an important first step toward its elimination. Among the hundreds of thousands who served in the American military during World War II, a significant number of men had married during their overseas duty. With the war concluded in an Allied victory, the War Brides Act permitted these soldiers to return with their immigrant wives, who received an exemption from national origins quotas. Since about twelve thousand Chinese Americans had also served the United States through military assignment, the law enabled these men to bring wives from China.

Chinese women responded dramatically to this new offer of nonquota status. By the end of the Korean War in 1953, the number of war brides from China exceeded

Filipino American World War II-era war brides and their husbands, Seattle, circa 1955. (Filipino American National Historical Society)

seven thousand. Many married Anglo-American soldiers, but most followed Chinese husbands to the United States. While failing to overturn the policy of discrimination to which this segment of its population had been subjected for generations, the United States had at least ended its policy against Chinese American family development. The pattern of substantial female immigration continued through the early 1960's, helping the Chinese American community move steadily toward gender parity. Thus, the War Brides Act made a significant contribution to the process of building permanence and a sense of belonging among Americans of Chinese ancestry.

War Relocation Authority (WRA): U.S. government agency created in 1942 to administer the Japanese American RELOCATION CENTERS of World War II. During the internment Japanese Americans, whether immigrant or American-born, were removed from the West Coast without a hearing or a trial. They were placed in what the government officially called "relocation camps" but unofficially referred to as "CONCENTRATION CAMPS." The internees were not free to leave on their own. They were confined under armed guard, in barracks surrounded by barbed wire fences and guard towers.

The WRA was the agency in charge of the relocation centers. Japanese were removed from the West Coast under EXECUTIVE ORDER 9066, issued by President Franklin D. Roosevelt on February 19, 1942, extending to the military the authority to take whatever measures necessary to secure the safety of the West Coast. Under the argument of "military necessity," all persons of Japanese ancestry were required to leave their homes.

Formation of the WRA. On March 18 Roosevelt issued Executive Order 9102 authorizing the formation of a civilian agency, the WRA, to administer the camps. Milton S. Eisenhower became the national director of the WRA in March, 1942. Its national headquarters was based in Washington, D.C. In order to supervise the formation of the ten relocation centers, regional offices were utilized in San Francisco, Denver, and Little Rock until the fall of 1942.

Initially Eisenhower had planned to confine Japanese Americans in camps until they could be resettled in areas outside the West Coast. On April 7, 1942, however, in a conference of governors, attorneys general, and state and federal officials of ten Western states, Eisenhower found that the governors opposed such a plan, whereupon Eisenhower and the WRA decided to confine 110,000 Japanese Americans in centers or camps with no intention of resettlement. By June 5, 1942, ten sites for the camps were chosen on federal lands, reservations, and lands purchased by the federal government in isolated areas and difficult climates. The centers were: TOPAZ in Utah; POSTON and GILA RIVER in Arizona; GRANADA in Colorado; HEART MOUNTAIN in Wyoming; JEROME and ROHWER in Arkansas; MINIDOKA in Idaho; and MANZANAR and TULE LAKE in California. The WRA was responsible for the day-to-day operation of the camps. In the initial formation of each center, the WRA staff, numbering less than a hundred, relied upon Japanese Americans to

Japanese American mother and child wait for the bus that will take them to the Tanforan assembly center near San Francisco. (National Archives)

perform the necessary functions in the mess halls, hospitals, police stations, and other offices. The Army was in charge of securing the perimeters of the centers and quelling disturbances and demonstrations that could not be handled by the WRA staff.

Japanese Americans were first placed in so-called ASSEMBLY CENTERS under the direction of the WARTIME CIVIL CONTROL ADMINISTRATION (WCCA). By June 6, 1942, every person of Japanese ancestry living in Military Area No. 1, whether citizen or immigrant, had been placed in assembly centers.

Eisenhower resigned as director on June 17, 1942. Although he had misgivings about the removal of Japanese Americans from the West Coast, he did not make those feelings public. Roosevelt appointed Dillon S. Myer, an administrator for the Agriculture Department, to replace Eisenhower.

All Japanese Americans had been moved from the assembly centers to the relocation centers by November 1, 1942. By the end of 1942, almost 107,000 Japanese Americans had been interned. The WRA would ultimately be in charge of more than 120,000 people.

Policies, Procedures, and Programs. The WRA established policies and procedures regulating the lives of the internees. It determined housing and facilities, the distribution of food, clothing, and medical care, employment and jobs, schooling, recreation, the structure of day-to-day activities, religious worship, a form of internee government, and policing. The WRA set wages at $12, $16, and $19 a month depending upon the type of work. The agency was also in charge of releasing Japanese Americans from the camps, initially for specific reasons such as to pursue a college education or to work as seasonal farm laborers.

Beginning on October 1, 1942, the WRA instituted procedures allowing some Japanese Americans to leave the centers. Those applying for a leave clearance had to complete a loyalty check and had to be assessed

At Tanforan Race Track (south of San Francisco), horse stalls were converted to living quarters for evacuated Japanese Americans during World War II. (National Japanese American Historical Society)

World War II Japanese American combat units were highly decorated. (Library of Congress)

President Reagan speaks at the signing ceremony for the Japanese American internment compensation bill in 1988. (Ronald Reagan Library)

by the WRA on their ability to support themselves and the general acceptance by the community.

One of the most controversial programs of the authority was the registration program and the use of a questionnaire, entitled "Application for Leave Clearance," beginning on February 10, 1943. The U.S. Army had proposed to form a unit consisting of Nisei, second-generation Japanese Americans, from Hawaii and the internment camps. In order to establish those who were acceptable, the Army ordered that a questionnaire be used to confirm the loyalty of the Japanese American recruits. The authority expanded the purpose of the questionnaire to establish the loyalty of all Japanese Americans over the age of seventeen including the Issei, the immigrant generation, as well as the Nisei.

Beyond the descriptive questions, two questions, number 27 and 28, caused great confusion among the internees. QUESTION 27 stated: "Are you willing to serve in the armed forces of the United States on combat duty, wherever ordered?" The questionnaire for the Issei and Nisei women asked them if they would serve in the WACs or the Army Nurse Corps. QUESTION 28 asked: "Will you swear unqualified allegiance to the United States of America and faithfully defend the United States from any or all attack by foreign or domestic forces, and forswear any form of allegiance or obedience to the Japanese emperor, to any other foreign government, power or organization?" Such questions raised fears and angered some Japanese Americans who felt that the questions were not fair and because it was not clear to the internees how their responses would be used. The Issei were already ineligible for U.S. citizenship, and to answer question 28 affirmatively would be tantamount to renouncing their Japanese citizenship. For the Nisei, question 27 could be interpreted as indicating their desire to volunteer. Some of the Nisei questioned whether it was fair to expect the Nisei to serve in the military when their citizenship rights had been and continued to be violated.

Eventually more than twelve hundred Nisei volunteered to serve in the military. In addition the responses by the internees to questions 27 and 28, particularly those who answered in the negative to both questions, were interpreted by the WRA as indications of disloyalty. The WRA decided to consolidate the "disloyal" at one relocation center, TULE LAKE.

Other Consequences. There were a number of important demonstrations, protests, strikes, and riots challenging WRA authority in the centers. WRA policies had divided the Japanese American internees, resulting in conflict and fighting among Japanese Americans and between Japanese Americans and the WRA administration. For example there was a riot at Manzanar on December 6, 1942, initiated by protests over the arrest of Harry Ueno and others who had been accused of attacking a member of the JAPANESE AMERICAN CITIZENS LEAGUE (JACL), an organization that had taken the stance of cooperation with the WRA. In addition, there were protests at Tule Lake in 1943-1944 and at HEART MOUNTAIN in October and November of 1942 and early 1943 over the registration issue.

On February 16, 1944, Roosevelt issued Executive Order 9423, placing the WRA under the authority of the Department of the Interior and the direction of Interior Secretary Harold L. Ickes. The WRA also took over the operation of a shelter for one thousand refugees at Fort Ontario in Oswego, New York.

The U.S. government subsequently announced that the exclusion orders would be rescinded on January 2, 1945. The last center, Tule Lake, closed on March 21, 1946. On June 30, 1946, the WRA closed its doors.— *Alexander Y. Yamato*

SUGGESTED READINGS: • Daniels, Roger. *Concentration Camps, North America: Japanese in the United States and Canada During World War II*. Malabar, Fla.: Robert E. Krieger, 1981. • Drinnon, Richard. *Keeper of Concentration Camps: Dillon S. Meyer and American Racism*. Berkeley: University of California Press, 1987. • Myer, Dillon S. *Uprooted Americans: The Japanese Americans and the War Relocation Authority During World War II*. Tucson: University of Arizona Press, 1971. • U.S. Commission on Wartime Relocation and Internment of Civilians. *Personal Justice Denied*. Washington, D.C.: Government Printing Office, 1992. • U.S. War Relocation Authority. *Administrative Highlights of the WRA Program*. Washington,

D.C.: Government Printing Office, 1946. • Weglyn, Michi. *Years of Infamy: The Untold Story of America's Concentration Camps*. New York: William Morrow, 1976.

Wartime Civil Control Administration (WCCA): U.S. Army-controlled civilian affairs unit created within the Western Defense Command in 1942. It was established to handle the forced relocation and incarceration of Japanese Americans in temporary assembly centers during World War II. Later it was also asked to supervise the movement of internees from the ASSEMBLY CENTERS to RELOCATION CENTERS.

Watanabe, Gedde (Gary Watanabe; b. June 26, 1955, Ogden, Utah): Actor. He appeared in several major motion pictures in the 1980's, including *Sixteen Candles* (1984) and *Gung Ho* (1986). His roles, especially in the former, have been criticized for perpetuating stereotypical roles depicting Asian Americans as nerds and foreigners.

Watsonville incident (1930): Anti-Filipino riot lasting five days that broke out January 19 in Watsonville, California, when mobs of predominantly white men terrorized local Filipinos. The causes of the Watsonville incident involved three interwoven themes. First, there was growing hostility toward Filipino laborers who worked cheaply and under poor conditions in local fields. Second, local white laborers reacted to the growing stereotype that Filipino social, sexual, and health habits were a danger to the community. Third, opportunistic politicians used anti-Filipino rhetoric to increase their voter appeal. The Watsonville incident demonstrated the hostile racial attitudes of the community and the duplicity of the police and politicians in covering up the murder of a Filipino farmworker.

Judge D. W. Rohrback of the Northern Pajaro Township Court was partly the catalyst to the Watsonville anti-Filipino riot. He delivered a series of xenophobic speeches about the dangers of Filipino labor and followed these with a lengthy interview in the *Watsonville Evening Pajaronian*. This interview used pseudoscientific evidence to suggest that Filipinos worked too cheaply and were a health hazard. As a result, the Northern Monterey Chamber of Commerce passed a series of anti-Filipino resolutions.

The flames of local discontent were fanned further when a taxi-dance hall opened in nearby Palm Beach. The young dance-hall girls and their Filipino partners were met by opposition from unruly street mobs. The

Watsonville Evening Pajaronian, caught up in the frenzy of the moment, ran the following headline: "State Organizations Will Fight the Filipino Influx into the County." Immediately after the newspaper's inflammatory story, five days of rioting broke out in Watsonville.

From Sunday, January 19, until early Tuesday, January 23, angry mobs of two hundred to seven hundred white youths searched for Filipinos in the Watsonville streets. After raiding the Palm Beach dance hall, the mob formed a car caravan and drove out to San Juan Road and John Murphy's ranch. The eight-car caravan cornered a twenty-five-year-old Filipino worker, Fermin Tovera, and shot him dead.

The eight men police arrested for the murder had also raided a bunkhouse on the Andrew Storm Ranch down the road from the Murphy Ranch and only two miles from town. Rohrback ruled that the evidence indicated that the eight men should be turned over to the superior court for trial. In the Monterey Superior Court in Salinas, the men pleaded guilty and received thirty days in jail and two years of probation and were told to "refrain from agitation against the darker race." Filipinos viewed the sentence as a mandate for legalized murder.

The Watsonville incident prompted local vigilantes to form a law-and-order committee to prevent future violence. In an unexpected turn of events, there was as much hostility toward the vigilantes as there was toward Filipinos.

Responsible members of the local Filipino community attempted to educate local citizens on the positive side of using Filipino labor. A. Antenor Cruz, a local Filipino leader, called a meeting of the Monterey Bay Filipino Club at Palm Beach. A resolution was passed condemning politicians and businesspersons for inciting anti-Filipino sentiment. Another Filipino leader, A. E. Magsuci, pointed out that Rohrback's self-serving comments had helped create the white mobs that attacked Filipino farmworkers.

Because of changes in immigration laws, Filipinos replaced Japanese and Chinese workers in the fields. Immediately, there was opposition to Filipino labor. Congressman Richard J. Welch and V. S. McClatchy, chairperson of the California Joint Immigration Committee, lobbied for exclusion of Filipino labor.

The Watsonville incident intensified labor-union organization by local Filipinos and prompted Filipino newspapers such as the Los Angeles-based *Ang Bantay* and Stockton's *The Torch* and *The Three Stars* to protest the negative racial attitudes of Californians.

Watumull, G. J. [Gobindram Jhamandas] (June 26, 1891, Hyderabad, Sind, now Pakistan, India—Aug., 1959, Honolulu, Hawaii): Businessperson, political activist, community leader, and philanthropist. Watumull was the eighth child in a family of four sons and five daughters. When he was very young, his father, who had been a brick contractor, suffered an accident which left him an invalid for life. A wealthy landlord, recognizing the boy's intelligence, paid his school fees. When the landlord forgot to pay, Watumull was sent to the back of the class to sit in humiliation. Later Gobindram's mother pawned her last jewels in order to send him to Karachi University. After earning an engineering degree he worked on dams and irrigation projects on the Indus River.

In 1917 G. J.'s brother Jhamandas WATUMULL summoned him to Honolulu to help manage the East India Store, a small business that Jhamandas and a partner had started in 1913. After his arrival, Jhamandas left to attend to other business matters in Asia. Under G. J.'s management, the East India Store in downtown Honolulu prospered, starting as a small bazaar and flourishing into a major department store that sold the first raw silk and Hawaiian aloha shirts offered in the islands. In 1937 G. J. erected an impressive new structure, the Watumull Building, in Honolulu to house the headquarters of the growing Watumull Brothers business enterprise. Shortly thereafter he opened additional branch stores in Waikiki and the downtown Honolulu area. By 1947 the Watumull businesses were grossing $2.6 million annually. The brothers continued to expand their holdings until by 1957 their properties included ten stores, a Waikiki apartment house, and assorted commercial developments. Jhamandas returned to Honolulu in 1956. After G. J.'s death in 1959, Jhamandas continued to expand operations in the islands. In 1973 there were twenty-nine Watumull stores offering a wide variety of products.

Back in 1922 G. J. had married Ellen Jensen, an American of Danish extraction who taught music at Hanahauoli School. He had also applied for U.S. citizenship, but a court ruling (*United States v. Bhagat Singh Thind*) the following year prevented him from becoming a citizen. Moreover, his wife also lost her citizenship because she was now married to a noncitizen. Determined to regain her citizenship, Ellen worked with the League of Women Voters in Hawaii to lobby for amendment of the CABLE ACT of 1922 to enable American-born women—even those of foreign descent—to keep their citizenship regardless of whom they married. When the act was repealed in 1931, she

G. J. Watumull as photographed by Ansel Adams. (Ansel Adams)

was the first woman naturalized. G. J. himself did not become a naturalized U.S. citizen until passage of the LUCE-CELLER BILL OF 1946, restoring naturalization rights to nationals of India.

Watumull cared deeply for his mother country and used the wealth that he had acquired through business to support India's struggle for independence. His activity on the Committee for India's Independence from 1942 to 1947 included visiting Washington, D.C., several times, supporting Indians such as Syed Hussain, Krishnalal Shridharani, and Anup Singh who publicized India's cause through their writings and lectures, and financing the movement generally.

In 1942 Gobindram established the WATUMULL FOUNDATION. Its three stated objectives were to help improve the national efficiency of India, to help citizens of India and of the United States to understand one another better, and to support cultural, educational, and philanthropic activity in Hawaii. The foundation supports many projects in India which include providing technical equipment, scholarships, and wells. It has also sponsored an ongoing exchange of prominent lecturers between the two countries. In

1952 Ellen Watumull, through the foundation, worked with Margaret Sanger, founder of the American birth-control movement, to organize the first International Planned Parenthood Conference ever held in India. Also, biennial book awards are given by the foundation through the American Historical Association to the author of the best book on India published in the United States.

Watumull, Jhamandas (Feb. 14, 1885, Hyderabad, Sind, now Pakistan, India—198?, Honolulu, Hawaii): Merchant and philanthropist. Jhamandas Watumull came from a large family—four sons and five daughters. His father had been a brick contractor before an accident left him an invalid. The family then depended on relatives until the older sons were able to work and support them. When Watumull was fourteen, he moved to Manila to live with an older brother and to work in the textile mills.

Later Watumull started a retail business in Manila that specialized in imports from the Orient. World War I severely hurt the Philippine economy, so in 1913 Watumull moved to Hawaii in search of better opportunities. He and a partner, Dharamdas, opened a retail store in Honolulu that same year. The following year they renamed it the "East India Store." In 1917 his partner returned to India, and Watumull's brother, Gobindram (G. J.), arrived to help with the store. With his brother as his only partner, Jhamandas was free to attend to business in Asia.

Over the years the East India Store in downtown Honolulu prospered, starting as a small bazaar and flourishing into a major department store. In 1937 G. J. erected an impressive new structure, the Watumull Building, in Honolulu to house the headquarters of the growing Watumull Brothers business enterprise. Shortly thereafter he opened additional branch stores in Waikiki and the downtown Honolulu area. By 1947 the Watumull businesses were grossing $2.6 million annually. The brothers continued to expand their holdings until by 1957 their properties included ten stores, a Waikiki apartment house, and assorted commercial developments. Jhamandas returned to Honolulu in 1956. After Gobindram's death in 1959, Jhamandas continued to expand operations in the islands. In 1973, there were twenty-nine Watumull stores offering a wide variety of products.

When his wife Radhibai died in 1955, Jhamandas established a hospital in her name in Bombay. This same year Jhamandas and his brother divided their business interests. His brother took over the real estate, and Jhamandas kept the seven retail stores and the Royal Hawaiian Manufacturing Company. He then made Hawaii, or in his words, "paradise," his permanent residence.

Jhamandas established two family foundations, the Rama Watumull Fund (named for his late son) and the J. Watumull Estate, to benefit local charitable and educational institutions. Having had little formal education, he valued it highly and gave large endowments to the University of Hawaii, Hawaii Pacific College, Chaminade College, and the Honolulu Academy of Arts. Also, the Watumull College of Engineering was established in Bombay.

Watumull Foundation: Foundation established by G. J. WATUMULL in Honolulu in 1942 to benefit India and the United States. Its three-fold mission was to increase India's national efficiency, promote better understanding between India and the United States, and support educational, philanthropic, and cultural work in Hawaii. Watumull had come to Hawaii in 1917 to become a partner in his brother's retail business. The business thrived, and in 1942 Watumull decided to place some of his wealth in a foundation to benefit

Ellen Jensen Watumull worked with Margaret Sanger to hold the first Planned Parenthood Conference in India in 1952. (Watumull Foundation)

both his mother country and his adopted home.

In order to achieve the first goal of increasing India's efficiency, the Watumull Foundation grants scholarships to Indian students, distributes books to hundreds of Indian libraries, and contributes technical equipment to hospitals. A revolving fund in India provides rehabilitation for displaced persons and hundreds of sewing machines to individuals seeking retraining. Also, many wells have been installed in order to raise the standard of living and to increase the amount of tillable land. Through the Watumull Foundation, Watumull's wife, Ellen Jensen Watumull, worked with Margaret Sanger, founder of the American birth-control movement, to hold the first International Planned Parenthood Conference ever in India. It was convened in Bombay in 1952. The foundation contributes contraceptives and books to family planning centers. Aid has also been given through the Cooperative for American Relief to Everywhere (CARE) and Meals for Millions Foundation of Los Angeles for famine relief.

Projects undertaken in order to better the understanding between the two countries include sponsoring lecture exchanges, providing support to visiting Indian professors at universities in the United States, and donating funds to university, college, and public libraries to purchase books on India. The foundation also offers biennial awards through the American Historical Association to authors of the best books on India published in the United States. Some of the selected authors have been Ernest J. R. Mackay for *Chanhu-Daro Excavations, 1935-36* (1943), D. Mackenzie Brown for *White Umbrella: Indian Political Thought from Manu to Gandhi* (1953), Thomas R. Metcalf for *The Aftermath of Revolt* (1964), and M. N. Pearson for *Merchants and Rulers in Gujarat: The Response to the Portuguese in the Sixteenth Century* (1976).

In order to achieve its third objective, the foundation gives support to the University of Hawaii, numerous private schools, and the East-West Center in Honolulu. It also contributes to many local organizations such as the Young Men's Christian Association (YMCA) and Young Women's Christian Association (YWCA), the Asian and Pacific Affairs Council, and hospitals. Finally, the foundation has bought many works of art for the Honolulu Academy of Arts in addition to providing financial assistance to the academy for special exhibitions.

Webb-Heney Bill of 1913. *See* **Alien Land Law of 1913**

Webb v. O'Brien (1923): U.S. Supreme Court ruling that under the provisions of California's ALIEN LAND LAW OF 1920, sharecropping contracts between U.S. citizens and aliens ineligible for naturalization were unlawful. The statute itself prohibited aliens ineligible for U.S. citizenship (such as the Issei) from owning or leasing agricultural land. American citizen J. J. O'Brien and Issei farmer J. Inouye signed a contract allowing Inouye to plant, cultivate, and harvest crops grown on land owned by O'Brien. California attorney general U. S. Webb considered this a violation of the 1920 statute, however, and stepped in to prevent the contract's enforcement. O'Brien then filed suit in state court to enjoin Webb from confiscating his land, and the court issued an injunction.

On appeal, the Supreme Court overturned that decision, finding the land law to be constitutional. Before the bench, O'Brien claimed that his agreement with Inouye involved merely an arrangement between employer and employee to perform specified farm labor. Webb, however, argued that the contract as enforced would actually allow Inouye to enjoy the benefits of the land—thereby permitting precisely what the statute was enacted to prevent—and the Court agreed. The opinion also held that the statute did not conflict with the U.S.-JAPAN TREATY OF COMMERCE AND NAVIGATION (1911), which under federal regulations would have mandated annulment of the former.

Weglyn, Michi (Michiko Nishiura; b. Nov. 29, 1926, Stockton, Calif.): Writer and costume designer. Though a theatrical costume designer by profession, this Nisei is best known for writing *Years of Infamy: The Untold Story of America's Concentration Camps* (1976), after extensive research. Her book was the first to document the process by which the U.S. government decided to intern Japanese Americans during World War II.

Wei, William: Scholar. A professor at the University of Colorado, where he teaches in the Asian American Studies program, Wei is the author of *The Asian American Movement* (1993). The first full-scale history of the ASIAN AMERICAN MOVEMENT, it is an indispensable contribution to ASIAN AMERICAN STUDIES.

Wei Min Bao: Bilingual monthly community journal published by Wei Min She (Organization for the People) in San Francisco, California. The paper, published between 1971 and 1975, carried articles on Asian American history and China and featured news and in-depth analyses of the Chinese American community that mainstream newspapers neglected.

Wenyan (ancient script): Classical written Chinese language, that of the educated classes of premodern Chinese society. Prior to cultural and political developments occurring before 1920, the *wenyan* writing system had been promoted as the standard national language since the Han Dynasty (206 B.C.E.-220 C.E.). Into the twentieth century this system, with its antiquated script and vocabulary, was still in use. It was, however, complex and inaccessible and therefore impractical for everyday common usage. As advanced by China's New Culture movement (1917-1923), and following the May Fourth movement (1919), *wenyan* was eventually supplanted by the more modern *baihua* (colloquial spoken language) as the medium for general written communication, scholarly and otherwise. Over strong opposition the Ministry of Education in 1920 declared that *baihua* would be the language taught in public schools. By the 1930's almost all writing—textbooks, periodicals, newspapers, public documents—was published in *baihua*.

Western Samoa, Independent State of: Independent nation consisting of the islands of Savaii, Apolima, Manono, and Upolu and five uninhabited islets in the western portion of the Samoan archipelago in the southwest Pacific Ocean. These islands have much greater land area (1,093 square miles) and a larger population (159,000 in 1990) than American Samoa, the island chain to the east. The port of Apia on Upolu has a population of about 45,000.

John Williams of the London Missionary Society arrived in Western Samoa in 1830—an event that ultimately resulted in the Christianization of Samoans. Apia had been a commercial center with a European settlement since the 1840's. It was a major port of call for whaling ships; British, German, and American traders carried on a lucrative trade in copra, the source of coconut oil.

After several decades of political strife wherein American, British, and German commercial interests were in conflict, a tripartite convention in 1899 awarded the United States control over Tutuila, Aunuu, and the Manua Islands, and gave Germany control over the rest of Samoa. German dominion was terminated, however, in August of 1914 when German officials in Upolu surrendered to New Zealand troops at the outbreak of World War I. New Zealand maintained a trusteeship relationship over what had become known as "Western Samoa" until 1962, when the islands became independent. The country has a parliamentary system of government with a prime minister. There is also a ceremonial head of state, a position held by a member of one of the four royal family lines in Western Samoa.

In spite of its long history of European contact and the bustling activity of Apia with its hotels and shops, Western Samoa has retained the true flavor of the South Seas of an earlier era. The economy of Western Samoa is primarily agricultural—subsistence-level and some cash-cropping of taro, bananas, and cacao. Industrial development has been limited, but some light manufacturing of such products as soap and beer exists. Imports outweigh exports, and wages tend to be low. Many Western Samoans seek to improve their economic fortunes by migrating to New Zealand or to American Samoa, and then to the United States. The money (remittances) they send back to family members plays an important role in the Western Samoan economy.

White v. Chin Fong (1920): U.S. Supreme Court ruling that permitted a resident Chinese of the United States to reenter the country after finding that his rights had been violated. Chin Fong had been living in the United States for more than a year before traveling to China on business. Upon returning to the United States, he was denied readmission by the immigration commissioner and taken into custody on suspicion of being an illegal alien entrant. At trial in federal district court, the officer recommended that Chin be deported as an unlawful alien. Chin protested his lawful U.S. residence and his right to a judicial, as opposed to an executive, hearing on the issue of whether his initial entry was in fact legal. The district court's finding for the commissioner was overturned by a federal appellate court in Chin's favor.

The Supreme Court explained that Chinese living in the United States are entitled to a wider spectrum of legal rights than those persons merely hoping to secure entry. Resident Chinese must be given the opportunity for a court hearing where their rights are concerned. Aliens, by contrast, are owed nothing more than an executive determination of the rights available to them. Chin, as a lawful U.S. resident, fell into the former category. Denied his right to a judicial hearing, he was therefore to be admitted on the basis of a legal technicality.

Willoughby, Charles A. (Mar. 8, 1892, Heidelberg, Germany—Oct. 25, 1972, Naples, Fla.): Army officer.

Chief of intelligence on General Douglas MacArthur's staff in the Philippine campaign in 1941, he served in the southwest Pacific from 1941 to 1946. A veteran of Bataan and Corregidor, he represented MacArthur in negotiations to receive the surrender of the Imperial Japanese delegation in August, 1945. He wrote *The Economic and Military Participation of the United States in the World War* (1931) and *Maneuver in War* (1939).

Wing Luke Asian Museum: In 1965, Seattle city councilmember Wing Luke, the first Asian American elected official in the Northwest, died in a plane crash at the age of forty. In 1967, a museum in that city's International District was founded in Luke's name, honoring his legacy of tolerance, humanism, and cultural awareness.

The original site of the museum was the Wah Young Import Co., where a collection of Chinese artifacts was found; at the time, Luke commented that Seattle's long history of Asian immigration and folk art should be preserved. It was first dubbed the Wing Luke Memorial Museum, but the name was changed in September, 1986, to the Wing Luke Asian Museum in order to reflect the diversity of material found there. On January 29, 1987, the museum celebrated its grand opening at a larger facility one block away, in a garage renovated by the local Asian American community.

The Wing Luke Asian Museum is dedicated to the history, art, and culture of Asian Americans, past and present. The stories of Chinese, Japanese, Filipino, Korean, Vietnamese, Pacific Islander, Cambodian, Hawaiian, Balinese, and Indonesian immigrants and their descendants are told in words and photographs, and folk art and artifacts from all Asian cultures are displayed. One outstanding feature is an authentic re-creation of a barracks from a World War II internment camp for Japanese Americans. The facility also offers craft workshops by traditional artisans and literary readings by new Asian American writers. In the 1980's, the museum was awarded a grant from the National Endowment for the Humanities.

Women, Asian American: Asia is a vast region, encompassing the nations that make up East Asia, South Asia, and Southeast Asia and containing more than half the world's population. Asian immigration to the United States began in the mid-nineteenth century, starting with the Chinese, followed by the Japanese, the Koreans, and the Filipinos. Later immigrants have come from India and other South Asian nations and

Asian American women share a joyous moment at an Illinois graduation ceremony. (Jim Whitmer)

from Vietnam, Cambodia, Laos, and other Southeast Asian nations.

Women have played a vital role in Asian American history. Asian American women operate in a specific nexus of complex social and economic conditions characterized by class division, racial discrimination, and patriarchal tradition.

Early History of Immigration. Asian immigrants first came to California and Hawaii in response to demand for cheap labor in an emerging industrial nation. American economic growth depended upon frontier land, foreign resources, and abundant cheap labor. This expansionist policy was informed by a largely unquestioned belief in white racial superiority. Asians came to a nation of institutionalized racism, personified in the treatment of Native Americans and the enslavement of Africans.

Substantial Chinese immigration to the United States began with the California Gold Rush in 1849. Chinese immigrants worked in the mines, railroads, fisheries, farms, orchards, canneries, logging camps, and garment industries. Conditions were poor, wages

low. Most of the immigrant laborers left their families behind in China and dreamed of making enough money to return home wealthy.

This first wave of Chinese immigration was almost exlusively male. However, both Chinese and American men brought young women from China to be prostitutes. In 1870, seven out of ten Chinese women in California were prostitutes. Most prostitutes lived and worked as slaves to their owners and did not survive in America for more than six years. They were sold by poor parents for $70 to $150, imported to the United States as indentured servants, and then resold for $350 to $1,000. Upon arrival in San Francisco, these young women, generally between the ages of sixteen and twenty-five, were sold to the highest bidder. They were treated like commodities and subjected to physical and mental abuse. Some of them were sent to the mining camps, where life for a Chinese woman was as harsh as it was short. For some, escape came by suicide or madness. While the practice of using Chinese prostitutes may have satisfied the sexual needs of the miners and male SOJOURNERS abroad, it hindered the development of a community.

The growth of a full-fledged Chinese American community was also hindered by anti-Chinese violence and discriminatory legislation. During the 1860's, thousands of Chinese laborers were recruited to build the transcontinental railroad. When a series of economic depressions followed in the 1870's, politicians, labor leaders, and assorted rabble-rousers blamed the Chinese for the economic ills. Anti-Chinese riots, lynchings, arson, and lootings occurred in many Western cities and towns. Chinese prostitutes were targeted in anti-Chinese campaigns as additional proof of Chinese immorality. This accusation ignored the obvious presence of prostitutes and brothels of numerous other foreign nationals. Nevertheless, specific legislation—such as the PAGE LAW OF 1875—was enacted against the "debauched Chinese women."

The U.S. Congress, under increasing pressure from the ANTI-CHINESE MOVEMENT, passed the CHINESE EXCLUSION ACT OF 1882, denying Chinese laborers entry to the United States for a period of ten years. The 1882 act, the first in a series of discriminatory laws intended to curtail Chinese immigration, was the first U.S. law to exclude would-be immigrants on the basis of race, ethnicity, or national origin. As a result of this campaign for exclusion, the number of Chinese Americans on the U.S. mainland declined between 1890 and 1920.

Exclusion from naturalization on the basis of race was another facet of anti-Chinese (and, more broadly, anti-Asian) discrimination. The NATURALIZATION ACT OF 1790 provided for citizenship by naturalization for any free white person with good moral character who had resided in the United States for two years. In 1870, eligibility for naturalization was extended to aliens of African birth and persons of African descent. Asian immigrants, however, unlike all other immigrants, were categorized as "aliens ineligible to citizenship." While their American-born children were American citizens by right of birth, these Asian immigrants were denied the right to full participation in American society.

In Hawaii, the sugar industry, followed by the rice and pineapple industries, had completely transformed the islands economically and politically. The MASTERS AND SERVANTS ACT OF 1850 authorized the Royal Hawaiian Agricultural Society to import sugar plantation workers from China, and Chinese contract laborers came to Hawaii in substantial numbers until the 1880's, when the planters began to shift to Japanese contract labor.

Unlike the mainland, Hawaii encouraged the immigration of women. The first group of ninety women and ten children arrived to work on agricultural plantations in Hawaii with their husbands in 1865. Both husbands and wives signed contracts with the planters, but women were to be paid three dollars per month while men were paid four dollars. The coming of women proved to be important to the morale of the male agricultural workers. By 1900, of the 25,767 Chinese in Hawaii, 3,471, or about 13 percent, were female.

Japanese immigrants to the United States, like the Chinese before them, had to contend with prejudice and discrimination. In 1907 and 1908, amid rising agitation against Japanese immigration, the United States and Japan exchanged a series of diplomatic notes that became known as the GENTLEMEN'S AGREEMENT. Japan agreed to stop issuing passports to new immigrant laborers who wished to go to the United States.

While the Gentlemen's Agreement reduced Japanese immigration, it did have some provisions that

Korean picture bride Kang Aie Park. (The Korea Society/Los Angeles)

Chinese American woman prepares fish for market as her child plays nearby, Monterey, California, 1948. (Asian American Studies Library, University of California at Berkeley)

were conducive to the formation of a Japanese American community. The agreement allowed spouses and family members of Japanese laborers who were already in the United States to join them there. It also allowed Japanese immigrants who had returned from the United States to Japan to reenter the United States (with spouses and families, if applicable). These provisions encouraged family building.

Most of the Japanese women who immigrated to the continental United States and Hawaii between 1908 and 1921 came as "PICTURE BRIDES," having been selected by their husbands via the mail. Upon the first meeting between a bride and groom, some disappointment was common. Many men lied about both their physical appearance and their economic status in order to secure wives. Some women were physically abused or sold into brothels. Most women persevered and endured because of family pressure and also for the sake of their children.

The picture brides worked beside their husbands in the cane fields of Hawaii's plantations, on the railroads, in the coal mines in Wyoming, in the sugar-beet fields in Utah, in the lumber camps and mills in the Pacific Northwest, and in the fish canneries in Alaska. In urban areas women worked in the service industries.

The entrance of the picture brides added fuel to the ANTI-JAPANESE MOVEMENT and affected Koreans as well. (Between 1910, when Japan annexed Korea, and 1945, Koreans were regarded as Japanese nationals.) The picture-bride system was regarded as an immoral social custom, contrary to American Christian traditions. The exclusionists denounced the practice as uncivilized, arguing that the women married without regard to morality or love. The exclusionists further argued that the children of picture brides were a dangerous addition to the Japanese population. Some opponents feared that these new citizens would one day be able to buy land for their alien parents. (See ALIEN LAND LAWS.)

The unrelenting attacks by the anti-Japanese movement and subsequent U.S. governmental pressure forced the Japanese government to discontinue sending picture brides in 1920. This left 40 percent of Japanese men and Korean men still single.

Korean picture brides came to Hawaii and California as well. Most of them were between the ages of eighteen and twenty-four. Most were illiterate; they came from poor rural farming communities and were accustomed to hard work. Immigrant Korean women came not only for economic reasons but also for political, personal, and religious freedom. Others considered marriage a chance for adventure, an escape to a foreign land. Some women even arranged their own marriages.

Most Koreans in California lived in boardinghouses and labor camps that were overcrowded and substandard. These women endured long hours of backbreaking and demeaning labor, meager wages, and lives of great loneliness in a strange land. They also worked in canneries, railways, fisheries, and laundries.

The IMMIGRATION ACT OF 1924 severely limited

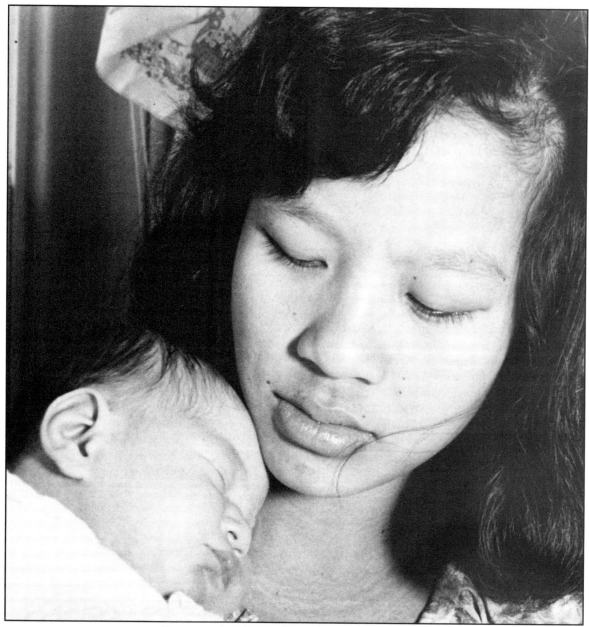

Vietnamese American mother and child. (Marilyn Nolt)

Fertility of Asian American Women, 1990

Group	Children born for every 1,000 married women, ages 15-44	Birthrate per woman
All American women	1,758	1.76
All Asian American women	1,680	1.68
Chinese American women	1,424	1.42
Filipino American women	1,712	1.71
Japanese American women	1,330	1.33
Korean American women	1,482	1.48
Asian Indian American women	1,590	1.59
Vietnamese American women	2,176	2.18

Source: U.S. Bureau of the Census, *1990 Census of Population: Asians and Pacific Islanders in the United States,* 1993.

new immigration from Japan and Korea. In conjunction with earlier legislation, including the Chinese Exclusions Acts, its intent was to halt Asian immigration and the growth of Asian American families and communities. Particularly burdensome were provisions that prevented wives from joining their husbands in the United States.

The pattern for Filipino immigration was similar in some respects and different in others. The Philippines was a U.S. territory, but Filipinos were not American citizens. (In contrast, persons born in Hawaii, which became a U.S. territory in 1900, were American citizens.) Filipinos, however, did have the status of U.S. NATIONALS. As such, they enjoyed unrestricted immigration. This made Filipino labor increasingly in demand as restrictions grew on immigration from China, Japan, Korea, and elsewhere in Asia.

Most of the early Filipino immigrants were young, single, uneducated men from farming villages. Many came to work in Hawaii and California in the 1920's. Large numbers of Filipino women did not immigrate until after World War II, but there were some women among the early immigrants.

In contrast to Japanese and Korean immigrant women, Filipina immigrants did not generally work with their husbands in the field. There were other cultural differences as well. It is a custom in the Philippines for wives to play a strong role in family decisions, especially with family finances. This tradition was carried over into family life in the United States. Some Filipinas continued to practice their skills in business management by raising vegetables and farm animals.

The TYDINGS-MCDUFFIE ACT OF 1934 ended unrestricted Filipino immigration to the United States, setting a quota of fifty persons a year for Filipino immigration. The act also changed the status of Filipinos from American nationals to "alien immigrants." Filipinos with travel funds, however, continued to immigrate to America after 1934. Most of the Filipino women learned that life in America was not easy for minority women. At times acting as the heads of their families, these women raised children, cared for relatives, and preserved cultural traditions while working one, two, and even three jobs to make ends meet. These women were a stabilizing force in Filipino American communities.

Proud of her ethnic heritage, Chinese American woman wears traditional costume at an Asian festival. (Jim Hays, Unicorn Stock Photos)

Contributions of the Early Immigrant Women. When Asian immigrant women first arrived, they were surprised at the harsh living conditions in Hawaii and California. It was not what they had dreamed about. They suffered from the multiple oppression of gender, race, and class. Many married men twice their age, were widowed early, and were compelled to raise young children by themselves.

Migration led to a gain in the status of Asian women, however, as a result of changes in the distribution of power within the family. It was the freedom from their mothers-in-law and the hope that their children would receive an education that made them determined to stay. Women were responsible for preserving their language and cultural heritage, which was considered one of the most important aspects of their identity. They were able to challenge the stereotypes of Asian women as passive and subservient. They participated in the labor force and focused on their families and community for survival. Such women became the dominant forces in their own homes.

The coming of Asian women and children to the United States transformed the character of the Asian immigrant significantly. The immigrants became settlers, no longer mere SOJOURNERS. Asian men did not have to live in enforced celibacy and deprivation. The immigrants were more content to integrate with the rest of the population in America. These early women made the Asian American family unit possible and played a vital role in the transition from a society of single male laborers into a multiethnic and multicultural community.

Exclusion, Internment, and Steps Toward Reform. After the passage of the Immigration Act of 1924, anti-Asian prejudice and political agitation continued until after World War II. Barriers to community development continued to exist. Asian Americans were confined through both legal and social segregation to congested, dilapidated areas in large cities. They were subjected to discriminatory laws that subjugated them economically and disenfranchised them politically. Nisei (second-generation Japanese) women with college educations frequently could find only menial jobs, mostly as domestics. Some worked in family businesses. Racial segregation limited their social activities to their own communities.

Despite the Exclusion Acts, some Chinese women immigrated by slipping through the loopholes of exempt categories to come to the United States. Most of the Chinese immigrants who arrived between 1910 and 1940 were detained at the ANGEL ISLAND IMMIGRATION STATION in San Francisco Bay, where immigration officials subjected them to physical examinations and intense interrogations. Following a twenty-to-thirty-day sea journey, this process could stretch from fourteen days to two years. Most of the women found their first experiences in America shocking and degrading. Upon their arrival, many wives went to live and work wherever their husbands lived. Immediately they assumed responsibilities as wife, mother, and provider. Some of them helped their husbands operate laundries, restaurants, and stores.

The language barrier, reinforced by cultural traditions, kept these Chinese immigrant women isolated from the larger society. After the 1920's, however, economic necessity compelled many of them to work outside their homes. This experience hastened the process of acculturation.

In 1942, President Franklin D. Roosevelt signed EXECUTIVE ORDER 9066, under which more than 110,000 Japanese Americans on the West Coast, aliens and citizens alike, were evacuated to temporary ASSEMBLY CENTERS. They were allowed to take only

During World War II, the evacuation camp experience changed the roles of Japanese American women. Manzanar relocation camp, California. (National Archives)

Educational Attainment of Asian American Women, 1991

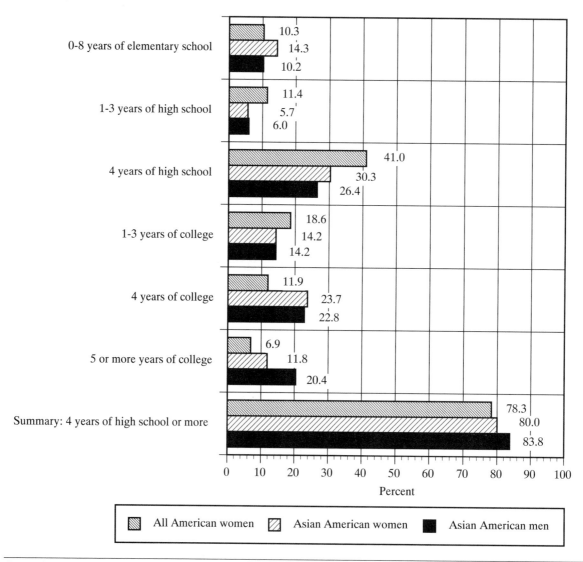

Source: Susan B. Gall and Timothy L. Gall, eds., *Statistical Record of Asian Americans.* Detroit: Gale Research, Inc., 1993.
Note: Data are for workers 25 years and older.

whatever clothing and bedding they could carry. Later, they were sent to RELOCATION CENTERS, where they lived in barracks, imprisoned by barbed-wired walls patrolled by armed guards.

The traumatic experience of evacuation and internment undermined the deeply patriarchal Japanese family system. Women were allowed to assume greater authority and were largely relieved of the demanding work of the household—freedoms which they had never before experienced. Traditional roles governing

relations between men and women and between generations were challenged. Many Japanese women began to take jobs as clerks and nurses. After World War II, some followed their children, who had found housing and work in Colorado, Illinois, New York, and other states, while others returned to California, Oregon, and Washington.

During the war and its aftermath, a number of laws were passed that cumulatively marked a change in U.S. policy toward Asian immigration and the naturalization of Asian immigrants. These laws had significant long-term consequences for Asian American women. The IMMIGRATION ACT OF 1943 repealed the Chinese Exclusion Acts and made Chinese immigrants eligible for naturalization. The LUCE-CELLER BILL OF 1946 established an annual immigration quota of 100 persons for Asian Indians (who had largely been denied entry since the BARRED ZONE ACT OF 1917) and made Asian Indian immigrants eligible for naturalization; the bill also increased the annual Filipino immigration quota to 100 (still a token figure) and made Filipino immigrants eligible for naturalization.

Moreover, as a result of other legislative provisions, actual immigration greatly exceeded the quotas; a majority of new immigrants during this period were nonquota immigrants. Under a 1947 amendment to the WAR BRIDES ACT OF 1945, for example, ten thousand wives of Chinese American servicemen came to the United States. Two thousand separated wives joined their husbands in 1950. Filipinos who served as stewards in the U.S. Navy during World War II were allowed to bring their wives, several thousand of whom came to the United States.

The MCCARRAN-WALTER ACT OF 1952 removed the virtual ban on immigration from Japan and made Japanese and Korean immigrants—and other Asian immigrants not covered by previous reforms—eligible for naturalization. Aging Issei (first-generation Japanese immigrants) who had spent their entire adult lives in the United States finally had the opportunity to become citizens.

The IMMIGRATION AND NATIONALITY ACT OF 1965 finally abolished the national-origins quota system that had been in place since 1924 and admitted foreign nationals based on preference categories. It opened the door to a new wave of Asian immigration that transformed the diverse Asian American communities. The majority of Japanese women in the United States are native-born, while a large number of Asian Indian, Chinese, Filipino, Korean, and Southeast Asian women are foreign-born. This disparity reflects the patterns of Asian immigration to the United States between 1970 and 1990.

Education, Employment, and Occupations. Asian American women are high educational achievers compared to women of other nationalities living in the United States. The public education system has been the most potent force for acculturation among all eth-

Female student studies in college library. (Hazel Hankin)

nic groups. Asian immigrants have brought from their former societies strong cultural values: an emphasis on education, respect for elders and authority, industriousness, and personal discipline. At the same time, they have been flexible, adapting to American society, which itself has undergone great change.

For example, after World War II, when educational and employment opportunities increased for women, Asian American parents began to place greater emphasis on education for daughters. These parents realized that better-paying jobs were available to educated women, and that daughters could fulfill the cherished dream of bringing honor to the family through education.

There were many opportunities for occupational participation for all ethnic groups in the 1950's. Well-educated Asian American women welcomed the chance to enter the work force. Nevertheless, racial discrimination and gender bias made it difficult for

them to break into well-paid or decision-making positions. The occupational distribution of women's work was gender-segregated. For the most part, they ended up in sales, clerical and domestic services, as seamstresses, or in family businesses. Later, they entered the technical and professional fields.

Most Asian American women who work are employed in periphery occupations. Native-born women tend to be concentrated in professional and clerical occupations, whereas foreign-born women tend to be concentrated in service and blue-collar occupations. The one exception is the category of foreign-born Filipino women, who constitute a higher proportion in the nursing and health-care professions. On average, Asian American women earn a little more than white women and far less than white men. For Asian American women, better educational qualifications, residence in higher-paying regions, and greater propensity to work full-time have helped spur the rise in pay. Some of the

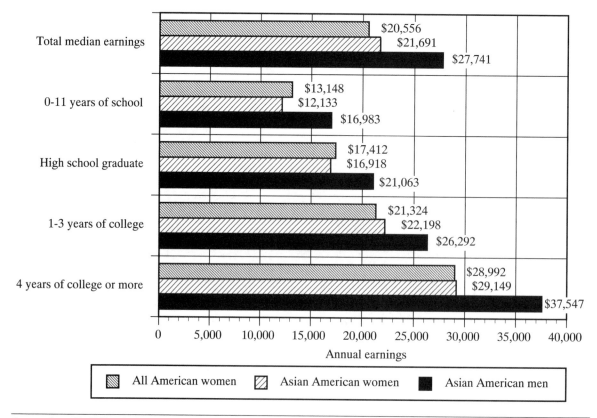

Median Earnings of Asian American Women by Education, 1990

Education	All American women	Asian American women	Asian American men
Total median earnings	$20,556	$21,691	$27,741
0-11 years of school	$13,148	$12,133	$16,983
High school graduate	$17,412	$16,918	$21,063
1-3 years of college	$21,324	$22,198	$26,292
4 years of college or more	$28,992	$29,149	$37,547

Annual earnings

Source: Susan B. Gall and Timothy L. Gall, eds., *Statistical Record of Asian Americans.* Detroit: Gale Research, Inc., 1993.
Note: Data are for workers 25 years and older.

Occupational Distribution of Employed Asian American Women, 1991

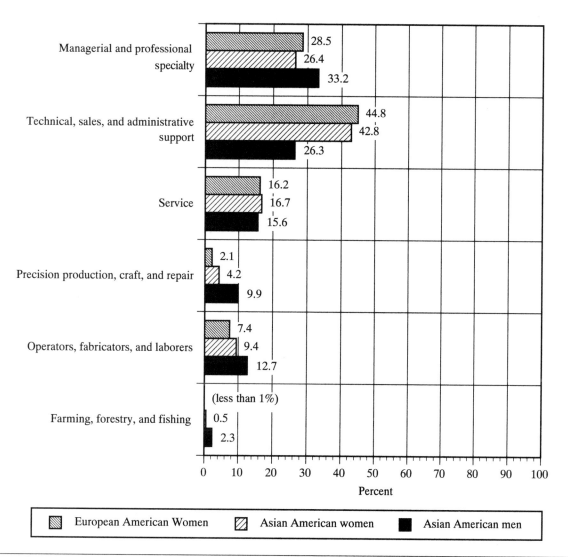

Source: Susan B. Gall and Timothy L. Gall, eds., *Statistical Record of Asian Americans.* Detroit: Gale Research, Inc., 1993.

recent Asian women immigrants are highly skilled professionals, but many are also employed in sweatshops, working very long hours for low pay.

Identity and Images. The coming of large numbers of Asian women produced a generation of American-born Asians. Most of the second-generation Asian girls were brought up in America, despised and oppressed by the dominant society but exposed to American values through the public schools. They were torn between wanting to fulfill their parents' expectations and being American. Cultural conflict and identity crises inevitably followed. They were taught at home not to

question their elders, while at school they were encouraged to be individualistic and assertive. Asian tradition places family and group interest above individual needs and feelings. Many Asian American families slowly advanced into the middle class and moved out of inner cities or rural areas. Although they became acculturated, their physical features and home life were constant reminders of their racial and cultural differences. Looking different inevitably suggests being different. Asian women are caught in a terrible bind. They are being asked to hide their differences, but at the same time they are being told that they must

Filipino American women are highly represented in health care fields. (Jim Whitmer)

and will always be different.

Asian American women have been invisible and silent for too long. They are influenced by how others see them; of more importance is how they see themselves. Racist and sexist stereotypes set the Asian and Asian American woman up for victimization, regardless of her place of birth. Indeed, over the decades the American media has consistently projected images of Asian women as either docile, sensuous, passive, and mysterious or sinister, unscrupulous, and amoral.

This cultural construction of Asian women has its roots in the wartime experiences of American males in Asia. During World War II, the Korean War, and the Vietnam War, Asian women were viewed as the spoils of war or as objects of love and comfort for lonely American soldiers. In the popular media, white men are routinely pictured as having free and unfettered sexual access to Asian women.

Asian women as portrayed in American media are interchangeable in appearance, generally saying little. Several generations of Americans have been raised with racist, sexist, and cartoonlike images of Asian women. The models for passivity and servility in films, television programs, and Western literature fit neatly into the stereotypes imposed on Asian women and contrast sharply with the more liberating ideals of independence and activism. Asian women should take an active role in changing these images and the dehumanization implicit in the stereotypes of expendability and invisibility.—*Carol C. Fan*

SUGGESTED READINGS:

• Asian Women United of California, ed. *Making Waves: An Anthology of Writings By and About Asian American Women.* Boston, Mass.: Beacon Press, 1989. A collection of autobiographical writings, short stories, poetry, essays, and photographs by and about the experiences and history of Asian American women. It tries to expose the realities hidden by the tendency to ignore and stereotype Asian American women.

• Barringer, Herbert R., Robert W. Gardner, and Michael J. Levin. *Asians and Pacific Islanders in the United States.* National Committee for Research on the 1980 Census. New York: Russell Sage Foundation, 1993. This monograph gives a history of Asian immigration to the United States and then does a demographic profile of Asian Americans. It deals with fertility, mortality, age and sex composition, residence and migration, education, employment, and socioeconomic status, all based on the 1980 census results. This is a good source of statistics, especially for the post-World War II period. Pacific Islanders are profiled separately in the final chapter and are also included in some comparisons in the sections on education, occupation, and socioeconomic status.

• Kikumura, Akemi. *Through Harsh Winters: The Life of a Japanese Immigrant Woman.* Novato, Calif.: Chandler and Sharp, 1981. The author presents an oral life history of her mother, a Japanese woman who came to America with her husband in 1923, based on taped interviews and research. The mother discusses her experiences as a girl in Japan, in California in the 1920's and 1930's, in the internment camps in Arizona during World War II, and starting over after the war. The author comments in the appendices on several cultural issues important to understanding this story and on the methodology for doing the history.

• Kwong, Peter. *The New Chinatown.* New York: Hill & Wang, 1987. A writer and community activist, Kwong lived for many years in New York's Chinatown, the subject of this book. Revealing the underside of the new Chinatown (exploitation of recent immigrants; influence of organized crime) as well as its success stories, Kwong's book provides a valuable corrective to other accounts. Also useful for background coverage of post-1965 Chinese immigration.

• Lee, Mary Paik. *Quiet Odyssey: A Pioneer Korean*

Japanese American women now participate in taiko drum groups, traditionally a male pursuit. (Ben Klaffke)

Woman in America. Edited by Sucheng Chan. Seattle: University of Washington Press, 1990. An edited autobiography of a Korean woman who emigrated with her family to Hawaii at age five in 1910 and eventually operated a vegetable farm in California with her husband and children. The introduction covers the historical context for this story in Korea and in the United States. The appendices give further detailed information on Korean immigrant farming in California.

• McCunn, Ruthanne Lum. *Thousand Pieces of Gold*. Boston, Mass.: Beacon Press, 1981. A slightly fictionalized account of the life history of a Mongolian woman, Lalu Nathoy, later known as Polly Bemis, who was sold by her family in China in 1871 to procurers who brought her to America, where she was sold to a saloon keeper in a frontier town in Idaho. The story tells of her struggle against slavery and prostitution to survive and keep her dignity, and about how she eventually gains her freedom and creates a new life on the frontier.

South Asian American woman with child, New York City. (Hazel Hankin)

• Nakano, Mei. *Japanese American Women: Three Generations, 1890-1990*. With *Okaasan* by Grace Shibata. San Francisco: National Japanese American Historical Society, 1990. This book gives an easy-to-read generalized sociological/historical account of conditions for the Issei, Nisei, and Sansei generations of Japanese American women, mostly on the West Coast, illustrated by quotes and examples from individual stories. There are a number of good photographs. Also included in the text is *Okaasan*, a life history of an Issei woman written by her daughter Grace Shibata.

• Yung, Judy. *Chinese Women of America: A Pictorial History*. Published for the Chinese Culture Foundation of San Francisco. Seattle: University of Washington Press, 1986. Makes good use of historical photographs and prints to illustrate the history of Chinese women in America and also to explore the images and stereotypes about them. Combines factual and statistical information with lots of anecdotes about individual women to give the reader a feel for what life was like for these women in each period, covering the years from 1834 to 1985.

Women of South Asian Descent Collective: Group formed in the San Francisco Bay Area in 1991 to produce an anthology of works by South Asian Indian women writers. The organization, consisting of South Asian Indian women, published its results in 1993. *Our Feet Walk the Sky: Women of the South Asian Diaspora* (1993) is the first volume to chronicle the emigration experiences of South Asian Indian women.

Wong, Anna May (Wong Liu Tsong; Jan. 3, 1907, Los Angeles, Calif.—Feb. 3, 1961, Santa Monica, Calif.): Actor. At a time when race and sex discrimination made it difficult for Chinese Americans to find meaningful work in Hollywood and aspire to stardom, Wong became the first well-known Chinese American actor, starring in more than a hundred films in her forty-year career.

Born the second of eight children to Wong Sam Sing and Lee Gon Toy, she was named Liu Tsong (frosted yellow willow) by her parents, who operated a laundry business, and Anna by the doctor who delivered her. Although the family lived outside Chinatown, Anna May Wong attended Chinese school after public school in the evenings. In her early teens she frequented local nickelodeons and aspired to become a movie actor such as Theda Bara or Gloria Swanson. Despite her father's objections she began making the

Screen actor Anna May Wong. (AP/Wide World Photos)

rounds of the casting offices, landing a part as an extra in *Red Lantern* (1919) at the age of twelve.

Wong's first leading role was in *The Toll of the Sea* (1922) as a Chinese Madame Butterfly who commits suicide after her white lover leaves her. She made her mark as an actress in the role of a "Mongol slave" in the lavish production *The Thief of Bagdad* (1924), starring with Douglas Fairbanks. From then, she became Hollywood's favorite Chinese flapper, often photographed as an exotic yet glamorous figure. Her success coincided with Hollywood's interest in Chinatown's aura of mystery and treachery. By 1928 she had appeared in more than twenty silent films typecast as an oriental villain including *Mr. Wu* (1927), *The Devil Dancer* (1927), and *Chinatown Charlie* (1928).

In 1928 Wong left for Europe in search of international fame. There she learned to speak English, German, and French and received acclaim for her performance in the films *Song* (1928), *Piccadilly* (1929), and *The Flame of Love* (1930). In 1929 she made her stage debut in *Circle of Chalk* with Laurence Olivier in London.

In 1930 Wong returned to the United States and, under contract with Paramount, took on leading roles in suspenseful melodramas such as *Daughter of the Dragon* (1931), *Shanghai Express* (1932), *A Study in Scarlet* (1933), *Limehouse Blues* (1934), and *Java Head* (1934). Although these roles made her a popular actor in Hollywood, they also promoted stereotypes of Chinese women as the exotic China doll or treacherous villain. In 1936, when she went to China to study acting there and was chastised by Chinese officials for her negative portrayals, she responded that those were the only roles open to her. Nevertheless she later refused to play the role of the vindictive concubine in *The Good Earth* (1937).

As the war of resistance against Japan began in China, Wong returned to the United States and performed in the first film sympathetic to the Chinese, *Daughter of Shanghai* (1937), which reflected improved relations between China and the United States. With the outbreak of World War II, Wong announced her retirement from acting and volunteered for the war effort. Seventeen years later she made a final comeback as Lana Turner's maid in the box-office success *Portrait in Black* (1960).

Wong never married, choosing to devote her life to her acting career. In 1961 she died of a heart attack at the Santa Monica home she shared with her brother Richard. Tragically, because of racial discrimination, she never realized her full potential as an actor; the film industry's policy was to reserve major roles in class A films for white performers. Yet she made a name for herself in Asian American history as the first successful Asian American movie actor.

Wong, B. D. (b. Oct. 24, 1962, San Francisco, Calif.): Actor. In 1988 Wong became the first Asian American actor to receive a Tony Award, for his performance as Song Liling in David Henry HWANG's *M. Butterfly*.

Tony award-winning actor B. D. Wong signs autographs. (Asian Week)

Wong also received the Drama Desk, Theatre World, Outer Critics' Circle, and Clarence Derwent awards for that performance; no other American actor has been so honored. A confirmed trailblazer, in 1992 Wong became both the first male performer and the first actor of color to star in the musical *Peter Pan*, at Kansas City's Starlight Theatre. Wong distinguished himself as an outspoken advocate for Asian American performers, leading the 1990 protest against casting policies for the Broadway production of *MISS SAIGON* and becoming a founding member of the Asian Pacific Alliance for Creative Equality (APACE). Wong's film credits include *Family Business*, *The Freshman*, *Father of the Bride*, *Jurassic Park*, and the film version of *And the Band Played On*, based on Randy Shilts's book about the acquired immune deficiency syndrome (AIDS) epidemic.

Wong, Bernard P. (b. Feb. 12, 1941, Guangdong Province, China): Scholar. A faculty member at San Francisco State University, in 1991 he became the first Chinese American to chair its Department of Anthropology. He has conducted research on the Chinese in the Philippines, China, Peru, Singapore, and the United States, and he is the author of *A Chinese Ameri-*

can Community: Ethnicity and Survival Strategies (1979), *Chinatown* (1982), and *Patronage, Brokerage, Entrepreneurship, and the Chinese Community of New York* (1988).

Wong, Diane Yen-Mei (b. Feb. 12, 1950, Seattle, Wash.): Writer. A columnist for the *Hawaii Herald* newspaper and a contributor to *USA Weekend Magazine*, she writes extensively on Asian American issues. Through ASIAN WOMEN UNITED of California, she coedited *Making Waves: An Anthology of Writings By and About Asian American Women* (1989) and authored two question-and-answer books, *Dear Diane: Questions and Answers for Asian American Women* (1983) and *Dear Diane: Letters from Our Daughters* (1983). She served as executive director of the ASIAN AMERICAN JOURNALISTS ASSOCIATION (1987-1992), edited *East/West*, a San Francisco-based Asian American newspaper, and served as consultant to Unity '94, a coalition of national minority journalism associations (1992-1994). In 1992, she began writing plays about Asian Americans.

Wong, Elizabeth (b. June 6, 1958, South Gate, Calif.): Playwright and journalist. Educated at the University of Southern California and New York University, she turned her attention to playwriting after a successful career in journalism. Her *Letters to a Student Revolutionary* (pr. 1991), the first American script to consider the 1989 Tiananmen Square incident, won the 1990 Playwrights' Forum Award and a 1992 Margo Jones New Play Citation. Her other plays include *Bu and Bun* (pr. 1991), *Reveries of an Amorous Woman* (pr. 1991), and *Kimchee and Chitlins* (pr. 1992), about conflicts between African Americans and Korean Americans.

Wong, H. K. [Henry Kwock] (Apr., 1907, San Francisco, Calif.—Jan. 13, 1985): Community advocate. Wong founded the "MISS CHINATOWN USA" pageant in 1958 and the CHINESE HISTORICAL SOCIETY OF AMERICA (CHSA) in 1963. He served as executive secretary of the CHINESE CONSOLIDATED BENEVOLENT ASSOCIATION (CCBA) and as technical director for the film *Flower Drum Song* (1961). He also wrote for numerous community newspapers and edited the book *San Francisco Chinatown on Parade in Picture and Story* (1961).

Wong, Jade Snow (b. Jan. 21, 1922, San Francisco, Calif.): Ceramist and writer. Snow was the fifth daugh-

ter of Hong and Hing Kwai Wong. Her father operated a garment factory out of the family home while she was growing up in San Francisco. From her father, Wong acquired her skills in calligraphy and her knowledge of ancient Chinese culture and history. As a Chinese daughter she was not encouraged to pursue a college education. Nevertheless she managed to work her way through school and earned a B.A. degree from Mills College. While at college she discovered her talents in design and ceramics. Primarily a potter, Wong has seen her pieces exhibited at the Chicago Art Institute and as part of exhibits sponsored by the Metropolitan Museum of Art and the Syracuse Museum of Fine Arts.

Wong's autobiography *Fifth Chinese Daughter*, was published in 1945. The work, told in the third person, depicts the "collision of worlds" between the traditions of the old world and the lure of American values and lifestyles. *Fifth Chinese Daughter* is one of the earlier works by Asian Americans where the dilemma of bridging two different cultures is addressed. This also meant that she had to adjust to two distinctly different models of womanhood. In her later work *No Chinese Stranger* (1975), the conflict appears resolved: She

Jade Snow Wong. (Asian Week)

observed that she was able to act Chinese with her tradition-bound father, but that in the "new American world" she had "learned to act like an American." *Fifth Chinese Daughter* enjoyed widespread popularity and was subsequently translated into several languages. Another work *The Immigrant Experience*, was published in 1971.

The popularity of *Fifth Chinese Daughter* outside the United States attracted the attention of the State Department. In 1951 Wong was sent on a four-month world tour through the department's Leaders and Specialists Exchange Program as an example of a Chinese American woman who had succeeded professionally in America. Wong has also been a columnist for the *San Francisco Examiner* and a regular contributor to several periodicals.

Wong, Nellie (b. 1934, Oakland, Calif.): Poet. Wong has become a powerful voice for Asian American writers in general and Chinese American writers in particular. Her poems have been collected in *Dreams in Harrison Railroad Park* (1977) and *The Death of Long Steam Lady* (1986) and in such anthologies as *This Bridge Called My Back: Writings by Radical Women of Color* (1981) and *Breaking Silence: An Anthology of Contemporary Asian American Poets* (1983). In 1981, she was featured in the documentary film *Mitsuye and Nellie, Asian-American Poets* with Japanese American Mitsuye Yamada. Wong has also served as an analyst in affirmative action at the University of California, San Francisco.

Wong, Richard S. H. "Dickie" (b. June 10, 1933, Honolulu, Territory of Hawaii): State senator. Wong is on the five-member board controlling Princess Bernice Pauahi Bishop's $8 billion estate, the largest private landowner in Hawaii. He served in the state legislature for twenty-six years, the longest tenure in Hawaii state history, and retired at the age of fifty-nine in 1992.

Part Hawaiian and part Chinese, Wong attended Catholic Maryknoll High School. He was graduated with a bachelor's degree from the University of Hawaii in 1956. He took part in civil rights marches in Selma, Alabama, in the 1960's.

Wong was a former United Public Workers business agent, Oahu division director. In 1962 he got his first job with the state as a detention home counselor for the juvenile court. He won election to the state house in 1966 and to the senate in 1974. Wong served as senate president from 1979 to 1992, an unprecedented span of time for that office.

Wong's power-sharing tactics enabled him to win cooperation from opponents. When confronted with a struggle in the senate, Wong allowed people to voice their frustrations; once the grievances were out in the open, he carefully steered discussions toward solutions. His understanding of power enabled him to share it liberally, giving other lawmakers wide latitude to pursue their own agendas and set their own committee priorities. As a legislator he remained firmly anchored to the working-class values of the community.

Wong, Sau-ling Cynthia: Scholar. An associate professor in the Department of Ethnic Studies at the University of California, Berkeley and director of the ASIAN AMERICAN STUDIES program there, Wong is the author of the influential study *Reading Asian American Literature: From Necessity to Extravagance (1993)*.

Wong, Shawn (b. 1949, Oakland, Calif.): Novelist. Wong received acclaim with his first novel, *Homebase* (1979). He has also coedited the Asian American anthologies *Aiieeeee! An Anthology of Asian-American Writers* (1974) and *The Big Aiiieeeee! An Anthology of Chinese American and Japanese American Literature* (1991), as well as the multicultural collections *The Before Columbus Foundation Fiction Anthology: Selections from the American Book Awards, 1980-1990* (1992) and *The Before Columbus Foundation Poetry Anthology: Selections from the American Book Awards, 1980-1990* (1992). Wong has served as the director of the ASIAN AMERICAN STUDIES program at the University of Washington.

Wong, Stella (b. Mar. 30, 1914, Oakland, Calif.): Painter. She attended the California College of Arts and Crafts as well as the University of California, Berkeley. Her postgraduate studies took her to Mexico City and Dublin, Ireland. She also lived in New York City, designing jewelry for Helena Rubinstein before returning to the San Francisco Bay Area in 1940. She was a member of the Chinese Art Association when they exhibited at the M. H. de Young Memorial Museum in 1935.

Wong Wing v. United States (1896): U.S. Supreme Court ruling that granted a petition for *habeus corpus* filed by four illegal Chinese immigrants after finding that they had been denied due process of law. Adopting a rationale reminiscent of the earlier Supreme Court case of YICK WO v. HOPKINS (1886), the opinion announced that all persons living in the United States— aliens as well as citizens—are entitled to the due process protections afforded by the U.S. Constitution.

In 1892, Wong Wing and three other Chinese immigrants were found to have entered the United States unlawfully. Responding to a recommendation by the customs inspector, a Michigan federal court ordered them imprisoned at hard labor for a time and then deported pursuant to the GEARY ACT OF 1892. Arguing that the court had no jurisdiction to prosecute them for illegal entry, the four men filed for a writ of *habeus corpus*, a federal constitutional right that allows an individual held in some form of custody to allege that he or she is being detained unlawfully and to have the courts decide the matter quickly. The prisoners contended that the act violated the Constitution's Fifth and Sixth amendments guaranteeing formal court indictments and speedy jury trials. The petition was, however, denied, and the men were sent back to prison. Shortly thereafter, they issued an appeal to the Supreme Court.

The Court agreed with the Chinese that they had been convicted and imprisoned at hard labor without due process of law (no judicial finding of innocence or guilt) and that their sentence was therefore unconstitutional. The ruling struck down that section of the Geary Act deemed to have infringed the Fifth and Sixth amendments. Without a court indictment and a fair trial, the men would have to be freed. The justices underscored the rule expressed in the earlier Supreme Court cases of CHAE CHAN PING V. UNITED STATES (1889) and FONG YUE TING V. UNITED STATES (1893): that Congress has plenary constitutional authority to expel, deport, or exclude aliens. Even so, the Court declared, the latter are entitled to due process of law—a constitutional right with which federal and state authorities must comply.

Woo, Gilbert Gang Nam (Hu Jingnan; Dec. 25, 1911, Taishan, China—Nov. 17, 1979, San Francisco, Calif.): Journalist. For forty years, Woo's columns made him a major voice in the CHINESE AMERICAN PRESS.

In the 1930's, during the war between China and Japan, he wrote propaganda dramas and patriotic songs for radio and became an editor for the CHINESE TIMES under Walter U. Lum. After the entry of the United States into World War II, Woo began a controversial column called "Qizhe" (I wish to inform you); one of his essays condemned the treatment of Japanese Americans, who were being sent to INTERNMENT CAMPS. Such views caused trouble with Lum, and Woo quit the newspaper after a disagreement. Woo also worked as a radio news commentator and wrote for

The Chinese Hour, which broadcast Chinese opera and news segments.

After World War II ended, Woo focused on racial discrimination in the United States. He founded a newspaper to address such issues in the Chinese American community and called it *Chinese Pacific Weekly*. It was nonpartisan, refusing to support either side, the Nationalists or the communists, in the political turmoil in China. When civil war broke out, *Chinese Pacific Weekly* was one of the few objective sources of information about the conflict, since the Nationalists controlled the media in Chinatown. After the communists under MAO ZEDONG were victorious, Woo was one of many accused of procommunist sympathies both by Chinese Americans loyal to the Nationalists and by McCarthyites. With the start of the Korean War, in which the United States and the new People's Republic of China squared off on Korean soil, Chinese Americans feared the same kind of treatment faced by Japanese Americans before them. *Chinese Pacific Weekly* played a crucial role in these troubled times by keeping the Chinese American community informed.

Woo continued to expand the readership and influence of his newspaper, founding the United Outing Association for youth groups and promoting Chinese American writing by soliciting stories. In 1960, *Chinese Pacific Weekly* was granted membership in the San Francisco Press Club. The 1960's brought new levels of activism to Chinatown and a pride in Chinese heritage on the part of young American-born Chinese people, both of which Woo sought to support through his commentaries. After Woo's death in 1979, *Chinese Pacific Weekly* lost much of its heart, and it was slowly subsumed into *East-West*, a bilingual weekly published by his friend David Shew.

A fuller account of Woo's life can be found in Him Mark LAI's "A Voice of Reason: Life and Times of Gilbert Woo, Chinese American Journalist," in *Chinese America: History and Perspectives (1992): 83-123.*

Woo, John (b. 1946, Canton, China): Filmmaker. With his stylishly violent, artistic, and often comic films, Hong Kong director Woo is considered one of the finest action directors of his generation. He began in the 1970's with martial-arts pictures and slapstick comedies, but by the 1980's, Woo's admiration for such directors as Sergio Leone, Sam Peckinpah, and Martin Scorsese became apparent as his films took on a bloodier, darker cast.

This change was first evident in *A Better Tomorrow* (1986), a gangster epic, and he sharpened his political and (ironically) antiviolence message in one of that film's prequels, the Vietnam War-era *Bullet in the Head* (1989). Woo caught the attention of American audiences with his 1989 masterpiece *The Killer*, an almost sentimental film about a hitman who accidentally blinds a nightclub singer and falls in love with her. His feature *Hard-Boiled* (1991) edged closer to camp with its extended gun battle in a hospital, the hero firing his weapon with one hand and cradling a newborn baby with the other.

Film director John Woo. (Asian Week)

Woo moved to Los Angeles in 1992 (partly to escape Hong Kong before it reverted to Chinese control in 1997) and directed his first Hollywood film, the Jean-Claude Van Damme vehicle *Hard Target*, in 1993. His style of melodramatic gore and violent humor was not appreciated, however, by the rating board of the Motion Picture Association of America, which initially labeled the film NC-17; Woo cut footage seven times before *Hard Target* was awarded an R rating. Moreover, instead of casting Chinese actor Chow Yun-fat, the popular star of many of Woo's action films, he had to direct a proven box-office draw in American cinema. Ironically, it is Woo's Hong Kong epics, with their stylized violence and Asian stars, that have proved most influential with such young American directors as Quentin Tarantino, Abel Ferrara, and Sam Raimi.

Los Angeles political activist Mike Woo. (AP/Wide World Photos)

Woo, Michael (b. Oct. 8, 1951, Los Angeles, Calif.): Government official. In 1985 Woo became the first Asian American on the Los Angeles City Council. A native Los Angeleno born in the Crenshaw community, Woo attended public schools and earned a B.A. degree from the University of California, Santa Cruz and an M.A. degree in urban planning at the University of California, Berkeley. He is the first of his parents' children to be born in the United States. His father is a prominent Chinese American banker who has been active in Republican Party politics.

After working briefly for a nonprofit urban-planning research center in San Francisco, Woo was hired by state senate majority leader David Roberti as a key speechwriter and policy advisor. In 1981 Woo campaigned for the Thirteenth District city council seat held by Peggy Stevenson and won. A liberal Democrat and Vietnam War protester, he lost the Los Angeles mayoral election to Richard Riordan in June, 1993, when Tom Bradley retired after twenty years in office.

Some critics, assessing Woo's mayoral defeat, suggested that his long career in politics since his graduation in 1975 had branded him as a "professional" politician at a time when public disenchantment with politicians was running high. An adult life spent almost entirely inside government agencies did not win him credit.

As city councilman for Hollywood, Woo achieved a great deal. In March, 1991, he called on Los Angeles police chief Daryl Gates to resign in the wake of the Rodney King beating. Woo led the fight to strengthen tenants' rights and pushed for a new law extending sick-leave benefits to city employees who are members of nontraditional families. He was instrumental in both limiting overdevelopment on Ventura Boulevard and preserving Fryman Canyon. A $1 billion redevelopment program for Hollywood was also the result of Woo's effort.

In 1986 Woo married Susan Fong, who worked for the California Community Foundation.

Woo, S. B. (b. Aug. 13, 1937, Shanghai, China): Politician. As lieutenant governor of Delaware (1985-1989), he became the highest-ranking Asian American state official in the continental United States. He was principal of the Chinese School of Delaware (1973), board chair and chief executive officer of the Chinese American Community Center (1982-1983), and national board member (1977-1979) and later national president (1990-1991) of the ORGANIZATION OF CHINESE AMERICANS. He was graduated with a Ph.D. degree from Washington University in St. Louis, Missouri, in 1964 and has taught physics at the University of Delaware.

Woo Yee-bew (1864, Fat San, near Canton, China—1930): Christian missionary. After becoming a Christian, Woo enrolled at a Lutheran school in Canton, where he studied Chinese classics, German, and religion. He left home to study theology at St. Stephen's College in Hong Kong in 1880. He later traveled to San Francisco and then Hawaii, where he started a camp for Chinese plantation laborers. He began to evangelize the Chinese community at Kohala, Hawaii, in 1887, later assisting the founding of the St. Paul Chinese Mission. Other mission work followed in Honolulu, where he moved in 1915. Woo was the first Chinese cleric of the Episcopal church in Hawaii.

Workingmen's Party of California: Political organization founded in 1877 and a major catalyst in the anti-Chinese and exclusion movements. In California thousands of laborers migrating as part of the "Forty-Niner" gold rush belonged to a variety of workingmen's parties, which had existed in the East since the

S. B. Woo speaks on the day of his election to the position of lieutenant governor of Delaware. (AP/Wide World Photos)

late 1820's. After failing to realize their dreams of instant wealth, many of these migrants chose to stay in the new state as wage workers—and to form their own political movement. Charging that Chinese immigrants created unfair competition by accepting substandard wages, they formed a number of "anticoolie" groups and organized the California Anti-Chinese Convention in 1870. As an effort to gain additional influence, they also affiliated with the Workingmen's Party of the United States, which held a rally at San Francisco in 1877 but refused to endorse a single-issue campaign against Chinese workers.

Frustrated by this unsatisfactory level of support, California activists under the leadership of Denis KEARNEY separated from the national organization and formed an independent political party. On December 12, 1877, the Workingmen's Party of California petitioned both Congress and the president to revise treaty relations with China for the purpose of stopping further immigration. Such aggressive action aroused growing voter support for the infant party, prompting both Democrats and Republicans to call for a general referendum on the Chinese issue. In 1879, still trying to neutralize this new political threat, the major parties also produced a revised and patently anti-Chinese California state constitution. The following year California's congressional representatives spearheaded renegotiation of the 1868 BURLINGAME TREATY. Its successor, ANGELL'S TREATY (1880), permitted the restriction of Chinese immigrants. Finally, the CHINESE EXCLUSION ACT OF 1882 virtually eliminated the immigration of laborers from China.

In the wake of exclusion, most California voters decided that a radical third party was not necessary to protect their interests. The Workingmen's Party of California faded in importance during the 1880's, and later ANTI-CHINESE MOVEMENTS did not rely on its leadership. Still Kearney's organization had played a major role in the nineteenth century process that made the oppression of Chinese Americans a formal part of both California and U.S. law.

World Theater: Film theater founded in San Francisco's Chinatown in the 1960's. It featured films from the People's Republic of China. Later it began to offer mainstream motion pictures.

World War II, China and: For China World War II began in 1937, when Japan launched its large-scale invasion of the country on July 7. Japan had a long-range plan to expand into China beginning with the Manchuria invasion in September, 1931, when Japan occupied the four provinces in northeast China and later established the Manchukuo (the Manchu Kingdom) in 1932. This was the prelude to its aggression against China proper below the Great Wall.

After the Japanese occupation of Manchuria, China appealed to the League of Nations for justice. The league set up the Lytton Commission of Inquiry, which submitted an unfavorable report about Japan to the league. It recommended a denial of diplomatic recognition to Manchukuo. As a protest Japan withdrew from the league in 1933.

Early Years of the Sino-Japanese War (1937-1945). Internal domination by the military in Japan and the lack of effective action by the international community to stop Japanese aggression in China encouraged Japan further to encroach upon China's sovereignty. It forced China to recognize special Japanese interests in north China. Japanese ambition eventually led to the Marco Polo Bridge incident in July, 1937, which started the long Sino-Japanese War. Japan was defeated by Allied forces in 1945 and officially surrendered to the Allied Powers, including China, on September 2, 1945.

During the initial period of the war against Japan, the Chinese people rallied to the Nationalist government headed by CHIANG KAI-SHEK, leader of the GUOMINDANG (the Nationalist Party) to fight the Japanese. Even the Chinese Communist Party officially supported Chiang and abolished its Soviet government in China and its Red Army. At least nominally the Communists put their forces under the control of the Nationalist government. National solidarity did not, however, last long. The first major clash between the Nationalist and Communist forces occurred in 1941, when in the New Fourth Army incident Nationalist forces liquidated the Communist New Fourth Army. The anti-Japanese alliance of all parties and groups soon fell apart, and civil strife between the Nationalists and the Communists started again, which seriously undermined China's fight against Japanese invasion.

Communist Expansion. The Japanese invasion of China greatly helped the Chinese Communists in expanding their influence in China. Before Japan had invaded China, the Nationalists succeeded in destroying the main Communist force in Jiangxi in south China and encircled the remnants of the Communist force in northern Shaanxi Province after the Long March of 1934 to 1935. Japanese invasion forced Chiang Kai-shek to abandon his military campaign against the Communists and to organize a national

U.S.-trained Chinese air force pilots, veterans of many air battles with Japanese fighter planes, 1943. (AP/Wide World Photos)

united front which included the Communists, against Japan. This gave the Communists an opportunity to expand their forces in the countryside in the Japanese-occupied areas. The result was that Chiang fought a two-front war against both the Japanese and the Communists. The Communists also fought a two-front war against the Japanese and the Nationalists. By the end of World War II the Communists increased their party membership from about 40,000 in 1937 to about 1.2 million in 1945. The Communists expanded their armed forces to more than half a million. They claimed that they controlled 90 million people in the several hundred counties in their "liberated areas." This paved the way for the full-scale civil war in China after World War II and the eventual triumph of Communism in China in 1949.

During the early years of World War II, China did not receive substantial assistance from any country except the Soviet Union. The United States and other Western countries were too timid to intervene effectively on China's behalf. To make things worse, many American companies were still selling strategic materials, such as iron and oil, to Japan, thereby strengthening Japan's war capacity. Poverty, loss of lives and territories, economic devastation, and international isolation forced Chiang to retreat to the hinterland of China with Chongqing as his wartime capital. Chiang hoped that eventually the United States and other Western powers would enter the war against Japan.

U.S. Involvement. The PEARL HARBOR attack on the United States on December 7, 1941, was a turning point for China in its fight against Japan. After a declaration of war by the United States, China immediately became an ally. China began to receive much economic and military assistance.

The international position of China was improved because of efforts by U.S. president Franklin D. Roosevelt. The United States led the way in abolishing its unequal treaties with China. Other Western allies followed suit. In 1943 the United States abolished its Chinese exclusion laws as a symbolic gesture of goodwill toward the Chinese people. China was given superpower status when the United Nations was organized.

During the war against Japan, China suffered enormous losses in terms of human lives and property. It was estimated that China lost about $31 billion in public and private property as a direct result of the war. China also suffered millions of casualties to both soldiers and civilians. (The infamous Rape of NANJING by Japanese troops in 1937 has been documented.) This does not include indirect losses of lives and prop-

erty, the physical and emotional suffering of the Chinese people in the eight years of war against Japan, or the loss of lives and property from 1931 to 1937.

China's major contribution to World War II was its determination to continue the fight against Japan regardless of the cost. A large number of Japanese troops were trapped in China, thus reducing Japanese military pressure on Allied Forces elsewhere. Japan was also forced to allocate a great deal of its resources to support its military campaigns in China. China's participation in the Anglo-American-Chinese campaign in Burma in 1944 also helped the Allied Forces win the war.—*George P. Jan*

SUGGESTED READINGS: • Chen, Yung-fa. *Making Revolution: The Communist Movement in Eastern and Central China, 1937-1945.* Berkeley: University of California Press, 1986. • Eastman, Lloyd. *Seeds of Destruction: Nationalist China in War and Revolution, 1937-1949.* Stanford, Calif.: Stanford University Press, 1984. • Fairbank, John King. *The United States and China.* 4th ed. Cambridge, Mass.: Harvard University Press, 1979. • Jones, F. C., Hugh Borton, and B. R. Pearn. *The Far East: 1942-1946.* New York: Oxford University Press, 1955. • Michael, Franz H., and George E. Taylor. *The Far East in the Modern World.* New York: Henry Holt, 1956. • U.S. Department of State. *United States Relations with China, with Special Reference to the Period 1944-1949.* Department of State Publication 3573. Washington, D.C.: Government Printing Office, 1949.

World War II, Japan and: Japan's establishment of a puppet state in Manchuria in 1932 was the first of a series of encroachments upon Chinese territory that led to the formal outbreak of war in July, 1937. The fighting remained regional until December 7, 1941, when Japan simultaneously attacked Hawaii, Hong Kong, Malaya, Singapore, and the Philippines. During the following seven months Japan gained control of most of Southeast Asia, the East Indies, and the western Pacific before its advance was halted at the Battle of MIDWAY (June 3-6, 1942). During the final twenty-six months of the war, the Japanese tenaciously defended their overextended empire against twin American thrusts across the Pacific and a Nationalist Chinese army revitalized by American assistance. By May, 1945, Japan had lost its Pacific empire. Massive American bombing of the mainland culminated in the destruction of Hiroshima (August 6) and Nagasaki (August 9) by atomic bombs. Japan formally surrendered on September 2.

Causes. Japanese economic and military aggression was the fundamental cause of the Pacific war. The modernization of the country following the MEIJI RESTORATION (1868-1912) led to industrialization, which demanded natural resources not available in Japan. Through war with China (1894-1895) and Russia (1904-1905), and by means of a number of international agreements, by the 1920's the Japanese Empire formally included the Ryukyu Islands, Taiwan, and Korea and practically involved heavy military and economic influence throughout Manchuria and northern China.

Facing an economy threatened by rising protective tariffs in the wake of international depression (1929) and a rapidly expanding population, the Japanese public gave increasing support to the expansionistic militarists, who effectively destroyed democratic politics during the 1930's. In 1931 the mineral-rich Chinese province of Manchuria was occupied, and a year later the puppet-state of Manchukuo was proclaimed. During the following five years, Japan gained increasing control of the five northern provinces. Fearing strengthened Chinese organization, the Japanese invaded the area around Beijing on July 7, 1937, and within three weeks captured the city. This is usually considered the formal beginning of World War II in Asia.

War Against China. The first phase of the war (1937-1941) was fought militarily against China and diplomatically against the West. In China the invasion led to an unenthusiastic rapprochement between the Nationalist government and Communist forces. In the United States it began to undermine the almost universal isolationism that had diplomatically smoothed Japan's aggression during the 1930's. Japan's initial goal was to secure a raw material base in China from which to spur further industrial development, which in turn would force Communist and Nationalist forces in western China to cooperate with Japan as the predominant partner in a "Greater East Asian Co-Prosperity Sphere." By October, 1938, this process was complete, Beijing, Shanghai, Tsingtao, Nanjing, Xiamen, Canton, and the intervening countryside having been secured. In the process, however, Japan outraged world opinion by the merciless bombing of Chinese cities and widespread acts of brutality, most notably the in-

Captured Japanese photograph taken aboard a Japanese carrier before the attack on Pearl Harbor, December 7, 1941. (National Archives)

USS Shaw *explodes during the Japanese air raid on Pearl Harbor, December 7, 1941.* (National Archives)

discriminate massacre of some 100,000 civilians and the rape of innumerable women during the Rape of NANJING (December, 1937).

The beginning of war in Europe in September, 1939, led to a new wave of Japanese aggression, including the occupation of French Indochina (September, 1940) and the signing of the Tripartite Pact with Germany and Italy during the same month. Although the Asian and European wars were never coordinated, it was hoped that the Axis agreement would forestall American interference in Asia. The United States, however, progressively utilized its diplomatic muscle to freeze Japanese assets abroad and to limit severely exports of petroleum and scrap iron vital to Japanese war production. By July, 1941, the embargo was virtually complete. Japan was then faced with either a humiliating retreat from China or an invasion of the resource-rich Netherlands East Indies, which would certainly bring war.

Right-wing elements prevailed, and on December 7, 1941, the Japanese destroyed most of the U.S. Pacific fleet at Pearl Harbor, Hawaii, and began the conquest of Hong Kong, the Philippines, Malaya, and Singapore in preparation for the invasion of the Netherlands East Indies, which commenced in January, 1942. In March, Nationalist loan requests of $500 million and $50 million were approved by the United States and Great Britain, fortifying Chinese military resistance. During the remaining three-and-a-half years of the Asian war, China's greatest contribution was to engage approximately 40 percent of Japanese troops at a time when Japanese planners had expected to be utilizing puppet troops.

War in the Pacific. In the seven months after neutralizing the United States at PEARL HARBOR, Japan expanded rapidly. Meeting ineffective British and Dutch resistance, by June, 1942, the Japanese occupied Burma, Hong Kong, Malaya, Singapore, the Netherlands East Indies, the Philippines, northern New

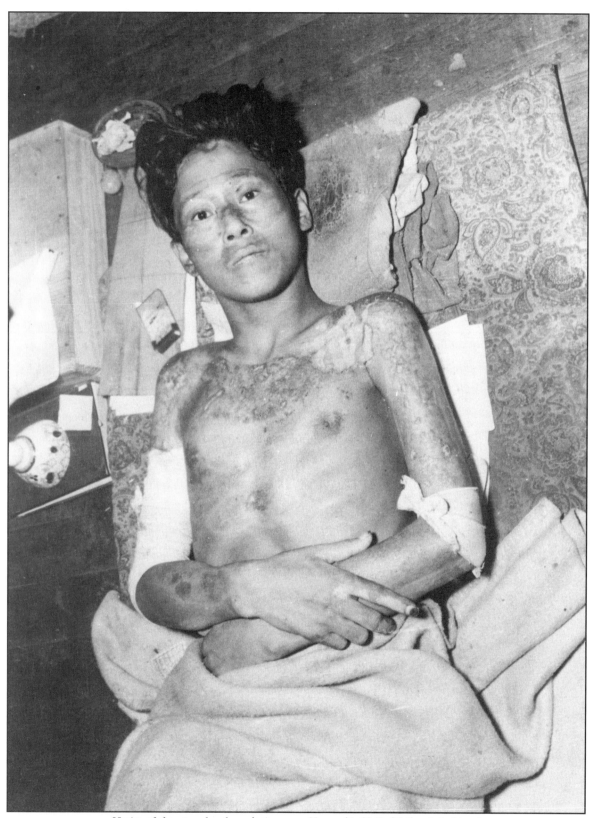

Victim of the atom bomb explosion over Nagasaki, 1945. (National Archives)

Guinea, and all major Pacific islands behind a line extending from Guadalcanal and the Gilbert Islands in the South Pacific to Attu and Kiska in the Aleutian Islands in the North Pacific. The Japanese southern advance, however, was halted in the Battle of Coral Sea (May 7) and its eastern advance in the decisive Battle of MIDWAY, in which the Japanese lost four aircraft carriers and dozens of highly trained pilots.

Beginning in July, 1943, American and Australian troops under the command of General Douglas MacArthur opened a concerted offensive beginning in the Solomon Islands. By the end of 1944 New Guinea, much of the Netherlands East Indies, and most of the Philippines had been reconquered. In February, 1944, another force of principally naval troops under the direction of Admiral Chester W. Nimitz began sweeping Japanese troops from the central Pacific. By November American forces were using the Mariana Islands as a base for widespread bombing of the Japanese mainland and six months later were staging massive bombing raids of the Japanese mainland from Okinawa, less than four hundred miles away. By May, 1945, British and American troops under Admiral Lord Louis Mountbatten had reconquered Burma and were rapidly pushing the Japanese back throughout Southeast Asia. Though Japanese resistance everywhere was fierce, with troops frequently fighting to the last man, their emaciated military machine was no match for the burgeoning industrial might of the United States. Still refusing to surrender, Japan suffered the destruction of HIROSHIMA (August 6) and Nagasaki (August 9) in the United States' first uses of the nuclear technology that had been developed during the war. By August 14 terms of surrender were agreed upon and on September 2 were formally signed on board the USS *Missouri* in Tokyo Bay.

Results. U.S. occupation forces landed in Japan on August 26, 1945, and would stay until April 28, 1952,

Japanese dignitaries aboard the USS Missouri *in Tokyo Bay to participate in surrender ceremonies, September, 1945.* (National Archives)

when Japan formally resumed its independence. The Japanese Empire was reduced to its home islands, its military capacities were hugely circumscribed, and the divinity accorded the emperor by the huge majority of Japanese citizens was stripped away. Unexpectedly friendly relations between occupiers and occupied led to the general renunciation of militarism under the protection of the United States, which coveted Japan's strategic position in the Cold War defense against communism in Asia.—*John Powell*

Suggested Readings: • Boyle, John. *China and Japan at War, 1937-1945: The Politics of Collaboration*. Stanford, Calif.: Stanford University Press, 1972. • Harries, Meirion, and Susie Harries. *Soldiers of the Sun: The Rise and Fall of the Imperial Japanese Army*. New York: Random House, 1991. • Iriye, Akira. *The Origins of the Second World War in Asia and the Pacific*. New York: Longman, 1987. • Iriye, Akira. *Power and Culture: The Japanese-American War, 1941-1945*. Cambridge, Mass.: Harvard University Press, 1981. • Shillony, Ben-Ami. *Politics and Culture in Wartime Japan*. Oxford, England: Clarendon Press, 1981. • Thorne, Christopher. *The Issue of War: States, Societies, and the Far Eastern Conflict of 1941-1945*. New York: Oxford University Press, 1985.

World War II, The Philippines and: Ever since the United States claimed control of the Philippine archipelago in late 1898, American policymakers had feared a possible Japanese takeover of the islands. When the territory became a commonwealth in 1935, General Douglas MacArthur, retired U.S. Army chief of staff, became military adviser to President Manuel QUEZON. MacArthur developed a defense plan that he said would protect the Philippines for eternity. The Japanese invasion of the islands in December, 1941, proved MacArthur wrong, and the war would have important consequences for future Philippine national development.

Resisting the Japanese Invasion (December, 1941-June, 1942). Not long after the attack on PEARL HARBOR, which occurred December 7, 1941, Japanese forces landed on the northern island group of Batanes. By the end of December, they had also landed forces at Aparri, Vigan, Lingayen Gulf, Lamon Bay, and Legazpi on Luzon, Davao on Mindanao, and Jolo in the Sulu archipelago. Shortly before Christmas, MacArthur had decided to move his combined Filipino and American forces on Luzon to Bataan Peninsula and Corregidor Island to await reinforcements from the United States. Manila was declared an open city, and

Japanese forces occupied it on January 2, 1942.

Because of the debacle at Pearl Harbor, reinforcements would never arrive. Filipino and American forces at Bataan resisted as long as they could until General Edward King ordered the surrender of Luzon forces on April 9. Those troops that had withdrawn to Corregidor held out until, after one month of almost continual shelling, they surrendered on May 6. The following day, General Jonathan Wainwright ordered Filipino and American troops throughout the islands to surrender. Many of those who survived the fighting and shelling on Bataan and Corregidor would not survive the infamous BATAAN DEATH MARCH that followed.

Two months earlier, MacArthur had escaped from Corregidor to Australia, and President Quezon and Vice President Sergio Osmeña soon joined him. MacArthur took command over the Southwest Pacific area, while Quezon and Osmeña proceeded to Washington, D.C., where they set up a Philippine government-in-exile.

Guerrilla Activities (May, 1942-September, 1944). Filipinos soon confronted a harsh and oppressive rule, as the Japanese treated them with disdain. As a result, many Filipinos fled to the mountains and either formed their own guerrilla outfits or joined existing ones. The latter were composed of Filipino troops who had refused to follow Wainwright's surrender order, and American military leaders accepted these outfits as part of the U.S. Army. In reprisal for Filipino guerrilla attacks, the Japanese executed several innocent villagers as part of a policy of controlling the countryside.

Liberation (September, 1944-July, 1945). On July 26, 1944, MacArthur, Admiral Chester Nimitz, and President Franklin D. Roosevelt met in Honolulu to discuss a future strategy for the Pacific theater. Nimitz wanted to bypass the Philippines and attack Taiwan. MacArthur argued for retaking the Philippines first, and Roosevelt agreed.

As a prelude to the invasion, U.S. bombers from Task Force Thirty-eight attacked Japanese airfields in Mindanao, the Visayan Islands, and Luzon throughout September. By mid-September, Leyte Island had replaced Mindanao as the invasion point because Japanese defenses were weaker there. American troops started landing on the east coast of Leyte on October 20, gaining control of Tacloban the following day. Meanwhile, Japanese strategists had decided to concentrate all their naval and air power against the U.S. invasion at Leyte. This led to the Battle of Leyte Gulf on October 23-26, the largest naval battle in history, and a serious defeat for the Japanese. It also saw the first use of *kamikaze* pilots by the Japanese in the Pacific war.

Leyte was secured by mid-December, and the American invasion of Luzon began on January 2, 1945. American forces landed at Lingayen Gulf and made their way toward Manila, copying the Japanese tactic of 1941. The bulk of Japanese forces on Luzon retreated into the northern mountains, but those that remained in Manila put up fierce resistance. They bayoneted, shot, and burned thousands of men, women, and children as the American pincer tightened around the city. Manila was finally secured on March 3.

The liberation of the rest of the Visayan Islands and Mindanao had started at the end of February. Denied the means of maintaining an effective defense, Japanese forces lost more territory and men. On July 5, 1945, MacArthur announced the completion of the Philippines' liberation, except for a few small pockets of resistance. Such resistance would end when the Japanese Empire surrendered on August 15. (One Japanese straggler, however, stayed in the mountains until coming out from hiding in the mid-1970's.)

Consequences. On March 2, 1942, several members of prewar labor and peasant organizations had formed a guerrilla unit to fight the Japanese. They took the name "*Hukbalahap*," and when the war ended, the Huks controlled much of central Luzon. Accused of being communists when the war ended, the Huks fought a guerrilla war with Philippine troops from 1946 to 1954. This war would consume much of the government's resources, complicating economic rehabilitation.

The collaboration issue was another important consequence of the war. Acting on orders from President QUEZON, many Filipino politicians had collaborated with their new Japanese rulers. This was an effort to try to lessen the harshness of the occupation, an effort that failed. After liberation, the collaboration issue would muddle Philippine politics for four years. It would cause division just when the country needed unity to deal with problems left over from the war.

These problems were many. They included financing the rebuilding of damaged property, reestablishing trade relations with the United States and other countries, and providing for future defense. Solutions to these needs and problems included the Philippine Rehabilitation Act (1946), which included the unfortunate "tie-in" provision with the Bell Trade Act (1946).

The "tie-in" provision said that no individual war damage claims of more than five hundred dollars would be settled until Filipinos amended their constitution, giving parity rights to American citizens. Parity meant the right to exploit Philippine natural resources and own public utilities as though Americans were Philippine citizens. Other provisions of the Bell Trade Act gave the United States control over certain sectors of the Philippine economy. Then in March, 1947, Philippine President Manuel Roxas signed the Military Bases Agreement with the United States. Because of the presence of these military bases, and the restricting provisions of the Bell Trade Act, many Filipinos thought they had less than complete independence after July 4, 1946.—*Donald L. Platt*

SUGGESTED READINGS: • Breuer, William B. *Retaking the Philippines: America's Return to Corregidor and Bataan, October 1944-March 1945*. New York: St. Martin's Press, 1986. • Cannon, M. Hamlin. *Leyte: The Return to the Philippines*. Washington, D.C.: Department of the Army, 1954. • Morton, Louis. *The Fall of the Philippines*. Washington, D.C.: Department of the Army, 1953. • Schaller, Michael. *Douglas MacArthur: The Far Eastern General*. New York: Oxford University Press, 1989. • Smith, Robert Ross. *Triumph in the Philippines*. Washington, D.C.: Department of the Army, 1963.

WRA. *See* **War Relocation Authority**

Wu, Chien-shiung (b. May 31, 1912, Shanghai, China): Physicist. Wu attended China's National Central University and the University of California, Berkeley. There she studied under Nobel Prize-winner Ernest Orlando Lawrence and earned her Ph.D. degree in physics in 1940. She taught nuclear physics at Princeton University for a time, then went to Columbia University, working for the Manhattan Project during World War II.

Wu also assisted Chinese American physicists Tsung-dao LEE and Chen Ning YANG, who with her help would make a fundamental theoretical breakthrough by demonstrating the nonconservation of parity. Wu and a team of scientists conducted experiments that confirmed this theory. The success of these discoveries produced Nobel Prizes for Lee and Yang and led to greater understanding of the physics of elementary particles. In 1958 she helped perform experiments that confirmed a theory advanced by American physicists Richard Feynman and Murray Gell-Mann. This collaboration also served to advance nuclear theory significantly.

Wu's contributions brought her many worldwide honors and awards. She became, in 1958, the first female winner of the Research Corporation Award, and she was also the first woman ever awarded an honorary doctorate in physics by Princeton.

Community arts advocate Robin Wu. (Asian Week)

Wu, Robin (b. June 3, 1956, New York, N.Y.): Community arts advocate. A pioneer in promoting Asian American performing arts to mainstream America and numerous overseas Chinese communities, she researched and prepared an exhibition entitled, "The Chinese of America, 1785-1980." She also cochaired a national symposium on Chinese American performance arts held in San Francisco in 1984. She has traveled outside the United States to promote cultural exchanges of various artists between the People's Republic of China and the United States.

Wu Dingfang (July 9, 1842, Singapore—1922): Diplomat. At about age three, Wu moved to Guangdong Province, China, and received a traditional Chinese education. He later attended a British boarding school in Hong Kong, where in 1877 he began practicing law. Five years later he accepted a post at Tianjin in the service of the Chinese government. As a government representative, in 1885 he helped negotiate a treaty between China and France, and later he helped build railroads in China as well. At the conclusion of the

Sino-Japanese War (1894-1895), Wu assisted in the drafting of the treaty with Japan.

From 1897 until 1902 and 1907 to 1909, Wu was based in Washington, D.C., serving as Chinese minister to the United States—the first English-speaking foreign government official in Washington. In this post, he visited numerous U.S. cities in an effort to persuade the American public to end all discriminatory practices against the Chinese. He also composed newspaper articles extolling the good personal qualities of the Chinese people, hoping to bolster the image of the Chinese in America.

Wuhan Revolution (1911): Rising that marked the beginning of the Chinese Revolution of 1911, which spread across China, culminating in the toppling of China's last dynasty, the Qing (1644-1911). Wuhan represents the tri-cities of Wuchang, Hankou, and Hanyang on the Yangtze River in Hubei Province.

The events that came to be known as the Chinese Revolution of 1911 began on October 9, 1911, in Hankou. On that day, the clandestine revolutionary organization at Hankou, together with its membership list, was uncovered by the government authorities. In a preemptive move, the revolutionaries decided to move up their rising, originally scheduled for October 16. On October 10, revolutionary soldiers of the military garrison in Wuchang rebelled and, together with civilian revolutionaries, quickly took over the city.

Three days later, a military government of a new Republic of China had been installed in Wuchang with Li Yuanhong, a brigade commander with no connection to the revolution, as military governor. Hankou and Hanyang had also been taken by the revolutionaries. All of this was accomplished by about five thousand civilian revolutionaries and six thousand to seven thousand sympathetic soldiers in the Wuhan military. From Wuhan, the revolution quickly spread across China. Within a month, fifteen provinces encompassing two-thirds of China declared their independence from the QING DYNASTY.

The Qing authorities put General Yuan Shikai in charge of the suppression of the Wuhan Revolution. On November 1, the government forces succeeded in reclaiming Hankou; the revolutionary army with Huang Hsing as commander-in-chief retreated to Wuchang. It was not until a month later that the two sides agreed to a cease-fire in Wuhan.

On December 4, a provisional government was established in Nanjing by representatives of the newly independent provinces. On December 18, the Qing Dynasty agreed to conduct peace talks with the revolutionaries. On December 25, SUN YAT-SEN arrived in Shanghai from France and was elected provisional president of the new Republic of CHINA. Sun took office on January 1, 1912, only to hold the post for less than two months before he resigned in favor of Yuan Shikai.

X

Xian incident (1936): Kidnapping at Xian of CHIANG KAI-SHEK, head of the Nationalist government of China, in December by Chinese troops from Manchuria. The incident forced Chiang to agree to negotiations between the Guomindang (GMD) and the Chinese Communist Party (CCP) to form a united effort in the war against Japan. ZHOU ENLAI intervened to release Chiang.

Xiedou: Chinese designation for communal feuding. Meaning literally "armed affray" or "fighting with weapons," this term began to appear only in eighteenth century reports of feuds between lineages and surname groups in southeastern China, although similar forms of private redress and organized violence had prevailed in China since antiquity. Frequent reports of *xiedou* outbreaks indicated an escalation of the already intense competition over land and other resources. This strife involved not only destructive battles but also heavy expenses. Adequate funds had to be collected by each feuding community in order to secure weapons, hire mercenaries, and pay for the bribes and litigation necessitated by homicides and other crimes committed during the fighting.

Xiedou conflicts varied in scale. Brawls between discrete communities often attracted dozens of armed combatants on each side. As feuds were perpetuated, however, local alliances sometimes drew neighboring communities into the disputes until hundreds or thousands of fighting men from many districts became engaged in extensive battles. *Xiedou* also grew more deadly when modern weapons were employed. Rifles and even cannon began to replace muskets and sharp-tipped poles during the nineteenth century, while machine guns were reportedly used by some Guangdong villages in the 1920's.

Xiedou strife was prevalent in the coastal provinces of Fujian and Guangdong until at least the 1930's. Taiwan, situated across the Taiwan Strait from Fujian, experienced endemic outbreaks as well until near the end of the nineteenth century. Extensive armed battles developed there between rival Chinese-speaking groups and among communities claiming different southern Fujian and eastern Guangdong origins. These conflicts featured not only numerous combatants but also hoards of hangers-on who participated in the widespread pillaging.

Moreover, the *xiedou* designation was applied to armed disputes between rival communities of overseas Chinese who likewise hailed from Fujian and Guangdong and had congregated abroad in separate speech and native-place groupings. Such strife occurred in both rural and urban areas of North America and Southeast Asia and lasted until around 1930. This included notorious TONG WARS waged in San Francisco and other North American Chinatowns by gangs or brotherhoods representing rival community interests. The overseas Chinese were also affected by *xiedou* outbreaks in China; they were called upon to furnish money, along with weapons and ammunition, for brawls staged by their respective ancestral villages and lineages back home.

Xingzhonghui (Revive China Society; as of 1912, Tongmenghui): China's first political party, founded in 1894. It was established in Hawaii by SUN YAT-SEN and later spread throughout the world. In the United States, it was a direct competitor with the BAO-HUANGHUI (Chinese Empire Reform Association; later the Constitutionalist Party), led by KANG YOUWEI. Partly for this reason, the Revive China Society was not a strong force in America's Chinese communities until 1910-1911, when events in China and internal problems within the Constitutionalist Party gave the Revive China Society (by then called the TONG-MENGHUI) the upper hand. In 1912, after the success of China's republican revolution, the party was merged into the newly established GUOMINDANG (GMD).

The Revive China Society was the first organization that Sun Yat-sen established to work for revolution in China, and it was closely identified with him. Sun's organizing, however, was not always successful. For example, the party's first branch in Hawaii did well in the beginning, but this was because Sun's older brother was an influential resident of Hawaii. After this brother decided against revolution and joined the rival China Reform Association, most other members of Hawaii's Revive China Society branch also went over to the China Reform Association. When Sun traveled to the continental United States in 1895 and again in 1904, he was unable to attract many adherents to the Revive China Society. What little success he did achieve came mostly from the Chinese Christian community.

Starting in 1908, however, internal weaknesses developing in Kang's organization and, in 1910 and 1911, some impressive revolutionary attempts in China helped Sun greatly in the United States. (By this time, the society had been superseded by the Tongmenghui, a coalition of revolutionary groups at least theoretically led by Sun.) The China Reform Association's cadet training school went over to Sun and the Tongmenghui in 1908, and in 1911, when Sun toured the United States on behalf of the Tongmenghui, he raised thousands of dollars and attracted hundreds of new adherents. When the revolution actually broke out in October of 1911, the overwhelming majority of the Chinese communities in the United States backed it and joined the Tongmenghui.

The Revive China Society/Tongmenghui in the United States stood first of all for revolution and loyalty to Sun. In addition, the party espoused the ideals of self-rule (that is, Chinese rather than Manchu rule of China) and, to a lesser extent, social justice, including a measure of individual autonomy and an adequate distribution of wealth. The social ideals had some effect on the structure of American CHINATOWNS, especially in 1910 and 1911.

Y

Yak phab: Korean dessert of sweetened rice cooked with fruits and nuts.

Yamada, Mitsuye Yasutake (b. 1923, Kyushu, Japan): Poet and educator. Born in Japan to Jack and Hide Yasutake, Mitsuye was reared in Seattle, Washington. Her father had served as an interpreter for the U.S. Immigration Service. During World War II, she and her family were incarcerated at the MINIDOKA relocation center in Idaho. She left Minidoka along with her brother in 1944 in order to take courses at the University of Cincinnati. Once they were released from the camp, Mitsuye's parents joined her and her brother in Cincinnati. Mitsuye went on to study at New York University in 1945 before completing a master's degree at the University of Chicago. After the war, she was married to Yoshikazu Yamada, a research chemist; the couple eventually settled in Irvine, California.

In 1976, Yamada published *Camp Notes and Other Poems*, a book of poetry based on her wartime experiences at Minidoka. A professor at Cypress College in Southern California for twenty years, Yamada taught various courses in ethnic literature, children's literature, and creative writing. In 1981, her poetry was featured along with that of Chinese American poet Nellie Wong in the film *Mitsuye and Nellie: Asian American Poets*, broadcast on public television. Yamada was a writer in residence at the Yaddo writer's colony in New York in 1984. Her other publications included *The Webs We Weave* (1986) and *Desert Run: Poems and Stories* (1988). In 1988, she was named to the national board of directors for Amnesty International.

Yamada, Waka (Asaba Waka; Dec. 1, 1879, Kanagawa Prefecture, Japan—Sept. 6, 1956, Japan): Writer and social critic. Forced into prostitution after arriving in Seattle, Yamada eventually returned to Japan, where she became a key player in the Japanese feminist movement.

Asaba began attending elementary school in 1886, earning excellent grades. After four years of schooling, which was all that parents were legally required to give their children, her father, a farmer, withdrew her so that she could work on the farm. At age sixteen, she married a naval shipyard broker. Unhappy in her marriage, and more concerned about her family's failing financial condition, she went to Yokohama determined to find a job. There she was tricked into sailing for America based on the promise of a lucrative job, the details of which were never explained. She left Japan sometime after 1895.

Asaba landed in North America—possibly in Seattle but more likely in Victoria, British Columbia, Canada, where she was seized and taken to Seattle to work in a brothel. Working at the Eastern Hotel, which catered exclusively to white customers, she was known only by her nickname, the "Arabian Oyae." After about six years, she managed to escape to San Francisco with the help of Tachii Nobusaburo, an Issei journalist for a Seattle Japanese newspaper. A short time later, however, Tachii's insistence that she resume prostitution caused her to flee to the city's Presbyterian Mission House for Chinese Girls (later to become the Donaldina CAMERON HOUSE). There Asaba converted to Christianity and served as an interpreter for other Japanese immigrant girls at the house.

As part of her rehabilitation, the staff sent her to a nearby school for English lessons. The school was run by Yamada Kakichi, an Issei teacher. After the two were married in about 1905, the devoted Kakichi began to tutor her in a variety of subjects. They returned to Japan following the San Francisco earthquake and fire of 1906 and moved into a house in the Yotsuya district, a residential section of Tokyo. Operating a private school from the house, he continued to teach foreign languages. Meanwhile, he encouraged his wife to become an earnest student of the women's movement in Japan.

Waka joined the Seitosha, a feminist organization, and from 1914 to 1916 wrote continuously for its journal, *Seito*. Her literary output, consisting of translations and original pieces, was prolific. In the role of social critic, she confronted such issues as abortion and free love, boldly expressing a feminist perspective on such matters. Years after *Seito* ceased publication, she joined the New Women's Association and formed her own magazine, *Women and the New Society*, writing for it while continuing to publish pieces in assorted other newspapers and magazines as well. A collection of her essays appeared in 1920. In 1931 the *Tokyo Asahi Shimbun* made her its advice columnist, a move that boosted the newspaper's circulation.

Kristi Yamaguchi. (AP/Wide World Photos)

Subsequently, Yamada began to embrace the concept of maternalism, ardently defending the extension of special rights and privileges to mothers in Japanese society. Beginning in the late 1930's she chaired the Motherhood Protection League and lobbied the government to enact legislation favorable to mothers. Such a law was passed in 1937. Later she erected a shelter and nursery school for mothers and their children, a project completed in 1939. In late 1937, under the sponsorship of the magazine *Shufunotomo*, Yamada embarked on a lecture tour of the United States. That December she visited First Lady Eleanor Roosevelt in the White House and was received by members of the U.S. Congress.

Yamaguchi: It is located on the southern part of Honshu, the largest island of Japan, and was the region of origin of many Japanese who immigrated to the United States from the 1880's to 1924. Many of these Japanese landed in Hawaii because of a U.S.-Japanese agreement to import laborers. The agreement was arranged by Robert Walker IRWIN, whose friends, the Japanese foreign minister Inoue Kaoru and the importer Masuda Takashi—both from Yamaguchi Prefecture—suggested attracting laborers from that area. About 2,358 square miles in size, it reported a 1991 population of about 1.57 million people.

Yamaguchi, Kristi (b. July 12, 1971, Hayward, Calif.): Figure skater. Despite being born with severely clubbed feet, Yamaguchi, a Yonsei (fourth-generation Japanese American), began skating at age five and competing three years later. She competed successfully in pairs skating (1983-1990) with Rudi Galindo before skating solo exclusively. She earned a measure of worldwide prominence in 1989 by finishing second at the U.S. figure skating championships. She then became a national hero when she won the gold medal in women's figure skating at the 1992 Winter Olympics in Albertville, France. There she defeated Midori Ito of Japan and teammate Nancy Kerrigan to become the first American woman to "strike gold" in the event since Dorothy Hamill in 1976. In addition to the Olympic gold, Yamaguchi also captured the U.S. national and the world championship figure skating titles, all in 1992.

Yamamoto, Hisaye (b. 1921, Redondo Beach, Calif.): Writer. A Nisei, Yamamoto was interned with her parents and siblings during World War II at the Poston relocation center. One of her brothers was killed in Italy while serving with the 442nd Regimental Combat Team. Yamamoto had begun publishing pieces in *Kashu Mainichi*, a Japanese American newspaper in Los Angeles, while she was still a teenager, and she contributed regularly to the camp paper, the *Poston Chronicle*, during the internment.

After the war she worked for several years as a journalist and published several highly regarded essays and stories. In 1950 she received a John Hay Whitney Foundation Opportunity Fellowship. Her story "Yoneko's Earthquake" was included in *Best American Short Stories, 1952*. From 1953 to 1955 she was a volunteer with Dorothy Day's Catholic Worker movement. Married to Anthony DeSoto, she has five children.

A collection of Yamamoto's stories, *"Seventeen Syllables" and Other Stories*, was published in 1988. The title story of that volume, first published in 1949, and the story "Yoneko's Earthquake" were adapted by Emiko Omori for a 1991 American Playhouse production (PBS), *Hot Summer Winds*. In 1986 Yamamoto

Kristi Yamaguchi takes first place in the Ladies' Singles Original Program competition in the 1992 U.S. Figure Skating Championships. (AP/Wide World Photos)

Architect Minoru Yamasaki. (AP/Wide World Photos)

received an American Book Award for Lifetime Achievement from the Before Columbus Foundation.

Yamasaki, Minoru (Dec., 1912, Seattle, Wash.—Feb. 6, 1986, Detroit, Mich.): Architect. He was chief designer of the World Trade Center's twin towers in New York, the world's two tallest buildings at the time of their construction. He gained fame as head of his own firm, producing well in excess of 250 residential, commercial, and industrial buildings. Some of Yamasaki's notable structures include the St. Louis Airport Terminal (completed in 1956), the Federal Science Pavilion at the World's Fair in Seattle (1962), the Woodrow Wilson School of Public and International Affairs at Princeton University (1965), and the Century Plaza Hotel (1966) and the Century Plaza Towers (1975), both in Los Angeles. In 1962 the JAPANESE AMERICAN CITIZENS LEAGUE (JACL) honored him as its Nisei of the Biennium for "artfully blending" Japanese art and culture with the architecture of the West.

Yamashita, Karen Tei (b. 1951): Writer. Her writings explore environmental, cultural, and political issues from a Japanese Brazilian perspective. Her first published book, *Through the Arc of the Rainforest* (1990), earned for her widespread recognition and a place in the field of Asian American literature. Styled after a Brazilian soap opera, the book is a complex black comedy decrying environmental destruction. She has also written *Brazil-Maru* (1992), a novel that portrays the experience of the Japanese in Brazil.

Yamashita, Soen (b. 1898, Yasuura, Hiroshima Prefecture, Japan): Journalist. Yamashita came to the United States in 1914 and was enrolled at the Iolani School of Honolulu. Later he was a reporter for the *Nippu Jiji*, a Hawaii Japanese newspaper, becoming its Japan correspondent in 1933. While stationed in Japan, he also worked on behalf of Nisei living there and later, under the direction of Japan's Foreign Ministry, oversaw an umbrella association of Nisei organizations in Japan. In 1942 he published a book supporting Japan's territorial claim to the Hawaiian Islands and its colonization of them as a logical step in the formation of a new order uniting the nations of East Asia.

Yamataya v. Fisher (1903): U.S. Supreme Court ruling that denied entrance into the United States to a Japanese immigrant deemed to be a pauper and therefore one likely to become a public charge in America. The U.S. Congress had passed a law in March, 1891,

permitting exclusion of such individuals in the interest of public security. Yamataya Kaoru arrived in Seattle, Washington, in 1901, but she was denied entry by port inspector Thomas Fisher based on the 1891 statute. Before authorities could deport her, however, she filed for a writ of habeus corpus; after a lower court denied her petition, she appealed to the Supreme Court, which affirmed the dismissal. The opinion found that her arrest for deportation had been justifiable under law but warned that in compliance with the requirements of due process every alien must first be accorded a proper hearing before being deported.

Yamato Colony: Japanese farming community founded in the early twentieth century. The Yamato Colony was the result of a series of corporate land investment purchases initiated by Kyutaro Abiko, a San Francisco newspaper publisher and businessman. It was his dream to establish a Japanese Christian colony in California. The first plot of barren desert land was purchased in Livingston in 1906 by the Japanese American Industrial Corporation. The first settlers were believed to be Nobuchika Minabe and Tajiro Kishi. By 1910 forty-six Japanese had come to the community to establish farms and families.

By 1907 the land purchases had spread into Cressey, the neighboring farming community. In 1914 the farmers of the community organized under the Livingston Cooperative Society with Shichiro Noda as the first manager. This organization served as the first Japanese farmers' cooperative for this community.

In 1918 the Livingston Japanese Church of Christ was organized. The church site was the center of all community activities including sporting events and Japanese films. In 1929 the church joined the Methodist Conference, changing its name to the Livingston Japanese Methodist Church.

The original cash crops were sweet potatoes, which provided income until the newly planted grapes and other fruit orchards began to produce.

In 1927 the farmers' cooperative divided into the Livingston Fruit Exchange and the Livingston Fruit Growers Association.

Through the growth of families the 1940 population of the Yamato Colony was approximately three hundred, with about fifty-five families.

World War II and the removal of the Japanese disrupted the community as many families lost their land and did not return. The postwar years brought about changes as the young adults left farming to find their future in the cities or chose to work in nonfarming jobs. The original population of Issei had retired and/or died. New families had joined the community.

In 1957 the Livingston Fruit Exchange and the Livingston Fruit Growers merged under one name—the Livingston Farmers Association.

The Grace Methodist Church became integrated with the First Methodist Church of Livingston in 1969 to form the Livingston United Methodist Church at the Japanese church site.

In the Yamato Colony there still remains a core of familiar names and third-generation families engaged in farming. Grapes are no longer the dominating crop as the cost of labor has forced farmers to convert to less labor-intensive crops.

Community activities now include the broad spectrum of a diverse Japanese American community.

Yamauchi, Wakako (Wakako Nakamura; b. Oct. 25, 1924, Westmoreland, Calif.): Playwright and short-story writer. Wakako Nakamura was born in California's Imperial Valley, the Nisei daughter of a farmer. During World War II, she and her family were incarcerated at the Poston relocation center in western Arizona. There she worked as a staff artist for the camp newspaper and became good friends with Nisei writer Hisaye YAMAMOTO.

Recipient of three Rockefeller Foundation grants and an American Theatre Critics Award for Outstanding Playwriting, Yamauchi is noted for her short story "And the Soul Shall Dance." The work depicts the struggles faced by Issei farmers in California. After reading the story, MAKO, formerly artistic director of Los Angeles' EAST WEST PLAYERS, urged her to adapt the piece as a full-length drama. Premiering in 1977 at East West Players, with Mako directing, *And the Soul Shall Dance* became a classic of the Asian American stage. It was honored as the best new play of that year by the Los Angeles Critics Circle. Later it was developed for public television. The first Asian American play to dramatize the Asian American search for cultural identity, it has been called the most honored and celebrated work in Asian American theater history.

Yamauchi's subsequent dramatic works, including *The Music Lessons* (1980), *12-1-A* (1982), *The Memento* (1984), *The Chairman's Wife* (1990), and *Not a Through Street* (1991), were produced across the United States at numerous theaters and universities, such as East West Players, Kumu Kahua, Yale Repertory Theatre Winterfest, Pan Asian Repertory Theatre, New York Public Theatre, and Asian Exclusion Act. Her essays and short stories have appeared in *Southwest Review*, RAFU SHIMPO, *Christian Science Monitor*, AMERASIA JOURNAL, and numerous anthologies.

Yan, Martin (b. 1949, Guangzhou, China): Chef, television personality, and writer. Host of the syndicated television program *Yan Can Cook*, he began his formal apprenticeship in Hong Kong, continuing his training in Canada and the United States. He has also written columns and published books, including *The Yan Can Cook Book* (1981), *The Joy of Wokking: A Chinese Cookbook* (1983), *Martin Yan: The Chinese Chef* (1985), *A Wok for All Seasons* (1988), *Everybody's Wokking* (1991), and *The Well-Seasoned Wok* (1993).

Martin Yan shops in Chinatown, San Francisco. (Asian Week)

Yan Wo Company: Association formed in 1852 in San Francisco to help newly arrived immigrants find housing and employment, settle member disputes, and represent the general interests of its members. This "fifth district" association later joined the other five district associations to form the Chung Wah Hui Guan in 1882, which was incorporated in 1901 as the Chinese Consolidated Benevolent Association, better known as the Chinese Six Companies.

Yanagisako, Sylvia (b. July 11, 1945, Honolulu, Territory of Hawaii): Scholar. She began teaching anthropology in 1975 and was director of the Feminist Studies Program at Stanford University from 1988 to 1991. She obtained her Ph.D. degree in anthropology from the University of Washington in 1975 and is best known for her study of kinship among Japanese Americans. In addition to articles in scholarly journals, she has authored the books *Transforming the Past: Kinship and Tradition Among Japanese Americans* (1985) and *Towards a Unified Analysis of Gender and Kinship* (1987, coedited with Jane F. Collier).

Yanehiro, Jan (b. Jan. 4, 1948, Honolulu, Territory of Hawaii): Broadcast journalist. As cohost of *Evening Magazine* (1976-1990), she became the first Asian American to host a magazine-style entertainment television show at KPIX, the Columbia Broadcasting System (CBS) affiliate in San Francisco, California. The winner of numerous Emmy awards for on-air talent and entertainment programming, she is a member of the ASIAN AMERICAN JOURNALISTS ASSOCIATION (AAJA) and the San Francisco chapter of the JAPANESE AMERICAN CITIZENS LEAGUE (JACL).

Yang, Chen Ning (b. Sept. 22, 1922, Hefei, Anhui Province, China): Physicist. The eldest of five children, Yang was brought up in the atmosphere of Quinghua University, outside Beijing, where his father was an eminent mathematician. Yang received his college education at the National Southwest Associated University of Kunming, Yunnan Province, where he met Tsung-Dao Lee. In 1944, he received his master of science degree from Qinghua University. On a Qinghua fellowship Yang entered the University of Chicago in 1946 to study under Enrico Fermi. Yang completed his Ph.D. degree in less than two years.

Yang adopted "Franklin" as his first name out of admiration for American statesman, scientist, and philosopher, Benjamin Franklin. Known to his friends as "Frank," Yang married Chih-Li Tu in 1950, who had been a former student of his in China but who was now studying at Princeton. They have two sons and a daughter. Yang went on to the Institute of Advanced Study in Princeton, where in 1955 he became one of

President Reagan presents National Science Medal to Chen Ning Yang. (Asian Week)

the very small number of professors on the institute's permanent staff. He became a U.S. citizen in 1964.

Yang shared the 1957 Nobel Prize in Physics with Tsung-Dao Lee for their penetrating investigations of the parity laws, which disproved a principle that had been accepted for three decades and which led to revolutionary discoveries regarding subatomic particles.

In addition to the Nobel Prize, Yang received numerous other honors and awards, including the Albert Einstein Commemorative Award (1957), Rumford Prize (1980), National Medal of Science (1986), and Liberty Award (1986).

Yang received honorary doctorates from Princeton University (1958), Polytechnic Institute of Brooklyn (1965), University of Wroclaw (1974), University of Durham, England (1979), Fudan University, People's Republic of China (1984), and Eidg Technische Hochschule, Switzerland (1987). He is honorary professor at numerous universities in China and distinguished professor-at-large at the Chinese University of Hong Kong.

In 1966 Yang became Albert Einstein Professor of Physics and director of the Institute of Theoretical Physics at the State University of New York at Stony Brook. Yang has visited China frequently since 1971, helping to promote mutual understanding and friendship between his native country and the United States.

Yang, Linda Tsao (b. Sept. 5, 1926, Shanghai, China): Economist. She was the first Asian American to serve on the Board of Administration of the California Public Employees Retirement System (1977-1980) and the first minority and woman to serve as California Sav-

Economist Linda Yang. (San Francisco Chronicle)

ings and Loan commissioner (1980-1982). A regular contributor to the *Hong Kong Economic Journal*, she was a board member of California Blue Cross and a three-time delegate to the Democratic National Convention (1984, 1988, and 1992).

Yano, Rodney J. T. (1943, Kona, Territory of Hawaii—1969): Vietnam War hero. Yano was one of only four Japanese Americans ever awarded the Congressional Medal of Honor. A sergeant attached to the Air Cavalry Troop, he was on a helicopter mission when a grenade detonated aboard ship. Despite suffering severe wounds, he bravely attempted to jettison the rest of the explosives from the ship before they could explode. He later died of his injuries.

Yappie: Abbreviation for "young Asian professional," in imitation of the term "yuppie," which stands for "young urban professional."

Yashima, Taro (Iwamatsu Jun Atsushi; b. Sept. 21, 1908, Kagoshima, Japan): Writer, artist, and illustrator. Taro Yashima—the pen name under which he is known—is an internationally acclaimed author and illustrator of children's books. Among his many books for children are *Crow Boy* (1955), *Umbrella* (1958), *The Golden Footprints* (1960), *Youngest One* (1962), and *Seashore Story* (1967). Another side of his work is not as well known: his powerful autobiographical books *The New Sun* (1943) and *Horizon Is Calling* (1947) anticipated by several decades the vogue for serious use of a "picture book" or comic book format. Yashima's wife, Mitsu Yashima, was a well-respected artist in her own right; their son is the distinguished actor and theater director, Mako, while their daughter, Momo, is an actor as well.

Yasui, Minoru (Oct. 19, 1916, Hood River, Oreg.—Nov. 14, 1986, Denver, Colo.): Curfew order violator. Yasui was not an ideal candidate to test the World War II (1939-1945) curfew order as it applied to Japanese Americans. He had worked at the Japanese consulate in Chicago before the bombing of Pearl Harbor. Following the attack his father was arrested based on frivolous evidence of aiding Japan in the war effort. For Yasui, a man who considered himself a patriotic American citizen, the circumstances were not favorable. He attempted to enlist in the Army but was rejected on racial grounds. To the United States, the country of his birth and loyalty, he was considered an "enemy alien."

Minoru Yasui tested the curfew law for Japanese Americans during World War II. (Asian Week)

Yasui's training as a lawyer, his father's arrest, and his rejection by the Army convinced him on March 28, 1942, to challenge the curfew order that applied to everyone of Japanese ancestry. At 11:00 P.M. in the city of Portland, Oregon, he purposely broke the curfew law, hoping to be arrested. He tried to get a policeman to detain him but was told to go home before he got into trouble. Finally he went to a police station and was granted his request.

Yasui's trial began on June 12, 1942. At issue was the curfew order; however, the WAR RELOCATION AUTHORITY (WRA) viewed this case as instrumental in successfully defending the rationale for imprisoning Japanese Americans. On November 16, 1942, after hearing arguments from the defense and the prosecution, the judge issued his opinion. In an unorthodox ruling he decided that the curfew order, as it applied to American citizens, was unconstitutional. He also found, however, that Yasui had forfeited his U.S. citizenship by working at the Japanese consulate. For this reason the judge ruled that Yasui (as a non-U.S. citizen) was guilty of violating the curfew order. Two days later the court sentenced Yasui to one year in prison and a fine of $5,000. An appeal was immediately filed.

On February 19, 1943, the one-year anniversary of EXECUTIVE ORDER 9066, Yasui joined fellow resisters Fred T. KOREMATSU and Gordon K. HIRABAYASHI at the court of appeals. Everyone argued their cases and then prepared for an appeal to the Supreme Court. The U.S. government, eager for the cases to be heard before an all but certain defeat for the government in the Mitsuye ENDO case, urged the appeals court to use a procedure called "certification" to accelerate the process. In essence the appeals court would ask the Supreme Court to rule on Yasui's citizenship status.

On June 21, 1943, the Supreme Court reversed the lower court ruling that the curfew order was unconstitutional in its application to American citizens and also found that the trial judge had wrongly decided that Yasui forfeited his citizenship by working at the Japanese consulate. The case was returned to the trial court for resentencing with a strong hint that a one-year penalty was too harsh. More than forty years later, in 1984, Yasui's conviction was vacated by the U.S. district court upon a motion by the government.

Yatabe, Thomas T. (1897, San Francisco, Calif.—?): Community leader and administrator. Yatabe was best known as one of the founders of the JAPANESE AMERICAN CITIZENS LEAGUE (JACL). He grew up in San Francisco. Since his family lived outside the Japanese

Thomas T. Yatabe was one of the founders of the Japanese American Citizens League. (Pacific Citizen)

American community, he was the only Asian child at his school. When he was eight years old, Yatabe was forced to leave because of the San Francisco Board of Education's decision to segregate its schools. While a compromise solution was being negotiated in Washington, D.C., Yatabe and other students of Japanese ancestry attended a private school organized by their Issei parents. Five months later, the issue was resolved and Yatabe was allowed to reenter public school. Though he was young, the experience with segregation had a profound effect on his life.

In 1918, fresh out of dental school, Yatabe and a group of other white-collar Nisei began to meet informally to discuss issues concerning Japanese Americans. By the fall of 1919, they were holding formal meetings at the San Francisco Japanese Young Men's Christian Association (YMCA) as the American Loyalty League (ALL). By 1923 the organization had disbanded as a result of the small pool of adult-aged Nisei, the rigors of surviving everyday life, and Yatabe's departure to Fresno, California. Once in Fresno, Yatabe opened up his dental practice and once again organized the ALL. Naturally, Yatabe was the group's first president. With the help of other Nisei, the group with-stood many lean years in the 1920's and eventually managed to grow to fifteen chapters throughout California (though most of them were dormant). In 1930 Yatabe and the league joined other like-minded Nisei organizations to form the JACL. Four years later he became the first elected president of the organization.

During World War II Yatabe was interned at the Jerome concentration camp in Arkansas. While in camp, he continued his dental practice as well as his leadership role in the JACL. In 1943 he resettled in Chicago, Illinois, and founded a JACL chapter.

Yau, John (b. 1950, Lynn, Mass.): Poet and art critic. Yau has combined a productive career as a poet with a career in the visual arts, writing criticism and curating; in addition, he has taught at the Pratt Institute, the University of California, Berkeley, and other institutions. He has frequently collaborated with visual artists on books and other projects.

Yau received a bachelor's degree from Bard College and an M.F.A. from Brooklyn College. His first book of poetry, *Crossing Canal Street*, was published in 1976. Yau is often described as an offshoot of John Ashbery and the New York School. While Yau studied under Ashbery, and while it is true that his poetry, like Ashbery's, often seems to elude paraphraseable meaning, there are other currents in his work; many of his poems and prose poems are darker and less distanced by irony than Ashbery's customary performances. Often, as in the ongoing sequence "Genghis Chan: Private Eye," Yau appropriates images from familiar narratives for subversive use in his surreal fragments.

Among Yau's many later volumes of poetry are *Corpse and Mirror* (1983), selected by Ashbery for the National Poetry Series, *Radiant Silhouette: New and Selected Work 1974-1988* (1989), and *Edificio Sayonara* (1993). His art criticism includes *In the Realm of Appearances: The Art of Andy Warhol* (1993) and *A. R. Penck* (1993), the first full-length study of the contemporary German artist, who fuses the iconography of primitive art with images from the contemporary world. Yau has received numerous fellowships and awards, including the Academy of American Poets' Lavan Award for Younger Poets (1988) and the General Electric Foundation Award for Younger Writers (1988).

Yee Fow: Chinese name for the city of Sacramento, California. The phrase also means "second city," second in importance to San Francisco, commonly known as Dai Fow (or "first city"). Early nineteenth century Chinese settlers went to the second city to work on farms and in the railroad, manufacturing, and liquor industries. They also opened the Overseas Chinese School in 1908 and built the Confucius Church, a cultural and religious landmark.

Yellow peril: English translation of a term attributed to German Kaiser William II, who forewarned of a European invasion from Asia during the 1890's. Even before the specific term was coined, however, a xenophobic fear of Asia already existed in the United States and had turned into hostility toward Chinese immigrants. By 1905 "yellow peril" had become a familiar phrase in the United States primarily in reference to a threat from Japan and Japanese immigrants.

The five major categories of threat from yellow peril to Caucasian European-Americans are perceived to be large population increases, un-American activities, miscegenation, economic competition, and military invasion.

As the population of Asian immigrants increased in America, racial tolerance changed to antagonism, and the notion of a yellow peril emerged. The increase in Chinese immigrants during the 1870's led to the enactment of the CHINESE EXCLUSION ACT OF 1882. Likewise the increase in Japanese immigration during the first decade of the twentieth century led to the GENTLEMEN'S AGREEMENT (1907-1908), which restricted new immigration of Japanese laborers.

Racial prejudice towards Asian immigrants fostered an intolerance of Asian culture and a presumption of the inability of the Asian immigrant to assimilate into American culture. The Asian ways were criticized as heathen. The argument suggested that Asian immigrants could no more change their values and behavior than they could their physical features.

Antimiscegenation laws prohibiting the marriage of whites to nonwhites were aimed at preventing interracial relationships so as to protect the purity of the white race. In such laws, Chinese and Japanese were categorized as Mongolian while Filipinos were separately described as Malay.

Early Asian American workers were viewed as economic competitors by white laborers and labor organizations. First the Chinese and then the Japanese and other Asian immigrants were considered a menace for their willingness to work longer hours for lower wages. At the same time accounts of the rapid industrialization of Asian countries in the early twentieth century were distorted to give the false image of Asia as a worldwide economic threat.

The 1905 defeat of the Russian navy by Japan gave alarmists concern that Japan would try to attack America. American writer Homer Lea wrote in 1909 of a war with Japan, while in 1908 U.S. representative Richmond Hobson warned of a race war. The *San Francisco Examiner* in 1906 ran an article suggesting that Japanese immigrants were actually soldiers in disguise.

Such fears, reinforced by stereotypes in literature, the newly born film industry, and other cultural media and fueled by anti-Asian agitation, contributed to the discriminatory treatment of Asian Americans that persisted even into the post-World War II era.

Yeong Wo Company: Association formed in 1852 in San Francisco to help newly arrived immigrants from China's Heungshan area find housing and employment, settle member disputes, and represent the general interests of its members. This "fourth district" association later joined the other five district associations to form the Chung Wah Hui Guan in 1882, which was incorporated in 1901 as the Chinese Consolidated Benevolent Association, better known as the Chinese Six Companies.

Yep, Laurence (b. June 14, 1948, San Francisco, Calif.): Novelist. Yep is the most underrated of all the major contemporary Asian American writers. Since the early 1970's, he has written more than thirty novels and plays dealing with core issues facing Asian America, yet because most of his work is directed toward young adults, it has seldom been taken seriously.

Yep grew up in an African American neighborhood near San Francisco's Chinatown. He describes his early years in his autobiography, *The Lost Garden* (1991). He received a Ph.D. degree in Faulkner studies and at the same time began publishing his first stories in science fiction. His interest in this genre, he later realized, was attributable in part to his identification with the alien or outsider and to his affinity for the sense of wonder that children possess.

In 1975, Yep published the award-winning *Dragonwings*, the book for which he is best known. Set in San Francisco in the first decade of the twentieth century, the novel concerns a newly arrived boy and his father, who wants to build and fly an airplane. The climactic scene of the flight suggests the power of the imagination and celebrates the freedom of the individual. Also memorable is the earlier scene in which the leader of their company or family association breaks into a railroad work song to inspire the members of the company to help haul the airplane up the mountain. Yep adapted

Laurence Yep. (K. Yep)

this novel into a play, which has toured the United States with the Berkeley Repertory Theatre.

In addition to novels about Mark Twain and Twain's fictional characters, Yep produced a fantasy trilogy. The series, which begins with *Dragons of the Lost Sea* (1982), is based on Chinese myths and centers on a dragon princess who, with a small band of outcasts, embarks on a quest for revenge. Other Yep novels focus on young Chinese Americans dealing with their unique identities: the popular *Child of the Owl* (1977) and *Sea Glass* (1979), perhaps Yep's finest work. He has retold traditional Chinese folktales in two collections, *Rainbow People* (1989) and *Tongues of Jade* (1991), taken from material gathered from Chinese Americans in the 1930's as part of a Works Progress Administration (WPA) project. Yep has also edited the anthology *American Dragons: Twenty-Five Asian American Voices* (1993).

Yep's most ambitious work is a projected series of five historical novels, the first two of which are *Serpent's Children* (1984) and *Mountain Light* (1985). This *Roots*-like saga traces succeeding generations of Chinese American pioneers, from farmers in south China after the Opium Wars to gold prospectors on their transpacific journeys to railroad crews tunneling through the Sierras. These books eventually link up with characters featured in *Dragonwings*, creating Yep's own rich Yoknapatawpha.

Yep's novels feature a variety of well-drawn protagonists. Feisty young women are profiled in *Seademons* (1977) and *Serpent's Children*. *Dragon Cauldron* (1991) depicts a monkey wizard reminiscent of the hero of the Ming Dynasty classic *Xiyou ji* (1592; *The Journey to the West*, 1977-1983). The central character of *Sea Glass* is an unathletic, overweight child. Many of the situations in Yep's books are somber, dealing with cultural conflicts, prejudice, and—notably in the pioneers' saga—violence and death. At the heart of the stories are the internal struggles of Yep's protagonists as they seek their places within their families and their communities. To an increasingly multicultural America, Yep offers the hard message of *Sea Glass*: that a clear-eyed but often grudging respect for another's differences is the true basis for any relationship.

Yi Dynasty (1392-1910): The line of hereditary rulers in the CHOSON Kingdom founded by Yi Song-gye in 1392. The Yi Dynasty, which consisted of twenty-seven kings, ruled the kingdom for 518 years, until the Japanese annexation of Korea in 1910.

Incensed by the widely prevailing misconducts and worldliness of the Buddhist temple, Yi Song-gye adopted an oppressive policy toward Buddhism. Consequently Buddhism ceased to be the state religion of the Yi Dynasty. The Yi Dynasty named Confucianism as its state creed and eventually created an orthodox Confucian state in Asia. The Korean value system and social practices were restructured along Confucian principles. In order to promote Confucian learning and to train Confucian-oriented officials, Yi Song-gye established a college and five municipal schools in Seoul. He then recruited his officials from among the graduates of these schools through the civil service examination system. The written language in schools and government continued to be Chinese throughout the Yi Dynasty period, although HANGUL (the Korean phonetic alphabet) was invented in 1443.

The Yi Dynasty adopted the Chinese governmental structure: a state council, a royal secretariat, six ministries, and the board of censors. The country was divided into eight provinces, which were in turn subdivided into prefectures, counties, and districts. Social classes in the Yi Kingdom consisted of hereditary ruling families known as the *yangban*, or "the two groups," which monopolized both the civil and the military branches of the bureaucracy; common people, known as *yangmin* (good people), predominantly peasants who paid

taxes and performed unpaid labor; and *chonmin* (base people), private or government slaves who worked in mines, factories, or other industries.

In foreign relations the Yi Dynasty established a suzerain-tributary relationship with China, in which the Yi pledged its loyalty to China while China claimed suzerainty over the Choson Kingdom. This Sino-Korean relationship continued to exist for five centuries, until 1895.

In 1592 Japan launched a full-scale invasion of Korea but was eventually turned back. Another Japanese invasion in 1597 was ultimately repelled, but as the Japanese troops withdrew from Korea, they left behind a country devastated by war.

From the mid-seventeenth century onward, Europeans began to arrive in Korea. There they launched futile attempts to "open" up the country. The Korean rulers were opposed to any kind of contact with the Western world, primarily because Catholicism was incompatible with Confucianism. The Yi rulers were strongly opposed to Catholic rejection of ancestral worship as idolatry. Consequently the government began to persecute Christians.

Korea was able to maintain its policy of isolationism until the later nineteenth century. Beginning with the completion of a treaty with Japan in 1876, Korea's doors to the Western powers were ajar for the first time. As a result Korea soon became the focus of economic and other competition between the more powerful nations of the world. Japanese influence, in particular, intensified considerably, especially after Japanese victories over China (the Sino-Japanese War of 1894-1895) and Russia (the Russo-Japanese War of 1904-1905). Japan formally annexed Korea in 1910, bringing the Yi Dynasty to a close. (See CHOSON.)

Yi Tong-hwi (1873, Hamgyong Province, Korea—1935, near Vladivostok, Soviet Union): Political leader and revolutionary. He urged armed conflict as the means to defeat the Japanese colonialist policies. Japan had disbanded the Korean army in 1907. In 1909, however, he attempted, without success, to stage an armed insurrection. He founded the first pro-Bolshevik Korean political party, the Han in Sahoedang (Korean People's Socialist Party) in 1918. It was later renamed the Koryo Kongsandang (Korean Communist Party). He also held important offices in the Korean provisional government (1919-1945).

Yi Wan-yong (1858—1926): Government official. He was born to a family of *yangban*, the scholar-official ruling class of traditional Korea. During the later years of the YI DYNASTY (1392-1910), he served the Korean government in a variety of posts. He was appointed ambassador to the United States in 1888, becoming foreign minister in 1896. With political inclinations that were strongly pro-Japan, he was a signatory to the Protectorate Treaty of 1905. In 1907 he became prime minister. Later he helped negotiate the TREATY OF ANNEXATION of 1910.

Yick Wo v. Hopkins (1886): U.S. Supreme Court ruling that no state may use its police powers to violate the equal protection guarantees of the Constitution's Fourteenth Amendment. That amendment, moreover, protects all persons, whether citizens or aliens.

In July, 1880, the San Francisco Board of Supervisors passed an ordinance requiring a license to operate a laundry in a wooden building. Ostensibly for the purpose of preventing fires, it was in fact aimed at driving the Chinese out of the laundry business and ultimately out of California and the United States. The board granted licenses to 79 whites and 1 Chinese; 200 other applications by persons of Chinese lineage were denied. Yick Wo, a Chinese resident alien and a laundryman for more than twenty years, had his application rejected. He defied the ordinance and, along with approximately 150 other Chinese, was arrested and convicted for violating the licensing law.

Yick Wo's case was appealed from the California tribunals to the Supreme Court. In a unanimous opinion, written by Justice Stanley Matthews, the Court struck down the San Francisco law as a violation of the equal protection clause of the Fourteenth Amendment to the Constitution.

To Matthews it was clear that the ordinance, despite its declared intent, was being administered in such a manner as to reveal an oppressive animus against Chinese aliens. The Fourteenth Amendment, he pointed out, protected not only American citizens but also "persons . . . without regard to any differences of race, of color, or of nationality." If the San Francisco ordinance, though "fair on its face, and impartial in appearance," was being enforced "with an evil eye and an unequal hand," then it offended the guaranties of the Constitution. There was no reason given for the denial of the licenses; the ordinance gave complete and unbridled discretion to the board to grant or reject license applications. "The conclusion," Matthews stated, "cannot be resisted that no reason for it exists except hostility to the race and nationality to which the petitioners belong."

The Court's decision in *Yick Wo* is significant because it extended the Constitution's equal protection clause, which was originally intended to secure the civil rights of African Americans, to all persons, citizens and aliens alike and irrespective of race.

Yip, Wai-lim (Yeh Wei-lien; b. June 20, 1937, Guangdong Province, China): Poet, translator, and scholar. One of the leading contemporary Chinese poets of Taiwan, Yip has also enjoyed a long and productive career as a translator and literary scholar in the United States. A professor of Chinese and comparative literature at the University of California, San Diego, where he has been since 1967, he is the author of more than thirty books in Chinese and English, including *Ezra Pound's "Cathay"* (1969), *Chinese Poetry: Major Modes and Genres* (1976), and *Diffusion of Distances: Dialogues Between Chinese and Western Poetics* (1993).

Yobiyose jidai: Japanese phrase referring to the years—generally between 1906 and 1924—during which Japanese immigration took place under U.S. laws allowing the reunification of Japanese families. *Yobiyose* refers to Japanese immigrants who came to the United States as children during this period, rejoining family members who had immigrated earlier. While technically Issei, this group shared many experiences with the Nisei.

Yoga: One of the six systems of classical Hindu philosophy. The term "yoga" is a Sanskrit word meaning "union" or "harnessing." The Yoga practitioner (*yogi*) attempts to harness or control the body to such an extent as to allow the mind freedom to unite with the Universal Soul, *Brahman*, the yogi's ultimate goal.

The origin of Yoga is unclear, although it possibly had its precursor in the Indus Valley civilization in northwest India, which flourished from about 2500 B.C.E. to 1700 B.C.E. In the *Vedas*, the classical religious texts of Hinduism written between 1800 B.C.E. and 1100 B.C.E., mention is made of certain ecstatics who are most likely the predecessors of the yogi.

Yoga was organized into a system of philosophy by Patanjali, an Indian sage who composed the *Yoga-sutra* in the second century B.C.E. Using Samkhya philosophy as his foundation, Patanjali systemically described the theory of Yoga and formalized its techniques and methods as they are practiced today.

The Yoga path to salvation, or union with Brahman, consists of eight stages of moral, physical, and meditational practices. The first two stages are ethical practices of restraint and behavior that prepare the yogi for further asceticism. The third and fourth stages are concerned with controlling the body and breath by assuming static postures and stabilizing the rhythm of breath. In the fifth stage, the yogi withdraws attention from the outward world of sense objects. In the sixth, the yogi focuses attention on only one object and does not allow other distractions to enter the mind. The seventh stage directs the yogi to have an uninterrupted state of pure meditation on an object, until the sense of "self" or "ego" is dissolved. When this happens, the yogi has entered the eighth stage of *samadhi*, in which distinctions between the yogi and the object of meditation have disappeared and only oneness remains. Once the yogi has attained *samadhi*, union with Brahman has been achieved.

Instruction in Yoga, once confined to India, arrived in the West in the early twentieth century. Most Yoga classes taught in the West, however, place emphasis on the physical benefits of the practice, with little or no attention given to its spiritual aspects.

Yoneda, Karl Goso (b. 1906, Calif.): Journalist, educator, and labor activist. Born in Southern California, Karl Yoneda moved to Japan with his family in 1917. A voracious reader who was attracted to Marxism as a teenager, Yoneda left Japan for China in order to seek out a Russian author whose works he admired. Faced with the prospect of conscription into the Japanese army if he returned to Japan, Yoneda chose to return to the United States instead. After settling in California, he joined the Communist Party and became active in the local labor movement. During the 1930's, Yoneda worked as editor of *Rodo Shimbun*, a Japanese-language newspaper known for its leftist ideological stance. He also worked as a labor organizer in California and in Alaska. In 1933, he was married to Elaine Black, a Caucasian woman who was a fellow communist.

After the Japanese attack on Pearl Harbor in 1941, Yoneda was incarcerated at the relocation center in MANZANAR, California; although she was not of Japanese descent, his wife joined him and their young son at the camp. During the war, Yoneda and other Japanese Americans were stripped of their membership in the American Communist Party. Undeterred, Yoneda worked hard to improve conditions at Manzanar, cooperating with members of the JAPANESE AMERICAN CITIZENS LEAGUE (JACL) as well as the camp's administrators. Yoneda believed that such cooperation was necessary in order to achieve victory against fascism abroad; once that victory was secure, there would

be time to seek redress for injustices suffered by Japanese Americans. Facing threats against his life because of his stance, Yoneda was removed from the camp and later served as a volunteer intelligence officer and translator with U.S. Army forces in the Pacific theater.

After the war, Yoneda rejoined the American Communist Party and resumed his efforts as a labor activist, this time working with the International Longshoreman's and Warehouseman's Union. As an active participant in the redress movement during the 1970's and 1980's, Yoneda received greater attention within the Japanese American community for his wartime efforts. Yoneda also worked as a teacher and lecturer on the subject of Asian American studies. His autobiography, *Ganbatte: Sixty-Year Struggle of a Kibei Worker*, was published by the Asian American Studies Center at the University of California, Los Angeles, in 1983.

Yonsei: Fourth-generation Americans of Japanese ancestry. This terminology continues a tradition among Japanese immigrants to North America of identifying each generation of persons of Japanese ancestry. The Yonsei are American-born children of the Sansei, third-generation Japanese Americans. Because immigration to Hawaii occurred much earlier than to the mainland United States, Yonsei are more frequently found there. In some Japanese American communities, such as in Honolulu, San Francisco, Sacramento, and San Jose, there are preschools where Yonsei children are sent to learn about Japanese and Japanese American cultures. While some of the Nisei, second-generation Japanese Americans, grew up in communities before World War II that were segregated, and other Nisei were reared in internment camps during World War II, many of the Sansei, except for the few who were born in the internment camps, and the Yonsei were not raised in Japanese American communities or with other Japanese Americans.

Very little is known about the Yonsei, as they are coming of age in the 1990's. From the experience of the Sansei, the third generation, it is known that the degree to which the Yonsei were exposed to the Japanese American cultural heritage varies widely within the generational group. Some of the Nisei chose not to rear their Sansei children in a Japanese American community or to become active in Japanese American community groups and activities. Other Nisei, by contrast, have reared their children in Japanese American community institutions, sending their children to Japanese American churches or Buddhist temples and being actively involved in Japanese American children's

Amanda (left) and Josina Morita are fourth-generation Japanese Americans. (National Japanese American Historical Society)

athletic leagues. Likewise, some Sansei parents, many of whom have married non-Japanese, choose to continue Japanese American traditions while others choose not to. The extent to which the Yonsei will identify culturally with their Japanese ancestry and heritage has yet to be determined.

Yoshi: Japanese term referring to an adopted child or son-in-law. A son-in-law can be adopted into a family and take on the wife's name, usually taking the place of the *chonan*, or oldest son, in order to carry on the family name.

Yoshida, Jim (b. July 28, 1921, Seattle, Wash.): Translator and writer. A Nisei, in April, 1941, he and his family went to Japan to return his father's ashes and for a short visit. Following the Pearl Harbor attack on December 7, 1941, his family was stranded in Japan, and he was conscripted into the Japanese Imperial

Army and served in central China. After the war, he worked as a translator for the U.S. Army in Korea. His efforts to regain U.S. citizenship were rewarded in court in April, 1954. His autobiography, written with Bill Hosokawa, has been published under the title *The Two Worlds of Jim Yoshida* (1972).

Yoshimura, Wendy (b. Jan., 1943, Manzanar, Calif.): Antiwar activist and artist. Yoshimura was born at MANZANAR, a World War II relocation center for Japanese Americans. After the war her father, Frank Yoshimura, renounced his American citizenship and moved the family to Hiroshima, Japan. They returned to the United States when Wendy was eleven years old and settled in Fresno, California. At age nineteen she moved to the San Francisco Bay Area to attend junior college and art school in Oakland. There she was affected by the Vietnam War and became involved in antiwar activities.

Wendy Yoshimura, former roommate of Patricia Hearst, appears in Pleasanton, California, after her release from jail in 1975. (AP/Wide World Photos)

Yoshimura, a Japanese American Sansei artist, gained national attention when she was arrested along with Patty Hearst in San Francisco in September, 1975. Hearst, the daughter of the head of the Hearst Corporation, previously had been abducted from her Berkeley apartment by members of the radical Symbionese Liberation Army (SLA). After the kidnapping Hearst changed from victim to self-professed "urban guerrilla" and joined her captors. She was convicted for her involvement in a San Francisco bank robbery and served time in a federal prison.

While Hearst claimed that Yoshimura also was a member of the SLA, no such charges were ever brought against Yoshimura. Instead Yoshimura was convicted of possession of explosives and a machine gun based on felony charges resulting from a March, 1972, raid on a garage in Berkeley. Inside were materials to make homemade bombs, part of an alleged plan to bomb the Navy Reserve Officers' Training Corps (ROTC) building on the University of California, Berkeley campus.

Soon after Yoshimura's arrest, the Japanese American community in the San Francisco Bay Area rallied to her support by establishing a fair trial committee that raised her $25,000 bail and funds for her legal defense and conducted a survey of potential jurors.

During her trial Yoshimura refused to divulge any information on her whereabouts during the three years she spent underground. The defense argued that being raised with Japanese cultural values had instilled in her an obligation not to betray those who had assisted her. She was convicted of the charges and served six months in state prison followed by another eight months in a work-release program.

Young, Victor Sen (1915, San Francisco, Calif.—Nov. 9, 1980, North Hollywood, Calif.): Actor. Young's father was a businessman who had left Canton to start an importing business in San Francisco. Young supported himself through high school and the University of California, Berkeley, earning a B.A. degree in economics there in 1937. After working on *The Good Earth* (1937), he landed the role of Charlie CHAN's number-two son in *Charlie Chan in Honolulu* (1938). As a Hollywood actor for more than forty years, Young appeared in numerous Chan films and in such films as *The Letter* (1940) with Bette Davis, *Across the Pacific* (1942) with Humphrey Bogart, and *Flower Drum Song* (1961). In television, Young had a recurring role (1961-1962) on *Bachelor Father* (1957-1962) and appeared in such series as *Hawaii Five-O*

(1968-1980) and *Kung Fu* (1972-1975). His longest-running role was in *Bonanza* (1959-1973), in which he played the part of Hop Sing, the Chinese cook at the Cartwright ranch.

Young Buddhist Association (YBA): Organization consisting of young people belonging to various Buddhist temples in the United States. It was established in 1900 and serves a variety of functions according to the changing times. Buddhist temples in Hawaii and the mainland United States were established primarily in the early twentieth century as centers of Japanese immigrant life, providing a bulwark against racial, social, and legal discrimination.

The first YBA, formed in Hawaii in 1900, when the Issei (Japanese immigrants to the United States) were young adults, provided social, cultural, and spiritual sustenance, as well as links to the homeland. As the Nisei (sons or daughters of Japanese immigrants and born and reared in the United States) population grew in numbers, all Buddhist temples formed a YBA or its variations.

From the late 1920's to the post-World War II era, these associations sponsored conferences, retreats, and oratorical contests, as well as baseball, basketball, and bowling leagues. Subsequently, as the Issei population declined, other YBA members took over the leadership of Buddhist temples and began to make BUDDHISM a part of American life.

Some of the groups' early accomplishments include the approval of the official inscription of "B" for "Buddhist" on armed forces identification tags and the use of various Buddhist insignia. Other accomplishments are granting the Sangha Award for the Buddhist Boy Scouts and establishing Buddhist chaplaincy for the armed forces and the Wheel of Dharma for grave markers for fallen U.S. soldiers. With the emergence of the Sansei (children of the Nisei), the YBA experienced a decrease in membership but an increase in cultural and religious awareness of the Buddhist tradition, reflecting a greater understanding and appreciation of Buddhism among the general American public.

Young China Association: Nationalist Chinese organization founded in San Francisco and existing briefly between 1909 and 1913. It was important in garnering Chinatown's support for SUN YAT-SEN's republican revolution. The Young China Association was founded by an American-born Chinese, Li Gongxia (also known as Lee See-nam), and was to serve as a front for the Chinese Nationalist revolution in the United States.

Since 1644 (and until 1911), China had been ruled by an ethnic minority from the northeastern part of China, commonly known as the MANCHUS. In the mid-nineteenth century, the Manchu government became a cumbersome bureaucracy, and the nation was beset with countless rebellions and disasters. As a consequence, great powers such as Great Britain, France, and Germany began to encroach on China's territorial integrity and to undermine Chinese sovereignty. It was against this background that Sun and his Nationalist comrades vowed to save China by first overthrowing the alien Manchu Dynasty and then establishing a republic and expelling imperialism from their motherland.

It took Sun, however, more than a decade to inspire more and more Chinese to follow his example by deed. Among his followers was Li, who made a trip to Hong Kong in 1907 and joined Sun's revolutionary organization the TONGMENGHUI (Chinese United League). Two years later, Li founded the Young China Association with its headquarters in San Francisco and branches in Berkeley, Chicago, New York City, and other cities. Though the membership of the association remained small, consisting mostly of Chinese students, it provided energy and enthusiasm for the revolutionary movement. The association also raised money and recruited a suicide squad ready for action in China. It then stepped up propaganda for nationalism and republicanism by publishing a weekly journal called the *Youth*. The journal proved to be so effective that the association decided to expand it into a daily newspaper, hence the beginning of the *Young China*. Its first issue was published on August 19, 1910. The paper was to evolve into a major voice in Chinatown, helping to shape public opinion among Chinese in the United States.

After the Republic was established in China, the Young China Association publicly merged with other Nationalist organizations into the umbrella Chinese Nationalist League of America in January, 1913, and Li was named the new organization's deputy director.

Young India: Weekly journal founded in 1915 by freedom fighter Lala Lajpat Rai, who served as publisher until 1919. He was succeeded as editor and publisher by nationalist leader Mahatma GANDHI. Based in Ahmadadbad, India, the journal strove to advance the ideals of achieving justice, promoted civic responsibility, and later served as the foundation for Gandhi's Free India movement. Under Gandhi, *Young India* ran from 1919 until 1931; it ceased publication in January, 1932.

Young Men's Organization to Serve the Mother Country. *See* **Hokoku Seinen-dan**

Yu, Connie Young (b. June 19, 1941, Los Angeles, Calif.): Scholar. The daughter of John C. and Mary Lee Young, Connie earned an English degree from Mills College in 1963. With an interest in writing that began in high school, she has published numerous materials on Chinese American history in various books and journals and has lectured widely. Her books include *Chinatown, San Jose, USA* (1991) and *Profiles in Excellence: Chinese Americans on the Peninsula* (1986). Other activities have included consulting on educational history projects being developed for public broadcast and teaching fencing. Yu was honored for her service to the Asian American community in 1987, 1990, and 1993.

Yu-Ai Kai (Japanese American Community Senior Service): Nonprofit organization founded in San Jose, California in 1974 to benefit elderly Japanese Americans. The name "Yu-Ai Kai" means "organization for friendship and love."

Yu-Ai Kai traces its origin to the efforts, in the 1970's, of Sansei (third-generation Japanese American) students from San Jose State University to promote an understanding of the traditions and cultures of Asian Americans in Santa Clara County. The Sansei formed Asians for Community Action (ACA). The group found that there was a need to provide services for Japanese American seniors. It organized activities, such as providing a traditional Japanese New Year's food, *ozoni*, to the Issei and visiting the Issei at convalescent hospitals. Although the ACA was discontinued in 1972, its members participated in community meetings to plan a temporary senior center. Funded by a donation from ACA, the senior center opened in July, 1973, at a building once known as Kuwabara Hospital in the Japantown area of San Jose. The center provided recreational activities, such as *shogi* and *go*, and social activities for Japanese American seniors.

In April, 1974, the Japanese American Community Senior Service (JACSS) of San Jose was established as an organization to operate the permanent senior center. With the support and effort of volunteers, Yu-Ai Kai— as the organization came to be known—offered activities such as singing, learning English, taking day trips, fishing, and shopping and organized important celebrations such as Bonen Kai, which is a party at the end of the year, and the Keiro Kai, which honors seniors. Yu-Ai Kai became a nonprofit organization in June,

1977. It was also able to hire paid staff in that year. Yu-Ai Kai initiated a nutrition program in February, 1978, with federal support from the Older Americans Act of 1965. With the help of Comprehensive Employment Training Act (CETA) funding from 1978 to 1981, six full-time staff were hired. One of the projects was an oral history of the Issei, resulting in the publication of *Beginnings: Japanese Americans in San Jose* (1981).

Yu-Ai Kai is licensed as an adult day-care program and has been providing senior day services since March, 1984. In 1985 Yu-Ai Kai began fund-raising efforts for a new building. The group was awarded grants from the state of California and the city of San Jose, and land was purchased in 1986. The new center was built with contributions from the state, city, county, foundations and corporations, and community. It opened on March 20, 1993.

Yuey, Joe (b. 1906, Hoiping, China): Entrepreneur. After immigrating to the United States in July, 1923, he was detained at the ANGEL ISLAND IMMIGRATION STATION in San Francisco Bay for almost a month. He chaired the Suey Sing Tong for more than twenty terms, founded the Chinese Culture Foundation of San Francisco (1963), and became owner of the Imperial Palace Restaurant, one of the first elegant dining establishments in San Francisco's Chinatown.

Yum cha: Cantonese phrase that means "drinking tea." It refers to eating *dim sum*, a light meal—usually breakfast, brunch, or lunch—consisting of Chinese dumplings and appetizers.

Yun Chi-ho (1865-1945): Aristocrat, reformer, and Christian leader in Korea. He was sent to Japan for special training in foreign languages, returning in 1883 to serve as interpreter for the first American minister to Korea. He became a Christian in 1887—the first Korean nobleman to convert to Protestantism. His impressive skill with languages earned for him a succession of key posts at the Korean royal court. In 1896, however, risking his career but fueled by his convictions, he helped found the Tongnip Hyophoe (Independence Club). In reaction the government reassigned him, and the Independence Club folded in 1898. From 1915 to 1920 he served as general secretary of the Young Men's Christian Association (YMCA).

Yune, Johnny (b. Choongbook Province, Korea): Comedian. Yune became a U.S. citizen in 1968. His career as a comic entertainer took off following an ap-

pearance on *The Tonight Show Starring Johnny Carson*. He has also enjoyed roles in feature films.

Yung, Judy (b. San Francisco, Calif.): Scholar. A faculty member of the American Studies department at the University of California, Santa Cruz, and the coordinator of the Asian American Studies program there, Yung is the author of *Chinese Women of America: A Pictorial History* (1986) and coeditor of *Island: Poetry and History of Chinese Immigrants on Angel Island, 1910-1940* (1980), with Him Mark LAI and Genny LIM. In addition, Yung was the project director for the pathbreaking anthology *Making Waves: An Anthology of Writings By and About Asian American Women* (1989).

Judy Yung, coordinator of Asian American Studies at the University of California at Santa Cruz. (Asian Week)

Yung Wing (Nov. 17, 1828, Nam Ping, Pedro Island, China—Apr. 21, 1912, Hartford, Conn.): Government official and educator. Yung attended missionary schools in Hong Kong and Macao and in 1847 was one of the first three Chinese to come to study in the United States. He also converted to Christianity and, in October, 1852, became a naturalized U.S. citizen. Upon earning his degree at Yale University in 1854, he became the first Chinese to graduate from an American university. Yung was persuaded that an American education was the answer to China's sociopolitical problems. After returning home, he encouraged the Chinese government to send students to the United States to attend American schools.

After that, Yung was involved with various commercial transactions in the United States and China. Eventually, he returned to China to enter the tea industry and then went into government service. During this time he led commercial, educational, and diplomatic missions to America for the Chinese government, becoming the first Chinese to conduct a cultural exchange between the two nations.

As the first commissioner of the Chinese Educational Mission of 1872 to 1881, Yung brought 120 Chinese to study in the United States under Chinese government sponsorship. The plan called for the group to study for fifteen years and then return to China to assist in the nation's modernization drive. Yung planned their Western curriculum. The mission was housed at Hartford, where it remained until being recalled because of conflicts over its operation.

While heading the mission, Yung and his colleague Chen Lanbin also engaged in diplomatic negotiations for China with Spain and Peru. Their efforts eventually resulted in the abolishment of the infamous COOLIE TRADE to Cuba and Peru. Later, they were appointed the first Chinese foreign ministers to the United States, Spain, and Peru. A permanent U.S. legation was established in Washington, D.C., in 1875. After 1881 Yung continued his involvement in U.S.-China business affairs but relinquished all government posts.

Equally important as Yung's service to China was his commitment to making a life in the United States. He had married Mary L. Kellogg, an American, in 1875. After her death in 1886, he reared their two sons and occasionally traveled to China at the request of Chinese officials. Around 1898 the U.S. government revoked his American citizenship on the basis of federal legislation prohibiting Chinese naturalization. Somehow he managed to return to the United States. Yung spent his final years in retirement in Hartford, writing his memoirs and corresponding with family and friends. His autobiography, *My Life in China and America*, was published in 1909.

Some modern scholars of Asian American history cite the life of Yung Wing as evidence that some Chinese, at least, attempted to assimilate into American society and succeeded. This runs counter to the posture taken by the early proponents of Chinese exclusion, who insisted that the Chinese would never really become part of American life.

Yuriko (Yuriko Kikuchi; b. Feb. 2, 1920, San Jose, Calif.): Modern dancer and choreographer. Following internment at Gila River relocation center, she became a major soloist in Martha Graham's Dance Company, originating significant roles in the Graham repertory, including *Appalachian Spring* (pr. 1944) and *Cave of the Heart* (pr. 1946). She created the role of Eliza in the original Broadway production of *The King and I* (pr. 1951) and restaged Jerome Robbins' original choreography of that play in numerous revivals. She also directed The Martha Graham Ensemble, taught at the Martha Graham School of Contemporary Dance, and choreographed more than forty original modern dance works.

Z

Zhang Yinhuan (Chang Yin-Huan; Feb. 8, 1837, Foshan, Canton, China—1900, Xinjiang Province, China): Diplomat, scholar, and poet. Reared in Canton, Zhang began his government career when he attempted to pass a state examination in order to join the scholarly ranks of Chinese officials. After failing the examination, he managed to purchase a title as a student of the Chinese Imperial Academy and later reached the rank of magistrate. When Japan invaded the island of Formosa in 1875, Zhang was one of the key architects of a plan to fortify and protect other trading ports on the Chinese mainland.

After receiving a diplomatic appointment as his country's minister to the United States, Zhang traveled to Washington, D.C., in March of 1886. During his term as minister, he negotiated important settlements between China and the United States on behalf of Chinese miners killed in an 1885 massacre at Rock Springs, Wyoming (see ROCK SPRINGS RIOT), and on behalf of other miners killed at the Log Cabin Bar near the Snake River in Idaho (see SNAKE RIVER MASSACRE). As part of the terms of the latter treaty, Zhang agreed to a clause in which the Chinese government would voluntarily prohibit the immigration of Chinese laborers to the United States for a period of twenty years in exchange for greater protection for Chinese citizens against mob attacks. This clause disturbed many residents of Canton who profited from such immigration, and they exerted strong pressure on officials in Peking to reject the treaty. Reluctant to alienate Cantonese interests, the Chinese government delayed ratification of the treaty—a tactic that was interpreted by the U.S. government as indication of complete rejection of the treaty. As a result of this misunderstanding, Congress took action to pass a bill proposed by Representative William L. Scott of Pennsylvania in 1888 that called for the cancellation of all certificates of identity issued to Chinese laborers and the complete exclusion of such laborers attempting to reenter the United States after visiting their homeland (see SCOTT ACT OF 1888).

Zhang was recalled to Peking in 1889 by the Chinese government to signal their displeasure that President Cleveland signed the bill into law. Zhang continued to serve in a variety of governmental positions and was named to the Board of Revenue in 1892 as senior vice president. Zhang's contacts abroad brought him into disfavor, however, as anti-foreign sentiment grew within China; he was banished to Xinjiang Province in western China before being executed in 1900.

Zhongguo-ren: Mandarin term for a person from Zhongguo—The Middle Kingdom, the ancient name for China among the Chinese people.

Chinese premier Zhou Enlai (right) greets U.S. envoy Henry Kissinger in Beijing, 1971. (National Archives)

Zhou Enlai (Mar. 5, 1898, near Shaoxing, Zhejiang Province, China—Jan. 8, 1976, Beijing, People's Republic of China): Politician and diplomat. As premier of China from its establishment in 1949 to his death in 1976, he was a key figure in the negotiations to restore diplomatic relations with the United States during President Richard M. Nixon's trip in 1972. He was a leading figure in the Chinese Communist Party (CCP), becoming director of the CCP Central Committee's military department and the CCP's chief negotiator during the civil war between the GUOMINDANG (GMD) and the CCP. He was instrumental in the downfall of CHIANG KAI-SHEK and in resisting Guomindang influence.

Zoroastrians: Religious and ethnic group whose members are followers of Zoroastrianism, a religion that began in Persia (modern-day Iran) between 1000 and 700 B.C.E. The worldwide Zoroastrian community numbers about 125,000, centered in India (80,000) and Iran (30,000). In 1990 there were approximately 3,000 Zoroastrians in the United States, half of whom lived in Southern California.

The group takes its name from its prophet, Zoroaster (who is called Zarathustra in the *Avesta*, the holy book of Zoroastrianism). He taught that there is only one true god, Ahura Mazda. Fire is the symbol of Ahura Mazda, and Zoroastrian ceremonies generally incorporate the use of fire, usually the burning of sandalwood (thus the popular misconception that Zoroastrians are "fire-worshipers").

Zoroastrianism is a form of monotheism, with the forces of both good and evil under the control of Ahura Mazda. Zoroastrians believe that people are born with free will and serve either good or evil. They are responsible for their own choices; there is no savior to help them, nor can they pray or make offerings to expiate any sin.

Zoroastrianism became the official religion of the Achaemenid (559-330 B.C.E.), Parthian (247 B.C.E.-224 C.E.), and Sasanid (224-651 C.E.) rulers of Persia. After the Muslim conquest of Persia, most Zoroastrians converted to Islam. Some, however, continued to practice their religion in Persia, where they were excluded from the mainstream of society, while others fled Muslim persecution. Beginning in the tenth century, Zoroastrians migrated from Persia to India, first settling in the Gujarat region, then shifting to Bombay.

In India, Zoroastrians are known as Parsis (that is, people from Persia). Over the centuries, they have adopted many Hindu practices (the women wear saris, for example) while retaining their distinctive beliefs. Today, as a result of this long process, there are significant differences in outlook and in customs between Parsis and Iranian Zoroastrians.

While small numbers of Zoroastrians emigrated from India and Iran to the United States before 1970, the Zoroastrian community in the United States is largely of recent origin. Of the approximately 1,500 Zoroastrians in Southern California, about two-thirds are from Iran and one-third from India. Typically, Zoroastrian immigrants are well educated (education and public service are highly valued in their community) and include many professionals, businesspeople, and entrepreneurs.

Like other immigrant communities, Zoroastrians must confront questions of assimilation and cultural continuity. For Zoroastrians those questions are par-

ticularly acute, since traditionally they have foresworn converting others to their faith: Membership in the group is by birth only. While out-marriage is permitted, the spouse of a believer remains an outsider. Traditionally, children of mixed marriages in which the father is Zoroastrian have the option to join the community when they reach adulthood, but the same privilege is not extended to children of marriages in which only the mother is Zoroastrian.

In Southern California, some Iranian Zoroastrians, while still rejecting active proselytizing, accept converts who choose—without any pressure—to embrace the Zoroastrian faith. Others in the community, including a majority of the Parsis, maintain the orthodox definition of membership.

Zuzu Ben: Folk designation of the phonological characteristics of the Tohoku dialects which are spoken in the northeastern region of Honshu, the main island of Japan. Immigrants to Hawaii who used these dialects were frequently ridiculed and looked down upon by immigrants from other regions of Japan whose dialects became the standard for the Japanese community in Hawaii.

In certain areas in the Miyagi, Fukushima, and Yamagata prefectures as well as in the Niigata region, the distinction is not made between the pairs of speech sounds /shi/ and /su/, /chi/ and /tsu/, and /ji/ and /zu/. Consequently, /shi/, /chi/, and /ji/ sounds which occur in Standard Japanese words are replaced by /su/, /tsu/, and /zu/, respectively. For example, such words as *nasi* "pear" and *nasu* "eggplant" are both pronounced as /nasu/, Standard Japanese for eggplant. *Chizu* "map" and *tsuji* "crossroad" both become /tsuzu/, which has no corresponding form in Standard Japanese. *Susu* "soot" and *sushi* "vinegared rice" both become /susu/, Standard Japanese for soot. In addition, the high front vowel /i/ tends to be lowered to /e/ after a consonant. Thus the words *shijimi* "corbicula, a kind of shellfish" and *suzume* "sparrow" have the same pronunciation, both coming to sound like /suzume/, which means sparrow in Standard Japanese.

These sound alterations together with such dialectal features as the nasalization of homo-organic consonants (e.g., *mado*/mando/ "window" and *tobi*/tombi/ "kite") are referred to as Zuzu Ben, which means literally the /zuzu/ accent. Of all the regional dialects in Japan, Zuzu Ben was singled out as an extreme linguistic deviant. Social prejudice against Zuzu Ben may have derived in part from a general perception of the Tohoku region as economically and culturally backward. The entertainment media has helped perpetuate the image of Zuzu Ben speakers as good-natured but rustic and slow-witted; comedians often mimic their speech in a mocking way. On the other hand, it is also a common practice in Japanese translations of foreign-language literature to represent the rural speech of the original text with Zuzu Ben as a prototypical Japanese dialect.

Time Line

1521	Portuguese explorer Ferdinand Magellan claims the Philippines in the name of the Spanish crown. Colonial rule begins in 1565.
1587	First Filipinos reportedly arrive in California.
1600's	Chinese and Filipinos arrive in the New World via the ships of the Manila galleon trade.
1761	Great Britain assumes colonial control over the Indian subcontinent.
	Filipinos arrive in America, jump ship in New Orleans, and remain in Louisiana.
1778	English navigator Captain James Cook discovers the Hawaiian Islands, which he names the "Sandwich Islands."
1784	The *Empress of China*, the first American ship to reach China, drops anchor at Canton.
1785	Three Chinese sailors set foot in Baltimore, Maryland, the first known Chinese to visit the United States
1786	Major Samuel Shaw becomes the first American consul sent to China. Appointed by President George Washington and charged with promoting U.S.-China trade, he helps to increase greatly the export of porcelain from China.
1788	Chinese sailors land in Hawaii, the first known Chinese to visit the islands.
1790	First visitor from India reportedly arrives in Salem, Massachusetts. Over the next ten years, more Asian Indians sail to the United States in the course of trade
	Congress passes the Naturalization Act extending U.S. citizenship to all "free white persons."
1818	First five Chinese students in the United States arrive to attend school. They are enrolled at the Foreign Mission School in Cornwall, Connecticut, until 1825.
1820	First American missionaries from New England sail to Hawaii.
1830	Three Chinese living in the United States, according to the first U.S. census to report on the Asian population.
1834	Afong Moy, the first Chinese woman known to have visited the United States, is exhibited in a theater in New York.
1835	In Hawaii, Americans organize the islands' first sugar plantation.
1839-1842	First Opium War between China and Great Britain. China signs the Treaty of Nanjing opening Chinese ports to foreign trade by Western and later Japanese powers.
1843	Japanese citizen Nakahama Manjiro (John Mung) is rescued and brought to the United States. He is the first known Japanese to land in the United States.
1844	The United States and China sign the Treaty of Wangxia, whereby American citizens in China are granted extraterritorial rights. First treaty ever concluded between the two nations.
1847	Chinese student Yung Wing arrives in the United States to attend the Monson Academy in Massachusetts. In 1854 he becomes the first Chinese to be graduated from a U.S. college, Yale.
1848	First Chinese (two men, one woman) immigrate to the United States, embarking in San Francisco.
	Gold is discovered in California, bringing more Chinese to the United States.
1850	California enacts the Foreign Miners' Tax to discourage Chinese miners.
	Hamada Hikozo (Joseph Heco) is brought to America after being rescued. He later becomes the first U.S. citizen of Japanese ancestry.

1850 (cont.)	In Hawaii, the Masters and Servants Act is passed. The state also establishes the Royal Hawaiian Agricultural Society to recruit plantation workers.
	California's year-end Chinese population is estimated at about 4,000.
1851	Sam Yup and Sze Yup associations are founded by San Francisco Chinese.
	Within one year, California's Chinese population rises from 4,000 to 25,000.
1852	Several hundred Chinese contract laborers arrive in Hawaii to work the sugar plantations.
	Lured by the gold rush, more than 20,000 Chinese arrive in California.
	William Speer starts a Presbyterian mission for Chinese in San Francisco.
1853	Several hundred years of Tokugawa isolation end as Commodore Matthew C. Perry of the United States forces Japan to open its doors to foreign commerce.
1854	*People v. Hall*, a California case, rules that Chinese cannot testify for or against white persons in court. The case is abrogated in 1872.
	First Chinese newspaper in America begins publication.
	The United States and Japan conclude first treaty, the Treaty of Kanagawa.
	California Chinese establish the Chinese Six Companies.
1856-1860	Second Opium War.
1857	In San Francisco, missionary A. W. Loomis begins his ministry to the Chinese.
1858	California enacts a law to keep Chinese and "Mongolians" from immigrating to the state.
	The United States and Japan sign the Yedo Treaty.
	France invades Vietnam and establishes colonial rule across Indochina by 1884.
	Fraser River gold rush in British Columbia, Canada, brings Chinese immigrants further north.
1859	The Qing court, in the Treaty of Tianjin, allows Chinese to travel abroad and to emigrate.
	In San Francisco, Chinese are barred from attending public schools.
1860	A Japanese diplomatic mission arrives in the United States.
	California passes a law to tax Chinese engaged in fishing.
	A California law bars Chinese Americans, Indians, and African Americans from public schools.
	The U.S. census records 34,933 Chinese residents.
1862	California enacts a Police Tax on Chinese in the state.
1863	*Lin Sing v. Washburn* holds the Police Tax to be unconstitutional.
1864	In Hawaii, the planters' society and the Bureau of Immigration are created by plantation owners.
1865	As plans unfold for the building of the first transcontinental railroad, the Central Pacific Railroad begins hiring Chinese laborers.
1866	Work begins on the western portion of the transcontinental railroad, linking the United States' Pacific and Atlantic coasts. At its peak the project employs more than 10,000 Chinese.
1867	2,000 Chinese railroad laborers stage a week-long strike.
	A U.S. district court rules that Chinese may not become American citizens.
	Fukuzawa Yukichi, who first introduced Japan to the West, visits the United States.

1868	The earliest Japanese contract laborers to Hawaii, the Gannen-mono, arrive after having been illegally recruited by Eugene Van Reed. Following reports that these workers are being mistreated, the Japanese government halts emigration for the next 17 years.
	The United States and China conclude the Burlingame Treaty allowing free emigration for citizens of both countries but barring the Chinese from the right to become U.S. citizens.
1868-1920	62 strikes on the sugar plantations of Hawaii involve 72,000 Japanese laborers.
1869	The Wakamatsu Tea and Silk Farm Colony is established at Gold Hill, California.
	Work on the western portion of the transcontinental railroad is completed, leaving thousands of Chinese laborers out of work.
1870	Builders of the Alabama and Chattanooga Railroad hire hundreds of Chinese laborers for the task.
	Congress allows a dozen Japanese students to enroll at the U.S. Naval Academy at Annapolis, Maryland.
	California law declares illegal the importation of Chinese, Japanese, and "Mongolian" women for prostitution.
	San Francisco's anti-Chinese Cubic Air Ordinance requires that each city tenement have at least 500 cubic feet of air per inhabitant. The law's true intent is to harass Chinatown residents, for whom crowded living conditions are the norm.
	In San Francisco the Reverend Otis Gibson forms a rescue agency, the Women's Missionary Society, to aid Chinese prostitutes.
1871	In Los Angeles, an outbreak of anti-Chinese violence occurs.
	A friendship treaty is concluded between Japan and Hawaii.
1872	The Iwakura Mission brings 53 Japanese students to the United States.
	The Chinese Educational Mission brings thirty Chinese students to the United States.
	California law is amended to allow Chinese to testify in state courts.
1873	San Francisco's anti-Chinese Laundry Ordinance penalizes Chinese laundrymen for not using horses or horse-drawn delivery vehicles. The law's true intent is to halt the spread of Chinese laundries.
1875	Under the Page Law, Chinese, Japanese, and "Mongolian" prostitutes, felons, and contract laborers are barred from entering the United States.
1876	The Reciprocity Treaty between the United States and Hawaii allows Hawaiian sugar to enter the United States duty-free.
	In San Francisco, the city's Queue Ordinance authorizes the sheriff to cut off the queues of Chinese prisoners—a condition that in China is punishable by execution. The law's purpose is to keep Chinese from passing through or settling in San Francisco.
	Japan forces Korea to open its harbors to trade by foreign powers.
1877	In San Francisco, the Gospel Society, the first immigrant association formed by Japanese, is established by Japanese Christians.
	Denis Kearney helps form the Workingmen's Party of California and agitates for Chinese exclusion.
	Anti-Chinese violence breaks out in Chico, California.
1879	California's second constitution contains many measures that discriminate against the Chinese.
	President Rutherford B. Hayes vetoes the Fifteen Passenger Bill, under which no ship may carry more than 15 Chinese.
1870's	Economic recession across the United States leads to West Coast labor shortages and protests against "cheap Chinese labor."

1880	A California law prohibits mixed marriages between Caucasians and "Mongolians, Negroes, mulattoes and persons of mixed blood." The law is amended in 1933 to include Filipinos. Repealment of the statute follows in 1948.
	Under a new U.S.-China treaty, China agrees to limit and restrict Chinese immigration to the United States, while the latter promises better treatment and protection for Chinese living in the United States.
	The U.S. Census Bureau reports that 149 Japanese immigrated to the United States from 1871 to 1880.
	Anti-Chinese violence occurs in Denver, Colorado.
1881	Japan receives King David Kalakaua of Hawaii during his world tour.
	California's governor announces that March 4 will be a legal holiday set aside for anti-Chinese protests.
1882	Congress passes the Chinese Exclusion Act barring Chinese laborers from coming to the United States for 10 years and prohibiting Chinese already in the country from becoming naturalized American citizens. The act is repealed in 1943.
	The first treaty between the United States and Korea is concluded. It brings about 100 Korean students and government officials to the United States for training.
	Congress passes the first general immigration law setting federal guidelines for immigration to the United States.
	The Chinese Consolidated Benevolent Association (CCBA) is established in San Francisco. A branch is started in New York the following year.
1883	A Korean diplomatic mission arrives in San Francisco.
1884	Under a new amendment to the Chinese Exclusion Act of 1882, Chinese must present certificates in order to reenter the United States.
	Korean citizen So Chae-pil (Philip Jaisohn) arrives in the United States and is eventually naturalized.
	Joseph and Mary Tape file a lawsuit challenging the racist policies of the San Francisco school board.
	In Honolulu, the United Chinese Society is founded.
1885	Large-scale immigration of Japanese to the United States begins with the arrival of the first shipment of Japanese laborers in Honolulu, the result of the Irwin Convention.
	In Rock Springs, Wyoming, an incident of anti-Chinese violence occurs.
	Congress passes a bill to outlaw contract labor.
	The segregated Oriental Public School is built in San Francisco.
	Following passage of Exclusion Acts in the United States, Canada institutes discriminatory taxes and other measures designed to discourage Chinese immigration.
1886	The Japanese government rescinds the law that prevented Japanese citizens from emigrating. The first Japanese arrive in Victoria, British Columbia, Canada.
	Forcible expulsion of Chinese begins in many areas in the western United States.
	Yick Wo v. Hopkins annuls discriminatory New York law enacted against Chinese laundrymen.
	Chinese immigration to Hawaii ends.
1888	Under the Scott Act, as many as 20,000 Chinese outside the United States are left holding reentry certificates that are now nullified by law.
1889	Chinese exclusion laws are upheld as constitutional in *Chae Chan Ping v. United States*.
	First two Korean women, wives of Korean diplomats, enter the United States.
	The San Francisco *Bulletin* initiates its "yellow peril" campaign against Japanese immigration.

1890	The U.S. Census Bureau reports 107,488 Chinese living in the United States.
1891	*Chinese World*, the first bilingual daily published in both English and Chinese, debuts in San Francisco.
1892	The Geary Act extends the Chinese Exclusion Act of 1882 (exclusion of Chinese laborers) for another ten years and institutes mandatory registration by all Chinese.
1893	*Fong Yue Ting v. United States* upholds the constitutionality of the Geary Act.
	The first Japanese trade association, the Japanese Shoemakers' League, is established in San Francisco.
	At the World's Columbian Exposition in Chicago, Swami Vivekananda addresses the Parliament of Religions.
	San Francisco's school board orders that all Japanese children attend a segregated Chinese school. After protest by Japanese consul Chinda Sutemi, the order is rescinded.
1894	Under the Gresham-Yang Treaty, China agrees to halt Chinese immigration to the United States, while the U.S. allows Chinese holding valid reentry certificates to return.
	In Honolulu, Sun Yat-sen establishes the Revive China Society.
	In re Saito declares Japanese ineligible for U.S. citizenship.
1895	The Hawaiian Sugar Planters' Association (HSPA) is created.
	The Native Sons of the Golden State is formed, later becoming the Chinese American Citizens Alliance (CACA).
1898	Following the decision to annex Hawaii, Congress adopts a ruling barring further Chinese immigration to Hawaii. Moreover, Chinese living there cannot move to the mainland United States.
	Wong Kim Ark v. United States guarantees the citizenship of Chinese born in the United States.
	In San Francisco, Abiko Kyutaro founds the *Nichibei Shimbun*.
	The United States annexes Hawaii, which becomes a U.S. possession.
	The Spanish-American War. The United States annexes the Philippines at the close of the war by virtue of the Treaty of Paris. The pact permits Filipinos to travel to the United States freely and grants entry to all Filipino war brides.
	China leases the New Territories to Great Britain for 99 years, giving Hong Kong its present dimensions.
1899	Buddhist priests from Japan form the Buddhist Churches of America.
1899-1902	The Philippine Insurrection.
1900	Congress passes the Organic Act; the act, stipulating that all U.S. laws are enforceable in Hawaii, outlaws contract labor in the islands. Japanese contract laborers now head for the U.S. mainland to seek work.
	Hawaii becomes a U.S. territory, the Territory of Hawaii
	The number of Japanese living in America climbs to about 25,000.
	The Boxer Rebellion erupts—a violent uprising against foreigners in Beijing.
1901	The first Korean immigrant arrives in Hawaii on a Japanese ship.
1902	Congress enacts legislation that extends Chinese exclusion for another 10 years.
	The Philippine Organic Act is approved by the U.S. Senate and forms the basis of U.S. Philippine policy during the Taft era.
	The Hawaiian Sugar Planters' Association (HSPA) initiates the recruitment of Korean laborers.

1903	Earliest group of Korean contract laborers sets foot in Hawaii to work the sugar plantations—the beginning of Korean immigration to the United States. The Japanese colonial government in Korea halts all emigration in 1905; before that happens, however, about 7,000 Koreans arrive in the islands.
	In Oxnard, California, Japanese and Mexican sugar-beet workers stage a strike.
	Filipino *pensionados* arrive in America to begin their education.
	The Korean Evangelical Society is established in Hawaii.
1904	First organized strike by Japanese plantation workers in Hawaii is launched.
	South Asian Indians begin coming to North America. Punjabi Sikhs, in particular, begin arriving in British Columbia, Canada. Through 1924 as many as fifteen thousand South Asians, mostly from the Punjab, settle along the Pacific Coast of Canada and the United States. By 1923, about seven thousand South Asians are living in the United States, mostly on the West Coast.
	Korean citizen Syngman Rhee arrives in Hawaii and begins gathering support among Korean immigrants there for the Korean independence movement.
1905	Koreans start Episcopal and Methodist churches in Hawaii and California, respectively.
	The Asiatic Exclusion League is formed in San Francisco to eliminate immigration from Asia.
	In China, a nationwide boycott of American goods is staged to protest American discrimination against Chinese.
	As the Russo-Japanese War ends, Japan occupies Korea and stops Korean immigration to Hawaii.
1906	The San Francisco earthquake and fire devastates the city and its Chinatown.
	The San Francisco school board crisis creates international headlines.
	In Vancouver, British Columbia, an anti-Asian riot breaks out.
	Asian Indian Lajpat Rai arrives in the United States. He later establishes the India Home Rule League of America.
	Filipino contract laborers recruited by the Hawaiian Sugar Planters' Association (HSPA) arrive in Hawaii.
1907	The Gentlemen's Agreement between Japan and the United States helps end the San Francisco school board crisis and requires Japan to bar further contract labor immigration to the United States. Consequently, labor contractors in Alaskan fisheries and on California and Hawaiian farms and plantations begin recruiting Filipinos.
	In the Bellingham, Washington, incident, Asian Indians are driven from the city by white lumbermill workers.
	The United Korean Society is formed in Hawaii.
	More than 200 Filipinos land in Hawaii to work the sugar plantations. By 1924, 46,000 men and 7,000 women have journeyed to the islands.
1908	In an effort to combat racial discrimination, the Japanese Association of America is founded.
	The Hankuk Puin Hoe is established in San Francisco as the first cultural and social organization for Korean women.
	In Canada, Asian Indians who have not reached Canada by "continuous journey" from their homelands are denied entry.
	Asian Indians are driven out of Live Oak, California.
	Japanese picture brides begin arriving in the United States.

1909	The Korean National Association (KNA) is established.
	On Oahu, Hawaii, 7,000 Japanese sugar plantation laborers begin a four-month-long strike—the first major strike by Japanese laborers in the islands.
	My Life in China and America, the autobiography of former U.S. citizen Yung Wing, is published.
1910	Three South Asian Indian women sail into San Francisco. The number of South Asian women living on the Pacific Coast now stands at six.
	California legislators devise ways to restrict the flow of Asian Indians into the state.
	The U.S. immigration service establishes the Angel Island immigration station on the West Coast.
	Japan annexes Korea, which does not regain its independence until the end of World War II in 1945.
1911	Pablo Manlapit creates the Filipino Higher Wages Association in Hawaii.
	Asian Indian political leader Har Dayal arrives in the United States.
1912	The Republic of China is established by Sun Yat-sen, its first president.
	In Stockton, California, Sikhs erect a *gurdwara* and found the Khalsa Diwan Society.
1913	California enacts the Alien Land Law to keep aliens ineligible for U.S. citizenship from buying or leasing land.
	Under the leadership of Har Dayal, the Hindu Association of the Pacific Coast is formed. The association later becomes the Ghadr Party, a revolutionary movement to free India from British rule. Headquartered in San Francisco, the party begins publishing the *Hindustan Gadar*.
	Pablo Manlapit establishes the Filipino Unemployed Association in Hawaii.
	Korean farm laborers are forcibly expelled from Hemet Valley, California.
1914	Sakaram Ganesh Pandit, claiming to be white, becomes a U.S. citizen.
	In Vancouver, Canada, immigration officials deny entry to Asian Indians who had arrived by "continuous journey."
	Korean activist Park Yong-man, persuaded that Korea's liberation from Japan will come only from military overthrow, forms the Korean Military Corps.
	At the University of California, Berkeley, Padma Chandra is the first Asian Indian woman to attend.
	World War I begins.
1915	The Central Japanese Association and the Japanese Chamber of Commerce are established.
1916	Kanta Gupta is the first Asian Indian woman to file for American citizenship.
	The San Francisco Chinese Young Women's Christian Association is founded.
1917	Arizona enacts an Alien Land Law.
	The Barred Zone Act further restricts immigration to the United States from almost all of Asia except for Japan.
	In Hawaii, Syngman Rhee establishes the Korean Christian Church.
	Pan Asiatic League founder Chandra K. Chakravarty is arrested in connection with the Hindu Conspiracy case. Ram Chandra is also tried in the case but is shot to death by one of his countrymen during the hearings.
	The United States enters World War I.

1918	World War I veterans of Asian ancestry are granted U.S. citizenship.
	In the Imperial and Coachella valleys of Southern California, Asian Indians create the Hindustani Welfare Reform Association.
	Koreans in Hawaii establish the New Church, led by Syngman Rhee.
	World War I ends. In its aftermath, the United States, Great Britain, and Japan jockey for control of China. In Asia, Communist influence begins to spread.
1919	The Korean independence movement, with Koreans in the United States vigorously protesting the Japanese presence in Korea, is in full swing. During the March First movement in Korea, many protesters are killed by Japanese police.
	The First Korean Liberty Congress is held in Philadelphia in order to draw worldwide attention to the situation in Korea.
	V. S. McClatchy creates the California Joint Immigration Committee. He uses it to further his anti-Japanese policies and goals.
	In San Francisco, Nisei form the American Loyalty League (ALL).
	In Hawaii, Japanese form the Federation of Japanese Labor.
1920	A Hawaii sugar plantation strike involves ten thousand Japanese and Filipino laborers demanding that racially discriminatory pay scales be abolished.
	The Kim Brothers Company is established in Reedley, California.
1920-1921	Under pressure from rising anti-Japanese hostility toward the picture-bride system, Japan refuses to issue any more passports to picture brides.
1921	Alien Land Laws are enacted in Washington and Louisiana.
	Filipinos open a branch of the Caballeros de Dimas-Alang in San Francisco and a branch of the Legionarios del Trabajo in Honolulu.
	The first Filipino newspaper to be published in the mainland United States, the *Philippine Independent News*, debuts in Salinas, California.
	Congress enacts the Quota Immigration Act, the first quota immigration law passed by the government.
	In an effort to combat racial discrimination, Nisei form the Seattle Progressive Citizens League.
1922	Under the Cable Act, a female U.S. citizen can be stripped of her citizenship for marrying an alien ineligible for citizenship. Repealed in 1931.
	Japanese are made ineligible for U.S. citizenship in *Ozawa v. United States*.
	New Mexico enacts an Alien Land Law.
	The Asian Pacific American Labor Alliance founded by Asian Pacific American labor activists and the AFL-CIO and designed to address the needs of Asian Pacific American labor by organizing workers and training union leaders. Chapters located in Washington, California, New York, the District of Columbia, Massachusetts, and Hawaii.
1923	*United States v. Bhagat Singh Thind* rules that Asian Indians cannot become naturalized U.S. citizens. The American government then tries to annul the citizenship of seventy Asian Indians, including Sakaram Ganesh Pandit, previously naturalized. Not until 1946 are Asian Indians granted citizenship and property rights in the United States.
	Alien Land Laws are passed in Idaho, Montana, and Oregon.
	Canada imposes more severe restrictions on Chinese immigration.

1924	A major new Immigration Act bars all Asians ineligible for American citizenship (Hawaiians and Filipinos are the exceptions) from entering the United States.
	In Hawaii, 1,600 Filipinos stage a bloody strike that lasts eight months.
1925	U.S. legislation requires that Filipinos must serve three years in the U.S. Navy in order to become eligible for American citizenship.
	Truce is declared by warring *tongs* in North American Chinatowns.
	Hilario Moncado establishes the Filipino Federation of America.
1927	Amid the Great Depression, incidents of anti-Asian violence occur.
	James Sakamoto is the first Nisei to box professionally at New York's Madison Square Garden.
	The American Federation of Labor (AFL) adopts a resolution urging Congress to halt Filipino immigration.
1928	In Seattle, James Sakamoto begins publishing the *Japanese American Courier*.
	Filipino farm laborers are forcibly expelled from the Yakima Valley, Washington.
1930	An anti-Filipino riot erupts in Watsonville, California.
	The Japanese American Citizens League (JACL) is formed in Seattle.
	The Grass Roof, by Korean American writer Younghill Kang, is published.
1931	Hari G. Govil founds the India Society of America in New York.
	Filipino veterans of the U.S. armed forces become eligible for American citizenship.
1933	The Hare-Hawes-Cutting Act sets a date for Philippine independence from U.S. control. The Philippine Senate, however, refuses to ratify the act.
	The Filipino Labor Union (FLU) is created in central California.
1934	The Tydings-McDuffie Act sets a goal of complete independence for the Philippines on July 4, 1946, and establishes a Philippine immigration quota of 50 admissions per year.
	In the Salinas Valley, California, Filipino lettuce pickers stage a strike.
	Morrison v. California rules that Filipinos cannot qualify for American citizenship.
1935	Under the Filipino Repatriation Act, the U.S. government will pay the transportation expenses for all Filipinos wishing to return to the Philippines but will not thereafter allow them to return to the United States. Roughly 2,000 Filipinos accept this offer.
	The Philippine Commonwealth is established.
	My Country and My People, by Chinese author and scholar Lin Yutang, is published.
	U.S. Public Law 162 extends naturalization rights to certain veterans of World War I residing in the United States.
1936	A Filipino-Mexican labor union wins a charter from the AFL.
1938	More than 1,000 female Japanese workers join cannery unions affiliated with the Congress of Industrial Organizations (CIO).
	National Dollar Stores is the target of a three-month strike by Chinese women garment workers, who establish the first Chinese chapter of the International Ladies' Garment Workers Union (ILGWU).
	In Sacramento, California, the first Filipino National Conference takes place.
1939	World War II begins.

1941	The U.S. government breaks off treaty relations with Japan and freezes the assets of Japanese nationals living in the United States.
	Japan attacks Pearl Harbor.
	The U.S. government declares war on Japan.
	U.S. Justice Department officials begin rounding up suspected Japanese collaborators on the West Coast.
	Japanese American Citizens League (JACL) president Saburo Kido assures the U.S. government of the loyalty and cooperation of the Nisei.
	Of the Filipinos living in the United States, one-third join the U.S. military to fight the Japanese, who earlier had invaded the Philippines.
1942	Executive Order 9066, signed by President Franklin D. Roosevelt, triggers the chain of events leading to full evacuation and incarceration of Japanese on the West Coast. The directive authorizes the Army to designate militarily sensitive zones from which certain individuals may be forcibly removed. Eventually, more than 110,000 Japanese Americans on the West Coast are imprisoned in 10 relocation centers in the United States.
	The U.S. government establishes the Wartime Civil Control Administration (WCCA).
	The U.S. government, pursuant to Executive Order 9102, organizes the War Relocation Authority (WRA).
	Under the direction of the U.S. War Department, the 1st Filipino Infantry Regiment is assembled.
1943	The U.S. military decides to form all-Nisei combat regiments. Later that year, the 100th Infantry Battalion begins its Africa campaign.
	The U.S. government's registration of Japanese internees for the draft or the resettlement programs provokes a crisis in the relocation camps.
	California law is amended to allow Philippine nationals and Filipino citizens of the United States to hold real property in the state.
	A new Immigration Act repeals the exclusion laws, grants Chinese the right of American citizenship, and sets a quota of 105 immigrants from China per year.
1944	The U.S. government begins drafting relocation-center Nisei for service in the 442nd Regimental Combat Team.
	U.S. Public Law 405 gives American citizens the right to renounce their citizenship in time of war.
	The WRA declares that all relocation centers will be closed by the end of 1945.
1945	On August 6, the U.S. military detonates an atomic bomb over Hiroshima, Japan.
	On August 9, the U.S. military detonates a hydrogen bomb over Nagasaki, Japan.
	On September 2, World War II ends as Japan formally surrenders. Korea regains independence.
	The U.S. government cancels all exclusion orders and military restrictions pertaining to Japanese in the country.
	The last relocation center closes.
	Under the War Brides Act, the GI Fiancees Act, and legislation passed the following year, Asian wives, fiancees, and children of American servicemen are allowed entry into the United States. As a result, about 200,000 Asian war brides enter the country.
1946	More than 400 persons of Japanese ancestry are deported to Japan for being disloyal American citizens.
	The Filipino Naturalization Act offers citizenship to all Filipinos in the United States.
	The Luce-Celler Bill grants U.S. citizenship rights to Asian Indians while limiting to 100 per year the number of persons immigrating from India to the United States.

1946 (cont.)	The Philippines becomes an independent nation, as promised in the Tydings-McDuffie Act of 1934. The annual Filipino immigration quota is raised to 100.
	The Philippine Trade Act extends nonquota immigrant status to Philippine citizens and their spouses and children residing in the United States, with certain restrictions.
	In the United States, the first Asian American to hold a state office, Wing Ong, joins the Arizona House of Representatives.
	The French (First) Indochina War begins.
1947	In an amendment to the War Brides Act of 1945, Chinese American war veterans may now bring their brides to the United States.
	India becomes an independent nation, and Pakistan is created. Between 1947 and 1957, about 2,500 Indians and Pakistanis enter the United States.
1948	Under the Displaced Persons Act, 15,000 Chinese in the United States earn the right to adjust their legal status.
	Under the Japanese American Evacuation Claims Act, the U.S. government must compensate former internees for financial losses occasioned by the evacuation.
	At the London Olympics, Vicki Manalo Draves, a Filipino American, is the first woman ever to win gold medals in both the high- and low-diving events.
	The U.S. Supreme Court finds unconstitutional a California law prohibiting interracial marriage.
	The Korean peninsula is partitioned into South and North Korea.
	Canada loosens restrictions against Chinese immigration after the United States enacts similar legislation in 1943.
1949	Following civil war in China, the victorious Communist forces under Mao Zedong establish the mainland People's Republic of China. Chiang Kai-shek and the Guomindang (GMD) establish a new base in Taiwan.
	After the Communists seize power in China, the United States confers refugee status on 5,000 highly educated Chinese in the United States.
	Japanese American Tokyo Rose (Iva Toguri d'Aquino) is convicted of treason and sentenced to 10 years in prison. Released in 1956, she is eventually pardoned by President Gerald Ford in 1977.
1950	The Korean War begins.
	New U.S. legislation brings to the United States 6,423 Asian war brides over the next 15 years.
1950's	Korean War brides begin emigrating to the United States.
1952	The McCarran-Walter Act repeals the Immigration Act of 1924. The new law promises naturalization and eventual citizenship for Asian immigrants and sets a U.S. limit of 105 emigrants annually for each Asian country.
1953	The Refugee Relief Act brings Chinese political refugees to the United States.
	The Korean War ends with the signing of the Mutual Defense Treaty reestablishing the status quo along the 38th parallel.
1954	The French Indochina War ends with the signing of the Geneva Conference peace accords. Vietnam is partitioned into South and North Vietnam. Laos and Cambodia become independent.
	In the United States, Chinese having technical knowledge are permitted to move to mainland China.
1956	Chinese American James Wong Howe wins the first of two Academy Awards in cinematography, for *The Rose Tattoo* (1955).
	California voters choose to repeal the state's Alien Land Laws.

1956 (cont.)	Dalip Singh Saund, an Asian Indian American from California, wins a seat in Congress—the first Asian American elected to Congress.
1957	Japanese American actor Sessue Hayakawa stars in the motion picture *The Bridge on the River Kwai*, for which he earns an Academy Award nomination.
	Chinese Americans Chen Ning Yang and Tsung-Dao Lee share the Nobel Prize in Physics.
1959	The U.S. government institutes the "Confession Program" under which illegal aliens may change their immigration status by informing on other illegal aliens.
	Hawaii becomes the fiftieth and last U.S. state.
	Daniel Inouye of Hawaii becomes the first Japanese American U.S. representative.
	Hiram Fong of Hawaii becomes the first Chinese American U.S. senator.
1962	Inouye is elected U.S. senator from Hawaii, while Spark Matsunaga, another Japanese American, is elected to the U.S. House of Representatives.
1964	Japanese American Patsy Mink, elected as a U.S. representative, becomes the United States' first Asian American woman in Congress.
	North Vietnamese troops bomb two U.S. intelligence ships in the Gulf of Tonkin, escalating Ameri-can involvement in the war.
	Congress passes a Civil Rights Act to combat racial discrimination; it passes another in 1965.
1965	Under the Immigration and Nationality Act, larger numbers of Asian immigrants are allowed to enter the United States.
	Large influx of Korean immigrants to the United States triggers the emergence of Koreatowns in Los Angeles and Chicago.
	The Delano grape strike is launched.
	The Voting Rights Act gives all American citizens equal access to the electoral process.
	President Lyndon B. Johnson deploys the first U.S. military combat troops to South Vietnam to fight the Viet Cong.
	President Johnson orders the bombing of Hanoi, escalating the rise of the antiwar movement in the United States.
1967	A ruling issued by the U.S. Supreme Court prohibits the states from erecting bans on interracial marriages.
	Canada's Immigration Act triggers rapid increase in Chinese immigration. The new law parallels the major reforms instituted by the United States' Immigration and Nationality Act of 1965.
1968	San Francisco State College strike involves Third World students demanding that an ethnic studies program be created.
	Asian Indian American Har Gobind Khorana, Robert Holley, and Marshall Nirenberg share the Nobel Prize in Physiology or Medicine.
1969	Third World students at the University of California, Berkeley, also strike for the formation of an ethnic studies program. As a result of the demonstrations, Asian American Studies programs are established.
	The United States begins withdrawing troops from Vietnam.
1971	More Koreans emigrate to the United States after martial law is imposed in South Korea.
	East Pakistan becomes the independent nation of Bangladesh.

1972	More Filipinos immigrate to the United States after martial law is declared in the Philippines.
	Title VII of the Civil Rights Act makes it unlawful for employers to discriminate against their workers because of race or other reasons.
	Direct U.S. military intervention in Vietnam ends with the signing of a peace agreement.
1974	California voters elect March Fong Eu as secretary of state.
	Under *Lau v. Nichols*, school districts must sponsor bilingual education for students in their jurisdiction with limited English skills.
1975	Pol Pot comes to power in Phnom Penh, capital of Cambodia, following a coup by the Khmer Rouge. During the atrocities that ensue, more than one million Cambodian civilians are killed.
	The South Vietnamese capital of Saigon falls to the Viet Cong. U.S. forces withdraw from the region.
	As Communist regimes come to power in South Vietnam, Cambodia, and Laos, about 125,000 refugees from these countries find their way to the United States. About 2,200 enter Canada.
	The Indochina Migration and Refugee Assistance Act authorizes U.S. government funding in support of refugee resettlement programs.
1976	Chinese American Samuel Ting is named a cowinner (with Burton Richter) of the Nobel Prize in Physics.
	The Indochinese Refugee Children's Assistance Act provides money to support the education of children from Vietnam, Cambodia, and Laos.
	As the mayor of Kauai, Hawaii, Eduardo Manlapit becomes the United States' first Filipino American county executive.
	President Gerald Ford rescinds Executive Order 9066.
	In *Hampton v. Mow Sun Wong*, the U.S. Supreme Court rules that aliens residing in the United States are entitled to compete for jobs with the federal government.
	Vietnam announces unification of South and North Vietnam.
1976-1985	More than 762,000 refugees from Southeast Asia are resettled in the United States.
1978	At a national convention of the Japanese American Citizens League (JACL), conferees adopt a resolution demanding redress and reparations for Japanese interned during World War II.
	As conditions in Vietnam become more intolerable, massive numbers of "boat people" flee the country.
1979	The Carter Administration establishes diplomatic relations with the People's Republic of China and breaks off official relations with Taiwan.
	The Orderly Departure Program, initiated by the Vietnamese government and the United Nations (UN), allows refugees to emigrate legally.
1980	In response to the flow of refugees to America, Congress passes the Refugee Act to ease the admission process.
	U.S. census figures indicate that the country's Asian and Pacific American population is 3.5 million, or 1.5 percent of the entire U.S. population.
1981	About 120,000 Southeast Asian refugees arrive in the United States. U.S. government spending on refugee-assistance programs peaks at $902 million.
	In Texas, the Ku Klux Klan (KKK) sets fire to the boats of Vietnamese fishermen.
	The congressional Commission on Wartime Relocation and Internment of Civilians (CWRIC) finds that the Japanese internment was unjustified and the result of racist hysteria and an absence of political leadership.
	In the Philippines, martial law is ended.

1982	In Detroit, Michigan, Chinese American Vincent Chin is beaten to death by two white men, neither one of whom will be convicted for the crime.
	A strike staged by 10,000 Asian garment workers in New York wins important concessions for the strikers.
	The American Immigration Act extends immigration priority to children from specified Southeast Asian countries who are known to have been fathered by American citizens. Vietnamese refugee admissions into the United States and Canada decline sharply and remain that way over the next eight years.
1983	The National Committee for Japanese American Redress (NCJAR) asks the federal courts to authorize monetary compensation for World War II internees.
	Three Japanese Americans convicted of violating the curfew/evacuation orders of World War II ask the federal courts to vacate their convictions. All three are successful.
	Asian Indian American Subramanyan Chandrasekhar and William Fowler share the Nobel Prize in Physics.
1984	China and Great Britain sign an agreement establishing the conditions under which Hong Kong will revert to Chinese control in 1997.
1985	The first Asian American to fly a U.S. space-shuttle mission is Ellison Onizuka, a Japanese American mission specialist aboard the *Discovery*.
	The income level of first-wave Vietnamese Americans matches the U.S. average.
1986	Congress passes the Immigration Reform and Control Act.
	In the Philippines, President Ferdinand Marcos is ousted from office. Corazon Aquino is elected president.
	The U.S. Civil Rights Commission releases a study chronicling the rise of anti-Asian violence in the country.
	English is the official language in California, according to a new state initiative.
	Congress allocates to Hong Kong an annual immigration quota of 5,000 admissions.
	Canadian census figures report 63,000 Vietnamese living in Canadian provinces.
1987	Under the Amerasian Homecoming Act, children in Vietnam born of American fathers are allowed to immigrate to the United States.
	Congress enacts new federal legislation that penalizes employers who knowingly hire undocumented aliens and offers amnesty for illegal aliens entering the United States prior to 1982.
	At the University of California, Berkeley, admissions officials come under fire for allegedly discriminating against Asian American applicants.
	Martial law is suspended in Taiwan.
1988	President Ronald Reagan signs into law the Civil Liberties Act, under which the government will issue an official apology for the internment and pay each surviving internee $20,000.
	Southeast Asian countries of first asylum begin closing their doors to boat people by means of a screening process that denies them refugee status and assistance.
1989	The Chinese government deploys troops to suppress prodemocracy demonstrations in Beijing's Tiananmen Square.
	Five Southeast Asian schoolchildren are killed in the Stockton, California, schoolyard incident.
	Vietnamese troops withdraw from Cambodia.

1990	Congress passes legislation reaffirming the principles of the 1965 immigration reform and authorizing additional increase in immigration.
	Congress raises Hong Kong's annual immigration quota to 10,000 admissions, with an additional increase to 20,000 yearly by 1995.
	Litigation by the Vietnamese Fishermen's Association secures for noncitizens the right to own and operate commercial fishing boats off the California coast.
	As many as 100,000 Vietnamese boat people languish in refugee camps in Southeast Asia, the highest total since 1979.
	First group of 150 former South Vietnamese political prisoners comes to the United States under a new government program.
	U.S. census; the results, as they become available, show that Asian Americans are the fastest-growing ethnic minority group in the United States, with a 1990 population exceeding 7.2 million.
1991	Korean American Won So is the first student member of the New York City School Board, as well as the first Asian American to ever serve on the Board.
	The first 194 (of the some 50,000 eligible) Filipino veterans of World War II finally become naturalized U.S. citizens, under the Immigration Reform Act of 1990. After a 45-year struggle with the U.S., they have made the government honor its promise of citizenship to Filipinos who fought under the U.S. flag during the war.
1992	In four days of rioting following the verdict in the first trial of four Los Angeles Police Department officers accused of using excessive force in the arrest of motorist Rodney King, the Korean community in Los Angeles suffers devastating losses; between 2,000 and 2,500 Korean businesses are damaged or destroyed.
	Jay Kim, a Korean-born businessperson in California, is elected to the U.S. House of Representatives, becoming the first Asian immigrant to serve in Congress.
	In the wake of the 1989 Tiananmen Square incident, Congress passes the Chinese Student Protection Act, permitting Chinese students and other Chinese in the U.S to adjust their visa status, becoming permanent residents.
1993	The National Asian Pacific American Legal Consortium, the first national civil rights organization for Asian Americans, is founded.
	In response to protests by Asian American students, professors, and other activists, the University of California, Irvine, agrees to establish an Asian American Studies program.
1994	The United States ends its 19-year embargo on trade with Vietnam, the first step toward establishing full diplomatic relations; response in the Vietnamese American community is mixed but predominantly favorable.

Organizations

ASIAN AMERICAN, GENERAL

Asian American Arts Alliance, Inc.
339 Lafayette Street
New York, NY 10012

Asian American Journalists Association (AAJA)
1765 Sutter Street, Suite 1000
San Francisco, CA 94115

Asian American Legal Defense and Education Fund (AALDEF)
99 Hudson Street
New York, NY 10013

Asian American Political Coalition
P.O. Box 113
Mount Freedom, NJ 07970

Asian CineVision (ACV)
32 East Broadway
New York, NY 10002

Asian Law Caucus
468 Bush Street, 3d Floor
San Francisco, CA 94108

Asian Pacific American Labor Alliance
1444 Eye Street NW, Suite 702
Washington, D.C. 20005

Asian Pacific American Legal Center of Southern California
1010 South Flower Street, Suite 302
Los Angeles, CA 90015

Asian/Pacific American Librarians Association
Ohio State University, University Libraries
1858 Neil Avenue Mall
Columbus, OH 43210

Asian/Pacific Women's Network
1300 Markham Way
Sacramento, CA 98518

Asia Society, The (TAS)
725 Park Avenue
New York, NY 10021

Coalition of Asian Pacific American Associations
240 East 76th Street, Suite 3F
New York, NY 10021

Leadership Education for Asian Pacifics, Inc.
327 East 2d Street, Suite 226
Los Angeles, CA 90012

Media Action Network for Asian Americans
P.O. Box 1881
Santa Monica, CA 90406

National Asian American Telecommunications Association (NAATA)
346 9th Street, 2d Floor
San Francisco, CA 94103

National Asian Pacific American Legal Consortium
1629 K Street NW, Suite 1010
Washington, D.C. 20006

Organization of Pan Asian American Women
Meyer Foundation
1400 16th Street NW, Suite 360
Washington, D.C. 20016

ASIAN INDIAN AMERICAN

Association of Indians in America
8636 Red Coat Lane
Potomac, MD 20854

National Association of Canadians of Origin in India
P.O. Box 2308, Station D
Ottawa, ON KIP 5W5 Canada

CHINESE AMERICAN

Chinese American Citizens Alliance
Los Angeles Lodge
415 Bamboo Lane
Los Angeles, CA 90012

Chinese American Democratic Club
915 Grant Avenue
San Francisco, CA 94108

Chinese-American Librarians Association (CALA)
Auraria Library
Lawrence and 11th Streets
Denver, CO 80204

Chinese for Affirmative Action (CAA)
17 Walter U. Lum Place
San Francisco, CA 94108

Chinese Historical Society of America
650 Commercial Street
San Francisco, CA 94108

Organization of Chinese American Women
Los Angeles Chapter
P.O. Box 3278
Alhambra, CA 91803

Organization of Chinese Americans
2025 I Street NW, Suite 926
Washington, D.C. 20006

FILIPINO AMERICAN

Pilipino American Network and Advocacy
1720 West Beverly Boulevard, #200
Los Angeles, CA 90026

JAPANESE AMERICAN

Japanese American Citizens League (JACL)
1765 Sutter Street
San Francisco, CA 94115

Japanese American Curriculum Project
234 Main Street
P.O. Box 1587
San Mateo, CA 94401

KOREAN AMERICAN

Korean Society, The
412 1st Street SE
Washington, D.C. 20003

Korean Youth and Community Center
3470 Wilshire Boulevard, Suite 1110
Los Angeles, CA 90010

Museums

ASIAN AMERICAN, GENERAL

Amerasia Bookstore and Gallery
174 Japanese Village Plaza
Los Angeles, CA 90012

Asian American Arts Centre
26 Bowery Street
New York, NY 10013

Asian Arts Institute
26 Bowery Street
New York, NY 10013

House of Pacific Relations, The
Balboa Park
San Diego, CA 92101

Kamuela Museum
Kawaihae-Kohala Junction
Routes 19 and 250
P.O. Box 507
Kamuela, HI 96743

Lyman House Memorial Museum
276 Haili Street
Hilo, HI 96720

Pacific Heritage Museum
608 Commercial
San Francisco, CA 94111

Roger Williams Park
Museum of Natural History
Roger Williams Park
Providence, RI 02905

Wing Luke Asian Museum
407 7th Avenue
Seattle, WA 98104

CHINESE AMERICAN

Captain Robert Bennet Forbes House
Charitable Trust
215 Adams Street
Milton, MA 02186

Chico Museum
2d and Salem Streets
Chico, CA 95926

Chinese Historical Society Museum
650 Commercial Street
San Francisco, CA 94111

Chinese Museum
P.O. Box 12
Fiddletown, CA 95629

Chinese Museum, Chew Kee Store
Main Street
P.O. Box 12
Fiddletown, CA 95629

Columbia State Historic Park
P.O. Box 151
Columbus, CA 95310

Del Norte County Historical Society
577 H Street
Crescent City, CA 95531

Ellis Island Immigraton Museum
52 Vanderbilt Avenue
New York, NY 10007

Hawaii Immigrant Heritage
Preservation Center
Bernice Pauahi Bishop Museum
1525 Bernice Street
P.O. Box 19000-A
Honolulu, HI 96817

Institute of Texan Cultures
801 South Bowie
San Antonio, TX 78205

Kam Wah Chung and Company
Museum
City Park NW Canton
HCR 56, Box 290
John Day, OR 97845

Kearney Mansion Museum
7160 West Kearney Boulevard
Fresno, CA 93706

Taoist Temple and Museum
Hanford, CA 93230

Tombstone Courthouse State Historic
Park
P.O. Box 216
Tombstone, AZ 85638

University of Hawaii at Manoa Art
Gallery
Honolulu, HI 96822

Weaverville Joss House State Historic
Park
State Historic Park
P.O. Box 1217
Weaverville, CA 96093

FILIPINO AMERICAN

Hawaii Immigrant Heritage
Preservation Center
Bernice Pauahi Bishop Museum
1525 Bernice Street
P.O. Box 19000-A
Honolulu, HI 96817

Institute of Texan Cultures
801 South Bowie
San Antonio, TX 78205

JAPANESE AMERICAN

Eastern California Museum
155 Grant Street
P.O. Box 206
Independence, CA 93526

Hanalei Museum
P.O. Box 91
Hanalei, HI 96714

Hawaii Immigrant Heritage
Preservation Center
Bernice Pauahi Bishop Museum
1525 Bernice Street
P.O. Box 19000-A
Honolulu, HI 96817

Institute of Texan Cultures
801 South Bowie
San Antonio, TX 78205

Japan Society Gallery
333 East 47th Street
New York, NY 10017

Japanese American National Museum
941 East 3d Street, Suite 201
Los Angeles, CA 90013

Kearney Mansion Museum
7160 West Kearney Boulevard
Fresno, CA 93706

Morikami Museum of Japanese
Culture
Japanese Gardens
4000 Morikami Park Road
Delray Beach, FL 33446

Sweetwater County Historical
Museum
80 West Flaming Gorge Way
Green River, WY 82935

Tacoma Art Museum
12th and Pacific Avenues
Tacoma, WA 98402

PACIFIC ISLANDER AMERICAN

Alexander and Baldwin Sugar Museum
3957 Hansen Road
P.O. Box 125
Puunene, HI 96784

Amy B. Greenwell Ethnobotanical
Garden
P.O. Box 1053
Captain Cook, HI 96704

Bailey House Museum
2375-A Main Street
Wailuku, HI 96793

Bernice Pauahi Bishop Museum
1525 Bernice Street
P.O. Box 19000-A
Honolulu, HI 96817

Contemporary Museum, The
2411 Makiki Heights Drive
Honolulu, HI 96822

Hawaii Children's Museum
650 Iwilei Road
Honolulu, HI 96817

Hawaii Immigrant Heritage Preservation Center
Bernice Pauahi Bishop Museum
1525 Bernice Street
P.O. Box 19000-A
Honolulu, HI 96817

Hawaii Maritime Center
Pier 7, Honolulu Harbor
Honolulu, HI 96813

Kamuela Museum
Kawaihae-Kohala Junction
Routes 19 and 250
P.O. Box 507
Kamuela, HI 96743

Kokee Museum
Kokee State Park
P.O. Box 400
Waimea, HI 96796

Maui Historical Society
2375-A Main Street
Wailuku, HI 96793

Mission Houses Museum
553 South King Street
Honolulu, HI 96813

Queen Emma Summer Place
2913 Pali Highway
Honolulu, HI 96813

Queen's Medical Center Historical Room
1301 Punchbowl Street
P.O. Box 861
Honolulu, HI 96808

Roger Williams Park Museum of Natural History
Roger Williams Park
Providence, RI 02905

University of Northern Iowa Museum
3219 Hudson Road
Cedar Falls, IA 50614

Waipahu Cultural Garden Park
P.O. Box 103
94695 Waipahu Street
Waipahu, HI 96797

VIETNAMESE AMERICAN

Institute of Texan Cultures
801 South Bowie
San Antonio, TX 78205

Research Centers and Libraries

ASIAN AMERICAN, GENERAL

Asian American Studies Center
University of California, Los Angeles
3232 Campbell Hall
Los Angeles, CA 90024

Asian American Studies Center Reading Room
University of California, Los Angeles
3232 Campbell Hall
Los Angeles, CA 90024

Asian American Studies Library
Institute of East Asian Studies
University of California, Berkeley
2223 Fulton Street, 6th Floor
Berkeley, CA 94720

Asian Branch Library
Oakland Public Library
449 9th Street
Oakland, CA 94607

Asian Pacific American Photographic Archives
Visual Communications
263 South Los Angeles Street, Room 307
Los Angeles, CA 90012

Asian Pacific Resource Center
Los Angeles County Public Library
1550 West Beverly Boulevard
Montebello, CA 90640

Asian Studies Center
4650 Arrow Highway, Suite D-6
Montclair, CA 91763

Asian Studies Center
Heritage Foundation
214 Massachusetts Avenue NE
Washington, D.C. 20002

Asian Studies Program
University of Pittsburgh
4E35 Forbes Quadrangle
Pittsburgh, PA 15260

Brown University Center for Race and Ethnicity
82 Waterman
Box 1886
Providence, RI 02912

Center for Immigrant and Population Studies
College of Staten Island of the City University of New York
130 Stuyvesant Place, Room 1-932
Staten Island, NY 10301

Center for Immigrant's Rights
48 Street Marks Place
New York, NY 10003

Center for Immigration Policy and Refugee Assistance Library
Georgetown University
Hoya Station, Box 2298
Washington, D.C. 20057

Center for Immigration Research
Balch Institute of Ethnic Studies
18 South 7th Street
Philadelphia, PA 19106

Center for Migration Studies of New York Library
209 Flagg Place
Staten Island, NY 10304

Center for Research on Women
Memphis State University
Clement Hall-339
Memphis, TN 38152

Center for Studies of Ethnicity and Race in America
University of Colorado, Boulder
Ketchum 30
Campus Box 339
Boulder, CO 80309

Center for Third World Organizing
1218 East 21st Street
Oakland, CA 94606

Church World Service Immigration and Refugee Program
475 Riverside Drive, Room 656
New York, NY 10115

EAPI/PI/RSI Research Materials Collection
East-West Center
1777 East-West Road
Honolulu, HI 96848

East Asian Institute
Columbia University
420 West 118th Street
New York, NY 10027

East-West Center
1777 East-West Road
Honolulu, HI 96848

Ethnic American Council Library
820 Lathrop
River Forest, IL 60305

Ethnic Materials Information Exchange
Queens College of the City University of New York
Graduate School of Library and Information Studies
NSF 300
65-30 Kissena Boulevard
Flushing, NY 11367

International Theatre Studies Center
University of Kansas
339 Murphy Hall
Lawrence, KS 66045

Midwest Asia Center
245 East 6th Street
St. Paul, MN 55101

National Archives and Records Administration
National Archives
Great Lakes Region
7358 South Pulaski Road
Chicago, IL 60629

National Immigration Law Center
1636 West 8th Street,
Suite 215
Los Angeles, CA 90017

Pacific Studies Center
222 B View Street
Mountain View, CA 94041

Population and Development Program Research Library
Cornell University
218 Warren Hall
Ithaca, NY 14853

School of Hawaiian, Asian and Pacific Studies
University of Hawaii, Manoa
Moore Hall 416
1890 East-West Road
Honolulu, HI 96822

Special Collections
Leeward Community College Library
96-045 Ala Ike
Pearl City, HI 96782

United States Committee for Refugees Library
1025 Vermont Avenue NW,
Suite 920
Washington, D.C. 20005

CHINESE AMERICAN

Chatham Square Regional Branch Library
New York Public Library
33 East Broadway
New York, NY 10002

Chinese Collection
Los Angeles Public Library,
Chinatown Branch
536 West College Street
Los Angeles, CA 90012

Chinese Historical Society of America Archives
650 Commercial Street
San Francisco, CA 94111

Hawaii Chinese History Center Library
111 North King Street, Suite 410
Honolulu, HI 96817
Oral History Program
California State University, Fullerton, Library
800 North State College Boulevard
Fullerton, CA 92634

JAPANESE AMERICAN

Donald B. Gordon Memorial Library
Morikami Museum of Japanese Culture
4000 Morikami Park Road
Delray Beach, FL 33446
Franklin D. Murphy Library
Japanese American Cultural and Community Center
244 South San Pedro Street, 2nd Floor, Room 505
Los Angeles, CA 90012
Gordon W. Prange Collection
McKeldin Library
University of Maryland, College Park,
Libraries
College Park, MD 20742
Honolulu Heart Program
Kuakini Medical Center
347 North Kuakini Street
Honolulu, HI 96817
Institute for Intercultural Studies
Our Lady of the Lake University
411 SW 24th Street
San Antonio, TX 78207
Japanese American National Library
1619 Sutter Street
P.O. Box 590598
San Francisco, CA 94159
Oral History Program
California State University, Fullerton, Library
800 North State College Boulevard
Fullerton, CA 92634
Special Collections Department Oviatt Library
California State University, Northridge
18111 Nordhoff Street
Northridge, CA 91330

PACIFIC ISLANDER AMERICAN

Alvin Seale South Seas Collection
Pacific Grove Public Library
550 Central Avenue
Pacific Grove, CA 93950

Asian Pacific Resource Center
Los Angeles County Public Library
1550 West Beverly Boulevard
Montebello, CA 90640
Curriculum Research and Development Group
College of Education
University of Hawaii, Manoa
1776 University Avenue
Honolulu, HI 96822
EAPI/PI/RSI Research Materials Collection
East-West Center
1777 East-West Road
Honolulu, HI 96848
Edna Allyn Room
Hawaii State Library
Hawaii State Public Library System
634 Pensacola Street
Honolulu, HI 96814
Hawaii and Pacific Section I
Hawaii State Library
Hawaii State Public Library System
634 Pensacola Street
Honolulu, HI 96814
Hawaii Newspaper Agency Library
605 Kapiolani Boulevard
Honolulu, HI 96813
Hawaiian Mission Children's Society Library
553 South King Street
Honolulu, HI 96813
Institute for Polynesian Studies
Brigham Young University, Hawaii
Laie, HI 96762
Kathryn E. Lyle Memorial Library
Lyman House Memorial Museum
276 Haili Street
Hilo, HI 96720
Mission-Historical Library
Hawaii Historical Society
560 Kawaiahao Street
Honolulu, HI 96813
Pacific/Asian American Mental Health Research Center
University of Illinois, Chicago
1033 West Van Buren Street, Suite 7N
Chicago, IL 60607
Pacific Collection
Hamilton Library Special Collections
University of Hawaii, Honolulu
2550 The Mall
Honolulu, HI 96822
Pacific Islands Development Program
East-West Center
1777 East-West Road
Honolulu, HI 96848

School of Hawaiian, Asian and Pacific Studies
University of Hawaii, Manoa
Moore Hall 315
1890 East-West Road
Honolulu, HI 96822
Social Science Research Institute
University of Hawaii, Honolulu
Porteus Hall 704
2424 Maile Way
Honolulu, HI 96822
Special Collections
Leeward Community College Library
96-045 Ala Ike
Pearl City, HI 96782
State Archives
Hawaii Department of Accounting and General Services
Iolani Palace Grounds
Honolulu, HI 96813
Young Adult Section
Hawaii State Library
Hawaii State Public Library System
634 Pensacola Street
Honolulu, HI 96814

VIETNAMESE AMERICAN

Reference Collection
Southeast Asia Rescue Foundation
Hangar 6, Taxiway Lindy Loop
Spruce Creek Airport
Daytona Beach, FL 32124
Vietnam Refugee Fund Library
6433 Nothana Drive
Springfield, VA 22150

OTHER ASIAN AMERICAN

American Institute of Indian Studies
(Asian Indian)
1130 East 59th Street
Chicago, IL
Southeast Asian Archive (Southeast Asians)
University of California, Irvine
University of California Library
P.O. Box 19557
Irvine, CA 92713
Southeast Asian Refugee Studies Project (primarily Hmong and Cambodian American)
University of Minnesota
330 Humphrey Center
301 19th Avenue South
Minneapolis, MN 55455

Asian American Studies Programs

Brown University
American Civilization Department
Box 1892
Brown University
Providence, RI 02912
(401) 863-1693; 863-2896
Director: Robert Lee

California State University, Fresno
Asian American Studies
Department of Anthropology
Fresno, CA 93740-0016
(209) 278-2200
Director: Franklin Ng

**California State University,
Long Beach**
Department of Asian and Asian
American Studies
1250 Bellflower Blvd.
Long Beach, CA 90840
(213) 985-4645
Founded: 1970
Director: Arnold Kaminsky

California State University, Northridge
Asian American Studies Department
18111 Nordhoff St.
California State University
Northridge, CA 91330
(818) 885-4966
Founded: 1990
Director: Kenyon S. Chan

Cornell University
Asian American Studies Program
292 Caldwell Hall
Ithaca, NY 14853
(607) 225-3320
Founded: 1985
Director: Gary Y. Okihiro

**Hunter College, City University of
New York**
Asian American Studies
695 Park Ave.
New York, NY 10021
(212) 772-5559
Founded: 1993
Director: Peter Kwong

Queens College
Asian/Asian American Center
163-03 Horace Harding Expressway,
Room 507
Flushing, NY 11365
(718) 670-4226
Founded: 1987
Director: Jack Tchen

San Francisco State University
Asian American Studies
School of Ethnic Studies
1600 Holloway Ave., PSY Room 103
San Francisco, CA 94132
(415) 338-1054; 338-2698
Founded: 1969
Director: Marlon K. Hom

San Jose State University
Asian American Studies Program
One Washington Square
San Jose, CA 95192-0121
(408) 924-5750
Founded: 1970
Director: Alexander Yamato

Santa Clara University
Ethnic Studies Program
Santa Clara, CA 95053
(408) 554-6880
Director: Stephen Fugita

University of California, Berkeley
Asian American Studies
Ethnic Studies Department
3407 Dwinelle Hall
Berkeley, CA 94720
(501) 642-6555]
Founded: 1969
Director: Sau-ling C. Wong

University of California, Davis
Asian American Studies Program
AOB IV, Room 156
Davis, CA 95616
(916) 752-3625
Founded: 1969
Acting Director: Isao Fujimoto

University of California, Irvine
Asian American Studies Program
University of California
Irvine, CA 92717
(714) 856-4196
Acting Director: R. Bin Wong

University of California, Los Angeles
Asian American Studies Center
3232 Campbell Hall
Los Angeles, CA 90024-1546
(310) 825-2974
Founded: 1970
Director: Don T. Nakanishi

University of California, Riverside
Ethnic Studies Department
University of California
Riverside, CA 92521

(909) 787-4579
Director: Clifford Trafzer

University of California, San Diego
Ethnic Studies Department
9500 Gilman Dr.
University of California, San Diego
La Jolla, CA 92093-0414
(619) 534-3276
Director: Ramon Guitierrez

**University of California,
Santa Barbara**
Asian American Studies Program
Ellison Hall 2843
Santa Barbara, CA 93106
(805) 893-2371
Founded: 19??
Director: Sucheng Chan

**University of California,
Santa Cruz**
American Studies Department
Oakes College
University of California
Santa Cruz, CA 92132-0763
(408) 459-4725
Director: Judy Yung

University of Colorado
Asian American Studies
Center for the Study of Race and
Ethnicity in America
University of Colorado
Boulder, CO 80309
(303) 492-8852
Director: Evelyn Hu-DeHart

University of Connecticut
Asian American Studies Institute
241 Glenbrook Road
Storrs, CT 06269-2103
(203) 486-3560
Founded: 1993
Interim Director: Roger N. Buckley

University of Hawaii, Manoa
Ethnic Studies Program
East-West Road 4, Room 4D
Honolulu, HI 96822
(808) 956-8975
Director: Franklin Odo

University of Michigan
American Culture Department
410 Mason Hall
Ann Arbor, MI 48109-1027
(313) 763-5559
Director: Gail M. Nomura

University of Washington
Asian American Studies
Department of American Ethnic
  Studies
B 501 Padelford Hall
Seattle, WA 98195
(206) 543-5401
Director: Shawn Wong

University of Wisconsin, Madison
Asian American Studies Program
1600 North Park St.
7185 Helen C. White
Madison, WI 53705-252
(608) 263-3658
Founded: 1990
Acting Director: Michael Thornton

Washington State University
Asian/Pacific American Studies
Department of Comparative American
  Cultures
Pullman, WA 99164-5910
(509) 335-2605
Director: William Willard

Newspapers, Newsletters, Magazines, and Journals

ASIAN AMERICAN, GENERAL

NEWSPAPERS

Asian News of Florida, The
1140 NE 163d, Suite 28
North Miami Beach, FL 33162

Asianweek
Pan Asia Venture Capital Corp.
809 Sacramento Street
San Francisco, CA 94108
First published: 1979

Centre Daily News
Chang Newspaper, Ltd.
620 Washington Street
San Francisco, CA
First published: 1982

East Is East Newspaper
P.O. Box 95247
Seattle, WA 98145

Eastern Times
2315 Wilson Boulevard, Suite D
Arlington, VA 22201

International Examiner
622 South Washington
Seattle, WA 98104
First published: 1973

New Asian Times
Box 1435
New York, NY 10013
First published: 1988

World Daily News
724 Monterey Pass Road
Monterey Park, CA 91754

NEWSLETTERS

American Buddhist News
American Buddhist Movement
New York, NY
First published: 1981

Asia and Pacific Population Forum
East-West Population Institute
East-West Center
Honolulu, HI
First published: 1974

Asian American Educators Association Newsletter
Los Angeles, CA

Asian American News
National Federation of Asian
American United Methodists
New York, NY

Asian American Studies Center—Newsletter
Asian American Studies Center
University of California, Los Angeles
Los Angeles, CA
First published: 1970

Asian/Pacific American Librarians Association—Newsletter
Asian/Pacific American Librarians
Association
Brooklyn, NY
First published: 1980

Asian Pacific Health Project
Los Angeles, CA

Asian Pacific Lifeline
USC Asian Pacific Student Outreach,
Student Union
University of Southern California
Los Angeles, CA

Asian Rehabilitation Services, Inc.
Los Angeles, CA

Asian Studies Newsletter
Association for Asian Studies
University of Ann Arbor
Ann Arbor, MI
First published: 1955

Center for East Asian Studies—Newsletter
Center for East Asian Studies
University of Kansas
Lawrence, KS
First published: 1965

Center for Southeast Asia Studies—Newsletter
Center for Southeast Asia Studies
University of California, Berkeley
Berkeley, CA

Chicago South Asia Newsletter
South Asia Language and Area Center
University of Chicago
Chicago, IL
First published: 1977

Committee on Women in Asian Studies Newsletter
Asian Studies Program
University of Pittsburgh
Pittsburgh, PA
First published: 1982

East Asian Studies Center—Newsletter
East Asian Studies Center
Indiana University
Bloomington, IN

East West Newsletter
East West Players
Los Angeles, CA

East-West Report
United States Pan Asian American
Chamber of Commerce
Washington, D.C.

Echoes from Gold Mountain
Asian American Student Association
California State University, Long Beach
Long Beach, CA

Inside Moves
Association of Asian/Pacific
American Artists
Los Angeles, CA
First published: 1976

New Life News
South-East Asia Center
Chicago, IL
First published: 1984

New Saayer
Services for Asian American Youth
Los Angeles, CA

Outreach
South Asian Area Center
University of Wisconsin, Madison
Madison, WI

P/AAMHRC Research Review
Pacific/Asian American Mental
Health Research Center
Chicago, IL

PACE Newsletter
Pacific Asian Consortium on
Employment
Los Angeles, CA

Pan Asia News
Organization of Pan Asian Women
Washington, D.C.

Rice Paper
Asian American Drug Abuse Program
Los Angeles, CA

Warrior, The
Zen-Do Kai Martial Arts Association
Johnstown, NY

Washington Buddhist
Buddhist Vihara Society
Washington, D.C.

Zen Bow
Rochester Zen Center
Rochester, NY
First published: 1967

MAGAZINES

Asia Today
17230 Bothell Way, NE
Seattle, WA 98155

Asia Today
2020 National Press Building
Washington, D.C. 20045
First published: 1989

Asian Affairs: An American Review
Heldref Publications
Helen Dwight Reid Educational
Foundation
4000 Albemarle Street, NW
Washington, D.C. 20016
First published: 1973

Asian Riza Magazine
6290 Sunset Boulevard, #1801
Los Angeles, CA 90028
First published: 1988

Asian Times
3425 Payne Street
Falls Church, VA 22041

Asian Week
321 South San Vicente Boulevard, #504
Los Angeles, CA 90048

Balitaan
2352 West 3d Street
Los Angeles, CA 90057
First published: 1975

Bridge: Asian American Perspectives
Asian CineVision, Inc.
32 East Broadway
New York, NY 10002
First published: 1971

CrossCurrents
University of California, Los Angeles
Asian American Studies Center
Resource Development and
Publications
3232 Campbell Hall
405 Hilgard Avenue
Los Angeles, CA 90024
First published: 1977

Jade
6464 Sunset Boulevard
Los Angeles, CA 90027
First published: 1974

New Life Magazine
6125 Carlos Avenue
Hollywood, CA 90028

Pacific Ties
112-B Kerkhoff Hall
308 Westwood Plaza
Los Angeles, CA 90024
First published: 1985

PAN NET
United States Pan Asian American
Chamber of Commerce
1625 K Street NW, Suite 380
Washington, D.C. 20006

Rice
P.O. Box 25723
Los Angeles, CA 90025
First published: 1987

Transpacific
Asiam Publishing
22653 Pacific Coast Highway, #297
Malibu, CA 90265
First published: 1986

JOURNALS

Amerasia Journal
Asian American Studies Center
University of California, Los Angeles
Resource Development and
Publications
3232 Campbell Hall
405 Hilgard Avenue
Los Angeles, CA 90024
First published: 1971

Bulletin of Concerned Asian Scholars
3239 9th Street
Boulder, CO 80304
First published: 1968

Journal of Asian Studies, The
Association for Asian Studies, Inc.
1 Lane Hall
University of Michigan
Ann Arbor, MI 48109
First published: 1947

Modern Asian Studies
Cambridge University Press
40 West 20th Street
New York, NY 10011
First published: 1967

ASIAN INDIAN AMERICAN

NEWSPAPERS

Hinduism Today
Himalayan Academy
1819 2d Street
Concord, CA 94519
First published: 1978

India Globe
820 North Pollard Street
Arlington, VA 22203
First published: 1989

India Tribune
India Tribune Publications
2702 West Peterson Avenue
Chicago, IL 60659

India-West
5901 Christie Avenue, Suite 301
Emeryville, CA 94608
First published: 1975

Indo-American Business News
P.O. Box 33364, Farragut Station
Washington, D.C. 20033

NEWSLETTER

**American Society of Engineers from
India—Newsletter**
American Society of Engineers
from India
Troy, MI

MAGAZINE

India Currents
P.O. Box 21285
San Jose, CA
First published: 1987

CHINESE AMERICAN

NEWSPAPERS

American Chinese News
737 South San Pedro
Los Angeles, CA 90014

American Chinese World
396 Broadway, Suite 301-A
New York, NY 10013

Cheng Yen Pao
809 Sacramento Street
San Francisco, CA 94108
First published: 1967

China Daily News
Young China Daily Publishing Co.
1400 Monterey Pass Road
Monterey Park, CA 91754
First published: 1910

China Daily News
657 Mission Street
San Francisco, CA 94105

China Post
85 White Street
New York, NY 10013
First published: 1972

China Spring
P.O. Box 243
New York, NY 10185
First published: 1988

China Times
445 Madera Street
San Gabriel, CA 91776

China Times
952 National Press Building
Washington, D.C. 20045
First published: 1985

China Tribune
396 Broadway, #1002
New York, NY 10013
First published: 1943

Chinese Outreach
1238 North Edgemont Avenue
Los Angeles, CA 90029

Chinese Times
686 Sacramento Street
San Francisco, CA 94111
First published: 1924

Dong A Il Bo
2703 Geary Boulevard
San Francisco, CA 94118
International Daily News
870 Monterey Pass Road
Monterey Park, CA 91754
First published: 1981
New China Daily Press
P.O. Box 1656
Honolulu, HI 96806
First published: 1900
Newcomer News, The
755-A Commercial Street
San Francisco, CA 85818
Sampan
90 Tyler Street
Boston, MA 02111
First published: 1982
Seattle Chinese Post
414 8th Avenue, S
Seattle, WA 98104
First published: 1982
Sing Tao Daily (*Hsing Tao Jih Pao*)
185 Canal Street
New York, NY 10013
Sing Tao Daily (*Hsing Tao Jih Pao*)
625 Kearney Street
San Francisco, CA 94108
Sino Express
449 Broadway
New York, NY 10013
Taiwan Tribune
P.O. Box 1527
Long Island, NY 11101
First published: 1981
Truth
809 Sacramento Street
San Francisco, CA 94108
First published: 1882
United Journal
83-85 White Street
New York, NY 10013
First published: 1952
U.S. Eastern Times
133-36 41st Road, #CS-9
Flushing, NY 11355
Vietnam-Chinese Newspaper
403 West College Street
Los Angeles, CA 90012
Wor Kuen
P.O. Box 26229
San Francisco, CA 94126
World Journal
231 Adrian Road
Millbrae, CA 94030
Young China Daily, The
49-51 Hang-Ah Street
San Francisco, CA 94108
First published: 1910

NEWSLETTERS
Challenger
Chinese Christian Mission
Petaluma, CA
China Notes
Office of East Asia and the
Pacific, China Program
National Council of the
Churches of Christ
in the USA
New York, NY
First published: 1950
Chinatown Service Center Newsletter
Chinatown Service Center
Los Angeles, CA
**Chinese American Medical
Society—Newsletter**
Chinese American Publishing
Medical Society
Teaneck, NJ
First published: 1985
**Chinese for Affirmative Action
Newsletter**
Chinese for Affirmative Action
San Francisco, CA
First published: 1971
**Chinese Historical Society of
America—Bulletin**
Chinese Historical Society of America
San Francisco, CA
First published: 1966
Notes from the National Committee
National Committee on U.S.-China
Relations
New York, NY
First published: 1970
OCA Image
Organization of Chinese Americans
Washington, D.C.
First published: 1977
So-Cal Chinese Community News
San Gabriel, CA
Taiwan Economic News
U.S.A.-Republic of China Economic
Council
Crystal Lake, IL
First published: 1978
Taiwan Today
Friends of Free China
1629 K Street
Washington, D.C. 20006
First published: 1978

MAGAZINES
Chinese American Forum
606 Brantford Avenue
Silver Spring, MD 20904
First published: 1984

Chinese American Progress
Chinese American Civic Council
2249 Wentworth Avenue, 2d Floor
Chicago, IL 60616
First published: 1951
Dan Chung Weekly
P.O. Box 4658
Irvine, CA 92716
Linh San Jose Magazine
524 Hassinger Road
San Jose, CA 95111
Pamir Magazine
8122 Mayfield Road
P.O. Box 8
Chesterland, OH 44026
First published: 1964
Sinorama Magazine
Kwang Hwa Publishing Co.
5 Greenway Plaza, Suite 216
Houston, TX 77046
T'ai Chi
Wayfarer Publications
P.O. Box 26156
Los Angeles, CA 90026
First published: 1977
Taiwan Culture
Taiwan-United States Cultural Exchange
301 North Harrison Street, Suite 4B
Princeton, NJ 08540
First published: 1986
Vajra Bodhi Sea
Dharma Realm Buddhist Association
City of 10,000 Buddhas
Talmage, CA 95481
First published: 1970

JOURNALS
Chinese Culture Association Journal
Chinese Culture Association
P.O. Box 1272
Palo Alto, CA 94302
First published: 1966
Chinese United Journal
85 White Street
New York, NY 10013
First published: 1952
East West Chinese American Journal
838 Grant Avenue, Suite 307
San Francisco, CA 94108

FILIPINO AMERICAN

NEWSPAPERS
California Examiner
2901 West Beverly Boulevard
Los Angeles, CA 90057
Filipino-American Herald, The
508 Maynard Avenue South
P.O. Box 14240
Seattle, WA 98114
First published: 1942

Filipino Reporter
 1457 Broadway
 New York, NY 10036
Los Angeles Philippine News
 1052 West 6th Street, Suite 420
 Los Angeles, CA 90017
Philippine American News
 3301 Beverly Boulevard
 Los Angeles, CA 90004
Philippine News
 P.O. Box 2767
 San Francisco, CA 94083
 First published: 1961
Philippine News—Los Angeles
 1052 West 6th Street, #420
 Los Angeles, CA 90017
Philippine Virginia Chronicle
 5660 Indian River Road, #104
 Virginia Beach, VA 22464

NEWSLETTERS
Philippine News Survey
 Church Coalition for Human Rights
  in the Philippines
 Washington, D.C.
 First published: 1988
Philippine Studies Newsletter
 Philippine Studies Group
 Association for Asian Studies
 University of Hawai'i
 Honolulu, HI
 First published: 1978
Philippine Witness
 Church Coalition for Human Rights
  in the Philippines
 Washington, D.C.
 First published: 1985

MAGAZINES
Katipunan
 P.O. Box 8477
 Berkeley, CA 94707
 First published: 1987
Laging Una
 3003 Future Place
 Los Angeles, CA 90065
 First published: 1949

JAPANESE AMERICAN

NEWSPAPERS
Chicago Shimpo
 4670 North Manor Avenue
 Chicago, IL 60625
 First published: 1945
Gateway, U.S.A.
 1411 West Olympic Boulevard,
  Suite 511
 Los Angeles, CA 90015

Hawaii Hochi
 P.O. Box 17429
 Honolulu, HI 96817
 First published: 1912
Hokubei Mainichi
 1746 Post Street
 San Francisco, CA 94115
 First published: 1948
Japan Times, The
 3151 Airay Avenue, #K105
 Costa Mesa, CA 92626
**Kashu Mainichi—California Daily
 News**
 706 East 1st Street
 Los Angeles, CA 90012
 First published: 1931
New York Nichibei, The
 Japanese American News Corp.
 396 Broadway, Suite 301-B
 New York, NY 10013
 First published: 1945
New York Yomiuri Press
 500 5th Avenue, #1927
 New York, NY 10110
Nichi Bei Times
 P.O. Box 193098
 San Francisco, CA 94119
 First published: 1946
Nihon Kiezai Shimbun
 725 South Figueroa
 Los Angeles, CA 90017
North American Post
 662½ South Jackson Street
 Seattle, WA 98144
 First published: 1946
Pacific Citizen
 Japanese American Citizens League
 941 East 3d Street, Suite 200
 Los Angeles, CA 90012
 First published: 1929
Rafu Shimpo
 259 South Los Angeles Street
 Los Angeles, CA 90012
 First published: 1903
Rocky Mountain Jiho
 1215 19th Street
 Denver, CO 80202
 First published: 1962
Tozai Times
 5810 East Olympic Boulevard
 Los Angeles, CA 90022
Utah Nippo
 52 North 1000 West
 Salt Lake City, UT 84116
 First published: 1914

NEWSLETTERS
**Center for Japanese Studies—
 Newsletter**
 Center for Japanese Studies
 University of Michigan
 Ann Arbor, MI
 First published: 1974
Community Center News
 San Fernando Valley Japanese-
  American Community Center
 Pacoima, CA
**East San Gabriel Valley Japanese
 Community Center—Newsletter**
 West Covina, CA
Geppo Haiki Journal
 Yuki Teikei Haiku Society of the
  United States and Canada
 Chabot College, Valley Campus
 Livermore, CA
Impressions
 Ukiyo-e Society of America
 New York, NY
 First published: 1976
Japan Society—Newsletter
 New York, NY
 First published: 1952
**Japanese Investment in U.S. Real
 Estate Review**
 Mead Ventures
 Phoenix, AZ
 First published: 1988
**Japanese Sword Society of the United
 States—Newsletter**
 Japanese Sword Society of the United
  States
 Breckenridge, TX
 First published: 1969
**Kagi: The Japanese Guide to
 California**
 Los Angeles, CA
LTSC News
 Little Tokyo Service Center
 Los Angeles, CA
Nikkei Senior Citizens
 Japanese Community Pioneer Center
 Los Angeles, CA
Nikkei-Sentinel
 Little Tokyo People's Rights Organi-
  zation
 Los Angeles, CA
**United States-Japan Foundation—
 Forum**
 United States-Japan Foundation
 New York, NY
 First published: 1985

MAGAZINE

Postal Bell
Japanese-American Society for Philately
P.O. Box 1049
El Cerrito, CA 94530
First published: 1939

KOREAN AMERICAN

NEWSPAPERS

Christian Herald
260 South Los Angeles Street
Los Angeles, CA 90012

Dong A Daily News
1035 Crenshaw Boulevard
Los Angeles, CA 90019

Hae Oe Han Win Bo
192 Cow Neck Road
Port Washington, NY 11050

Hanguk Ilbo
3418 West 1st Street
Los Angeles, CA 90004
First published: 1965

Joong-Ang Daily News
690 Wilshire Place
Los Angeles, CA 90017
First published: 1965

Korea Central Daily
13749 Midvale North
Seattle, WA 98133

Korea News
42-22 27th Street
Long Island City, NY 11101
First published: 1980

Korea Post
2720 El Camino Real
Santa Clara, CA 95051

Korea Times, The
Korean Daily News
141 North Vermont Avenue
Los Angeles, CA 90004
First published: 1991

Korea Times, The
430 Yale Avenue North
Seattle, WA 98109
First published: 1984

Korea Times Boston
Korea News, Inc.
425 Broadway
Somerville, MA 02144

Korean Central Daily
4546 North Kedzie Avenue
Chicago, IL 60625

Korean Street Journal
1321 West 11th Street
Los Angeles, CA 90015
First published: 1981

Korean Sunday Post, The
730 South Western Avenue
Los Angeles, CA 90005

Korean Times
2248 Delaware
Ann Arbor, MI 48103

Unification News of Korea, The
3171 West Olympic Boulevard
Los Angeles, CA 90006

NEWSLETTERS

Center for Korean Studies—Newsletter
Center for Korean Studies
University of Hawai'i, Manoa
Honolulu, HI
First published: 1974

Korea Report
Korea Information and Resource Center
Washington, D.C.
First published: 1987

Korea Update
North American Coalition for Human Rights in Korea
Washington, D.C.
First published: 1990

Korean Philately
Korea Stamp Society
Grand Junction, CO
First published: 1951

MAGAZINES

Korean Culture
Korean Cultural Service
5505 Wilshire Boulevard
Los Angeles, CA 90036
First published: 1980

Korean People, The
2605 West Olympic Boulevard
Los Angeles, CA 90005
First published: 1984

New Korea, The
2936 West 8th Street
Los Angeles, CA 90005
First published: 1905

PACIFIC ISLANDER AMERICAN

NEWSLETTERS

A/PI Task Force News
Asian/Pacific Island Task Force on High Blood Pressure, Education and Control
Los Angeles, CA

Centernews
Public Affairs Office of the East-West Center
East-West Center
Honolulu, HI

Literary Arts in Hawaii
Honolulu, HI
First published: 1974

Pacific Information and Library Services—Newsletter
Pacific Information and Library Services
Graduate School of Library Studies
University of Hawai'i
Honolulu, HI
First published: 1977

VIETNAMESE AMERICAN

NEWSPAPERS

Chinh Nghia
685 Singleton Road
San Jose, CA 95111
First published: 1986

Da Hieu
1646 Sandwich Road
San Jose, CA 95112

Dac San Hoi Ngo
2103 Alum Rock Avenue
San Jose, CA 95116

Dai Nam News
3790 El Camino Real, #290
San Jose, CA 95113

Nguoi Viet
3111 Martin Luther King Jr. Way South
Seattle, WA 98144

Nguoi Viet
14841 Moren Street
Westminster, CA 92683
First published: 1978

Tha Huong
641 Iris Avenue
Sunnyvale, CA 94086

Thang Mo San Francisco-Oakland
619 Hyde Street
San Francisco, CA 94109

Thoi Luan
1685 Beverly Boulevard
Los Angeles, CA 90026

Tin Bien
422 Park Avenue
San Jose, CA 95110

Tin Viet
9872 Chapman Avenue, Suite 12
Garden Grove, CA 92641

Truyen Hinh Rang Dong
18 East Empire Street
San Jose, CA 95113

Truyen Hinh Viet Nam
345 East Santa Clara Street, Suite 105
San Jose, CA 95113

Viet Press Weekly
P.O. Box 2264
Westminster, CA 92683

Vietnam-Chinese Newspaper
403 West College Street
Los Angeles, CA 90012

Vietnam Daily Newspaper
575 Tully Road
San Jose, CA 95111

Yeu Weekly Newspaper
675 North 1st Street, Suite 611
San Jose, CA 95112

NEWSLETTERS

Hoi Cong Dong Nguoi Viet Tai Orange County/Vietnamese Community of Orange County Bilingual Newsletter
Vietnamese Community of Orange County
Santa Ana, CA

Vietnam Culture Newsletter
Asia Books
Carbondale, FL
First published: 1987

MAGAZINES

Chuong Viet Magazine
728 North 9th Street
San Jose, CA 95112

Duc Tin Magazine
888 East Santa Clara Street
San Jose, CA 95116

Gia Dinh Moi (New Family)
P.O. Box 7009
Mountain View, CA 94039

Hon Viet
P.O. Box 4279
Garden Grove, CA 91202

Khang Chien Magazine
P.O. Box 7826
San Jose, CA 95150
First published: 1983

Nguon Song Magazine
2070 Flint Avenue
San Jose, CA 95148

Nguyen Tu A: Viet Press Weekly
P.O. Box 2264
Westminster, CA 92683

Thoung Mai Vietnam
2339 West 1st Street
Santa Ana, CA 92703

Tien Phong Magazine
15 North Highland Street
Arlington, VA 22201
First published: 1976

Trai Tim Duc Me
1900 Grand Avenue
Carthage, MO 64836
First published: 1949

Trieu Thanh Magazine
40 North 4th Stret
San Jose, CA 95112

Truyen Thong Magazine
282 North 1st Street
San Jose, CA 95113

Van Nghe Tien Phong
15 North Highland Street
Arlington, VA 22201
First published: 1976

Viet Nam Hai Ngoai
P.O. Box 33627
San Diego, CA 92103
First published: 1977

OTHER ASIAN AMERICAN

NEWSPAPERS

Pakistan Herald (Pakistani American)
Five Star Press
41-37 52d Street
Woodside, NY 11377
First published: 1989

Siam Media Weekly Newspaper
(Thai American)
Siam Media
4214 West Beverly Boulevard, Suite 221
Los Angeles, CA 90004

Siam Post
3341 North Federal Highway
Ft. Lauderdale, FL 33306

Tai Diep Newspaper, The
403 West College Street, #108
Los Angeles, CA 90012

MAGAZINE

Thai Magazine
5619 Hollywood Boulevard
Los Angeles, CA 90028

Films and Videos

ASIAN AMERICAN, GENERAL

DOCUMENTARIES/EDUCATIONAL FILMS AND VIDEOS

Afterbirth. Jason Hwang. 1982. 34 minutes.

All Orientals Look the Same. Valerie Soe. 1986. 1 minute 30 seconds.

Angel Island. 1980. 30 minutes.

Asian American New Wave. Nancy Tong. 1985. 18 minutes.

Asians Now. KTVU-TV. 1975. 30 minutes.

Asians Now: International Women's Day. KTVU-TV. 1975. 30 minutes.

Banana Split. Kip Fulbeck. 1990. 37 minutes.

Black Sheep. Valerie Soe. 1990. 6 minutes.

Children of the Railroad Workers. Richard Gong. 1981. 40 minutes.

Claiming a Voice. Arthur Dong. 1990. 60 minutes.

Color Schemes. Shu Lee Chang. 1989. 28 minutes.

East of Occidental. Maria Gargiulo. 1988. 29 minutes.

East + West = Music. Chinese Media Project. 1970. 60 minutes.

En Ryo Identity. Paul Mayeda Berges. 1991. 23 minutes.

Facets. San Francisco State University. 1974. 30 minutes.

Framed Out: The Challenges of the Asian American Actor. John Esaki. 1983. 28 minutes.

Immigration. Chinese Cultural Center. 1974. Two parts, 30 minutes each.

Loose Pages Bound. Christine Choy. 1978. 56 minutes.

Mitsue and Nellie: Asian American Poets. Allie Light. 1981. 58 minutes.

Ourselves. Jon Wing Lum. 1979. 60 minutes.

Pacific Bridges. Noel Izon. 1978. 6 programs, 30 minutes each.

Perceptions: A Question of Justice. Sandra Gin Yep. 1984. 25 minutes.

Perceptions: The New Yellow Peril. Sandra Gin Yep. 1984. 25 minutes.

Pieces of a Dream. Eddie Wong. 1974. 30 minutes.

Slaying the Dragon. Deborah Gee. 1988. 60 minutes.

Who Killed Vincent Chin? Christine Choy and Renee Tajima. 1988. 87 minutes.

With Silk Wings: Asian American Women at Work. A series of four films: **Four Women** (1982), **On New Ground** (1982), and **Frankly Speaking** (1982), by Loni Ding, and **Talking History** (1984), by Spencer Nakasako. 30 minutes each.

Yellow Portrait, The. Nancy Tong. 1985. 18 minutes.

Yellow Tale Blues: Two American Families. Christine Choy and Renee Tajima. 1990. 28 minutes.

NARRATIVE FILMS AND VIDEOS/FEATURES

Fool's Dance. Robert A. Nakamura. 1983. 30 minutes.

I'm on a Mission from Buddha. Deborah Gee. KQED-TV. 1991. 60 minutes.

ASIAN INDIAN

DOCUMENTARIES/EDUCATIONAL FILMS AND VIDEOS

Floating in the Air, Followed by the Wind. 1973. 34 minutes.

Khush Refugees. Nidhi Singh. 1991. 32 minutes.

Memory Pictures. 1989. 24 minutes.

New Puritans: The Sikhs of Yuba City, The. Ritu Sarin and Tenzing Sonam. 1985. 27 minutes.

One Dream: A Few Voices. Manoj Bhaumik. 1984. 55 minutes.

Shrandajali. Cecile Guidote. 1982. 28 minutes.

So Far from India. Mira Nair. 1982. 49 minutes.

Sweet Jail; The Sikhs of Yuba City. Beheroze F. Shroff. 1984. 48 minutes.

Time to Rise, A. Anand Patwardhan. 1982. 40 minutes.

CHINESE AMERICAN

DOCUMENTARIES/EDUCATIONAL FILMS AND VIDEOS

American Chinatown. Todd Carrel. 1982. 30 minutes.

Asian Community Press Conference on the "Triad Report." CMC Productions. 1974. 30 minutes.

Bean Sprouts. Loni Ding. 1978. Five programs, 30 minutes each.

Carved in Silence. Felicia Lowe. 1987. 45 minutes.

Boat People of Vietnam [ethnic Chinese refugees from Vietnam]. J. Michael Hagopian. 1982. 20 minutes.

Chiang Ching: A Dance Journey. Lana Pih Jokel. 1982. 30 minutes.

China: Land of My Father. Felicia Lowe. 1979. 28 minutes.

Chinatown: Immigrants in America. John Alpert. 1976. 60 minutes.

Chinatown Report: Lee Mah Strike. KQED-TV. 1974. 60 minutes.

Chinatown 2-Step. Eddie Wong. 1975. 17 minutes.

Chinese-American: The Early Immigrants, The. 1973. 20 minutes.

Chinese-American: The Twentieth Century, The. 1973. 20 minutes.

Chinese American Artists. 1985. 30 minutes.

Chinese Americans: The Second Century. Shirley Sun. 1980. 30 minutes.

Chinese Gold: The Chinese of the Monterey Bay Region. Mark Schwartz and Geoffrey Dunn. 1987. 42 minutes.

Eight-Pound Livelihood. Yuet-Fong Ho. 1984. 27 minutes.

First Tuesday: Secrets of Chinatown. NBC-TV. 1973. 30 minutes.

Forbidden City, U.S.A. Arthur Dong. 1989. 56 minutes.

From Spikes to Spindles. Christine Choy. 1976. 50 minutes.

Gam Saan Haak. Henry Der. 1974. Six parts, 30 minutes each.

Gin and Don. Jon Wing Lum. 1979. 29 minutes.

Golden Mountain on Mott Street, The. WCBS-TV. 1975. 34 minutes.

History of Boston's Chinatown. Peter Kiang. 1983. 28 minutes.

How We Got Here. Loni Ding. 1976. 30 minutes.

In Transit: The Chinese in California. Lillian Wu. 1977. 26 minutes.

Inside Chinatown. Michael Chin. 1977. 43 minutes.

James Wong Howe: The Man and His Movies. Beulah Kwoh. 1975. 25 minutes.

Jung Sai—Chinese American. Frieda Lee Mack. 1977. 29 minutes.

Legal Aid in Chinatown. Nancy Tong. 1985. 18 minutes.

Living Music for Golden Mountains. Arthur Dong. 1982. 27 minutes.

Made in China: A Search for Roots. Lisa Hsia. 1986. 28 minutes.

Maxine Hong Kingston: Talking Story. Joan Saffa. 1990. 60 minutes.

Mississippi Triangle. Christine Choy. 1983. 110 minutes.

My Name Is Susan Yee. Beverly Shaffer. 1975. 12 minutes.

Overseas Chinese. Lisa Hsia. 1985. 30 minutes.

Reaching for the Stars. Nancy Tong. 1984. 24 minutes.

Sewing Woman. Arthur Dong. 1982. 14 minutes.

World of Dong Kingman, The. James Wong Howe. 1954. 15 minutes.

Year of the Dragon. Chinese for Affirmative Action. 1985. 60 minutes.

NARRATIVE FILMS AND VIDEOS/FEATURES

Big Trouble in Little China. John Carpenter. Twentieth Century-Fox. 1986. 100 minutes.

Brighter Moon, A. Keith Lock. 1987. 25 minutes.

Chan Is Missing. Wayne Wang. New Yorker Films. 1982. 80 minutes.

Charlie Chan Carries On. Hamilton MacFadden. Twentieth Century-Fox. 1931. 76 minutes.

China Girl. Abel Ferrara. Vestron Entertainment. 1987. 88 minutes.

Combination Platter. Tony Chan. Bluehorse Film. 1993. 84 minutes.

Dim Sum: A Little Bit of Heart. Wayne Wang. Orion Classics. 1984. 89 minutes.

Dragon: The Bruce Lee Story. Rob Cohen. Universal Pictures. 1993. 121 minutes.

Eat a Bowl of Tea. Wayne Wang. Columbia Pictures/American Playhouse. 1989. 104 minutes.

Enter the Dragon. Robert Clouse. Warner Bros. 1973. 97 minutes.

Flower Drum Song. Henry Koster. Universal Studios. 1961. 133 minutes.

Fei Tien: Goddess in Flight. Christine Choy. 1983. 22 minutes.

Fine Line. Ang Lee. 1984. 30 minutes.

Freckled Rice. Stephen C. Ning. 1983. 48 minutes.

Golden Gate. John Madden. Samuel Goldwyn Company. 1994. 95 minutes.

Great Wall, A. Peter Wang. Orion Classics. 1986. 100 minutes.

Jade Snow. Ron Finley. 1976. 27 minutes.

Joy Luck Club, The. Wayne Wang. Hollywood Pictures. 1993. 138 minutes.

Kind of Yellow. David Chan. 1983. 20 minutes.

Liru. Henry Chow. 1987. 25 minutes.

New Wife, The. Renee Cho. 1978. 30 minutes.

New Year. Valerie Soe. 1987. 23 minutes.

Only Language She Knows, The. Stephen Okazaki. 1983. 17 minutes.

Q It Up. Chinatown Youth Center. 1985. 16 minutes.

Wedding Banquet, The. Ang Lee. Samuel Goldwyn Company. 1993. 104 minutes.

Year of the Dragon. Michael Cimino. Metro-Goldwyn-Mayer/United Artists. 1985. 136 minutes.

FILIPINO AMERICAN

DOCUMENTARIES/EDUCATIONAL FILMS AND VIDEOS

Dollar a Day, Ten Cents a Dance, A. Geoffrey Dunn and Mark Schwartz. 1984. 29 minutes.

Dreaming Filipinos. Manny Reyes. 1990. 52 minutes.

Fall of the I-Hotel, The. Curtis Choy. 1983. 57 minutes.

Filipino Immigrant, The. Leonardo F. Ignacio, Jr. 1974. 30 minutes.

In No One's Shadow: Filipinos in America. Naomi De Castro. 1988. 28 minutes.

Manong. Linda Mabalot. 1979. 30 minutes.

Perceptions: The Vanishing Heroes. Sandra Gin Yep. 1984. 25 minutes.

Pinoy. Deborah Bock. 1979. 29 minutes.

JAPANESE AMERICAN

DOCUMENTARIES/EDUCATIONAL FILMS AND VIDEOS

Color of Honor: The Japanese American Soldier in World War II, The. Loni Ding. 1988. 90 minutes.

Conversations: Before the War/After the War. Robert A. Nakamura. 1986. 29 minutes.

Cruisin' J-Town. Duane Kubo. 1976. 30 minutes.

Days of Waiting. Steven Okazaki. 1990. 18 minutes.

Emi. Michael Toshiyuki Uno. 1978. 28 minutes.

Emiko. Emiko Omori. 1969. 5 minutes.

Family Gathering. Lisa Yasui. 1988. 30 minutes.

Fujikawa. Michael Toshiyuki Uno and Frank Nesbitt. 1979. 30 minutes.

Guilty by Reason of Race. Fred Flamenhaft. 1972. 51 minutes.

History and Memory. Rea Tajiri. 1991. 30 minutes.

I Told You So. Alan Kondo. 1974. 18 minutes.

Invisible Citizens. Keiko Tsuno. 1983. 59 minutes.

Issei, Nisei, Sansei. 1971. 30 minutes.

Issei Wahine. Ann Moriyasu. 1991. 22 minutes.

Japanese-Americans, The. Handel Film Corporation. 1974. 30 minutes.

Japanese Americans in Concentration Camps [testimony from federal hearings held in Boston]. Asian American Resource Workshop. 1981. 120 minutes.

Japanese American in Concentration Camps [testimony from federal hearings held in Los Angeles]. Visual Communications. 1981. 120 minutes.

Jazz Is My Native Language: A Portrait of Toshiko Akiyoshi. Renee Cho. 1983. 58 minutes.

Mako. Frank Nesbitt. 1979. 29 minutes.

Manzanar. Robert A. Nakamura. 1971. 16 minutes.

Memories from the Department of Amnesia. Janice Tanaka. 1989. 14 minutes.

Nisei Soldier: Standard Bearer for an Exiled People. Loni Ding. 1983. 29 minutes.

Perceptions: Japanese American Redress. Sandra Gin Yep. 1982. 25 minutes.

Personal Matter: Gordon Hirabayashi v. the United States, A. John de Graaf. 1992. 30 minutes.

Quiet Passages: The Japanese American War Bride Experience. Tim DePaepe. 1991. 26 minutes.

Reason to Remember. KRON-TV. 1975. 30 minutes.

Shinzen. Patricia Soika. 1981. Eight programs, 30 minutes each.

Subversion. Barry Brown. 1970. 28 minutes.

Survivors. Steven Okazaki. 1982. 30 minutes.

Taiko: The Music of the japanese Drums. David Kimura. 1980. 24 minutes.

Topaz. Ken Verdoia. 1987. 58 minutes.

Unfinished Business: The Japanese American Internment Camps. Steven Okazaki. 1986. 58 minutes.

Wataridori: Birds of Passage. Robert A. Nakamura. 1976. 37 minutes.

Yuki Shimoda: Asian American Actor. John Esaki. 1985. 30 minutes.

NARRATIVE FILMS AND VIDEOS/FEATURES

Come See the Paradise. Alan Parker. Twentieth Century-Fox. 1990. 138 minutes.

Departure, The. Emiko Omori. 1983. 14 minutes.

Farewell to Manzanar. NBC. 1976. 130 minutes.

Gung Ho. Ron Howard. Paramount Pictures. 1986. 120 minutes.

Hito-Hata: Raise the Banner. Duane Kubo and Robert A. Nakamura. 1980. 90 minutes.

Karate Kid, The. John G. Avildsen. Columbia Pictures. 1984. 126 minutes.

Living on Tokyo Time. Steven Okazaki. Skouras Pictures. 1987. 83 minutes.

Relocations. Mark Tang. 1991. 15 minutes.

Rising Sun. Philip Kaufman. Twentieth Century-Fox. 1993. 129 minutes.

KOREAN AMERICAN

DOCUMENTARIES/EDUCATIONAL FILMS AND VIDEOS

Christine Choy. Women in the Director's Chair. 1985. 30 minutes.

Sa-I-Gu. Dai Sil Kim-Gibson and Christine Choy. 1993. 39 minutes.

PACIFIC ISLANDER

DOCUMENTARIES/EDUCATIONAL FILMS AND VIDEOS

Makua Homecoming [Hawaiian]. Abe Ahmand. 1983. 30 minutes.

Ohana [Hawaiian]. George Tahara. 1980. 30 minutes.

Oko Mau Sai Pe: We're Alright [Tongan]. Solomona Aoelva. 1983. 30 minutes.

Omai Fa'atasi: Samoa Mo Samoa [Samoan]. Takashi Fujii. 1974. 30 minutes.

Pacific Islanders: The Forgotten Americans. Solomon Aoevla. 1983. 30 minutes.

Samoans: Coming of Age in America. Pacific Educational Network. 1984. 30 minutes.

Troubled Paradise [Hawaiian]. Steven Okazaki. 1991. 58 minutes.

NARRATIVE FILMS AND VIDEOS/FEATURES

Vaitafe [Samoan]. Alo Foe. 1981. 30 minutes

VIETNAMESE AMERICAN

DOCUMENTARIES/EDUCATIONAL FILMS AND VIDEOS

Fire on the Water. Robert Hillman. 1982. 56 minutes.

Footnotes to a War. 1984. 23 minutes.

From Hollywood to Hanoi. Tiana. 1993. 78 minutes.

Monterey's Boat People. Spencer Nakasako and Vincent DiGirolamo. 1982. 29 minutes.

One of Many: Dr. Nhan. 1987. 17 minutes.

Overture: Linh from Vietnam. Elaine Sperber. 1981. 26 minutes.

Phans of Jersey City, The. Stephen Forman and Dennis Lanson. 1979. 49 minutes.

Story of Vinh, The. Keiko Tsuno. 1990. 60 minutes.

Thanh's War. 1990. 58 minutes.

Way of the Willow, The. John Kent Harrison. 1982. 30 minutes.

NARRATIVE FILMS AND VIDEOS/FEATURES

Apocalypse Now. Francis Ford Coppola. United Artists. 1979. 153 minutes.

Casualties of War. Brian DePalma. Columbia Pictures. 1989. 113 minutes.

Deer Hunter, The. Michael Cimino. Universal Studios. 1978. 180 minutes.

Good Morning Vietnam. Barry Levinson. Touchstone Pictures. 1987. 120 minutes.

Heaven and Earth. Oliver Stone. Ixtlan Corporation. 1993. 135 minutes.

Platoon. Oliver Stone. Orion Pictures. 1986. 120 minutes

OTHER ASIAN AMERICAN

DOCUMENTARIES/EDUCATIONAL FILMS AND VIDEOS

Animal Appetites [Cambodian]. Michael Cho. 1991. 20 minutes.

Becoming American [Hmong]. Ken Levine and Ivory Waterworth Levine. 1982. 58 minutes.

Bittersweet Survival [Southeast Asian]. Christine Choy. 1981. 30 minutes.

Blue Collar and Buddha [Laotian]. Taggart Siegel. 1988. 57 minutes.

Cutting Edge, The [Vietnamese, Hmong, and Laotian]. Judith Mann. 1983. 29 minutes.

Farewell to Freedom [Hmong]. WCCO/CBS-TV. 1981. 55 minutes.

Freedom of Our Own [Southeast Asian]. Sumiko Hennessey. 1982. 28 minutes.

Great Branches, New Roots: The Hmong Family. Rita LaDoux. 1983. 42 minutes.

Pak Bueng on Fire [Thai]. Supachai Surongsain. 1987. 25 minutes.

Price You Pay, The [Cambodian and Laotian]. Christine Keyser. 1988. 29 minutes.

Refugees from Laos—A Hill Tribe in West Oakland [Iu Mien]. Art Nomura. 1981. 28 minutes.

NARRATIVE FILMS AND VIDEOS/FEATURES

Killing Fields, The [Cambodian]. Roland Joffe. Warner Bros. 1984. 139 minutes.

Bibliography

Sources by Population Groups

ASIAN AMERICANS (PANETHNIC)

Asian Women United of California, eds. *Making Waves: An Anthology of Writings By and About Asian American Women.* Boston: Beacon Press, 1989. *Change: The Magazine of Higher Learning* 28 (November/December, 1989). Special issue on Asian Americans.

Backus, Karen, and Julia C. Furtaw, eds. *Asian Americans Information Directory.* Detroit: Gale Research, 1992.

Baron, Dennis. *The English-Only Question: An Official Language for Americans?* New Haven, Conn.: Yale University Press, 1990.

Barry, Kathleen, Charlotte Bunch, and Shirley Castley, eds. *International Feminism: Networking Against Female Sexual Slavery.* New York: International Women's Tribune Centre, 1984.

Berkson, Issac B. *Theories of Americanization: A Critical Study, with Special Reference to the Jewish Group.* 1920. Reprint. New York: Arno Press, 1969.

Boucher, Sandy. *Turning the Wheel: American Women Creating the New Buddhism.* San Francisco: Harper & Row, 1988.

Center for Integration and Improvement of Journalism. *Project Zinger: A Critical Look at News Media Coverage of Asian Pacific Americans.* San Francisco: Asian American Journalists Association, 1992.

Chan, Sucheng. *Asian Americans: An Interpretive History.* Boston: Twayne, 1991.

Colangelo, Nicholas, Dick Dustin, and Cecelia H. Foxley, eds. *Multicultural Nonsexist Education: A Human Relations Approach.* 2d ed. Dubuque, Iowa: Kendall/Hunt, 1985.

Conference on Anti-Asian Violence. *Break the Silence: A Conference on Anti-Asian Violence.* San Francisco: Break the Silence Coalition, 1986.

Cretser, Gary A., and Joseph J. Leon, eds. *Intermarriage in the United States.* New York: Haworth, 1982.

Cummins, James. *Bilingualism and Minority-Language Children.* Toronto: Ontario Institute for Studies in Education, 1981.

Daniels, Roger. *Asian Americans: Chinese and Japanese in the United States Since 1850.* Seattle: University of Washington Press, 1988.

De Bary, William T., ed. *The Buddhist Tradition in India, China, and Japan.* New York: Vintage Books, 1972.

Espiritu, Yen Le. *Asian American Panethnicity: Bridging Institutions and Identities.* Philadelphia: Temple University Press, 1992.

Fields, Rick. *How the Swans Came to the Lake: A Narrative History of Buddhism in America.* 3d ed. Boston: Shambhala, 1992.

Fuchs, Lawrence H. *The American Kaleidoscope: Race, Ethnicity, and the Civic Culture.* Hanover, N.H.: Wesleyan University Press, 1990.

Gall, Susan B., and Timothy L. Gall, eds. *Statistical Record of Asian Americans.* Detroit: Gale Research, 1993.

Glazer, Nathan. *Affirmative Discrimination: Ethnic Inequality and Public Policy.* New York: Basic Books, 1975.

Goodwin, Clarissa Garland. *The International Marriage: Or, The Building of a Nation.* Los Angeles: UCLA Special Collections, 1931.

Hartmann, Edward George. *The Movement to Americanize the Immigrant.* 1948. Reprint. New York: AMS Press, 1967.

Hayslip, Le Ly, with Jay Wurts. *When Heaven and Earth Changed Places.* New York: Doubleday, 1989.

Higham, John. *Strangers in the Land: Patterns of American Nativism, 1860-1925.* New Brunswick, N.J.: Rutgers University Press, 1955.

Ho, Man Keung. "Family Therapy with Asian/Pacific Americans." In *Family Therapy with Ethnic Minorities.* Newbury Park, Calif.: Sage, 1987.

Hundley, Norris, Jr., ed. *The Asian American: The Historical Experience.* Santa Barbara, Calif.: ABC-Clio, 1976.

Hune, Shirley, et al., eds. *Asian Americans: Comparative and Global Perspectives.* Pullman: Washington State University Press, 1991.

Imamura, Anne E. *Strangers in a Strange Land: Coping with Marginality in International Marriage.* East Lansing: Women in International Development, Michigan State University, 1987.

Josey, E. J., and Marva L. DeLoach, eds. *Ethnic Collections in Libraries.* New York: Neal-Schuman, 1983.

Kauz, Herman. *The Martial Spirit: An Introduction to the Origin, Philosophy, and Psychology of the Martial Arts.* Woodstock, N.Y.: The Overlook Press, 1977.

Kim, Elaine H. *Asian American Literature: An Introduction to the Writings and Their Social Context.* Philadelphia: Temple University Press, 1982.

Konvitz, Milton R. *The Alien and the Asiatic in American Law.* Ithaca, N.Y.: Cornell University Press, 1946.

Kotkin, Joel. *Tribes: How Race, Religion, and Identity Determine Success in the New Global Economy.* New York: Random House, 1993.

Kulka, Richard A., et al. *Trauma and the Vietnam War Generation.* New York: Brunner/Mazel, 1990.

Light, Ivan. *Ethnic Enterprise in America.* Berkeley: University of California Press, 1972.

Lu Yu. *The Classic of Tea.* Translated by Francis Ross Carpenter. Boston: Little, Brown, 1974.

Manuel, Peter. *Popular Musics of the Non-Western World.* New York: Oxford University Press, 1988.

May, Elizabeth, ed. *Musics of Many Cultures: An Introduction.* Berkeley: University of California Press, 1980.

Miller, Wayne Charles, with Faye Nell Vowell, Gary K. Crist, et al. *A Comprehensive Bibliography for the Study of American Minorities.* 2 vols. New York: New York University Press, 1976.

Mindel, Charles H. and Robert W. Habenstein, eds. *Ethnic Families in America: Patterns and Variations.* New York: Elsevier, 1976.

Morreale, Don, ed. *Buddhist America: Centers, Retreats, Practices.* Santa Fe, N. Mex.: John Muir, 1988.

Moynihan, Daniel P. *Pandaemonium: Ethnicity in International Politics.* New York: Oxford University Press, 1993.

Neff, Fred. *Basic Jujitsu Handbook.* Minneapolis: Lerner Publications, 1976.

Nieto, Sonia. *Affirming Diversity: The Sociopolitical Context of Multicultural Education.* New York: Longman, 1992.

Nomura, Gail, et al., eds. *Frontiers of Asian American Studies.* Pullman: Washington State University Press, 1989.

Okihiro, Gary, et al., eds. *Reflections on Shattered Windows: Promises and Prospects for Asian American Studies.* Pullman: Washington State University Press, 1988.

Omi, Michael, and Howard Winant. *Racial Formation in the United States: From the 1960s to the 1980s.* New York: Routledge & Kegan Paul, 1986.

Poon, Wei Chi. *The Directory of Asian American Collections in the United States.* Berkeley: Asian American Studies Library, University of California, 1982.

Poon, Wei Chi. *A Guide for Establishing Asian American Core Collections.* Berkeley: Asian American Studies Library, University of California, 1989.

Pratt, James Norwood. *The Tea Lover's Treasury.* San Francisco: 101 Productions, 1982.

Robinson, Richard H., and Willard L. Johnson. *The Buddhist Religion: A Historical Introduction.* 3d ed. Belmont Calif.: Wadsworth, 1982.

Root, Maria P. P., ed. *Racially Mixed People in*

America. Newbury Park, Calif.: Sage Publications, 1992.

Rose, Peter I. "Asian Americans: From Pariahs to Paragons." In *Clamor at the Gates: The New American Immigration*, edited by Nathan Glazer. San Francisco: Institute for Contemporary Studies Press, 1985.

Saravia-Shore, Marietta, and Steven F. Arvizu, eds. *Cross-Cultural Literacy: Ethnographies of Communication in Multiethnic Classrooms.* New York: Garland, 1992.

Scarborough, Katharine T. A., ed. *Developing Library Collections for California's Emerging Majority: A Manual of Resources for Ethnic Collection Development.* Berkeley, Calif.: Bay Area Library and Information System, 1990.

Schumann, Hans W. *The Historical Buddha.* Translated by M. Walshe. London: Arkana/Penguin, 1989.

Shon, Steven, and Davis Ja. "Asian Families." In *Ethnicity and Family Therapy*, by Monica McGoldrick, John Pearce, and Joseph Giordano. New York: Guilford Press, 1982.

Soet, John Steven. *Martial Arts Around the World.* Burbank: Unique Publications, 1991.

Spickard, Paul R. *Mixed Blood: Intermarriage and Ethnic Identity in Twentieth-Century America.* Madison: University of Wisconsin Press, 1989.

Sue, Stanley, and James Morishima. *The Mental Health of Asian Americans.* San Francisco: Jossey-Bass, 1982.

Tajima, Renee. *The Anthology of Asian Pacific American Film and Video.* New York: Film News Now Foundation, 1985.

Takaki, Ronald. *Strangers from a Different Shore: A History of Asian Americans.* Boston: Little, Brown, 1989.

Tan, Alexis S. *Why Asian American Journalists Leave Journalism and Why They Stay.* San Francisco: Asian American Journalists Association, 1990.

Taylor, Carol. "Mail-Order Bride." *Good Housekeeping* 210 (February 1, 1990): 62.

Thernstrom, Stephen, ed. *Harvard Encyclopedia of American Ethnic Groups.* Cambridge, Mass.: The Belknap Press of Harvard University Press, 1980.

U.S. Commission on Civil Rights. *Civil Rights Issues Facing Asian Americans in the 1990s: A Report of the United States Commission on Civil Rights.* Washington, D.C.: Government Printing Office, 1992.

U.S. Commission on Civil Rights. *Recent Activities Against Citizens and Residents of Asian Descent.* Washington, D.C.: Government Printing Office, 1986.

Wei, William. *The Asian American Movement.* Philadelphia: Temple University Press, 1993.

Williams, Bryn. *Martial Arts of the Orient.* New York: Hamlyn, 1975.

Yun, Grace, ed. *A Look Beyond the Model Minority Image: Critical Issues in Asian America.* New York: Minority Rights Group, 1989.

ASIAN INDIAN AMERICANS AND THE INDIAN DIASPORA *(See also INDIA; SOUTH ASIA; SOUTH ASIAN AMERICANS)*

Asian Women United of California, ed. *Making Waves: An Anthology By and About Asian American Women.* Boston: Beacon Press, 1989.

Bagai, Leona B. *The East Indians and the Pakistanis in America.* Rev. ed. Minneapolis: Lerner, 1972.

Barrier, N. Gerald, and Verne A. Dusenbery. *The Sikh Diaspora: Migration and the Experience Beyond Punjab.* Columbia, Mo.: South Asia Publications, 1989.

Boucher, Sandy. *Turning the Wheel: American Women Creating the New Buddhism.* San Francisco: Harper & Row, 1988.

Brown, Emily C. *Har Dayal: Hindu Revolutionary and Rationalist.* Tucson: University of Arizona Press, 1975.

Bruce J. Campbell. "Our Congressman from India." *Reader's Digest* 73 (September, 1958): 175-177.

Buchignani, Norman, Doreen M. Indra, and Ram Srivastiva. *Continuous Journey: A Social History of South Asians in Canada.* Toronto, Ontario, Canada: McClelland and Stewart in association with Dept. of the Secretary of State and the Govt. Pub. Centre, Supply and Services, Canada, 1985.

Chadney, James G. *The Sikhs of Vancouver.* New York: AMS Press, 1984.

Chandrasekhar, S., ed. *From India to America: A Brief History of Immigration, Problems of Discrimination, Admission, and Assimilation.* La Jolla, Calif.: A Population Review Book, 1982.

Copley, Anthony. *Gandhi: Against the Tide.* New York: Basil Blackwell, 1987.

Dignan, Don K. "The Hindu Conspiracy in Anglo-American Relations During World War I." *Pacific Historical Review* 40, no. 1 (1971): 57-76.

Duley, Margot, and Mary I. Edwards, eds. *The Cross-Cultural Study of Women.* New York: Feminist Press, 1986.

Fields, Rick. *How the Swans Came to the Lake: A Narrative History of Buddhism in America.* 3d ed. Boston: Shambhala, 1992.

Gandhi, Mahatma. *An Autobiography: The Story of Experiments with Truth.* Translated by Mahadev Desai. Harmondsworth, Middlesex, England: Penguin Books, 1982.

Gibson, Margaret A. *Accommodation Without Assimilation: Sikh Immigrants in an American High School.* Ithaca, N.Y.: Cornell University Press, 1988.

Helweg, Arthur W. "The Indian Diaspora: Influence on International Relations." In *Modern Diasporas in International Politics*, edited by Gabriel Sheffer. New York: St. Martin's Press, 1986.

Helweg, Arthur W., and Usha M. Helweg. *An Immigrant Success Story: East Indians in America.* Philadelphia: University of Pennsylvania Press, 1990.

Hughes, Peter. *V. S. Naipaul.* New York: Routledge, 1988.

Jain, Usha R. *The Gujaratis of San Francisco.* New York: AMS Press, 1989.

Jeffrey, Robin. *What's Happening to India? Punjab, Ethnic Conflict, Mrs. Gandhi's Death, and the Test of Federalism.* New York: Holmes & Meier, 1986.

Jensen, Joan M. *Passage from India: Asian Indian Immigrants in North America.* New Haven, Conn.: Yale University Press, 1988.

Johnston, Hugh J. M. *The East Indians in Canada.* Ottawa, Ontario, Canada: Canadian Historical Association, 1984.

Joy, Annamma. *Ethnicity in Canada: Social Accommodation and Cultural Persistence Among the Sikhs and the Portuguese.* New York: AMS Press, 1989.

Judah, J. Stillson. *The History and Philosophy of the Metaphysical Movements in America.* Philadelphia: The Westminster Press, 1967.

Kanungo, Rabindra N., ed. *South Asians in the Canadian Mosaic.* Montreal, Quebec, Canada: Kala Bharati, 1984.

King, Ralph, Jr. "From Bombay to L.A." *Forbes* 146 (November 12, 1990): 124.

La Brack, Bruce. *The Sikhs of Northern California, 1904-1975.* New York: AMS Press, 1988.

Leonard, Karen Isaksen. *Making Ethnic Choices: California's Punjabi Mexican Americans.* Philadelphia: Temple University Press, 1992.

Lorch, Donatella. "Between Two Worlds: New York's Bangladeshis." *New York Times*, October 10, 1991.

Lorch, Donatella. "An Ethnic Road to Riches: The Immigrant Job Specialty." *New York Times*, January 12, 1992.

MacKaye, Milton. "U.S. Congressman from Asia." *The Saturday Evening Post* 231 (August 2, 1958): 25.

Mandel, Michael J., and Christopher Farrell. "The Immigrants: How They're Revitalizing the U.S. Economy." *Business Week*, no. 3274 (July 13, 1992): 116-122.

Mazumdar, Sucheta. "Punjabi Agricultural Workers in California, 1905-1945." In *Labor Immigration Under Capitalism: Asian Workers in the United States Before World War II*, edited by Lucie Cheng and Edna Bonacicih. Berkeley: University of California Press, 1984.

Mazumdar, Sucheta. "South Asians in the United States with a Focus on Asian Indians." In *The State of Asian Pacific America: A Public Policy Report, Policy Issues to the Year 2020.* Los Angeles: LEAP Asian Pacific American Public Policy Institute and UCLA Asian American Studies Center, 1993.

Melendy, H. Brett. *Asians in America: Filipinos, Koreans, and East Indians.* Boston: Twayne, 1977.

Melton, J. Gordon. *The Encyclopedia of American Religions.* 2d ed. Detroit: Gale Research, 1987.

Migration and Modernization: The Indian Di-

aspora in Comparative Perspective. Williamsburg, Va.: Department of Anthropology, College of William and Mary, 1987.

Miller, Timothy, ed. *America's Alternative Religions*. Albany: State University of New York Press, 1993.

Miller, Timothy, ed. *When Prophets Die: The Postcharismatic Fate of New Religious Movements*. Albany: State University of New York Press, 1991.

Morreale, Don, ed. *Buddhist America: Centers, Retreats, Practices*. Santa Fe, N. Mex.: John Muir, 1988.

Palmer, Norman D. *The United States and India: The Dimensions of Influence*. New York: Praeger, 1984.

Papademetriou, Demetrios G., and Mark J. Miller, eds. *The Unavoidable Issue: U.S. Immigration Policy in the 1980's*. Philadelphia: Institute for the Study of Human Issues, 1983.

Puri, Harish K. *Ghadar Movement: Ideology, Organization and Strategy*. 2d ed. Amritsar, Punjab: Guru Nanak Dev University Press, 1993.

Ramcharan, Subhas. *Racism: Nonwhites in Canada*. Toronto, Ontario, Canada: Butterworths, 1982.

Rustomji-Kerns, Roshni, ed. Special issue. "South Asian Women Writers: The Immigrant Experience." *The Journal of South Asian Literature* 21 (Winter/Spring, 1986).

Saran, Parmatma. *The Asian Indian Experience in the United States*. Cambridge, Mass.: Schenkman, 1985.

Saran, Parmatma, and Edwin Eames, eds. *The New Ethnics: Asian Indians in the United States*. New York: Praeger, 1980.

Saund, Dalip Singh. *Congressman from India*. New York: E. P. Dutton, 1960.

Shulman, Albert M. *The Religious Heritage of America*. San Diego: A. S. Barnes & Company, 1981.

Singer, Milton. *When a Great Tradition Modernizes: An Anthropological Approach to Indian Civilization*. New York: Praeger, 1972.

Singh, Jane, et al. *South Asians in North America: An Annotated and Selected Bibliography*. Berkeley: Center for South and Southeast Asia Studies, University of California, Berkeley, 1988.

South Asians in North America: An Annotated and Selected Bibliography. Berkeley: Center for South and Southeast Asia Studies, University of California, Berkeley, 1988.

Takaki, Ronald. *Strangers from a Different Shore: A History of Asian Americans*. New York: Penguin Books, 1990.

Thaker, Suvarna, and Sucheta Mazumdar. "The Quality of Life of Asian Indian Women in the Motel Industry." *South Asia Bulletin* 2, no. 1 (1982): 68-73.

Thomas, Raju G. C. *Indian Security Policy*. Princeton, N.J.: Princeton University Press, 1986.

Tinker, Hugh. *A New System of Slavery: The Export of Indian Labour Overseas, 1830-*

1920. New York: Oxford University Press, 1974.

Vassanji, M. G., ed. *A Meeting of Streams: South Asian Canadian Literature*. Toronto: Toronto South Asia Review Publications, 1985.

Wolpert, Stanley. *A New History of India*. 4th ed. New York: Oxford University Press, 1993.

Women of South Asian Descent Collective, eds. *Our Feet Walked the Sky: Women of the South Asian Diaspora*. San Francisco: Aunt Lute Books, 1993.

Zaretsky, Irving I. and Mark P. Leone, eds. *Religious Movements in Contemporary America*. Princeton, N.J.: Princeton University Press, 1974.

Ziring, Lawrence, ed. *The Subcontinent in World Politics: India, Its Neighbors, and the Great Powers*. Rev. ed. New York: Praeger, 1982.

CHINA (See also CHINESE AMERICANS AND THE CHINESE DIASPORA)

Anderson, Eugene. *The Food of China*. New Haven, Conn.: Yale University Press, 1988.

Barnett, A. Doak. *Communist China and Asia: A Challenge to American Policy*. New York: Vintage Books, 1960.

Blofeld, John. *The Chinese Art of Tea*. Boston: Shambhala, 1985.

Campbell, P. C. *Chinese Coolie Emigration to Countries Within the British Empire*. Taipei: Ch'eng Wen Publishing, 1970.

Chang, Hsin-pao. *Commissioner Lin and the Opium War*. Cambridge, Mass.: Harvard University Press, 1964.

Chang, K. C., ed. *Food in Chinese Culture: Anthropological and Historical Perspectives*. New Haven, Conn.: Yale University Press, 1977.

Chang, Sidney H., and Leonard H. D. Gordon. *All Under Heaven: Sun Yat-sen and His Revolutionary Thought*. Stanford, Calif.: Hoover Institution Press, 1991.

Chao, Yuen Ren. *A Grammar of Spoken Chinese*. Berkeley: University of California Press, 1968.

Char, Tin-Yuke. *The Hakka Chinese: Their Origin and Folk Songs*. Translated by C. H. Kwock. San Francisco: Jade Mountain Press, 1969.

Chen, Kenneth. *Buddhism in China: A Historical Survey*. Princeton, N.J.: Princeton University Press, 1964.

Chen, Ta. *Emigrant Communities in South China*. Edited by Bruno Lasker. New York: Institute of Pacific Relations, 1940.

Chen, Yung-fa. *Making Revolution: The Communist Movement in Eastern and Central China, 1937-1945*. Berkeley: University of California Press, 1986.

Cheng, Chu-yuan. *Behind the Tiananmen Massacre: Social, Political, and Economic Ferment in Modern China*. Boulder, Colo.: Westview, 1990.

Cheng, Chu-yuan, ed. *Sun Yat-sen's Doctrine in*

the Modern World. Boulder, Colo.: Westview Press, 1989.

Chew, Sock Foon. *Ethnicity and Nationality in Singapore*. Athens: Ohio University Center for International Studies, 1987.

Claiborne, Craig, and Virginia Lee. *The Chinese Cookbook*. Philadelphia: J. B. Lippincott, 1972.

Cohen, Marc J. *Taiwan at the Crossroads: Human Rights, Political Development, and Social Change on the Beautiful Island*. Washington, D.C.: Asia Resource Center, 1988.

Conwell, R. H. *Why and How: Why the Chinese Emigrate and the Means They Adopt for the Purpose of Reaching America*. Boston: Lee and Shepard, 1871.

Copper, John F. *China Diplomacy: The Washington-Taipei-Beijing Triangle*. Boulder, Colo.: Westview Press, 1992.

DeFrancis, John. *The Chinese Language: Fact and Fantasy*. Honolulu: University of Hawaii Press, 1984.

DeWoskin, Kenneth J. *A Song for One or Two: Music and the Concept of Art in Early China*. Ann Arbor: University of Michigan, Center for Chinese Studies, 1982.

Downen, Robert L. *The Taiwan Pawn in the China Game: China to the Rescue*. Washington, D.C.: Centre for Strategic and International Studies, 1979.

Dreyer, June Teufel. *China's Forty Millions: Minority Nationalities and National Integration in the People's Republic of China*. Cambridge, Mass.: Harvard University Press, 1976.

Dreyer, June Teufel. *China's Political System: Modernization and Tradition*. New York: Paragon House, 1993.

Eastman, Lloyd. *Seeds of Destruction: Nationalist China in War and Revolution, 1937-1949*. Stanford, Calif.: Stanford University Press, 1984.

Fairbank, John K. *China: A New History*. Cambridge, Mass.: Harvard University Press, 1992.

Fairbank, John K. *Trade and Diplomacy on the China Coast: The Opening of the Treaty Ports, 1842-1854*. Cambridge, Mass.: Harvard University Press, 1953.

Fairbank, John K. *The United States and China*. 4th ed. Cambridge, Mass.: Harvard University Press, 1983.

Fay, Peter Ward. *The Opium War, 1840-1842*. Cambridge, England: Cambridge University Press, 1975.

Feuchtwang, Stephan D. R. *An Anthropological Analysis of Chinese Geomancy*. Vientiane, Laos: Editions Vithagna, 1974.

Finn, Michael. *Martial Arts: A Complete Illustrated History*. Woodstock, N.Y.: Overlook Press, 1988.

Fitzgerald, C. P. *The Southern Expansion of the Chinese People*. New York: Praeger, 1972.

Fitzgerald, Stephen. *China and the Overseas Chinese*. Cambridge: Cambridge University Press, 1972.

Forrest, R. A. D. *The Chinese Language*. 2d rev. ed. London: Faber & Faber, 1965.

Fu, Jen-kun. *Taiwan and the Geopolitics of the Asian-American Dilemma*. New York: Praeger, 1992.

Gernet, Jacques. *A History of Chinese Civilization*. Cambridge: Cambridge University Press, 1982.

Gregor, A. James, and Maria H. Chang. *The Republic of China and U.S. Policy: A Study in Human Rights*. Washington, D.C.: Ethics and Public Policy Center, 1983.

Guillermaz, Jacquez. Translated by Anne Oesteray. *A History of the Chinese Communist Party*. New York: Random House, 1972.

Harding, Harry. *Fragile Relationship: The United States and China Since 1972*. Washington, D.C.: Brookings Institution, 1992.

Ho, Ping-ti. *The Cradle of the East: An Inquiry into the Indigenous Origins of Techniques and Ideas of Neolithic and Early Historic China, 5000-1000 B.C.* Chicago: University of Chicago Press, 1975.

Hsieh, Chiao-min. *Taiwan—Ilha Formosa: A Geography in Perspective*. Washington, D.C.: Butterworths, 1964.

Hsiung, James C., et al., eds. *The Taiwan Experience, 1950-1980: Contemporary Republic of China*. New York: American Association of Chinese Studies, 1981.

Hsu, Immanuel. *China Without Mao: The Search for a New Order*. New York: Oxford University Press, 1983.

Hsu, Immanuel C. Y. *The Rise of Modern China*. 4th ed. New York: Oxford University Press, 1990.

Hurd, Douglas. *The Arrow War: An Anglo-Chinese Confusion, 1856-1860*. New York: Macmillan, 1967.

Jansen, Marius B. *The Japanese and Sun Yatsen*. Cambridge; Mass.: Harvard University Press, 1954.

Jones, F. C., Hugh Borton, and B. R. Pearn. *The Far East: 1942-1946*. New York: Oxford University Press, 1955.

Kauz, Herman. *The Martial Spirit: An Introduction to the Origin, Philosophy, and Psychology of the Martial Arts*. Woodstock, N.Y.: Overlook Press, 1988.

Kerr, George H. *Formosa: Licensed Revolution and the Home Rule Movement, 1895-1945*. Honolulu: University Press of Hawaii, 1974.

Kiang, Clyde. *The Hakka Odyssey and Their Taiwan Homeland*. Elgin, Pa.: Allegheny Press, 1992.

Knapp, Ronald G., ed. *Chinese Landscapes: The Village as Place*, chapter 12. Honolulu: University of Hawaii Press, 1992.

Kratochvil, Paul. *The Chinese Language Today*. London: Hutchinson University Library, 1968.

Ladany, Laszlo. *The Communist Party of China and Marxism, 1921-1985: A Self Portrait*. Stanford, Calif.: Hoover Institution Press, 1988.

Lao-tzu. *The Way of Lao Tzu*. Translated by Wing-tsit Chan. Indianapolis, Ind.: Bobbs-Merrill, 1963.

Lasater, Martin L. *Policy in Evolution: The U.S. Role in China's Reunification*. Boulder, Colo.: Westview Press, 1988.

Leung, Benjamin K. P. *Social Issues in Hong Kong*. Hong Kong: Oxford University Press, 1990.

Levesque, Leonard. *Hakka Beliefs and Customs*. Translated by J. Maynard Murphy. Taichung: Kuang Chi Press, 1969.

Lewis, Peter. *Martial Arts of the Orient*. New York: Gallery Books, 1985.

Liang, Ming-Yueh. *Music of the Billion: An Introduction to Chinese Musical Culture*. New York: Heinrichschofen, 1985.

Lo, Kenneth. *Chinese Regional Cooking*. New York: Pantheon Books, 1979.

Ma, L. Eve Armentrout. *Revolutionaries, Monarchists, and Chinatowns*. Honolulu: University of Hawaii Press, 1990.

McGurn, William. *Perfidious Albion: The Abandonment of Hong Kong, 1997*. Washington, D.C.: Ethics and Public Policy Center, 1992.

Mackerras, Colin P. *The Rise of the Peking Opera, 1770-1870*. Oxford, England: Clarendon Press, 1972.

Mackie, J. A. C., ed. *The Chinese in Indonesia*. Honolulu: University Press of Hawaii, 1976.

Meisner, Maurice. *Mao's China and After: A History of the People's Republic*. New York: Free Press, 1986.

Michael, Franz H., and George E. Taylor. *The Far East in the Modern World*. New York: Henry Holt, 1956.

Mosher, Steven W. *China Misperceived: American Illusions and Chinese Reality*. New York: Basic Books, 1990.

Myers, Ramon H., ed. *Two Chinese States: U.S. Foreign Policy and Interests*. Stanford, Calif.: Hoover Institution Press, 1978.

Needham, Joseph. *Science and Civilisation in China: History of Scientific Thought*. Vol. 2. Cambridge, England: Cambridge University Press, 1956.

Norman, Jerry. *Chinese*. New York: Cambridge University Press, 1988.

Pepper, Suzanne. *China's Education Reform in the 1980s: Policies, Issues, and History*. Berkeley: Center for Chinese Studies, 1990.

Ramsey, S. Robert. *The Languages of China*. Princeton, N.J.: Princeton University Press, 1987.

Rodzinski, Witold. *The People's Republic of China*. New York: Free Press, 1988.

Rossbach, Sarah. *Interior Design with Feng Shui*. New York: E. P. Dutton, 1987.

Scalapino, Robert A., and George T. Yu. *Modern China and Its Revolutionary Process: Recurrent Challenges to the Traditional Order, 1859-1920*. Berkeley: University of California Press, 1985.

Schiffrin, Harold Z. *Sun Yat-sen: Reluctant Revolutionary*. Boston: Little, Brown, 1980.

Schwartz, Benjamin I. *Chinese Communism and the Rise of Mao*. Cambridge, Mass.: Harvard University Press, 1951.

Scott, Ian. *Political Change and the Crisis of Legitimacy in Hong Kong*. Honolulu: University of Hawaii Press, 1989.

Skinner, G. W. *Chinese Society in Thailand: An Analytical History*. Ithaca, N.Y.: Cornell University Press, 1957.

Soet, John Steven. *Martial Arts Around the World*. Burbank, Calif.: Unique Publications, 1991.

Spence, Jonathan D. *The Search for Modern China*. New York: W. W. Norton, 1990.

Sutter, Robert G. *The China Quandary: Domestic Determinants of U.S. China Policy, 1972-1982*. Boulder, Colo.: Westview Press, 1983.

Tsai, Shih-shan H. *China and the Overseas Chinese in the United States, 1868-1911*. Fayetteville: University of Arkansas Press, 1983.

Uhalley, Stephen. *A History of the Chinese Communist Party*. Stanford, Calif.: Hoover Institution Press, 1988.

U.S. Department of State. *United States Relations with China, with Special Reference to the Period 1944-1949*. Department of State Publication 3573. Washington, D.C.: Government Printing Office, 1949.

Waley, Arthur. *The Opium War Through Chinese Eyes*. London: Allen & Unwin, 1958.

Wang, Dee. *Chinese Cooking the Easy Way*. New York: Elsevier/Nelson Books, 1979.

Wang, K'o-fen. *History of Chinese Dance*. Beijing: Foreign Language Press, 1885.

Weinstein, Stanley. *Buddhism Under the Tang*. Cambridge, England: Cambridge University Press, 1987.

Welch, Holmes. *The Parting of the Way: Lao Tzu and the Taoist Movement*. Boston: Beacon Press, 1957.

Welch, Holmes, and Anna Seidel, eds. *Facets of Taoism: Essays in Chinese Religion*. New Haven, Conn.: Yale University Press, 1979.

Wheatley, Paul. *The Pivot of the Four Quarters: A Preliminary Enquiry Into the Origins and Character of the Ancient Chinese City*. Chicago: Aldine, 1971.

Wheeler, Jimmy W., and Perry L. Wood. *Beyond Recrimination: Perspectives on U.S.-Taiwan Trade Tensions*. Indianapolis: Hudson Institute, 1987.

Whyte, Martin K., and William Parish. *Urban Life in Contemporary China*. Chicago: University of Chicago Press, 1984.

Wilbur, C. Martin. *Sun Yat-sen: Frustrated Patriot*. New York: Columbia University Press, 1976.

Winzeler, Robert. *Ethnic Relations in Kelantan*. Singapore: Oxford University Press, 1985.

Wong, Doc-Fai, and Jane Hallander. *Tai Chi Chuan's Internal Secrets*. Burbank, Calif.: Unique Publications, 1991.

Wong, Richard Y. C., and Joseph Y. S. Cheng, eds. *The Other Hong Kong Report, 1990*. Hong Kong: Chinese University Press, 1990.

Wright, Arthur. *Buddhism in Chinese History*. Stanford, Calif.: Stanford University Press, 1988.

Yen, Ching-Hwang. *Coolies and Mandarins: China's Protection of Overseas Chinese During the Late Ch'ing Period (1851-1911).* Singapore: Singapore University Press, 1985.

Yung, Bell. *Cantonese Opera: Performance as Creative Process.* Cambridge, England: Cambridge University Press, 1989.

Zürcher, Erich. *Buddhist Conquest of China: The Spread and Adaptation of Buddhism in Early Medieval China.* Leiden, The Netherlands: E. J. Brill, 1959.

CHINESE AMERICANS AND THE CHINESE DIASPORA (See also CHINA)

Anderson, Kay J. *Vancouver's Chinatown: Racial Discourse in Canada, 1875-1980.* Montreal: McGill-Queen's University Press, 1991.

Axon, Gordon. *The California Gold Rush.* New York: Mason/Charter, 1976.

Barth, Gunther. *Bitter Strength: A History of the Chinese in the United States, 1850-1870.* Cambridge, Mass.: Harvard University Press, 1964.

Beck, Louis. *New York's Chinatown.* New York: Bohemia Publishing Company, 1898.

Cayton, Horace R., and Anne Q. Lively. *The Chinese in the United States and the Chinese Christian Church.* New York: National Council of Churches, 1955.

Chan, Sucheng. *Asian Americans: An Interpretive History.* Boston: Twayne, 1991.

Chan, Sucheng, ed. *Entry Denied: Exclusion and the Chinese Community in America, 1882-1943.* Philadelphia: Temple University Press, 1991.

Chan, Sucheng. *This Bittersweet Soil: The Chinese in California Agriculture, 1860-1910.* Berkeley: University of California Press, 1986.

Char, Tin-Yuke. *The Hakka Chinese: Their Origin and Folk Songs.* Translated by C. H. Kwock. San Francisco: Jade Mountain Press, 1969.

Chen, Jack. *The Chinese of America: From the Beginnings to the Present.* New York: Harper and Row/San Francisco, 1980.

Chen, Ta. *Emigrant Communities in South China.* Edited by Bruno Lasker. New York: Institute of Pacific Relations, 1940.

Cheung, King-Kok. *Articulate Silences: Hisaye Yamamoto, Maxine Hong Kingston, Joy Kogawa.* Ithaca, N.Y.: Cornell University Press, 1993.

Chew, Sock Foon. *Ethnicity and Nationality in Singapore.* Athens: Ohio University Center for International Studies, 1987.

Chin, Frank, et al., eds. *The Big Aiiieeeee! An Anthology of Chinese American and Japanese American Literature.* New York: Meridian Books, 1991.

Chin, Ko-lin. *Chinese Subculture and Criminality.* New York: Greenwood Press, 1990.

Chinese Historical Society of America, Publication Committee, eds. *Chinese America: History and Perspectives, 1990.* San Francisco: Chinese Historical Society of America, 1990.

Chinn, Thomas W., H. Mark Lai, and Philip P. Choy, eds. *A History of the Chinese in California: A Syllabus.* San Francisco: Chinese Historical Society of America, 1969.

Chiu, Ping. *Chinese Labor in California, 1850-1880: An Economic Study.* Madison, Wis.: State Historical Society of Wisconsin, 1963.

Chou, Michaelyn P. *Oral History Interview with Hiram L. Fong, Senator from Hawaii, 1959 to 1977.* Washington, D.C.: Former Members of Congress, Inc., 1979, 1980.

Claiborne, Craig, and Virginia Lee. *The Chinese Cookbook.* Philadelphia: J. B. Lippincott, 1972.

Colman, Elizabeth. *Chinatowns U.S.A.* New York: Asia Press in association with John Day Company, 1946.

Coolidge, Mary R. *Chinese Immigration.* New York: Henry Holt, 1909.

Daniels, Roger. *Asian America: Chinese and Japanese in the United States Since 1850.* Seattle: University of Washington Press, 1988.

Dong, Lorraine. "The Forbidden City Legacy and Its Chinese American Women." *Chinese America: History and Perspectives* (1992): 125-148.

Finn, Michael. *Martial Arts: A Complete Illustrated History.* Woodstock, N.Y.: Overlook Press, 1988.

Fitzgerald, Stephen. *China and the Overseas Chinese.* Cambridge: Cambridge University Press, 1972.

Freedman, Maurice. *Chinese Lineage and Society: Fukien and Kwangtung.* New York: Humanities Press, 1966.

Glick, Clarence E. *Sojourners and Settlers: Chinese Migrants in Hawaii.* Honolulu: University Press of Hawaii, 1980.

Greever, William. *The Bonanza West: The Story of the Western Mining Rushes, 1848-1900.* Norman: University of Oklahoma Press, 1963.

Hamilton, Mildred. "Ethnic TV, the Multi-Lingual Tube." *San Francisco Examiner & Chronicle,* Scene/Arts section, October 8, 1978.

Hirata, Lucie Cheng. "Chinese Immigrant Women in Nineteenth-Century California." In *Women of America,* edited by Carol Ruth Berkin and Mary Beth Norton. Boston: Houghton Mifflin, 1979.

Hoy, William. *The Chinese Six Companies.* San Francisco: Chinese Consolidated Benevolent Association, 1942.

Hsu, Kai-yu, and Helen Palubinskas, eds. *Asian-American Authors.* Boston: Houghton Mifflin, 1972.

Kauz, Herman. *The Martial Spirit: An Introduction to the Origin, Philosophy, and Psychology of the Martial Arts.* Woodstock, N.Y.: Overlook Press, 1988.

Kiang, Clyde. *The Hakka Odyssey and Their Taiwan Homeland.* Elgin, Pa.: Allegheny Press, 1992.

Kifner, John. "New Immigrant Wave from Asia Gives the Underworld New Faces." *The New York Times,* January 6, 1991, p. 1.

Kim, Elaine H. *Asian American Literature: An Introduction to the Writings and Their Social Context.* Philadelphia: Temple University Press, 1982.

Kingston, Maxine Hong. *The Woman Warrior: Memoirs of a Girlhood Among Ghosts.* New York: Alfred A. Knopf, 1976.

Kinkead, Gwen. *Chinatown: A Portrait of a Closed Society.* New York: HarperCollins, 1992.

Kung, S. W. *Chinese in American Life: Some Aspects of Their History, Status, Problems, and Contributions.* Westport, Conn.: Greenwood Press, 1962.

Kwong, Peter. *Chinatown, New York: Labor and Politics, 1930-1950.* New York: Monthly Review Press, 1979.

Kwong, Peter. *The New Chinatown.* New York: Hill and Wang, 1987.

Lai, Chuenyan David. *Chinatowns: Towns Within Cities in Canada.* Vancouver: University of British Columbia Press, 1988.

Lai, Him Mark. "The Chinese American Press." In *The Ethnic Press in the United States: A Historical Analysis and Handbook.* edited by Sally M. Miller, pp. 27-43. New York: Greenwood Press, 1987.

Lai, Him Mark. "Island of Immortals: Chinese Immigrants and the Angel Island Immigration Station." *California History* 57 (Spring, 1978): 88-103.

Lai, Him Mark. "The Ups and Downs of the Chinese Press in the U.S." *East/West,* Nov. 20, 1986.

Lai, Him Mark, Genny Lim, and Judy Yung. *Island: Poetry and History of Chinese Immigrants on Angel Island, 1910-1940.* 1980. Reprint. Seattle: University of Washington Press, 1991.

Lee, Rose Hum. *The Chinese in the United States of America.* Hong Kong: Hong Kong University Press, 1960.

Lee Lai To, ed. *Early Chinese Immigrant Societies: Case Studies from North America and British Southeast Asia.* Singapore: Heinemann, 1988.

Leung, Edwin Pak-wah. "The Making of the Chinese Yankees: School Life of the Chinese Educational Mission Students in New England." "China and the West: Studies in Education, Nationalism, and Diplomacy." Special issue of *Asian Profile* 16 (October, 1988): 401-412.

Leung, Peter C. Y. *One Day, One Dollar: Locke, California, and the Chinese Farming Experience in the Sacramento Delta.* Edited by L. Eve Armentrout Ma. El Cerrito, Calif.: Chinese/Chinese American History Project, 1984.

Lewis, Peter. *Martial Arts of the Orient.* New York: Gallery Books, 1985.

Li, Peter S. *The Chinese in Canada.* Toronto: Oxford University Press, 1988.

Lim, Christina, and Sheldon Lim. *In the Shadow of the Tiger*. San Mateo, Calif.: Japanese American Curriculum Project, 1993.

Lim, Genny, ed. *The Chinese American Experience: Papers from the Second National Conference on Chinese American Studies* (1980). San Francisco: Chinese Historical Society of America: Chinese Culture Foundation of San Francisco, 1984.

Ling, Amy. *Between Worlds: Women Writers of Chinese Ancestry*. Elmsford, N.Y.: Pergamon Press, 1990.

Linking Our Lives: Chinese American Women of Los Angeles. Los Angeles: Chinese Historical Society of Southern California, 1984.

Liu, Melinda. "The New Slave Trade: Chinese Gangs Are Smuggling Illegal Immigrants by the Thousands into America Often Forcing Them into a Life of Servitude." *Newsweek* 121 (June 21, 1993).

Liu, Pei Chi. *A History of Chinese in the United States of America, II*. In Chinese. Taipei: Liming Wenhua Shiye Youxian Gongsi, 1982.

Lo, Karl. "Kim Shan Jit San Luk: The First Chinese Newspaper Published in America." *Chinese Historical Society of America Bulletin* 6 (October, 1971): 1-4.

Loewen, James W. *The Mississippi Chinese: Between Black and White*. 2d ed. Prospect Heights, Ill.: Waveland Press, 1988.

Lum, Arlene, ed. *Sailing for the Sun: The Chinese in Hawaii 1789-1989*. Honolulu: Three Heroes, 1989.

Lydon, Sandy. *Chinese Gold: The Chinese in the Monterey Bay Region*. Capitola, Calif.: Capitola Book Company, 1985.

Lyman, Stanford. *Chinese Americans*. New York: Random House, 1974.

Ma, L. Eve Armentrout, ed. *Chinese America: History and Perspectives*. San Francisco: Chinese Historical Society of America, 1987.

Ma, L. Eve Armentrout. *Revolutionaries, Monarchists, and Chinatowns*. Honolulu: University of Hawaii Press, 1990.

McCunn, Ruthanne Lum. *An Illustrated History of the Chinese in America*. San Francisco: Design Enterprises of San Francisco, 1979.

McCunn, Ruthanne Lum. *Thousand Pieces of Gold*. Boston, Mass.: Beacon Press, 1981.

Mackie, J. A. C., ed. *The Chinese in Indonesia*. Honolulu: University Press of Hawaii, 1976.

MacNair, H. F. *The Chinese Abroad, Their Position and Protection*. Shanghai, China: Commercial Press, 1924.

Mark, Diane Mei Lin, and Ginger Chih. *A Place Called Chinese America*. Dubuque, Iowa: Kendall-Hunt, 1982.

Miller, Stuart C. *The Unwelcome Immigrant: The American Image of the Chinese, 1752-1882*. Berkeley: University of California Press, 1969.

Nagasawa, Richard. *Summer Wind: The Story of an Immigrant Chinese Politician*. Tucson, Ariz.: Westernlore Press, 1986.

Nee, Victor, and Brett Nee. *Longtime Californ': A Documentary Study of an American Chinatown*. New York: Pantheon Books, 1973.

Ong, Paul M. "An Ethnic Trade: The Chinese Laundries in Early California." *Journal of Ethnic Studies* 8, no. 4 (1981): 95-113.

Orleans, Leo. *Chinese Students in America: Policies, Issues, and Numbers*. Washington, D.C.: National Academy Press, 1988.

Overseas Chinese Affairs Commission, the Republic of China. *We Always Stay Together: A Report on Overseas Chinese Affairs*. Taipei, Taiwan: Overseas Chinese Affairs Commission, 1991.

Pang, Wing Ning. *Build Up the Kingdom: A Study of the North American Chinese Church*. Pasadena: North American Congress of Chinese Evangelicals, 1980.

Pang, Wing Ning. *The Chinese and the Chinese Church in America*. Houston: National Convocation on Evangelizing Ethnic America, 1985.

Quan, R. S. *Lotus Among the Magnolias: The Mississippi Chinese*. Jackson University Press of Mississippi, 1982.

Rossbach, Sarah. *Interior Design with Feng Shui*. New York: E. P. Dutton, 1987.

Sandmeyer, Elmer C. *The Anti-Chinese Movement in California*. Urbana: University of Illinois Press, 1939.

Saxton, Alexander. *The Indispensable Enemy: Labor and the Anti-Chinese Movement in California*. Berkeley: University of California Press, 1971.

Seward, George. *Chinese Immigrants: Its Social and Economic Aspects*. New York: Arno Press, 1970.

Siu, Paul. *The Chinese Laundryman: A Study in Social Isolation*. New York: New York University Press, 1987. Edited by John Tchen.

Skinner, G. W. *Chinese Society in Thailand: An Analytical History*. Ithaca, N.Y.: Cornell University Press, 1957.

Smith, Sidonie. *A Poetics of Women's Autobiography: Marginality and the Fictions of SelfRepresentation*. Bloomington: Indiana University Press, 1987.

Soet, John Steven. *Martial Arts Around the World*. Burbank, Calif.: Unique Publications, 1991.

Stellmam, Louis J. "Yellow Journals: San Francisco's Oriental Newspapers." *Sunset* 24 (February, 1910): 197-201.

Sung, Betty Lee. *Mountain of Gold: The Story of the Chinese in America*. New York: Macmillan, 1967.

Sung, Betty Lee. *A Survey of Chinese American Manpower and Employment*. New York: Praeger Publishers, 1976.

Takaki, Ronald. *Iron Cages: Race and Culture in Nineteenth Century America*. New York: Alfred A. Knopf, 1979.

Takaki, Ronald. *Strangers from a Different Shore: A History of Asian Americans*. Boston: Little, Brown, 1989.

Tow, J. S. *The Real Chinese in America*. New York: Academic Press, 1923.

Tsai, Shih-shan Henry. *China and the Overseas Chinese in the United States, 1868-1911*. Fayetteville: University of Arkansas Press, 1983.

Tsai, Shih-shan Henry. *The Chinese Experience in America*. Bloomington: Indiana University Press, 1986.

U.S. Commission on Civil Rights. *Civil Rights Issues Facing Asian Americans in the 1990s*. Washington, D.C.: Government Printing Office, 1992.

Wang, Y. C. *Chinese Intellectuals and the West, 1872-1949*. Chapel Hill: University of North Carolina Press, 1966.

Ward, W. Peter. *White Canada Forever: Popular Attitudes and Public Policy Toward Orientals in British Columbia*. 2d ed. Montreal: McGill-Queen's University Press, 1990.

Wells, Marianne Kaye. *Chinese Temples in California*. San Francisco: R and E Research Associates, 1971.

Wickberg, Edgar. *The Chinese in Philippine Life, 1850-1898*. New Haven, Conn.: Yale University Press, 1965.

Wickberg, Edgar, ed. *From China to Canada: A History of the Chinese Communities in Canada*. Toronto: McClelland and Stewart, 1982.

Winzeler, Robert. *Ethnic Relations in Kelantan*. Singapore: Oxford University Press, 1985.

Wong, Bernard P. *Chinatown: Economic Adaptation and Ethnic Identity of the Chinese*. New York: Holt, Rinehart and Winston, 1982.

Wong, Jade Snow. *Fifth Chinese Daughter*. 1945. New ed. Seattle: University of Washington Press, 1989.

Wu, Cheng-Tsu, ed. *"Chink!": A Documentary History of Anti-Chinese Prejudice in America*. New York: World, 1972.

Yee, Min. "Chinatown in Crisis." *Newsweek* 75 (February 23, 1970): 57-58.

Yen, Ching-Hwang. *Coolies and Mandarins: China's Protection of Overseas Chinese During the Late Ch'ing Period (1851-1911)*. Singapore: Singapore University Press, 1985.

Yu, Connie Young: "Rediscovered Voices: Chinese Immigrants and Angel Island." *Amerasia Journal* 4, no. 2 (1977): 123-139.

Yu, Renqiu. *To Save China, To Save Ourselves: The Chinese Hand Laundry Alliance of New York*. Philadelphia: Temple University Press, 1992.

Yung, Judy. *Chinese Women of America: A Pictorial History*. Published for the Chinese Culture Foundation of San Francisco. Seattle: University of Washington Press, 1986.

Zhou, Min. *Chinatown: The Socioeconomic Potential of an Urban Enclave*. Philadelphia: Temple University Press, 1992.

FILIPINO AMERICANS AND THE
FILIPINO DIASPORA (See also THE
PHILLIPINES)

Agoncillo, Teodoro A. *History of the Filipino People*. 8th ed. Quezon City: R. P. Garcia, 1990.

Alcantara, Ruben R. *Sakada: Filipino Adaptation in Hawaii*. Washington, D.C.: University Press of America, 1981.

Almirol, E. B. *Ethnic Identity and Social Negotiation: A Study of a Filipino Community in California*. New York: AMS Press, 1985.

Buaken, Manuel. *I Have Lived with the American People*. Caldwell, Idaho: Caxton Printers, 1948.

Bulosan, Carlos. *America Is in the Heart*. Seattle: University of Washington Press, 1946.

Bulosan, Carlos. *If You Want to Know What We Are: A Carlos Bulosan Reader*. Albuquerque, N.Mex.: West End Press, 1983.

Bulosan, Carlos. *The Philippines Is in the Heart*. Quezon City: New Day Publishers, 1978.

Bulosan, Carlos. *The Power of the People*. Manila: National Book Store, 1986.

Bulosan, Carlos. *The Sound of Falling Light*. Edited by Dolores Feria. Quezon City: University of the Philippines Press, 1960.

Cabezas, Amado, Larry Shinagawa, and Gary Kawaguchi. "New Inquiries into the Socioeconomic Status of Filipino Americans in California." *Amerasia Journal* 13, no. 1 (1986-1987): 1-21.

Carino, B. V., J. T. Fawcett, R. W. Gardner, and Fred Arnold. "The New Filipino Immigrants to the United States: Increasing Diversity and Change." *Papers of the East-West Population Institute*, no. 115 (May, 1990).

Cordova, Dorothy. "Voices from the Past." In *Making Waves*, edited by Asian Women United of California. Boston: Beacon Press, 1989.

Cordova, Fred. *Filipinos: Forgotten Asian Americans, A Pictorial Essay, 1763-1963*. Edited by Dorothy L. Cordova and Albert A. Acena. Dubuque: Kendall/Hunt, 1983.

Crouchett, Lorraine Jacobs. *Filipinos in California: From the Days of the Galleons to the Present*. El Cerrito, Calif.: Downey Place Publishing House, 1982.

DeWitt, Howard A. *Anti-Filipino Movements in California: A History, Bibliography and Study Guide*. San Francisco: R and E Research Associates, 1976.

DeWitt, Howard A. *Images of Ethnic and Radical Violence in California Politics, 1917-1930: A Survey*. San Francisco: R and E Research Associates, 1975.

DeWitt, Howard A. *Violence in the Fields: Filipino Farm Labor Unionization During the Great Depression*. Saratoga, Calif.: Century Twenty One Publishing, 1980.

Dionisio, Juan C., ed. *Filipinos in Hawaii . . . the First 75 Years*. Honolulu: Hawaii Filipino News Specialty Publications, 1981.

Filipino American Experience in Hawaii: Social Process in Hawaii, The 33 (1991).

Hooson, David, ed. *Geography and National Identity*. Vol. 29 in the Institute of British Geographers Special Service Publications Series. Cambridge, Mass.: Blackwell, 1993.

Jocano, F. Landa. *Growing up in a Philippine Barrio*. New York: Holt, Rinehart and Winston, 1969.

Kushner, Sam. *Long Road to Delano*. New York: International Publishers, 1975.

Lasker, Bruno. *Filipino Immigration to Continental United States and to Hawaii*. Chicago: University of Chicago Press for the American Council, Institute of Pacific Relations, 1931.

Lynch, Frank, ed. *Social Acceptance: Four Readings on Philippine Values*. Quezon City: Ateneo de Manila University, 1964.

McWilliams, Carey. *Brothers Under the Skin*. Rev. ed. Boston: Little, Brown, 1964.

Manlapit, Pablo. *Filipinos Fight for Justice: Case of the Filipino Laborers in the Big Strike of 1924*. Honolulu: Kumalee Publishing, 1933.

Melendy, H. Brett. *Asians in America: Filipinos, Koreans and East Indians*. Boston: Twayne, 1977.

1924 Filipino Strike on Kauai, The. Manoa: Ethnic Studies Program, University of Hawaii, Manoa, 1979.

Okamura, Jonathan Y., et al., eds. *The Filipino American Experience in Hawaii*. Social Process in Hawaii, vol. 33. Manoa: Department of Sociology, University of Hawaii, Manoa, 1991.

Pido, Antonio J. A. *The Filipinos in America: Macro/Micro Dimensions of Immigration and Integration*. New York: Center for Migration Studies, 1986.

Posadas, Barbara M., and Roland L. Guyotte. "Unintentional Immigrants: Chicago's Filipino Foreign Students Become Settlers." *Journal of American Ethnic History* 9 (Spring, 1990): 26-48.

Quinsaat, Jesse. *Letters in Exile*. Los Angeles: UCLA Asian American Studies Center, 1976.

Ringrose, Marjorie, and Adam Lerner, eds. *Reimagining the Nation*. Bristol, Pa.: Taylor & Francis, 1993.

Saniel, J. M., ed. *The Filipino Exclusion Movement*. Quezon City, Philippines: Institute of Asian Studies, University of the Philippines, 1967.

San Juan, E., Jr. *Bulosan: An Introduction with Selections*. Manila: National Book Store, 1983.

San Juan, E., Jr. *Carlos Bulosan and the Imagination of the Class Struggle*. Quezon City: University of the Philippines Press, 1972.

Santos, Bienvenido. *Scent of Apples*. Seattle: University of Washington Press, 1979.

Scharlin, Craig, and Lillia Villanueva. *Philip Vera Cruz: A Personal History of Filipino Immigrants and the Farmworkers Movement*. Edited by Glenn Omatsu and Augusto Espiritu. Los Angeles: UCLA Labor Center Institute of Industrial Relations and UCLA Asian American Studies Center, 1992.

Sharma, Miriam. "The Philippines: A Case of Migration to Hawai'i, 1906 to 1946." In *Labor Immigration Under Capitalism: Asian Workers in the United States before World War II*, edited by L. Cheng and E. Bonacich. Berkeley: University of California Press, 1984.

Takaki, Ronald. "Dollar a Day, Dime a Dance: The Forgotten Filipinos." In *Strangers from a Different Shore: A History of Asian Americans*. New York: Penguin Books, 1990.

Teodoro, Luis, ed. *Out of This Struggle: The Filipinos in Hawaii*. Honolulu: University of Hawaii Press, 1981.

U.S. Commission on Civil Rights. *Civil Rights Issues Facing Asian Americans in the 1990's*. Washington, D.C.: Author, 1992.

Vera Cruz, Philip. "Sour Grapes: Symbol of Oppression." In *Roots: An Asian American Reader*, edited by Amy Tachiki. Los Angeles: Continental Graphics, 1971.

HAWAII; HAWAIIANS; PACIFIC ISLANDS; PACIFIC ISLANDER AMERICANS

Alcantara, Ruben R. *Sakada: Filipino Adaptation in Hawaii*. Washington, D.C.: University Press of America, 1981.

Allen, Gwenfread. *Hawaii's War Years: 1941-1945*. Edited by Aldyth V. Morris. Honolulu: University of Hawaii Press, 1952.

Anthony, J. Garner. *Hawaii Under Army Rule*. Stanford, Calif.: Stanford University Press, 1955.

Barringer, H. R., R. W. Gardner, and M. J. Levin. *Asians and Pacific Islanders in the United States*. New York: Russell Sage Foundation, 1993.

Beechert, Edward D. *Working in Hawaii: A Labor History*. Ethnic Studies Oral History Project, University of Hawaii at Manoa. Honolulu: University of Hawaii Press, 1985.

Beekman, Allan. *Crisis: The Japanese Attack on Pearl Harbor and Southeast Asia*. Honolulu, Hawaii: Heritage Press of the Pacific, 1992.

Beekman, Take, and Allan Beekman. "Hawaii's Great Japanese Strike." In *Kodomo No Tame Ni: For the Sake of the Children*, by Dennis Ogawa. Honolulu: University of Hawaii Press, 1978.

Blaisdell, Kekuni, and Noreen Mokuau. "Kanaka Maoli: Indigenous Hawaiians" In *Handbook of Social Services for Asian and Pacific Islanders*, edited by Noreen Mokuau. New York: Greenwood Press, 1991.

Brower, Kenneth. *Micronesia: The Land, the People and the Sea*. Edited by Gregory Vitiello. Baton Rouge: Louisiana State University Press, 1981.

Callies, David L. *Regulating Paradise: Land Use Controls in Hawaii*. Honolulu: University of Hawaii Press, 1984.

Carano, Paul, and Pedro C. Sanchez. *A Complete History of Guam*. Rutland, Vt.: Charles E. Tuttle, 1964.

Chaplin, George, and Glenn D. Paige, eds. *Hawaii 2000*. Honolulu: University of Hawaii Press, 1973.

Chapman, Murray, and Philip S. Morrison, eds. *Mobility and Identity in the Island Pacific*. A special issue of *Pacific Viewpoint*. Wellington, New Zealand: Department of Geography and Victoria University of Wellington, 1985.

Chou, Michaelyn P. *Oral History Interview with Hiram L. Fong, Senator from Hawaii, 1959 to 1977*. Washington, D.C.: Former Members of Congress, Inc., 1979, 1980.

Clifford, Sister Mary Dorita. "The Hawaiian Sugar Planter[s] Association and Filipino Exclusion." In *The Filipino Exclusion Movement*, edited by J. M. Saniel. Quezon City, Philippines: Institute of Asian Studies, University of the Philippines, 1967.

Daws, Gavan. *Shoal of Time: A History of the Hawaiian Islands*. New York: Macmillan, 1968.

Del Valle, Teresa. *Social and Cultural Change in the Community of Umatac, Southern Guam*. Agana, Guam: Micronesian Area Research Center, University of Guam, 1979.

Dionisio, Juan C., ed. *Filipinos in Hawaii . . . the First 75 Years*. Honolulu: Hawaii Filipino News Specialty Publications, 1981.

Dudley, Michael Kioni. *Man, Gods, and Nature*. Honolulu: Na Kane O Ka Malo Press, 1990.

Dudley, Michael Kioni, and Keoni Kealoha Agard. *A Call for Hawaiian Sovereignty*. Honolulu: Na Kane O Ka Malo Press, 1990.

Ellis, William. *Journal of William Ellis*. Honolulu: Advertiser Publishing, 1963.

Emerson, Nathaniel B. *The Unwritten Literature of Hawaii: The Sacred Songs of the Hula*. Rutland, Vt.: Charles E. Tuttle, 1965.

Feis, Herbert. *Road to Pearl Harbor*. New York: Atheneum, 1950.

Forbes, David W. *Encounters with Paradise: Views of Hawaii and Its People, 1778-1941*. Honolulu: Honolulu Academy of Arts, 1992.

Ford, Douglas. *The Pacific Islanders*. New York: Chelsea House, 1989.

Glazer, Sarah Jane. *Ralph Nader Congress Project. Citizens Look at Congress. Spark M. Matsunaga: Democratic Representative from Hawaii*. Washington: Grossman, 1972.

Gledhill, Marion. *Growing Up: Child Development in the Pacific Islands*. Suva, Fiji: Lotu Pasifika Productions, 1974.

Goodwin, Bill. *Frommer's South Pacific '92-'93*. Englewood Cliffs, N.J.: Prentice-Hall, 1992.

Grattan, F. J. H. *An Introduction to Samoan Custom*. Apia: Samoan Printing and Publishing Company, 1948.

Gray, J. A. C. *Amerika Samoa*. Annapolis, Md.: U.S. Naval Institute, 1960.

Hall, Carla. "The Senator and His Space Refrain: Hawaii's Spark Matsunaga Pushing the Potential of Mars." *The Washington Post*, August 13, 1986.

Handy, E. S. Craighill, and Mary Kawena Pukui. *The Polynesian System in Ka'u,*

Hawai'i. Rutland, Vt.: Charles E. Tuttle, 1972.

Hawaii Advisory Committee to the U.S. Commission on Civil Rights. *A Broken Trust: The Hawaiian Homelands Program—Seventy Years of Failure of the Federal and State Governments to Protect the Civil Rights of Native Hawaiians*. Author, 1991.

Hazama, Dorothy Ochiai, and Jane Okamoto Komeiji. *Okage Sama De: The Japanese in Hawaii, 1885-1985*. Honolulu: Bess Press, 1986.

Holmes, Lowell D., and Ellen Rhoads Holmes. *Samoan Village: Then and Now.* 2d ed. Fort Worth: Harcourt Brace Jovanovich, 1992.

Horwitz, Robert H., and Norman Meller. *Land and Politics in Hawaii*. 3d ed. Honolulu: University of Hawaii Press, 1966.

Ike, Nobutake. *Japan's Decision for War: Records of the 1941 Policy Conferences*. Stanford, Calif.: Stanford University Press, 1967.

Johnson, Dwight L., Michael J. Levin, and Edna L. Paisano. *We, the Asian and Pacific Islander Americans*. Washington, D.C.: Government Printing Office, 1988.

Jolly, Margaret, and Martha Macintyre, eds. *Family and Gender in the Pacific: Domestic Contradictions and the Colonial Impact*. Cambridge, England: Cambridge University Press, 1989.

Kamakau, Samuel. *Ruling Chiefs of Hawaii*. Rev. ed. Honolulu: Kamehameha Schools Press, 1992.

Kameeleihiwa, Lilikala. *Native Land and Foreign Desires*. Honolulu: Bishop Museum Press, 1992.

Kanahele, George, ed. *Hawaiian Music and Musicians: An Illustrated History*. Honolulu: University Press of Hawaii, 1979.

Kanahele, George. *Hawaiian Renaissance*. Honolulu: Project Waiaha, 1982.

Kanahele, George. *Ku Kanaka, Stand Tall: A Search for Hawaiian Values*. Honolulu: University of Hawaii Press, 1986.

Keesing, Felix, and Marie M. Keesing. *Elite Communication in Samoa*. Stanford, Calif.: Stanford University Press, 1956.

Kent, Noel J. *Hawaii: Islands Under the Influence*. New York: Monthly Review Press, 1983.

Kimura, Yukiko. *Issei: Japanese Immigrants in Hawaii*. Honolulu: University of Hawaii Press, 1988.

Kotani, Roland. *The Japanese in Hawaii: A Century of Struggle*. Honolulu: Hawaii Hochi, 1985.

Kuykendall, R. S. *The Hawaiian Kingdom*. 3 vols. Honolulu: University of Hawaii Press, 1938-1967.

Lasaqa, Isireli. *The Fijian People Before and After Independence*. Canberra: Australian National University Press, 1984.

Lawson, Stephanie. *The Failure of Democratic Politics in Fiji*. New York: Oxford University Press, 1991.

Liliuokalani, Queen of Hawaii. *Hawaii's Story.*

Reprint. Rutland, Vt.: Charles E. Tuttle, 1962.

Lind, Andrew. *Hawaii's Japanese: An Experiment in Democracy*. Princeton, N.J.: Princeton University Press, 1946.

Lord, Walter. *Day of Infamy*. New York: Holt, 1957.

MacKenzie, Melody Kapilialoha. *Native Hawaiian Rights Handbook*. Honolulu: Native Hawaiian Legal Corporation, 1991.

Macpherson, Cluny, Bradd Shore, and Robert Franco, eds. *New Neighbors—Islanders in Adaptation*. Santa Cruz, Calif.: Center for South Pacific Studies, University of California, 1978.

Manlapit, Pablo. *Filipinos Fight for Justice: Case of the Filipino Laborers in the Big Strike of 1924*. Honolulu: Kumalee Publishing, 1933.

Matsunaga, Spark, and Ping Chen. *Rulemakers of the House*. Champaign-Urbana: University of Illinois Press, 1976.

Mead, Margaret. *Coming of Age in Samoa*. New York: William Morrow, 1928.

Minister of Education. *Report of the Ministry of Education for the Year 1990*. Nukualofa: Government of Tonga, 1991.

Moriyama, Alan T. *Imingaisha: Japanese Emigration Companies and Hawaii, 1894-1908*. Honolulu: University of Hawaii Press, 1985.

Mulholland, John F. *Hawaii's Religions*. Rutland, Vt.: Charles Tuttle, 1970.

1924 Filipino Strike on Kauai, The. Manoa: Ethnic Studies Program, University of Hawaii, Manoa, 1979.

Odo, Franklin, and Kazuko Sinoto. *A Pictorial History of the Japanese in Hawaii, 1885-1924*. Edited by Bonnie Tocher Clause. Honolulu: Bishop Museum, 1985.

Ogawa, Dennis M. *Kodomo No Tame Ni: For the Sake of the Children: The Japanese American Experience in Hawaii*. Honolulu: University Press of Hawaii, 1978.

Okamura, Jonathan, and Amefil Agbayani. "Filipino Americans." In *Handbook of Social Services for Asian and Pacific Islanders*, edited by Noreen Mokuau. New York: Greenwood Press, 1991.

Okihiro, Gary Y. *Cane Fires: The Anti-Japanese Movement in Hawaii, 1865-1945*. Philadelphia: Temple University Press, 1991.

Osborne, Thomas J. *"Empire Can Wait": American Opposition to Hawaiian Annexation, 1893-98*. Kent, Ohio: Kent State University Press, 1981.

Pai, Margaret K. *The Dreams of Two Yi-Min*. Honolulu: University of Hawaii Press, 1989.

Patterson, Wayne. *The Korean Frontier in America: Immigration to Hawaii, 1896-1910*. Honolulu: University of Hawaii Press, 1988.

Prange, Gordon W. *At Dawn We Slept*. New York: Penguin Books, 1982.

Pulea, Mere. *The Family, Law and Population in the Pacific Islands*. Suva, Fiji: Institute of

Pacific Studies, University of the South Pacific, 1986.

Puyo, Ana Maria. *The Acceptance of Americanization by the Chamorros and Carolinians of Saipan.* St. Louis: St. Louis University, 1964.

Rayson, Ann. *Modern Hawaiian History.* Honolulu: Bess Press, 1984.

Roberts, Helen Heffron. *Ancient Hawaiian Music.* New York: Dover Publications, 1967.

Roth, G. K. *Fijian Way of Life.* 2d ed. Melbourne: Oxford University Press, 1973.

Russ, William A., Jr. *The Hawaiian Revolution, 1893-94.* Selinsgrove, Pa.: Susquehanna University Press, 1959.

Rutherford, Noel. *Friendly Islands: A History of Tonga.* Melbourne: Oxford University Press, 1977.

Sanchez, Pedro C. *Guahan Guam: The History of Our Island.* Agana, Guam: Sanchez Publishing House, 1986.

Santos, Bienvenido. *Scent of Apples.* Seattle: University of Washington Press, 1979.

Shu, Ramsay Leung-Hay. "Kinship System and Migrant Adaptation: Samoans of the United States." *Amerasia Journal* 12, no. 1 (1985-1986): 23-47.

Spencer, Mary L., ed. *Chamorro Language Issues and Research on Guam: A Book of Readings.* Mangilao, Guam: University of Guam Press, 1987.

Stagner, Ishmael W. *Hula!* Laie, Haw.: Institute for Polynesian Studies, Brigham Young University-Hawaii, 1985.

Stannard, David E. *Before the Horror: The Population of Hawaii on the Eve of Western Contact.* Honolulu: Social Science Research Institute, University of Hawaii, 1989.

Stoneburner, Bryan C., comp. *Hawaiian Music: An Annotated Bibliography.* New York: Greenwood Press, 1986.

Tatar, Elizabeth. *Nineteenth Century Hawaiian Chant.* Honolulu: Department of Anthropology, Bernice P. Bishop Museum, 1982.

Thompson, Laura. *Guam and Its People.* New York: Greenwood Press, 1969.

Thomson, Basil. *The Fijians: A Study of the Decay of Custom.* 1908. Reprint. London: Dawsons, 1968.

Tippett, Alan Richard. *Fijian Material Culture.* Honolulu: Bishop Museum Press, 1968.

Trask, Haunani-Kay. *From a Native Daughter: Colonialism and Sovereignty in Hawaii.* Monroe, Maine: Common Courage Press, 1993.

Tremblay, Edward A. *When You Go to Tonga.* Derby, N.Y.: Daughters of St. Paul, Apostolate of the Press, 1954.

Tributes to the Honorable Hiram L. Fong of Hawaii in the United States Senate, upon the Occasion of His Retirement from the Senate. Washington, D.C.: U.S. Government Printing Office, 1977.

Uemoto, Shuzo. *Nana Iho Loea Hula.* Honolulu: Kalihi-Palama Culture and Arts Society, 1984.

U.S. Bureau of the Census. *We, the Asian and Pacific Islander Americans.* Washington, D.C.: Government Printing Office, 1980.

U.S. Congress. House. Committee on the Territories. *Proposed Amendments to the Organic Act of the Territory of Hawaii.* 66th Congress, 2d session, 1920.

U.S. Congress. House. Committee on the Territories. *Proposed Amendments to the Organic Act of the Territory of Hawaii.* 67th Congress, 1st session, 1921. House Report 7257.

U.S. Congress. House. *President's Message Relating to the Hawaiian Islands.* 53rd Congress, 2d Session, 1893. Executive Document 47.

U.S. Congress. Office of Technology Assessment. *Current Health Status and Population Projections of Native Hawaiians Living in Hawaii.* Washington, D.C.: Government Printing Office, 1987.

U.S. Congress. Senate. *Senate Report 227 ("Morgan Report").* 53rd Congress, 2d session, 1894.

Valeri, Valerio. *Kingship and Sacrifice.* Chicago: University of Chicago Press, 1985.

Van Peenen, Mavis Warner. *Chamorro Legends on the Island of Guam.* Agana, Guam: Micronesian Area Research Center, University of Guam, 1974.

Wakukawa, Ernest Katsumi. *A History of the Japanese People in Hawaii.* Honolulu: The Toyo Shoin, 1938.

Wohlstetter, Robert. *Pearl Harbor: Warning and Decision.* Stanford, Calif.: Stanford University Press, 1962.

Wong, Diane Yen-Mei. "Media Policy: Will the Real Asian Pacific American Please Stand Up?" In *The State of Asian Pacific America: Policy Issues to the Year 2020.* Los Angeles: LEAP Asian Pacific American Public Policy Institute and UCLA Asian American Studies Center, 1993.

Wright, Ronald. *On Fiji Islands.* New York: Viking, 1986.

Wright, Theon. *The Disenchanted Isles: The Story of the Second Revolution in Hawaii.* New York: Dial Press, 1972.

INDIA (See also ASIAN INDIAN AMERICANS AND THE INDIAN DIASPORA; SOUTH ASIA; SOUTH ASIAN AMERICANS)

Basham, A. L. *The Origins and Development of Classical Hinduism.* Boston: Beacon Press, 1989.

Basham, A. L. *The Wonder That Was India: A Survey of the Culture of the Indian Subcontinent Before the Coming of the Muslims.* London: Sidgwick and Jackson, 1954.

Brands, H. W. *India and the United States: The Cold Peace.* Boston: Twayne, 1990.

Brass, Paul. *The Politics of India Since Independence.* New York: Cambridge University Press, 1990.

Brown, Emily C. *Har Dayal: Hindu Revolutionary and Rationalist.* Tucson: University of Arizona Press, 1975.

Brown, Judith M. *Gandhi: Prisoner of Hope.* New Haven, Conn.: Yale University Press, 1989.

Carnegie Task Force on Non-Proliferation and South Asian Security. *Nuclear Weapons and South Asian Security.* Washington, D.C.: Carnegie Endowment for International Peace, 1988.

Chatterjee, Margaret. *Gandhi's Religious Thought.* Notre Dame, Ind.: University of Notre Dame Press, 1983.

Chitrabhanu, Gurudev Shree. *Twelve Facets of Reality: The Jain Path to Freedom.* New York: Dodd, Mead, 1980.

Cole, W. Owen. *The Guru in Sikhism.* London: Darton, Longman & Todd, 1982.

Cole, W. Owen, and Piara Singh Sambhi. *The Sikhs: Their Religious Beliefs and Practices.* London: Routledge & Kegan Paul, 1978.

Dalal, Tarla. *Low Calorie Healthy Cooking.* Bombay, India: Sanjay, 1989.

De Bary, William T., ed. *The Buddhist Tradition in India, China, and Japan.* New York: Vintage Books, 1972.

De Souza, Alfred, ed. *Women in Contemporary India.* Delhi: Manohar Book Service, 1975.

Devi, Yamuna. *The Best of Lord Krishna's Cuisine: Favorite Recipes from the Art of Indian Vegetarian Cooking.* California: Bala Books, 1991.

Dignan, Don K. *The Indian Revolutionary Problem in British Diplomacy, 1914-1919.* New Delhi, India: Allied Publishers, 1983.

Edwardes, Michael. *A History of India from the Earliest Times to the Present Day.* New York: Farrar, Straus and Cudahy, 1961.

Embree, Ainslie T., ed. *The Hindu Tradition.* New York: Random House, 1966.

Embree, Ainslie T., and Stephen Hay, eds. *Sources of Indian Tradition,* 2d ed. 2 vols. New York: Columbia University Press, 1988.

Everett, Jana Matson. *Women and Social Change in India.* Delhi: Heritage, 1979.

Fischer, Louis. *The Life of Mahatma Gandhi.* New York: Harper & Row, 1983.

Fox, Richard. *Lions of the Punjab: Culture in the Making.* Berkeley: University of California Press, 1985.

Gandhi, Mahatma. *Essential Gandhi: An Anthology of His Writings on His Life, Work, and Ideas.* Edited by Louis Fischer. New York: Vintage Books, 1962.

Ganguly, Sumit. *The Origins of War in South Asia: Indo-Pakistani Conflicts Since 1947.* Boulder, Colo.: Westview Press, 1986.

Gilmartin, David. *Empire and Islam: Punjab and the Making of Pakistan.* Berkeley: University of California Press, 1988.

Grewal, J. S. *The Sikhs of the Punjab.* New York: Cambridge University Press, 1990.

Gross, Susan Hill, and Mary Hill Rojas. *Contemporary Issues for Women in South Asia: India, Pakistan, Bangladesh, Sri Lanka, Nepal, and Bhutan.* St. Louis Park, Minn.: Glenhurst, 1989.

Hopkins, Thomas J. *The Hindu Religious Tradition*. Encino, Calif.: Dickenson, 1971.

"India and Pakistan: Collision or Compromise?" In *Great Decisions*, edited by the Foreign Policy Association. New York: Foreign Policy Association, 1993.

Jackson, Robert. *South Asian Crisis: India, Pakistan and Bangla Desh: A Political and Historical Analysis of the 1971 War*. New York: Praeger, 1975.

Jaffrey, Madhur. *Madhur Jaffrey's World-of-the-East Vegetarian Cooking*. New York: Alfred A. Knopf, 1981.

Jahan, Rounaq, and Hanna Papanek, eds. *Women and Development: Perspectives from South and Southeast Asia*. Dacca: The Bangladesh Institute of Law and International Affairs, 1979.

Jaini, Padmanabh S. *The Jaina Path of Purification*. Berkeley: University of California Press, 1979.

Jayakar, Pupul. *Krishnamurti: A Biography*. San Francisco: Harper & Row, 1986.

Jeffrey, Robin. *What's Happening to India? Punjab, Ethnic Conflict, Mrs. Gandhi's Death, and the Test of Federalism*. New York: Holmes & Meier, 1986.

Josh, Sohan Singh. *The Hindustan Gadar Party: A Short History*. 2 vols. New Delhi: People's Publishing House, 1977-1978.

Kinsley, David R. *Hinduism: A Cultural Perspective*. Englewood Cliffs, N.J.: Prentice-Hall, 1982.

Kirchner, Bharati. *The Healthy Cuisine of India: Recipes from the Bengal Region*. Los Angeles: Lowell House, 1992.

Krishnamurti, Jiddu. *Krishnamurti on Education*. New Delhi: Orient Longman, 1974.

Krishnamurti, Jiddu. *Krishnamurti's Notebook*. New York: Harper & Row, 1976.

Kumar, Acharya Sushil. *Song of the Soul*. Blairstown, N.J.: Siddhachalam, 1987.

Lutyens, Mary. *Krishnamurti: The Years of Awakening*. London: John Murray, 1975.

Lutyens, Mary. *Krishnamurti: The Years of Fulfillment*. London: John Murray, 1983.

Lutyens, Mary. *Krishnamurti: The Open Door*. London: John Murray, 1988.

McLeod, W. H. *The Evolution of the Sikh Community*. Oxford, England: Clarendon Press, 1976.

McLeod, W. H., ed. and trans. *Textual Sources for the Study of Sikhism*. Totowa, N.J.: Barnes & Noble Books, 1984.

Manuel, Peter. *Popular Musics of the Non-Western World*. New York: Oxford University Press, 1988.

Mason, Philip. *The Guardians*. Vol. 2 in *The Men Who Ruled India*. London: Jonathan Cape, 1963.

Nixon, Rob. *London Calling: V. S. Naipaul, Postcolonial Mandarin*. New York: Oxford University Press, 1992.

Nyrop, Richard F., ed. *India: A Country Study*. Washington, D.C.: U.S. Government Printing Office, 1986.

Palmer, Norman D. *The United States and India: The Dimensions of Influence*. New York: Praeger, 1984.

Puri, Harish K. *Ghadar Movement: Ideology, Organization and Strategy*. 2d ed. Amritsar, Punjab: Guru Nanak Dev University Press, 1993.

Ray, Sumana. *Indian Regional Cooking*. New Jersey: Chartwell Books, 1986.

Roach, James R., ed. *India 2000: The Next Fifteen Years*. Riverdale, Md.: Riverdale, 1986.

Robinson, Richard H., and Willard L. Johnson. *The Buddhist Religion: A Historical Introduction*. 3d ed. Belmont Calif.: Wadsworth, 1982.

Rothermund, Dietmar. *Mahatma Gandhi: An Essay in Political Biography*. New Delhi: Manohar, 1991.

Rudolph, Lloyd I., et al. *The Regional Imperative: The Administration of U.S. Foreign Policy Towards South Asian States Under Presidents Johnson and Nixon*. Atlantic Highlands, N.J.: Humanities Press, 1980.

Rudolph, Susanne Hoeber, and Lloyd I. Rudolph. *Gandhi: The Traditional Roots of Charisma*. Chicago: University of Chicago Press, 1983.

Sakala, Carol. *Women of South Asia: A Guide to Resources*. Millwood, N.Y.: Kraus International, 1980.

Sambamoorthy, P. *South Indian Music*. (6 vols.) Madras: Indian Music Publishing House, 1958-1969.

Sarabhai, Mrinalini. *Understanding Bharata Natyam*. 3d ed. Ahmedabad, India: Darpana Academy of Performing Arts, 1981.

Sarma, D. S. *Studies in the Renaissance of Hinduism in the Nineteenth and Twentieth Centuries*. Benares: Benares Hindu University, 1944.

Schumann, Hans W. *The Historical Buddha*. Translated by M. Walshe. London: Arkana/Penguin, 1989.

Shankar, Ravi. *My Music, My Life*. New York: Simon & Schuster, 1968.

Singer, Milton. *Traditional India: Structure and Change*. Philadelphia: American Folklore Society, 1959.

Singh, Mohinder, ed. *History and Culture of Punjab*. New Delhi, India: Atlantic Publishers and Distributors, 1988.

Sitaramayya, B. Pattabhi. *History of the Indian National Congress*. 2 vols. Bombay: Padma, 1946-1947.

Smith, Vincent A. *The Oxford History of India*. Edited by Percival Spear. 3d ed. Oxford, England: Clarendon Press, 1967.

Stevenson, Margaret. *The Heart of Jainism*. London: Oxford University Press, 1915.

Theroux, Paul. "V. S. Naipaul." In *Sunrise with Seamonsters: A Paul Theroux Reader*. Boston: Houghton Mifflin, 1985.

Thomas, Raju G. C. *Indian Security Policy*. Princeton, N.J.: Princeton University Press, 1986.

Wade, Bonnie C. *Music in India: The Classical Traditions*. Englewood Cliffs, N.J.: Prentice-Hall, 1979.

Weber, Max. *The Religion of India*. Glencoe, Ill.: Free Press, 1958.

Williams, Raymond Brady. *Religions of Immigrants from India and Pakistan: New Trends in the American Tapestry*. New York: Cambridge University Press, 1988.

Wolpert, Stanley. *A New History of India*. 4th ed. New York: Oxford University Press, 1993.

Zaehner, R. C. *Hinduism*. New York: Oxford University Press, 1971.

Ziring, Lawrence, ed. *The Subcontinent in World Politics: India, Its Neighbors, and the Great Powers*. Rev. ed. New York: Praeger, 1982.

JAPAN (See also JAPANESE AMERICANS AND THE JAPANESE DIASPORA)

Asahi Shimbun, ed. *The Pacific Rivals: A Japanese View of Japanese-American Relations*. New York: Weatherhill Asahi, 1972.

Beasley, W. G. *The Meiji Restoration*. Stanford, Calif.: Stanford University Press, 1972.

Beekman, Allan. *Crisis: The Japanese Attack on Pearl Harbor and Southeast Asia*. Honolulu, Hawaii: Heritage Press of the Pacific, 1992.

Belleme, John, and Jan Belleme. *Culinary Treasures of Japan*. Garden City Park, N.J.: Avery Publishing Group, 1992.

Blaker, Michael, ed. *The Politics of Trade: U.S. and Japanese Policymaking for the GATT Negotiations*. New York: Columbia University, 1978.

Boxer, Charles R. *The Christian Century in Japan, 1549-1650*. Berkeley: University of California Press, 1951.

Boxer, Charles R. *Jan Compagnie in Japan, 1600-1850*. 2d rev. ed. The Hague: Martinus Nijhoff, 1950.

Boyle, John. *China and Japan at War, 1937-1945: The Politics of Collaboration*. Stanford, Calif.: Stanford University Press, 1972.

Cooper, Michael. *They Came to Japan*. Berkeley: University of California Press, 1965.

Donohue, John J. *The Forge of the Spirit: Structure, Motion, and Meaning in the Japanese Martial Tradition*. New York: Garland, 1991.

Eliot, Charles. *Japanese Buddhism*. London: Routledge & Kegan Paul, 1969.

Ernst, Earle. *The Kabuki Theatre*. New York: Oxford University Press, 1956.

Feis, Herbert. *Road to Pearl Harbor*. New York: Atheneum, 1950.

Finn, Richard B., ed. *U.S.-Japan Relations: Learning from Competition*. New Brunswick, N.J.: Transaction Books, 1986.

Gunji, Masakatsu. *Buyo: The Classical Dance*. Translated by Don Kenny. New York: Weatherhill, 1970.

Hall, John W., and Richard K. Beardsley. *Twelve Doors to Japan*. New York: McGraw-Hill, 1965.

Hamada, Hiroyuki Teshin. *Spirit of Japanese*

Classical Martial Arts: Historical and Philosophical Perspectives. Dubuque, Iowa: Kendall/Hunt, 1990.

Haradda, Tetsuo. *Outlines of Modern Japanese Linguistics.* Tokyo: Nihon University/Tateshina Publishing, 1966.

Hardacre, Helen. *Shinto and the State, 1868-1988.* Princeton, N.J.: Princeton University Press, 1989.

Harries, Meirion, and Susie Harries. *Soldiers of the Sun: The Rise and Fall of the Imperial Japanese Army.* New York: Random House, 1991.

Harrison, E. J. *The Fighting Spirit of Japan.* Woodstock, N.Y.: The Overlook Press, 1982.

Holtom, Daniel C. *The National Faith of Japan: A Study in Modern Shinto.* London: Kegan Paul, 1938.

Huber, Thomas M. *The Revolutionary Origins of Modern Japan.* Stanford, Calif.: Stanford University Press, 1981.

Ike, Nobutake. *Japan's Decision for War: Records of the 1941 Policy Conferences.* Stanford, Calif.: Stanford University Press, 1967.

Inoguchi, Takashi. *Japan's International Relations.* Boulder, Colo.: Westview Press, 1991.

Inoguchi, Takashi, and Daniel I. Okimoto. *The Political Economy of Japan.* Vol. 2. Stanford, Calif.: Stanford University Press, 1988.

Iriye, Akira. *The Origins of the Second World War in Asia and the Pacific.* New York: Longman, 1987.

Iriye, Akira. *Power and Culture: The Japanese-American War, 1941-1945.* Cambridge, Mass.: Harvard University Press, 1981.

Iriye, Akira, and Warren Cohen, eds. *The United States and Japan in the Postwar World.* Lexington: University Press of Kentucky, 1989.

Ishinomori, Shotaro. *Japan, Inc.: An Introduction to Japanese Economics (The Comic Book).* Translated by Betsey Scheiner. Berkeley: University of California Press, 1988.

Japan Travel Bureau. *Illustrated Eating in Japan.* Volume 3 in *JTB Illustrated Books.* Tokyo: Japan Travel Bureau, 1989.

Japanese Classics Translation Committee. *The Noh Drama.* Tokyo: Charles E. Tuttle, 1960.

Jensen, Marius B., and Gilbert Rozman, eds. *Japan in Transition: From Tokugawa to Meiji.* Princeton, N.J.: Princeton University Press, 1986.

Kawai, Kazuo. *Japan's American Interlude.* Chicago: University of Chicago Press, 1960.

Keene, Donald, ed. *Anthology of Japanese Literature: From the Earliest Era to the Mid-Nineteenth Century.* New York: Grove Press, 1955.

Kerr, George H. *Okinawa: The History of an Island People.* Rutland, Vt.: Charles E. Tuttle, 1958.

Kindaichi, Haruhiko. *The Japanese Language.* Translated by Umeyo Hirano. Rutland, Vt.: Charles E. Tuttle, 1978.

Kitagawa, Joseph M. *Religion in Japanese History.* New York: Columbia University Press, 1966.

Lebra, William P. *Okinawan Religion: Belief, Ritual, and Social Structure.* Honolulu: University of Hawaii Press, 1966.

Lincoln, Edward J. *Japan's Unequal Trade.* Washington, D.C.: Brookings Institution, 1990.

Lord, Walter. *Day of Infamy.* New York: Holt, 1957.

Malm, William. *Japanese Music and Musical Instruments.* Tokyo: Charles E. Tuttle, 1959.

Miller, Roy Andrew. *The Japanese Language.* Chicago: University of Chicago Press, 1967.

Morley, James W., ed. *The Pacific Basin: New Challenges for the United States.* New York: Academy of Political Science, Columbia University, 1986.

Nagai, Yonosuke, and Akira Iriye, eds. *The Origins of the Cold War in Asia.* New York: Columbia University Press, 1977.

Nakane, Chie. *Japanese Society.* Berkeley: University of California Press, 1970.

Okutsu, Keichiro, and Akio Tanaka. *Invitation to the Japanese Language.* Tokyo: Bonjinsha, 1989.

Ono Sokyo. *Shinto the Kami Way.* Rutland, Vt.: Charles E. Tuttle, 1962.

Patrick, Hugh T., and Ryuichiro Tachi, eds. *Japan and the United States Today.* New York: Center on Japanese Economy and Business, Columbia University, 1986.

Prange, Gordon W. *At Dawn We Slept.* New York: Penguin Books, 1982.

Ratti, Oscar, and Adele Westbrook. *Secrets of the Samurai: A Survey of the Martial Arts of Feudal Japan.* Rutland, Vt.: Charles E. Tuttle, 1973.

Reischauer, Edwin O. *Japan: The Story of a Nation.* 4th ed. New York: McGraw-Hill, 1990.

Reischauer, Edwin O. *The Japanese.* Cambridge, Mass.: The Belknap Press of Harvard University Press, 1977.

Ross, Floyd H. *Shinto, the Way of Japan.* Boston: Beacon Press, 1965.

Sakai, Robert. "The Ryukyu Islands as a Fief of Satsuma." In *The Chinese World Order,* edited by John K. Fairbank. Cambridge, Mass.: Harvard University Press, 1968.

Sansom, G. B. *Japan: A Short Cultural History.* Rev. ed. New York: Appleton-Century-Crofts, 1962.

Sansom, George. *A History of Japan, 1615-1867.* Stanford, Calif.: Stanford University Press, 1963.

Shaner, David Edward. *The Bodymind Experience in Japanese Buddhism: A Phenomenological Perspective of Kukai and Dogen.* Albany: State University of New York Press, 1985.

Shillony, Ben-Ami. *Politics and Culture in Wartime Japan.* Oxford, England: Clarendon Press, 1981.

Soet, John S. *Martial Arts Around the World.* Burbank, Calif.: Publications, 1991.

Sugano, Kimiko. *Kimiko's World.* San Francisco: Strawberry Hill Press, 1982.

Sugawara, Makoto. *Nihongo: A Japanese Approach to Japanese.* Tokyo: The East Publications, 1985.

Suzuki, Daisetz Taitaro. *Japanese Spirituality.* 1972. Reprint. New York: Greenwood Press, 1988.

Suzuki, Daisetz Taitaro. *The Training of the Zen Buddhist Monk.* 1934. Reprint. New York: Globe Press, 1991.

Suzuki, Takao. *Japanese and the Japanese: Words in Culture.* Translated by Akira Miura. Tokyo: Kodansha International, 1978.

Thorne, Christopher. *The Issue of War: States, Societies, and the Far Eastern Conflict of 1941-1945.* New York: Oxford University Press, 1985.

Totman, Conrad. *The Collapse of the Tokugawa Bakufu, 1862-1868.* Honolulu: University Press of Hawaii, 1980.

Totman, Conrad D. *Politics in the Tokugawa Bakufu, 1600-1843.* Cambridge, Mass.: Harvard University Press, 1967.

Tsuji, Shizuo. *Japanese Cooking, A Simple Art.* Tokyo: Kodansha International, 1980.

Varley, Paul, and Kumakura Isao. *Tea in Japan.* Honolulu: University of Hawaii Press, 1989.

Vogel, Ezra F. *Japan as Number One: Lessons for America.* Cambridge, Mass.: Harvard University Press, 1979.

Webb, Herschel. *The Japanese Imperial Institution in the Tokugawa Period.* New York: Columbia University Press, 1968.

Weinstein, Franklin B., ed. *U.S.-Japan Relations and the Security of East Asia.* Boulder, Colo.: Westview Press, 1978.

Williams, Bryn. *Martial Arts of the Orient.* New York: Hamlyn, 1975.

Wohlstetter, Robert. *Pearl Harbor: Warning and Decision.* Stanford, Calif.: Stanford University Press, 1962.

Wolferen, Karel van. *The Enigma of Japanese Power.* New York: Vintage Books, 1990.

Yamamura, Kozo, ed. *Policy and Trade Issues of the Japanese Economy.* Seattle: University of Washington Press, 1982.

JAPANESE AMERICANS AND THE JAPANESE DIASPORA (See also JAPAN)

Adachi, Ken. *The Enemy That Never Was: A History of the Japanese Canadians.* Toronto: McClelland and Stewart, 1991.

Adams, Ansel. *Manzanar.* With photographs by Ansel Adams and commentary by John Hersey. Compiled by John Armor and Peter Wright. New York: Times Books, 1988.

Anthony, J. Garner. *Hawaii Under Army Rule.* Stanford, Calif.: Stanford University Press, 1955.

Anzovin, Steven, ed. *The Problem of Immigration.* New York: H.W. Wilson, 1985.

Barkan, Elliott Robert. *Asian and Pacific Islander Migration to the United States: A Model of New Global Patterns.* Westport, Conn.: Greenwood Press, 1992.

Broadfoot, Barry. *Years of Sorrow, Years of Shame: The Story of Japanese Canadians in World War II*. Garden City, N.Y.: Doubleday, 1977.

Bruchac, Joseph, ed. *Breaking Silence: An Anthology of Contemporary Asian American Poets*. New York: Greenfield Review Press, 1983.

Buddhist Churches of America. *Buddhist Churches of America*. 2 vols. Chicago: Nobart, 1974.

Chan, Jeffrey Paul, Frank Chin, Lawson Fusao Inada, and Shawn Wong, eds. *The Big Aiiieeeee! An Anthology of Chinese American and Japanese American Literature*. New York: Meridian Books, 1991.

Chan, Sucheng. *Asian Americans: An Interpretive History*. Boston: Twayne Publishers, 1991.

Cheung, King-Kok. *Articulate Silences: Hisaye Yamamoto, Maxine Hong Kingston, Joy Kogawa*. Ithaca, N.Y.: Cornell University Press, 1993.

Chuman, Frank. *The Bamboo People: Japanese Americans, Their History, and the Law*. Chicago: Japanese American Research Project and Japanese American Citizens League, 1981.

Clary, Mike. "Dream Turns to Tragedy." *Los Angeles Times*. February 2, 1993.

Collins, Donald E. *Native American Aliens: Disloyalty and the Renunciation of Citizenship by Japanese Americans During World War II*. Westport, Conn.: Greenwood Press, 1985.

Commission on Wartime Relocation and Internment of Civilians. *Personal Justice Denied*. Washington, D.C.: Government Printing Office, 1982.

Conroy, Hilary, and T. Scott Miyakawa, eds. *East Across the Pacific: Historical and Sociological Studies of Japanese Immigration and Assimilation*. Santa Barbara, Calif.: Clio Press, 1972.

Cretser, Gary A., and Joseph J. Leon, eds. *Intermarriage in the United States*. New York: Haworth, 1982.

Daniels, Roger. *Asian America: Chinese and Japanese in the United States Since 1850*. Seattle: University of Washington Press, 1988.

Daniels, Roger. *Concentration Camps, North America: Japanese in the United States and Canada During World War II*. Malabar, Fla.: Robert E. Krieger, 1981.

Daniels, Roger. *The Politics of Prejudice: The Anti-Japanese Movement in California and the Struggle for Japanese Exclusion*. 1962. 2d ed. Berkeley: University of California Press, 1978.

Daniels, Roger, Sandra C. Taylor, and Harry H. L. Kitano, eds. *Japanese Americans: From Relocation to Redress*. Rev. ed. Seattle: University of Washington Press, 1991.

Daws, Gavan. *Shoal of Time: A History of the Hawaiian Islands*. New York: Macmillan, 1968.

Divine, Robert A. *American Immigration Policy, 1924-1952*. New Haven, Conn.: Yale University Press, 1957.

Dolan, Jay P., ed. *The American Catholic Parish: A History from 1850 to the Present*. Vol. 2. Mahwah, N.J.: Paulist Press, 1987.

Drinnon, Richard. *Keeper of Concentration Camps: Dillon S. Meyer and American Racism*. Berkeley: University of California Press, 1987.

Ehrlich, Paul R., Loy Bilderback, and Anne H. Ehrlich. *The Golden Door: International Migration, Mexico, and the United States*. New York: Ballantine Books, 1979.

Embrey, Sue Kunitomi, ed. *The Lost Years: 1942-1946*. Los Angeles: Moonlight Publications, 1972.

Embrey, Sue Kunitomi, Arthur A. Hansen, and Betty Kulberg Mitson, eds. *Manzanar Martyr: An Interview with Harry Y. Ueno*. Fullerton, Calif.: Japanese American Project, Oral History Program, California State University, Fullerton, 1986.

Emi, Frank. "Draft Resistance at the Heart Mountain Concentration Camp and the Fair Play Committee." In *Frontiers of Asian American Studies: Writing, Research and Commentary*, edited by Gail M. Nomura, Russell Endo, Stephen H. Sumida, and Russell C. Leong. Pullman: Washington State University Press, 1989.

Ethnic Studies Oral History Project. *Uchinanchu: A History of Okinawans in Hawaii*. Honolulu: Ethnic Studies Program, University of Hawaii at Manoa, 1981.

Fawcett, James T., and Benjamin V. Carino, eds. *Pacific Bridges: The New Immigration from Asia and the Pacific Islands*. Staten Island, N.Y.: Center for Migration Studies of New York, 1987.

Fujita, Stephen S., and David J. O'Brien. *Japanese American Ethnicity: The Persistence of Community*. Seattle: University of Washington Press, 1991.

Fukuda, Moritoshi. *Legal Problems of Japanese-Americans*. Tokyo: Keio Tsushin, 1980.

Garrett, Jessie A., and Ronald C. Larson, eds. *Camp and Community: Manzanar and the Owens Valley*. Fullerton, Calif.: Japanese American Project, Oral History Program, California State University, Fullerton, 1977.

Glazer, Sarah Jane. *Ralph Nader Congress Project. Citizens Look at Congress. Spark M. Matsunaga: Democratic Representative from Hawaii*. Washington: Grossman, 1972.

Glenn, Evelyn Nakano. *Issei, Nisei, War Bride: Three Generations of Japanese American Women in Domestic Service*. Philadelphia: Temple University Press, 1986.

Grodzins, Morton. *Americans Betrayed: Politics and the Japanese Evacuation*. Chicago: University of Chicago Press, 1949.

Hall, Carla. "The Senator and His Space Refrain: Hawaii's Spark Matsunaga Pushing the Potential of Mars." *The Washington Post*, August 13, 1986.

Hansen, Arthur A., and Betty E. Mitson, eds. *Voices Long Silent: An Oral Inquiry into the Japanese American Evacuation*. Fullerton, Calif.: Japanese American Project, Oral History Program, California State University, Fullerton, 1974.

Harrison, E. J. *The Fighting Spirit of Japan*. Woodstock, N.Y.: The Overlook Press, 1982.

Hartmann, Edward George. *The Movement to Americanize the Immigrant*. 1948. Reprint. New York: AMS Press, 1967.

Hazama, Dorothy Ochiai, and Jane Okamoto Komeiji. *Okage Sama De: The Japanese in Hawaii, 1885-1985*. Honolulu: Bess Press, 1986.

Herman, Masako. *The Japanese in America: 1843-1973*. Dobbs Ferry, N.Y.: Oceana Publications, 1974.

Higham, John. *Strangers in the Land: Patterns of American Nativism, 1860-1925*. New Brunswick, N.J.: Rutgers University Press, 1955.

Hing, Bill Ong. *Making and Remaking Asian America Through Immigration Policy, 1850-1990*. Stanford, Calif.: Stanford University Press, 1993.

Hohri, William Minoru. *Repairing America*. Pullman: Washington State University Press, 1988.

Hosokawa, Bill. *JACL in Quest of Justice*. New York: William Morrow, 1982.

Hosokawa, Bill. *Nisei: The Quiet Americans*. New York: William Morrow, 1969.

Houston, Jeanne Wakatsuki, and James D. Houston. *Farewell to Manzanar*. Boston: Houghton Mifflin, 1973.

Hsu, Kai-yu, and Helen Palubinskas, eds. *Asian-American Authors*. Boston: Houghton Mifflin, 1972.

Hutchinson, E. P. *Legislative History of American Immigration Policy, 1798-1965*. Philadelphia: University of Pennsylvania Press, 1981.

Ichihashi, Yamato. *Japanese in the United States*. Stanford, Calif.: Stanford University Press, 1932. Reprint. New York: Arno Press, 1969.

Ichioka, Yuji. *The Issei: The World of the First Generation Japanese Immigrants, 1885-1924*. New York: Free Press, 1988.

Irons, Peter H. *Justice at War: The Inside Story of the Japanese American Internment Cases*. New York: Oxford University Press, 1983.

Iwata, Masakazu. *Planted in Good Soil: A History of the Issei in United States Agriculture*. Vols. 1 and 2. New York: Peter Lang, 1992.

Johnson, Terry E. "Immigrants: New Victims." *Newsweek* 107 (May 12, 1986): 57.

Jones, Maldwyn Allen. *American Immigration*. 2d ed. Chicago: University of Chicago Press, 1992.

Kashima, Tetsuden. *Buddhism in America: The Social Organization of an Ethnic Religious Institution*. Westport, Conn.: Greenwood Press, 1977.

Kikumura, Akemi. *Through Harsh Winters: The Life of a Japanese Immigrant Woman*. Novato, Calif.: Chandler and Sharp, 1981.

Kimura, Yukiko. *Issei: Japanese Immigrants in Hawaii*. Honolulu: University of Hawaii Press, 1988.

Kitano, Harry H. L. *Japanese Americans: The Evolution of a Subculture*. 2d ed. Englewood Cliffs, N.J.: Prentice-Hall, 1976.

Kogawa, Joy. *Obasan*. Boston: David R. Godine, 1981.

Konvitz, Milton R. *The Alien and the Asiatic in American Law*. Ithaca, N.Y.: Cornell University Press, 1946.

Kumamoto, Bob. "The Search for Spies: American Counterintelligence and the Japanese American Community 1931-1942." *Amerasia Journal* 6, no. 2 (1979): 45-76.

Lind, Andrew. *Hawaii's Japanese: An Experiment in Democracy*. Princeton, N.J.: Princeton University Press, 1946.

Masaoka, Mike, and Bill Hosokawa. *They Call Me Moses Masaoka*. New York: William Morrow, 1987.

Matsunaga, Spark, and Ping Chen. *Rulemakers of the House*. Champaign-Urbana: University of Illinois Press, 1976.

Miyamoto, S. Frank. "Problems of Interpersonal Style Among the Nisei." *Amerasia Journal* 13, no. 2 (1986-1987): 29-45.

Miyamoto, S. Frank. *Social Solidarity Among the Japanese in Seattle*. Seattle: University of Washington Press, 1939.

Moriyama, Alan Takeo. *Imingaisha: Japanese Emigration Companies and Hawaii, 1894-1908*. Honolulu: University of Hawaii Press, 1985.

Morrow, Lance, et al. "Nation: America in the Mind of Japan." *Time* 139 (February 10, 1992): 16.

Myer, Dillon S. *Uprooted Americans: The Japanese Americans and the War Relocation Authority During World War II*. Tucson: University of Arizona Press, 1971.

Nakano, Mei. *Japanese American Women: Three Generations, 1890-1990*. With *Okaasan* by Grace Shibata. San Francisco: National Japanese American Historical Society, 1990.

Namias, June. *First Generation: In the Words of Twentieth-Century American Immigrants*. Rev. ed. Urbana: University of Illinois Press, 1992.

Negoro, Motoyuki. *Meiji Yonjuichi, ni-nen Hawaii Hojin Katsuyakushi*. Honolulu: Taisho 4, 1915.

Nelson, Douglas W. *Heart Mountain: The History of an American Concentration Camp*. Madison: The State Historical Society of Wisconsin, 1976.

O'Brien, David J., and Stephen S. Fujita. *The Japanese American Experience*. Bloomington: Indiana University Press, 1991.

Oda, James. *Heroic Struggles of Japanese Americans*. North Hollywood, Calif.: J. Oda, 1980.

Ogawa, Dennis M. *Kodomo No Tame Ni: For the Sake of the Children, the Japanese American Experience in Hawaii*. Honolulu: University of Hawaii Press, 1978.

Okihiro, Gary Y. *Cane Fires: The Anti-Japa-*

nese Movement in Hawaii, 1865-1945. Philadelphia: Temple University Press, 1991.

Petersen, William. *Japanese Americans: Oppression and Success*. New York: Random House, 1971.

Petersen, William. "Success Story: Japanese American Style." *The New York Times Magazine* (January 6, 1966).

Root, Maria P. P., ed. *Racially Mixed People in America*. Newbury Park, Calif.: Sage Publications, 1992.

Scott, Esther, and Calvin Naito. *Against All Odds: The Japanese Americans' Campaign for Redress*. Cambridge, Mass.: Case Program, Harvard Kennedy School of Government, 1990.

Shutt, Harry. *The Myth of Free Trade: Patterns of Protectionism Since 1945*. New York: Blackwell, 1985.

Sone, Monica. *Nisei Daughter*. Boston: Little, Brown, 1953.

Spickard, Paul R. *Mixed Blood: Intermarriage and Ethnic Identity in Twentieth-Century America*. Madison: University of Wisconsin Press, 1989.

Stroup, Dorothy Anne. *The Role of the Japanese-American Press in Its Community*. Berkeley: University of California Press, 1960.

Sugano, Kimiko. *Kimiko's World*. San Francisco: Strawberry Hill Press, 1982.

Sunahara, Ann Gomer. *The Politics of Racism: The Uprooting of Japanese Canadians During the Second World War*. Toronto: Lorimer, 1981.

Takaki, Ronald. *Strangers from a Different Shore: A History of Asian Americans*. New York: Penguin Books, 1990.

Tamura, Eileen H. *Americanization, Acculturation, and Ethnic Identity: The Nisei Generation in Hawaii*. Urbana: University of Illinois Press, 1994.

TenBroek, Jacobus, et al. *Prejudice, War and the Constitution*. Berkeley: University of California Press, 1954.

Thomas, Dorothy Swaine, and Richard S. Nishimoto. *The Spoilage*. Berkeley: University of California Press, 1946.

Tuck, Donald R. *Buddhist Churches of America: Jodo Shinshu*. Lewiston, N.Y.: Edwin Mellen Press, 1987.

United Japanese Society of Hawaii, Publications Committee, ed. *A History of Japanese in Hawaii*. Honolulu: United Japanese Society of Hawaii, 1971.

United States Commission on Civil Rights. *Civil Rights Issues Facing Asian Americans in the 1990s*. Washington, D.C.: Government Printing Office, 1992.

U.S. Commission on Wartime Relocation and Internment of Civilians. *Personal Justice Denied: Report of the Commission on Wartime Relocation and the Internment of Civilians*. Washington, D.C.: Government Printing Office, 1983.

U.S. Congress. House. Committee on Interior and Insular Affairs. *Personal Justice De-*

nied: Report of the Commission on Wartime Relocation and Internment of Civilians. 102d Congress, 2d session, 1983. Washington, D.C.: Government Printing Office, 1992.

U.S. War Relocation Authority. *Administrative Highlights of the WRA Program*. Washington, D.C.: Government Printing Office, 1946.

Van Wolferen, Karl. *The Enigma of Japanese Power*. New York: Alfred A. Knopf, 1989.

Vogel, Ezra. *Japan As Number One: Lessons for America*. New York: Harper Colophon, 1979.

Wakukawa, Ernest Katsumi. *A History of the Japanese People in Hawaii*. Honolulu: The Toyo Shoin, 1938.

Walls, Thomas K. *The Japanese Texans*. San Antonio: University of Texas Institute of Texan Cultures at San Antonio, 1987.

Ward, W. Peter. *White Canada Forever: Popular Attitudes and Public Policy Toward Orientals in British Columbia*. Montreal: McGill-Queen's University Press, 1990.

Weglyn, Michi. *Years of Infamy: The Untold Story of America's Concentration Camps*. New York: William Morrow, 1976.

Wilson, Robert A., and Bill Hosokawa. *East to America: A History of the Japanese in the United States*. New York: William Morrow, 1980.

Yamamoto, Hisaye. *Seventeen Syllables and Other Stories*. Latham, N.Y.: Kitchen Table—Women of Color Press, 1988.

Yamaoka, Seigen H. *Jodo Shinshu: An Introduction*. San Francisco: Buddhist Churches of America, 1989.

KOREA (See also KOREAN AMERICANS AND THE KOREAN DIASPORA; SOUTHEAST ASIA; SOUTHEAST ASIAN AMERICANS AND THE SOUTHEAST ASIAN DIASPORA)

Alexander, Bevin. *Korea: The First War We Lost*. New York: Hippocrene Books, 1986.

Allen, Richard C. *Korea's Syngman Rhee: An Unauthorized Portrait*. Rutland, Vt.: Charles E. Tuttle, 1960.

Appleman, Roy E. *South to the Naktong, North to the Yalu*. Washington, D.C.: Department of the Army, 1961.

Bridges, Brian. *Korea and the West*. New York: Routledge & Kegan Paul, 1986.

Buswell, Robert. "Buddhism in Korea." In *Buddhism and Asian History*, edited by Joseph Kitagawa and Mark Cummings. New York: Macmillan, 1989.

Choe, Sang-Su. *Annual Customs of Korea: Notes on the Rites and Ceremonies of the Year*. Seoul: Seomun-dang, 1983.

Chryssides, George D. *The Advent of Sun Myung Moon: The Origins, Beliefs, and Practices of the Unification Church*. New York: St. Martin's Press, 1991.

Clark, Donald N. *Christianity in Modern Korea*. Lanham, Md.: University Press of America, 1986.

Clark, Donald N., ed. *Korea Briefing, 1993*. Boulder, Colo.: Westview Press, 1993.

Conroy, Hilary. *The Japanese Seizure of Korea, 1868-1910: A Study of Realism and Idealism in International Relations*. Philadelphia: University of Pennsylvania Press, 1960.

Cumings, Bruce. *The Origins of the Korean War*. Princeton, N.J.: Princeton University Press, 1990.

Dennett, Tyler. *Americans in Eastern Asia*. New York: Barnes & Noble Books, 1941.

Eckert, Carter J., et al. *Korea Old and New: A History*. Seoul, Korea: Ilchokak, 1990; distributed in U.S. by Harvard University Press.

Fichter, Joseph H. *The Holy Family of Father Moon*. Kansas City, Mo.: Leaven Press, 1985.

Haas, Michael, ed. *Korean Reunification: Alternative Pathways*. New York: Praeger, 1989.

Henthorn, William E. *A History of Korea*. New York: Free Press, 1971.

Hoji, Jajime, ed. *Japanese/Korean Linguistics*, Stanford, Calif.: Center for the Study of Language and Information, 1990.

International Cultural Foundation, ed. *Customs and Manners in Korea*. Seoul: Si-sa-yong-o-sa Publishers, 1982.

Janelli, Roger, and Dawnhee Yim Janelli. *Ancestor Worship and Korean Society*. Stanford, Calif.: Stanford University Press, 1982.

Kendall, Laurel. *Shamans, Housewives, and Other Restless Spirits*. Honolulu: University of Hawaii Press, 1985.

Kim, Gi Pal. *The Third Republic*. Seoul: Hyundai Culture, 1986.

Kim, Man-Kil. "Korean." In *The World's Major Languages*, edited by Bernard Comrie. New York: Oxford University Press, 1987.

Koo, Hagen, and Eui-Young Yu. *Korean Immigration to the United States: Its Demographic Pattern and Social Implications for Both Societies*. Papers of the East-West Population Institute 74, Honolulu: East-West Center, 1981.

Koo, Youngnok, and Sung-joo Han, eds. *The Foreign Policy of the Republic of Korea*. New York: Columbia University Press, 1985.

Korea: Its People and Culture. Seoul: Hakwonsa. 1970.

Korean National Commission for UNESCO, ed. *The Korean Language*. Seoul: Si-sa-yong-o-sa, 1983.

Korean Overseas Information Service. *A Handbook of Korea*, 6th ed. Seoul: Seoul International Publishing House, 1987.

Kwak, Tae-Hwan, Chonghan Kim, and Hong Nack Kim, eds. *Korean Reunification: New Perspectives and Approaches*. Seoul, Korea: Kyungnam University Press, 1984.

Kwon, Ik Whan. "Japanese Agricultural Policy on Korea; 1910-1945." *Koreana Quarterly* 7 (Autumn, 1965): 96-112.

Kwon, Ik Whan. "Japanese Industrialization in Korea, 1930-1945: Idealism or Realism?" *Koreana Quarterly* 8 (Summer, 1966): 80-95.

Lautensach, Hermann. *Korea: A Geography Based on the Author's Travels and Literature*. Translated and edited by Katherine and Eckart Dege. Berlin: Springer-Verlag, 1988.

Lee, Chong-sik, ed. *Korea Briefing, 1990*. Boulder, Colo.: Westview Press, 1991.

Lee, Chong-sik. *The Politics of Korean Nationalism*. Berkeley: University of California Press, 1963.

Lee, Ki-baik. *A New History of Korea*. Cambridge, Mass.: Harvard University Press, 1984.

Lee, Peter, et al., eds. *Sourcebook of Korean Civilization*. Vol. 1. New York: Columbia University Press, 1993.

Lee, Sun K. *Korean History, Modern Times*. Seoul: Eul U Publishing, 1963.

McCune, Shannon. *Korea's Heritage: A Regional and Social Geography*. Rutland, Vt.: Charles E. Tuttle, 1956.

Macdonald, Donald S. *The Koreans: Contemporary Politics and Society*. Boulder, Colo.: Westview Press, 1990.

McKenzie, Frederick A. *Korea's Fight for Freedom*. New York: Fleming H. Revell, 1920.

Martin, Samuel E. *Korean in a Hurry: A Quick Approach to Spoken Korean*. Rutland, Vt.: Charles E. Tuttle, 1954.

Martin, Samuel E., and Young-Sook C. Lee. *Beginning Korean*. 1969. Reprint. Rutland, Vt.: Charles E. Tuttle, 1986.

Matray, James I., ed. *Historical Dictionary of the Korean War*. New York: Greenwood Press, 1991.

Mazarr, Michael, et al., eds. *Korea 1991: The Road to Peace*. Boulder, Colo.: Westview Press, 1991.

Merrill, John. *Korea: The Peninsular Origins of the War*. Newark: University of Delaware Press, 1989.

Moffett, Samuel Hugh. *The Christians of Korea*. New York: Friendship Press, 1962.

Moon, Sun Myung. *A Prophet Speaks Today*. New York: HSA Publications, 1975.

Nahm, Andrew C. *Korea, Tradition and Transformation: A History of the Korean People*. Elizabeth, N.J.: Hollym, 1988.

Nahm, Andrew C., ed. *Korea Under Japanese Colonial Rule: Studies of the Policy and Techniques of Japanese Colonialism*. Kalamazoo: Center for Korean Studies, Western Michigan University, 1973.

Nilsen, Robert. *South Korea Handbook*. Chico, Calif.: Moon Publications, 1988.

Ohn, Chang-Il. "The Basic Nature of U.S.-Korean Relations." *Korea and World Affairs* 12 (Fall, 1988).

Oliver, Robert T. *Korea: Forgotten Nation*. Washington: Public Affairs Press, 1944.

Oliver, Robert T. *Syngman Rhee: The Man Behind the Myth*. New York: Dodd, Mead, 1954.

Oliver, Robert T. *Syngman Rhee and American Involvement in Korea, 1942-1960*. Seoul: Panmun Book Co., 1978.

Palmer, Spencer J. *Korea and Christianity*. Seoul, Korea: Hollym, 1967.

Phillips, E. H., and E. Y. Yu, eds. *Religions in Korea: Beliefs and Cultural Values*. Los Angeles: Center for Korean-American and Korean Studies, California State University, Los Angeles, 1982.

Pou Kuksa. *A Buddha from Korea: The Zen Teachings of T'aego*. Translated by J. C. Cleary. Boston: Shambhala, 1988.

Ro, Bong-Rin, and Marlin L. Nelson, eds. *Korean Church Growth Explosion*. Seoul, Korea: Word of Life Press, 1985.

Shearer, Roy E. *Wildfire: Church Growth in Korea*. Grand Rapids, Mich.: William B. Eerdmans, 1966.

Soet, John S. *Martial Arts Around the World*. Burbank: Unique Publications, 1991.

Sontag, Frederick. *Sun Myung Moon and the Unification Church*. Nashville: Abingdon Press, 1977.

Spear, Robert K. *Hapkido: The Integrated Fighting Art*. Burbank: Unique Publications, 1988.

Sunoo, Harold H. *America's Dilemma in Asia: The Case of South Korea*. Chicago: Nelson-Hall, 1979.

Williams, Boyn. *Martial Arts of the Orient*. New York: Hamlyn, 1975.

Yates, Keith D. *The Complete Book of Taekwon Do Forms*. Boulder, Colo.: Paladin Press, 1982.

Yates, Keith D. *Tae Kwon Do Basics*. New York: Sterling Publishing Company, 1987.

Yoon, Hong-key. *Geomantic Relations Between Culture and Nature in Korea*. Taipei: Chinese Association for Folklore, 1976.

Yoon, In-Jin. *The Social Origins of Korean Immigration to the United States from 1965 to the Present*. Papers of the East-West Population Institute 121, Honolulu: East-West Center, 1993.

KOREAN AMERICANS AND THE KOREAN DIASPORA (See also KOREA; SOUTHEAST ASIA; SOUTHEAST ASIAN AMERICANS AND THE SOUTHEAST ASIAN DIASPORA)

Allen, Richard C. *Korea's Syngman Rhee: An Unauthorized Portrait*. Rutland, Vt.: Charles E. Tuttle, 1960.

Berwick, Stephen W. F. "From Chongnyangni to Northfield: The Story of a Korean Immigrant to America." *Korean Culture* 12, no. 1 (1991): 34-38.

Cha, Theresa Hak Kyung. *Dictee*. New York: Tanam Press, 1982.

Cheng, Lucie, and Yen Le Espiritu. "Korean Business in Black and Hispanic Neighborhoods: A Study of Intergroup Relations." *Sociological Perspectives* 32 (1989): 521-534.

Choy, Bong-youn. *Koreans in America*. Chicago: Nelson-Hall, 1979.

Chryssides, George D. *The Advent of Sun Myung Moon: The Origins, Beliefs, and Practices of the Unification Church*. New York: St. Martin's Press, 1991.

Clark, Donald N., ed. *Korea Briefing, 1993*. Boulder, Colo.: Westview Press, 1993.

Fichter, Joseph H. *The Holy Family of Father Moon*. Kansas City, Mo.: Leaven Press, 1985.

Houchins, Lee, and Chang-su Houchins. "The Korean Experience in America, 1903-1924." *Pacific Historical Review* 43 (November, 1974): 584-75.

Hurh, Won Moo, and Kwang Chung Kim. *Korean Immigrants in America: A Structural Analysis of Ethnic Confinement and Adhesive Adaptation*. Madison, N.J.: Fairleigh Dickinson University Press, 1984.

Hurh, Won Moo, and Kwang Chung Kim. "Religious Participation of Korean Immigrants in the United States." *Journal of the Scientific Study of Religion* 29 (1990): 19-34.

Kang, Younghill. *East Goes West: The Making of an Oriental Yankee*. New York: Charles Scribner's Sons, 1937.

Kim, Bok-Lim. "Asian Wives of U.S. Servicemen: Women in Shadows." *Amerasia Journal* 4 (November 1, 1977): 91-111.

Kim, Bok-Lim C. *Korean-American Child at School and at Home*. Washington, D.C.: Administration for Children, Youth, and Families, U.S. Department of Health, Education, and Welfare, 1980.

Kim, Elaine H. *Asian American Literature: An Introduction to the Writings and Their Social Context*. Philadelphia: Temple University Press, 1982.

Kim, Hyun Sook, and Pyong Gap Min. "The Post-1965 Korean Immigrants: Their Characteristics and Settlement Patterns." *Korea Journal of Population and Development* 21 (1992): 121-143.

Kim, Illsoo. "Korea and East Asia: Preimmigration Factors and U.S. Immigration Policy." In *Pacific Bridges: The New Immigration from Asia and the Pacific Islands*, edited by James Fawcett and Bejamin Carino. Staten Island: Center for Migration Studies, 1987.

Kim, Illsoo. *New Urban Immigrants: The Korean Community in New York*. Princeton, N.J.: Princeton University Press, 1981.

Kim, Kwang Chung, and Won Moo Hurh. "Ethnic Resource Utilization of Korean Immigrant Entrepreneurs in the Chicago Minority Area." *International Migration Review* 19 (Spring, 1985): 82-111.

Kim, Kwang Chung, and Won Moo Hurh. "Korean Americans and the 'Success' Image: A Critique." *Amerasia Journal* 10 (October 2, 1983): 3-21.

Kim, Ronyoung. *Clay Walls*. New York: Permanent Press, 1986.

"Koreans in Mexico." *Korea Times*, April 28, 1974.

Lee, Chong-sik. *The Politics of Korean Nationalism*. Berkeley: University of California Press, 1963.

Lee, Mary Paik. *Quiet Odyssey: A Pioneer Korean Woman in America*. Edited by Sucheng Chan. Seattle: University of Washington Press, 1990.

Light, Ivan, and Edna Bonacich. *Immigrant Entrepreneurs: Koreans in Los Angeles, 1965-1982*. Berkeley: University of California Press, 1988.

Light, Ivan, Hadas Har-Chvi, and Kenneth Kan. "Black-Korean Conflict in Los Angeles." In *Managing Divided Cities*, edited by Seamus Dunn. Newbury Park, Calif. Sage Publications, 1994.

Light, Ivan, Jung-Kwuon Im, and Zhong Deng. "Korean Rotating Credit Associations in Los Angeles." *Amerasia* 16 (1990): 35-54.

Lyu, Kingsley K. "Korean Nationalist Activities in Hawaii and the Continental United States, 1900-1945." *Amerasia Journal* 4: 1-2 (1977).

Min, Pyong Gap. "The Cultural and Economic Boundaries of Korean Ethnicity: A Comparative Analysis." *Ethnic and Racial Studies* 14 (1991): 225-241.

Min, Pyong Gap. *Ethnic Business Enterprise: Korean Small Business in Atlanta*. New York: Center for Migration Studies, 1988.

Min, Pyong Gap. "Korean Immigrants in Los Angeles." In *Immigration and Entrepreneurship*, edited by Ivan Light and Parminder Bhachu. New York: Transaction Publishers, 1993.

Min, Pyong Gap. "The Structure and Social Functions of Korean Immigrant Churches in the United States." *International Migration Review* 26 (1992): 1370-1394.

Moon, Sun Myung. *A Prophet Speaks Today*. New York: HSA Publications, 1975.

Oliver, Robert T. *Syngman Rhee: The Man Behind the Myth*. New York: Dodd, Mead, 1954.

Oliver, Robert T. *Syngman Rhee and American Involvement in Korea, 1942-1960*. Seoul: Panmun Book Co., 1978.

Pai, Margaret K. "The Tragic Split." In *The Dreams of Two Yi-min*. Honolulu: University of Hawaii Press, 1989.

Park, Insook Han, James T. Fawcett, Fred Arnold, and Robert W. Gardner. *Korean Immigrants and U.S. Immigration Policy: A Predeparture Perspective*. Papers of the East-West Population Institute 114. Honolulu: East-West Center, 1990.

Patterson, Wayne. *The Korean Frontier in America: Immigration to Hawaii, 1896-1910*. Honolulu: University of Hawaii Press, 1988.

Shim, Steve. *Korean Immigrant Churches Today in Southern California*. San Francisco: R and E Research Associates, 1977.

Soet, John S. *Martial Arts Around the World*. Burbank: Unique Publications, 1991.

Song, Cathy. *Picture Bride*. New Haven, Conn.: Yale University Press, 1983.

Sontag, Frederick. *Sun Myung Moon and the Unification Church*. Nashville: Abingdon Press, 1977.

Spear, Robert K. *Hapkido: The Integrated Fighting Art*. Burbank: Unique Publications, 1988.

Sunoo, Sonia S. "Korean Women Pioneers of the Pacific Northwest." *Oregon Historical Quarterly* 79 (Spring, 1978): 51-63.

Sutton, R. Anderson. "Korean Music in Hawaii." *Asian Music* 19 (1987): 99-120.

Thamos, John Alsop. *Korean Students in Southern California: Factors Influencing Their Plans Toward Returning Home*. Ann Arbor: UMI, 1981.

United States Commission on Civil Rights. *Civil Rights Issues Facing Asian Americans in the 1990s*. Washington, D.C.: Government Printing Office, 1992.

Yoon, In-Jin. "The Changing Significance of Ethnic and Class Resources in Immigrant Businesses: The Case of Korean Immigrant Businesses in Chicago." *International Migration Review* 25 (Summer, 1991): 303-331.

Yoon, In-Jin. *The Social Origins of Korean Immigration to the United States from 1965 to the Present*. Papers of the East-West Population Institute 121. Honolulu: East-West Center, 1993.

Young, Philip K. Y. "Family Labor, Sacrifice, and Competition: Korean Greengrocers in New York City." *Amerasia Journal* 10 (Fall/Winter, 1983): 53-71.

Yu, Eui-Young. "'Koreatown' Los Angeles: Emergence of a New Inner-City Ethnic Community." *Bulletin of Population and Development Studies* 14 (1985): 29-44.

Yu, Eui-Young, and Earl Phillips, eds. *Korean Women in Transition: At Home and Abroad*. Los Angeles: Center for Korean-American and Korean Studies, California State University, Los Angeles, 1987.

Yu, Eui-Young, Earl Phillips, and Eun Sik Yang, eds. *Koreans in Los Angeles: Prospects and Promises*. Los Angeles: Center for Korean-American and Korean Studies, California State University, Los Angeles, 1982.

THE PHILIPPINES (See also FILIPINO AMERICANS AND THE FILIPINO DIASPORA)

Agoncillo, Teodoro A. *History of the Filipino People*. 8th ed. Quezon City: R. P. Garcia, 1990.

Agoncillo, Teodoro A. *Introduction to Filipino History*. Manila: Radiant Star Publishing, 1974.

Agoncillo, Teodoro A. *A Short History of the Philippines*. New York: New American Library, 1975.

Anderson, Gerald H. *Studies in Philippine Church History*. Ithaca, N.Y.: Cornell University Press, 1969.

Bonner, Raymond. *Waltzing with a Dictator: The Marcoses and the Making of American Policy*. New York: Times Books, 1987.

Brands, H. W. *Bound to Empire: The United States and the Philippines*. New York: Oxford University Press, 1992.

Bresnan, John, ed. *Crisis in the Philippines*. Princeton, N.J.: Princeton University Press, 1986.

Breuer, William B. *Retaking the Philippines: America's Return to Corregidor and Bataan, October 1944-March 1945*. New York: St. Martin's Press, 1986.

Broad, Robin. *Unequal Alliance: The World Bank, the International Monetary Fund, and the Philippines*. Berkeley: University of California Press, 1988.

Burton, Sandra. *Impossible Dream: The Marcoses, the Aquinos, and the Unfinished Revolution*. New York: Warner Books, 1989.

Cannon, M. Hamlin. *Leyte: The Return to the Philippines*. Washington, D.C.: Department of the Army, 1954.

Colbert, Evelyn. *The United States and the Philippine Bases*. Washington, D.C.: Foreign Policy Institute, The Johns Hopkins University Press, 1987.

Constantino, Renato. *The History of the Philippines: From the Spanish Colonization to the Second World War*. New York: Monthly Review Press, 1975.

Constantino, Renato, and Letizia R. Constantino. *The Philippines: The Continuing Past*. Quezon City: The Foundation for Nationalist Studies, 1978.

Doronila, Amando. *The State, Economic Transformation, and Political Change in the Philippines, 1946-1972*. New York: Oxford University Press, 1992.

Friend, Theodore. *Between Two Empires: The Ordeal of the Philippines, 1929-1946*. New Haven, Conn.: Yale University Press, 1965.

Graff, Henry, ed. *American Imperialism and the Philippine Insurrection*. Boston: Little, Brown, 1969.

Greene, Fred, ed. *The Philippine Bases: Negotiating for the Future: American and Philippine Perspectives*. New York: Council on Foreign Relations, 1988.

Grunder, Garel A., and William E. Livezey. *The Philippines and the United States*. Norman: University of Oklahoma Press, 1951.

Hart, Donn, ed. *Philippine Studies: Political Science, Economics, and Linguistics*. De Kalb: Northern Illinois University, Center for Southeast Asian Studies, 1981.

Hessel, Eugene A. *The Religious Thought of Jose Rizal*. Rev. ed. Quezon City: New Day Publishers, 1983.

Jocano, F. Landa. *Growing up in a Philippine Barrio*. New York: Holt, Rinehart and Winston, 1969.

Karnow, Stanley. *In Our Image: America's Empire in the Philippines*. New York: Random House, 1989.

Kikuchi, Yasuchi. *Uncrystallized Philippine Society: A Social Anthropological Analysis*. Detroit: Cellar Book Shop, 1992.

LeBar, Frank, ed. *Ethnic Groups of Insular Southeast Asia*, Vol. I. New Haven, Conn.: HRAF Press, 1972.

Linn, Brian McAllister. *The U.S. Army and Counterinsurgency in the Philippine War, 1899-1902*. Chapel Hill: University of North Carolina Press, 1989.

Ludszuweit, Daniel. *The Philippines: Cockatoo's Handbook*. Manila: Cockatoo Press, 1988.

Lynch, Frank, ed. *Social Acceptance: Four Readings on Philippine Values*. Quezon City: Ateneo de Manila University, 1964.

McDougald, Charles C. *The Marcos File: Was He a Philippine Hero or Corrupt Tyrant?* San Francisco: San Francisco Publishers, 1987.

Maceda, Jose. "Drone and Melody in Philippine Music Instruments." In *Traditional Drama and Music of Southeast Asia*, edited by Mohd. Taib Osman. Kuala Lumpur: Kementerian Pelajaran Malaysia, 1974.

McFarland, Curtis, comp. *A Linguistic Atlas of the Philippines*. Tokyo: Institute for the Study of Languages and Cultures of Asia and Africa, 1980.

McWilliams, Carey. *Brothers Under the Skin*. Rev. ed. Boston: Little, Brown, 1964.

Miller, Edward S. *War Plan Orange: The U.S. Strategy to Defeat Japan, 1897-1945*. Annapolis, Md.: Naval Institute Press, 1991.

Miller, Stuart C. *"Benevolent Assimilation": The American Conquest of the Philippines, 1899-1903*. New Haven, Conn.: Yale University Press, 1982.

Molina, A. J. *Music of the Philippines*. Manila: The Philippine Press, 1967.

Morton, Louis. *The Fall of the Philippines*. Washington, D.C.: Department of the Army, 1953.

National Security Council. "A Report to the President on the Position of the United States with Respect to the Philippines." A secret National Security Council policy report recommending U.S. policies toward Philippines. Declassified, October 10, 1975.

Nurge, Ethel. *Life in a Leyte Village*. Seattle: University of Washington Press, 1965.

Nydegger, William F., and Corinne Nydegger. "Tarong: An Ilocos Barrio in the Philippines." In *Six Cultures—Studies of Childrearing*, edited by Beatrice B. Whiting. New York: John Wiley & Sons, 1963.

Paredes, Ruby R., ed. *Philippine Colonial Democracy*. New Haven, Conn.: Yale University, Southeast Asia Studies, 1988.

Pomeroy, William. *The Philippines: Colonialism, Collaboration, and Resistance*. New York: International Publishers, 1993.

Quinsaat, Jesse. *Letters in Exile*. Los Angeles: UCLA Asian American Studies Center, 1976.

Ramos, Teresita. *Tagalog Structures*. Honolulu: University of Hawaii Press, 1971.

Rempel, William C. *Delusions of a Dictator: The Mind of Marcos as Revealed in His Secret Diaries*. Boston: Little, Brown, 1993.

Romulo, Beth Day. *Inside the Palace: The Rise and Fall of Ferdinand and Imelda Marcos*. New York: Putnam, 1987.

Russell, Charles Edward. *The Outlook for the Philippines*. New York: Century, 1922.

Russell, Charles Edward, and E. B. Rodriguez. *The Hero of the Filipinos: The Story of Jose Rizal—Poet, Patriot and Martyr*. New York: Century, 1923.

Sanchez-Arcilla Bernal, Jose. *Rizal and the Emergence of the Philippine Nation*. Quezon City: Office of Research and Publications, Ateneo de Manila University, 1991.

Schachter, Paul, and Fe T. Otanes. *Tagalog Reference Grammar*. Berkeley: University of California Press, 1972.

Schaller, Michael. *Douglas MacArthur: The Far Eastern General*. New York: Oxford University Press, 1989.

Schirmer, Daniel B. *Republic or Empire: American Resistance to the Philippine War*. Cambridge, Mass.: Schenkman, 1972.

Schirmer, Daniel B., and Stephen Rosskamm Shalom, eds. *The Philippines Reader: A History of Colonialism, Neocolonialism, Dictatorship, and Resistance*. Boston: South End Press, 1987.

Seagrave, Sterling. *The Marcos Dynasty*. New York: Harper & Row, 1988.

Shalom, Stephen Rosskamm. *The United States and the Philippines: A Study of Neocolonialism*. Philadelphia: Institute for the Study of Human Issues, 1981.

Simbulan, Roland G. *The Bases of Our Insecurity: A Study of the US Military Bases in the Philippines*. 2d ed. Metro Manila: BALAI Fellowship, 1985.

Smith, Robert Ross. *Triumph in the Philippines*. Washington, D.C.: Department of the Army, 1963.

Terranel, Quintin C. *Jose Rizal: Lover of Truth and Justice*. Metro Manila: National Book Store, 1984.

Walton, Charles. "A Philippine Language Tree." In *Anthropological Linguistics: An Introduction*. By Joseph H. Greenberg. New York: Random House, 1968.

Youngblood, Robert L. *Marcos Against the Church: Economic Development and Political Repression in the Philippines*. Ithaca, N.Y.: Cornell University Press, 1990.

Zaide, Gregorio F. *Rizal: His Martyrdom*. Santa Cruz, Manila: Saint Mary's Publishing, 1976.

Zaide, Gregorio F., and Sonia M. Zaide. *Jose Rizal: Life, Works and Writings of a Genius, Writer, Scientist, and National Hero*. Metro Manila: National Book Store, 1984.

Zaide, Gregorio F., and Sonia M. Zaide. *Rizal and Other Great Filipinos*. Metro Manila: National Book Store, 1988.

SOUTH ASIA *(See also ASIAN INDIAN AMERICANS AND THE INDIAN DIASPORA; INDIA; SOUTH ASIAN AMERICANS)*

Ahmed, Akbar S. *Pakistan Society: Islam, Ethnicity, and Leadership in South Asia*. New York: Oxford University Press, 1986.

Ali, Ahmed, tr. *Al-Quran: A Contemporary Translation*. 1984. Rev. ed. Princeton, N.J.: Princeton University Press, 1988.

Bhatia, Tej K. *A History of the Hindi Grammatical Tradition*. Leiden, The Netherlands: E. J. Brill, 1987.

Bhatia, Tej K. "Transplanted South Asian Languages: An Overview." *Studies in the Linguistic Sciences* 11, no. 2 (Fall, 1981): 129-134.

Brands, H. W. *India and the United States: The Cold Peace.* Boston: Twayne, 1990.

Burki, Shahid Javed. *Pakistan: A Nation in the Making.* Boulder, Colo.: Westview Press, 1986.

Carnegie Task Force on Non-Proliferation and South Asian Security. *Nuclear Weapons and South Asian Security.* Washington, D.C.: Carnegie Endowment for International Peace, 1988.

Chantavanich, Supang, and E. Bruce Reynolds, eds. *Indochinese Refugees: Asylum and Resettlement.* Bangkok: Institute of Asian Studies, Chulalongkorn University, 1988.

Cohn, Bernard S. *India: The Social Anthropology of a Civilization.* Englewood Cliffs, N.J.: Prentice-Hall, 1971.

Duley, Margot, and Mary I. Edwards, eds. *The Cross-Cultural Study of Women.* New York: Feminist Press, 1986.

Endress, Gerhard. *An Introduction to Islam.* Translated by Carole Hillenbrand. New York: Columbia University Press, 1988.

Esposito, John. "Islam." In *World Religions in America: An Introduction,* edited by Jacob Neusner. Louisville, Ky.: Westminster/John Knox Press, 1994.

Fox, Richard. *Lions of the Punjab: Culture in the Making.* Berkeley: University of California Press, 1985.

Ganguly, Sumit. *The Origins of War in South Asia: Indo-Pakistani Conflicts Since 1947.* Boulder, Colo.: Westview Press, 1986.

Gilmartin, David. *Empire and Islam: Punjab and the Making of Pakistan.* Berkeley: University of California Press, 1988.

Grant, Bruce. *The Boat People: An "AGE" Investigation.* Harmondsworth, Middlesex, England: Penguin Books, 1979.

Grewal, J. S. *The Sikhs of the Punjab.* New York: Cambridge University Press, 1990.

Gross, Susan Hill, and Mary Hill Rojas. *Contemporary Issues for Women in South Asia: India, Pakistan, Bangladesh, Sri Lanka, Nepal, and Bhutan.* St. Louis Park, Minn.: Glenhurst, 1989.

Harrison, Selig S. "South Asia and the United States: A Chance for a Fresh Start." *Current History* 91 (March, 1992): 97-105.

Hewitt, Venon Marston. *The International Politics of South Asia.* New York: Manchester University Press, 1992.

"India and Pakistan: Collision or Compromise?" In *Great Decisions,* edited by the Foreign Policy Association. New York: Foreign Policy Association, 1993.

Jackson, Robert. *South Asian Crisis: India, Pakistan and Bangla Desh: A Political and Historical Analysis of the 1971 War.* New York: Praeger, 1975.

Jahan, Rounaq, and Hanna Papanek, eds. *Women and Development: Perspectives from South and Southeast Asia.* Dacca: The Bangladesh Institute of Law and International Affairs, 1979.

Jalal, Ayesha. *The State of Martial Rule: The Origins of Pakistan's Political Economy of Defence.* Cambridge, England: Cambridge University Press, 1990.

Malik, Iftikhar H. "The Pakistan-U.S. Security Relationship." *Asian Survey* 30 (March, 1990).

Maloney, Clarence. *Peoples of South Asia.* New York: Holt, Rinehart and Winston, 1974.

Masica, Colin. *The Indo-Aryan Languages.* Cambridge, England: Cambridge University Press, 1991.

Maududi, Abul Ala. *Fundamentals of Islam.* 1975. 7th ed. Lahore, Pakistan: Islamic Publications, 1986.

Noman, Omar. *Pakistan: Political and Economic History Since 1947.* London: Kegan Paul, 1990.

Perkovich, George. "A Nuclear Third Way in South Asia." *Foreign Policy* no. 91 (Summer, 1993).

Rahman, Fazlur. *Islam.* 1966. 2d ed. Chicago: University of Chicago Press, 1979.

Rogge, John R., ed. *Refugees: A Third World Dilemma.* Totowa, N.J.: Rowman & Littlefield, 1987.

Rudolph, Lloyd I., et al. *The Regional Imperative: The Administration of U.S. Foreign Policy Towards South Asian States Under Presidents Johnson and Nixon.* Atlantic Highlands, N.J.: Humanities Press, 1980.

St. Cartmail, Robert Keith. *Exodus Indochina.* Auckland, New Zealand: Heinemann, 1983.

Sakala, Carol. *Women of South Asia: A Guide to Resources.* Millwood, N.Y.: Kraus International, 1980.

Schimmel, Annemarie. *Islam: An Introduction.* Albany: State University of New York Press, 1992.

Schwartzberg, Joseph E., et al. *A Historical Atlas of South Asia.* Chicago: University of Chicago Press, 1978.

Singer, Milton. *When a Great Tradition Modernizes: An Anthropological Approach to Indian Civilization.* New York: Praeger, 1972.

Singh, Mohinder, ed. *History and Culture of Punjab.* New Delhi, India: Atlantic Publishers and Distributors, 1988.

Thomas, Raju G. C. *Indian Security Policy.* Princeton, N.J.: Princeton University Press, 1986.

Tinker, Hugh. *The Banyan Tree: Overseas Emigrants from India, Pakistan, and Bangladesh.* New York: Oxford University Press, 1977.

Watt, William Montgomery. *Muhammad, Prophet and Statesman.* 1961. Reprint. Oxford: Oxford University Press, 1964.

Ziring, Lawrence, ed. *The Subcontinent in World Politics: India, Its Neighbors, and the Great Powers.* Rev. ed. New York: Praeger, 1982.

Zograph, G. A. *Languages of South Asia: A Guide.* London: Routledge & Kegan Paul, 1982.

SOUTH ASIAN AMERICANS (*See also* ASIAN INDIAN AMERICANS AND THE INDIAN DIASPORA; INDIA; SOUTH ASIA)

Bagai, Leona B. *The East Indians and the Pakistanis in America.* Minneapolis: Lerner, 1972.

Buchignani, Norman, Doreen M. Indra, and Ram Srivastiva. *Continuous Journey: A Social History of South Asians in Canada.* Toronto, Ontario, Canada: McClelland and Stewart in association with Dept. of the Secretary of State and the Govt. Pub. Centre, Supply and Services, Canada, 1985.

Chadney, James G. *The Sikhs of Vancouver.* New York: AMS Press, 1984.

Chandrasekhar, S., ed. *From India to America: A Brief History of Immigration, Problems of Discrimination, Admission, and Assimilation.* La Jolla, Calif.: A Population Review Book, 1982.

Clarke, Colin, Ceri Peach, and Steven Vertovec, eds. *South Asians Overseas: Migration and Ethnicity.* New York: Cambridge University Press, 1990.

Gregory, Robert G. *South Asians in East Africa: An Economic and Social History, 1890-1980.* Boulder, Colo.: Westview Press, 1993.

Helweg, Arthur W., and Usha M. Helweg. *An Immigrant Success Story: East Indians in America.* Philadelphia: University of Pennsylvania Press, 1990.

Jensen, Joan M. *Passage from India: Asian Indian Immigrants in North America.* New Haven, Conn.: Yale University Press, 1988.

Johnston, Hugh J. M. *The East Indians in Canada.* Ottawa, Ontario, Canada: Canadian Historical Association, 1984.

Joy, Annamma. *Ethnicity in Canada: Social Accommodation and Cultural Persistence Among the Sikhs and the Portuguese.* New York: AMS Press, 1989.

Kanungo, Rabindra N., ed. *South Asians in the Canadian Mosaic.* Montreal, Quebec, Canada: Kala Bharati, 1984.

Katrak, Ketu H., and R. Radhakrishnan, eds. Special issue. "Desh-Videsh: South Asian Expatriate Writing and Art." *The Massachusetts Review* 29 (Winter, 1988-1989).

Kotkin, Joel. *Tribes: How Race, Religion, and Identity Determine Success in the New Global Economy.* New York: Random House, 1993.

La Brack, Bruce. *The Sikhs of Northern California, 1904-1975.* New York: AMS Press, 1988.

Larmer, Brook. "Sri Lankan Ethnic Strife Troubles Tamils in the U.S." *Christian Science Monitor* 78 (May 9, 1986): 1, 36.

Lorch, Donatella. "Between Two Worlds: New York's Bangladeshis." *The New York Times,* October 10, 1991, p. B1, B10.

Malik, Iftikhar Haider. *Pakistanis in Michigan: A Study of Third Culture and Acculturation.* New York: AMS Press, 1989.

Mazumdar, Sucheta. "Colonial Impact and Punjabi Emigration to the United States." In

Labor Immigration Under Capitalism: Asian Workers in the United States Before World War II, edited by Lucie Cheng and Edna Bonacich. Berkeley: University of California Press, 1984.

Mazumdar, Sucheta. "Punjabi Agricultural Workers in California, 1905-1945." In *Labor Immigration Under Capitalism: Asian Workers in the United States Before World War II*, edited by Lucie Cheng and Edna Bonacich. Berkeley: University of California Press, 1984.

Mazumdar, Sucheta. "South Asians in the United States with a Focus on Asian Indians: Policy on New Communities." In *The State of Asian Pacific America: A Public Policy Report, Policy Issues to the Year 2020*. Los Angeles: LEAP Asian Pacific American Public Policy Institute and UCLA Asian American Studies Center, 1993.

Melendy, H. Brett. *Asians in America: Filipinos, Koreans, and East Indians*. Boston: Twayne, 1977.

Ramcharan, Subhas. *Racism: Nonwhites in Canada*. Toronto, Ontario, Canada: Butterworths, 1982.

Rustomji-Kerns, Roshni, ed. Special issue. "South Asian Women Writers: The Immigrant Experience." *The Journal of South Asian Literature* 21 (Winter/Spring, 1986).

Saran, Parmatma. *The Asian Indian Experience in the United States*. Cambridge, Mass.: Schenkman, 1985.

Singh, Jane, et al. *South Asians in North America: An Annotated and Selected Bibliography*. Berkeley: Center for South and Southeast Asia Studies, University of California, Berkeley, 1988.

Takaki, Ronald. *Strangers from a Different Shore: A History of Asian Americans*. Boston: Little, Brown, 1989.

Tinker, Hugh. *The Banyan Tree: Overseas Emigrants from India, Pakistan, and Bangladesh*. New York: Oxford University Press, 1977.

Vassanji, M. G., ed. *A Meeting of Streams: South Asian Canadian Literature*. Toronto: Toronto South Asia Review Publications, 1985.

Women of South Asian Descent Collective, eds. *Our Feet Walked the Sky: Women of the South Asian Diaspora*. San Francisco: Aunt Lute Books, 1993.

SOUTHEAST ASIA (See also KOREA; KOREAN AMERICANS AND THE KOREAN DIASPORA; SOUTHEAST ASIAN AMERICANS AND THE SOUTHEAST ASIAN DIASPORA; VIETNAM; VIETNAMESE AMERICANS)

Adams, Nina S., and Alfred W. McCoy, eds. *Laos: War and Revolution*. New York: Harper & Row, 1970.

Benedict, Paul. *Austro-Thai Language and Culture*. New Haven, Conn.: HRAF Press, 1975.

Bliatout, Bruce T. *Hmong Sudden, Unexpected Nocturnal Death Syndrome: A Cultural Study*. Portland, Oreg.: Sparkle Publications, 1982.

Bui, Diana D. *Hong Kong: The Other Story*. Washington, D.C.: Indochina Resource Action Center, 1990.

Bunge, Frederica M., ed. *Thailand: A Country Study*. Washington, D.C.: U.S. Government Printing Office, 1981.

Butler-Diaz, Jacqueline. *Yao Design of Northern Thailand*. Rev. ed. Bangkok, Thailand: The Siam Society, 1981.

Carrison, Muriel P. *Cambodian Folk Stories from the Gatiloke*. Translated by Kong Chhean. Rutland, Vt.: Charles E. Tuttle, 1987.

Catlin, Amy, ed. *APSARA: The Feminine in Cambodian Art*. Los Angeles: Woman's Building, 1987.

Chandler, David P. *Brother Number One: A Political Biography of Pol Pot*. Boulder, Colo.: Westview Press, 1992.

Chandler, David P. *A History of Cambodia*. 2d ed. Boulder, Colo.: Westview Press, 1992.

Chandler, David. *The Land and People of Cambodia*. New York: HarperCollins, 1991.

Chandler, David P. *The Tragedy of Cambodian History: Politics, War, and Revolution Since 1945*. New Haven, Conn.: Yale University Press, 1991.

Chantavanich, Supang, and E. Bruce Reynolds, eds. *Indochinese Refugees: Asylum and Resettlement*. Bangkok: Institute of Asian Studies, Chulalongkorn University, 1988.

Condominas, Georges. "Lao Religion." In *The Encyclopedia of Religion*, edited by Mircea Eliade. Vol. 8. New York: Collier Macmillan, 1987.

Crystal, Eric. "Champa and the Study of Southeast Asia." In *Le Champa et le monde malais*, edited by P. LaFont. Berkeley, Calif.: Conference on Champa and the Malay World, 1992.

Davidson, Jeremy H. C. S., and Helen Cordell, eds. *The Short Story in South East Asia*. London: School of Oriental and African Studies, University of London, 1982.

Davidson, Jeremy H. C. S., R. H. Robins, and Helen Cordell, eds. *South-East Asian Linguistics: Essays in Honour of Eugenie J. A. Henderson*. London: School of Oriental and African Studies, University of London, 1989.

Davis, Leonard. *Hong Kong and the Asylum-Seekers from Vietnam*. Basingstoke: Macmillan, 1991.

De Berval, René, ed. *Kingdom of Laos: The Land of the Million Elephants and of the White Parasol*. Translated by Mrs. Teissier du Cros et al. Saigon, Vietnam: France-Asie, 1959.

De Blij, Harm J., and Peter O. Muller. *Geography: Regions and Concepts*. 6th ed. New York: John Wiley & Sons, 1992.

Dommer, Arthur J. *Conflict in Laos: The Politics of Neutralization*. New York: Praeger, 1971.

Doore, Gary, ed. and comp. *Shaman's Path: Healing, Personal Growth and Empowerment*. Boston: Shambhala Press, 1988.

Downing, Bruce, Bruce Olney, and Douglas Olney, eds. *The Hmong in the West: Observations and Reports*. Minneapolis: Center for Urban and Regional Affairs, University of Minnesota, 1982.

Endress, Gerhard. *An Introduction to Islam*. Translated by Carole Hillenbrand. New York: Columbia University Press, 1988.

Esposito, John. "Islam." In *World Religions in America: An Introduction*, edited by Jacob Neusner. Louisville, Ky.: Westminster/John Knox Press, 1994.

Fisher, James S., ed. *Geography and Development: A World Regional Approach*. 4th ed. New York: Macmillan, 1992.

Geddes, William. *Migrants of the Mountains*. Oxford, England: Clarendon Press, 1976.

Girling, John L. S. *Thailand: Society and Politics*. Ithaca, N.Y.: Cornell University Press, 1981.

Goldstein, Martin E. *American Policy Toward Laos*. Rutherford, N.J.: Fairleigh Dickinson University Press, 1973.

Grant, Bruce. *The Boat People: An "AGE" Investigation*. Harmondsworth, Middlesex, England: Penguin Books, 1979.

Haas, Michael. *Genocide by Proxy: Cambodian Pawn on a Superpower Chessboard*. New York: Praeger, 1991.

Hall, Daniel George Edward. *A History of South East Asia*. New York: St. Martin's Press, 1961.

Hamilton-Merritt, Jane. *Tragic Mountains: The Hmong, the Americans, and the Secret Wars for Laos, 1942-1992*. Bloomington: Indiana University Press, 1993.

Harles, John C. "Politics in an American Lifeboat: The Case of Laotian Immigrants." *Journal of American Studies* 25 (December, 1991): 419-441.

Harrison, B. *South-East Asia: A Short History*. London: Macmillan, 1954.

Hassan, Riaz, ed. *Singapore: Society in Transition*. New York: Oxford University Press, 1976.

Hendricks, Glenn, Bruce Downing, and Amos Deinard, eds. *The Hmong in Transition*. Staten Island, N.Y.: Center for Migration Studies of New York, 1986.

Herbert, Patricia, and Anthony Milner, eds. *South-East Asia Languages and Literatures: A Select Guide*. Honolulu: University of Hawaii Press, 1989.

Hoke, Donald, ed. *The Church in Asia*. Chicago: Moody Press, 1975.

Huffman, Franklin. *Bibliography and Index of Mainland Southeast Asian Languages and Linguistics*. New Haven, Conn.: Yale University Press, 1986.

Jackson, Karl D., comp. *Cambodia, 1975-1978: Rendezvous with Death*. Princeton, N.J.: Princeton University Press, 1989.

Jolly, Margaret, and Martha Macintyre, eds. *Family and Gender in the Pacific: Domestic Contradictions and the Colonial Impact*.

Cambridge, England: Cambridge University Press, 1989.

Keyes, Charles F. *The Golden Peninsula: Culture and Adaptation in Mainland Southeast Asia*. New York: Macmillan, 1977.

Keyes, Charles F. *Thailand: Buddhist Kingdom as Modern Nation-State*. Boulder, Colo.: Westview Press, 1987.

Krause, Lawrence B., Ai Tee Koh, and Yuan Lee. *The Singapore Economy Reconsidered*. Singapore: Institute of Southeast Asian Studies, 1987.

Kunstadter, Peter, ed. *Southeast Asian Tribes, Minorities, and Nations*. 2 vols. Princeton, N.J.: Princeton University Press, 1967.

LeBar, Frank, ed. *Ethnic Groups of Insular Southeast Asia*. Vol. 1. New Haven, Conn.: HRAF Press, 1972.

LeBar, Frank M., G. C. Hickey, and J. K. Musgrave. *Ethnic Groups of Mainland Southeast Asia*. New Haven, Conn.: Human Relations Area Files Press, 1964.

LeBar, Frank M. and Adrienne Suddard, eds. *Laos: Its People, Its Society, Its Culture*. New Haven, Conn.: Human Relations Area Files, 1960.

Lemoine, Jacques. *Yao Ceremonial Paintings*. Bangkok, Thailand: White Lotus, 1982.

LePoer, Barbara Leitch, ed. *Singapore: A Country Study*. Washington, D.C.: Government Printing Office, 1991.

Lewis, Judy, ed. *Minority Cultures of Laos: Kammu, Laua, Lahu, Hmong, and Mien*. Rancho Cordova, Calif.: Southeast Asia Community Resource Center, 1992.

Lindell, Kristina, Hakan Lundstrom, Jan-Olof Svantesson, and Damrong Tayanin. *The Kammu Year: Its Lore and Music*. Scandinavian Institute of Asian Studies: Studies on Asian Topics 4. London: Curzon Press, 1982.

Lutheran Immigration and Refugee Service. *Cambodia: The Land and Its People*. New York: Lutheran Council in the USA, 1983.

McCoy, Alfred W. *The Politics of Heroin: CIA Complicity in the Global Drug Trade*. New York: Lawrence Hill Books, 1991.

Majumdar, Ramesh Chandra. *Champa: History and Culture of an Indian Colonial Kingdom in the Far East, Second to Sixteenth Century A.D.* Delhi, India: Gian Publishing House, 1985.

Manikam, R. B., and L. T. Thomas. *The Church in South-East Asia*. New York: Friendship Press, 1956.

Matisoff, James A. *The Dictionary of Lahu*. Berkeley: University of California Press, 1988.

Matisoff, James A. *The Grammar of Lahu*. Berkeley: University of California Press, 1973. Reprinted 1982.

Maududi, Abul Ala. *Fundamentals of Islam*. 1975. 7th ed. Lahore, Pakistan: Islamic Publications, 1986.

Moffett, Samuel Hugh. *A History of Christianity in Asia*. San Francisco: Harper San Francisco, 1992.

Neher, Clark D. *Southeast Asia in the New International Era*. Boulder, Colo.: Westview Press, 1991.

Osborne, Milton. *Southeast Asia: An Illustrated Introductory History*. Exp. ed. Boston: Allen & Unwin, 1988.

Osman, Mohd. Taib, ed. *Traditional Drama and Music of Southeast Asia*. Kuala Lumpur: Kementerian Pelajaran Malaysia, 1974.

Peacock, James. *Indonesia: An Anthropological Perspective*. Pacific Palisades, Calif.: Goodyear Publishing, 1973.

Prasad, Ram Chandra. *Archaeology of Champa and Vikramasila*. Delhi, India: Rammanand Vidya Bhawan, 1987.

Provencher, Ronald. *Mainland Southeast Asia: An Anthropological Perspective*. Pacific Palisades, Calif.: Goodyear Publishing, 1975.

Quah, Jon S. T., Heng Chee Chan, and Chee Meow Seah. *Government and Politics of Singapore*. Singapore: Oxford University Press, 1985.

Rahman, Fazlur. *Islam*. 1966. 2d ed. Chicago: University of Chicago Press, 1979.

Rigg, Jonathan. *Southeast Asia: A Region in Transition*. Boston: Unwin Hyman, 1991.

Rogge, John R., ed. *Refugees: A Third World Dilemma*. Totowa, N.J.: Rowman & Littlefield, 1987.

Rudolph, Lloyd I., et al. *The Regional Imperative: The Administration of U.S. Foreign Policy Towards South Asian States Under Presidents Johnson and Nixon*. Atlantic Highlands, N.J.: Humanities Press, 1980.

St. Cartmail, Robert Keith. *Exodus Indochina*. Auckland, New Zealand: Heinemann, 1983.

SarDesai, D. R. *Southeast Asia: Past and Present*. 2d ed. Basingstoke, England: Macmillan, 1989.

Schanberg, Sydney H. *The Death and Life of Dith Pran*. New York: Penguin Books, 1985.

Schimmel, Annemarie. *Islam: An Introduction*. Albany: State University of New York Press, 1992.

Shawcross, William. *Sideshow: Kissinger, Nixon, and the Destruction of Cambodia*. London: The Hogarth Press, 1986.

Shu, Ramsay Leung-Hay. "Kinship System and Migrant Adaptation: Samoans of the United States." *Amerasia Journal* 12, no. 1 (1985-1986): 23-47.

Singapore Ministry of Communications and Information. *Singapore Facts and Pictures, 1989*. Singapore: Information Division, Ministry of Communications and Information, 1989.

Smith, Jeffrey Merrill. *Cultural Comparison Chart: American and Cambodian Cultures*. Rev. Ed. Portland, Maine: Portland Public Schools, 1988.

Stanton, Shelby. *Green Berets at War: U.S. Army Special Forces in Southeast Asia, 1956-1975*. Novato, Calif.: Presidio Press, 1985.

Stevenson, Charles A. *The End of Nowhere: American Policy Towards Laos Since 1954*. Boston: Beacon Press, 1972.

Strand, Paul J. *Indochinese Refugees in America: Problems of Adaptation and Assimilation*. Durham, N.C.: Duke University Press, 1985.

Stuart-Fox, Martin, ed. *Contemporary Laos: Studies in the Politics and Society of the Lao People's Democratic Republic*. New York: St. Martin's Press, 1982.

Stuart-Fox, Martin. *Laos: Politics, Economics, and Society*. London: Frances Pinter, 1986.

Swearer, Donald. *Buddhism and Society in Southeast Asia*. Chambersburg, Pa.: Anima, 1981.

Tambiah, Stanley Jeyaraja. *Buddhism and the Spirit Cults in North-East Thailand*. Cambridge, England: Cambridge University Press, 1970.

Tapp, Nicholas. *Sovereignty and Rebellion: The White Hmong of Northern Thailand*. Singapore: Oxford University Press, 1989.

Tarling, Nicholas, ed. *The Cambridge History of Southeast Asia*. Cambridge, England: Cambridge University Press, 1992.

Thomas, David, Ernest W. Lee, and Nguyen Dang Liem, eds. *Chamic Studies*. Canberra: Department of Linguistics, Research School of Pacific Studies, Australian National University, 1977.

Turnbull, Constance M. *A History of Singapore, 1810-1975*. Kuala Lumpur, Malaysia: Oxford University Press, 1977.

U.S. Congress. House. Committee on International Relations. *Proposal to Control Opium from the Golden Triangle and Terminate the Shan Opium Trade*. Washington, D.C.: Government Printing Office, 1975.

Velazquez, Elaine. *Moving Mountains: The Story of the Yiu Mien*. New York: Filmmakers Library, 1989. Film.

Voegelin, C. F., and F. M. Voegelin. *Classification and Index of the World's Languages*. New York: Elsevier, 1977.

Walker, Anthony R., ed. *Farmers in the Hills*. Penang: Universiti Sains Malaysia, 1975.

Westermeyer, Joseph. *Poppies, Pipes, and People: Opium and Its Use in Laos*. Berkeley: University of California Press, 1982.

Whitaker, Donald P. et al. *Area Handbook for Laos*. Washington, D.C.: Foreign Area Studies, U.S. Government Press, 1972.

Whitaker, Donald P. et al. *Laos: A Country Study*. Washington D.C.: Government Printing Office, 1986.

Whitmore, John K., ed. *An Introduction to Indochinese History, Culture, Language, and Life*. Ann Arbor: Center for South and Southeast Asian Studies, University of Michigan, 1979.

Wyatt, David K. *Thailand: A Short History*. New Haven, Conn.: Yale University Press, 1984.

SOUTHEAST ASIAN AMERICANS AND THE SOUTHEAST ASIAN DIASPORA (See also KOREA; KOREAN AMERICANS AND THE KOREAN DIASPORA; SOUTHEAST ASIA; VIETNAM; VIETNAMESE AMERICANS)

Arax, Mark. "Lost in L.A." *Los Angeles Times Magazine*, December 13, 1987, pp. 10-16.

Barkan, Elliott Robert. *Asian and Pacific Islander Migration to the United States: A Model of New Global Patterns*. Westport, Conn.: Greenwood Press, 1992.

Bliatout, Bruce T. *Hmong Sudden, Unexpected Nocturnal Death Syndrome: A Cultural Study*. Portland, Oreg.: Sparkle Publications, 1982.

Butler-Diaz, Jacqueline. *Yao Design of Northern Thailand*. Rev. ed. Bangkok, Thailand: The Siam Society, 1981.

Caplan, Nathan, John K. Whitmore, and Marcella H. Choy. *The Boat People and Achievement in America: Family Life, Hard Work, and Cultural Values*. Ann Arbor: University of Michigan Press, 1989.

Catlin, Amy, ed. *APSARA: The Feminine in Cambodian Art*. Los Angeles: Woman's Building, 1987.

Catlin, Amy. *Music of the Hmong: Singing Voices and Talking Reeds*. Providence, R.I.: Center for Hmong Lore, Museum of Natural History, 1981.

Chan, Sucheng. *Asian Americans: An Interpretive History*. Boston: Twayne, 1991.

Chantavanich, Supang, and E. Bruce Reynolds, eds. *Indochinese Refugees: Asylum and Resettlement*. Bangkok: Institute of Asian Studies, Chulalongkorn University, 1988.

Dannen, Fredric. "Revenge of the Green Dragons." *The New Yorker* 68 (November 16, 1992): 76-99.

Doore, Gary, ed. and comp. *Shaman's Path: Healing, Personal Growth and Empowerment*. Boston: Shambhala Press, 1988.

Downing, Bruce, Bruce Olney, and Douglas Olney, eds. *The Hmong in the West: Observations and Reports*. Minneapolis: Center for Urban and Regional Affairs, University of Minnesota, 1982.

Fuchs, Lawrence. "Xenophobia, Racism, and Bigotry." In *The American Kaleidoscope: Race, Ethnicity, and the Civic Culture*. Hanover, N.H.: Wesleyan University Press/University Press of New England, 1990.

Garrett, W. E. "Thailand: Refuge from Terror." *National Geographic Magazine* 157 (May, 1980): 633-642.

Geddes, William R. *Migrants of the Mountains: The Cultural Ecology of the Blue Miao (Hmong Njua) of Thailand*. Oxford, England: Clarendon Press, 1976.

Grant, Bruce. *The Boat People: An "AGE" Investigation*. Harmondsworth, Middlesex, England: Penguin Books, 1979.

Gupta, Udayan. "From Other Shores." In *The Problem of Immigration*, edited by Steven Anzovin. New York: H.W. Wilson, 1985.

Haines, David W., ed. *Refugees as Immigrants: Cambodians, Laotians, and Vietnamese in America*. Totokwa, N.J.: Rowman & Littlefield, 1989.

Hall, Daniel George Edward. *A History of South East Asia*. New York: St. Martin's Press, 1961.

Hamilton-Merritt, Jane. *Tragic Mountains: The Hmong, the Americans, and the Secret Wars for Laos, 1942-1992*. Bloomington: Indiana University Press, 1993.

Hammond, Ruth E. "Sad Suspicions of a Refugee Rip-off: The Hmong Are Paying to Free Laos—but What's Happening to the Money (Contributions to the Neo Hom)?" *The Washington Post*, April 16, 1991, p. B1.

Harles, John C. "Politics in an American Lifeboat: The Case of Laotian Immigrants." *Journal of American Studies* 25 (December, 1991): 419-441.

Hendricks, Glenn, Bruce Downing, and Amos Deinard, eds. *The Hmong in Transition*. Staten Island, New York: Center for Migration Studies, 1986.

Hitchcox, Linda. "Why They Had to Leave." In *Vietnamese Refugees in Southeast Asian Camps*. Oxford, England: St. Antony's College, 1990.

Huang, Larke Nahme. "Southeast Asian Refugee Children and Adolescents." In *Children of Color*, by Jewelle Taylor Gibbs, et al. San Francisco: Jossey-Bass, 1989.

Johnson, Terry E. "Immigrants: New Victims." *Newsweek* 107 (May 12, 1986): 57.

Kifner, John. "New Immigrant Wave from Asia Gives the Underworld New Faces." *The New York Times*, January 6, 1991, p. 1.

Kitano, Harry H. L., and Roger Daniels. *Asian Americans: Emerging Minorities*. Englewood Cliffs, N.J.: Prentice-Hall, 1988.

Kunstadter, Peter, ed. *Southeast Asian Tribes, Minorities and Nations*. 2 vols. Princeton, N.J.: Princeton University Press, 1967.

Larsen, Wanwadee. *Confessions of a Mail Order Bride: American Life Through Thai Eyes*. Far Hills, N.J.: New Horizon Press, 1989.

LeBar, Frank M., G. C. Hickey, and J. K. Musgrave. *Ethnic Groups of Mainland Southeast Asia*. New Haven, Conn.: Human Relations Area Files Press, 1964.

Lemoine, Jacques. *Yao Ceremonial Paintings*. Bangkok, Thailand: White Lotus, 1982.

Lewis, Judy, ed. *Minority Cultures of Laos: Kammu, Laua, Lahu, Hmong, and Mien*. Rancho Cordova, Calif.: Southeast Asia Community Resource Center, 1992.

Lindell, Kristina, Hakan Lundstrom, Jan-Olof Svantesson, and Damrong Tayanin. *The Kammu Year: Its Lore and Music*. Scandinavian Institute of Asian Studies: Studies on Asian Topics 4. London: Curzon Press, 1982.

Miller, Terry E. *The Survival of Lao Traditional Music in America: Selected Reports in Ethnomusicology*. Vol. 6. Los Angeles: University of California Press, 1985.

Ngor, Haing. *A Cambodian Odyssey*. New York: Macmillan, 1987.

Quincey, Keith. *Hmong: History of a People*. Cheney: Eastern Washington University Press, 1988.

St. Cartmail, Keith. *Exodus Indochina*. Auckland, New Zealand: Heinemann, 1983.

Sam, Sam-Ang, and Patricia Shehan Campbell. *Silent Temples, Songful Hearts: Traditional Music of Cambodia*. Danbury, Conn.: World Music Press, 1991.

Schanberg, Sydney. *The Life and Death of Dith Pran*. New York: Penguin Books, 1985.

Seigel, Taggart. *Blue Collar and Buddha*. San Francisco: CrossCurrent Media, 1987. Film.

Shaw, Clifford R., and Henry D. McKay. *Juvenile Delinquency and Urban Areas: A Study of Rates of Delinquency in Relation to Differential Characteristics of Local Communities in American Cities*. Rev. ed. Chicago: University of Chicago Press, 1972.

Shawcross, William. *The Quality of Mercy: Cambodia, Holocaust, and Modern Conscience*. New York: Simon & Schuster, 1984.

Shawcross, William. *Sideshow: Kissinger, Nixon, and the Destruction of Cambodia*. New York: Simon & Schuster, 1979.

Smalley, William A. *Mother of Writing: The Origin and Development of a Hmong Messianic Script*. Chicago: University of Chicago Press, 1990.

Smith, Jeffrey Merrill. *Cultural Comparison Chart: American and Cambodian Cultures*. Rev. Ed. Portland, Maine: Portland Public Schools, 1988.

Stengel, Richard. "Resentment Tinged with Envy." *Time* 126 (July 8, 1985): 56-57.

Strand, Paul J. *Indochinese Refugees in America: Problems of Adaptation and Assimilation*. Durham, N.C.: Duke University Press, 1985.

Takaki, Ronald. *Strangers from a Different Shore: A History of Asian Americans*. Boston: Little, Brown, 1989.

Tepper, Eliot L., ed. *Southeast Asian Exodus: From Tradition to Resettlement, Understanding Refugees from Laos, Kampuchea and Vietnam in Canada*. Ottawa: The Canadian Asian Studies Association, 1980.

Thomas, David, Ernest W. Lee, and Nguyen Dang Liem, eds. *Chamic Studies*. Canberra: Department of Linguistics, Research School of Pacific Studies, Australian National University, 1977.

United States Commission on Civil Rights. *Civil Rights Issues Facing Asian Americans in the 1990s*. Washington, D.C.: Government Printing Office, 1992.

Velazquez, Elaine. *Moving Mountains: The Story of the Yiu Mien*. New York: Filmmakers Library, 1989. Film.

Viviani, Nancy. *The Long Journey: Vietnamese Migration and Settlement in Australia*. Carlton, Victoria: Melbourne University Press, 1984.

Waters, Tony, and Lawrence E. Cohen. *Laotians in the Criminal Justice System*. Berkeley, Calif.: California Policy Seminar, 1993.

Whitaker, Donald P. et al. *Area Handbook for Laos.* Washington, D.C.: Foreign Area Studies, U.S. Government Press, 1972.

Zinsmeister, Karl. "Prejudice Against Asians: Anxiety and Acceptance." *Current* 297 (November, 1987): 37-40.

VIETNAM (See also SOUTHEAST ASIA; SOUTHEAST ASIAN AMERICANS AND THE SOUTHEAST ASIAN DIASPORA; VIETNAMESE AMERICANS)

Chantavanich, Supang, and E. Bruce Reynolds, eds. *Indochinese Refugees: Asylum and Resettlement.* Bangkok: Institute of Asian Studies, Chulalongkorn University, 1988.

Cohen, Barbara. *The Vietnam Guidebook.* Teaneck, N.J.: Eurasia Press, 1990.

Condominas, Georges. *We Have Eaten the Forest: The Story of a Montagnard Village in the Central Highlands of Vietnam.* New York: Hill & Wang, 1977.

Crawford, A. C. *Customs and Culture of Vietnam.* Rutland, Vt.: Charles E. Tuttle, 1966.

Davis, Leonard. *Hong Kong and the Asylum-Seekers from Vietnam.* Basingstoke: Macmillan, 1991.

Engelmann, Larry. *Tears Before the Rain: An Oral History of the Fall of South Vietnam.* New York: Oxford University Press, 1990.

Grant, Bruce. *The Boat People: An "AGE" Investigation.* Harmondsworth, Middlesex, England: Penguin Books, 1979.

Hawthorne, Lesleyanne, ed. *Refugee: The Vietnamese Experience.* New York: Oxford University Press, 1982.

Hayslip, Le Ly, with Jay Wurts. *When Heaven and Earth Changed Places.* New York: Doubleday, 1989.

Hickey, Gerald. *Free in the Forest: Ethnohistory of the Vietnamese Central Highlands, 1954-1976.* New Haven, Conn.: Yale University Press, 1982.

Hickey, Gerald. *Sons of the Mountains: Ethnohistory of the Vietnamese Central Highlands to 1954.* New Haven, Conn.: Yale University Press, 1982.

Huynh Dinh Te. "Tet, The Vietnamese New Year Festival." In *Introduction to Cambodian Culture.* 2d ed. San Diego: Multifunctional Service Center, San Diego State University, 1989.

Jamieson, Neil. *Understanding Vietnam.* Berkeley: University of California Press, 1993.

Kahin, George McT. *Intervention: How Ameri-can Became Involved in Vietnam.* New York: Alfred A. Knopf, 1986.

Karnow, Stanley. *Vietnam: A History.* New York: Viking Press, 1983.

Kissinger, Henry S. *Years of Upheaval.* London: Weidenfeld & Nicolson, 1982.

Kulka, Richard A., et al. *Trauma and the Vietnam War Generation.* New York: Brunner/Mazel, 1990.

Le Quang Vinh. *Moon Festival (Tet Trung Thu).* Bassendean, Western Australia: Avery Publishing Company, 1990.

McCoy, Alfred W. *The Politics of Heroin in Southeast Asia.* New York: Harper & Row, 1972.

Mole, Robert. *The Montagnards of South Vietnam: A Study of Nine Tribes.* Rutland, Vt.: Charles E. Tuttle, 1970.

Nguyen, Thuyet Phong, and Patricia Shehan Campbell. *From Rice Paddies and Temple Yards: Traditional Music of Vietnam.* Danbury, Conn.: World Music Press, 1990.

Nguyen Phan, Kim-Anh, ed. and comp. *Tet: The Vietnamese New Year.* San Jose: San Jose Unified School District, 1986.

Nguyen Trieu Dan. *A Vietnamese Family Chronicle: Twelve Generations on the Banks of the Hat River.* Jefferson, N.C.: McFarland, 1991.

Rogge, John R., ed. *Refugees: A Third World Dilemma.* Totowa, N.J.: Rowman & Littlefield, 1987.

St. Cartmail, Robert Keith. *Exodus Indochina.* Auckland: Heinemann, 1983.

Scruggs, Jan C., and Joel L. Swerdlow. *To Heal a Nation: The Vietnam Veterans Memorial.* New York: Harper & Row, 1985.

Sheehan, Neil. *A Bright Shining Lie: John Paul Vann and America in Vietnam.* New York: Random House, 1988.

Whitfield, Danny J. *Historical and Cultural Dictionary of Vietnam.* Metuchen, N.J.: Scarecrow Press, 1976.

Woodside, A. B. *Community and Revolution in Modern Vietnam.* Boston: Houghton Mifflin, 1976.

VIETNAMESE AMERICANS (See also SOUTHEAST ASIA; SOUTHEAST ASIAN AMERICANS AND THE SOUTHEAST ASIAN DIASPORA; VIETNAM)

Amerasians' Special Needs Report. Sacramento: State of California, Health and Welfare Agency, Department of Social Services, 1989.

Auerbach, Susan. *Vietnamese Americans.* American Voices. Vero Beach, Fla.: Rourke, 1991.

Caplan, Nathan, et al. *The Boat People and Achievement in America: A Study of Family Life, Hard Work, and Cultural Values.* Ann Arbor: University of Michigan Press, 1989.

Crawford, A. C. *Customs and Culture of Vietnam.* Rutland, Vt.: Charles E. Tuttle, 1966.

Felsman, J. Kirk, Mark C. Johnson, Frederick T. L. Leong, and Irene C. Felsman. *Vietnamese Amerasians: Practical Implications of Current Research.* Washington, D.C.: Office of Refugee Resettlement, Family Support Administration, Department of Health and Human Services, 1989.

Freeman, James A. *Hearts of Sorrow: Vietnamese-American Lives.* Stanford, Calif.: Stanford University Press, 1989.

Hayslip, Le Ly, with Jay Wurts. *When Heaven and Earth Changed Places: A Vietnamese Woman's Journey from War to Peace.* New York: Doubleday, 1989.

Huynh Dinh Te. "Tet, The Vietnamese New Year Festival." In *Introduction to Cambodian Culture.* 2d ed. San Diego: Multifunctional Service Center, San Diego State University, 1989.

Lacey, Marilyn. *In Our Father's Land: Vietnamese Amerasians in the United States.* Washington, D.C.: Migration and Refugee Services, United States Catholic Conference, 1985.

Le Quang Vinh. *Moon Festival (Tet Trung Thu).* Bassendean, Western Australia: Avery Publishing Company, 1990.

Newell, Jean F. *Vietnamese Amerasians: A Needs Assessment.* Ann Arbor, Mich.: University Microfilms International, 1993.

Rutledge, Paul James. *The Vietnamese Experience in America.* Bloomington: Indiana University Press, 1992.

Strand, Paul J., and Woodrow Jones, Jr. *Indochinese Refugees in America: Problems of Adaptation and Assimilation.* Durham, N.C.: Duke University Press, 1985.

U.S. Department of State. Bureau of Public Affairs. *Amerasians in Vietnam.* Washington, D.C.: Government Printing Office, 1988.

Valverde, Kieu-Linh Caroline. "From Dust to Gold: The Vietnamese Amerasian Experience." In *Racially Mixed People in America,* edited by Maria P. P. Root. Newbury Park, Calif.: Sage, 1992.

Sources by Subject Areas

ARTS, ENTERTAINMENT, AND MEDIA

Asian Women United of California, eds. *Making Waves: An Anthology of Writings By and About Asian American Women.* Boston: Beacon Press, 1989.

Bruchac, Joseph, ed. *Breaking Silence: An Anthology of Contemporary Asian American Poets.* New York: Greenfield Review Press, 1983.

Bulosan, Carlos. *If You Want to Know What We Are: A Carlos Bulosan Reader.* Albuquerque, N.Mex.: West End Press, 1983.

Bulosan, Carlos. *The Philippines Is in the Heart.* Quezon City: New Day Publishers, 1978.

Bulosan, Carlos. *The Power of the People.* Manila: National Book Store, 1986.

Bulosan, Carlos. *The Sound of Falling Light.* Edited by Dolores Feria. Quezon City: University of the Philippines Press, 1960.

Carrison, Muriel P. *Cambodian Folk Stories from the Gatiloke.* Translated by Kong

Chhean. Rutland, Vt.: Charles E. Tuttle, 1987.

Catlin, Amy. *Music of the Hmong: Singing Voices and Talking Reeds*. Providence, R.I.: Center for Hmong Lore, Museum of Natural History, 1981.

Center for Integration and Improvement of Journalism. *Project Zinger: A Critical Look at News Media Coverage of Asian Pacific Americans*. San Francisco: Asian American Journalists Association, 1992.

Center for Integration and Improvement of Journalism. *Project Zinger: The Good, the Bad and the Ugly*. San Francisco: Asian American Journalists Association, 1991.

Cha, Theresa Hak Kyung. *Dictee*. New York: Tanam Press, 1982.

Chan, Jeffrey Paul, Frank Chin, Lawson Fusao Inada, and Shawn Wong, eds. *The Big Aiiieeeee! An Anthology of Chinese American and Japanese American Literature*. New York: Meridian Books, 1991.

Char, Tin-Yuke. *The Hakka Chinese: Their Origin and Folk Songs*. Translated by C. H. Kwock. San Francisco: Jade Mountain Press, 1969.

Cheung, King-Kok. *Articulate Silences: Hisaye Yamamoto, Maxine Hong Kingston, Joy Kogawa*. Ithaca, N.Y.: Cornell University Press, 1993.

Chinese Historical Society of America, Publication Committee, ed. *Chinese America: History and Perspectives, 1990*. San Francisco: Chinese Historical Society of America, 1990.

DeWoskin, Kenneth J. *A Song for One or Two: Music and the Concept of Art in Early China*. Ann Arbor: University of Michigan, Center for Chinese Studies, 1982.

Emerson, Nathaniel B. *The Unwritten Literature of Hawaii: The Sacred Songs of the Hula*. Rutland, Vt.: Charles E. Tuttle, 1965.

Ernst, Earle. *The Kabuki Theatre*. New York: Oxford University Press, 1956.

Gunji, Masakatsu. *Buyo: The Classical Dance*. Translated by Don Kenny. New York: Weatherhill, 1970.

Hamilton, Mildred. "Ethnic TV, the Multi-Lingual Tube." *San Francisco Examiner & Chronicle*, Scene/Arts section, October 8, 1978.

Hsu, Kai-yu, and Helen Palubinskas, eds. *Asian-American Authors*. Boston: Houghton Mifflin, 1972.

Ichioka, Yuji. *The Issei: The World of the First Generation Japanese Immigrants, 1885-1924*. New York: Free Press, 1988.

Japanese Classics Translation Committee. *The Noh Drama*. Tokyo: Charles E. Tuttle, 1960.

Kanahele, George S., ed. *Hawaiian Music and Musicians: An Illustrated History*. Honolulu: University Press of Hawaii, 1979.

Kanahele, George S. *Hawaiian Renaissance*. Honolulu: Project Waiaha, 1982.

Kang, Younghill. *East Goes West: The Making of an Oriental Yankee*. New York: Charles Scribner's Sons, 1937.

Kim, Elaine H. *Asian American Literature: An Introduction to the Writings and Their Social Context*. Philadelphia: Temple University Press, 1982.

Kim, Ronyoung. *Clay Walls*. New York: Permanent Press, 1986.

Lai, H. M. "Chinese-Language TV Flourishes in Bay Area: 36 Hours Weekly in Cantonese and Mandarin." *East/West*, July 10, 1986.

Lai, Him Mark. "The Ups and Downs of the Chinese Press in the U.S." *East/West*, Nov. 20, 1986.

Lai, Him Mark. "A Voice of Reason: Life and Times of Gilbert Woo, Chinese American Journalist." *Chinese America: History and Perspectives* (1992): 83-123.

Lee, Mary Paik. *Quiet Odyssey: A Pioneer Korean Woman in America*. Seattle: University of Washington Press, 1990.

Lee Byongwon. "Contemporary Korean Musical Cultures." In *Korea Briefing, 1993*, edited by Donald N. Clark. Boulder, Colo.: Westview Press, 1993.

Lemoine, Jacques. *Yao Ceremonial Paintings*. Bangkok, Thailand: White Lotus, 1982.

Liang, Ming-Yueh. *Music of the Billion: An Introduction to Chinese Musical Culture*. New York: Heinrichschofen, 1985.

Ling, Amy. *Between Worlds: Women Writers of Chinese Ancestry*. Elmsford, N.Y.: Pergamon Press, 1990.

Lo, Karl. "Kim Shan Jit San Luk: The First Chinese Newspaper Published in America." *Chinese Historical Society of America Bulletin* 6 (October, 1971): 1-4.

Mackerras, Colin P. *The Rise of the Peking Opera, 1770-1870*. Oxford, England: Clarendon Press, 1972.

Malm, William. *Japanese Music and Musical Instruments*. Tokyo: Charles E. Tuttle, 1959.

Manuel, Peter. *Popular Musics of the Non-Western World*. New York: Oxford University Press, 1988.

May, Elizabeth, ed. *Musics of Many Cultures: An Introduction*. Berkeley: University of California Press, 1980.

Miller, Sally M., ed. *The Ethnic Press in the United States: A Historical Analysis and Handbook*. New York: Greenwood Press, 1987.

Miller, Terry E. *The Survival of Lao Traditional Music in America: Selected Reports in Ethnomusicology*. Vol. 6. Los Angeles: University of California Press, 1985.

Molina, A. J. *Music of the Philippines*. Manila: The Philippine Press, 1967.

Mukherjee, Bharati. "Writers of the Indian Commonwealth." *The Literary Review* 29 (Summer, 1986): 400-401.

Nguyen, Thuyet Phong, and Patricia Shehan Campbell. *From Rice Paddies and Temple Yards: Traditional Music of Vietnam*. Danbury, Conn.: World Music Press, 1990.

Oda, James. *Heroic Struggles of Japanese Americans*. North Hollywood, Calif.: J. Oda, 1980.

Osman, Mohd. Taib, ed. *Traditional Drama and Music of Southeast Asia*. Kuala Lumpur: Kementerian Pelajaran Malaysia, 1974.

Roberts, Helen Heffron. *Ancient Hawaiian Music*. New York: Dover Publications, 1967.

Sam, Sam-Ang, and Patricia Shehan Campbell. *Silent Temples, Songful Hearts: Traditional Music of Cambodia*. Danbury, Conn.: World Music Press, 1991.

Sambamoorthy, P. *South Indian Music*. (6 vols.) Madras: Indian Music Publishing House, 1958-1969.

Sarabhai, Mrinalini. *Understanding Bharata Natyam*. 3d ed. Ahmedabad, India: Darpana Academy of Performing Arts, 1981.

Shankar, Ravi. *My Music, My Life*. New York: Simon & Schuster, 1968.

Smith, Sidonie. *A Poetics of Women's Autobiography: Marginality and the Fictions of Self-Representation*. Bloomington: Indiana University Press, 1987.

South Asians in North America: An Annotated and Selected Bibliography, edited by Jane Singh. Berkeley: Center for South and Southeast Asia Studies, University of California, Berkeley, 1988.

Stagner, Ishmael W. *Hula!* Laie, Haw.: Institute for Polynesian Studies, Brigham Young University-Hawaii, 1985.

Stannard, David E. *Before the Horror: The Population of Hawaii on the Eve of Western Contact*. Honolulu: Social Science Research Institute, University of Hawaii, 1989.

Stellmam, Louis J. "Yellow Journals: San Francisco's Oriental Newspapers." *Sunset* 24 (February, 1910): 197-201.

Stoneburner, Bryan C., comp. *Hawaiian Music: An Annotated Bibliography*. New York: Greenwood Press, 1986.

Stroup, Dorothy Anne. *The Role of the Japanese-American Press in Its Community*. Berkeley: University of California Press, 1960.

Tajima, Renee. *The Anthology of Asian Pacific American Film and Video*. New York: Film News Now Foundation, 1985.

Tan, Alexis S. *Why Asian American Journalists Leave Journalism and Why They Stay*. San Francisco: Asian American Journalists Association, 1990.

Tatar, Elizabeth. *Nineteenth Century Hawaiian Chant*. Honolulu: Department of Anthropology, Bernice P. Bishop Museum, 1982.

Uemoto, Shuzo. *Nana Iho Loea Hula*. Honolulu: Kalihi-Palama Culture and Arts Society, 1984.

United Japanese Society of Hawaii, Publications Committee, ed. *A History of Japanese in Hawaii*. Honolulu: United Japanese Society of Hawaii, 1971.

Vassanji, M. G., ed. *A Meeting of Streams: South Asian Canadian Literature*. Toronto: Toronto South Asia Review Publications, 1985.

Wade, Bonnie C. *Music in India: The Classical Traditions*. Englewood Cliffs, N.J.: Prentice-Hall, 1979.

Wang, K'o-fen. *History of Chinese Dance*. Beijing: Foreign Language Press, 1885.

Women of South Asian Descent Collective, eds. *Our Feet Walked the Sky: Women of the*

South Asian Diaspora. San Francisco: Aunt Lute Books, 1993.

Yung, Bell. *Cantonese Opera: Performance as Creative Process*. Cambridge, England: Cambridge University Press, 1989.

Zhang, Wei-hua. "Fred Ho and Jon Jang: Profiles of Two Chinese American Jazz Musicians." *Chinese America: History and Perspectives* (1994): 175-199.

CUISINE, CUSTOMS, AND CULTURAL TRADITIONS

Anderson, Eugene. *The Food of China*. New Haven, Conn.: Yale University Press, 1988.

Belleme, John, and Jan Belleme. *Culinary Treasures of Japan*. Garden City Park, N.J.: Avery Publishing Group, 1992.

Blofeld, John. *The Chinese Art of Tea*. Boston: Shambhala, 1985.

Catlin, Amy, ed. *APSARA: The Feminine in Cambodian Art*. Los Angeles: Woman's Building, 1987.

Chang, K. C., ed. *Food in Chinese Culture: Anthropological and Historical Perspectives*. New Haven, Conn.: Yale University Press, 1977.

Choe, Sang-Su. *Annual Customs of Korea: Notes on the Rites and Ceremonies of the Year*. Seoul: Seomun-dang, 1983.

Claiborne, Craig, and Virginia Lee. *The Chinese Cookbook*. Philadelphia: J. B. Lippincott, 1972.

Cohen, Barbara. "Holidays and Festivals." In *The Vietnam Guidebook*. Teaneck, N.J.: Eurasia Press, 1990.

Crawford, A. C. *Customs and Culture of Vietnam*. Rutland, Vt.: Charles E. Tuttle, 1966.

Dalal, Tarla. *Low Calorie Healthy Cooking*. Bombay, India: Sanjay, 1989.

De Berval, René, ed. *Kingdom of Laos: The Land of the Million Elephants and of the White Parasol*. Translated by Mrs. Teissier du Cros et al. Saigon, Vietnam: France-Asie, 1959.

Devi, Yamuna. *The Best of Lord Krishna's Cuisine: Favorite Recipes from the Art of Indian Vegetarian Cooking*. California: Bala Books, 1991.

Donohue, John J. *The Forge of the Spirit: Structure, Motion, and Meaning in the Japanese Martial Tradition*. New York: Garland, 1991.

Feuchtwang, Stephan D. R. *An Anthropological Analysis of Chinese Geomancy*. Vientiane, Laos: Editions Vithagna, 1974.

Finn, Michael. *Martial Arts: A Complete Illustrated History*. Woodstock, N.Y.: Overlook Press, 1988.

Grattan, F. J. H. *An Introduction to Samoan Custom*. Apia: Samoan Printing and Publishing Company, 1948.

Hamada, Hiroyuki Teshin. *Spirit of Japanese Classical Martial Arts: Historical and Philosophical Perspectives*. Dubuque, Iowa: Kendall/Hunt, 1990.

Harler, Campbell R. *The Culture and Marketing of Tea*. 3d ed. London: Oxford University Press, 1964.

Harrison, E. J. *The Fighting Spirit of Japan*. Woodstock, N.Y.: The Overlook Press, 1982.

Huynh Dinh Te. *Introduction to Cambodian Culture*. 2d ed. San Diego: Multifunctional Service Center, San Diego State University, 1989.

International Cultural Foundation, ed. *Customs and Manners in Korea*. Seoul: Si-sa-yong-o-sa Publishers, 1982.

Jaffrey, Madhur. *Madhur Jaffrey's World-of-the-East Vegetarian Cooking*. New York: Alfred A. Knopf, 1981.

Japan Travel Bureau. *Illustrated Eating in Japan*. Volume 3 in *JTB Illustrated Books*. Tokyo: Japan Travel Bureau, 1989.

Jocano, F. Landa. *Growing up in a Philippine Barrio*. New York: Holt, Rinehart and Winston, 1969.

Kanahele, George S. *Hawaiian Renaissance*. Honolulu: Project Waiaha, 1982.

Kanahele, George S. *Ku Kanaka, Stand Tall: A Search for Hawaiian Values*. Honolulu: University of Hawaii Press, 1986.

Kauz, Herman. *The Martial Spirit: An Introduction to the Origin, Philosophy, and Psychology of the Martial Arts*. Woodstock, N.Y.: Overlook Press, 1988.

Kirchner, Bharati. *The Healthy Cuisine of India: Recipes from the Bengal Region*. Los Angeles: Lowell House, 1992.

Korea: Its People and Culture. Seoul: Hakwon-sa. 1970.

Korean Overseas Information Service. *A Handbook of Korea*, 6th ed. Seoul: Seoul International Publishing House, 1987.

Le Quang Vinh. *Moon Festival (Tet Trung Thu)*. Bassendean, Western Australia: Avery Publishing Company, 1990.

LeBar, Frank M. and Adrienne Suddard, eds. *Laos: Its People, Its Society, Its Culture*. New Haven, Conn.: Human Relations Area Files, 1960.

Levesque, Leonard. *Hakka Beliefs and Customs*. Translated by J. Maynard Murphy. Taichung: Kuang Chi Press, 1969.

Lewis, Peter. *Martial Arts of the Orient*. New York: Gallery Books, 1985.

Lindell, Kristina, Hakan Lundstrom, Jan-Olof Svantesson, and Damrong Tayanin. *The Kammu Year: Its Lore and Music*. Scandinavian Institute of Asian Studies: Studies on Asian Topics 4. London: Curzon Press, 1982.

Lo, Kenneth. *Chinese Regional Cooking*. New York: Pantheon Books, 1979.

Lu Yu. *The Classic of Tea*. Translated by Francis Ross Carpenter. Boston: Little, Brown, 1974.

Lynch, Frank, ed. *Social Acceptance: Four Readings on Philippine Values*. Quezon City: Ateneo de Manila University, 1964.

Needham, Joseph. *Science and Civilisation in China: History of Scientific Thought*. Vol. 2. Cambridge, England: Cambridge University Press, 1956.

Nguyen Phan, Kim-Anh, ed. and comp. *Tet: The Vietnamese New Year*. San Jose: San Jose Unified School District, 1986.

Nilsen, Robert. *South Korea Handbook*. Chico, Calif.: Moon Publications, 1988.

Nurge, Ethel. *Life in a Leyte Village*. Seattle: University of Washington Press, 1965.

Pratt, James Norwood. *The Tea Lover's Treasury*. San Francisco: 101 Productions, 1982.

Ratti, Oscar, and Adele Westbrook. *Secrets of the Samurai: A Survey of the Martial Arts of Feudal Japan*. Rutland, Vt.: Charles E. Tuttle, 1973.

Ray, Sumana. *Indian Regional Cooking*. New Jersey: Chartwell Books, 1986.

Rossbach, Sarah. *Interior Design with Feng Shui*. New York: E. P. Dutton, 1987.

Smith, Jeffrey Merrill. *Cultural Comparison Chart: American and Cambodian Cultures*. Rev. Ed. Portland, Maine: Portland Public Schools, 1988.

Soet, John Steven. *Martial Arts Around the World*. Burbank, Calif.: Unique Publications, 1991.

Spear, Robert K. *Hapkido: The Integrated Fighting Art*. Burbank: Unique Publications, 1988.

Stagner, Ishmael W. *Hula!* Laie, Haw.: Institute for Polynesian Studies, Brigham Young University-Hawaii, 1985.

Stannard, David E. *Before the Horror: The Population of Hawaii on the Eve of Western Contact*. Honolulu: Social Science Research Institute, University of Hawaii, 1989.

Sugano, Kimiko. *Kimiko's World*. San Francisco: Strawberry Hill Press, 1982.

Tambiah, Stanley Jeyaraja. *Buddhism and the Spirit Cults in North-East Thailand*. Cambridge, England: Cambridge University Press, 1970.

Tippett, Alan Richard. *Fijian Material Culture*. Honolulu: Bishop Museum Press, 1968.

Tsuji, Shizuo. *Japanese Cooking, A Simple Art*. Tokyo: Kodansha International, 1980.

Uemoto, Shuzo. *Nana Iho Loea Hula*. Honolulu: Kalihi-Palama Culture and Arts Society, 1984.

Varley, Paul, and Kumakura Isao. *Tea in Japan*. Honolulu: University of Hawaii Press, 1989.

Wang, Dee. *Chinese Cooking the Easy Way*. New York: Elsevier/Nelson Books, 1979.

Wheatley, Paul. *The Pivot of the Four Quarters: A Preliminary Enquiry Into the Origins and Character of the Ancient Chinese City*. Chicago: Aldine, 1971.

Whitaker, Donald P. et al. *Area Handbook for Laos*. Washington, D.C.: Foreign Area Studies, U.S. Government Press, 1972.

Whiting, Beatrice B., ed. *Six Cultures—Studies of Child-rearing*. New York: John Wiley & Sons, 1963.

Williams, Bryn. *Martial Arts of the Orient*. New York: Hamlyn, 1975.

Wong, Doc-Fai, and Jane Hallander. *Tai Chi Chuan's Internal Secrets*. Burbank, Calif.: Unique Publications, 1991.

Yates, Keith D. *The Complete Book of Taekwon*

Do Forms. Boulder, Colo.: Paladin Press, 1982.

Yates, Keith D. *Tae Kwon Do Basics*. New York: Sterling Publishing Company, 1987.

Yoon, Hong-key. *Geomantic Relations Between Culture and Nature in Korea*. Taipei: Chinese Association for Folklore, 1976.

COMMUNITY STUDIES

Adachi, Ken. *The Enemy That Never Was: A History of the Japanese Canadians*. Toronto: McClelland and Stewart, 1991.

Amerasians' Special Needs Report. Sacramento: State of California, Health and Welfare Agency, Department of Social Services, 1989.

Anderson, Kay J. *Vancouver's Chinatown: Racial Discourse in Canada, 1875-1980*. Montreal: McGill-Queen's University Press, 1991.

Arax, Mark. "Lost in L.A." *Los Angeles Times Magazine*, December 13, 1987, pp. 10-16.

Asian Women United of California, eds. *Making Waves: An Anthology of Writings By and About Asian American Women*. Boston: Beacon Press, 1989.

Barrier, N. Gerald, and Verne A. Dusenbery. *The Sikh Diaspora: Migration and the Experience Beyond Punjab*. Columbia, Mo.: South Asia Publications, 1989.

Barringer, H. R., R. W. Gardner, and M. J. Levin. *Asians and Pacific Islanders in the United States*. New York: Russell Sage Foundation, 1993.

Barth, Gunther. *Bitter Strength: A History of the Chinese in the United States, 1850-1870*. Cambridge, Mass.: Harvard University Press, 1964.

Beck, Louis. *New York's Chinatown*. New York: Bohemia Publishing Company, 1898.

Beechert, Edward D. *Working in Hawaii: A Labor History*. Honolulu: University of Hawaii Press, 1985.

Blaisdell, Kekuni, and Noreen Mokuau. "Kanaka Maoli: Indigenous Hawaiians" In *Handbook of Social Services for Asian and Pacific Islanders*, edited by Noreen Mokuau. New York: Greenwood Press, 1991.

Bliatout, Bruce T. *Hmong Sudden, Unexpected Nocturnal Death Syndrome: A Cultural Study*. Portland, Oreg.: Sparkle Publications, 1982.

Broadfoot, Barry. *Years of Sorrow, Years of Shame: The Story of Japanese Canadians in World War II*. Garden City, N.Y.: Doubleday, 1977.

Brower, Kenneth. *Micronesia: The Land, the People and the Sea*. Edited by Gregory Vitiello. Baton Rouge: Louisiana State University Press, 1981.

Buaken, Manuel. *I Have Lived with the American People*. Caldwell, Idaho: Caxton Printers, 1948.

Bulosan, Carlos. *America Is in the Heart*. Seattle: University of Washington Press, 1946.

Butler-Diaz, Jacqueline. *Yao Design of North-*

ern Thailand. Rev. ed. Bangkok, Thailand: The Siam Society, 1981.

Caplan, Nathan, et al. *The Boat People and Achievement in America: A Study of Family Life, Hard Work, and Cultural Values*. Ann Arbor: University of Michigan Press, 1989.

Carano, Paul, and Pedro C. Sanchez. *A Complete History of Guam*. Rutland, Vt.: Charles E. Tuttle, 1964.

Chan, Sucheng. *Asian Americans: An Interpretive History*. Boston: Twayne, 1991.

Chandrasekhar, S., ed. *From India to America: A Brief History of Immigration, Problems of Discrimination, Admission, and Assimilation*. La Jolla, Calif.: A Population Review Book, 1982.

Chapman, Murray, and Philip S. Morrison, eds. *Mobility and Identity in the Island Pacific*. A special issue of *Pacific Viewpoint*. Wellington, New Zealand: Department of Geography and Victoria University of Wellington, 1985.

Char, Tin-Yuke. *The Hakka Chinese: Their Origin and Folk Songs*. Translated by C. H. Kwock. San Francisco: Jade Mountain Press, 1969.

Chen, Jack. *The Chinese of America: From the Beginnings to the Present*. New York: Harper and Row/San Francisco, 1980.

Chen, Ta. *Emigrant Communities in South China*. Edited by Bruno Lasker. New York: Institute of Pacific Relations, 1940.

Cheng, Lucie, and Edna Bonacich, eds. *Labor Immigration Under Capitalism: Asian Workers in the United States Before World War II*. Berkeley: University of California Press, 1984.

Chew, Sock Foon. *Ethnicity and Nationality in Singapore*. Athens: Ohio University Center for International Studies, 1987.

Chin, Ko-lin. *Chinese Subculture and Criminality*. New York: Greenwood Press, 1990. Dannen, Fredric. "Revenge of the Green Dragons." *The New Yorker* 68 (November 16, 1992): 76-99.

Chinn, Thomas W., Him Mark Lai, and Philip P. Choy, eds. *A History of the Chinese in California: A Syllabus*. San Francisco: Chinese Historical Society of America, 1969.

Chiu, Ping. *Chinese Labor in California, 1850-1880: An Economic Study*. Madison, Wis.: State Historical Society of Wisconsin, 1963.

Colman, Elizabeth. *Chinatowns U.S.A.* New York: Asia Press in association with John Day Company, 1946.

Condominas, Georges. *We Have Eaten the Forest: The Story of a Montagnard Village in the Central Highlands of Vietnam*. New York: Hill & Wang, 1977.

Coolidge, Mary R. *Chinese Immigration*. New York: Henry Holt, 1909.

Cretser, Gary A., and Joseph J. Leon, eds. *Intermarriage in the United States*. New York: Haworth, 1982.

Daniels, Roger. *Asian America: Chinese and Japanese in the United States Since 1850*. Seattle: University of Washington Press, 1988.

Daniels, Roger, Sandra C. Taylor, and Harry H. L. Kitano, eds. *Japanese Americans: From Relocation to Redress*. Rev. ed. Seattle: University of Washington Press, 1991.

Dannen, Fredric. "Revenge of the Green Dragons." *The New Yorker* 68 (November 16, 1992): 76-99.

Del Valle, Teresa. *Social and Cultural Change in the Community of Umatac, Southern Guam*. Agana, Guam: Micronesian Area Research Center, University of Guam, 1979.

Dionisio, Juan C., ed. *Filipinos in Hawaii . . . the First 75 Years*. Honolulu: Hawaii Filipino News Specialty Publications, 1981.

Dreyer, June Teufel. *China's Forty Millions: Minority Nationalities and National Integration in the People's Republic of China*. Cambridge, Mass.: Harvard University Press, 1976.

Dudley, Michael Kioni, and Keoni Kealoha Agard. *A Call for Hawaiian Sovereignty*. Honolulu: Na Kane O Ka Malo Press, 1990.

Felsman, J. Kirk, Mark C. Johnson, Frederick T. L. Leong, and Irene C. Felsman. *Vietnamese Amerasians: Practical Implications of Current Research*. Washington, D.C.: Office of Refugee Resettlement, Family Support Administration, Department of Health and Human Services, 1989.

Fitzgerald, Stephen. *China and the Overseas Chinese*. Cambridge: Cambridge University Press, 1972.

Ford, Douglas. *The Pacific Islanders*. New York: Chelsea House, 1989.

Freeman, James A. *Hearts of Sorrow: Vietnamese-American Lives*. Stanford, Calif.: Stanford University Press, 1989.

Fujita, Stephen S., and David J. O'Brien. *Japanese American Ethnicity: The Persistence of Community*. Seattle: University of Washington Press, 1991.

Geddes, William R. *Migrants of the Mountains: The Cultural Ecology of the Blue Miao (Hmong Njua) of Thailand*. Oxford, England: Clarendon Press, 1976.

Gibson, Margaret A. *Accommodation Without Assimilation: Sikh Immigrants in an American High School*. Ithaca, N.Y.: Cornell University Press, 1988.

Gledhill, Marion. *Growing Up: Child Development in the Pacific Islands*. Suva, Fiji: Lotu Pasifika Productions, 1974.

Glick, Clarence E. *Sojourners and Settlers: Chinese Migrants in Hawaii*. Honolulu: University Press of Hawaii, 1980.

Goodwin, Bill. *Frommer's South Pacific '92-'93*. Englewood Cliffs, N.J.: Prentice-Hall, 1992.

Grattan, F. J. H. *An Introduction to Samoan Custom*. Apia: Samoan Printing and Publishing Company, 1948.

Gray, J. A. C. *Amerika Samoa*. Annapolis, Md.: U.S. Naval Institute, 1960.

Haines, David, ed. *Refugees as Immigrants: Cambodians, Laotians, and Vietnamese in America*. Totowa, N.J.: Rowman & Littlefield, 1989.

Hamilton-Merritt, Jane. *Tragic Mountains: The*

Hmong, the Americans, and the Secret Wars for Laos, 1942-1992. Bloomington: Indiana University Press, 1993.

Handy, E. S. Craighill, and Mary Kawena Pukui. *The Polynesian System in Ka'u, Hawai'i*. Rutland, Vt.: Charles E. Tuttle, 1972.

Hayslip, Le Ly, with Jay Wurts. *When Heaven and Earth Changed Places: A Vietnamese Woman's Journey from War to Peace*. New York: Doubleday, 1989.

Hazama, Dorothy Ochiai, and Jane Okamoto Komeiji. *Okage Sama De: The Japanese in Hawaii, 1885-1985*. Honolulu: Bess Press, 1986.

Helweg, Arthur W., and Usha M. Helweg. *An Immigrant Success Story: East Indians in America*. Philadelphia: University of Pennsylvania Press, 1990.

Hendricks, Glenn, Bruce Downing, and Amos Deinard, eds. *The Hmong in Transition*. Staten Island, N.Y.: Center for Migration Studies of New York, 1986.

Hickey, Gerald. *Free in the Forest: Ethnohistory of the Vietnamese Central Highlands, 1954-1976*. New Haven, Conn.: Yale University Press, 1982.

Hickey, Gerald. *Sons of the Mountains: Ethnohistory of the Vietnamese Central Highlands to 1954*. New Haven, Conn.: Yale University Press, 1982.

Ho, Man Keung. "Family Therapy with Asian/Pacific Americans." In *Family Therapy with Ethnic Minorities*. Newbury Park, Calif.: Sage, 1987.

Holmes, Lowell D., and Ellen Rhoads Holmes. *Samoan Village: Then and Now*. 2d ed. Fort Worth: Harcourt Brace Jovanovich, 1992.

Hosokawa, Bill. *Nisei: The Quiet Americans*. New York: William Morrow, 1969.

Hsu, Immanuel C. Y. *The Rise of Modern China*. 4th ed. New York: Oxford University Press, 1990.

Gibbs, Jewelle Taylor, et al. *Children of Color*. San Francisco: Jossey-Bass, 1989.

Hurh, Won Moo, and Kwang Chung Kim. *Korean Immigrants in America: A Structural Analysis of Ethnic Confinement and Adhesive Adaptation*. Madison, N.J.: Fairleigh Dickinson University Press, 1984.

Ichioka, Yuji. *The Issei: The World of the First Generation Japanese Immigrants, 1885-1924*. New York: Free Press, 1988.

Jensen, Joan M. *Passage from India: Asian Indian Immigrants in North America*. New Haven, Conn.: Yale University Press, 1988.

Johnson, Dwight L., Michael J. Levin, and Edna L. Paisano. *We, the Asian and Pacific Islander Americans*. Washington, D.C.: Government Printing Office, 1988.

Jolly, Margaret, and Martha Macintyre, eds. *Family and Gender in the Pacific: Domestic Contradictions and the Colonial Impact*. Cambridge, England: Cambridge University Press, 1989.

Kameeleihiwa, Lilikala. *Native Land and Foreign Desires: Pehea La E Pono Ai?* Honolulu: Bishop Museum Press, 1992.

Kanahele, George H. S. *Ku Kanaka, Stand Tall: A Search for Hawaiian Values*. Honolulu: University of Hawaii Press and Waiaha Foundation, 1986.

Keesing, Felix, and Marie M. Keesing. *Elite Communication in Samoa*. Stanford, Calif.: Stanford University Press, 1956.

Kiang, Clyde. *The Hakka Odyssey and Their Taiwan Homeland*. Elgin, Pa.: Allegheny Press, 1992.

Kim, Bok-Lim C. *Korean-American Child at School and at Home*. Washington, D.C.: Administration for Children, Youth, and Families, U.S. Department of Health, Education, and Welfare, 1980.

Kim, Illsoo. *New Urban Immigrants: The Korean Community in New York*. Princeton, N.J.: Princeton University Press, 1981.

Kimura, Yukiko. *Issei: Japanese Immigrants in Hawaii*. Honolulu: University of Hawaii Press, 1988.

Kinkead, Gwen. *Chinatown: A Portrait of a Closed Society*. New York: HarperCollins, 1992.

Kitano, Harry H. L. *Japanese Americans: The Evolution of a Subculture*. 2d ed. Englewood Cliffs, N.J.: Prentice-Hall, 1976.

Kitano, Harry H. L., and Roger Daniels. *Asian Americans: Emerging Minorities*. Englewood Cliffs, N.J.: Prentice-Hall, 1988.

Knapp, Ronald G., ed. *Chinese Landscapes: The Village as Place*. Honolulu: University of Hawaii Press, 1992.

Kogawa, Joy. *Obasan*. Boston: David R. Godine, 1981.

Kung, S. W. *Chinese in American Life: Some Aspects of Their History, Status, Problems, and Contributions*. Seattle: University of Washington Press, 1962.

Kunstadter, Peter, ed. *Southeast Asian Tribes, Minorities and Nations*. 2 vols. Princeton, N.J.: Princeton University Press, 1967.

Kwong, Peter. *The New Chinatown*. New York: Hill and Wang, 1987.

La Brack, Bruce. *The Sikhs of Northern California, 1904-1975*. New York: AMS Press, 1988.

Lacey, Marilyn. *In Our Father's Land: Vietnamese Amerasians in the United States*. Washington, D.C.: Migration and Refugee Services, United States Catholic Conference, 1985.

Lai, Chuenyan David. *Chinatowns: Towns Within Cities in Canada*. Vancouver: University of British Columbia Press, 1988.

Lasaqa, Isireli. *The Fijian People Before and After Independence*. Canberra: Australian National University Press, 1984.

Lasker, Bruno. *Filipino Immigration*. Chicago: University of Chicago Press, 1931.

Lawson, Stephanie. *The Failure of Democratic Politics in Fiji*. New York: Oxford University Press, 1991.

LeBar, Frank M., G. C. Hickey, and J. K. Musgrave. *Ethnic Groups of Mainland Southeast Asia*. New Haven, Conn.: Human Relations Area Files Press, 1964.

Lee, Rose Hum. *The Chinese in the United States of America*. Hong Kong: Hong Kong University Press, 1960.

Leonard, Karen Isaksen. *Making Ethnic Choices: California's Punjabi Mexican Americans*. Philadelphia: Temple University Press, 1992

Levesque, Leonard. *Hakka Beliefs and Customs*. Translated by J. Maynard Murphy. Taichung: Kuang Chi Press, 1969.

Lewis, Judy, ed. *Minority Cultures of Laos: Kammu, Laua, Lahu, Hmong, and Mien*. Rancho Cordova, Calif.: Southeast Asia Community Resource Center, 1992.

Li, Peter S. *The Chinese in Canada*. Toronto: Oxford University Press, 1988.

Light, Ivan, and Edna Bonacich. *Immigrant Entrepreneurs: Koreans in Los Angeles, 1965-1982*. Berkeley: University of California Press, 1988.

Liliuokalani, Queen of Hawaii. *Hawaii's Story*. Reprint. Rutland, Vt.: Charles E. Tuttle, 1962.

Loewen, James W. *The Mississippi Chinese: Between Black and White*. 2d ed. Prospect Heights, Ill.: Waveland Press, 1988.

Lum, Arlene, ed. *Sailing for the Sun: The Chinese in Hawaii 1789-1989*. Honolulu: Three Heroes, 1989.

Mackie, J. A. C., ed. *The Chinese in Indonesia*. Honolulu: University Press of Hawaii, 1976.

MacNair, H. F. *The Chinese Abroad, Their Position and Protection*. Shanghai, China: Commercial Press, 1924.

Macpherson, Cluny, Bradd Shore, and Robert Franco, eds. *New Neighbors—Islanders in Adaptation*. Santa Cruz, Calif.: Center for South Pacific Studies, University of California, 1978.

Majumdar, Ramesh Chandra. *Champa: History and Culture of an Indian Colonial Kingdom in the Far East, Second to Sixteenth Century A.D.* Delhi, India: Gian Publishing House, 1985.

Mark, Diane M. L., and Ginger Chih. *A Place Called Chinese America*. Washington, D.C.: Organization of Chinese Americans, 1982.

Matisoff, James A. *The Dictionary of Lahu*. Berkeley: University of California Press, 1988.

Matisoff, James A. *The Grammar of Lahu*. Berkeley: University of California Press, 1973. Reprinted 1982.

Mead, Margaret. *Coming of Age in Samoa*. New York: William Morrow, 1928.

Melendy, H. Brett. *Asians in America: Filipinos, Koreans, and East Indians*. New York: Hippocrene, 1981.

Min, Pyong Gap. *Ethnic Business Enterprise: Korean Small Business in Atlanta*. Staten Island: Center for Migration Studies, 1988.

Mindel, Charles H., and Robert W. Habenstein, eds. *Ethnic Families in America: Patterns and Variations*. New York: Elsevier, 1976.

Minister of Education. *Report of the Ministry of Education for the Year 1990*. Nukualofa: Government of Tonga, 1991.

Mokuau, Noreen, ed. *Handbook of Social Ser-*

vices for Asian and Pacific Islanders. New York: Greenwood Press, 1991.

Mole, Robert. *The Montagnards of South Vietnam: A Study of Nine Tribes.* Rutland, Vt.: Charles E. Tuttle, 1970.

Moriyama, Alan T. *Imingaisha: Japanese Emigration Companies and Hawaii, 1894-1908.* Honolulu: University of Hawaii Press, 1985.

Nakano, Mei. *Japanese American Women: Three Generations, 1890-1990.* Berkeley, Calif.: Mina Press, 1990.

Nee, Victor, and Brett Nee. *Longtime Californ': A Documentary Study of An American Chinatown.* New York: Pantheon Books, 1973.

Newell, Jean F. *Vietnamese Amerasians: A Needs Assessment.* Ann Arbor, Mich.: University Microfilms International, 1993.

Ngor, Haing. *A Cambodian Odyssey.* New York: Macmillan, 1987.

O'Brien, David J., and Stephen S. Fugita. *The Japanese American Experience.* Bloomington: Indiana University Press, 1991.

Ogawa, Dennis M. *Kodomo No Tame Ni: For the Sake of the Children, the Japanese American Experience in Hawaii.* Honolulu: University of Hawaii Press, 1978.

Okihiro, Gary Y. *Cane Fires: The Anti-Japanese Movement in Hawaii, 1865-1945.* Philadelphia: Temple University Press, 1991.

Overseas Chinese Affairs Commission, the Republic of China. *We Always Stay Together: A Report on Overseas Chinese Affairs.* Taipei, Taiwan: Overseas Chinese Affairs Commission, 1991.

Pai, Margaret K. *The Dreams of Two Yi-Min.* Honolulu: University of Hawaii Press, 1989.

Patterson, Wayne. *The Korean Frontier in America: Immigration to Hawaii, 1896-1910.* Honolulu: University of Hawaii Press, 1988.

Pido, Antonio J. A. *The Pilipinos in America.* New York: Center for Migration Studies, 1986.

Prasad, Ram Chandra. *Archaeology of Champa and Vikramasila.* Delhi, India: Rammanand Vidya Bhawan, 1987.

Pulea, Mere. *The Family, Law and Population in the Pacific Islands.* Suva, Fiji: Institute of Pacific Studies, University of the South Pacific, 1986.

Puyo, Ana Maria. *The Acceptance of Americanization by the Chamorros and Carolinians of Saipan.* St. Louis: St. Louis University, 1964.

Quan, R. S. *Lotus Among the Magnolias: The Mississippi Chinese.* Jackson University Press of Mississippi, 1982.

Quincey, Keith. *Hmong: History of a People.* Cheney: Eastern Washington University Press, 1988.

Root, Maria P. P., ed. *Racially Mixed People in America.* Newbury Park, Calif.: Sage Publications, 1992.

Roth, G. K. *Fijian Way of Life.* 2d ed. Melbourne: Oxford University Press, 1973.

Rutherford, Noel. *Friendly Islands: A History of Tonga.* Melbourne: Oxford University Press, 1977.

Rutledge, Paul James. *The Vietnamese Experience in America.* Bloomington: Indiana University Press, 1992.

Sanchez, Pedro C. *Guahan Guam: The History of Our Island.* Agana, Guam: Sanchez Publishing House, 1986.

Saniel, J. M., ed. *The Filipino Exclusion Movement.* Quezon City, Philippines: Institute of Asian Studies, University of the Philippines, 1967.

Santos, Bienvenido. *Scent of Apples.* Seattle: University of Washington Press, 1979.

Saran, Parmatma. *The Asian Indian Experience in the United States.* Cambridge, Mass.: Schenkman, 1985.

Schanberg, Sydney. *The Life and Death of Dith Pran.* New York: Penguin Books, 1985.

Shaw, Clifford R., and Henry D. McKay. *Juvenile Delinquency and Urban Areas: A Study of Rates of Delinquency in Relation to Differential Characteristics of Local Communities in American Cities.* Rev. ed. Chicago: University of Chicago Press, 1972.

Shon, Steven, and Davis Ja. "Asian Families." In *Ethnicity and Family Therapy*, by Monica McGoldrick, John Pearce, and Joseph Giordano. New York: Guilford Press, 1982.

Singh, Jane, et al. *South Asians in North America: An Annotated and Selected Bibliography.* Berkeley: Center for South and Southeast Asia Studies, University of California, Berkeley, 1988.

Skinner, G. W. *Chinese Society in Thailand: An Analytical History.* Ithaca, N.Y.: Cornell University Press, 1957.

Spence, Jonathan D. *The Search for Modern China.* New York: W. W. Norton, 1990.

Spickard, Paul R. *Mixed Blood: Intermarriage and Ethnic Identity in Twentieth-Century America.* Madison: University of Wisconsin Press, 1989.

Stannard, David E. *Before the Horror: The Population of Hawaii on the Eve of Western Contact.* Honolulu: Social Science Research Institute, University of Hawaii, 1989.

State of Asian Pacific America: A Public Policy Report, Policy Issues to the Year 2020, The. Los Angeles: LEAP Asian Pacific American Public Policy Institute and UCLA Asian American Studies Center, 1993.

Strand, Paul J., and Woodrow Jones, Jr. *Indochinese Refugees in America: Problems of Adaptation and Assimilation.* Durham, N.C.: Duke University Press, 1985.

Sue, Stanley, and James Morishima. "Understanding the Asian American Family." In *The Mental Health of Asian Americans.* San Francisco: Jossey-Bass, 1982.

Sunahara, Ann Gomer. *The Politics of Racism: The Uprooting of Japanese Canadians During the Second World War.* Toronto: Lorimer, 1981.

Sung, Betty Lee. *Mountain of Gold: The Story of the Chinese in America.* New York: Macmillan, 1967.

Sung, Betty Lee. *A Survey of Chinese American Manpower and Employment.* New York: Praeger Publishers, 1976.

Takaki, Ronald. *Strangers from a Different Shore: A History of Asian Americans.* Boston: Little, Brown, 1989.

Thomas, David, Ernest W. Lee, and Nguyen Dang Liem, eds. *Chamic Studies.* Canberra: Department of Linguistics, Research School of Pacific Studies, Australian National University, 1977.

Thompson, Laura. *Guam and Its People.* New York: Greenwood Press, 1969.

Thomson, Basil. *The Fijians: A Study of the Decay of Custom.* 1908. Reprint. London: Dawsons, 1968.

Tippett, Alan Richard. *Fijian Material Culture.* Honolulu: Bishop Museum Press, 1968.

Tremblay, Edward A. *When You Go to Tonga.* Derby, N.Y.: Daughters of St. Paul, Apostolate of the Press, 1954.

Tsai, Henry Shih-shan. *The Chinese Experience in America.* Bloomington: Indiana University Press, 1986.

U.S. Bureau of the Census. *We, the Asian and Pacific Islander Americans.* Washington, D.C.: Government Printing Office, 1980.

U.S. Congress, Office of Technology Assessment. *Current Health Status and Population Projections of Native Hawaiians Living in Hawaii.* Washington, D.C.: Government Printing Office, 1987.

U.S. Department of State. Bureau of Public Affairs. *Amerasians in Vietnam.* Washington, D.C.: Government Printing Office, 1988.

Van Peenen, Mavis Warner. *Chamorro Legends on the Island of Guam.* Agana, Guam: Micronesian Area Research Center, University of Guam, 1974.

Walker, Anthony R., ed. *Farmers in the Hills.* Penang: Universiti Sains Malaysia, 1975.

Ward, W. Peter. *White Canada Forever: Popular Attitudes and Public Policy Toward Orientals in British Columbia.* 2d ed. Montreal: McGill-Queen's University Press, 1990.

Waters, Tony, and Lawrence E. Cohen. *Laotians in the Criminal Justice System.* Berkeley, Calif.: California Policy Seminar, 1993.

Weglyn, Michi. *Years of Infamy: The Untold Story of America's Concentration Camps.* New York: William Morrow, 1976.

Whitaker, Donald P. et al. *Laos: A Country Study.* Washington D.C.: Government Printing Office, 1986.

Wickberg, Edgar. *The Chinese in Philippine Life, 1850-1898.* New Haven, Conn.: Yale University Press, 1965.

Wickberg, Edgar, ed. *From China to Canada: A History of the Chinese Communities in Canada.* Toronto: McClelland and Stewart, 1982.

Wilson, Robert A., and Bill Hosokawa. *East to America: A History of the Japanese in the*

United States. New York: William Morrow, 1980.

Winzeler, Robert. *Ethnic Relations in Kelantan*. Singapore: Oxford University Press, 1985.

Wong, Bernard P. *Chinatown: Economic Adaptation and Ethnic Identity of the Chinese*. New York: Holt, Rinehart and Winston, 1982.

Wright, Ronald. *On Fiji Islands*. New York: Viking, 1986.

Yen, Ching-Hwang. *Coolies and Mandarins: China's Protection of Overseas Chinese During the Late Ch'ing Period (1851-1911)*. Singapore: Singapore University Press, 1985.

Yu, Eui-Young, Earl Phillips, and Eun Sik Yang, eds. *Koreans in Los Angeles: Prospects and Promises*. Los Angeles: Center for Korean-American and Korean Studies, California State University, Los Angeles, 1982.

Zhou, Min. *Chinatown: The Socioeconomic Potential of an Urban Enclave*. Philadelphia: Temple University Press, 1992.

EDUCATION AND SCHOLARSHIP

Asian Women United of California, eds. *Making Waves: An Anthology of Writings By and About Asian American Women*. Boston: Beacon Press, 1989.

Backus, Karen, and Julia C. Furtaw, eds. *Asian Americans Information Directory*. Detroit: Gale Research, 1992.

Baron, Dennis. *The English-Only Question: An Official Language for Americans?* New Haven, Conn.: Yale University Press, 1990.

Caplan, Nathan, John Whitmore, and Marcella H. Choy. *The Boat People and Achievement in America: A Study of Family Life, Hard Work, and Cultural Values*. Ann Arbor: University of Michigan Press, 1989.

Carrison, Muriel P. *Cambodian Folk Stories from the Gatiloke*. Translated by Kong Chhean. Rutland, Vt.: Charles E. Tuttle, 1987.

Chin, Frank, et al., eds. *The Big Aiiieeeee! An Anthology of Chinese American and Japanese American Literature*. New York: Meridian Books, 1991.

Choy, Bong-youn. *Koreans in America*. Chicago: Nelson-Hall, 1979.

Clausen, Edwin. "The Eagle's Shadow: Chinese Nationalism and American Educational Influence, 1900-1927" and "Nationalism and Political Challenge: Chinese Students, American Education and the End of an Era." In "China and the West: Studies in Education, Nationalism, Diplomacy." Special issue of *Asian Profile* (October, 1988): 413-440.

Colangelo, Nicholas, Dick Dustin, and Cecelia H. Foxley, eds. *Multicultural Nonsexist Education: A Human Relations Approach*. 2d ed. Dubuque, Iowa: Kendall/Hunt, 1985.

Cummins, James. *Bilingualism and Minority-*

Language Children. Toronto: Ontario Institute for Studies in Education, 1981.

Davidson, Jeremy H. C. S., and Helen Cordell, eds. *The Short Story in South East Asia*. London: School of Oriental and African Studies, University of London, 1982.

Davidson, Jeremy H. C. S., R. H. Robins, and Helen Cordell, eds. *South-East Asian Linguistics: Essays in Honour of Eugenie J. A. Henderson*. London: School of Oriental and African Studies, University of London, 1989.

Gall, Susan B., and Timothy L. Gall, eds. *Statistical Record of Asian Americans*. Detroit: Gale Research, 1993.

Herbert, Patricia, and Anthony Milner, eds. *South-East Asia Languages and Literatures: A Select Guide*. Honolulu: University of Hawaii Press, 1989.

Hsu, Kai-yu, and Helen Palubinskas, eds. *Asian-American Authors*. Boston: Houghton Mifflin, 1972.

Hune, Shirley, et al., eds. *Asian Americans: Comparative and Global Perspectives*. Pullman: Washington State University Press, 1991.

Josey, E. J., and Marva L. DeLoach, eds. *Ethnic Collections in Libraries*. New York: Neal-Schuman, 1983.

Kim, Elaine H. *Asian American Literature: An Introduction to the Writings and Their Social Context*. Philadelphia: Temple University Press, 1982.

Kim, Hyung-chan. "American Influence on Korean Education." *Educational Perspectives* 21, no. 4 (Winter, 1982): 27-32.

Kung, S. W. *Chinese in American Life: Some Aspects of Their History, Status, Problems, and Contributions*. Westport, Conn.: Greenwood Press, 1962.

Lee Lai To, ed. *Early Chinese Immigrant Societies: Case Studies from North America and British Southeast Asia*. Singapore: Heinemann, 1988.

Leung, Edwin Pak-wah. "The Making of the Chinese Yankees: School Life of the Chinese Educational Mission Students in New England." "China and the West: Studies in Education, Nationalism, and Diplomacy." Special issue of *Asian Profile* 16 (October, 1988): 401-412.

Ling, Amy. *Between Worlds: Women Writers of Chinese Ancestry*. Elmsford, N.Y.: Pergamon Press, 1990.

Miller, Wayne Charles, with Faye Nell Vowell, Gary K. Crist, et al. *A Comprehensive Bibliography for the Study of American Minorities*. 2 vols. New York: New York University Press, 1976.

Nguyen, Ngoc Bich. "Can the Southeast Asian Americans Play a Leading Role in the Current Revolution in American Education?" The 13th Annual Conference on Indochinese Education and Social Services, San Francisco, April, 1992.

Nieto, Sonia. *Affirming Diversity: The Sociopolitical Context of Multicultural Education*. New York: Longman, 1992.

Nomura, Gail, et al., eds. *Frontiers of Asian American Studies*. Pullman: Washington State University Press, 1989.

Okihiro, Gary, et al., eds. *Reflections on Shattered Windows: Promises and Prospects for Asian American Studies*. Pullman: Washington State University Press, 1988.

Orleans, Leo. *Chinese Students in America: Policies, Issues, and Numbers*. Washington, D.C.: National Academy Press, 1988.

Pepper, Suzanne. *China's Education Reform in the 1980s: Policies, Issues, and History*. Berkeley: Center for Chinese Studies, 1990.

Poon, Wei Chi. *The Directory of Asian American Collections in the United States*. Berkeley: Asian American Studies Library, University of California, 1982.

Poon, Wei Chi. *A Guide for Establishing Asian American Core Collections*. Berkeley: Asian American Studies Library, University of California, 1989.

Rodríguez, Fred. *Equity in Education: Issues and Strategies*. Dubuque: Kendall/Hunt, 1990.

Saravia-Shore, Marietta, and Steven F. Arvizu, eds. *Cross-Cultural Literacy: Ethnographies of Communication in Multiethnic Classrooms*. New York: Garland, 1992.

Scarborough, Katharine T. A., ed. *Developing Library Collections for California's Emerging Majority: A Manual of Resources for Ethnic Collection Development*. Berkeley, Calif.: Bay Area Library and Information System, 1990.

Thamos, John Alsop. *Korean Students in Southern California: Factors Influencing Their Plans Toward Returning Home*. Ann Arbor: UMI, 1981.

Thernstrom, Stephen, ed. *Harvard Encyclopedia of American Ethnic Groups*. Cambridge, Mass.: The Belknap Press of Harvard University Press, 1980.

Wang, Y. C. *Chinese Intellectuals and the West, 1872-1949*. Chapel Hill: University of North Carolina Press, 1966.

Wei, William. *The Asian American Movement*. Philadelphia: Temple University Press, 1993.

EMPLOYMENT, BUSINESS, LABOR, AND THE ECONOMY

Alcantara, Ruben R. *Sakada: Filipino Adaptation in Hawaii*. Washington, D.C.: University Press of America, 1981.

Asahi Shimbun, ed. *The Pacific Rivals: A Japanese View of Japanese-American Relations*. New York: Weatherhill Asahi, 1972.

Axon, Gordon. *The California Gold Rush*. New York: Mason/Charter, 1976.

Barth, Gunther. *Bitter Strength: A History of the Chinese in the United States, 1850-1870*. Cambridge, Mass.: Harvard University Press, 1964.

Beechert, Edward D. *Working in Hawaii: A Labor History*. Ethnic Studies Oral History Project, University of Hawaii at Manoa.

Honolulu: University of Hawaii Press, 1985.

Beekman, Take, and Allan Beekman. "Hawaii's Great Japanese Strike." In *Kodomo No Tame Ni: For the Sake of the Children*, by Dennis Ogawa. Honolulu: University of Hawaii Press, 1978.

Blaker, Michael, ed. *The Politics of Trade: U.S. and Japanese Policymaking for the GATT Negotiations*. New York: Columbia University, 1978.

Broad, Robin. *Unequal Alliance: The World Bank, the International Monetary Fund, and the Philippines*. Berkeley: University of California Press, 1988.

Campbell, P. C. *Chinese Coolie Emigration to Countries Within the British Empire*. Taipei: Ch'eng Wen Publishing, 1970.

Chan, Sucheng. *Asian Americans: An Interpretive History*. Boston: Twayne, 1991.

Chan, Sucheng. *This Bittersweet Soil: The Chinese in California Agriculture, 1860-1910*. Berkeley: University of California Press, 1986.

Chinn, Thomas. *A History of the Chinese in America*. San Francisco: Chinese Historical Society 1973.

Chinn, Thomas W., H. Mark Lai, and Philip P. Choy, eds. *A History of the Chinese in California: A Syllabus*. San Francisco: Chinese Historical Society of America, 1969.

Conwell, R. H. *Why and How: Why the Chinese Emigrate and the Means They Adopt for the Purpose of Reaching America*. Boston: Lee and Shepard, 1871.

Cooper, George, and Gavan Daws. *Land and Power in Hawaii: The Democratic Years*. Honolulu: Benchmark Press, 1985.

Crouchett, Lorraine Jacobs. *Filipinos in California: From the Days of the Galleons to the Present*. El Cerrito, Calif.: Downey Place Publishing House, 1982.

Daniels, Roger. *Asian America: Chinese and Japanese in the United States Since 1850*. Seattle: University of Washington Press, 1988.

DeWitt, Howard A. *Anti-Filipino Movements in California: A History, Bibliography and Study Guide*. San Francisco: R and E Research Associates, 1976.

DeWitt, Howard A. *Images of Ethnic and Radical Violence in California Politics, 1917-1930: A Survey*. San Francisco: R and E Research Associates, 1975.

DeWitt, Howard A. *Violence in the Fields: Filipino Farm Labor Unionization During the Great Depression*. Saratoga, Calif.: Century Twenty One Publishing, 1980.

Dunn, Seamus, ed. *Managing Divided Cities*. Newbury Park, Calif.: Sage Publications, 1994.

Fugita, Stephen S., and David J. O'Brien. *Japanese American Ethnicity: The Persistence of Community*. Seattle: University of Washington Press, 1991.

Greenwald, John. "Finding Niches in a New Land." *Time* 126 (July 8, 1985): 72-73.

Greever, William. *The Bonanza West: The Story of the Western Mining Rushes, 1848-1900*. Norman: University of Oklahoma Press, 1963.

Hsiao, Michael, and Chung-Chen Lin. "Investment and Saving Pattern of Taiwanese." In *Survey Report of General Social Survey in Taiwan*. Taiwan: Academica Sinica, Institute for Social Science, 1992.

Hundley, Norris, Jr., ed. *The Asian American: The Historical Experience*. Santa Barbara, Calif.: ABC-Clio, 1976.

Inoguchi, Takashi. *Japan's International Relations*. Boulder, Colo.: Westview Press, 1991.

Inoguchi, Takashi, and Daniel I. Okimoto. *The Political Economy of Japan*. Vol. 2. Stanford, Calif.: Stanford University Press, 1988.

Ishinomori, Shotaro. *Japan, Inc.: An Introduction to Japanese Economics (The Comic Book)*. Translated by Betsey Scheiner. Berkeley: University of California Press, 1988.

Iwata, Masakazu. *Planted in Good Soil: A History of the Issei in United States Agriculture*. Vols. 1 and 2. New York: Peter Lang, 1992.

Kent, Noel. *Hawaii: Islands Under the Influence*. New York: Monthly Review Press, 1983.

Kim, Illsoo. *New Urban Immigrants: The Korean Community in New York*. Princeton, N.J.: Princeton University Press, 1981.

Kushner, Sam. *Long Road to Delano*. New York: International Publishers, 1975.

Lee, Rose Hum. *The Chinese in the United States of America*. Hong Kong: Hong Kong University Press, 1960.

Leung, Peter C. Y. *One Day, One Dollar: Locke, California, and the Chinese Farming Experience in the Sacramento Delta*. Edited by L. Eve Armentrout Ma. El Cerrito, Calif.: Chinese/Chinese American History Project, 1984.

Light, Ivan. *Ethnic Enterprise in America*. Berkeley: University of California Press, 1972.

Light, Ivan, and Edna Bonacich. *Immigrant Entrepreneurs: Koreans in Los Angeles, 1965-1982*. Berkeley: University of California Press, 1988.

Lincoln, Edward J. *Japan's Unequal Trade*. Washington, D.C.: Brookings Institution, 1990.

Loewen, James W. *The Mississippi Chinese: Between Black and White*. 2d ed. Prospect Heights, Ill.: Waveland Press, 1988.

Lydon, Sandy. *Chinese Gold: The Chinese in the Monterey Bay Region*. Capitola, Calif.: Capitola Book Company, 1985.

Ma, L. Eve Armentrout. "The Big Business Ventures of Chinese in North America, 1850-1930." In *The Chinese American Experience: Papers from the Second National Conference on Chinese American Studies*, edited by Genny Lim. San Francisco; Chinese Historical Society of America and Chinese Culture Foundation of San Francisco, 1982.

McCunn, Ruthanne Lum. *An Illustrated History of the Chinese in America*. San Francisco: Design Enterprises of San Francisco, 1979.

MacNair, H. F. *The Chinese Abroad, Their Position and Protection: A Study in International Law and Relations*. Taipei: Ch'eng Wen Publishing, 1971.

Mandel, Michael J., and Christopher Farrell. "The Immigrants: How They're Revitalizing the U.S. Economy." *Business Week*, no. 3274 (July 13, 1992): 116-122.

Manlapit, Pablo. *Filipinos Fight for Justice: Case of the Filipino Laborers in the Big Strike of 1924*. Honolulu: Kumalee Publishing, 1933.

Melendy, H. Brett. *Asians in America: Filipinos, Koreans and East Indians*. Boston: Twayne, 1977.

Min, Pyong Gap. *Ethnic Business Enterprise: Korean Small Business in Atlanta*. New York: Center for Migration Studies, 1988.

1924 Filipino Strike on Kauai, The. Manoa: Ethnic Studies Program, University of Hawaii, Manoa, 1979.

Okamura, Jonathan Y., et al., eds. *The Filipino American Experience in Hawaii*. Social Process in Hawaii, vol. 33. Manoa: Department of Sociology, University of Hawaii, Manoa, 1991.

Papademetriou, Demetrios G., and Mark J. Miller, eds. *The Unavoidable Issue: U.S. Immigration Policy in the 1980's*. Philadelphia: Institute for the Study of Human Issues, 1983.

Quan, R. S. *Lotus Among the Magnolias: The Mississippi Chinese*. Jackson University Press of Mississippi, 1982.

Saxton, Alexander. *The Indispensable Enemy: Labor and the Anti-Chinese Movement in California*. Berkeley: University of California Press, 1971.

Scharlin, Craig, and Lillia Villanueva. *Philip Vera Cruz: A Personal History of Filipino Immigrants and the Farmworkers Movement*. Edited by Glenn Omatsu and Augusto Espiritu. Los Angeles: UCLA Labor Center Institute of Industrial Relations and UCLA Asian American Studies Center, 1992.

Seward, George. *Chinese Immigrants: Its Social and Economic Aspects*. New York: Arno Press, 1970.

Shutt, Harry. *The Myth of Free Trade: Patterns of Protectionism Since 1945*. New York: Blackwell, 1985.

Siu, Paul. *The Chinese Laundryman: A Study in Social Isolation*. New York: New York University Press, 1987. Edited by John Tchen.

Smith, Jared G. *The Big Five*. Honolulu: Advertiser Publishing, 1942.

Soga, Keiho. *Gojunenkan No Hawai Kaiko*. Honolulu: Kankokai, 1953.

Sung, Betty L. *Mountain of Gold*. New York: Macmillan, 1967.

Sung, Betty Lee. *A Survey of Chinese American Manpower and Employment*. New York: Praeger Publishers, 1976.

Takaki, Ronald T. *Iron Cages: Race and Cul-*

ture in Nineteenth Century America. New York: Alfred A. Knopf, 1979.

Takaki, Ronald. *Strangers from a Different Shore: A History of Asian Americans*. Boston: Little, Brown, 1989.

U.S. Immigration and Naturalization Service. *Guide to Immigration Benefits*. Rev. ed. Washington, D.C.: Government Printing Office, 1982.

Van Wolferen, Karl. *The Enigma of Japanese Power*. New York: Alfred A. Knopf, 1989.

Vogel, Ezra. *Japan As Number One: Lessons for America*. New York: Harper Colophon, 1979.

Wakukawa, Ernest Katsumi. *A History of the Japanese People in Hawaii*. Honolulu: The Toyo Shoin, 1938.

Yamamura, Kozo, ed. *Policy and Trade Issues of the Japanese Economy*. Seattle: University of Washington Press, 1982.

Yen, Ching-Hwang. *Coolies and Mandarins: China's Protection of Overseas Chinese During the Late Ch'ing Period (1851-1911)*. Singapore: Singapore University Press, 1985.

Young, Philip K. Y. "Family Labor, Sacrifice, and Competition: Korean Greengrocers in New York City." *Amerasia Journal* 10 (Fall/Winter, 1983): 53-71.

IMMIGRATION

Adachi, Ken. *The Enemy That Never Was: A History of the Japanese Canadians*. Toronto: McClelland and Stewart, 1991.

Anderson, Kay J. *Vancouver's Chinatown: Racial Discourse in Canada, 1875-1980*. Montreal: McGill-Queen's University Press, 1991.

Asian Women United of California, ed. *Making Waves: An Anthology By and About Asian American Women*. Boston: Beacon Press, 1989.

Bagai, Leona B. *The East Indians and the Pakistanis in America*. Rev. ed. Minneapolis: Lerner, 1972.

Baker, Susan Gonzalez. *The Cautious Welcome: The Legalization Programs of the Immigration Reform and Control Act*. Santa Monica, Calif.: RAND, 1990.

Barkan, Elliott Robert. *Asian and Pacific Islander Migration to the United States: A Model of New Global Patterns*. Westport, Conn.: Greenwood Press, 1992.

Barrier, N. Gerald, and Verne A. Dusenbery. *The Sikh Diaspora: Migration and the Experience Beyond Punjab*. Columbia, Mo.: South Asia Publications, 1989.

Barringer, Herbert R., Robert W. Gardner, and Michael J. Levin. *Asians and Pacific Islanders in the United States*. National Committee for Research on the 1980 Census.

Barth, Gunther. *Bitter Strength: A History of the Chinese in the United States, 1850-1870*. Cambridge, Mass.: Harvard University Press, 1964.

Bean, Frank D., Georges Vernez, and Charles B. Keely. *Opening and Closing the Doors: Evaluating Immigration Reform and Control*. Santa Monica, Calif.: RAND, 1989.

Beechert, Edward D. *Working in Hawaii: A Labor History*. Honolulu: University of Hawaii Press, 1985.

Broadfoot, Barry. *Years of Sorrow, Years of Shame: The Story of Japanese Canadians in World War II*. Garden City, N.Y.: Doubleday, 1977.

Buaken, Manuel. *I Have Lived with the American People*. Caldwell, Idaho: Caxton Printers, 1948.

Buchignani, Norman, Doreen M. Indra, and Ram Srivastiva. *Continuous Journey: A Social History of South Asians in Canada*. Toronto, Ontario, Canada: McClelland and Stewart in association with Dept. of the Secretary of State and the Govt. Pub. Centre, Supply and Services, Canada, 1985.

Bulosan, Carlos. *America Is in the Heart*. Seattle: University of Washington Press, 1946.

Calavita, Kitty. *Inside the State: The Bracero Program, Immigration, and the I.N.S.* New York: Routledge, 1992.

Caplan, Nathan, John K. Whitmore, and Marcella H. Choy. *The Boat People and Achievement in America: Family Life, Hard Work, and Cultural Values*. Ann Arbor: University of Michigan Press, 1989.

Carino, B. V., J. T. Fawcett, R. W. Gardner, and F. Arnold. *The New Filipino Immigrants to the United States: Increasing Diversity and Change*. Papers of the East-West Population Institute, No. 115. Honolulu: East-West Center, 1990.

Chadney, James G. *The Sikhs of Vancouver*. New York: AMS Press, 1984.

Chan, Sucheng. *Asian Americans: An Interpretive History*. Boston: Twayne Publishers, 1991.

Chantavanich, Supang, and E. Bruce Reynolds, eds. *Indochinese Refugees: Asylum and Resettlement*. Bangkok: Institute of Asian Studies, Chulalongkorn University, 1988.

Chen, Jack. *The Chinese of America: From the Beginnings to the Present*. New York: Harper and Row/San Francisco, 1980.

Chen, Ta. *Emigrant Communities in South China*. Edited by Bruno Lasker. New York: Institute of Pacific Relations, 1940.

Cheng, Lucie, and Edna Bonacich, eds. *Labor Immigration Under Capitalism: Asian Workers in the United States Before World War II*. Berkeley: University of California Press, 1984.

Chew, Sock Foon. *Ethnicity and Nationality in Singapore*. Athens: Ohio University Center for International Studies, 1987.

Chinn, Thomas W., Him Mark Lai, and Philip P. Choy, eds. *A History of the Chinese in California: A Syllabus*. San Francisco: Chinese Historical Society of America, 1969.

Chiu, Ping. *Chinese Labor in California, 1850-1880: An Economic Study*. Madison, Wis.: State Historical Society of Wisconsin, 1963.

Choy, Bong-youn. *Koreans in America*. Chicago: Nelson-Hall, 1979.

Chuman, Frank F. *The Bamboo People: The Law and Japanese-Americans*. Del Mar, California: Publisher's Inc., 1976.

Clarke, Colin, Ceri Peach, and Steven Vertovec, eds. *South Asians Overseas: Migration and Ethnicity*. New York: Cambridge University Press, 1990.

Conroy, Hilary, and T. Scott Miyakawa, eds. *East Across the Pacific: Historical and Sociological Studies of Japanese Immigration and Assimilation*. Santa Barbara, Calif.: Clio Press, 1972.

Coolidge, Mary R. *Chinese Immigration*. New York: Henry Holt, 1909.

Cordova, Fred. *Filipinos: Forgotten Asian Americans*. Dubuque, Iowa: Kendall/Hunt, 1983.

Cose, Ellis. *A Nation of Strangers: Prejudice, Politics, and the Populating of America*. New York: William Morrow, 1992.

Daniels, Roger. *Asian America: Chinese and Japanese in the United States Since 1850*. Seattle: University of Washington Press, 1988.

Daniels, Roger. *The Politics of Prejudice: The Anti-Japanese Movement in California and the Struggle for Japanese Exclusion*. 1962. 2d ed. Berkeley: University of California Press, 1978.

Daniels, Roger, Sandra C. Taylor, and Harry H. L. Kitano, eds. *Japanese Americans: From Relocation to Redress*. Rev. ed. Seattle: University of Washington Press, 1991.

Davis, Leonard. *Hong Kong and the Asylum-Seekers from Vietnam*. Basingstoke: Macmillan, 1991.

Dionisio, Juan C., ed. *Filipinos in Hawaii . . . the First 75 Years*. Honolulu: Hawaii Filipino News Specialty Publications, 1981.

Divine, Robert A. *American Immigration Policy, 1924-1952*. New Haven, Conn.: Yale University Press, 1957.

Dorita, Sister Mary. *Filipino Immigration to Hawaii*. Master's thesis, University of Hawaii, 1954. San Francisco: R and E Research Associates, 1975.

Ehrlich, Paul R., Loy Bilderback, and Anne H. Ehrlich. *The Golden Door: International Migration, Mexico, and the United States*. New York: Ballantine Books, 1979.

Espiritu, Yen Le. *Asian American Panethnicity: Bridging Institutions and Identities*. Philadelphia: Temple University Press, 1992.

Ethnic Studies Oral History Project. *Uchinanchu: A History of Okinawans in Hawaii*. Honolulu: Ethnic Studies Program, University of Hawaii at Manoa, 1981.

Fawcett, James T., and Benjamin V. Carino, eds. *Pacific Bridges: The New Immigration from Asia and the Pacific Islands*. Staten Island, N.Y.: Center for Migration Studies of New York, 1987.

Fitzgerald, Stephen. *China and the Overseas Chinese*. Cambridge: Cambridge University Press, 1972.

Fuchs, Lawrence H. *The American Kaleidoscope: Race, Ethnicity, and the Civic Culture*. Hanover, N. H.: Wesleyan University Press, 1990.

Gibson, Margaret A. *Accommodation Without Assimilation: Sikh Immigrants in an American High School*. Ithaca, N.Y.: Cornell University Press, 1988.

Glazer, Nathan, ed. *Clamor at the Gates: The New American Immigration*. San Francisco: ICS Press, 1985.

Glick, Clarence E. *Sojourners and Settlers: Chinese Migrants in Hawaii*. Honolulu: University Press of Hawaii, 1980.

Grant, Bruce. *The Boat People: An "AGE" Investigation*. Harmondsworth, Middlesex, England: Penguin Books, 1979.

Gregory, Robert G. *South Asians in East Africa: An Economic and Social History, 1890-1980*. Boulder, Colo.: Westview Press, 1993.

Gupte, Pranay. *The Crowded Earth: People and the Politics of Population*. New York: W. W. Norton, 1984.

Haines, David W., ed. *Refugees as Immigrants: Cambodians, Laotians, and Vietnamese in America*. Totowa, N.J.: Rowman & Littlefield, 1989.

Haines, David W., ed. *Refugees in the United States: A Reference Handbook*. Westport, Conn.: Greenwood Press, 1985.

Hawthorne, Lesleyanne, ed. *Refugee: The Vietnamese Experience*. New York: Oxford University Press, 1982.

Hazama, Dorothy O., and Jane O. Komeiji. *Okage Sama De: The Japanese in Hawaii, 1885-1985*. Honolulu: Bess Press, 1986.

Helweg, Arthur W., and Usha M. Helweg. *An Immigrant Success Story: East Indians in America*. Philadelphia: University of Pennsylvania Press, 1990.

Herman, Masako. *The Japanese in America: 1843-1973*. Dobbs Ferry, N.Y.: Oceana Publications, 1974.

Higham, John. *Strangers in the Land: Patterns of American Nativism, 1860-1925*. New Brunswick, N.J.: Rutgers University Press, 1955.

Hing, Bill Ong. *Making and Remaking Asian America Through Immigration Policy, 1850-1990*. Stanford, Calif.: Stanford University Press, 1993.

Hutchinson, Edward P. *Legislative History of American Immigration Policy, 1798-1965*. Philadelphia: University of Pennsylvania Press, 1981.

Ichioka, Yuji. *The Issei: The World of the First Generation Japanese Immigrants, 1885-1924*. New York: Free Press, 1988.

Immigration and Nationality Act. Washington, D.C.: Government Printing Office, 1980.

Jain, Usha R. *The Gujaratis of San Francisco*. New York: AMS Press, 1989.

Jensen, Joan M. *Passage from India: Asian Indian Immigrants in North America*. New Haven, Conn.: Yale University Press, 1988.

Johnston, Hugh J. M. *The East Indians in Canada*. Ottawa, Ontario, Canada: Canadian Historical Association, 1984.

Jones, Maldwyn Allen. *American Immigration*. 2d ed. Chicago: University of Chicago Press, 1992.

Joy, Annamma. *Ethnicity in Canada: Social Accommodation and Cultural Persistence Among the Sikhs and the Portuguese*. New York: AMS Press, 1989.

Kanungo, Rabindra N., ed. *South Asians in the Canadian Mosaic*. Montreal, Quebec, Canada: Kala Bharati, 1984.

Kim, Illsoo. *New Urban Immigrants: The Korean Community in New York*. Princeton, N.J.: Princeton University Press, 1981.

Kimura, Yukiko. *Issei: Japanese Immigrants in Hawaii*. Honolulu: University of Hawaii Press, 1988.

Kitano, Harry H. L. *Japanese Americans: The Evolution of a Subculture*. 2d ed. Englewood Cliffs, N.J.: Prentice-Hall, 1976.

Kogawa, Joy. *Obasan*. Boston: David R. Godine, 1981.

Koo, Hagen, and Eui-Young Yu. *Korean Immigration to the United States: Its Demographic Pattern and Social Implications for Both Societies*. Papers of the East-West Population Institute 74, Honolulu: East-West Center, 1981.

Kotkin, Joel. *Tribes: How Race, Religion, and Identity Determine Success in the New Global Economy*. New York: Random House, 1993.

Kung, S. W. *Chinese in American Life: Some Aspects of Their History, Status, Problems, and Contributions*. Seattle: University of Washington Press, 1962.

La Brack, Bruce. *The Sikhs of Northern California, 1904-1975*. New York: AMS Press, 1988.

Lai, Chuenyan David. *Chinatowns: Towns Within Cities in Canada*. Vancouver: University of British Columbia Press, 1988.

Lai, Him Mark, Genny Lim, and Judy Yung. *Island: Poetry and History of Chinese Immigrants on Angel Island, 1910-1940*. 1980. Reprint. Seattle: University of Washington Press, 1991.

Lasker, Bruno. *Filipino Immigration to Continental United States and to Hawaii*. Chicago: University of Chicago Press for the American Council, Institute of Pacific Relations, 1931.

Lee, Rose Hum. *The Chinese in the United States of America*. Hong Kong: Hong Kong University Press, 1960.

Lee Lai To, ed. *Early Chinese Immigrant Societies: Case Studies from North America and British Southeast Asia*. Singapore: Heinemann, 1988.

Leonard, Karen Isaksen. *Making Ethnic Choices: California's Punjabi Mexican Americans*. Philadelphia: Temple University Press, 1992.

Li, Peter S. *The Chinese in Canada*. Toronto: Oxford University Press, 1988.

Light, Ivan, and Edna Bonacich. *Immigrant Entrepreneurs: Koreans in Los Angeles, 1965-1982* Berkeley: University of California Press, 1988.

Lorch, Donatella. "Between Two Worlds: New York's Bangladeshis." *New York Times*, October 10, 1991.

Lorch, Donatella. "An Ethnic Road to Riches: The Immigrant Job Specialty." *New York Times*, January 12, 1992.

Lum, Arlene, ed. *Sailing for the Sun: The Chinese in Hawaii 1789-1989*. Honolulu: Three Heroes, 1989.

Mackie, J. A. C., ed. *The Chinese in Indonesia*. Honolulu: University Press of Hawaii, 1976.

MacNair, H. F. *The Chinese Abroad, Their Position and Protection*. Shanghai, China: Commercial Press, 1924.

McWilliams, Carey. *Brothers Under the Skin*. Rev. ed. Boston: Little, Brown, 1964.

Malik, Iftikhar Haider. *Pakistanis in Michigan: A Study of Third Culture and Acculturation*. New York: AMS Press, 1989.

Mark, Diane M. L., and Ginger Chih. *A Place Called Chinese America*. Washington, D.C.: Organization of Chinese Americans, 1982.

Melendy, H. Brett. *Asians in America: Filipinos, Koreans, and East Indians*. New York: Hippocrene, 1981.

Migration and Modernization: The Indian Diaspora in Comparative Perspective. Williamsburg, Va.: Department of Anthropology, College of William and Mary, 1987.

Miller, Stuart C. *The Unwelcome Immigrant: The American Image of the Chinese, 1752-1882*. Berkeley: University of California Press, 1969.

Miyamoto, S. Frank. *Social Solidarity Among the Japanese in Seattle*. Seattle: University of Washington Press, 1939.

Moriyama, Alan Takeo. *Imingaisha: Japanese Emigration Companies and Hawaii, 1894-1908*. Honolulu: University of Hawaii Press, 1985.

Namias, June. *First Generation: In the Words of Twentieth-Century American Immigrants*. Rev. ed. Urbana: University of Illinois Press, 1992.

Nee, Victor, and Brett Nee. *Longtime Californ': A Documentary Study of An American Chinatown*. New York: Pantheon Books, 1973.

O'Brien, David J., and Stephen S. Fugita. *The Japanese American Experience*. Bloomington: Indiana University Press, 1991.

Ogawa, Dennis M. *Kodomo No Tame Ni: For the Sake of the Children, the Japanese American Experience in Hawaii*. Honolulu: University of Hawaii Press, 1978.

Okihiro, Gary Y. *Cane Fires: The Anti-Japanese Movement in Hawaii, 1865-1945*. Philadelphia: Temple University Press, 1991.

Orleans, Leo. *Chinese Students in America: Policies, Issues, and Numbers*. Washington, D.C.: National Academy Press, 1988.

Overseas Chinese Affairs Commission, the Republic of China. *We Always Stay Together: A Report on Overseas Chinese Affairs*. Taipei, Taiwan: Overseas Chinese Affairs Commission, 1991.

Papademetriou, Demetrios G., and Mark J. Miller, eds. *The Unavoidable Issue: U.S. Immigration Policy in the 1980's*. Philadelphia: Institute for the Study of Human Issues, 1983.

Park, Insook Han, James T. Fawcett, Fred Arnold, and Robert W. Gardner. *Korean Immigrants and U.S. Immigration Policy: A Predeparture Perspective.* Papers of the East-West Population Institute 114. Honolulu: East-West Center, 1990.

Patterson, Wayne. *The Korean Frontier in America: Immigration to Hawaii, 1896-1910.* Honolulu: University of Hawaii Press, 1988.

Pido, Antonio J. A. *The Filipinos in America.* New York: Center for Migration Studies, 1986.

Quinsaat, Jesse. *Letters in Exile.* Los Angeles: UCLA Asian American Studies Center, 1976.

Ramcharan, Subhas. *Racism: Nonwhites in Canada.* Toronto, Ontario, Canada: Butterworths, 1982.

Reimers, David M. *Still the Golden Door: The Third World Comes to America.* New York: Columbia University Press, 1985.

Riggs, Frederick Warren. *Pressures on Congress: A Study of the Repeal of Chinese Exclusion.* New York: King's Crown Press, 1950.

Rogge, John R., ed. *Refugees: A Third World Dilemma.* Totowa, N.J.: Rowman & Littlefield, 1987.

Rolph, Elizabeth S. *Immigration Policies: Legacy from the 1980s and Issues for the 1990s.* Santa Monica, Calif.: RAND, 1992.

St. Cartmail, Robert Keith. *Exodus Indochina.* Auckland, New Zealand: Heinemann, 1983.

Sandmeyer, Elmer C. *The Anti-Chinese Movement in California.* Urbana: University of Illinois Press, 1939.

Saniel, J. M., ed. *The Filipino Exclusion Movement.* Quezon City, Philippines: Institute of Asian Studies, University of the Philippines, 1967.

Santos, Bienvenido. *Scent of Apples.* Seattle: University of Washington Press, 1979.

Saran, Parmatma, and Edwin Eames, eds. *The New Ethnics: Asian Indians in the United States.* New York: Praeger, 1980.

Saxton, Alexander. *The Indispensable Enemy: Labor and the Anti-Chinese Movement in California.* Berkeley: University of California Press, 1971.

Sheffer, Gabriel, ed. *Modern Diasporas in International Politics.* New York: St. Martin's Press, 1986.

Skinner, G. W. *Chinese Society in Thailand: An Analytical History.* Ithaca, N.Y.: Cornell University Press, 1957.

State of Asian Pacific America: A Public Policy Report, Policy Issues to the Year 2020, The. Los Angeles: LEAP Asian Pacific American Public Policy Institute and UCLA Asian American Studies Center, 1993.

Sunahara, Ann Gomer. *The Politics of Racism: The Uprooting of Japanese Canadians During the Second World War.* Toronto: Lorimer, 1981.

Sung, Betty Lee. *Mountain of Gold: The Story of the Chinese in America.* New York: Macmillan, 1967.

Takaki, Ronald. *Strangers from a Different Shore: A History of Asian Americans.* New York: Penguin Books, 1990.

Thamos, John Alsop. *Korean Students in Southern California: Factors Influencing Their Plans Toward Returning Home.* Ann Arbor: UMI, 1981.

Tinker, Hugh. *The Banyan Tree: Overseas Emigrants from India, Pakistan, and Bangladesh.* New York: Oxford University Press, 1977.

Tinker, Hugh. *A New System of Slavery: The Export of Indian Labour Overseas, 1830-1920.* New York: Oxford University Press, 1974.

Tsai, Henry Shih-shan. *The Chinese Experience in America.* Bloomington: Indiana University Press, 1986.

U.S. Immigration and Naturalization Service. *Guide to Immigration Benefits.* Rev. ed. Washington, D.C.: Government Printing Office, 1982.

Ward, W. Peter. *White Canada Forever: Popular Attitudes and Public Policy Toward Orientals in British Columbia.* 2d ed. Montreal: McGill-Queen's University Press, 1990.

Wickberg, Edgar. *The Chinese in Philippine Life, 1850-1898.* New Haven, Conn.: Yale University Press, 1965.

Wickberg, Edgar, ed. *From China to Canada: A History of the Chinese Communities in Canada.* Toronto: McClelland and Stewart, 1982.

Wilson, Robert A., and Bill Hosokawa. *East to America: A History of the Japanese in the United States.* New York: William Morrow, 1980.

Winzeler, Robert. *Ethnic Relations in Kelantan.* Singapore: Oxford University Press, 1985.

Yen, Ching-Hwang. *Coolies and Mandarins: China's Protection of Overseas Chinese During the Late Ch'ing Period (1851-1911).* Singapore: Singapore University Press, 1985.

Yoon, In-Jin. *The Social Origins of Korean Immigration to the United States from 1965 to the Present.* Papers of the East-West Population Institute 121, Honolulu: East-West Center, 1993.

Yu, Eui-Young, and Earl H. Phillips, eds. *Korean Women in Transition: At Home and Abroad.* Los Angeles: Center for Korean-American and Korean Studies, California State University, Los Angeles, 1987.

LANGUAGE AND LANGUAGES

Baron, Dennis. *The English-Only Question: An Official Language for Americans?* New Haven, Conn.: Yale University Press, 1990.

Benedict, Paul. *Austro-Thai Language and Culture.* New Haven, Conn.: HRAF Press, 1975.

Bhatia, Tej K. *A History of the Hindi Grammatical Tradition.* Leiden, The Netherlands: E. J. Brill, 1987.

Bickerton, Derek. *Roots of Language.* Ann Arbor: Karoma Publishers, 1981.

Carr, Elizabeth Ball. *Da Kine Talk: From Pidgin to Standard English in Hawaii.* Honolulu: University of Hawaii Press, 1972.

Carrison, Muriel P. *Cambodian Folk Stories from the Gatiloke.* Translated by Kong Chhean. Rutland, Vt.: Charles E. Tuttle, 1987.

Chao, Yuen Ren. *A Grammar of Spoken Chinese.* Berkeley: University of California Press, 1968.

Colangelo, Nicholas, Dick Dustin, and Cecelia H. Foxley, eds. *Multicultural Nonsexist Education: A Human Relations Approach.* 2d ed. Dubuque, Iowa: Kendall/Hunt, 1985.

Comrie, Bernard, ed. *The World's Major Languages.* New York: Oxford University Press, 1987.

Cummins, James. *Bilingualism and Minority-Language Children.* Toronto: Ontario Institute for Studies in Education, 1981.

Davidson, Jeremy H. C. S., and Helen Cordell, eds. *The Short Story in South East Asia.* London: School of Oriental and African Studies, University of London, 1982.

Davidson, Jeremy H. C. S., R. H. Robins, and Helen Cordell, eds. *South-East Asian Linguistics: Essays in Honour of Eugenie J. A. Henderson.* London: School of Oriental and African Studies, University of London, 1989.

DeFrancis, John. *The Chinese Language: Fact and Fantasy.* Honolulu: University of Hawaii Press, 1984.

Forrest, R. A. D. *The Chinese Language.* 2d rev. ed. London: Faber & Faber, 1965.

Greenberg, Joseph H. *Anthropological Linguistics: An Introduction.* New York: Random House, 1968.

Haradda, Tetsuo. *Outlines of Modern Japanese Linguistics.* Tokyo: Nihon University/Tateshina Publishing, 1966.

Hart, Donn, ed. *Philippine Studies: Political Science, Economics, and Linguistics.* De Kalb: Northern Illinois University, Center for Southeast Asian Studies, 1981.

Herbert, Patricia, and Anthony Milner, eds. *South-East Asia Languages and Literatures: A Select Guide.* Honolulu: University of Hawaii Press, 1989.

Hoji, Jajime, ed. *Japanese/Korean Linguistics,* Stanford, Calif.: Center for the Study of Language and Information, 1990.

Huffman, Franklin. *Bibliography and Index of Mainland Southeast Asian Languages and Linguistics.* New Haven, Conn.: Yale University Press, 1986.

Hymes, Dell, ed. *Pidginization and Creolization of Languages.* Cambridge, England: Cambridge University Press, 1971.

Kindaichi, Haruhiko. *The Japanese Language.* Translated by Umeyo Hirano. Rutland, Vt.: Charles E. Tuttle, 1978.

Korean National Commission for UNESCO,

ed. *The Korean Language*. Seoul: Si-sa-yong-o-sa, 1983.

Kratochvil, Paul. *The Chinese Language Today*. London: Hutchinson University Library, 1968.

Lao-tzu. *The Way of Lao Tzu*. Translated by Wing-tsit Chan. Indianapolis, Ind.: Bobbs-Merrill, 1963.

LeBar, Frank, ed. *Ethnic Groups of Insular Southeast Asia*. Vol. 1. New Haven, Conn.: HRAF Press, 1972.

LeBar, Frank, et al. *Ethnic Groups of Mainland Southeast Asia*. New Haven, Conn.: HRAF Press, 1964.

McFarland, Curtis, comp. *A Linguistic Atlas of the Philippines*. Tokyo: Institute for the Study of Languages and Cultures of Asia and Africa, 1980.

Martin, Samuel E. *Korean in a Hurry: A Quick Approach to Spoken Korean*. Rutland, Vt.: Charles E. Tuttle, 1954.

Martin, Samuel E., and Young-Sook C. Lee. *Beginning Korean*. 1969. Reprint. Rutland, Vt.: Charles E. Tuttle, 1986.

Masica, Colin. *The Indo-Aryan Languages*. Cambridge, England: Cambridge University Press, 1991.

Miller, Roy Andrew. *The Japanese Language*. Chicago: University of Chicago Press, 1967.

Nagara, Susumu. *Japanese Pidgin English in Hawaii: A Bilingual Description*. Honolulu: University of Hawaii Press, 1972.

Norman, Jerry. *Chinese*. New York: Cambridge University Press, 1988.

Okutsu, Keichiro, and Akio Tanaka. *Invitation to the Japanese Language*. Tokyo: Bonjinsha, 1989.

Peacock, James. *Indonesia: An Anthropological Perspective*. Pacific Palisades, Calif.: Goodyear Publishing, 1973.

Provencher, Ronald. *Mainland Southeast Asia: An Anthropological Perspective*. Pacific Palisades, Calif.: Goodyear Publishing, 1975.

Ramos, Teresita. *Tagalog Structures*. Honolulu: University of Hawaii Press, 1971.

Ramsey, S. Robert. *The Languages of China*. Princeton, N.J.: Princeton University Press, 1987.

Saravia-Shore, Marietta, and Steven F. Arvizu, eds. *Cross-Cultural Literacy: Ethnographies of Communication in Multiethnic Classrooms*. New York: Garland, 1992.

Schachter, Paul, and Fe T. Otanes. *Tagalog Reference Grammar*. Berkeley: University of California Press, 1972.

Smalley, William A. *Mother of Writing: The Origin and Development of a Hmong Messianic Script*. Chicago: University of Chicago Press, 1990.

Spencer, Mary L., ed. *Chamorro Language Issues and Research on Guam: A Book of Readings*. Mangilao, Guam: University of Guam Press, 1987.

Sugawara, Makoto. *Nihongo: A Japanese Approach to Japanese*. Tokyo: The East Publications, 1985.

Suzuki, Takao. *Japanese and the Japanese: Words in Culture*. Translated by Akira Miura. Tokyo: Kodansha International, 1978.

Voegelin, C. F., and F. M. Voegelin. *Classification and Index of the World's Languages*. New York: Elsevier, 1977.

Zograph, G. A. *Languages of South Asia: A Guide*. London: Routledge & Kegan Paul, 1982.

ORGANIZATIONS

Alcantara, Ruben. *Sakada: Filipino Adaptation in Hawaii*, pp. 57-59, 146-151. Washington, D.C.: University Press of America, 1981.

Ave, Mario. *Characteristics of Filipino Social Organizations in Los Angeles*. Master's thesis, University of Southern California, 1956. San Francisco: R and E Research Associates, 1974.

Chan, Sucheng. *Asian Americans: An Interpretive History*. Boston: Twayne, 1991.

Chen, Jack. *The Chinese of America*. San Francisco: Harper & Row, 1980.

Crouchett, Lorraine Jacobs. *Filipinos in California: From the Days of the Galleons to the Present*. El Cerrito, Calif.: Downey Place Publishing House, 1982.

Daniels, Roger. *Asian America: Chinese and Japanese in the United States Since 1850*. Seattle: University of Washington Press, 1988.

Daniels, Roger, Sandra C. Taylor, and Harry H. L. Kitano, eds. *Japanese Americans: From Relocation to Redress*. Rev. ed. Seattle: University of Washington Press, 1991.

DeWitt, Howard A. *Anti-Filipino Movements in California: A History, Bibliography and Study Guide*. San Francisco: R and E Research Associates, 1976.

DeWitt, Howard A. *Images of Ethnic and Radical Violence in California Politics, 1917-1930: A Survey*. San Francisco: R and E Research Associates, 1975.

DeWitt, Howard A. *Violence in the Fields: Filipino Farm Labor Unionization During the Great Depression*. Saratoga, Calif.: Century Twenty One Publishing, 1980.

Ethnic Studies Oral History Project. *Uchinanchu: A History of Okinawans in Hawaii*. Honolulu: Ethnic Studies Program, University of Hawaii at Manoa, 1981.

Freedman, Maurice. *Chinese Lineage and Society: Fukien and Kwangtung*. New York: Humanities Press, 1966.

Fugita, Stephen S., and David J. O'Brien. *Japanese American Ethnicity: The Persistence of Community*. Seattle: University of Washington Press, 1991.

Hosokawa, Bill. *JACL in Quest of Justice*. New York: William Morrow, 1982.

Hoy, William. *The Chinese Six Companies*. San Francisco: Chinese Consolidated Benevolent Association, 1942.

Ichioka, Yuji. *The Issei: The World of the First Generation Japanese Immigrants, 1885-1924*. New York: Free Press, 1988.

Iwata, Masakazu. *Planted in Good Soil: A History of the Issei in United States Agriculture*. Vols. 1 and 2. New York: Peter Lang, 1992.

Kitano, Harry H. L. *Japanese Americans: The Evolution of a Subculture*. 2d ed. Englewood Cliffs, N.J.: Prentice-Hall, 1976.

Lai, Him Mark. "Historical Development of the Chinese Consolidated Benevolent Association/Huiguan System." In *Chinese America: History and Perspectives, 1987*, edited by the Publication Committee, pp. 13-51. San Francisco: Chinese Historical Society of America, 1987.

Lyman, Stanford. *Chinese Americans*. New York: Random House, 1974.

Masaoka, Mike, and Bill Hosokawa. *They Call Me Moses Masaoka*. New York: William Morrow, 1987.

Melendy, H. Brett. *Asians in America: Filipinos, Koreans and East Indians*. Boston: Twayne, 1977.

Miyamoto, S. Frank. *Social Solidarity Among the Japanese in Seattle*. Seattle: University of Washington Press, 1939.

Nee, Victor G., and Brett de Bary. *Longtime Californ': A Documentary Study of an American Chinatown*. New York: Pantheon Books, 1973.

O'Brien, David J., and Stephen S. Fugita. *The Japanese American Experience*. Bloomington: Indiana University Press, 1991.

Sung, Betty Lee. *Mountain of Gold: The Story of the Chinese in America*. New York: Macmillan, 1967.

Tsai, Shih-shan Henry. *The Chinese Experience in America*. Bloomington: Indiana University Press, 1986.

Yee, Min. "Chinatown in Crisis." *Newsweek* 75 (February 23, 1970): 57-58.

POLITICS, GOVERNMENT, COMMUNITY LEADERSHIP, LAW, AND THE MILITARY

Adams, Ansel. *Manzanar*. With photographs by Ansel Adams and commentary by John Hersey. Compiled by John Armor and Peter Wright. New York: Times Books, 1988.

Adams, Nina S., and Alfred W. McCoy, eds. *Laos: War and Revolution*. New York: Harper & Row, 1970.

Agoncillo, Teodoro. *Introduction to Filipino History*. Quezon City: R. P. Garcia, 1985.

Ahmed, Akbar S. *Pakistan Society: Islam, Ethnicity, and Leadership in South Asia*. New York: Oxford University Press, 1986.

Alexander, Bevin. *Korea: The First War We Lost*. New York: Hippocrene Books, 1986.

Allen, Gwenfread. *Hawaii's War Years: 1941-1945*. Edited by Aldyth V. Morris. Honolulu: University of Hawaii Press, 1952.

Allen, Richard C. *Korea's Syngman Rhee: An Unauthorized Portrait*. Rutland, Vt.: Charles E. Tuttle, 1960.

Anthony, J. Garner. *Hawaii Under Army Rule*. Stanford, Calif.: Stanford University Press, 1955.

Appleman, Roy E. *South to the Naktong, North to the Yalu*. Washington, D.C.: Department of the Army, 1961.

Asahi Shimbun, ed. *The Pacific Rivals: A Japanese View of Japanese-American Relations.* New York: Weatherhill Asahi, 1972.

Baker, Susan Gonzalez. *The Cautious Welcome: The Legalization Programs of the Immigration Reform and Control Act.* Santa Monica, Calif.: RAND, 1990.

Barnett, A. Doak. *Communist China and Asia: A Challenge to American Policy.* New York: Vintage Books, 1960.

Baron, Dennis. *The English-Only Question: An Official Language for Americans?* New Haven, Conn.: Yale University Press, 1990.

Bean, Frank D., Georges Vernez, and Charles B. Keely. *Opening and Closing the Doors: Evaluating Immigration Reform and Control.* Santa Monica, Calif.: RAND, 1989.

Beasley, W. G. *The Meiji Restoration.* Stanford, Calif.: Stanford University Press, 1972.

Beekman, Allan. *Crisis: The Japanese Attack on Pearl Harbor and Southeast Asia.* Honolulu, Hawaii: Heritage Press of the Pacific, 1992.

Blaker, Michael, ed. *The Politics of Trade: U.S. and Japanese Policymaking for the GATT Negotiations.* New York: Columbia University, 1978.

Bonner, Raymond. *Waltzing with a Dictator: The Marcoses and the Making of American Policy.* New York: Times Books, 1987.

Boxer, Charles R. *The Christian Century in Japan, 1549-1650.* Berkeley: University of California Press, 1951.

Boxer, Charles R. *Jan Compagnie in Japan, 1600-1850.* 2d rev. ed. The Hague: Martinus Nijhoff, 1950.

Boyle, John. *China and Japan at War, 1937-1945: The Politics of Collaboration.* Stanford, Calif.: Stanford University Press, 1972.

Brands, H. W. *Bound to Empire: The United States and the Philippines.* New York: Oxford University Press, 1992.

Brands, H. W. *India and the United States: The Cold Peace.* Boston: Twayne, 1990.

Brass, Paul. *The Politics of India Since Independence.* New York: Cambridge University Press, 1990.

Bresnan, John, ed. *Crisis in the Philippines.* Princeton, N.J.: Princeton University Press, 1986.

Breuer, William B. *Retaking the Philippines: America's Return to Corregidor and Bataan, October 1944-March 1945.* New York: St. Martin's Press, 1986.

Bridges, Brian. *Korea and the West.* New York: Routledge & Kegan Paul, 1986.

Brown, Emily C. *Har Dayal: Hindu Revolutionary and Rationalist.* Tucson: University of Arizona Press, 1975.

Brown, Judith M. *Gandhi: Prisoner of Hope.* New Haven, Conn.: Yale University Press, 1989.

Bunge, Frederica M., ed. *Thailand: A Country Study.* Washington, D.C.: U.S. Government Printing Office, 1981.

Burki, Shahid Javed. *Pakistan: A Nation in the*

Making. Boulder, Colo.: Westview Press, 1986.

Burton, Sandra. *Impossible Dream: The Marcoses, the Aquinos, and the Unfinished Revolution.* New York: Warner Books, 1989.

Calavita, Kitty. *Inside the State: The Bracero Program, Immigration, and the I.N.S.* New York: Routledge, 1992.

Callies, David L. *Regulating Paradise: Land Use Controls in Hawaii.* Honolulu: University of Hawaii Press, 1984.

Cannon, M. Hamlin. *Leyte: The Return to the Philippines.* Washington, D.C.: Department of the Army, 1954.

Carnegie Task Force on Non-Proliferation and South Asian Security. *Nuclear Weapons and South Asian Security.* Washington, D.C.: Carnegie Endowment for International Peace, 1988.

Chan, Sucheng. *Asian Americans: An Interpretive History.* Boston: Twayne Publishers, 1991.

Chandler, David P. *Brother Number One: A Political Biography of Pol Pot.* Boulder, Colo.: Westview Press, 1992.

Chandler, David P. *A History of Cambodia.* 2d ed. Boulder, Colo.: Westview Press, 1992.

Chandler, David. *The Land and People of Cambodia.* New York: HarperCollins, 1991.

Chandler, David P. *The Tragedy of Cambodian History: Politics, War, and Revolution Since 1945.* New Haven, Conn.: Yale University Press, 1991.

Chang, Hsin-pao. *Commissioner Lin and the Opium War.* Cambridge, Mass.: Harvard University Press, 1964.

Chang, Sidney H., and Leonard H. D. Gordon. *All Under Heaven: Sun Yat-sen and His Revolutionary Thought.* Stanford, Calif.: Hoover Institution Press, 1991.

Chaplin, George, and Glenn D. Paige, eds. *Hawaii 2000.* Honolulu: University of Hawaii Press, 1973.

Chatterjee, Margaret. *Gandhi's Religious Thought.* Notre Dame, Ind.: University of Notre Dame Press, 1983.

Chen, Jack. *The Chinese of America.* San Francisco: Harper & Row, 1980.

Chen, Yung-fa. *Making Revolution: The Communist Movement in Eastern and Central China, 1937-1945.* Berkeley: University of California Press, 1986.

Cheng, Chu-yuan. *Behind the Tiananmen Massacre: Social, Political, and Economic Ferment in Modern China.* Boulder, Colo.: Westview, 1990.

Cheng, Chu-yuan, ed. *Sun Yat-sen's Doctrine in the Modern World.* Boulder, Colo.: Westview Press, 1989.

Chinese Historical Society of America, Publication Committee, ed. *Chinese America: History and Perspectives, 1987.* San Francisco: Chinese Historical Society of America, 1987.

Chou, Michaelyn P. *Oral History Interview with Hiram L. Fong, Senator from Hawaii, 1959 to 1977.* Washington, D.C.: Former Members of Congress, Inc., 1979, 1980.

Choy, Bong-youn. *Koreans in America.* Chicago: Nelson-Hall, 1979.

Chuman, Frank. *The Bamboo People: Japanese Americans, Their History, and the Law.* Chicago: Japanese American Research Project and Japanese American Citizens League, 1981.

Chuman, Frank F. *The Bamboo People: The Law and Japanese-Americans.* Del Mar, California: Publisher's Inc., 1976.

Clark, Donald, ed. *Korea Briefing, 1992.* Boulder, Colo.: Westview Press, 1992.

Cohen, Marc J. *Taiwan at the Crossroads: Human Rights, Political Development, and Social Change on the Beautiful Island.* Washington, D.C.: Asia Resource Center, 1988.

Colbert, Evelyn. *The United States and the Philippine Bases.* Washington, D.C.: Foreign Policy Institute, The Johns Hopkins University Press, 1987.

Collins, Donald E. *Native American Aliens: Disloyalty and the Renunciation of Citizenship by Japanese Americans During World War II.* Westport, Conn.: Greenwood Press, 1985.

Commission on Wartime Relocation and Internment of Civilians. *Personal Justice Denied.* Washington, D.C.: Government Printing Office, 1982.

Conroy, Hilary. *The Japanese Seizure of Korea, 1868-1910: A Study of Realism and Idealism in International Relations.* Philadelphia: University of Pennsylvania Press, 1960.

Coolidge, Mary. *Chinese Immigration.* New York: Henry Holt, 1909.

Cooper, Michael. *They Came to Japan.* Berkeley: University of California Press, 1965.

Copley, Anthony. *Gandhi: Against the Tide.* New York: Basil Blackwell, 1987.

Copper, John F. *China Diplomacy: The Washington-Taipei-Beijing Triangle.* Boulder, Colo.: Westview Press, 1992.

Cordova, Fred. *Filipinos: Forgotten Asian Americans.* Dubuque, Iowa: Kendall/Hunt, 1983.

Cose, Ellis. *A Nation of Strangers: Prejudice, Politics, and the Populating of America.* New York: William Morrow, 1992.

Cretser, Gary A., and Joseph J. Leon, eds. *Intermarriage in the United States.* New York: Haworth, 1982.

Cumings, Bruce. *The Roaring of the Cataract, 1947-1950.* Vol. 2 in *The Origins of the Korean War.* Princeton, N.J.: Princeton University Press, 1990.

Daniels, Roger. *Asian America: Chinese and Japanese in the United States Since 1850.* Seattle: University of Washington Press, 1988.

Daniels, Roger. *Concentration Camps, North America: Japanese in the United States and Canada During World War II.* Malabar, Fla.: Robert E. Krieger, 1981.

Daniels, Roger. *The Politics of Prejudice: The Anti-Japanese Movement in California and the Struggle for Japanese Exclusion.* 1962.

2d ed. Berkeley: University of California Press, 1978.

Daws, Gavan. *Shoal of Time: A History of the Hawaiian Islands*. New York: Macmillan, 1968.

De Berval, Rene, ed. *Kingdom of Laos*. Saigon: France-Asie, 1959.

Dennett, Tyler. *Americans in Eastern Asia*. New York: Barnes & Noble Books, 1941.

Dignan, Don K. *The Indian Revolutionary Problem in British Diplomacy, 1914-1919*. New Delhi, India: Allied Publishers, 1983.

Divine, Robert A. *American Immigration Policy, 1924-1952*. New Haven, Conn.: Yale University Press, 1957.

Dommer, Arthur J. *Conflict in Laos: The Politics of Neutralization*. New York: Praeger, 1971.

Doronila, Amando. *The State, Economic Transformation, and Political Change in the Philippines, 1946-1972*. New York: Oxford University Press, 1992.

Downen, Robert L. *The Taiwan Pawn in the China Game: China to the Rescue*. Washington, D.C.: Centre for Strategic and International Studies, 1979.

Dreyer, June Teufel. *China's Political System: Modernization and Tradition*. New York: Paragon House, 1993.

Drinnon, Richard. *Keeper of Concentration Camps: Dillon S. Myer and American Racism*. Berkeley: University of California Press, 1987.

Dudley, Michael Kioni. *A Call For Hawaiian Sovereignty*. Honolulu: Na Kane O Ka Malo Press, 1990.

Dudley, Michael Kioni. *Man, Gods, and Nature*. Honolulu: Na Kane O Ka Malo Press, 1990.

Eastman, Lloyd. *Seeds of Destruction: Nationalist China in War and Revolution, 1937-1949*. Stanford, Calif.: Stanford University Press, 1984.

Eckert, Carter J., et al. *Korea Old and New: A History*. Seoul, Korea: Ilchokak, 1990; distributed in U.S. by Harvard University Press.

Edwardes, Michael. *A History of India from the Earliest Times to the Present Day*. New York: Farrar, Straus and Cudahy, 1961.

Embrey, Sue Kunitomi, ed. *The Lost Years: 1942-1946*. Los Angeles: Moonlight Publications, 1972.

Embrey, Sue Kunitomi, Arthur A. Hansen, and Betty Kulberg Mitson, eds. *Manzanar Martyr: An Interview with Harry Y. Ueno*. Fullerton, Calif.: Japanese American Project, Oral History Program, California State University, Fullerton, 1986.

Engelmann, Larry. *Tears Before the Rain: An Oral History of the Fall of South Vietnam*. New York: Oxford University Press, 1990.

Enloe, Cynthia. *Bananas, Beaches and Bases: Making Feminist Sense of International Politics*. Berkeley: University of California Press, 1990.

Essential Gandhi: An Anthology of His Writings on His Life, Work, and Ideas, The. Ed-

ited by Louis Fischer. New York: Vintage Books, 1962.

Fairbank, John K. *Trade and Diplomacy on the China Coast: The Opening of the Treaty Ports, 1842-1854*. Cambridge, Mass.: Harvard University Press, 1953.

Fairbank, John K. *The United States and China*. 4th ed. Cambridge, Mass.: Harvard University Press, 1983.

Fay, Peter Ward. *The Opium War, 1840-1842*. Cambridge, England: Cambridge University Press, 1975.

Feis, Herbert. *Road to Pearl Harbor*. New York: Atheneum, 1950.

Finn, Richard B., ed. *U.S.-Japan Relations: Learning from Competition*. New Brunswick, N.J.: Transaction Books, 1986.

Fischer, Louis. *The Life of Mahatma Gandhi*. New York: Harper & Row, 1983.

Forbes, David W. *Encounters with Paradise: Views of Hawaii and Its People, 1778-1941*. Honolulu: Honolulu Academy of Arts, 1992.

Freedman, Maurice. *Chinese Lineage and Society: Fukien and Kwangtung*. New York: Humanities Press, 1966.

Freeman, James M. *Hearts of Sorrow: Vietnamese-American Lives*. Stanford, Calif.: Stanford University Press, 1989.

Friend, Theodore. *Between Two Empires: The Ordeal of the Philippines, 1929-1946*. New Haven, Conn.: Yale University Press, 1965.

Fu, Jen-kun. *Taiwan and the Geopolitics of the Asian-American Dilemma*. New York: Praeger, 1992.

Fukuda, Moritoshi. *Legal Problems of Japanese-Americans*. Tokyo: Keio Tsushin, 1980.

Gandhi, Mahatma. *An Autobiography: The Story of Experiments with Truth*. Translated by Mahadev Desai. Harmondsworth, Middlesex, England: Penguin Books, 1982.

Ganguly, Sumit. *The Origins of War in South Asia: Indo-Pakistani Conflicts Since 1947*. Boulder, Colo.: Westview Press, 1986.

Garrett, Jessie A., and Ronald C. Larson, eds. *Camp and Community: Manzanar and the Owens Valley*. Fullerton, Calif.: Japanese American Project, Oral History Program, California State University, Fullerton, 1977.

Girling, John L. S. *Thailand: Society and Politics*. Ithaca, N.Y.: Cornell University Press, 1981.

Glazer, Nathan, ed. *Clamor at the Gates: The New American Immigration*. San Francisco: ICS Press, 1985.

Glazer, Sarah Jane. *Ralph Nader Congress Project. Citizens Look at Congress. Spark M. Matsunaga: Democratic Representative from Hawaii*. Washington: Grossman, 1972.

Goldstein, Martin E. *American Policy Toward Laos*. Rutherford, N.J.: Fairleigh Dickinson University Press, 1973.

Graff, Henry, ed. *American Imperialism and the Philippine Insurrection*. Boston: Little, Brown, 1969.

Greene, Fred, ed. *The Philippine Bases: Negotiating for the Future: American and Philip-

pine Perspectives*. New York: Council on Foreign Relations, 1988.

Gregor, A. James, and Maria H. Chang. *The Republic of China and U.S. Policy: A Study in Human Rights*. Washington, D.C.: Ethics and Public Policy Center, 1983.

Grodzins, Morton. *Americans Betrayed: Politics and the Japanese Evacuation*. Chicago: University of Chicago Press, 1949.

Grunder, Garel A., and William E. Livezey. *The Philippines and the United States*. Norman: University of Oklahoma Press, 1951.

Guillermaz, Jacquez. *A History of the Chinese Communist Party*. Translated by Anne Oesteray. New York: Random House, 1972.

Haas, Michael. *Genocide by Proxy: Cambodian Pawn on a Superpower Chessboard*. New York: Praeger, 1991.

Haas, Michael, ed. *Korean Reunification: Alternative Pathways*. New York: Praeger, 1989.

Hall, John W., and Richard K. Beardsley. *Twelve Doors to Japan*. New York: McGraw-Hill, 1965.

Hansen, Arthur A., and Betty E. Mitson, eds. *Voices Long Silent: An Oral Inquiry into the Japanese American Evacuation*. Fullerton, Calif.: Japanese American Project, Oral History Program, California State University, Fullerton, 1974.

Harding, Harry. *Fragile Relationship: The United States and China Since 1972*. Washington, D.C.: Brookings Institution, 1992.

Harries, Meirion, and Susie Harries. *Soldiers of the Sun: The Rise and Fall of the Imperial Japanese Army*. New York: Random House, 1991.

Hassan, Riaz, ed. *Singapore: Society in Transition*. New York: Oxford University Press, 1976.

Hawaii Advisory Committee to the U.S. Commission on Civil Rights. *A Broken Trust: The Hawaiian Homelands Program—Seventy Years of Failure of the Federal and State Governments to Protect the Civil Rights of Native Hawaiians*. Author, 1991.

Hayslip, Le Ly, with Jay Wurts. *When Heaven and Earth Changed Places*. New York: Doubleday, 1989.

Hazama, Dorothy Ochiai, and Jane Okamoto Komeiji. *Okage Sama De: The Japanese in Hawaii, 1885-1985*. Honolulu: Bess Press, 1986.

Henthorn, William E. *A History of Korea*. New York: Free Press, 1971.

Herman, Masako. *The Japanese in America: 1843-1973*. Dobbs Ferry, N.Y.: Oceana Publications, 1974.

Hewitt, Venon Marston. *The International Politics of South Asia*. New York: Manchester University Press, 1992.

Higham, John. *Strangers in the Land: Patterns of American Nativism, 1860-1925*. New Brunswick, N.J.: Rutgers University Press, 1955.

Hitchcox, Linda. *Vietnamese Refugees in Southeast Asian Camps*. Oxford, England: St. Antony's College, 1990.

Hohri, William Minoru. *Repairing America*. Pullman: Washington State University Press, 1988.

Hooson, David, ed. *Geography and National Identity*. Vol. 29 in the Institute of British Geographers Special Service Publications Series. Cambridge, Mass.: Blackwell, 1993.

Horwitz, Robert H., and Norman Meller. *Land and Politics in Hawaii*. 3d ed. Honolulu: University of Hawaii Press, 1966.

Hosokawa, William. *JACL: In Quest of Justice*. New York: William Morrow, 1982.

Houston, Jeanne Wakatsuki, and James D. Houston. *Farewell to Manzanar*. Boston: Houghton Mifflin, 1973.

Hoy, William. *The Chinese Six Companies*. San Francisco: Chinese Consolidated Benevolent Association, 1942.

Hsieh, Chiao-min. *Taiwan—Ilha Formosa: A Geography in Perspective*. Washington, D.C.: Butterworths, 1964.

Hsiung, James C., et al., eds. *The Taiwan Experience, 1950-1980: Contemporary Republic of China*. New York: American Association of Chinese Studies, 1981.

Hsu, Immanuel. *China Without Mao: The Search for a New Order*. New York: Oxford University Press, 1983.

Huber, Thomas M. *The Revolutionary Origins of Modern Japan*. Stanford, Calif.: Stanford University Press, 1981.

Hurd, Douglas. *The Arrow War: An Anglo-Chinese Confusion, 1856-1860*. New York: Macmillan, 1967.

Hutchinson, Edward P. *Legislative History of American Immigration Policy, 1798-1965*. Philadelphia: University of Pennsylvania Press, 1981.

Ichihashi, Yamato. *Japanese in the United States*. Stanford, Calif.: Stanford University Press, 1932. Reprint. New York: Arno Press, 1969.

Ichioka, Yuji. *The Issei: The World of the First Generation of Japanese Immigrants, 1885-1924*. New York: Free Press, 1988.

Ike, Nobutake. *Japan's Decision for War: Records of the 1941 Policy Conferences*. Stanford, Calif.: Stanford University Press, 1967.

Immigration and Nationality Act. Washington, D.C.: Government Printing Office, 1980.

"India and Pakistan: Collision or Compromise?" In *Great Decisions*, edited by the Foreign Policy Association. New York: Foreign Policy Association, 1993.

Inoguchi, Takashi. *Japan's International Relations*. Boulder, Colo.: Westview Press, 1991.

Inoguchi, Takashi, and Daniel I. Okimoto. *The Political Economy of Japan*. Vol. 2. Stanford, Calif.: Stanford University Press, 1988.

Iriye, Akira. *The Origins of the Second World War in Asia and the Pacific*. New York: Longman, 1987.

Iriye, Akira. *Power and Culture: The Japanese-American War, 1941-1945*. Cambridge, Mass.: Harvard University Press, 1981.

Iriye, Akira, and Warren Cohen, eds. *The United States and Japan in the Postwar World*. Lexington: University Press of Kentucky, 1989.

Irons, Peter. *Justice at War: The Inside Story of the Japanese American Internment Cases*. New York: Oxford University Press, 1983.

Ishinomori, Shotaro. *Japan, Inc.: An Introduction to Japanese Economics (The Comic Book)*. Translated by Betsey Scheiner. Berkeley: University of California Press, 1988.

Jackson, Karl D., comp. *Cambodia, 1975-1978: Rendezvous with Death*. Princeton, N.J.: Princeton University Press, 1989.

Jackson, Robert. *South Asian Crisis: India, Pakistan and Bangla Desh: A Political and Historical Analysis of the 1971 War*. New York: Praeger, 1975.

Jalal, Ayesha. *The State of Martial Rule: The Origins of Pakistan's Political Economy of Defence*. Cambridge, England: Cambridge University Press, 1990.

Jamieson, Neil. *Understanding Vietnam*. Berkeley: University of California Press, 1993.

Jansen, Marius B. *The Japanese and Sun Yat-sen*. Cambridge; Mass.: Harvard University Press, 1954.

Jensen, Joan M. *Passage from India: Asian Indian Immigrants in North America*. New Haven, Conn.: Yale Unviersity Press, 1988.

Jensen, Marius B., and Gilbert Rozman, eds. *Japan in Transition: From Tokugawa to Meiji*. Princeton, N.J.: Princeton University Press, 1986.

Jones, F. C., Hugh Borton, and B. R. Pearn. *The Far East: 1942-1946*. New York: Oxford University Press, 1955.

Josh, Sohan Singh. *The Hindustan Gadar Party: A Short History*. 2 vols. New Delhi: People's Publishing House, 1977-1978.

Kahin, George McT. *Intervention: How America Became Involved in Vietnam*. New York: Alfred A. Knopf, 1986.

Karnow, Stanley. *In Our Image: America's Empire in the Philippines*. New York: Random House, 1989.

Karnow, Stanley. *Vietnam: A History*. New York: Viking Press, 1983.

Kawai, Kazuo. *Japan's American Interlude*. Chicago: University of Chicago Press, 1960.

Kent, Noel J. *Hawaii: Islands Under the Influence*. New York: Monthly Review Press, 1983.

Kerr, George H. *Formosa: Licensed Revolution and the Home Rule Movement, 1895-1945*. Honolulu: University Press of Hawaii, 1974.

Keyes, Charles F. *The Golden Peninsula: Culture and Adaptation in Mainland Southeast Asia*. New York: Macmillan, 1977.

Keyes, Charles F. *Thailand: Buddhist Kingdom as Modern Nation-State*. Boulder, Colo.: Westview Press, 1987.

Kikuchi, Yasuchi. *Uncrystallized Philippine Society: A Social Anthropological Analysis*. Detroit: Cellar Book Shop, 1992.

Kim, Gi Pal. *The Third Republic*. Seoul: Hyundai Culture, 1986.

Kissinger, Henry S. *Years of Upheaval*. London: Weidenfeld & Nicolson, 1982.

Konvitz, Milton R. *The Alien and the Asiatic in American Law*. Ithaca, N.Y.: Cornell University Press, 1946.

Koo, Youngnok, and Sung-joo Han, eds. *The Foreign Policy of the Republic of Korea*. New York: Columbia University Press, 1985.

Kotani, Roland. *The Japanese in Hawaii: A Century of Struggle*. Honolulu: Hawaii Hochi, 1985.

Krause, Lawrence B., Ai Tee Koh, and Yuan Lee. *The Singapore Economy Reconsidered*. Singapore: Institute of Southeast Asian Studies, 1987.

Kulka, Richard A., et al. *Trauma and the Vietnam War Generation*. New York: Brunner/Mazel, 1990.

Kunstadter, Peter, ed. *Southeast Asian Tribes, Minorities, and Nations*. 2 vols. Princeton, N.J.: Princeton University Press, 1967.

Kuykendall, R. S. *The Hawaiian Kingdom*. 3 vols. Honolulu: University of Hawaii Press, 1938-1967.

Kwak, Tae-Hwan, Chonghan Kim, and Hong Nack Kim, eds. *Korean Reunification: New Perspectives and Approaches*. Seoul, Korea: Kyungnam University Press, 1984.

Kwong, Peter. *Chinatown, New York: Labor and Politics, 1930-1950*. New York: Monthly Review Press, 1979.

Ladany, Laszlo. *The Communist Party of China and Marxism, 1921-1985: A Self Portrait*. Stanford, Calif.: Hoover Institution Press, 1988.

Lasater, Martin L. *Policy in Evolution: The U.S. Role in China's Reunification*. Boulder, Colo.: Westview Press, 1988.

Lautensach, Hermann. *Korea: A Geography Based on the Author's Travels and Literature*. Translated and edited by Katherine and Eckart Dege. Berlin: Springer- Verlag, 1988.

Lee, Chong-sik, ed. *Korea Briefing, 1990*. Boulder, Colo.: Westview Press, 1991.

Lee, Chong-sik. *The Politics of Korean Nationalism*. Berkeley: University of California Press, 1963.

Lee, Ki-baik. *A New History of Korea*. Cambridge, Mass.: Harvard University Press, 1984.

Lee, Sun K. *Korean History, Modern Times*. Seoul: Eul U Publishing, 1963.

Leonard, Karen Isaksen. *Making Ethnic Choices: California's Punjabi Mexican Americans*. Philadelphia: Temple University Press, 1992.

LePoer, Barbara Leitch, ed. *Singapore: A Country Study*. Washington, D.C.: Government Printing Office, 1991.

Leung, Benjamin K. P. *Social Issues in Hong Kong*. Hong Kong: Oxford University Press, 1990.

Liliuokalani, Queen of Hawaii. *Hawaii's Story by Hawaii's Queen*. Boston: Lothrop, Lee and Shepard Co., 1898.

Lim, Christina, and Sheldon Lim. *In the Shadow of the Tiger*. San Mateo, Calif.: Japanese American Curriculum Project, 1993.

Lim, Genny, ed. *The Chinese American Experience: Papers from the Second National Conference on Chinese American Studies*. San Francisco: Chinese Historical Society of America, 1984.

Lincoln, Edward J. *Japan's Unequal Trade*. Washington, D.C.: Brookings Institution, 1990.

Lind, Andrew. *Hawaii's Japanese: An Experiment in Democracy*. Princeton, N.J.: Princeton University Press, 1946.

Linn, Brian McAllister. *The U.S. Army and Counterinsurgency in the Philippine War, 1899-1902*. Chapel Hill: University of North Carolina Press, 1989.

Lord, Walter. *Day of Infamy*. New York: Holt, 1957.

Ludszuweit, Daniel. *The Philippines: Cockatoo's Handbook*. Manila: Cockatoo Press, 1988.

Lutheran Immigration and Refugee Service. *Cambodia: The Land and Its People*. New York: Lutheran Council in the USA, 1983.

Lyman, Stanford. *Chinese Americans*. New York: Random House, 1974.

Ma, L. Eve Armentrout. *Revolutionaries, Monarchists, and Chinatowns*. Honolulu: University of Hawaii Press, 1990.

McCoy, Alfred W. *The Politics of Heroin in Southeast Asia*. New York: Harper & Row, 1972.

McCune, Shannon. *Korea's Heritage: A Regional and Social Geography*. Rutland, Vt.: Charles E. Tuttle, 1956.

Macdonald, Donald Stone. *The Koreans: Contemporary Politics and Society*. 2d ed. Boulder, Colo.: Westview Press, 1990.

McDougald, Charles C. *The Marcos File: Was He a Philippine Hero or Corrupt Tyrant?* San Francisco: San Francisco Publishers, 1987.

McGurn, William. *Perfidious Albion: The Abandonment of Hong Kong, 1997*. Washington, D.C.: Ethics and Public Policy Center, 1992.

McKenzie, Frederick A. *Korea's Fight for Freedom*. New York: Fleming H. Revell, 1920.

MacKenzie, Melody Kapilialoha. *Native Hawaiian Rights Handbook*. Honolulu: Native Hawaiian Legal Corporation, 1991.

McWilliams, Carey. *Brothers Under the Skin*. Rev. ed. Boston: Little, Brown, 1964.

Mason, Philip. *The Guardians*. Vol. 2 in *The Men Who Ruled India*. London: Jonathan Cape, 1963.

Matray, James I., ed. *Historical Dictionary of the Korean War*. New York: Greenwood Press, 1991.

Matsunaga, Spark, and Ping Chen. *Rulemakers of the House*. Champaign-Urbana: University of Illinois Press, 1976.

Mazarr, Michael, et al., eds. *Korea 1991: The Road to Peace*. Boulder, Colo.: Westview Press, 1991.

Meisner, Maurice. *Mao's China and After: A History of the People's Republic*. New York: Free Press, 1986.

Melendy, H. Brett. *Asians in America: Filipinos, Koreans, and East Indians*. Boston: Twayne, 1977.

Merrill, John. *Korea: The Peninsular Origins of the War*. Newark: University of Delaware Press, 1989.

Michael, Franz H., and George E. Taylor. *The Far East in the Modern World*. New York: Henry Holt, 1956.

Miller, Edward S. *War Plan Orange: The U.S. Strategy to Defeat Japan, 1897-1945*. Annapolis, Md.: Naval Institute Press, 1991.

Miller, Stuart C. *"Benevolent Assimilation": The American Conquest of the Philippines, 1899-1903*. New Haven, Conn.: Yale University Press, 1982.

Miller, Stuart C. *The Unwelcome Immigrant: The American Image of the Chinese, 1752-1882*. Berkeley: University of California Press, 1969.

Morley, James W., ed. *The Pacific Basin: New Challenges for the United States*. New York: Academy of Political Science, Columbia University, 1986.

Morton, Louis. *The Fall of the Philippines*. Washington, D.C.: Department of the Army, 1953.

Mosher, Steven W. *China Misperceived: American Illusions and Chinese Reality*. New York: Basic Books, 1990.

Moynihan, Daniel P. *Pandaemonium: Ethnicity in International Politics*. New York: Oxford University Press, 1993.

Myer, Dillon S. *Uprooted Americans: The Japanese Americans and the War Relocation Authority During World War II*. Tucson: University of Arizona Press, 1971.

Myers, Ramon H., ed. *Two Chinese States: U.S. Foreign Policy and Interests*. Stanford, Calif.: Hoover Institution Press, 1978.

Nagai, Yonosuke, and Akira Iriye, eds. *The Origins of the Cold War in Asia*. New York: Columbia University Press, 1977.

Nagasawa, Richard. *Summer Wind: The Story of an Immigrant Chinese Politician*. Tucson, Ariz.: Westernlore Press, 1986.

Nahm, Andrew C. *Korea, Tradition and Transformation: A History of the Korean People*. Elizabeth, N.J.: Hollym International, 1988.

Nahm, Andrew C., ed. *Korea Under Japanese Colonial Rule: Studies of the Policy and Techniques of Japanese Colonialism*. Kalamazoo: Center for Korean Studies, Western Michigan University, 1973.

Nakane, Chie. *Japanese Society*. Berkeley: University of California Press, 1970.

Nee, Victor G., and Brett de Bary. *Longtime Californ': A Documentary Study of an American Chinatown*. New York: Pantheon Books, 1973.

Nelson, Douglas W. *Heart Mountain: The History of an American Concentration Camp*. Madison: The State Historical Society of Wisconsin, 1976.

Nguyen Trieu Dan. *A Vietnamese Family Chronicle: Twelve Generations on the Banks of the Hat River*. Jefferson, N.C.: McFarland, 1991.

Noman, Omar. *Pakistan: Political and Economic History Since 1947*. London: Kegan Paul, 1990.

Nyrop, Richard F., ed. *India: A Country Study*. Washington, D.C.: U.S. Government Printing Office, 1986.

O'Brien, David J., and Stephen S. Fugita. *The Japanese American Experience*. Bloomington: Indiana University Press, 1991.

Odo, Franklin, and Kazuko Sinoto. *A Pictorial History of the Japanese in Hawaii, 1885-1924*. Edited by Bonnie Tocher Clause. Honolulu: Bishop Museum, 1985.

Ogawa, Dennis M. *Kodomo No Tame Ni: For the Sake of the Children: The Japanese American Experience in Hawaii*. Honolulu: University Press of Hawaii, 1978.

Oliver, Robert T. *Korea: Forgotten Nation*. Washington: Public Affairs Press, 1944.

Oliver, Robert T. *Syngman Rhee: The Man Behind the Myth*. New York: Dodd, Mead, 1954.

Oliver, Robert T. *Syngman Rhee and American Involvement in Korea, 1942-1960*. Seoul: Panmun Book Co., 1978.

Osborne, Thomas J. *"Empire Can Wait": American Opposition to Hawaiian Annexation, 1893-98*. Kent, Ohio: Kent State University Press, 1981.

Palmer, Norman D. *The United States and India: The Dimensions of Influence*. New York: Praeger, 1984.

Patrick, Hugh T., and Ryuichiro Tachi, eds. *Japan and the United States Today*. New York: Center on Japanese Economy and Business, Columbia University, 1986.

Pedraza-Bailey, Silvia. *Political and Economic Migrants in America: Cubans and Mexicans*. Austin: University of Texas Press, 1985.

Phan, Peter. *Chinese America: History and Perspectives, 1993*. San Francisco: Chinese Historical Society of America, 1993.

Pomeroy, William. *The Philippines: Colonialism, Collaboration, and Resistance*. New York: International Publishers, 1993.

Prange, Gordon W. *At Dawn We Slept*. New York: Penguin Books, 1982.

Puri, Harish K. *Ghadar Movement: Ideology, Organization and Strategy*. 2d ed. Amritsar, Punjab: Guru Nanak Dev University Press, 1993.

Quah, Jon S. T., Heng Chee Chan, and Chee Meow Seah. *Government and Politics of Singapore*. Singapore: Oxford University Press, 1985.

Quinsaat, Jesse. *Letters in Exile*. Los Angeles: UCLA Asian American Studies Center, 1976.

Rayson, Ann. *Modern Hawaiian History*. Honolulu: Bess Press, 1984.

Reimers, David M. *Still the Golden Door: The*

Third World Comes to America. New York: Columbia University Press, 1985.

Reischauer, Edwin O. *Japan: The Story of a Nation*. 4th ed. New York: McGraw-Hill, 1990.

Reischauer, Edwin O. *The Japanese*. Cambridge, Mass.: The Belknap Press of Harvard University Press, 1977.

Rempel, William C. *Delusions of a Dictator: The Mind of Marcos as Revealed in His Secret Diaries*. Boston: Little, Brown, 1993.

Riggs, Frederick Warren. *Pressures on Congress: A Study of the Repeal of Chinese Exclusion*. New York: King's Crown Press, 1950.

Ringrose, Marjorie, and Adam Lerner, eds. *Reimagining the Nation*. Bristol, Pa.: Taylor & Francis, 1993.

Roach, James R., ed. *India 2000: The Next Fifteen Years*. Riverdale, Md.: Riverdale, 1986.

Rodríguez, Fred. *Equity in Education: Issues and Strategies*. Dubuque: Kendall/Hunt, 1990.

Rodzinski, Witold. *The People's Republic of China*. New York: Free Press, 1988.

Rolph, Elizabeth S. *Immigration Policies: Legacy from the 1980s and Issues for the 1990s*. Santa Monica, Calif.: RAND, 1992.

Romulo, Beth Day. *Inside the Palace: The Rise and Fall of Ferdinand and Imelda Marcos*. New York: Putnam, 1987.

Root, Maria P. P., ed. *Racially Mixed People in America*. Newbury Park, Calif.: Sage Publications, 1992.

Rothermund, Dietmar. *Mahatma Gandhi: An Essay in Political Biography*. New Delhi: Manohar, 1991.

Rudolph, Lloyd I., et al. *The Regional Imperative: The Administration of U.S. Foreign Policy Towards South Asian States Under Presidents Johnson and Nixon*. Atlantic Highlands, N.J.: Humanities Press, 1980.

Rudolph, Susanne Hoeber, and Lloyd I. Rudolph. *Gandhi: The Traditional Roots of Charisma*. Chicago: University of Chicago Press, 1983.

Russ, William A., Jr. *The Hawaiian Revolution, 1893-94*. Selinsgrove, Pa.: Susquehanna University Press, 1959.

Russell, Charles Edward. *The Outlook for the Philippines*. New York: Century, 1922.

Russell, Charles Edward, and E. B. Rodriguez. *The Hero of the Filipinos: The Story of Jose Rizal—Poet, Patriot and Martyr*. New York: Century, 1923.

Sanchez-Arcilla Bernal, Jose. *Rizal and the Emergence of the Philippine Nation*. Quezon City: Office of Research and Publications, Ateneo de Manila University, 1991.

Sandmeyer, Elmer C. *The Anti-Chinese Movement in California*. Urbana: University of Illinois Press, 1939.

Sansom, G. B. *Japan: A Short Cultural History*. Rev. ed. New York: Appleton-Century-Crofts, 1962.

Sansom, George. *A History of Japan, 1615-1867*. Stanford, Calif.: Stanford University Press, 1963.

Saund, Dalip Singh. *Congressman from India*. New York: E. P. Dutton, 1960.

Saxton, Alexander. *The Indispensable Enemy: Labor and the Anti-Chinese Movement in California*. Berkeley: University of California Press, 1971.

Scalapino, Robert A., and George T. Yu. *Modern China and Its Revolutionary Process: Recurrent Challenges to the Traditional Order, 1859-1920*. Berkeley: University of California Press, 1985.

Schaller, Michael. *Douglas MacArthur: The Far Eastern General*. New York: Oxford University Press, 1989.

Schanberg, Sydney H. *The Death and Life of Dith Pran*. New York: Penguin Books, 1985.

Schiffrin, Harold Z. *Sun Yat-sen: Reluctant Revolutionary*. Boston: Little, Brown, 1980.

Schwartz, Benjamin I. *Chinese Communism and the Rise of Mao*. Cambridge, Mass.: Harvard University Press, 1951.

Scott, Esther, and Calvin Naito. *Against All Odds: The Japanese Americans' Campaign for Redress*. Cambridge, Mass.: Case Program, Harvard Kennedy School of Government, 1990.

Scott, Ian. *Political Change and the Crisis of Legitimacy in Hong Kong*. Honolulu: University of Hawaii Press, 1989.

Scruggs, Jan C., and Joel L. Swerdlow. *To Heal a Nation: The Vietnam Veterans Memorial*. New York: Harper & Row, 1985.

Seagrave, Sterling. *The Marcos Dynasty*. New York: Harper & Row, 1988.

Shawcross, William. *The Quality of Mercy: Cambodia, Holocaust, and Modern Conscience*. New York: Simon & Schuster, 1984.

Shawcross, William. *Sideshow: Kissinger, Nixon, and the Destruction of Cambodia*. London: The Hogarth Press, 1986.

Sheehan, Neil. *A Bright Shining Lie: John Paul Vann and America in Vietnam*. New York: Random House, 1988.

Shillony, Ben-Ami. *Politics and Culture in Wartime Japan*. Oxford, England: Clarendon Press, 1981.

Shutt, Harry. *The Myth of Free Trade: Patterns of Protectionism Since 1945*. New York: Blackwell, 1985.

Simbulan, Roland G. *The Bases of Our Insecurity: A Study of the US Military Bases in the Philippines*. 2d ed. Metro Manila: BALAI Fellowship, 1985.

Singapore Ministry of Communications and Information. *Singapore Facts and Pictures, 1989*. Singapore: Information Division, Ministry of Communications and Information, 1989.

Sitaramayya, B. Pattabhi. *History of the Indian National Congress*. 2 vols. Bombay: Padma, 1946-1947.

Siu, Paul. *The Chinese Laundryman: A Study in Social Isolation*. New York: New York University Press, 1987. Edited by John Tchen.

Smith, Robert Ross. *Triumph in the Philippines*. Washington, D.C.: Department of the Army, 1963.

Smith, Vincent A. *The Oxford History of India*. Edited by Percival Spear. 3d ed. Oxford, England: Clarendon Press, 1967.

South Asians in North America: An Annotated and Selected Bibliography. Berkeley: Center for South and Southeast Asia Studies, University of California, Berkeley, 1988.

Spence, Jonathan D. *The Search for Modern China*. New York: W. W. Norton, 1990.

Spickard, Paul R. *Mixed Blood: Intermarriage and Ethnic Identity in Twentieth-Century America*. Madison: University of Wisconsin Press, 1989.

Stevenson, Charles A. *The End of Nowhere: American Policy Towards Laos Since 1954*. Boston: Beacon Press, 1972.

Stuart-Fox, Martin, ed. *Contemporary Laos: Studies in the Politics and Society of the Lao People's Democratic Republic*. New York: St. Martin's Press, 1982.

Stuart-Fox, Martin. *Laos: Politics, Economics, and Society*. London: Frances Pinter, 1986.

Sturdevant, Saundra Pollock, and Brenda Stoltzfus, eds. *Let the Good Times Roll: Prostitution and the U.S. Military in Asia*. New York: The New Press, 1992.

Sung, Betty Lee. *Mountain of Gold: The Story of the Chinese in America*. New York: Macmillan, 1967.

Sunoo, Harold H. *America's Dilemma in Asia: The Case of South Korea*. Chicago: Nelson-Hall, 1979.

Sutter, Robert G. *The China Quandary: Domestic Determinants of U.S. China Policy, 1972-1982*. Boulder, Colo.: Westview Press, 1983.

Takaki, Ronald T. *Iron Cages: Race and Culture in Nineteenth Century America*. New York: Alfred A. Knopf, 1979.

TenBroek, Jacobus, et al. *Prejudice, War and the Constitution*. Berkeley: University of California Press, 1954.

Terranel, Quintin C. *Jose Rizal: Lover of Truth and Justice*. Metro Manila: National Book Store, 1984.

Thomas, Dorothy Swaine, and Richard S. Nishimoto. *The Spoilage*. Berkeley: University of California Press, 1946.

Thomas, Raju G. C. *Indian Security Policy*. Princeton, N.J.: Princeton University Press, 1986.

Thorne, Christopher. *The Issue of War: States, Societies, and the Far Eastern Conflict of 1941-1945*. New York: Oxford University Press, 1985.

Totman, Conrad. *The Collapse of the Tokugawa Bakufu, 1862-1868*. Honolulu: University Press of Hawaii, 1980.

Totman, Conrad D. *Politics in the Tokugawa Bakufu, 1600-1843*. Cambridge, Mass.: Harvard University Press, 1967.

Trask, Haunani-Kay. *From a Native Daughter: Colonialism and Sovereignty in Hawaii*. Monroe, Maine: Common Courage Press, 1993.

Tributes to the Honorable Hiram L. Fong of Hawaii in the United States Senate, upon the Occasion of His Retirement from the Senate. Washington, D.C.: U.S. Government Printing Office, 1977.

Tsai, Shih-shan H. *China and the Overseas Chinese in the United States, 1868-1911.* Fayetteville: University of Arkansas Press, 1983.

Tsai, Shih-shan Henry. *The Chinese Experience in America.* Bloomington: Indiana University Press, 1986.

Turnbull, Constance M. *A History of Singapore, 1810-1975.* Kuala Lumpur, Malaysia: Oxford University Press, 1977.

Uhalley, Stephen. *A History of the Chinese Communist Party.* Stanford, Calif.: Hoover Institution Press, 1988.

U.S. Commission on Civil Rights. *Civil Rights Issues Facing Asian Americans in the 1990s.* Washington, D.C.: Government Printing Office, 1992.

U.S. Commission on Wartime Relocation and Internment of Civilians. *Personal Justice Denied: Report of the Commission on Wartime Relocation and the Internment of Civilians.* Washington, D.C.: Government Printing Office, 1983.

U.S. Congress. House. Committee on Interior and Insular Affairs. *Personal Justice Denied: Report of the Commission on Wartime Relocation and Internment of Civilians.* 102d Congress, 2d session, 1983. Washington, D.C.: Government Printing Office, 1992.

U.S. Congress. House. Committee on the Territories. *Proposed Amendments to the Organic Act of the Territory of Hawaii.* 66th Congress, 2d session, 1920.

U.S. Congress. House. Committee on the Territories. *Proposed Amendments to the Organic Act of the Territory of Hawaii.* 67th Congress, 1st session, 1921. House Report 7257.

U.S. Congress. House. *President's Message Relating to the Hawaiian Islands.* 53rd Congress, 2d Session, 1893. Executive Document 47.

U.S. Congress. Senate. *Senate Report 227 ("Morgan Report").* 53rd Congress, 2d session, 1894.

U.S. Department of State. *United States Relations with China, with Special Reference to the Period 1944-1949.* Department of State Publication 3573. Washington, D.C.: Government Printing Office, 1949.

U.S. War Relocation Authority. *Administrative Highlights of the WRA Program.* Washington, D.C.: Government Printing Office, 1946.

Van Wolferen, Karl. *The Enigma of Japanese Power.* New York: Alfred A. Knopf, 1989.

Vogel, Ezra F. *Japan as Number One: Lessons for America.* Cambridge, Mass.: Harvard University Press, 1979.

Von Glahn, Gerhard. *Law Among Nations: An Introduction to Public International Law.* 6th rev. ed. New York: Macmillan, 1992.

Waley, Arthur. *The Opium War Through Chinese Eyes.* London: Allen & Unwin, 1958.

Webb, Herschel. *The Japanese Imperial Institution in the Tokugawa Period.* New York: Columbia University Press, 1968.

Weglyn, Michi. *Years of Infamy: The Untold Story of America's Concentration Camps.* New York: William Morrow, 1976.

Weinstein, Franklin B., ed. *U.S.-Japan Relations and the Security of East Asia.* Boulder, Colo.: Westview Press, 1978.

Wheeler, Jimmy W., and Perry L. Wood. *Beyond Recrimination: Perspectives on U.S.-Taiwan Trade Tensions.* Indianapolis: Hudson Institute, 1987.

Whitfield, Danny J. *Historical and Cultural Dictionary of Vietnam.* Metuchen, N.J.: Scarecrow Press, 1976.

Whitmore, John K., ed. *An Introduction to Indochinese History, Culture, Language, and Life.* Ann Arbor: Center for South and Southeast Asian Studies, University of Michigan, 1979.

Whyte, Martin K., and William Parish. *Urban Life in Contemporary China.* Chicago: University of Chicago Press, 1984.

Wilbur, C. Martin. *Sun Yat-sen: Frustrated Patriot.* New York: Columbia University Press, 1976.

Wohlstetter, Robert. *Pearl Harbor: Warning and Decision.* Stanford, Calif.: Stanford University Press, 1962.

Wolferen, Karel van. *The Enigma of Japanese Power.* New York: Vintage Books, 1990.

Wolpert, Stanley. *A New History of India.* 4th ed. New York: Oxford University Press, 1993.

Wong, Richard Y. C., and Joseph Y. S. Cheng, eds. *The Other Hong Kong Report, 1990.* Hong Kong: Chinese University Press, 1990.

Woodside, A. B. *Community and Revolution in Modern Vietnam.* Boston: Houghton Mifflin, 1976.

Wright, Theon. *The Disenchanted Isles: The Story of the Second Revolution in Hawaii.* New York: Dial Press, 1972.

Wu, Cheng-Tsu, ed. *"Chink!": A Documentary History of Anti-Chinese Prejudice in America.* New York: World, 1972.

Wyatt, David K. *Thailand: A Short History.* New Haven, Conn.: Yale University Press, 1984.

Yamamura, Kozo, ed. *Policy and Trade Issues of the Japanese Economy.* Seattle: University of Washington Press, 1982.

Youngblood, Robert L. *Marcos Against the Church: Economic Development and Political Repression in the Philippines.* Ithaca, N.Y.: Cornell University Press, 1990.

Yu, E. Y., E. H. Phillips, and E. S. Yang, eds. *Korean Women in Transition: At Home and Abroad.* Los Angeles: Center for Korean-American and Korean Studies, California State University, Los Angeles, 1987.

Zaide, Gregorio F. *Rizal: His Martyrdom.* Santa Cruz, Manila: Saint Mary's Publishing, 1976.

Zaide, Gregorio F., and Sonia M. Zaide. *Jose Rizal: Life, Works and Writings of a Genius, Writer, Scientist, and National Hero.* Metro Manila: National Book Store, 1984.

Zaide, Gregorio F., and Sonia M. Zaide. *Rizal and Other Great Filipinos.* Metro Manila: National Book Store, 1988.

Ziring, Lawrence, ed. *The Subcontinent in World Politics: India, Its Neighbors, and the Great Powers.* Rev. ed. New York: Praeger, 1982.

PREJUDICE, DISCRIMINATION, CIVIL RIGHTS, AND INTERGROUP RELATIONS

Adams, Ansel. *Manzanar.* With photographs by Ansel Adams and commentary by John Hersey. Compiled by John Armor and Peter Wright. New York: Times Books, 1988.

Alcantara, Ruben R. *Sakada: Filipino Adaptation in Hawaii.* Washington, D.C.: University Press of America, 1981.

Anzovin, Steven, ed. *The Problem of Immigration.* New York: H.W. Wilson, 1985.

Asahi Shimbun, ed. *The Pacific Rivals: A Japanese View of Japanese-American Relations.* New York: Weatherhill Asahi, 1972.

Axon, Gordon. *The California Gold Rush.* New York: Mason/Charter, 1976.

Barth, Gunther. *Bitter Strength: A History of the Chinese in the United States, 1850-1870.* Cambridge, Mass.: Harvard University Press, 1964.

Beechert, Edward D. *Working in Hawaii: A Labor History.* Ethnic Studies Oral History Project, University of Hawaii at Manoa. Honolulu: University of Hawaii Press, 1985.

Brown, Judith M. *Gandhi: Prisoner of Hope.* New Haven, Conn.: Yale University Press, 1989.

Bulosan, Carlos. *If You Want to Know What We Are: A Carlos Bulosan Reader.* Albuquerque, N.Mex.: West End Press, 1983.

Bulosan, Carlos. *The Philippines Is in the Heart.* Quezon City: New Day Publishers, 1978.

Bulosan, Carlos. *The Power of the People.* Manila: National Book Store, 1986.

Bulosan, Carlos. *The Sound of Falling Light.* Edited by Dolores Feria. Quezon City: University of the Philippines Press, 1960.

Center for Integration and Improvement of Journalism. *Project Zinger: A Critical Look at News Media Coverage of Asian Pacific Americans.* San Francisco: Asian American Journalists Association, 1992.

Center for Integration and Improvement of Journalism. *Project Zinger: The Good, the Bad and the Ugly.* San Francisco: Asian American Journalists Association, 1991.

Chan, Sucheng. *Asian Americans: An Interpretive History.* Boston: Twayne Publishers, 1991.

Chatterjee, Margaret. *Gandhi's Religious Thought.* Notre Dame, Ind.: University of Notre Dame Press, 1983.

Chinn, Thomas. *A History of the Chinese in*

America. San Francisco: Chinese Historical Society 1973.

Chuman, Frank F. *The Bamboo People: The Law and Japanese-Americans.* Del Mar, California: Publisher's Inc., 1976.

Commission on Wartime Relocation and Internment of Civilians. *Personal Justice Denied.* Washington, D.C.: Government Printing Office, 1982.

Conference on Anti-Asian Violence. *Break the Silence: A Conference on Anti-Asian Violence.* San Francisco: Break the Silence Coalition, 1986.

Coolidge, Mary. *Chinese Immigration.* New York: Henry Holt, 1909.

Cooper, George, and Gavan Daws. *Land and Power in Hawaii: The Democratic Years.* Honolulu: Benchmark Press, 1985.

Copley, Anthony. *Gandhi: Against the Tide.* New York: Basil Blackwell, 1987.

Cordova, Fred. *Filipinos: Forgotten Asian Americans.* Dubuque, Iowa: Kendall/Hunt, 1983.

Cretser, Gary A., and Joseph J. Leon, eds. *Intermarriage in the United States.* New York: Haworth, 1982.

Crouchett, Lorraine Jacobs. *Filipinos in California: From the Days of the Galleons to the Present.* El Cerritos, Calif.: Downey Place Publishing House, 1982.

Daniels, Roger. *Asian America: Chinese and Japanese in the United States Since 1850.* Seattle: University of Washington Press, 1988.

Daniels, Roger. *Concentration Camps, North America: Japanese in the United States and Canada During World War II.* Malabar, Fla.: Robert E. Krieger, 1981.

Daniels, Roger. *The Politics of Prejudice: The Anti-Japanese Movement in California and the Struggle for Japanese Exclusion.* 1962. 2d ed. Berkeley: University of California Press, 1978.

Daniels, Roger, Sandra C. Taylor, and Harry H. L. Kitano, eds. *Japanese Americans: From Relocation to Redress.* Rev. ed. Seattle: University of Washington Press, 1991.

DeWitt, Howard A. *Anti-Filipino Movements in California: A History, Bibliography and Study Guide.* San Francisco: R and E Research Associates, 1976.

DeWitt, Howard A. *Images of Ethnic and Radical Violence in California's Politics, 1917-1930: A Survey.* San Francisco: R and E Research Associates, 1975.

DeWitt, Howard A. *Violence in the Fields: Filipino Farm Labor Unionization During the Great Depression.* Saratoga, Calif.: Century Twenty One Publishing, 1980.

Divine, Robert A. *American Immigration Policy, 1924-1952.* New Haven, Conn.: Yale University Press, 1957.

Drinnon, Richard. *Keeper of Concentration Camps: Dillon S. Meyer and American Racism.* Berkeley: University of California Press, 1987.

Dudley, Michael Kioni. *A Call For Hawaiian Sovereignty.* Honolulu: Na Kane O Ka Malo Press, 1990.

Dudley, Michael Kioni. *Man, Gods, and Nature.* Honolulu: Na Kane O Ka Malo Press, 1990.

Dunn, Seamus, ed. *Managing Divided Cities.* Newbury Park, Calif.: Sage Publications, 1994.

Embrey, Sue Kunitomi, ed. *The Lost Years: 1942-1946.* Los Angeles: Moonlight Publications, 1972.

Embrey, Sue Kunitomi, Arthur A. Hansen, and Betty Kulberg Mitson, eds. *Manzanar Martyr: An Interview with Harry Y. Ueno.* Fullerton, Calif.: Japanese American Project, Oral History Program, California State University, Fullerton, 1986.

Emi, Frank. "Draft Resistance at the Heart Mountain Concentration Camp and the Fair Play Committee." In *Frontiers of Asian American Studies: Writing, Research and Commentary,* edited by Gail M. Nomura, Russell Endo, Stephen H. Sumida, and Russell C. Leong. Pullman: Washington State University Press, 1989.

Espiritu, Yen Le. *Asian American Panethnicity: Bridging Institutions and Identities.* Philadelphia: Temple University Press, 1992.

Essential Gandhi: An Anthology of His Writings on His Life, Work, and Ideas, The. Edited by Louis Fischer. New York: Vintage Books, 1962.

Fischer, Louis. *The Life of Mahatma Gandhi.* New York: Harper & Row, 1983.

Fuchs, Lawrence. *The American Kaleidoscope: Race, Ethnicity, and the Civic Culture.* Hanover, N.H.: Wesleyan University Press/University Press of New England, 1990.

Fugita, Stephen S., and David J. O'Brien. *Japanese American Ethnicity: The Persistence of Community.* Seattle: University of Washington Press, 1991.

Fukuda, Moritoshi. *Legal Problems of Japanese-Americans.* Tokyo: Keio Tsushin, 1980.

Gandhi, Mahatma. *An Autobiography: The Story of Experiments with Truth.* Translated by Mahadev Desai. Harmondsworth, Middlesex, England: Penguin Books, 1982.

Garrett, Jessie A., and Ronald C. Larson, eds. *Camp and Community: Manzanar and the Owens Valley.* Fullerton, Calif.: Japanese American Project, Oral History Program, California State University, Fullerton, 1977.

Glazer, Nathan. *Affirmative Discrimination: Ethnic Inequality and Public Policy.* New York: Basic Books, 1975.

Glazer, Nathan, ed. *Clamor at the Gates: The New American Immigration.* San Francisco: Institute for Contemporary Studies Press, 1985.

Greever, William. *The Bonanza West: The Story of the Western Mining Rushes, 1848-1900.* Norman: University of Oklahoma Press, 1963.

Grodzins, Morton. *Americans Betrayed: Poli-tics and the Japanese Evacuation.* Chicago: University of Chicago Press, 1949.

Hansen, Arthur A., and Betty E. Mitson, eds. *Voices Long Silent: An Oral Inquiry into the Japanese American Evacuation.* Fullerton, Calif.: Japanese American Project, Oral History Program, California State University, Fullerton, 1974.

Hartmann, Edward George. *The Movement to Americanize the Immigrant.* 1948. Reprint. New York: AMS Press, 1967.

Hawaii Advisory Committee to the U.S. Commission on Civil Rights. *A Broken Trust: The Hawaiian Homelands Program—Seventy Years of Failure of the Federal and State Governments to Protect the Civil Rights of Native Hawaiians.* Author, 1991.

Herman, Masako. *The Japanese in America: 1843-1973.* Dobbs Ferry, N.Y.: Oceana Publications, 1974.

Higham, John. *Strangers in the Land: Patterns of American Nativism, 1860-1925.* New Brunswick, N.J.: Rutgers University Press, 1955.

Hohri, William Minoru. *Repairing America.* Pullman: Washington State University Press, 1988.

Hosokawa, William. *JACL: In Quest of Justice.* New York: William Morrow, 1982.

Houston, Jeanne Wakatsuki, and James D. Houston. *Farewell to Manzanar.* Boston: Houghton Mifflin, 1973.

Hutchinson, Edward P. *Legislative History of American Immigration Policy, 1798-1965.* Philadelphia: University of Pennsylvania Press, 1981.

Ichihashi, Yamato. *Japanese in the United States.* Stanford, Calif.: Stanford University Press, 1932. Reprint. New York: Arno Press, 1969.

Ichioka, Yuji. *The Issei: The World of the First Generation of Japanese Immigrants, 1885-1924.* New York: Free Press, 1988.

Immigration and Nationality Act. Washington, D.C.: Government Printing Office, 1980.

Irons, Peter. *Justice at War: The Inside Story of the Japanese American Internment Cases.* New York: Oxford University Press, 1983.

Iwata, Masakazu. *Planted in Good Soil: A History of the Issei in United States Agriculture.* Vols. 1 and 2. New York: Peter Lang, 1992.

Kanahele, George S. *Hawaiian Renaissance.* Honolulu: Project Waiaha, 1982.

Kanahele, George S. *Ku Kanaka, Stand Tall: A Search for Hawaiian Values.* Honolulu: University of Hawaii Press, 1986.

Karnow, Stanley. *In Our Image: America's Empire in the Philippines.* New York: Random House, 1989.

Kent, Noel J. *Hawaii: Islands Under the Influence.* New York: Monthly Review Press, 1983.

Konvitz, Milton R. *The Alien and the Asiatic in American Law.* Ithaca, N.Y.: Cornell University Press, 1946.

Leonard, Karen Isaksen. *Making Ethnic Choices: California's Punjabi Mexican*

Americans. Philadelphia: Temple University Press, 1992.

Loewen, James W. *The Mississippi Chinese: Between Black and White*. 2d ed. Prospect Heights, Ill.: Waveland Press, 1988.

MacKenzie, Melody Kapilialoha. *Native Hawaiian Rights Handbook*. Honolulu: Native Hawaiian Legal Corporation, 1991.

McWilliams, Carey. *Brothers Under the Skin*. Rev. ed. Boston: Little, Brown, 1964.

Manlapit, Pablo. *Filipinos Fight for Justice: Case of the Filipino Laborers in the Big Strike of 1924*. Honolulu: Kumalee Publishing, 1933.

Masaoka, Mike, and Bill Hosokawa. *They Call Me Moses Masaoka*. New York: William Morrow, 1987.

Melendy, H. Brett. *Asians in America: Filipinos, Koreans, and East Indians*. Boston: Twayne, 1977.

Miller, Stuart C. *The Unwelcome Immigrant: The American Image of the Chinese, 1752-1882*. Berkeley: University of California Press, 1969.

Myer, Dillon S. *Uprooted Americans: The Japanese Americans and the War Relocation Authority During World War II*. Tucson: University of Arizona Press, 1971.

Nelson, Douglas W. *Heart Mountain: The History of an American Concentration Camp*. Madison: The State Historical Society of Wisconsin, 1976.

1924 Filipino Strike on Kauai, The. Manoa: Ethnic Studies Program, University of Hawaii, Manoa, 1979.

Ogawa, Dennis. *Kodomo No Tame Ni: For the Sake of the Children*. Honolulu: University of Hawaii Press, 1978.

Okamura, Jonathan Y., et al., eds. *The Filipino American Experience in Hawaii*. Social Process in Hawaii, vol. 33. Manoa: Department of Sociology, University of Hawaii, Manoa, 1991.

Omi, Michael, and Howard Winant. *Racial Formation in the United States: From the 1960s to the 1980s*. New York: Routledge & Kegan Paul, 1986.

Osborne, Thomas J. *"Empire Can Wait": American Opposition to Hawaiian Annexation, 1893-98*. Kent, Ohio: Kent State University Press, 1981.

Quan, R. S. *Lotus Among the Magnolias: The Mississippi Chinese*. Jackson University Press of Mississippi, 1982.

Quinsaat, Jesse. *Letters in Exile*. Los Angeles: UCLA Asian American Studies Center, 1976.

Reimers, David M. *Still the Golden Door: The Third World Comes to America*. New York: Columbia University Press, 1985.

Root, Maria P. P., ed. *Racially Mixed People in America*. Newbury Park, Calif.: Sage Publications, 1992.

Rothermund, Dietmar. *Mahatma Gandhi: An Essay in Political Biography*. New Delhi: Manohar, 1991.

Rudolph, Susanne Hoeber, and Lloyd I. Rudolph. *Gandhi: The Traditional Roots of*

Charisma. Chicago: University of Chicago Press, 1983.

Russ, William A., Jr. *The Hawaiian Revolution, 1893-94*. Selinsgrove, Pa.: Susquehanna University Press, 1959.

Rutledge, Paul James. *The Vietnamese Experience in America*. Bloomington: Indiana University Press, 1992.

Sandmeyer, Elmer C. *The Anti-Chinese Movement in California*. Urbana: University of Illinois Press, 1939.

San Juan, E., Jr. *Bulosan: An Introduction with Selections*. Manila: National Book Store, 1983.

San Juan, E., Jr. *Carlos Bulosan and the Imagination of the Class Struggle*. Quezon City: University of the Philippines Press, 1972.

Saxton, Alexander. *The Indispensable Enemy: Labor and the Anti-Chinese Movement in California*. Berkeley: University of California Press, 1971.

Scott, Esther, and Calvin Naito. *Against All Odds: The Japanese Americans' Campaign for Redress*. Cambridge, Mass.: Case Program, Harvard Kennedy School of Government, 1990.

Seward, George. *Chinese Immigrants: Its Social and Economic Aspects*. New York: Arno Press, 1970.

Shutt, Harry. *The Myth of Free Trade: Patterns of Protectionism Since 1945*. New York: Blackwell, 1985.

Siu, Paul C. P. *The Chinese Laundryman: A Study of Social Isolation*. Edited by John K. W. Tchen. New York: New York University Press, 1987.

Smith, Jared G. *The Big Five*. Honolulu: Advertiser Publishing, 1942.

Soga, Keiho. *Gojunenkan No Hawai Kaiko*. Honolulu: Kankokai, 1953.

Spickard, Paul R. *Mixed Blood: Intermarriage and Ethnic Identity in Twentieth-Century America*. Madison: University of Wisconsin Press, 1989.

Stannard, David E. *Before the Horror: The Population of Hawaii on the Eve of Western Contact*. Honolulu: Social Science Research Institute, University of Hawaii, 1989.

State of Asian Pacific America: A Public Policy Report, Policy Issues to the Year 2020, The. Los Angeles: LEAP Asian Pacific American Public Policy Institute and UCLA Asian American Studies Center, 1993.

Takaki, Ronald T. *Iron Cages: Race and Culture in Nineteenth Century America*. New York: Alfred A. Knopf, 1979.

Takaki, Ronald. *Strangers from a Different Shore: A History of Asian Americans*. Boston: Little, Brown, 1989.

Tamura, Eileen H. *Americanization, Acculturation, and Ethnic Identity: The Nisei Generation in Hawaii*. Urbana: University of Illinois Press, 1994.

TenBroek, Jacobus, et al. *Prejudice, War and the Constitution*. Berkeley: University of California Press, 1954.

Thomas, Dorothy Swaine, and Richard S.

Nishimoto. *The Spoilage*. Berkeley: University of California Press, 1946.

Trask, Haunani-Kay. *From a Native Daughter: Colonialism and Sovereignty in Hawaii*. Monroe, Maine: Common Courage Press, 1993.

U.S. Commission on Civil Rights. *Civil Rights Issues Facing Asian Americans in the 1990s: A Report of the United States Commission on Civil Rights*. Washington, D.C.: Government Printing Office, 1992.

U.S. Commission on Civil Rights. *Recent Activities Against Citizens and Residents of Asian Descent*. Washington, D.C.: Government Printing Office, 1986.

U.S. Commission on Wartime Relocation and Internment of Civilians. *Personal Justice Denied: Report of the Commission on Wartime Relocation and the Internment of Civilians*. Washington, D.C.: Government Printing Office, 1983.

U.S. Congress. House. Committee on Interior and Insular Affairs. *Personal Justice Denied: Report of the Commission on Wartime Relocation and Internment of Civilians*. 102d Congress, 2d session, 1983. Washington, D.C.: Government Printing Office, 1992.

U.S. Congress. House. Committee on the Territories. *Proposed Amendments to the Organic Act of the Territory of Hawaii*. 67th Congress, 1st session, 1921. House Report 7257.

U.S. Congress. House. *President's Message Relating to the Hawaiian Islands*. 53rd Congress, 2d Session, 1893. Executive Document 47.

U.S. Congress. Senate. *Senate Report 227 ("Morgan Report")*. 53rd Congress, 2d session, 1894.

U.S. Reports. *Cases Adjudged in the Supreme Court at October Term 1922*. Vol. 261. Washington, D.C.: Government Printing Office, 1923.

U.S. War Relocation Authority. *Administrative Highlights of the WRA Program*. Washington, D.C.: Government Printing Office, 1946.

Unity '94. *Kerner Plus 25: A Call for Action*. Oakland, Calif.: Unity '94, 1993.

Van Wolferen, Karl. *The Enigma of Japanese Power*. New York: Alfred A. Knopf, 1989.

Vogel, Ezra. *Japan As Number One: Lessons for America*. New York: Harper Colophon, 1979.

Wakukawa, Ernest Katsumi. *A History of the Japanese People in Hawaii*. Honolulu: The Toyo Shoin, 1938.

Weglyn, Michi. *Years of Infamy: The Untold Story of America's Concentration Camps*. New York: William Morrow, 1976.

Wei, William. *The Asian American Movement*. Philadelphia: Temple University Press, 1993.

Wu, Cheng-Tsu, ed. *"Chink!": A Documentary History of Anti-Chinese Prejudice in America*. New York: World, 1972.

Yu, Renqiu. *To Save China, To Save Ourselves:*

The Chinese Hand Laundry Alliance of New York. Philadelphia: Temple University Press, 1992.

Yun, Grace, ed. *A Look Beyond the Model Minority Image: Critical Issues in Asian America*. New York: Minority Rights Group, 1989.

RELIGIOUS GROUPS AND RELIGION

Ali, Ahmed, tr. *Al-Quran: A Contemporary Translation*. 1984. Rev. ed. Princeton, N.J.: Princeton University Press, 1988.

Anderson, Gerald H. *Studies in Philippine Church History*. Ithaca, N.Y.: Cornell University Press, 1969.

Basham, A. L. *The Origins and Development of Classical Hinduism*. Boston: Beacon Press, 1989.

Basham, A. L. *The Wonder That Was India: A Survey of the Culture of the Indian Subcontinent Before the Coming of the Muslims*. London: Sidgwick and Jackson, 1954.

Boucher, Sandy. *Turning the Wheel: American Women Creating the New Buddhism*. San Francisco: Harper & Row, 1988.

Buddhist Churches of America. *Buddhist Churches of America*. 2 vols. Chicago: Nobart, 1974.

Cayton, Horace R., and Anne O. Lively. *The Chinese in the United States and the Chinese Christian Church*. New York: National Council of Churches, 1955.

Chen, Kenneth. *Buddhism in China: A Historical Survey*. Princeton, N.J.: Princeton University Press, 1964.

Chitrabhanu, Gurudev Shree. *Twelve Facets of Reality: The Jain Path to Freedom*. New York: Dodd, Mead, 1980.

Chryssides, George D. *The Advent of Sun Myung Moon: The Origins, Beliefs, and Practices of the Unification Church*. New York: St. Martin's Press, 1991.

Clark, Donald N. *Christianity in Modern Korea*. Lanham, Md.: University Press of America, 1986.

Cole, W. Owen. *The Guru in Sikhism*. London: Darton, Longman & Todd, 1982.

Cole, W. Owen, and Piara Singh Sambhi. *The Sikhs: Their Religious Beliefs and Practices*. London: Routledge & Kegan Paul, 1978.

Dearman, Marion. "Structure and Function of Religion in the Los Angeles Korean Community: Some Aspects." In *Koreans in Los Angeles: Prospects and Promises*, edited by E. Y. Yu, E. H. Phillips, and E. S. Yang. Los Angeles: Center for Korean-American and Korean Studies, California State University, Los Angeles, 1982.

De Bary, William T., ed. *The Buddhist Tradition in India, China, and Japan*. New York: Vintage Books, 1972.

Dolan, Jay P., ed. *The American Catholic Parish: A History from 1850 to the Present*. Vol. 2. Mahwah, N.J.: Paulist Press, 1987.

Doore, Gary, ed. and comp. *Shaman's Path: Healing, Personal Growth and Empowerment*. Boston: Shambhala Press, 1988.

Eliot, Charles. *Japanese Buddhism*. London: Routledge & Kegan Paul, 1969.

Ellis, William. *Journal of William Ellis*. Honolulu: Advertiser Publishing, 1963.

Embree, Ainslie T., ed. *The Hindu Tradition*. New York: Random House, 1966.

Embree, Ainslie T., and Stephen Hay, eds. *Sources of Indian Tradition*, 2d ed. 2 vols. New York: Columbia University Press, 1988.

Endress, Gerhard. *An Introduction to Islam*. Translated by Carole Hillenbrand. New York: Columbia University Press, 1988.

Fichter, Joseph H. *The Holy Family of Father Moon*. Kansas City, Mo.: Leaven Press, 1985.

Fields, Rick. *How the Swans Came to the Lake: A Narrative History of Buddhism in America*. 3d ed. Boston: Shambhala, 1992.

Fugita, Stephen S., and David J. O'Brien. *Japanese American Ethnicity: The Persistence of Community*. Seattle: University of Washington Press, 1991.

Hall, Daniel George Edward. *A History of South East Asia*. New York: St. Martin's Press, 1961.

Hardacre, Helen. *Shinto and the State, 1868-1988*. Princeton, N.J.: Princeton University Press, 1989.

Harrison, B. *South-East Asia: A Short History*. London: Macmillan, 1954.

Hoke, Donald, ed. *The Church in Asia*. Chicago: Moody Press, 1975.

Holtom, Daniel C. *The National Faith of Japan: A Study in Modern Shinto*. London: Kegan Paul, 1938.

Hopkins, Thomas J. *The Hindu Religious Tradition*. Encino, Calif.: Dickenson, 1971.

Jaini, Padmanabh S. *The Jaina Path of Purification*. Berkeley: University of California Press, 1979.

Janelli, Roger, and Dawnhee Yim Janelli. *Ancestor Worship and Korean Society*. Stanford, Calif.: Stanford University Press, 1982.

Jayakar, Pupul. *Krishnamurti: A Biography*. San Francisco: Harper & Row, 1986.

Judah, J. Stillson. *The History and Philosophy of the Metaphysical Movements in America*. Philadelphia: The Westminster Press, 1967.

Kamakau, Samuel. *Ruling Chiefs of Hawaii*. Rev. ed. Honolulu: Kamehameha Schools Press, 1992.

Kameeleihiwa, Lilikala. *Native Land and Foreign Desires*. Honolulu: Bishop Museum Press, 1992.

Kashima, Tetsuden. *Buddhism in America: The Social Organization of an Ethnic Religious Institution*. Westport, Conn.: Greenwood Press, 1977.

Kendall, Laurel. *Shamans, Housewives, and Other Restless Spirits*. Honolulu: University of Hawaii Press, 1985.

Kinsley, David R. *Hinduism: A Cultural Perspective*. Englewood Cliffs, N.J.: Prentice-Hall, 1982.

Kitagawa, Joseph M. *Religion in Japanese History*. New York: Columbia University Press, 1966.

Kitagawa, Joseph, and Mark Cummings, eds. *Buddhism and Asian History*. New York: Macmillan, 1989.

Kitano, Harry H. L. *Japanese Americans: The Evolution of a Subculture*. Englewood Cliffs, N.J.: Prentice-Hall, 1969.

Krishnamurti, Jiddu. *Krishnamurti on Education*. New Delhi: Orient Longman, 1974.

Krishnamurti, Jiddu. *Krishnamurti's Notebook*. New York: Harper & Row, 1976.

Kumar, Acharya Sushil. *Song of the Soul*. Blairstown, N.J.: Siddhachalam, 1987.

Lemoine, Jacques. "Shamanism in the Context of Hmong Resettlement." In *The Hmong in Transition*, edited by Glenn Hendricks, Bruce Downing, and Amos Deinard. Staten Island, New York: Center for Migration Studies of New York, 1986.

Lutyens, Mary. *Krishnamurti: The Years of Awakening*. London: John Murray, 1975.

Lutyens, Mary. *Krishnamurti: The Years of Fulfillment*. London: John Murray, 1983.

Lutyens, Mary. *Krishnamurti: The Open Door*. London: John Murray, 1988.

Ma, L. Eve Armentrout. "Chinese Traditional Religion in North America and Hawaii." In *Chinese America: History and Perspectives*. San Francisco: Chinese Historical Society of America, 1987.

McLeod, W. H. *The Evolution of the Sikh Community*. Oxford, England: Clarendon Press, 1976.

McLeod, W. H., ed. and trans. *Textual Sources for the Study of Sikhism*. Totowa, N.J.: Barnes & Noble Books, 1984.

Manikam, R. B., and L. T. Thomas. *The Church in South-East Asia*. New York: Friendship Press, 1956.

Mark, Diane Mei Lin, and Ginger Chih. *A Place Called Chinese America*. Dubuque, Iowa: Kendall-Hunt, 1982.

Maududi, Abul Ala. *Fundamentals of Islam*. 1975. 7th ed. Lahore, Pakistan: Islamic Publications, 1986.

Melton, J. Gordon. *The Encyclopedia of American Religions*. 2d ed. Detroit: Gale Research, 1987.

Miller, Timothy, ed. *America's Alternative Religions*. Albany: State University of New York Press, 1993.

Miller, Timothy, ed. *When Prophets Die: The Postcharismatic Fate of New Religious Movements*. Albany: State University of New York Press, 1991.

Moffett, Samuel Hugh. *The Christians of Korea*. New York: Friendship Press, 1962.

Moffett, Samuel Hugh. *A History of Christianity in Asia*. Vol. 1, *Beginnings to 1500*. San Francisco: Harper San Francisco, 1992.

Moon, Sun Myung. *A Prophet Speaks Today*. New York: HSA Publications, 1975.

Morreale, Don, ed. *Buddhist America: Centers, Retreats, Practices*. Santa Fe, N. Mex.: John Muir, 1988.

Mulholland, John F. *Hawaii's Religions*. Rutland, Vt.: Charles Tuttle, 1970.

Neusner, Jacob, ed. *World Religions in America: An Introduction*. Louisville, Ky.: Westminster/John Knox Press, 1994.

Ono Sokyo. *Shinto the Kami Way*. Rutland, Vt.: Charles E. Tuttle, 1962.

Palmer, Spencer J. *Korea and Christianity*. Seoul, Korea: Hollym, 1967.

Pang, Wing Ning. *Build Up the Kingdom: A Study of the North American Chinese Church*. Pasadena: North American Congress of Chinese Evangelicals, 1980.

Pang, Wing Ning. *The Chinese and the Chinese Church in America*. Houston: National Convocation on Evangelizing Ethnic America, 1985.

Phillips, E. H., and E. Y. Yu, eds. *Religions in Korea: Beliefs and Cultural Values*. Los Angeles: Center for Korean-American and Korean Studies, California State University, Los Angeles, 1982.

Pou Kuksa. *A Buddha from Korea: The Zen Teachings of T'aego*. Translated by J. C. Cleary. Boston: Shambhala, 1988.

Rahman, Fazlur. *Islam*. 1966. 2d ed. Chicago: University of Chicago Press, 1979.

Ro, Bong-Rin, and Marlin L. Nelson, eds. *Korean Church Growth Explosion*. Seoul, Korea: Word of Life Press, 1985.

Robinson, Richard H., and Willard L. Johnson. *The Buddhist Religion: A Historical Introduction*. 3d ed. Belmont, Calif.: Wadsworth, 1982.

Ross, Floyd H. *Shinto, the Way of Japan*. Boston: Beacon Press, 1965.

Sarma, D. S. *Studies in the Renaissance of Hinduism in the Nineteenth and Twentieth Centuries*. Benares: Benares Hindu University, 1944.

Schimmel, Annemarie. *Islam: An Introduction*. Albany: State University of New York Press, 1992.

Schumann, Hans W. *The Historical Buddha*. Translated by M. Walshe. London: Arkana/Penguin, 1989.

Scott, George, Jr. "A New Year in a New Land: Religious Change Among the Lao Hmong Refugees in San Diego." In *The Hmong in the West: Observations and Reports*, edited by Bruce Downing, Bruce Olney, and Douglas Olney. Minneapolis: Center for Urban and Regional Affairs, University of Minnesota, 1982.

Seigel, Taggart. *Blue Collar and Buddha*. San Francisco: CrossCurrent Media, 1987. Film.

Shaner, David Edward. *The Bodymind Experience in Japanese Buddhism: A Phenomenological Perspective of Kukai and Dogen*. Albany: State University of New York Press, 1985.

Shearer, Roy E. *Wildfire: Church Growth in Korea*. Grand Rapids, Mich.: William B. Eerdmans, 1966.

Shim, Steve. *Korean Immigrant Churches Today in Southern California*. San Francisco: R and E Research Associates, 1977.

Shulman, Albert M. *The Religious Heritage of America*. San Diego: A. S. Barnes & Company, 1981.

Singer, Milton. *Traditional India: Structure and Change*. Philadelphia: American Folklore Society, 1959.

Sontag, Frederick. *Sun Myung Moon and the Unification Church*. Nashville: Abingdon Press, 1977.

Stevenson, Margaret. *The Heart of Jainism*. London: Oxford University Press, 1915.

Suzuki, Daisetz Taitaro. *Japanese Spirituality*. 1972. Reprint. New York: Greenwood Press, 1988.

Suzuki, Daisetz Taitaro. *The Training of the Zen Buddhist Monk*. 1934. Reprint. New York: Globe Press, 1991.

Swearer, Donald. *Buddhism and Society in Southeast Asia*. Chambersburg, Pa.: Anima, 1981.

Takaki, Ronald. *Strangers from a Different Shore: A History of Asian Americans*. Boston: Little, Brown, 1989.

Tuck, Donald R. *Buddhist Churches of America: Jodo Shinshu*. Lewiston, N.Y.: Edwin Mellen Press, 1987.

Valeri, Valerio. *Kingship and Sacrifice*. Chicago: University of Chicago Press, 1985.

Velazquez, Elaine. *Moving Mountains: The Story of the Yiu Mien*. New York: Filmmakers Library, 1989. Film.

Watt, William Montgomery. *Muhammad, Prophet and Statesman*. 1961. Reprint. Oxford: Oxford University Press, 1964.

Weber, Max. *The Religion of India*. Glencoe, Ill.: Free Press, 1958.

Weinstein, Stanley. *Buddhism Under the Tang*. Cambridge, England: Cambridge University Press, 1987.

Wells, Marianne Kaye. *Chinese Temples in California*. San Francisco: R and E Research Associates, 1971.

Williams, Raymond Brady. *Religions of Immigrants from India and Pakistan: New Trends in the American Tapestry*. New York: Cambridge University Press, 1988.

Wright, Arthur. *Buddhism in Chinese History*. Stanford, Calif.: Stanford University Press, 1988.

Yamaoka, Seigen H. *Jodo Shinshu: An Introduction*. San Francisco: Buddhist Churches of America, 1989.

Zaehner, R. C. *Hinduism*. New York: Oxford University Press, 1971.

Zaretsky, Irving I. and Mark P. Leone, eds. *Religious Movements in Contemporary America*. Princeton, N.J.: Princeton University Press, 1974.

Zürcher, Erich. *Buddhist Conquest of China: The Spread and Adaptation of Buddhism in Early Medieval China*. Leiden, The Netherlands: E. J. Brill, 1959.

MARTIAL ARTS

Finn, Michael. *Martial Arts: A Complete Illustrated History*. Woodstock, N.Y.: Overlook Press, 1988.

Kauz, Herman. *The Martial Spirit: An Introduction to the Origin, Philosophy, and Psychology of the Martial Arts*. Woodstock, N.Y.: Overlook Press, 1988.

Lewis, Peter. *Martial Arts of the Orient*. New York: Gallery Books, 1985.

Neff, Fred. *Basic Jujitsu Handbook*. Minneapolis: Lerner Publications, 1976.

Soet, John Steven. *Martial Arts Around the World*. Burbank, Calif.: Unique Publications, 1991.

Spear, Robert K. *Hapkido: The Integrated Fighting Art*. Burbank: Unique Publications, 1988.

Tegner, Bruce, *Karate: Beginner to Black Belt*. Ventura, Calif.: Thor Publishing Company, 1982.

Williams, Bryn. *Martial Arts of the Orient*. New York: Hamlyn, 1975.

Wong, Doc-Fai, and Jane Hallander. *Tai Chi Chuan's Internal Secrets*. Burbank, Calif.: Unique Publications, 1991.

Yates, Keith D. *The Complete Book of Taekwon Do Forms*. Boulder, Colo.: Paladin Press, 1982.

Yates, Keith D. *Tae Kwon Do Basics*. New York: Sterling Publishing Company, 1987.

WOMEN'S ISSUES

Asian Women United of California, ed. *Making Waves: An Anthology By and About Asian American Women*. Boston: Beacon Press, 1989.

Barry, Kathleen, Charlotte Bunch, and Shirley Castley, eds. *International Feminism: Networking Against Female Sexual Slavery*. New York: International Women's Tribune Centre, 1984.

Berkin, Carol Ruth, and Mary Beth Norton, eds. *Women of America*. Boston: Houghton Mifflin, 1979.

Boucher, Sandy. *Turning the Wheel: American Women Creating the New Buddhism*. San Francisco: Harper & Row, 1988.

Catlin, Amy, ed. *APSARA: The Feminine in Cambodian Art*. Los Angeles: Woman's Building, 1987.

Chan, Sucheng. "The Exclusion of Chinese Women." In *Entry Denied: Exclusion and the Chinese Community in America, 1882-1943*, edited by Sucheng Chan. Philadelphia: Temple University Press, 1991.

Cretser, Gary A., and Joseph J. Leon, eds. *Intermarriage in the United States*. New York: Haworth, 1982.

De Souza, Alfred, ed. *Women in Contemporary India*. Delhi: Manohar Book Service, 1975.

Duley, Margot, and Mary I. Edwards, eds. *The Cross-Cultural Study of Women*. New York: Feminist Press, 1986.

Enloe, Cynthia. *Bananas, Beaches and Bases: Making Feminist Sense of International Politics*. Berkeley: University of California Press, 1990.

Everett, Jana Matson. *Women and Social Change in India*. Delhi: Heritage, 1979.

Glenn, Evelyn Nakano. *Issei, Nisei, War Bride: Three Generations of Japanese American*

Women in Domestic Service. Philadelphia: Temple University Press, 1986.

Goodwin, Clarissa Garland. *The International Marriage: Or, The Building of a Nation*. Los Angeles: UCLA Special Collections, 1931.

Gross, Susan Hill, and Mary Hill Rojas. *Contemporary Issues for Women in South Asia: India, Pakistan, Bangladesh, Sri Lanka, Nepal, and Bhutan*. St. Louis Park, Minn.: Glenhurst, 1989.

Hayslip, Le Ly, with Jay Wurts. *When Heaven and Earth Changed Places: A Vietnamese Woman's Journey from War to Peace*. New York: Doubleday, 1989.

Imamura, Anne E. *Strangers in a Strange Land: Coping with Marginality in International Marriage*. East Lansing: Women in International Development, Michigan State University, 1987.

Jahan, Rounaq, and Hanna Papanek, eds. *Women and Development: Perspectives from South and Southeast Asia*. Dacca: The Bangladesh Institute of Law and International Affairs, 1979.

Kikumura, Akemi. *Through Harsh Winters: The Life of a Japanese Immigrant Woman*. Novato, Calif.: Chandler and Sharp, 1981.

Kim, Bok-Lim C. *Korean-American Child at School and at Home*. Washington, D.C.: Administration for Children, Youth, and Families, U.S. Department of Health, Education, and Welfare, 1980.

Kingston, Maxine Hong. *The Woman Warrior: Memoirs of a Girlhood Among Ghosts*. New York: Alfred A. Knopf, 1976.

Larsen, Wanwadee. *Confessions of a Mail Order Bride: American Life Through Thai Eyes*. Far Hills, N.J.: New Horizon Press, 1989.

Lee, Mary Paik. *Quiet Odyssey: A Pioneer Korean Woman in America*. Edited by Sucheng Chan. Seattle: University of Washington Press, 1990.

Lim, Shirley Geok-lin. *Approaches to Teaching Kingston's "The Woman Warrior."* New York: Modern Language Association of America, 1991.

Ling, Amy. *Between Worlds: Women Writers of Chinese Ancestry*. New York: Pergamon Press, 1990.

Linking Our Lives: Chinese American Women of Los Angeles. Los Angeles: Chinese Historical Society of Southern California, 1984.

McCunn, Ruthanne Lum. *Thousand Pieces of Gold*. Boston, Mass.: Beacon Press, 1981.

Matsumoto, Valerie J. "Desperately Seeking 'Deirdre': Gender Roles, Multicultural Relations, and Nisei Women Writers of the 1930s." *Frontiers* 12, no. 1 (1991): 19-32.

Mindel, Charles H., and Robert W. Habenstein, eds. *Ethnic Families in America: Patterns and Variations*. New York: Elsevier, 1976.

Nakano, Mei. *Japanese American Women: Three Generations, 1890-1990*. With *Okaasan* by Grace Shibata. San Francisco: National Japanese American Historical Society, 1990.

Nomura, Gail M. "Tsugiki, a Grafting: A History of a Japanese Pioneer Woman in Washington State." *Women's Studies* 14 (1987): 15-37.

Root, Maria P. P., ed. *Racially Mixed People in America*. Newbury Park, Calif.: Sage Publications, 1992.

Sakala, Carol. *Women of South Asia: A Guide to Resources*. Millwood, N.Y.: Kraus International, 1980.

Smith, Sidonie. *A Poetics of Women's Autobiography: Marginality and the Fictions of Self-Representation*. Bloomington: Indiana University Press, 1987.

Sone, Monica. *Nisei Daughter*. Boston: Little, Brown, 1953.

Spickard, Paul R. *Mixed Blood: Intermarriage and Ethnic Identity in Twentieth-Century America*. Madison: University of Wisconsin Press, 1989.

Sturdevant, Saundra Pollock, and Brenda Stoltzfus, eds. *Let the Good Times Roll: Prostitution and the U.S. Military in Asia*. New York: The New Press, 1992.

Sue, Stanley, and James Morishima. "Understanding the Asian American Family." In *The Mental Health of Asian Americans*. San Francisco: Jossey-Bass, 1982.

Takaki, Ronald. *Strangers from a Different Shore*. Boston: Little, Brown, 1989.

U.S. Commission on Civil Rights. *Civil Rights Issues Facing Asian Americans in the 1990's*. Washington, D.C.: Author, 1992.

Weglyn, Michi. *Years of Infamy: The Untold Story of America's Concentration Camps*. New York: Morrow, 1976.

Women of South Asian Descent Collective, eds. *Our Feet Walked the Sky: Women of the South Asian Diaspora*. San Francisco: Aunt Lute Books, 1993.

Wong, Jade Snow. *Fifth Chinese Daughter*. 1945. New ed. Seattle: University of Washington Press, 1989.

Yamamoto, Hisaye. *Seventeen Syllables and Other Stories*. Latham, N.Y.: Kitchen Table—Women of Color Press, 1988.

Yu, Eui-Young, and Earl H. Phillips, eds. *Korean Women in Transition: At Home and Abroad*. Los Angeles: Center for Korean-American and Korean Studies, California State University, Los Angeles, 1987.

Yung, Judy. *Chinese Women of America: A Pictorial History*. Published for the Chinese Culture Foundation of San Francisco. Seattle: University of Washington Press, 1986.

Subject List

The following list categorizes the entries of this encyclopedia by various subject or topic areas. The first section alphabetically lists the entries by relevant population group: Asian Americans (panethnic); Asian Indian Americans and the Indian diaspora; China; Chinese Americans and the Chinese diaspora; Filipino Americans and the Filipino diaspora; Hawaii; Hawaiian and Pacific Islander Americans; India; Japan; Japanese Americans and the Japanese diaspora; Korea; Korean Americans and the Korean diaspora; Pacific Islands; The Philippines; South Asia; South Asian Americans; Southeast Asia; Southeast Asian Americans and the Southeast Asian diaspora; Vietnam; and Vietnamese Americans. The second section, beginning on page 1803, alphabetically lists the entries under fifteen subject areas: Arts, Entertainment, and the Media; Cuisine, Customs, and Cultural Traditions; Community Studies; Education and Scholarship; Employment, Business, Labor, and the Economy; Immigration; Language and Languages; Organizations; Politics, Government, Community Leadership, Law, and the Military; Prejudice, Discrimination, Civil Rights, and Intergroup Relations; Religious Groups and Religion; Science, Technology, Medicine and Health; Social Movements; Sports; and Women's Issues.

Entries by Population Group

ASIAN AMERICANS (PANETHNIC)

A. Magazine
Aion
Alien Land Law of 1913
Alien Land Law of 1920
Alien Land Laws
Aliens ineligible to citizenship
Amerasia Bookstore and Gallery
Amerasia Journal
American Citizens for Justice
American Civil Liberties Union
Americanization movement
Angel Island Asian American Theatre
  Company
Anti-Asian violence
Antimiscegenation laws
Asia-Pacific Economic Cooperation
Asia-Pacific Triangle
Asia Society
Asian American Arts Alliance
Asian American Arts Centre
Asian, Inc.
Asian American collections
Asian American Dance Performances
Asian American Dance Theatre
Asian American International Film
  Festival
Asian American Journalists Association
Asian American Movement
Asian American Political Coalition
Asian American population
Asian American Renaissance
Asian American Resource Workshop
Asian American Studies
Asian American Studies, University of
  California, Berkeley
Asian American Studies, University of
  California, Irvine
Asian American Studies Center, University of
  California, Los Angeles
Asian-American Theatre Company
Asian Americans for Community
  Involvement
Asian Americans for Equality
Asian CineVision
Asian Immigrant Women's Advocates

Asian Law Alliance
Asian Law Caucus
Asian Pacific American Labor Alliance
Asian Pacific American Legal Center
  of Southern California
Asian Pacific American Librarians
  Association
Asian Pacific Democratic Club
Asian Pacific Health Forum
Asian/Pacific Women's Network
Asian Week
Asian Women United
Asiaweek
Association for Asian American Studies
Association for Asian Performance
Association for Asian Studies
Association of Asian/Pacific American Artists
Austronesian languages
Bamboo Ridge: The Hawaii Writer's Quarterly
Bandung Conference
Barred Zone Act of 1917
Basement Workshop
Bilingual education
Bilingual Education Act of 1974
Bridge
Celler, Emanuel
Chin, Vincent, case
Cockrill v. People of State of California
Cold Tofu
Coloma
Combined Asian-American Resources Project
Commission on Asian American Affairs
CrossCurrent Media
Demonstration Project for Asian
  Americans
Displaced Persons Act of 1948
East West Players
English as a Second Language
English Standard Schools
Families
Feng shui
Filipinos and the Alaska canned salmon
  industry
Film
Foran Act of 1885
Frick v. Webb

Fujii Sei v. State of California
Gay and lesbian issues
Getting Together
Gidra
Godzilla
Grove Farm Plantation
Hall, Jack
Hampton v. Wong Mow Sun
Hawaii International Film Festival
Hua Long
I Wor Kuen
Immigration Act of 1882
Immigration Act of 1924
Immigration Act of 1990
Immigration and Nationality Act of 1965
Immigration policy
Imperial conferences
International District
International Examiner
Interracial marriage
Jade magazine
Johnson, Albert
Kearny Street Workshop
Leadership Education for Asian Pacifics
Light, Ivan
Local
Lodge, Henry Cabot
London, Jack
Los Angeles County Anti-Asiatic Society
Lyman, Stanford
McCarran-Walter Act of 1952
Mail-order brides
Martial arts
Masaoka v. State of California
Massie case
Media Action Network for Asian
  Americans
M.E.L.U.S.
Migration, primary
Migration, secondary
Miss Saigon controversy
Model Minority
National Asian American Telecommunications
  Association
National Asian Pacific American Bar
  Association

National Asian Pacific American Legal
    Consortium
National Democratic Council of Asian and
    Pacific Americans
Native Sons of the Golden West
Nativism
Naturalization Act of 1790
News Media and Asian Americans
Nirvana
Northwest Asian American Theatre
1.5 generation
Organization of PanAsian American Women
Oyama v. California
Pan Asian Repertory Theatre
Perez v. Sharp
Pidgin
Plessy v. Ferguson
Porterfield v. Webb
Racial formula
Ross, Edward Alsworth
Rotating credit associations
San Francisco State College strike
Shamanism
Sojourners
Suburbs
Sugar strike of 1946
Tea
Transpacific
U.S. Immigration Commission
Vietnam War and Asian Americans
Visual Communications
Waipahu Cultural Garden Park
Webb v. O'Brien
Wei, William
Wei Min Bao
Wing Luke Asian Museum
Women, Asian American
Yappie

*ASIAN INDIAN AMERICANS AND THE
INDIAN DIASPORA*

Adi Granth
American-Born Confused Deshis
Asian Indian businesses in the United States
Asian Indian women in the United States
Asian Indians in the motel/hotel business
Asian Indians in the United States
Association of Indians in America
Bellingham incident
Bose, Sudhindra
Chandrasekhar, Subrahmanyan
Cheema, Boona
Continuous voyage
Das, Tarak Nath
Dayal, Har
Diwali
Fijian Indians
Gandhi, Mahatma
German-Hindu Conspiracy
Ghadr movement
Gujarat
Gupta, Kanta Chandra
High-caste Hindus
Hindu Association of the Pacific Coast
Hindustan Gadar
HMCS *Rainbow*
India Abroad
India Currents

India League of America
India League of America, Madison,
    Wisconsin
India-West
Indian music and dance
Indian religious movements in the United
    States
Indian restaurants and cuisine
International Society for Krishna
    Consciousness
Jensen, Joan M.
Khalsa Diwan Society
Khan, Ali Akbar
Komagata Maru incident
Krishnamurti, Jiddu
La Brack, Bruce W.
Lal, Gobind Behari
Luce-Celler Bill of 1946
Mahesh Yogi, Maharishi
Marriage matchmaking, Asian Indians and
Mehta, Sonny [Ajay Singh]
Mehta, Ved [Parkash]
Mehta, Zubin
Mohanty, Chandra Talpade
Mukherjee, Bharati
Muzumdar, Haridas [Thakordas]
Naipaul, V. S. [Vidiadhar Surajprasad]
Nonresident Indians
Pandit, Sakaram Ganesh
Ram, Kanshi
Saund, Dalip Singh
Self-Realization Fellowship
Seth, Vikram
Shamakami
Shankar, Ravi
Shridharani, Krishnalal
Sikh Studies programs in North America
Sikhs in Canada
Sikhs in the United States
Sikhs in Yuba City
Singh, Gurdit
Singh, Jane
Singh, Jawala
South Asian American writers
South Asian diaspora
South Asian immigration to Canada
South Asian immigration to the United States
South Asian immigration to the United States,
    sources of
South Asian press in the United States
South Asian Studies centers
South Asians in the United States
Spivak, Gayatri Chakravorty
Stockton *gurdwara*
Subba Row, Yellapragada
United States v. Bhagat Singh Thind
Vivekananda
Watumull, G. J. [Gobindram Jhamandas]
Watumull, Jhamandas
Watumull Foundation
Women of South Asian Descent
    Collective
Zoroastrians

CHINA

Acupuncture and moxibustion
American Institute in Taiwan

Ancestor worship
Baohuanghui
Beijing
Boxer Rebellion
Buck, Pearl S.
Burlingame Treaty
Canton
Cantonese
Cathay
Chennault, Anna C.
Chiang Kai-shek
Chiang Soong Mei-ling
China
China, People's Republic of
China, People's Republic of—
    recognition
China, Republic of
China Books and Periodicals
China Institute in America
China lobby
China politics in the Chinese American
    community
China trade
China War Relief Association
Chinese almanac
Chinese boycott of 1905
Chinese Buddhism
Chinese calendar
Chinese Communist Party
Chinese contributions to the English
    language
Chinese Cultural Center of Visalia
Chinese Culture Foundation of San
    Francisco
The Chinese Diaspora
Chinese language
Chinese martial arts
Chinese music and dance
Chinese New Year
Chinese opera
Chinese popular religion
Chinese restaurants and cuisine
Chinese Revolution of 1911
Chinese romanization
Chinese zodiac
Chop suey
Confucianism
Coolie trade
Coordination Council for North
    American Affairs
Divination
Double Ten
Dragon Boat Festival
Dragon dance
Empress Dowager
Empress of China
Fan-Tan
February 28 incident
Feng shui
Fenollosa, Ernest Francisco
Foot-binding
Formosa
Fu Manchu
Fujian
Ginger and red egg party
Gresham-Yang Treaty
Guangdong
Guangong

Protectorate Treaty
Pyongyang
Restoration Association
Rhee, Syngman
Roh Tae Woo
Russo-Japanese War
Seoul
Shufeldt, Robert W.
Silla Dynasty
Sin Hanguk po
Sinhan Minbo
Sino-Japanese War of 1894-1895
Son Pyong-hui
Stevens, Durham White
Student uprisings of 1929-1930
Taedon Silop Jusik Hoesa
Taehan Tongnip Manse
Taewon-gun
Taft-Katsura Agreement
Thirty-eighth parallel
Tonghak movement
Tonghak rebellion
Tongji-hoe
Tongnip Sinmun
Tongnip Sinmun
Treaty of Annexation
Treaty of Chemulpo
Treaty of Kanghwa
Treaty of Portsmouth
Treaty of Shimonoseki
Treaty of Tientsin
Unification Church
U.S.-Korea relations
U.S. military bases in Asia
Yak phab
Yi Dynasty
Yi Tong-hwi
Yi Wan-yong
Yun Chii-ho

KOREAN AMERICANS AND THE KOREAN DIASPORA

Ahn Chang-ho
Ahn, Philip
Anti-Korean incidents
Asiatic Exclusion League
Association of Korean Political Studies in
  North America
Berger v. Bishop
Bul kogi
Cairo Declaration
Center for Korean Studies, University
  of Hawaii
Cha, Theresa Hak Kyung
Chang, Edward T.
Chang In-hwan
Chap chae
Chinmok-hoe
Cho, Henry
Choy, Christine
Choy, Herbert Young Cho
Christian Society for the Realization
  of Justice
Chung, Henry
Chung, Myung-Whun
Chusok
Declaration of the All-Korean
  Convention

Deshler, David W.
Dok guk
Dong-hoe
Dong-jang
Ese
Ewha Chinmok-hoe
First Korean Independence Air Force
Foreign Commission of the Korean Overseas
  Association
Gramm, Wendy Lee
Haan, Kil-soo
Hahn, Gloria
Hahn, Richard S.
Han, Maggie
Hanka Enterprise Company
Hanmi Bank
Harrison, Earl Grant
Hemet Valley incident
Holt International Children's Services
Hungsa-dan
Hurh, Won Moo
Hyun, Peter
Ilse
Immigration Act of 1907
Jaisohn, Philip
K. & S. Company
Kaeguk chinchwi
Kaibal Hoesa
Kalbi
Kang, Connie Kyonshill
Kang, Younghill
Kansas Camp
KCB Radio
Kim, Bok-lim C.
Kim, Charles
Kim, Elaine H.
Kim, Ernie
Kim, Eugene Eun-Chol
Kim, Haeryen
Kim, Hyung-chan
Kim, Illsoo
Kim, Jay C.
Kim, Kyu-sik
Kim, Randall Duk
Kim, Richard E.
Kim, Warren Y.
Kim, Willa
Kim, Willyce
Kim, Yongjeung
Kim, Young Oak
Kim, Young-ik
Kim Brothers Company
Kim chee
Kimm v. Rosenberg
Kongnip Hyop-hoe
Kongnip Sinpo
Korea Review
Korea Society
Korea Times
Koreagate
Korean American-African American
  relations
Korean American businesses
Korean American Coalition
Korean American Garment Industry
  Association
Korean American literature
Korean American Political Association

Korean American women
Korean Americans
Korean children, adoption of
Korean church in the United States
Korean Community Center of the
  East Bay
Korean Compound
Korean Evangelical Society
Korean Family Counseling and Legal Advice
  Center
Korean Girls' Seminary
Korean Immigrant Workers Advocates
Korean immigration to the United
  States
Korean immigration to the United
  States, sources of
Korean Independence League
Korean Liberty Congress
Korean martial arts
Korean Methodist Church of Honolulu
Korean Methodist Church of San
  Francisco
Korean music and dance
Korean National Association
Korean National Revolutionary Party
  of Los Angeles
Korean nationalist politics in the United States
Korean residents' associations
Korean special events
Korean students
Korean war brides
Korean Women's Patriotic Society
Korean Youth and Community Center
Korean Youth Military Academy
Koreans in China
Koreans in Hawaii
Koreans in Japan
Koreans in Mexico
Koreatown
KTAN-TV
Kwuon, Im Jung
Kye
Kyopo
Le Grand
Lee, Chol Soo
Lee, Chong-sik
Lee, David
Lee, Edward Jae Song
Lee, K. W. [Kyung Won]
Lee, Sammy
Los Angeles riots of 1992
McCarran-Walter Act of 1952
Mandu
Mi guk saram
Min, Pyong Gap
Min, Yong Soon
Moon, Henry
Moon, Sun Myung
Nahm, Andrew C.
Namul
New Korea
1.5 generation
Oriental Food Products of California
Pacific Times
Paik, Hark-joon
Paik, Naim June
Pak, Ty
Park, Joseph

Entries by Subject

Yau, John
Yep, Laurence
Yip, Wai-lim
Yoshida, Jim
Young, Victor Sen
Young India
Yune, Johnny
Yuriko

*CUISINE, CUSTOMS, AND
CULTURAL TRADITIONS*
Adobo
Aloha aina
Amae
Baisakhi Day
Baishakunin
Balut
Barrio
Bayanihan
Bindi
Birthday, first
Birthday, one-hundredth day
Birthday, sixtieth
Bishop Museum
Bon odori
Bul kogi
Burakumin
Burqah
Bushido
California roll
Caste
Chado
Chap chae
Cherry Blossom Festivals
Children's Day
Chinese almanac
Chinese calendar
Chinese martial arts
Chinese New Year
Chinese restaurants and cuisine
Chinese zodiac
Chonan
Chop suey
Chusok
Cockfighting
Confucianism
Daruma
Day of Remembrance
Divination
Diwali
Dok guk
Double Ten
Dragon Boat Festival
Dragon dance
Enryo
Fan-Tan
Feng shui
Fictive kinship
Filipino rites of passage
Filipino values
Filipino weddings
Foot-binding
Fortune cookie
Furo
Gaman
Ganbatte
Ginger and red egg party
Guanxi

Haji
Harijans
Hawaiian Renaissance
Hawaiian society, traditional
Hole hole bushi
Honen
Hula
Idul-Adha
Idul-Fitr
Iemoto
Indian restaurants and cuisine
Jan ken po
Japanese "Chinese" restaurants
Japanese martial arts
Japanese ornamental horticulture
Japanese restaurants and cuisine
Jati
Jizo
Kadomatsu
Kalbi
Kandodan brides
Kanreki
Kao
Kava ceremony
Khmer special events
Kim chee
Ko
Koden
Kodomo no tame ni
Korean martial arts
Korean special events
Kosai
Kumi
Land tenure in Hawaii
Lao special events
Lion dance
Lumpia
Mah-Jongg
Mandu
Marriage matchmaking, Asian Indians and
Miai
Miss Chinatown
Mochi
Mochitsuki
Moon cakes
Moon Festival
Namul
Narcissus Festival
Nisei Week
O-bon
Ohana
Oshogatsu
Osonae
Oyakoko
Ozoni
Paigow
Pancit
Perahera
Picture brides
Puja
Purdah
Qigong
Qing Ming
Ramadan
Ramnavami
Republic Day
Rizal Day
Salwar kameez

Samoan special events
Sari
Sea cucumber
Shushin
Sikh holidays
Spring Festival
Tea
Tea ceremony
Tet
Urasenke School of Tea
Varna
Vesak
Vietnamese special events
Vijayadashmi
Yak phab
Yan, Martin
Yoshi
Yum Cha

COMMUNITY STUDIES
Asian American population
Asian Indian women in the United States
Asian Indians in the United States
Cambodian Americans
Cham
Chamorros
Chinatowns
Chinese American nightclubs
Chinese Americans
The Chinese Diaspora
Chinese from Southeast Asia
Chinese gangs
Chinese in Canada
Chinese in the Mississippi Delta
District associations
Families
Fijian Indians
Fijians
Filipino Americans
Filipino immigration to the United States
Gardena
Guamanians
Hakka
Hawaiians
Hmong
Hmong Americans
Hood River
International District
Interracial marriage
Issei
Iu Mien
Japanese Americans
Japanese Americans in Hawaii
Japanese in Brazil
Japanese in Canada
Japanese in Peru
Khmu
Korean Americans
Koreans in China
Koreans in Hawaii
Koreans in Japan
Koreans in Mexico
Koreatown
Lahu
Laotian Americans
Locke
Miyakawa, T. Scott [Tetsuo]

Montagnards
Monterey Park
Nisei
Pacific Islander American families
Pacific Islanders
Samoans
Sansei
Sikhs in Canada
Sikhs in the United States
Sikhs in Yuba City
South Asian diaspora
South Asians in the United States
Southeast Asian diaspora
Southeast Asian gangs
Tai Dam
Terminal Island
Thai Americans
Tibetans
Tongans
Vietnamese Amerasians
Vietnamese Americans
Vietnamese in Westminster
Women, Asian American
Yamato Colony
Yonsei
Zoroastrians

EDUCATION AND SCHOLARSHIP
Amerasia Bookstore and Gallery
Amerasia Journal
Americanization movement
Asia Society
Asian American collections
Asian American Studies
Asian American Studies, University of
    California, Berkeley
Asian American Studies, University of
    California, Irvine
Asian American Studies Center, University of
    California, Los Angeles
Asian Pacific American Librarians
    Association
Association for Asian American Studies
Association for Asian Performance
Association of Asian Studies
Association of Chinese Teachers
Bamboo Ridge: The Hawaii Writer's Quarterly
Beekman, Alan
Bhachu, Parminder Kaur
Bilingual education
Bilingual Education Act of 1974
Bonacich, Edna
Bose, Sudhindra
Boxer Indemnity Fellowship
Bridge
Cameron, Donaldina Mackenzie
Cameron House
Cariaga, Roman Ruiz
Center for Korean Studies, University
    of Hawaii
Chan, Jeffery Paul
Chan, Kenyon Sing
Chan, Sucheng
Chan, Wing-tsit
Chandrasekhar, Subrahmanyan
Chang, Edward T.
Chang, Gordon

Chang, Yum Sinn
Chao, Yuen Ren
Char, Tin-Yuke
Chen, Jack
Chen, King C.
Cheng, Lucie
Cheung, King-Kok
Chin, Frank [Chew]
Chin, John Yehall
Chin, Marilyn
China Books and Periodicals
China Institute in America
Chinatown History Museum
Chinese-American Librarians
    Association
Chinese American literature
Chinese Cultural Center of Visalia
Chinese Culture Foundation of San
    Francisco
Chinese Historical Society of America
Chinese Historical Society of the Pacific
    Northwest
Chinese-language schools
Chinese students
Chinn, Thomas Wayne
Choy, Philip
Combined Asian-American Resources Project
Conroy, E. Francis Hilary
Coolidge, Mary Roberts
Coomaraswamy, Ananda Kentish
Cordova, Dorothy Laigo
Cordova, Fred
Daniels, Roger
Dayal, Har
Demonstration Project for Asian
    Americans
Eastwind Books and Arts
Emeneau, M. B. [Murray Barnson]
Endo, Russell
English as a Second Language
English Standard Schools
Espiritu, Yen Le
Farrington v. Tokushige
Fenollosa, Ernest Francisco
Filipino American National Historical Society
Fugita, Stephen S.
Fukuyama, Francis
Gong Lum v. Rice
Goto, Yasuo Baron
Hane, Mikiso
Hartmann, Carl Sadakichi
Hayakawa, S. I. [Samuel Ichiye]
Hirabayashi, James
Hirabayashi, Lane Ryo
Hokoyama, J. D.
Hongo, Florence M.
Hsu, Francis Lang Kwang
Hsu, Kai-yu
Hu-DeHart, Evelyn
Hune, Shirley
Hungsa-dan
Hurh, Won Moo
Ichihashi, Yamato
Ichioka, Yuji
India Studies Chair, University of
    California, Berkeley
Jan Ken Po Gakko
Japan Foundation

Japan Pacific Resource Network
Japanese American Curriculum Project
Japanese American Evacuation and
    Resettlement Study
Japanese American National Library
Japanese American National Museum
Japanese American Research Project
Japanese-language schools
Jensen, Joan M.
Joe, Kenneth
Kagiwada, George
Kamehameha Schools
Kang, Younghill
Kang Youwei
Khmer-language schools
Khmer literature
Kiang, Peter Nien-chu
Kikuchi, Charles
Kim, Bok-lim C.
Kim, Elaine H.
Kim, Eugene Eun-Chol
Kim, Hyung-chan
Kim, Illsoo
Kimura, Larry
Kitano, Harry H. L.
Korea Society
Korean Compound
Korean Girls' Seminary
Korean students
Kunitomo, George Tadao
Kwong, Peter
La Brack, Bruce W.
Lai, Him Mark
Lasker, Bruno
Lau v. Nichols
Lee, Chong-sik
Lee, Evelyn
Lee, Rose Hum
Leong, Russell Charles
Leung, Peter
Li, Victor H.
Light, Ivan
Lim, Shirley Geok-lin
Ling, Amy
Liu, Pei Chi
Liu, William T.
Loo, Chalsa M.
Loomis, Augustus Ward
Louie, David Wong
Lum, Kalfred Dip
Lyman, Stanford
Ma, L. Eve Armentrout
McCunn, Ruthanne Lum
McWilliams, Carey
Mass, Amy Iwasaki
Matsuda, Mari
Mazumdar, Sucheta
M.E.L.U.S.
Metcalf, Victor Howard
Min, Pyong Gap
Miyakawa, T. Scott [Tetsuo]
Miyamoto, Shotaro Frank
Miyoshi, Masao
Model Minority
Mohanty, Chandra Talpade
Mun Lun School
Muzumdar, Haridas [Thakordas]
Nahm, Andrew C.

Nakanishi, Don T.
Nakazawa, Ken
Nee, Victor
Nishimoto, Richard Shigeaki
Nitobe, Inazo
Nomura, Gail
Odo, Franklin S.
Ogawa, Dennis
Okamura, Jonathan Y.
Okihiro, Gary Y.
Omatsu, Glenn
Omi, Michael Allen
Ong, Paul
Ouchi, William George
Pak Un-sik
Patterson, Wayne
Pensionado Act of 1903
Philippine Expressions: Filipiniana Bookshop
Polynesian Cultural Center
Poon, Wei Chi
Pukui, Mary Abigail Kawena
Qinghua University
Reischauer, Edwin O.
Ross, Edward Alsworth
Saibara, Seito
San Francisco school board crisis
San Francisco State College strike
San Juan, E. [Epifanio], Jr.
Saxton, Alexander P.
Shushin
Sikh Studies programs in North America
Sindo haksaeng
Singh, Jane
South Asian Studies centers
Southeast Asian American educational
 issues
Spivak, Gayatri Chakravorty
Sue, Stanley
Sumida, Stephen H.
Sung, Betty Lee
Suzuki, Bob H.
Suzuki, Peter T.
Takagi, Paul
Takaki, Ronald
Tambiah, S. J. [Stanley Jeyaraja]
Tape v. Hurley
Tchen, John Kuo Wei
Tien, Chang-lin
Trask, Haunani-Kay
Tsai, Shih-shan Henry
Tuan, Yi-Fu
U.S.-China People's Friendship
 Association
Urasenke School of Tea
Vietnamese literature
Waipahu Cultural Garden Park
Wang, L. Ling-chi
Watumull Foundation
Wei, William
Wing Luke Asian Museum
Wong, Bernard P.
Wong, Sau-ling Cynthia
Yanagisako, Sylvia
Yang, Linda Tsao
Yip, Wai-lim
Yu, Connie Young
Yung, Judy
Yung Wing

EMPLOYMENT, BUSINESS, LABOR, AND THE ECONOMY

Abe, Tokunosuke
Abiko, Kyutaro
Agricultural Workers Organizing
 Committee
Alabama and Chattanooga Railroad
American Federation of Labor
Aoki, Hiroaki "Rocky"
Arai, Ryoichiro
Arakawa's
Argonauts
Asia-Pacific Economic Cooperation
Asian Indian businesses in the United States
Asian Indians in the motel/hotel business
Asian Pacific American Labor Alliance
Assing, Norman
Balch, John A.
Ban, Shinzaburo
Bango
Bank of the Orient
Big Five
Bishop, E. Faxon
Bishop Estate
British East India Company
California State Federation of Labor
Cannery Workers' and Farm Laborers' Union
Canton Bank of San Francisco
Central Pacific Bank
Chan, Gordon
Chao, Elaine L.
Chao, Stephen
Char, Tin-Yuke
Chick sexing
China Camp
China trade
Chinese American Bank
Chinese American businesses
Chinese banks
Chinese contract labor
Chinese garment workers
Chinese Hand Laundry Alliance
Chinese in agriculture
Chinese in fishing
Chinese in Mining
Chinese in railroad construction
Chinese in the Mississippi Delta
Chinese laundries
Chinese vegetable farms
Chinese Workers' Mutual Aid
 Association
Chinn, Thomas Wayne
Chun Quon
Chung, Kun Ai
Cigar Makers Union of California
City of Tokio
Coloma
Committee Against Nihonmachi
 Evictions
Confucius Plaza Project
Coolie trade
Cortez Colony
Credit-ticket system
Crocker, Charles
Dekaseginin
Deshler, David W.
Dillingham Commission
Dockworkers strike

Dong-hoe
Dong-jang
Donner Pass railroad tunnel
Eastern Bakery
El Monte berry strike
Emigration Convention of 1886
Empress of China
Exeter incident
Federated Agricultural Laborers
 Association
Filipino labor unions
Filipinos and the Alaska canned salmon
 industry
Fong, Walter
Foreign Miners' Tax
Forty-niners
Fresno Rodo Domei Kai
Fukuda, Mitsuyoshi
Fukuzawa Yukichi
Fun kung
Gannen-mono
Gardeners Associations
Gompers, Samuel
Goto, Yasuo Baron
Grove Farm Plantation
Guanxi
Guilds
Hall, Jack
Hampton v. Wong Mow Sun
Hanapepe massacre
Hanka Enterprise Company
Hanmi Bank
Harris, Townsend
Hawaiian Sugar Planters' Association
Higher Wage Association
Hilo massacre
Hing, Alex
Hinode Company
Hirasaki, Kiyoshi "Jimmy"
Ho, Chinn
Hole hole bushi
Hop pun
Huiguan
Hulugan
In re Ah Chong
In re Tiburcio Parrot
International Hotel controversy
International Longshoremen's and
 Warehousemen's Union, Local 142
Irwin, Robert Walker
Itliong, Larry Dulay
Jao, Frank
Japan bashing
Japanese Chamber of Commerce of Southern
 California
Japanese contract farming
Japanese Federation of Labor
Japanese gardeners
Japanese-Mexican Labor Association
Japanese sharecropping
Jiyu imin
Joe, Kenneth
K. & S. Company
Kagawa, Lawrence
Kaibal Hoesa
Kaisha
Kanyaku imin
Katayama, Sen

Asian American Arts Alliance
Asian American Arts Centre
Asian American Dance Performances
Asian American Journalists Association
Asian American Political Coalition
Asian American Renaissance
Asian American Resource Workshop
Asian Americans for Community
  Involvement
Asian Americans for Equality
Asian Immigrant Women's Advocates
Asian Law Alliance
Asian Law Caucus
Asian Pacific American Labor Alliance
Asian Pacific American Legal Center
  of Southern California
Asian Pacific American Librarians
  Association
Asian Pacific Democratic Club
Asian Pacific Health Forum
Asian/Pacific Women's Network
Asian Women United
Asiatic Exclusion League
Association for Asian American Studies
Association for Asian Performance
Association for Asian Studies
Association for the America-Bound
Association of Asian/Pacific American Artists
Association of Chinese Teachers
Association of Indians in America
Association of Korean Political Studies in
  North America
Basement Workshop
Bing Kung Tong (Bingkongtang)
Bow On Guk
California State Federation of Labor
Cannery Workers' and Farm Laborers' Union
Central Japanese Association of
  Southern California
Chee Kung Tong
Chinese American Citizens Alliance
Chinese American Democratic Club
Chinese-American Librarians
  Association
Chinese American Planning Council
Chinese Consolidated Benevolent
  Associations
Chinese Cultural Center of Visalia
Chinese Culture Foundation of San
  Francisco
Chinese for Affirmative Action
Chinese Historical Society of America
Chinese Historical Society of the Pacific
  Northwest
Chinese Workers' Mutual Aid
  Association
Chinmok-hoe
Christian Society for the Realization
  of Justice
Chung Lau Drama Club
Cigar Makers Union of California
Combined Asian-American Resources Project
Committee Against Nihonmachi
  Evictions
Coordination Council for North
  American Affairs
Daihyo Sha Kai
District associations

Emergency Service Committee
Family associations
Filipino American National Historical Society
Filipino Federation of America
Filipino labor unions
Filipino locality or hometown
  organizations
Fresno Rodo Domei Kai
Fujinkai
Gardeners Associations
Godzilla
Gospel Society
Guilds
Higher Wage Association
Hokoku Seinen-dan
Hua Long
Huiguan
Hulugan
Hungsa-dan
I Wor Kuen
India League of America
India League of America, Madison,
  Wisconsin
Japanese American Citizens League
Japanese associations
Japanese Chamber of Commerce of Southern
  California
Japanese Exclusion League of
  California
Japanese Federation of Labor
Japanese-Mexican Labor Association
Japanese Women's Society of Honolulu
Japantown Art and Media Workshop
Kaibal Hoesa
Kearny Street Workshop
Kenjinkai
Khalsa Diwan Society
Kimochi
Knights of Labor
Knights of St. Crispin
Kokuryukai
Kong Chow Company
Kongnip Hyop-hoe
Korean American Coalition
Korean American Garment Industry
  Association
Korean American Political Association
Korean Community Center of the East Bay
Korean Evangelical Society
Korean Family Counseling and Legal Advice
  Center
Korean Immigrant Workers Advocates
Korean Independence League
Korean National Association
Korean National Revolutionary Party
  of Los Angeles
Korean residents' associations
Korean Women's Patriotic Society
Korean Youth and Community Center
Leadership Education for Asian Pacifics
League of Deliverance
Los Angeles County Anti-Asiatic Society
Manoa Lin Yee Wui
Media Action Network for Asian
  Americans
M.E.L.U.S.
Min Qing
Moncado, Hilario Camino

Narika
National Asian American Telecommunications
  Association
National Asian Pacific American Bar
  Association
National Asian Pacific American Legal
  Consortium
National Chinese Welfare Council
National Coalition for Redress/
  Reparations
National Committee for Redress
National Council for Japanese American
  Redress
National Democratic Council of Asian and
  Pacific Americans
Native Sons of the Golden State
Native Sons of the Golden West
Neo Hom
Nihon Rikkokai
Nisei Farmers League
Organization of Chinese American Women
Organization of Chinese Americans
Organization of PanAsian American Women
Philippine News
Pilipino American Network and Advocacy
Protect Kahoolawe Ohana
Red Guard party
Reform Society
Restoration Association
Sam Yup Company
Samoan Civic Association
Secret societies
Sinmin-hoe
Sokuji Kikoku Hoshi-dan
Sonjinkai
Southern California Retail Produce Workers
  Union
Square and Circle Club
Tongji-hoe
United Cannery, Agricultural, Packing and
  Allied Workers of America
United Chinese Society
United Farm Workers Organizing
  Committee
United Japanese Society of Hawaii
United Okinawan Association
U.S.-China People's Friendship
  Association
VOLAGS
Women of South Asian Descent
  Collective
Workingmen's Party of California
Xingzhonghui
Yan Wo Company
Yeong Wo Company
Young China Association
Yu-Ai Kai

POLITICS, GOVERNMENT,
COMMUNITY LEADERSHIP,
LAW, AND THE MILITARY

Acheson v. Murakami
Aduja, Peter Aquino
Aguinaldo, Emilio
Ahn Chang-ho
Aiso, John
Akaka, Daniel Kahikina
Akali movement

Foreign Miners' Tax
Frick v. Webb
Fu Manchu
Fujii Sei v. State of California
Fukunaga, Myles
Gandhi, Mahatma
Gardeners Associations
Gay and lesbian issues
Geary Act of 1892
Gentlemen's Agreement
Gila River
Gompers, Samuel
Gong Lum v. Rice
Granada
Great *Mahele*
Gresham-Yang Treaty
Gulick, Sidney Lewis
Gullion, Allen
Hall, Jack
Hampton v. Wong Mow Sun
Hanapepe massacre
Hanihara Masanao
Hare-Hawes-Cutting Act of 1933
Hawaii, Annexation of
Hawaii, Republic of
Hawaii Seven
Hawaiian Homes Commission Act
    of 1920
Hawaiian Native Claims Settlement Bill
Hawaiian Renaissance
Hawaiian reparations
Hawaiian sovereignty
Hayashi, Dennis
Hearst, William Randolph
Heart Mountain
Heart Mountain Fair Play Committee
Hemet Valley incident
Heney, Francis J.
Herzig, John A. "Jack"
High-caste Hindus
Higher Wage Association
Hilo massacre
Hing, Alex
Hirabayashi, Gordon Kiyoshi
Ho Ah-kow v. Nunan
Hokoku Seinen-dan
Honouliuli
Hood River
House Select Committee to Investigate
    Un-American Activities
Immigration Act of 1907
Immigration Act of 1924
Immigration Act of 1943
Immigration and Nationality Act of 1965
In re Ah Chong
In re Ah Fong
In re Look Tin Sing
In re Tiburcio Parrot
Insular Cases
Internal Security Act of 1950
International District
International Hotel controversy
Internment camps
Inu
Irons, Peter
Irwin, Wallace
Ishigo, Estelle
Itliong, Larry Dulay

Jallianwala Bagh incident
Japan bashing
Japanese American Citizens League
Japanese American Evacuation and
    Resettlement Study
Japanese American Evacuation Claims Act of
    1948
Japanese American internment
Japanese internees from South America
Japanese-Mexican Labor Association
Japanese occupation of the Philippines
Jerome
Johnson, Albert
Kahoolawe
Kaohsiung incident
Kearney, Denis
Keetley Farms
Keihin Bank
Khalistan Declaration of Independence
Knights of Labor
Knights of St. Crispin
Knox, Frank
Kochiyama, Yuri
Komagata Maru incident
Korean American-African American
    relations
Korematsu, Fred Toyosaburo
Kurihara, Joseph Yoshisuke
Kwangju massacre
Laddaran v. Laddaran
Lau v. Nichols
Laundry Ordinances
League of Deliverance
Leasehold system in Hawaii
Lee, Chol Soo
Lee, Edward Jae Song
Lem Moon Sing v. United States
Leupp
Ligot, Cayetano
Lin Sing v. Washburn
Lippmann, Walter
Lodge, Henry Cabot
London, Jack
Lordsburg
Los Angeles County Anti-Asiatic Society
Los Angeles riot of 1871
Los Angeles riots of 1992
Loyalty oath
McCarran-Walter Act of 1952
McCarthyism
McClatchy, V. S. [Valentine Stuart]
McCloy, John Jay
McCreary Amendment of 1893
McWilliams, Carey
Manlapit, Pablo
Manzanar
Manzanar incident
Manzanar pilgrimages
Marysville labor camp
Masaoka v. State of California
Massie case
Matsuda, Mari
Media Action Network for Asian
    Americans
Merchant Marine Act of 1936
Minami, Dale
Minidoka
Miss Saigon controversy

Moab
Model Minority
Myer, Dillon S.
Nagae Lum, Peggy
Naichi
Nakamura, Gongoro
Nakanishi, Don T.
Nakayama, Joji
National Asian American Telecommunications
    Association
National Asian Pacific American Legal
    Consortium
National Chinese Welfare Council
National Coalition for Redress/
    Reparations
National Committee for Redress
National Council for Japanese American
    Redress
Native American Programs Act of 1974
Native Hawaiian Health Care Act
    of 1988
Native Hawaiian Legal Corporation
Native Hawaiians Study Commission
Native Sons of the Golden West
Nativism
News Media and Asian Americans
Nisei Farmers League
Nishikawa v. Dulles
Nishimura v. United States
No-no boys
Office of Hawaiian Affairs
Office of Redress Administration
Okimura v. Acheson
Oland, Warner
Olson, Culbert L.
Omatsu, Glenn
Omura, James Matsumoto
Organization of Chinese Americans
Ota Camp
Oyama v. California
Ozawa v. United States
Page Law of 1875
Pandit, Sakaram Ganesh
Patel, Marilyn
People v. Downer
People v. Hall
People v. McGuire
Perez v. Sharp
Phelan, James D.
Plessy v. Ferguson
Porterfield v. Webb
Poston
Powderly, Terence V. [Vincent]
Proposition 13
Proposition 15
Public Proclamation No. 1
Public Proclamation No. 2
Public Proclamation No. 3
Public Proclamation No. 4
Quakers
Question 27
Question 28
Queue Ordinance
Racial formula
Redress movement
Reinecke, John E., and Aiko Reinecke
Relocation centers
Reluctant Thirty-nine

Esaki, Leo
Gupta, Kanta Chandra
Hahn, Richard S.
Hayashi, Harvey Saburo
Herbal medicine
Ho, David
Jordan v. Tashiro
Kanamori, Hiroo
Lal, Gobind Behari
Le Grand
Lee, Evelyn
Lee, Sammy
Lee, Thomas Henry
Lee, Tsung-Dao
Li, Choh Hao
Lin, Maya Ying
Loo, Chalsa M.
Lue Gim Gong
Masuda, Minoru
Matsuda, Fujio
Matsudaira, Tadaatsu
Miyamoto, Kazuo
Moon, Henry
Murayama, Makio
Nakano, Yosuke W.
Native Hawaiian Health Care Act
    of 1988
Noguchi, Hideyo
Noguchi, Thomas [Tsunetomi]
Onizuka, Ellison
Palolo Chinese Home
Park, Joseph
Pei, I. M. [Ieoh Ming]
Qigong
Rangaku
Self-Help for the Elderly
South Asian Studies centers
Subba Row, Yellapragada
Sudden unexpected nocturnal death
    syndrome
Sue, Stanley
Survivor's guilt
Takamine, Jokichi
Ting, Samuel
Uyeda, Clifford
Wang, Taylor Gunjin
Wu, Chien-shiung
Yamasaki, Minoru
Yang, Chen Ning

SOCIAL MOVEMENTS

Akali movement
Americanization movement
Anti-Chinese movement
Anti-Japanese movement
April Revolution
Asian American Movement
Boxer Rebellion
Hawaiian Renaissance
Hong Xiuquan
Hungsa-dan

Khalsa
Local
Redress movement
San Francisco State College strike
Taft-Katsura Agreement

SPORTS

Asahis
Chang, Michael
Chinese martial arts
Draves, Victoria "Vickie" Manalo
Japanese martial arts
Kono, Tamio "Tommy"
Korean martial arts
Lee, Bruce
Lee, Sammy
Martial arts
Noda, Steere Gikaku
Olympics in Korea
Park Chan Ho
Sakata, Harold T.
Yamaguchi, Kristi

WOMEN'S ISSUES

Ai
Aoki, Brenda Wong
Asian Immigrant Women's Advocates
Asian Indian women in the United States
Asian/Pacific Women's Network
Asian Women United
Bandaranaike, Sirimavo Ratwatte Dias
Barroga, Jeannie
Berssenbrugge, Mei-mei
Bhachu, Parminder Kaur
Buck, Pearl S.
Cameron, Donaldina Mackenzie
Cameron House
Cha, Theresa Hak Kyung
Chan, Sucheng
Cheung, King-Kok
Chinese American women
Choy, Christine
Coboy-coboy
Ding, Loni
Families
Filipino American women
Foot-binding
Fujinkai
Gupta, Kanta Chandra
Hagedorn, Jessica Tarahata
Hahn, Gloria
Hayslip, Le Ly
Hill, Amy
Hirano, Irene Ann Yasutake
Houston, Jeanne [Toyo] Wakatsuki
Houston, Velina Hasu
Interracial marriage
Japanese American women
Korean American women
Korean Family Counseling and Legal Advice
    Center

Korean war brides
Korean Women's Patriotic Society
Kwuon, Im Jung
Leung, Tye
Lim, Genny
Lim, Shirley Geok-lin
Ling, Amy
Lord, Bette Bao
Louis, Nikki Nojima
Lowe, Felicia
Lum, Mary
McCunn, Ruthanne Lum
Mail-order brides
Marriage matchmaking, Asian
    Indians and
Mass, Amy Iwasaki
Matsuda, Mari
Mazumdar, Sucheta
Minh-ha, Trinh T.
Mirikitani, Janice
Mittwer, Mary Oyama
Model Minority
Mohanty, Chandra Talpade
Mukherjee, Bharati
Narika
Narita, Jude
Natividad, Irene
Ng, Fae Myenne
Nomura, Gail
Organization of Chinese American Women
Organization of PanAsian American Women
Page Law of 1875
Perez v. Sharp
Picture brides
Ramabai Sarasvati, Pandita
Salvador Roldan v. Los Angeles County
Schoolgirl
Shamakami
Sone, Monica
Song, Cathy
South Asian women
Spivak, Gayatri Chakravorty
Square and Circle Club
Sui Sin Far
Tajima, Renee
Ty-Casper, Linda
Uno, Roberta
Uyemoto, Holly
Women, Asian American
Women of South Asian Descent
    Collective
Wong, Diane Yen-Mei
Wong, Jade Snow
Wong, Nellie
Wong, Sau-ling Cynthia
Yamada, Waka
Yamamoto, Hisaye
Yanagisako, Sylvia
Yung, Judy

THE
ASIAN AMERICAN
ENCYCLOPEDIA

INDEX